Microsoft

SQL SERVER™ 2000
HIGH AVAILABILITY

Allan Hirt with Cathan Cook,
Kimberly L. Tripp, and Frank McBath

PUBLISHED BY
Microsoft Press
A Division of Microsoft Corporation
One Microsoft Way
Redmond, Washington 98052-6399

Library of Congress Cataloging-in-Publication Data
Microsoft SQL Server 2000 High Availability / Allan Hirt ... [et al.].
      p. cm.
   Includes index.
   ISBN 0-7356-1920-4
   1. SQL server. 2. Client/server computing. I. Hirt, Allan.

  QA76.9.C55M53215   2003
  005.75'85--dc21   2003051241

Printed and bound in the United States of America.

1 2 3 4 5 6 7 8 9   QWT   8 7 6 5 4 3

Distributed in Canada by H.B. Fenn and Company Ltd.

A CIP catalogue record for this book is available from the British Library.

Microsoft Press books are available through booksellers and distributors worldwide. For further information about international editions, contact your local Microsoft Corporation office or contact Microsoft Press International directly at fax (425) 936-7329. Visit our Web site at www.microsoft.com/mspress. Send comments to *mspinput@microsoft.com*.

BizTalk, Microsoft, Microsoft Press, Outlook, Visio, Visual SourceSafe, Windows, Windows NT, Windows Server, and Windows Server System are either registered trademarks or trademarks of Microsoft Corporation in the United States and/or other countries. Other product and company names mentioned herein may be the trademarks of their respective owners.

The example companies, organizations, products, domain names, e-mail addresses, logos, people, places, and events depicted herein are fictitious. No association with any real company, organization, product, domain name, e-mail address, logo, person, place, or event is intended or should be inferred.

Acquisitions Editor: Kathy Harding
Project Editor: Maureen Williams Zimmerman

Body Part No. X09-39086

Contents at a Glance

Table of Contents

Part IV   Putting the Pieces of the Puzzle Together

Foreword

How do we increase availability? Is planned downtime considered "unavailability"? What exactly is "high availability"? These are key questions that must be answered when discussing any high availability platform. However, to answer these questions, it is first important that one understands what availability is. There are many different definitions throughout the industry when it comes to the subject of availability or, more correctly, unavailability. The terms "high availability," "assured availability," "continuous availability," "unavailability," "five nines," and other expressions are widely used throughout the industry even though most people have little understanding of their meaning.

One of the most widely used terms in the industry today that relates to high availability is *nines* (which is discussed in detail in Chapter 1). One cannot walk the halls of any IS shop these days without hearing the terms "three nines," "four nines," and "five nines" bandied about. "How many nines are we at?," "Does that include planned downtime?," and "What can we do to reach five nines?" are questions often heard but seldom answered correctly because their answers are based on perspective.

For example, in a mission-critical environment where users only make use of their systems Monday through Friday, downtime is scheduled on the weekends for maintenance activities, and the unplanned downtime amounts to less than five minutes per year. Could one say that the availability of this system is five nines? From a user's perspective, this system could be defined as five nines, and probably rightfully so. However, from a platform perspective, the availability numbers reflect a much lower percentage.

Why? From an industry perspective, this system does not truly meet the criteria for five nines because in the world of high availability no differentiation is made between planned and unplanned downtime. The reasons for this are simple. Even though planned downtime is scheduled well in advance of any outage, and provisions are made to account for these outages, the system must be "available" during this time to perform maintenance. If the system is non-functional at the time maintenance is to be performed, then the time must be counted against normal availability requirements.

Given these requirements, how does one go about developing a highly available platform? What are the key factors that cause systems to be unavailable? How do you mitigate these factors? How do you develop a disaster recovery plan to maximize your system availability? The answers to these and other questions can vary widely, as every system is different. The answers lie in employing the concepts and best practices in *Microsoft SQL Server 2000 High Availability*.

In this book, Allan Hirt discusses the key drivers that affect availability of systems, particularly as they relate to Microsoft SQL Server. He discusses in depth the driving factors that can cause downtime and the best practices that can be employed to increase the availability of SQL Server environments. For the past several years, he has consulted with numerous corporations designing highly scalable and available SQL Server solutions, presented at conferences, and authored white papers on the subject of SQL Server availability. Within the realm of SQL Server, Allan has gained a reputation for being an authority on the subject of SQL Server availability.

My group is responsible for managing the SQL Server operations for Microsoft.com, the third-largest Web site in the world. Our world currently consists of more than 150 SQL Servers servicing almost 1,100 databases. Maintaining the highest availability on the Internet is our charter. The concepts and practices discussed in this book are what we live every day, and, thanks to the author, they can be brought to you.

Scott Gaskins
Group Operations Manager
Microsoft.com

Preface

Walt Disney once said, "It all started with a mouse." Walt's quotation, believe it or not, could apply to this book, except I can say, "It all started with a white paper." Take a trip in your time machine to the fall of 2000. I was going to write a white paper for Microsoft SQL Server on SQL Server 2000 failover clustering. I started it, but then it turned into a chapter for the *Microsoft SQL Server 2000 Resource Kit* (among others I wrote or had a hand in, including "Five Nines" and "Log Shipping") and finally became a white paper proper in 2001 (with more stuff than was in the Resource Kit chapter). But it did not end there——there were training courses, presentations, and so on. Like it or not, SQL Server 2000 high availability and I were joined at the hip. Thing is—I did like it.

Through it all, I have seen my own knowledge blossom (and be challenged) from focusing on just one specific technology to taking in the entire scene from a holistic point of view. What you have in your hands represents three years of work and research condensed into one volume. I certainly could not have written this book as it is a year or more ago, even though I wanted to and thought I could.

My main motivations for this book were not only painting the whole picture, but also the huge need I saw for a book like this in my interactions with customers over the years. Whether I was working with one customer or speaking to hundreds at a conference like TechEd or SQL PASS, it was clear to me that people wanted real (and practical) advice and guidance that spoke to them—not something that came from an ivory tower. I have both a DBA and a development/quality assurance background, so I could relate to that need. In fact, a lot of the documentation I create stems from that background. As the saying goes, keep it simple, stupid. Anything I create needs to explain things in a manner that not only makes sense but also talks to many audiences and helps people get their jobs done without wading through pages of information to find the one nugget they need. Practical always trumps theoretical.

The truth is, talking about high availability as it relates to SQL Server is hard to do in 40 pages of a white paper or one chapter of a Resource Kit, as I quickly found out. Topics need to breathe, like a fine wine. Microsoft Windows gets a small section in my failover clustering white paper or in most other SQL

Server only–based documents, but it gets a dedicated chapter here. And let's face it—it is sometimes impossible to track down multiple white papers, Microsoft Knowledge Base articles, and so on, to get that whole story. Until the release of this book, the best view of SQL Server 2000 high availability released to date has been the "Patterns and Practices" guide from the Prescriptive Architecture Group (PAG) at Microsoft. It's a great reference for those who want a concise look at high availability and SQL Server 2000.

No document—whether 10 pages or 1,000 pages—will cover everything. Many of the topics in this book could easily expand to be their own book (and maybe will be some day). Some of the topics are covered as far as they can be developed. The bottom line is that I want to make sure that with the information in the chapters and anything on the CD-ROM, you, the reader, get extreme value for your purchase and can use this book as a reference, and also that it proves useful in your daily tasks by providing job aids, worksheets, and so on.

Although SQL Server high availability material was published before this book and certainly will be again afterward, I hope you get as much from reading this book as we did from writing it.

Allan Hirt
May 2003

Acknowledgments

Allan Hirt

You do not create a book of this size and scope in a vacuum, and this book would not have come together without a lot of help. First and foremost, I need to thank my family (Mom, Dad, and Dorine), friends (Dave, Mike, Shelley [Dude], Becca, Becky, and Ken, to name a few), and bandmates old and new for putting up with my lack of availability during the writing of this book, as well as for their support. I would be remiss if I did not thank my local MCS management for their copious support during the writing of the book. From a historical perspective, I would like to thank people like Robert Schroyer, Jeff Lesser, Ricky Ford, and Bob Toth for seeing potential in me that needed just the right amount of push and cultivation.

Now that the book is in your hands, I can get back to composing and arranging for a big band album to be recorded in the fall of 2003. Who would have thought I would have a nearly 1,000-page book on store shelves before a jazz CD on a "real" label? Dave, you were right about that one!

From a book perspective, I must first thank Cathan Cook, Frank McBath, and Kimberly L. Tripp, who wrote or cowrote some portions of the book. There is no way I could have finished this book all on my own. They all sacrificed their time, so I would also like to thank their friends, family, and colleagues for putting up with them during those times, all because I asked them to contribute. Cathan and Kimberly have been friends for quite a while and have been there from nearly the beginning when this was just a white paper! Special thank you wishes need to go to Jeffrey Aven, Maria Balsamo, Todd Bonner, Thomas Casey, Patrick Conlan, Filo D'Souza, Scott Gaskins, Brian Goldstein, Matt Hollingsworth, Marc Ingle, Tom Lucas and the rest of his team, Max Myrick, Greg Page, Vaqar Pirzada, Mark Pohto, Dave Poole, Mike Ray, Greg Smith, Azhar Taj, Don Vilen, Dave Whitney, Logan Worley, and anyone else who has influenced, contributed, or helped along the way with the book. I also consider some of these people friends, and I am glad they are on my side.

There are many more people at Microsoft who should be thanked for their support of me these past few years or for their friendship (and sometimes even both!), but there is not enough space here. A quick attempt at a list other than the aforementioned: Donald Elliott, Rebecca Laszlo, Steve Murchie, Joe Yong, LeRoy Tuttle, Tim Wolff, Dave Wickert, Mark Souza, Bren Newman, Prem

Mehra, Alex Nayberg, Richard Waymire, Euan Garden, Will Sweeny, Steve Snyder, Howard Yin, and Lisa Pennington.

On the Microsoft Press side, I would like to thank Kathy Harding, Julie Miller, Michael Bolinger, and Maureen Zimmerman for putting up with me for all of these months. Maureen, in spite of me missing a few deadlines here and there, is an excellent editor who really knew when to push and when to let up. I would especially like to thank Kathy for her friendship during the past few years and for getting the book through the approval process and humoring me by talking about it much longer! I finally put my proverbial money where my mouth was. This book could not be in your hands without the team of editors from nSight, Inc., who did a yeoman's job editing the manuscript and preparing it for production: Tempe Goodhue, Teresa Horton, Joseph Gustaitis, Piotr Prussak, and Robert Saley.

Technical reviewers were crucial for this project. Without them you would not be reading this. They made sure that what you're holding in your hands is accurate and covers what it needs to. (Although, in a book this size, I am pretty sure that if something was forgotten, it will be covered in future editions.) The reviewers are Pankaj Agarwal, Rick Anderson, Pete Apple, Sandy Arthur, Ruud Baars, Tom Casey, Andrew Cencini, Brian Goldstein, Matt Hollingsworth, Michael Hotek, Jakub Kulesza, Ed Morrison, Max Myrick, Terrence Nevins, Vaqar Pirzada, Grigory Pogulsky, Ward Pond, Paul Randal, Steve Schmidt, Ray Schueler, Greg Smith, Xavier John Vetticappallil, Don Vilen, Landy Wang, Chris Whitaker, Dave Whitney, Mark Wistrom, and Michael Zwilling. If I accidentally left anyone off this list, my sincerest apologies!

Cathan Cook

Since we started collaborating on projects remotely several years ago, Allan and I have worked on many projects together. When Charlie Kindschi and Ann Beebe first brought me in on the *Microsoft SQL Server 2000 Resource Kit* project based on my real-world perspective, I never thought it would launch my career the way it did. Looking back on everything, I am amazed at the far-reaching effect a team united by dedication and enthusiasm can have, even when separated by thousands of miles and political boundaries in a large established company. This is a tribute to the difference you can make when you care about "doing things right," and to those we met along the way who really "get it."

My special appreciation goes to the people who sponsored my work on the first high availability project I worked on for Microsoft: Rebecca Laszlo, Billie Jo Murray, Steve Murchie, and Joe Yong. Well-deserved thank-yous go to

Tom Lucas and his team in Microsoft SSITOPS for their outstanding monitoring code and perpetual willingness to help, and to Filo D'Souza and Todd Bonner for precision performance and scalability tips, based on their work on the benchmarks. I also want to express my sincerest appreciation to my mentors (in chronological order): Kevin Cook (who was the start of it all), Arnie Carlson (who taught me the HA mindset), J.C. Armand (who put me in charge and let me take my own risks), Jim Carroll (who perpetually challenged me to challenge myself), and Dr. Jim Gray (who taught me to reach for the stars).

Of course, my list of thank-yous would be incomplete without saying how much I owe my MCS management for their support in this and other similar "global reach" projects, and for making them enlightening and character-building experiences. Most of all, I am deeply grateful and indebted to my family, who have kept me sane and who I love very much: Travis, the coolest kid I know; Selene, Rorden, and Augustan, who taught me the value of nuisance; Kevin, my personal hero; Martha and Cookie, who did my work at home so I was free to do this work for you; and Pat and Chuck (Mom and Dad), for teaching me I could do whatever I put my mind to.

Frank McBath

I would like to dedicate my contribution to this project to my wife, Nancy. To family and friends who were there along the way for me: Tom, Ginger, George, Marjorie, Courtney, and Martha Anne McBath. To great people who have given me opportunities at Microsoft: Bryan Krieger, Harry Merrill, and Peggy Seymour. To personal friends who helped me along in life: Tom Sanders, Bill Simon and Lynn Randolph, Clyde and Fay Moore. And to great people I've been able to work with: Harv Sidhu, Dan Ely, Dan Grant, Dave Sabaka, Paul van Wingerden, Lucy Fraser, Shrikant Parimi, Kay Johnston, Rick Stover, Kim Slee, Christoph Schuler, Jeff Collins, Hans Reutter, Mike Hatch, Juergen Thomas, Peter Scharlock, and Filo D'Souza.

Kimberly L. Tripp

I started working with databases in 1988 after an advertisement I produced for IBM (while working in marketing and advertising) went nationwide. It required customization for different IBM branch offices and therefore a database to track all these orders. It was a great project and introduced me to databases—DataEase, to be specific. One of my colleagues (Ward L. Christensen) recommended me for a FoxBASE project, and when they asked him how much I knew about FoxBASE, he said, "Nothing, but hire her anyway." Another nine months later, it was certain—working with databases was where I was going to stay. Thanks, Ward—you defined my career's direction!

In the 15 years that have followed, there have been so many wonderful influences in my career that I know I'm not going to have a chance to thank them all here . . . and really, this isn't my main work, it's Allan's, so I'll be brief. To start, I'd really like to thank Allan and Cathan for their dedication and inspiration to continuously make the book better—revision after revision after revision. And where would I be without the SQL Server Development team; thanks for making my career possible and for keeping it interesting! Specifically, special thanks go to Greg Smith, Don Vilen, Patrick Conlan, Steve Schmidt, Mike Zwilling, Lubor Kollar, Richard Waymire, Gert E.R. Drapers, Lale Divringi, Ted Hart, Richard Hughes, Gavin Jancke, and Rande Blackman. Outside of the SQL team there are so many others from high school to college to the present: Craig Shaw, Ross Naheedy, Jeffrey Starzec, Garry Foreman, Charlie Spencer, Marshall Olsen, Scott Gaskins, Stacey Dickenson, William R. Vaughn, Kalen Delaney, and all of my partners at Solid Quality Learning, who always amaze me with their dedication and skills. Finally, probably more influential than anyone: my students and conference/workshop attendees who have asked great questions—many of which I needed to research to answer, and I only learned more myself!

Above all, I would like to thank my family, my friends (Stacy, Jenn, Philo, Liz, Ken and Kristen, Bobbi and Bill), and my partner (P.C.) for all of their support and understanding when I had to work instead of going out or seeing a band. I owe you guys a few beers!

Part I

The High Availability Primer

1

Preparing for High Availability

The time:	4 A.M.
The place:	Your bedroom
The event:	Your pager and cellular phone start ringing, buzzing, and vibrating like crazy, waking you from a deep sleep.
The reason:	Your company's mission-critical Microsoft SQL Server is down, and has been for about an hour. The overnight operations staff was unable to bring it online.

Unfortunately, tomorrow is the busiest day of the week and the databases must be fully functional by 8 A.M. Can you not only get there in time, but also bring the server up by then? The last thing that you want to have is the CEO/ CTO/CFO/CIO (or other "chief") standing over your shoulder asking you, "When will it be up?"

Assuming you have a disaster recovery plan in place (which is crucial in any IT organization wanting high availability), the preparation, planning, and testing of that plan can mean the difference between seconds and minutes of downtime versus hours, days, or even weeks. You need to know how long it takes to execute the plan and, more importantly, *how* to execute it. In addition, if you're facing a truly worst-case disaster recovery scenario for your SQL Server, you need to know how long it would take to restore the database from backups, including the last known good (that means tested) backup and where it is located.

If this or a similar scenario is your recurring nightmare, the full gravity of making systems and solutions highly available is in the forefront of your mind. If this situation does not speak to you in any way, it might be that stress does not get to you or that you are unaware of the situation's implications. Your employer makes you carry a pager or cellular phone for a reason; he or she wants to be able to get in touch with you day or night in the event something catastrophic happens. There is one driver behind all of this: the risk of losing something critical to the company's business, whether it is revenue, productivity, both revenue and productivity, or an intangible such as industry credibility.

High Availability—What It Is and How to Get It

The simple definition of the availability of a system is the amount of time a system is up in a given year. In the past few years, the availability of a company's mission-critical systems has been a major focus point. Availability needs to be given the proper attention, in addition to performance and security, which have always been paramount in the mind of anyone who has interaction with the systems. End users and management are concerned when the system is down; they do not usually spend time worrying about availability or allocating additional money for availability when the system is up and running. Availability is not just a SQL Server issue, either—it is applicable to every aspect of a computing environment.

There are two main aspects to consider when thinking about high availability, *prevention* and *disaster recovery*, both of which have many more facets than just technology. Prevention is anything—including people, processes, and technology—that, when put in place, is designed to reduce the risk of a catastrophic occurrence. The harsh reality is that, despite planning, failures can occur. A highly available system is one that can potentially mask the effects of the failure and maintain availability to such a degree that end users are not affected by the failure.

Disaster recovery is exactly what it claims to be—a catastrophic event happened, and it must be dealt with. Achieving high availability must take into account both pieces of the proverbial puzzle to make the complete picture. High availability is not just the sigh of relief when the system comes back up. If you are a fighter pilot, would you rather be a daredevil and have fast planes with no safety precautions or fast planes with ejection seats? During World War I, it was thought of as a sign of weakness to carry a parachute, but obviously this attitude has changed. Taking precautions to save systems—or human lives—should never be viewed as extraneous.

Prevention

The basic tenets of prevention are deceptively simple:

- Deploy redundant systems in which one or more servers act as standbys for the primary servers.

- Reduce and try to eliminate single points of failure.

Both tenets provide a solution to only one aspect of the technology part of the equation—the server itself. What about the network connecting to the server? What about an application's ability to handle the switch to a secondary server during an outage? These are just two examples of possible problem areas; there will be more for your environment that you need to prepare for. The bottom line, though, is that planning, implementation, and administration of systems are equally important aspects of preventing an availability problem.

The more redundancy you have, the better off you are. However, there is a conundrum. No system is completely infallible in and of itself, but adding too many levels of redundancy might make an availability solution so complex that it becomes unmanageable.

The designers of the *Titanic* thought she was unsinkable, yet the ship went to the bottom of the ocean on her maiden voyage. For protection, the *Titanic* had 16 watertight compartments that could be sealed with 12 watertight doors. In theory, this would have kept the ship afloat despite flooding in three or four compartments. Unfortunately, the watertight compartments themselves only went to a certain level above the water line. When the iceberg struck the *Titanic*, the damage it caused was, in reality, only six noncontiguous small gashes totaling about 12 square feet. But they made it possible for water to overflow from one compartment into another (think of the way an ice cube tray fills with water) and eventually caused the ship to sink.

What turned out to be a fatal flaw was addressed to the best of the designers' ability at the time, but the unknown always lurks in the shadows. You must do your best when you are seeking to prevent a catastrophe.

Technology is only one part of the equation. Environmental and human aspects also contributed to the *Titanic*'s fate. She was caught in a set of circumstances—an ice field that affected most ships in the North Atlantic at that exact time, the lookout saw the iceberg too late, no other ships were close enough to assist after the *Titanic* struck the iceberg, and so on—for which no amount of technology could compensate.

Similarly, you might have two exact copies of your production database, but what happens if they are located in two data centers in the same state and are affected by an earthquake simultaneously? Do not overthink your availability solutions; there is only so much you can plan for.

Disaster Recovery

When the iceberg struck, the *Titanic* was unprepared. There had been no safety drills to test an emergency plan (if one existed), not enough lifeboats for all passengers, and so on. Survivor accounts of the chaos during the last few hours reinforce the importance of proper planning in ensuring that more good than harm occurs during a crisis. Consider that each database, or even the entire system, could need to be rescued but not have to be salvaged from the bottom of the ocean. Rash decisions for the solution could have dire consequences. The only way to execute a rescue or salvage operation is to have the right people in place with a complete, well-tested plan to direct them.

When the crisis has passed, a postmortem should be done to determine the lessons learned to prevent such an outage from occurring in the future. Chapter 12, "Disaster Recovery Techniques for Microsoft SQL Server," includes an in-depth discussion on disaster recovery and the plans needed.

Keep in mind that when it comes to disaster recovery, there can be another extreme. You can be proactive to the point of being negative. The person who is constantly worried about everything might be considered obsessed. There is a happy balance somewhere. If the crew of the *Titanic* made each passenger walk around with life preservers, a ration kit, and some sunblock, would that have been practical? No. Being prepared does not equate to paranoia. Assume that there is always something that could happen to your systems, anticipate and plan to the best of your ability, but go about your day knowing that you cannot control every factor.

If something happens—and something will happen at some point during your career—ensure that you will not go down with the ship. Whether you are the captain or just one of the passengers or crew, a disaster situation might make or break your career with your employer. Not being able to answer a question such as the one posed in the beginning of the chapter—"When will it be up?"— because, for example, the plan was never tested or the backups themselves were never tested and timed, is generally considered unacceptable. Keep in mind that fallout might still occur when the dust settles, but as long as you were prepared and handled the situation properly, all should be fine.

Agreeing on a Solution

Before starting on the design, purchase, and eventually roll out of any systems, the key players must meet to agree on the specifics of the solution that will eventually be deployed. This should be done for every deployment and solution desired, whether or not it is considered mission-critical.

The Project Team

Assemble a project team that will own the overall responsibility for the availability of the solution. The leader should be the business sponsor—a person from the management team who will ultimately answer for the success or failure of the operation and have the greatest influence on its budget. Representatives from all parts of the organization—from management to end users—should be part of the team, as each of them will be affected in one way or another by the availability of the systems or solution that will be put in place.

Guiding Principles for High Availability

Once the project team is assembled, it should meet to decide the principles that will govern how the solution will be designed and supported. The following are some sample questions to ask; there might be more for your environment.

- What type of application is being designed or purchased?

- How many users are expected to be supported concurrently by this solution in the short term? In the long term?

- How long is this solution, with its systems, supposed to stay in production?

- How much will the data grow over time? What is projected versus actual growth (if known)?

- What is acceptable performance from both an end user and administrative or management perspective? Keep in mind that performance can be defined in various ways—it might mean throughput, response time, or something else.

- What is the availability goal for the individual system? The entire solution?

- How is maintenance going to be executed on this system? Like performance, how you maintain your systems is specific to your particular environment.

- What are the security requirements for both the application and the systems for the solution? Are they in line with corporate policies?

- What is the short-term cost of developing, implementing, and supporting the solution? The long-term cost?

- How much money is available for the hardware?

- What is the actual cost of downtime for any one system? The entire solution?

- What are the dependencies of the components in the solution? For example, are there external data feeds into SQL Server that might fail as the result of an availability problem?

- What technologies will be used in the construction of the solution?

Some of the questions you ask might not have answers until other pieces of the puzzle are put in place, such as the specifications for each application, because they will drive how SQL Server and other parts of the solution (for example, Microsoft Windows 2000 Server) are used and deployed. Others might be answered right away. Ensure that both the business drivers and the more detailed "what if" scenarios are well documented, as they are crucial in every other aspect of planning for high availability. It might even be a good idea when documenting to divide the questions into separate lists: one that pertains to the requirements of the business independent of technology, and one that is technology-dependent.

Having listed questions, it is a safe assumption that each person in the room will have a different answer for each question. The goal is to have everyone on the same page from the start of the project; otherwise the proverbial iceberg might start ripping holes in the hull of your solution. Compromise will always be involved. Compromise can only be achieved if there is a business sponsor who is driving and ultimately owning the solution at all levels. It is the responsibility of this person to gather consensus and make decisions that result in the compromise that everyone can live with. As long as all parties agree on the compromise, the planning, implementation, and support of the solution will be much smoother than if the voices of those two steps down the road are not heard or are ignored.

Making Trade-Offs

High availability is not synonymous with other vital aspects of any production system, such as performance, security, feature sets, and graphical user interfaces (GUIs). Achieving high availability is ultimately some form of a trade-off of availability versus performance versus usability. All aspects also need to be considered when doing overall system, infrastructure, and application design. Designing a highly available system that is not usable will not satisfy anyone. This is where the trade-offs come into play.

Is buying a single 32-processor server to support a larger amount of concurrent users for a database that is used 24 hours a day the most important business factor, or is it more important to ensure that the server is going to be up 24 hours a day to support the continuous business? Chances are people will say both are equally as important, but in reality, a budget dictates that some sort of trade-off must occur. Having slightly lower performance to ensure availability might be a reasonable trade-off if the cost of downtime is greater than the ability to have 10 additional users on the system. The same could be said for security—if the system or solution is so secure that no one can use it, is it really available? Conversely, if a developer coded the database server's security administrator account and password into the application to make things more convenient, this may compromise security, as well as the application's ability to work with certain high-availability technologies.

Think of it another way: If money was no object and you had to purchase a car, would you buy a fast, sleek sports car or a sensible four-door sedan with airbags for all passengers? Many would choose style over substance—that is human nature. High availability is like buying the sedan; it might not be the best looking car on the block, but it is a solid, reliable investment. The airbags and sturdy roll bar, among other safety features, will make you as prepared as you can be for a possible accident.

For a clear example of a trade-off, briefly consider the *Titanic* again and that the White Star Line valued luxury over lifeboats. That was their trade-off, and at the time it made sense to the people funding the ship as well as the designers. That decision ultimately proved to be fatal. You need to determine what the acceptable trade-offs are for each situation so that the solution will meet the needs of everyone, especially those responsible for administering it and, most important, the end user or customer.

Identifying Risks

Once the basic principles governing the solution have been put into place, it is time to mitigate the known and unknown risks by asking the "what if" questions to the best of the group's ability. You might know what the risk and its associated questions are, but not the solution to mitigate them. Even more risks will become apparent as the solution moves from conception to planning, on through to implementation, and as more and more technology and application decisions are undertaken. Whenever a risk is identified, even if there is no answer at the time, make sure it is documented. Continually check the documented list of risks to see that there has been a corresponding answer to the question recorded. By the time the solution hits production, all identified risks should have a response, even if it is that nothing can be done to mitigate the risk.

Although there are many more possibilities, here are some common questions to jump-start the risk management process:

- What will you do if one disk fails? The entire disk subsystem?

- What will you do if a network card fails?

- What will you do if network connectivity is lost?

- What will you do if the entire system goes down or stops responding? Is loss of life involved (for example, a health system)? Although this is related to the overall cost of downtime, the specific result of downtime should be known.

- How does the application handle a hardware (including network) or software failure?

- Is there a corporate standard—what do we do now for availability on other systems—and is that plan working well?

- How will the proper people be notified in an emergency?

- How will a problem be detected?

Next Steps

Your guiding principles are now documented, along with some risks that might or might not have answers. At this point, the principles should be reviewed and debated to ensure that they are correct. If something is not right, now is the time to correct it, as these principles will live through the entire project life cycle. They can be modified and reassessed if necessary, but the initial principles should be the measuring stick against which the success or failure of a solution is measured. There should be a formal signing off by the entire team, because availability is the responsibility of everyone involved.

Availability Calculations and Nines

The definition of uptime and downtime is different in every computing environment. Technically, all downtime should count toward a final availability number, whether it is planned or unplanned, because both are service disruptions. Some environments do not count planned downtime, such as periods of normal maintenance, against an eventual system availability calculation. Although this is an individual decision each company makes, padding availability numbers by excluding planned downtime might send the wrong message to both management and end users. In fact, many enterprise customers pay for an external service to monitor the availability of their systems in comparison to their competitors' to ensure that the entire system's availability meets the guiding principles determined by the team.

Calculating Availability

Calculating availability is simple:

Availability = (Total Units of Time–Downtime)/Total Units of Time

For example, assume:

> Total units of time = 1 year (8760 hours)
>
> Downtime = 3 hours

Plug that into this formula:

> Availability = (8760 hours − 3 hours)/8760 hours

which results in .999658 availability of the individual system.

Keep in mind that the individual system rarely exists alone: it is part of a whole solution. You have now calculated the *individual* system's availability, but what is the entire solution's overall availability? That number is only as good as the weakest critical link, so if one of the essential servers in the solution only has .90497 uptime, that is the uptime of the entire solution. The number for the overall solution also has to factor in such things as network uptime, latency, and throughput. These critical distinctions bring the availability of a solution into focus. Having said that, qualify numbers when they are calculated and explained. This definition might be too simplistic for some environments—if the server that has .90497 uptime is not considered mission-critical and does not affect the end user's experience or the overall working of the solution, it might not need to be counted as the number for the overall solution. The bottom line is that multiple components in a solution can fail at the same time or at different times, and everything counts toward the end availability number.

There are also the related concepts of mean time between failures (MTBF) and mean time to recovery (MTTR). MTBF is the average expected time between failures of a specific component. A good example is a disk drive—every disk has an MTBF that is published in its corresponding documentation. If a drive advertises 10,000 hours as its MTBF, you then need to think about not only how long that is, but also how the usage patterns of your application will shorten or lengthen the life (that is, a highly used drive might have a shorter life than one that is used sparingly). An easy way to think of MBTF is predicted availability, whereas the calculation detailed earlier provides actual availability.

MTTR is the average time it takes to recover from a failure. Some define the MTTR for only nonfatal failures, but it should apply to all situations. MTTR fits into the disaster recovery phase of high availability.

What Is a Nine?

The calculation example yielded a result of 99.9 percent uptime. This equates to three nines of availability, but what exactly is a nine? A *nine* is the total number of consecutive nines in the percentage calculation for uptime, starting from the leftmost digit, and is usually measured up to five nines.

The following table shows the calculations from one to five nines.

Table 1-1.   Nines Calculations (Per Year), in Descending Order

Percentage	Downtime (Per Year)
100 percent	No downtime
99.999 percent (five nines)	Less than 5.26 minutes
99.99 percent (four nines)	5.26 minutes up to 52 minutes
99.9 percent (three nines)	52 minutes up to 8 hours, 45 minutes
99.0 percent (two nines)	8 hours, 45 minutes up to 87 hours, 36 minutes
90.0–98.9 percent (one nine)	87 hours, 36 minutes up to 875 hours, 54 minutes

What Level of Nines Is Needed?

Most environments desire the five nines level of availability. However, the gap between wanting and achieving that number is pretty large. How many companies can tolerate only 5.26 or less minutes of downtime—planned and unplanned—in a given calendar year? That number is fairly small. Good-quality, properly configured, reliable hardware should yield approximately two to three nines. Beyond that, achieving a higher level of nines comes from operational and design excellence. The cost of achieving more than three nines is high, not only in terms of money, but also effort. The cost might be exponential to go from three, to four, and ultimately, to five nines. Realistically, striving to achieve an overall goal of three or four nines for an individual system and its dependencies is very reasonable and something that, if sustained, can be considered an achievement.

Consider the following example: Microsoft SQL Server 2000 is installed in your environment. Assume that Microsoft releases a minimum of two service packs per year. Each service pack installation puts the SQL Server into single-user mode, which means it is unavailable for end user requests. Also assume that because of the speed of your hardware, the service pack takes 15 minutes to install. At the end of the install process, it might or might not require a reboot. For the sake of this example, assume it does. A reboot requires 7 minutes, for a total of 44 minutes of planned server downtime per year. This translates into 99.9916 percent uptime for the system, which is still four nines, but you can see how something as simple as installing a service pack can eliminate five nines of availability in short order. One possible way to mitigate this type of situation is to have one of the standby systems brought online to take requests, synchronize the primary server when the service pack is finished, and then switch back to the primary server. Each switch will result in a small outage, but it might wind up being less than the 22 minutes it takes for one service pack. That process also assumes that it has been tested and accurately timed on equivalent test hardware.

Negotiating Availability

If you ask the CEO, CFO, CIO, or CTO, each one will most likely tell you that they require five nines and 24/7 uptime. Down in the trenches, where the day-to-day battles of system administration are fought, the reality of achieving either of those goals is challenging, to say the least.

Keep in mind that the level of nines and the requirement might change during the day. If the company is, say, an 8-to-5 or a 9-to-6, Monday-to-Friday type of shop, those are the crucial hours of availability. Although the other hours might require the system to be up, there might not be a 100 percent uptime guarantee for the outlying hours. When the solution is designed, the goal should be to achieve the highest level of nines required, not shooting for the moon (five nines)—that might be overkill. When the question is asked during the business drivers meeting, such situations need to be taken into account. Five nines of availability from Monday to Friday might only mean 9 hours a day, which translates into 2340 hours per year. This number is well below the 8760 hours required for 24/7 support, 365 days a year. All of a sudden, what once seemed like a large problem might now seem much easier to tackle.

Also be mindful that each person—from members of management right down to each end user—will have different goals, work patterns, and agendas. In good times, the demand for high availability might be someone's priority, but if other factors and goals, such as high profitability, are currently driving the business, availability might not be number one on the list of priorities. This also relates to the nature of some industries or different organizations—financial and medical institutions by default require availability, whereas service or retail organizations might see availability only as an aspect of the business that might or might not be important. This could mean that in the negotiations, a variable rate of availability might be discussed, and might confuse people.

For example, if you need your systems to have five nines of availability from 8 A.M. to 8 P.M., that should be your target for availability. Stating different rates of availability for different hours can potentially lead to the design of an inferior system that will not be able to support the highest required availability number. In the end, it is important to understand all of the factors when putting together the business drivers and guiding principles that ultimately will govern the solution. Ignoring any one of the groups touching the systems is a mistake.

Types of Unavailability

Perception is reality, whether we like it or not. Because of this, it is important to make a distinction between the types of unavailability:

- **Actual unavailability** Anything that makes the system and its resulting solution unavailable to the people who are using it. There are varying degrees of total unavailability (complete system failure, site down, and data gone, all of which are described in more detail in Chapter 13, along with ways to mitigate them), and this is more often than not the catastrophic or unplanned failure. That said, things such as system maintenance—like service pack installs—might cause total unavailability of a system.

- **Perceived unavailability** When a system appears to be functioning properly from an administrative standpoint, but is unavailable to end users or customers. This can happen if only one aspect of the solution is down, for example, if the database administrators (DBAs) know SQL Server is up and running, but the front-end Web servers fielding the initial requests and serving up Active Server Page (ASP) pages are down. Another example is if someone outside has cut the network cable that goes from the data center to the outside world. Poor performance or lack of scalability can also lead to perceived unavailability, because an end user requires an answer back from your systems in a reasonable amount of time.

Each person in the availability equation sees a system or the entire solution differently. To mitigate issues caused by varied perceptions, service level agreements (SLAs) must be negotiated with all parties involved in the solution, including hosting companies, end users, contractors, administrators, and so on, to ensure that uptime and performance needs are met. Each SLA might state a different availability goal, but the overall availability is based on every component, not just one. Chapter 2, "The Basics of Achieving High Availability," delves further into SLAs.

Where Does Availability Start?

Take a mental poll of your current workplace or companies you have worked for in the past: how many applications and solutions were designed with availability in mind from inception? The reality is that in most—not all—development, test, and production environments, availability is an afterthought. In the minds of some application developers and management, availability is solely Information Technology's (IT's) concern—meaning not a design, just an end-of-line implementation issue—right? Wrong! Availability is not just a technology problem: it encompasses people, process, and technology, as well as end-to-end designs of applications, infrastructure, and systems. Chapter 2 gets into some of the specifics of the basics of high availability, from basic infrastructure to change control.

Assessing Your Environment for Availability

There are two approaches for assessing your environment for availability:

- **The application or solution is already in place.** Availability needs to be retrofitted to the environment. In the evaluation process of adding availability for the first time, or enhancing existing availability methods, new hardware might need to be purchased, new maintenance and other processes are added to the administrator's daily tasks, the application itself might need to be patched or redesigned, and more. Some of this might be the result of outgrowing current hardware capacity or scalability, causing a perceived unavailability problem.

- **The application or solution has not yet been implemented.** This more than likely means starting from the beginning, and the solution starts from a clean slate. In the evaluation of a completely new solution, planning is every bit as important, if not more important, than the final step of implementation. Planning ensures fewer problems over the solution's entire life cycle. It is much easier to get something right from the start than it is to take an existing solution and redesign it to be something else. Remember that scope creep is a problem for any planning, design, and implementation process—not just availability ones!

As noted earlier, Chapter 2 covers more specifics about the basics of high availability, but it is very important to keep in mind the differences in the two approaches and how they really are not the same. Keep this in mind as you go through each chapter in this book, as well as when you start to plan, design, and implement highly available solutions in your environment.

In assessing availability, it is important to keep in the forefront of everyone's mind that applications directly impact the availability of systems. One could even argue that in spite of massive amounts of other software and hardware redundancy, in the end the application might prove to be the weak point in the availability chain if it is not designed to handle such things as a server name change if it should be required during disaster recovery. The application drives the requirements of how each production server, its related hardware, and third-party software—such as database platforms and operating systems—will be selected and assembled; the infrastructure should not dictate the application. Designing the perfect infrastructure does no good if the one component accessing it cannot properly utilize the new multimillion-dollar infrastructure. This is also the reason that retrofitting high availability into an already existing environment is much more challenging than starting from scratch. Sometimes, it can be akin to putting a square peg into a round hole. A bad application means low availability.

The Cost of Availability

No ones likes the cost aspect of assessing availability and, to a large degree, it is the toughest aspect to handle. The question is not so much the cost of availability, but the cost of not having availability and, subsequently, the actual cost of downtime. Money is always a factor, as achieving availability is not cheap. Speaking realistically, achieving five nines of availability on a limited budget is just about impossible.

Consider the following example: A high volume e-commerce Web site generates, on average, $10,000 in sales per hour. For a day, that equates to $240,000, and weekly, $1,680,000. On the busiest day, the Web site encountered an unexpected availability problem around noon. When all was said and done, the Web site was down for six hours, which is the equivalent of $60,000 in sales. That was the surface cost of downtime.

Analyzing the downtime further, when the outage happened, no plan was in place, so an hour of that time was spent gathering the team together. This also meant that whomever was called in to work on the problem had to stop working on whatever they were doing. Because no plan was in place, there was no clear chain of command, resulting in many people attempting the same thing, further tying up system resources. This impacted other schedules and mission-critical timelines, a cost that must also be measured.

When the company went to call support, they realized that they never renewed their Microsoft Premier Support agreement because they did not really use support services in the past, so they felt it was not needed. Instead of getting the quick response engineers, they were left waiting in the queue with other pay-per-incident customers. Also hindering quick time to resolution, certain information was either not known about the systems or could not be gathered because of stringent processes. It took a committee a half hour to decide to allow the information to be gathered. The technical issue was eventually solved, but due to the delays caused by the lack of a support contract and the information problem, it took longer than it should have. These were tangible costs and direct problems.

Perhaps even more important than the tangibles are the intangibles: how many existing customers went to the Web site to buy something, could not access it, and did not come back because they knew they could get the item from another e-tailer that was up and running? Those users might be enticed by discount coupons to return—but perhaps not. An even bigger intangible was the loss of prospective customers who visited the site during the downtime, saw it was down, and never visited again. That might factor into the $10,000 hourly rate, but can you put a price on future business? Customer loyalty is directly associated with a brand name. A bad experience generates negative word of mouth. If word spreads that the site is unreliable, the more people that spread that message, the more potential there is of losing current and future business.

For this example, there are a few conclusions that should be highlighted as part of a postmortem to prevent the problem from happening again:

- A proper disaster recovery plan must be devised and implemented to avoid additional unnecessary downtime.

- A clear chain of command must be established to reduce confusion and duplicate efforts.

- Always have a support contract with appropriate vendors that provide the level of support and response needed.

- Support personnel need certain information sooner rather than later.

- Make sure customers are welcomed back with open arms after a significant outage.

Chapter 12 walks you through putting together a complete disaster recovery plan. Because the downtime cost at least $60,000 in this case (again, this is the only concrete number), would a $10,000 support contract have paid for itself? Most likely it would have. If the technical problem was found to be an issue of configuration, was it completely thought out during the planning process, or was the system rushed into production? Correcting these kinds of issues can save money and time to resolution.

Barriers to Availability

The preceding example shows that the lack of a proper disaster recovery plan, no support contract, and the possible missed configuration point are potential barriers to availability, or roadblocks to achieving the level of availability required. These barriers include, but are not limited to, the following:

- **People** Everything from improper staffing to too many chiefs mulling around and giving orders during downtime.

- **Process** Is there a plan? Are there normal company standards and processes that will impede the availability and possibly disaster recovery solutions?

- **Budget** Was enough money invested in all aspects of the solution (people, process, design, software, hardware, support, and so on)? Will cutting costs or restraining budgets cause *more* downtime in the end? Every solution obviously is not given carte blanche in terms of a budget, but an availability solution must fit a budget and the availability requirements. The two cannot be in direct conflict, otherwise there will not be a successful implementation.

- **Time** Are the goals set for coming back online unreasonable? Are maintenance windows too short, which means that if maintenance is not being done, it could cause availability problems down the road?

During the planning phase, you must take into account barriers to availability and mitigate any risks associated with them.

Summary

Achieving high availability is not as simple as installing a piece of software, a new piece of hardware, or using a /highavailability command-line switch when starting up a program. If it were that easy, you would not be reading this book. Constructing and testing an end-to-end solution that encompasses people, process, and technology is the only tried-and-true method of preparing for a potential disaster. Redundant technology for availability only provides the end physical manifestation of a larger, agreed-on goal that also takes into account security and performance. Trade-offs can be made to achieve the end result, but the end result should satisfy management, administrators, and end users. Each group should also formally buy into and share responsibility for high availability.

2

The Basics of Achieving High Availability

In every high availability solution, as alluded to in Chapter 1, "Preparing for High Availability," you must adhere to some fundamentals; otherwise, achieving the availability you need will be difficult. Even if you are in an IT shop or department that takes care of many of the basics listed in this chapter, you should still find a few nuggets of information here…or you might be bored. Either way, it would be inappropriate for a book on high availability to ignore the fundamentals.

This chapter addresses matters that relate to both the human and technological factors of the high availability equation. It includes such topics as data center best practices, staffing, service level agreements (SLAs), and change management.

Data Center Best Practices

This section starts with a few funny—and yet not so funny—stories that are not only based on real events, but more common than you would think.

■ A company was experiencing an availability problem intermittently. At approximately 2 A.M. a few nights a month, the main accounting database server went down and then automatically came back about an hour later. In some cases, at least one of the databases running was marked "suspect" in Enterprise Manager, causing it to be rebuilt. One occurrence would be an isolated incident, but this was clearly more than that. The CIO, CFO, and CTO launched a joint investigation. In the end, the culprit was not a denial of service attack, it was a janitor attack: the janitor was unplugging the system to plug in cleaning equipment.

■   SQL Server was experiencing intermittent failures with no apparent root cause or predictable timing. As in the first example, a joint investigation was launched to determine what was going on. The problem turned out to be that telephone maintenance workers were walking past the cabling, which was loose and tangled, shifting cable plugs a bit. To add insult to injury, in the main wiring room that contained the core networking and telephony wires, the telephone workers occasionally touched some of the network wiring in addition to the telephony ones, causing some network outages.

■   A junior database administrator (DBA), who was new to the company and did not know the systems, their purpose, or everything about how the company administered servers, started a backup process. The DBA did something incorrectly—such as backing up to the wrong disk volume and filling up a disk subsystem critical for another SQL server—and caused a serious availability problem until the situation was corrected.

Have any of these events, or something similar, happened where you currently work or have worked in the past? In most companies, at least, the first example is preventable by using qualified, professional, and trained cleaning staff. The others might not be as easily solved, especially the third one if, say, all the other DBAs are unavailable and the junior DBA is left at the helm. Proper training would not cover the improper backup situation, but it would eliminate the other problems (not knowing the systems, and so on).

Chances are, you inherently know the best practices that relate to your production environment—many books and sessions at conferences talk about them. But how many do you adhere to, and how many are barriers to your availability? Each topic in this section could be more detailed, but the ideas that follow will serve as guidelines.

As a database system engineer or administrator, you might not have complete authority over how your SQL Server is eventually hosted or managed, but you should be able to observe and document discrepancies you see. If problems persist, take your documentation, along with records of downtimes, to management to influence and change how the servers and systems you are responsible for are hosted and managed.

Even if you do not run the data center, have no direct involvement or access, or have no input on its potential construction, it is important to let the proper people know about the things listed next. Whether you are using a third-party hosting company or keeping everything in-house, consider location; security; cabling, power, communication systems, and networks; third-party hosting; support agreements; and the "under the desk" syndrome.

Location

The location of your data center will contribute to its availability. Do not locate or use a data center that is under plumbing lines, sewer lines, or anything similar—basically anything that could cause problems. What would happen if a pipe burst, sending water through the ceiling of the data center and flooding the server room? Think about what businesses are above and below your offices. If, for example, your offices are located under a kitchen, not only is the potential for fire increased, but also leaks could seep through the kitchen floor. Is it wise to put your data center near something that could go up in smoke at any minute?

If none of this can be avoided, consider the options listed throughout this section and see if they help mitigate risk to the data center. If they do not, or if some of them are not feasible due to high costs or other reasons, the risk will have to be documented and taken into account. Some situations are unavoidable, even in the best of IT shops.

■ Proper climate control of systems is crucial for availability. There is a *big* difference between hosting one server and hosting 1000 servers in the same location. Computers do not work well if they are overheating due to the climate, which might also cause anomalies such as condensation if the conditions in the room are just right. Make sure you have a properly installed heating, ventilation, and air conditioning (HVAC) system—with the emphasis on properly installed. This means that there will be sufficient air circulation to keep the entire room at a uniform, acceptable temperature. Conversely, if your data center is in an extremely cold geographic climate, you might also need a heating system because systems do not work well in extreme cold, either.

■ Make sure that the entire data center's airflow is even, otherwise there could be hot and cold spots. If certain areas are too cold, there's the risk of an administrator adjusting the air conditioning if he or she is cold while working in the room and raising the temperature in areas other than their own, causing system outages in the now-hot areas. Maintaining systems at the proper temperature extends their mean time between failures (MTBF) and the life of the hardware; in extreme temperatures some hardware might not function at all.

■ Electrical lines must be properly grounded. Failing to have this done can potentially result in some bizarre behaviors in electrical equipment. Newer buildings should, for the most part, be grounded, but some older buildings might not be. Computer components, especially small ones like CPUs and memory, do not react well when sudden power surges occur. Power conditioners might be needed to guarantee that there is a consistent, even amount of power flowing to all things electric.

■   Servers should be neatly and logically organized in racks (see Figure 2-1) where all equipment can be reached. The location of each server should be documented so that in the event of an emergency, an affected server can be easily located. Racks also help protect the equipment from damage, protect against most accidental situations (such as a person accidentally knocking a wire loose), and foster air circulation to assist with proper climate control.

Figure 2-1   A good example of servers arranged neatly in racks.

■   To enable the equipment to be rolled into the data center on racks, you might need specific clearance for both height and width; otherwise, you might not be able to get the equipment into the data center. Conversely, if you need to move the equipment out, you must account for that as well (for example, if you have custom racks built into the data center instead of brought in). Also, make sure that ramps can hold the weight of the equipment being rolled in and out, as well as accommodate people in wheelchairs. The ramps should not be too narrow.

■   Plan for growth on many levels. Much like capacity planning for your systems themselves, invest the time to assess how much physical space is currently needed and how much will be needed over the next few years. What is the planned life of the data center? One specific example of something small and seemingly insignificant is making sure there are enough electrical outlets in the room to allow for additional equipment over the years. In no case do you want to have to resort to power strips to expand the power, risking overload and outages. You must also take into account the increased power consumption and its affect on such things as the HVAC.

■ A fire suppression system should be installed in the data center. If at all possible, make sure that it will not further damage the computer systems and endanger human life. It's imperative that anyone who works in or near the server room reacts properly to a fire alarm and adheres to all building rules, including taking part in fire drills. If the fire alarm cannot be heard, there should be some other visual indicator in the data center to alert the staff. One concern about some fire systems is that they are just as dangerous to human beings as they are to computer systems. Halon depletes the ozone layer, and some fire suppression systems can turn artificial ceiling materials into a deadly weapon.

■ Make sure that there is enough room above and below the server racks to allow the cables and climate control system to be installed properly (see Figure 2-2). Also, make sure the racks will fit into the room—do not prepurchase racks only to find out that they will not fit your room, as well as allow for the clearance and airflow needed.

Figure 2-2   The proper amount of clearance above the racks as well as room for the cabling.

- Climate and geographic location are important factors in the placement of a data center. If you work in a place susceptible to volcanic eruptions, earthquakes, hurricanes, tsunamis, or other natural disasters, take that into account in your planning. Because of these limitations imposed by nature—you cannot stop a hurricane from flooding or, in a worst case scenario, destroying your data center—you might need to consider a second location in a separate geographical area to act as a secondary data center, or cold site.

Security

Security is no joke. Securing both the computer systems and the data center itself will not only protect the system, but increase your systems' availability. If it is not done, availability will decrease as a result of security breaches, viruses, or other attacks. According to two separate polls reported in *eWeek* (*http://www.eweek.com/article2/0,3959,930,00.asp* and *http://www.eweek.com/article2/0,3959,537304,00.asp*), many IT organizations were still struggling with securing their environments or thought they were doing just fine with their security plans, a shock in and of itself. Despite the fact that planning and implementing the security of your systems is a good thing, much like high availability, no matter how much you plan for security, there is always something you could miss. Although security is a book unto itself, its concepts are addressed throughout this book.

- No unauthorized users should be allowed physical access to the data center. To prevent this, access of all persons who enter the server room, and even those who enter the operations center, should be logged. For tighter security, only people with special entry cards should have access. At a bare minimum, invest in a clipboard, some paper, and a pen and make sure people walking in and out of the data center log their times.

- Install video monitoring equipment so that intruders can be identified in the event of unauthorized access. Store those tapes in a separate, secured location for the period of time specified by your corporate security policies.

- Along with allowing only authorized people to have access to the server room, make sure that no one needs to go through the server room or behind the racks to get to other equipment or areas, such as the telephone wiring system. The design of the data center should prevent such a situation.

- Locks, whether standard or electronic, should be installed where appropriate, starting with the doors, and possibly even down to the level of individual servers. This supports "authorized access only." If your data center has a clipboard, or even a live guard, to allow people to sign in or out (as previously mentioned) that might not be enough protection. Signing in does not stop someone from powering down a mission-critical server.

- After the server is moved into the data center, you should not need to physically touch the console, with rare exceptions, such as if a piece of hardware fails or software must be installed and installation cannot be done through some other method. Leave the server alone; forget it is there (well, do not forget, but only worry about it in other ways, such as backup and monitoring). Use a remote administration or access tool, such as SQL Server's Enterprise Manager or Windows Terminal Server, to manage and access the servers. Ensure that proper training is given to staff to prevent accidental shutdowns or reboots. If there is not a problem on the system, do not look for one.

- System auditing, both for physical logon to the operating system as well as auditing of events on Microsoft SQL Server, should be enabled if possible. This makes unauthorized accesses easier to track should they occur.

Cabling, Power, Communications Systems, and Networks

Very basic considerations in a data center—power and networking—are just as important as security.

- If your data center is located in an area that is prone to natural events such as tsunamis, earthquakes, tornados, and so on, or if you are worried about power interruptions, a power generator fueled by diesel should be connected to the data center to ensure a continuous power supply. These generators were very common in planning for Y2K efforts. Test the switch over to the generator and, if necessary, have a backup for the backup!

- Even if a power generator is not necessary, uninterruptible power supplies (UPSs)—at a bare minimum—should be attached to each system in the data center.

- Systems should not all be placed on the same power grid, especially if a primary server and its secondary or redundant server for high availability are in the same data center. This would be considered a single point of failure.

have direct access to qualified engineers, or is there a gated process that slows the time to resolution? This would be addressed by a proper SLA, which is discussed later in this chapter.

■   How secure is your equipment compared to that of another company? If someone is performing maintenance on another company's servers that are located next to yours, can the administrator accidentally dislodge a cable in your racks?

■   How will you monitor that the hosting company is actually doing the work it is required to (for example, swapping tapes in the backup digital linear tape [DLT] device)? How will you secure your backups? How will you access them quickly, if needed?

■   Make sure that the third-party vendor's support agreements are in place and meet your level of availability.

■   In conjunction with the previous point, check to see that the third-party hosting company itself is adhering to sound high availability and disaster recovery practices.

Support Agreements

Purchase support contracts for all software and hardware that will be hosted in the data center. This includes the operating system, application software, disk subsystem, network cards, switches, hubs, and routers—anything that is or is not nailed down! Support contracts are forms of SLAs. There is nothing worse than encountering the example described in Chapter 1 in which the system was down for a long time due to the lack of a proper support contract. If your availability requirement is three nines, make sure the hardware vendor or third-party hosting company and their vendors can meet that standard. Support contracts are insurance policies that any environment serious about high availability cannot be without.

Make sure you understand what type of agreements you have with each vendor your company has a contract with. Learn how to use their support services. Record their contact information in several safe but accessible places. Include your account number and any other information you need to open a case. Keep records of this information in your operations guide, and keep a copy of the operations guide offsite. It is critical that members of the team are well aware of the terms of these agreements, because many of them have specific restrictions on what you or your team can do to the system.

For example, many hardware vendor SLAs have clauses that permit only support personnel from the vendor or specific, certified persons from your team to open the server casing to replace defective components. Failure to comply could result in a violation of the SLA and potential nullification of any vendor warranties or liabilities. Something as simple as turning a screw on the case might violate the SLA, so be careful!

Also consider a product's support life cycle. This will not only help you determine the support contract that will need to be purchased, but will help the planners decide the life cycle of the solution without having to do a major upgrade. Microsoft publishes support life cycle, policies, and costs at *http://support.microsoft.com/lifecycle*. The Microsoft Support Life Cycle is a three-phase support approach:

- Most products will have a minimum of five years of mainstream support from the date they are generally available.

- Customers might have the ability to pay for two years of extended support for certain products.

- Online self-help for most products will be available for a minimum of eight years.

For any changes to policies in the program, please consult the Microsoft Web site just listed.

The "Under the Desk" Syndrome

Last but not least, the production servers should not be under the DBA or system administrator's desk. Sadly, this phenomenon still exists in some companies. Think about the way some applications make their way into production— someone releases a beta or prototype, people like it and start using it, and it becomes a production or mission-critical application. Most applications are planned for and do not get into production this way, but in companies small and large there are exceptions to the planning rule.

If a production server is "under the desk," the server does not have any of the protection (including monitoring and backups) it needs to be highly available, leaving it exposed to anyone who walks by. Another problem is that there is a good chance that because the application was not initially intended for production use or was a beta version, it might not have been fully tested and, more specifically, load tested to see if it can handle thousands of enterprise users hitting the server. The computer itself might have the right specifications to run the mission-critical application—the processor and memory might be more than you currently need, and it might work well on a desktop operating system—but once it becomes a mission-critical server that must be online, will it meet the needs and growth of the enterprise?

Keeping it in the data center does more than protect it from casual passersby or environmentally related accidents; it means that factors like needs and growth were accounted for. If there is no data center or its operations are not optimal to provide the protection and availability the server needs, other options should be explored, such as a hosting provider.

Staffing

Like the data center best practices already presented, this section covers another topic that could be a book in itself, database staff. The general principles apply to other types of IT groups as well.

Before getting into the specifics of what a DBA needs to do in a high availability environment, the company needs to determine whether it is properly staffed. Too often operational database administration work and other tasks, such as managing networks, disk backup and maintenance, and so on, are left to application developers and network operations people who are not only splitting their time, but are not experts. It can be argued that if a mission-critical database system needing four nines is deployed with no DBA or dedicated database staff onsite, the commitment to a highly available database system does not exist. Do not let staffing become a barrier to availability.

Creating a Database Team

Whether your team will support individual, highly available systems or an entire end-to-end solution, all team members must be able to function cohesively. The entire group should be responsible for the quality of the service it provides, with a focus on sharing information freely throughout the team. When issues arise, find root causes and identify process improvement solutions to address problems rather than worrying about who made each particular mistake. Shifting blame (or praise) from the individual to the group fosters an atmosphere of trust. Building such a team requires cycles of constant improvement with persons who are willing to do what is right for the good of the team, not just for individual gain. Regularly evaluate ways to improve the quality of your group's service, the interactions within your team, and the team's interactions with the rest of the company.

Team members should collectively own the database servers so that anyone can respond to issues for any server. If you have a system that only one person can administer, then that person becomes the single point of failure in the system. This is why it is so important for the DBA team to act as an integrated unit.

> **Note**   If you are currently the only DBA in the company, find another person (or several) to act as extra support for various aspects of the system when you will be absent.

Shared ownership in the team can be facilitated by rotation, effective use of spare time, lunchtime presentations, and reliable communications within the team. Rotation encourages cross-training, provides breadth of experience, encourages common practices, and leads to better documentation. Here are some examples of how your team can implement rotation practices:

- Assign a primary and at least one secondary DBA for each system, so that there are at least two people supporting each system.

- Rotate staff among projects, classes of servers, and different environments (development, test, and production).

- Rotate at long enough intervals to assure team comfort with new roles and individual knowledge and growth.

Proper training is crucial for the success of the individual and the team. Technical skills should be maintained and furthered. Whether someone is a junior administrator out of college or a senior administrator, if he or she is new to your environment, he or she should get acclimated to your systems before assuming full access and duties. The person should shadow someone who knows the ins and outs. Too small a training budget (or none at all) could be a barrier to availability.

In addition to technical training, team members should acquire "soft skills." Communication skills, both oral and written, enhance employees' long-term success in dealing with people at all levels. Writing and documentation are necessary for mentoring and knowledge transfer, and they also have historical value. Acquiring these communication skills might involve formal training or courses in presentation skills and technical writing, among other things.

The DBA's responsibilities are constantly evolving. He or she is expected to not only know how to twist knobs and optimize settings, but also to know about the culture and the business processes of the company. This includes understanding what he or she is doing and how it affects each person, the team, and the company as a whole. Conversely, understanding the big picture also helps the DBA understand the small picture. Things are not always simple. A successful DBA demonstrates good leadership when he or she aligns personal goals with the goals of the company and then takes others along for the ride.

By establishing a high level of communication and trust among team members, you will improve the response time of the team overall. As each DBA becomes familiar with other systems and environments, the number of issues that only one person can handle diminishes. As a result, the DBAs do not need to call each other as frequently for answers, which can save valuable minutes when a server needs extra attention or is unavailable. This also increases the availability of your DBA resources.

DBAs must be instantly available to each other during working hours using agreed-on methods (for example, cell phone, e-mail, pager, two-way radio) as well as during hours that the DBA is on call (should your company have such a policy), or if an emergency arises and you need to be contacted. Communication devices issued to DBAs must be tested on a regular basis, and contingency plans must be put in place in the event conventional methods fail.

Paramount to succeeding as a DBA is getting along with the other IT staff. Unfortunately, this can become a highly political push-and-pull situation. The long-term interpersonal goal should be to eliminate such tensions. This is easier said than done, because each group—whether it is the general Windows administrators, the people running the storage area network (SAN), the network gurus, or the build engineers—has its own daily duties. If you make a request, such as needing a domain account for the services for SQL Server, your request might be contrary to what they do or take time away from something they need to do. Be sensitive to and understanding of others. Be aware that the DBA's role as the gatekeeper and protector of the data might add stress to existing relationships.

A good example of working together is the planning, building, and deploying of a database system. The Windows administrators and the build engineers have in their minds what it takes to make a performing system, the network engineer has his or her requirements, and the database administrator also has his or her requirements. Each person must ultimately agree on the construction of the system, or it will be hard to maintain the system going forward for each group (they will all likely be involved).

Building a well-oiled team takes time—not just the passage of time, but also a commitment of time to team building that might seemingly be better spent in other ways. A racecar might normally go from 0 to 60 miles per hour in 4.6 seconds if it is properly maintained, unlike one with loose lug nuts and no motor oil. The principle is the same for a DBA team.

Service Level Agreements

An SLA is a list of system service requirements presented in a formal document or communication, with specific terms, roles, deliverables, responsibilities, and even liabilities (where applicable). It is not just a contract, say, between a company and a third-party hosting vendor. SLAs should exist between any two parties that will be using the system: the IT department and end users, the vendor and the IT department, the hosting company with its vendors, and so on. Without an SLA, service requests can quickly become nearly impossible to fulfill because no expectations are set, and the parties tend to adjust themselves to the state of the situation.

The goal of an SLA is to establish basic expectations between the two groups; anything else is negotiable. An SLA guarantees that a system will perform to specifications (this includes defining what performance means), support required growth, and be available to a given standard. Any regularly scheduled downtime windows (for data loads, invasive maintenance, and so on) must be noted in an SLA, as they will affect availability.

SLAs for database systems typically include the following (at minimum):

- Percentage of availability (defined as a percentage, such as 99.999 percent).

- Maximum number of concurrent users.

- Number of transactions to be supported per unit of time (such as 5000 per second).

- Method of contacting support personnel, and the maximum number of support calls permitted within a given period.

- Response time expected on support issues. This can also be defined at a higher level for the entire IT department.

An SLA can also include a section defining terms, limitations, and exceptions. The more experience the DBA has, the longer this additional section tends to be, which is a polite way of saying that the more trouble you have seen, the more likely you are to protect yourself from future trouble.

An SLA also includes staffing, server configuration, licensing, product support agreements, equipment utilized by the solution covered by the SLA, and finally, the cost of the service itself. If you cannot support an existing SLA as is, you need to either renegotiate the SLA or create a budget or a project before accepting the SLA. The DBAs should state the level of support that is possible without causing undue strain on the team or undue risk to other systems in the data center. Of course, this does not necessarily mean that you will not have to attempt to support the system that causes the risk, but you can at least quietly document the risk. Later, it cannot be said that management was uninformed of the risk. If repeated problems arise from the system because of this, you are more likely to see a revision of the SLA, or a budget increase for more staffing, new hardware, or other provisions.

An SLA must account for the weakest components of the system. For example, if your database vendor does not offer 24/7 technical support, do not guarantee 24/7 support to end users without taking this into account. If you have any doubts about an SLA, detail them immediately. If you develop doubts as time passes, renegotiate immediately, but keep in mind the delicacy of doing that. SLAs should never be renewed without detailed analysis of their content to determine if they still meet the requirements for the new period of coverage, or, in less common scenarios, if they are more than you require.

It is vital to keep SLAs current in a high availability environment. If you are unable to solve a system issue in a timely manner on your own, the absence of a vendor support agreement will probably threaten your uptime. The support service staffs of each vendor are troubleshooting professionals trained in their equipment or software. They have many more resources than anyone else available to them to find a solution for your problem.

However, all of this is useless if your staff does not know how to access the vendor's support center or does not have necessary account codes or contract numbers for verification when calling the support center.

Your goal is to manage the people, both internal and external to your company, who are involved in the systems you are supporting, the processes, and the technology with the expectation of meeting the terms of the SLA. Success should be measured in terms of customer satisfaction, as well as numeric values recorded over time and periodically compared to the SLA. If you miss your numbers, identify the points of failure and fix them. If you cannot fix the problem because of resources, processes, or technology, then renegotiate your SLA or create a report justifying the need for more resources. Attach a copy of your purchase orders to the report and send it to management. If you did not meet the agreed-on numbers, but the end users are still happy, also note that when the SLA comes up for renewal. It might be possible to renegotiate terms.

On the CD   A sample SLA can be found on the CD-ROM that accompanies this book. The file name is SLA.doc, and it can be customized to your environment or serve as a reference for an SLA you put together. Some SLAs might require the involvement of your company's legal counsel, so please check before sending such a document to someone else.

Manage Change or Be Managed by It

Change management is another important cog in the high availability works. *Change management* means different things to different people, but for the purposes of this book it is the process that allows changes to applications and systems to happen in a predictable fashion with minimal or no interruption in service. Change management applies to all phases, from development to production support.

> **More Info**   More information on change management can be found in the chapter "Managing Database Change" in the *Microsoft SQL Server 2000 Resource Kit* (available from Microsoft Press, ISBN 1-7356-1709-0), and the chapter "Change and Configuration Management" in the *SQL Server 2000 Operations Guide* on *http://www.microsoft.com*.

Change Management for Databases: The Basics

A lack of change management is a major cause of data center failures. From a database perspective, it must become a priority to document, test, and manage the deployment of all database changes. Database changes include stored procedures, functions, physical database structures (that is, indexes, constraints, stored procedures, and so on), the data, the storage components of the database, or even the server itself. This helps you avoid new errors and minimize the impact on the service level.

Besides having input into the design and planning stages, including the data access code, database objects, server architecture, and its configuration, the DBA must also be involved in evaluating and analyzing the proposed changes to any database system. The final stage in the change process is managing the implementation process, so that only known and tested factors are introduced into the system. The implementation process includes documented plans. A post implementation review, which includes the DBA team, allows learning from the change before it begins again.

Database work necessarily overlaps development and testing (Microsoft Solutions Framework, abbreviated MSF) with operations (Microsoft Operations Framework, abbreviated MOF). Change can be application driven or it can be operations driven. The DBA might begin in the design phase of the MSF cycle and end up going through MSF and part of MOF to implement the change. This same cyclical approach also applies to the way that a DBA maintains the database. By constantly evaluating the value of potential changes to either the database servers or the processes by which they are supported, the DBA is essentially continuously moving full circle through the Operations Framework. A formal process of quality assurance is essential to a stable production environment.

Keep in mind that the approaches to change management might differ depending on whether you are rolling out a packaged product or a custom-built application.

When you are making configuration and upgrade changes to your database environment, there are a number of tasks you should perform related to planning, user communication and coordination tasks, disaster recovery, testing, application and vendor issues, and many other considerations. Some of these issues are discussed in greater detail in Chapter 13, "Highly Available Upgrades."

Development, Testing, and Staging Environments

The optimal configuration for any environment implementing change management includes completely separate testing and staging environments that simulate or reproduce the production environment in the most faithful way possible. Why separate environments and not just one server, SQL Server instance, and so on, for all functionality? The problem is that they all have different purposes, and some environments are more transient than others. A development environment by nature is chaotic—changes are happening quickly. A testing environment is a bit more stable than a development environment; it is usually set up to test a particular version of the software or specific conditions and reconfigured accordingly for subsequent tests.

A staging environment, although similar to a testing environment, has a completely different use and purpose. Sure, it is for testing, but it is either a joint venture between the IT staff and product development or maintained by the IT staff only to test what will be rolled out in production. Staging, more often than not, is an exact copy of what is in production. You do not want to affect one environment at the expense of others.

Here are some sample questions to ask yourself.

- If development is always changing code on a server, does that invalidate any testing?

- What happens if a testing engineer accidentally deletes data needed by developers on a shared development and testing database?

- What happens if a developer or tester reboots a server in the middle of others testing or developing against it?

Although these issues sometimes occur in separate environments, they will be greatly minimized.

From a cost perspective, having three dedicated environments might not be possible—yet another barrier to availability. However, you have to ask yourself if not simulating your production environment in development, testing, and staging to save a few pennies will ultimately hurt more than it will help. Go back to the arguments posed in Chapter 1, "Preparing for High Availability" What is the cost of downtime versus any up-front investments, especially if you could have found an issue before releasing the software? As an example, production cluster systems and the disks that support them can be potentially expensive, so duplicating them might not be in the budget for one or two additional environments. If you do not have the budget, one option is to look for alternatives, such as spare hardware that can be reused in certain scenarios, or software like VMWare Workstation or Connectix VirtualPC that might help you simulate your environment.

The bottom line is that you should do the best you can to reduce the risk of failure and increase availability in your production environment by developing and testing environments properly before you need to support them on a daily basis. At the very least, try to maintain development and staging environments.

Maintaining Separate Environments

Maintaining separate environments also means more administrative work for everyone involved. How will you ensure a change to the production environment (such as a security patch) is reflected in development, testing, and staging so that when a new change is developed, it will not break production? Similarly, how will development be notified of any necessary changes to development or testing systems? These are only two possible scenarios. Processes must be devised and implemented to have changes flow from development to production and back. This requires a great deal of communication and synergy. It is potentially a huge pain to maintain these separate environments, but the efforts will pay themselves off with the first system failure that is caught in the test environment.

Change Request Form   Using a change request form is one way to manage the change process from development to production, or to make changes to the production environment. A change request form serves as an official document that is signed by the relevant parties prior to implementation. Otherwise, the implementation cannot occur. This document should be stored, and it can also be used to help measure success or failure, as well as satisfaction with the tasks performed. A change request form ensures accountability.

> **On the CD**   A sample change request form can be found on the CD-ROM with the title Change_Request.doc. The document can be used and altered for your environment.

Managing Change and Availability in Development

If you are developing custom applications or modifying and extending third-party or packaged applications, you must provide a change infrastructure to ensure availability by the time the application hits production. Change management also will encompass excellent high availability application development practices in the development space.

High Availability Is Not Just an IT Problem

Contrary to what many developers would like to think, high availability is not just an IT problem to be dealt with later. As mentioned briefly in the section "Where Does Availability Start?" in Chapter 1, decisions you make during the development life cycle absolutely impact how the solution will not only be deployed, but also maintained. Most important, these decisions impact the availability of the solution. Bad application decisions often lead to low availability applications even with a $10,000,000 back end. If you adhere to the MSF process, assessing risk will already be done on a regular basis. Developers should develop code with deployment and the eventual back end firmly in mind. If you are a DBA or an IT person, make your development counterparts aware of what they need to do from an application perspective. Remember, *you* are the one who will be supporting it in production!

> **More Info**   Specific tips about how you should think about coding applications for particular technologies are listed in some of the technology-specific chapters (such as Chapter 6, "Microsoft SQL Server 2000 Failover Clustering," and Chapter 7, "Log Shipping").

One topic not covered specifically in subsequent chapters is the development of the installation process for custom applications. This obviously affects the availability of any production rollout. There might be times when rebooting is completely unavoidable, but rebooting should be kept to a minimum. For example, the developer should think about making all changes and installing all files before requiring a reboot. Doing a reboot more than once could prove costly.

Equally important is the ability to uninstall the application or back out from the installation process (that is, cancel it in the middle of the installation) without adversely affecting the system, and to make sure it returns to its state prior to installation. Consider the following example. A contractor developed an updated version of an existing application. The application was supposedly tested and found to be as error-free as possible (meaning no "showstoppers") in the test environment, and it was installed during a maintenance window. All of a sudden, the process failed. When asked about the uninstall method, the developer shrugged and said, "What uninstall? This is a permanent change." In an IT shop, such a change would prove to be painful.

Version Control

Version control is the practice of being able to store and ultimately deploy multiple versions of an application, if necessary. Version control applies to application development and production environments.

From a development perspective, version control is absolutely critical to the success of the environment. It allows developers to check out and check in code so that no one developer can overwrite what someone else has done without creating a record of it. Version control also allows a development environment to trace the history and have code regression in case a bug is found in a current version. You do not want to ship a completed and compiled version of the application to customers without a way of rebuilding it exactly, should you need to. This situation does happen. Clearly identify the released version and make sure that it is made secure so that no one can modify or delete it.

Consider the uninstall example from the previous section. If that occurred, you would be relying on your backups and disaster recovery plans to get the system back into a usable state. With a version control tool or some other method, you might not have access to builds of a previous version of the application to restore the system to a working state if that is part of your disaster recovery plan. This would not increase your availability. In fact, without access to the proper bits, the process could be painful.

If there is no budget for a proper version control tool, the easiest way to start storing code is to put it in a protected, secure folder and use a simple directory structure with standardized file names to ensure uniqueness between version builds. However, you should use some form of version control software. This has some immediate advantages over directory storage, but it requires another process that needs to be managed and available. A great option for software is Visual SourceSafe. One limitation of SQL Server is that when database structures, functions, stored procedures, and so on are created or updated, they overwrite what was already there (that is, an existing object of the same type and name) without version control. You can mitigate this by maintaining the different versions of the database structures and updating scripts into a tool like Visual SourceSafe. Then give the proper script to the person executing the task to update or add the structure or stored procedure. Whatever method you use, be sure that everyone is trained in its use and committed to using it properly.

It is also useful to store related documents for application design, implementations, or server configurations in version control. Store e-mails outlining varying opinions, any design documents (whether they are used or not), and approvals from quality assurance. For example, if, in six months, someone asks you what happened to the AddressLine7 column where customer comments were stored, you will be able to get back to them with an intelligent and responsible answer. If later it becomes apparent that the design could have been better, you will have adequate documentation on any alternate designs that were suggested and the reasons (if any) that they were discarded. This can save valuable analysis time, which allows you to provide a timely answer even when you are busy with other tasks.

Testing Applications for High Availability

A great deal of testing is required before rolling out a change or update in a production environment. There are different types of testing—unit testing, regression testing, white box testing, black box testing, acceptance testing, and so on. This chapter is not going to redefine standard testing terminology. All types of tests are important. When it comes to testing for high availability, you must get beyond features and functions tested only in isolation. Three main questions must be addressed:

■ **How does the application perform in isolation with the technologies that will be deployed?**   It is crucial to document from testing for IT is how the application (by itself) behaves with respect to a specific technology (if it is not widely known). Packaged third-party applications should, in theory, be documenting this for you already.

■ **How does the application perform as part of the entire solution with respect to the failure of individual components?**   The problem really comes in when you start mixing software and technologies—how do they function together? Developers and testers can make IT's life difficult if they have no idea what to expect when they are handed the package to install and support. IT can make proper disaster recovery plans if everything is documented properly at this stage. Similarly, any findings that are discovered during the implementation process or in the support of the application or solution should flow back to development so test plans can be updated. Faulty, outdated, or unrealistic test plans should be considered unacceptable.

- ■ **What are the implementation pitfalls?**   Unfortunately, development does not always have the time to document how to properly or optimally set up an environment. This can lead to longer installation times as IT finds things out or—if something goes wrong— longer troubleshooting times. Developers and testers need to document, document, document!

Test plans with their specific test cases should take these points into account.

> **On the CD**   For a blank test plan form to fill in your test cases, use the document Blank_Test_Case.xls. See other chapters for sample test plans, based on this template, relating to technologies such as failover clustering.

Managing Change in Production

Now that you have addressed your development environment, it is time to tackle the change management process in a production environment.

Preparing for Change

Prior to rolling out a change or update in a production environment, a great deal of planning and work must be done. For any database–related change, whether to the system itself or to objects and data in the database, the database system engineer (DSE) or DBA should ensure that the changes developed will work well in the production environment. The DBA or DSE should develop or help develop, review, and test implementation scripts, rollback scripts, and testing scripts, as well as create or maintain related database documentation.

The Change Plan

Make sure that your change plan is as modular as possible. The ability to restart the entire process, stop at any point, and then continue, identifying exactly which changes have been made and which have not, is the best way to go. A good way to keep track of what you have done is to put auditing code in all of your implementation scripts, thereby recording success or failure to a database table.

Although each method of SQL code propagation serves a purpose, a script-based installation (if possible) best meets change management objectives. Scripts allow for repeated, controlled, and highly automated installations that can easily be rolled back at any state. Nonscript, graphical user interface (GUI)-based installations should cleanly uninstall if they are canceled at any point during the process, and they should be tested to ensure the system will be left in its previous state.

Contingency Plans

When making changes, even if they have been tested, always have a contingency plan ready. Never make a change without one, and raise a red flag if someone else attempts to make changes without one. Plan what to do if something goes wrong in the middle of the script sequence, or if the database scripts work but the application team encounters errors and has to remove the changes. Always plan for a minimum of two possibilities: complete removal of all changes (which could require rollback scripts, or a restore, if the application is not designed to support multiple versions running in the same database), or an alteration of your plan due to either predictable or unforeseen circumstances.

A highly available system should rarely, if ever, be altered without testing. Untested, non–standard production changes made to avert a crisis situation should be handled only by highly experienced DBAs or under the guidance of Microsoft Product Support Services (PSS).

During the planning stages, you should be thinking ahead to what could go wrong during this implementation. This risk analysis is vital to the success of your process, and might change what is implemented, or how it is done. If you can predict problems by thinking through the possibilities or recalling problems you have encountered in the past, make a chart showing these risks and what you could do to correct the problem. No matter what kind of risks you identify, even if you cannot identify any, you must have a rollback strategy for your production implementation. An experienced DBA can contribute a wealth of knowledge and guidance in this phase, even if he or she will not be doing the actual work. IT shops should not ignore DBA input for rollouts that, on the surface, might not seem to affect the database systems.

Your rollback strategy could be as simple as a script for how to undo every change you have made and restore everything to the way it was before you started. A script in this situation means a series of documented steps that you will perform to roll back your change. This will mostly consist of Transact-SQL scripts you will run. The strategy could also be much more complex, as in the case of a SQL Server service pack installation, because you cannot uninstall it; a service pack is a permanent change. Whatever the plan, it must be tested thoroughly.

Even if you have planned everything correctly, the need to roll back can still occur. You might have identified risks that could cause a catastrophic problem, or something might occur that you did not foresee. Developers or testers might even find some problem during the post implementation test that prevents them from approving the installation. When the call comes to roll it back, you will have a very short amount of time to undo all the changes.

If you have additional servers or instances involved in the implementation that are not all going to be upgraded simultaneously, you need to plan and script how these will also be changed. For example, assume you are making a major change to your database (say, you are merging several databases into one), and you want to delay implementation on your offsite standby, which is normally 24 hours behind the primary server. Once you have completed your production implementation, the offsite standby is merely serving as an easy way to restore to the point in time prior to the change. If you have a failure of the main site, however, and need to continue with the new system at the alternate site, then you have a large task to plan and immediately implement. The best practice is to think through all the possibilities and be as prepared as possible.

Implementation Team

The team deploying the change should have a good understanding of both the system in question and the change being made. The leader must have the authority to take drastic corrective action without undue delay, and he or she must know how to reach all the appropriate people in operations who can help with operational aspects that are outside his or her realm.

Determining an Implementation Window

Although minor changes to the system can be made without taking the system down, deploying a major change without incurring any outage takes planning and can involve the cooperation of more than one team. If this is a 24/7 system, your project team will have to negotiate an implementation window that is acceptable to all groups affected by the change. In a truly mission-critical system, even the shortest downtime might be unacceptable, so if your change is invasive you might need to provide another system or database for alternative access.

One option is to use a read-only database if that is the only thing needed. This clearly will not work in an e-commerce environment. In the case of a read-only database, interim support of the read-only system must also be provided, and the users and help desk personnel should be kept informed.

If, for any reason, you cannot keep the main system online during the change, you might instead have a manual switch to a standby system, especially for a read/write database. This ensures that the availability SLAs are met, but it might pose an administrative challenge in resynchronizing the data after the change is applied to the production server. If, for example, you are making extensive changes to the database schema, you cannot allow users to enter or change data on the standby system unless you have developed and tested a plan for capturing those changes and importing them into the new structure.

Planning the Implementation, Twice

You should compile an implementation plan and distribute it to everyone in the IT department who will be involved in or affected by the implementation. The plan is simply a list of the steps, who is responsible for each step, the times at which everything is expected to occur, and who to contact to initiate the next step. Be sure to include contact numbers for everyone on site or on call during that time frame.

Try to imagine likely events, and make a secondary plan that accommodates these variables. Once that is done, think of the improbable things that might occur, and accommodate those if possible. Experience with your application and infrastructure will help you gauge the level of detail required. Note any situations ("showstoppers") that would cancel the entire implementation and invoke the rollback plan.

As a group, the implementation team should create a backup plan. This is a little different than a simple rollback strategy for the database. If anyone's section fails, the group should have an overall plan for evaluating the situation, making a decision, and then proceeding with or canceling the implementation.

Testing the Implementation

No implementation should skip the testing stage. Important insights about the process come from testing, not to mention the confidence that the change plan works. A proper test environment is crucial. To make it useful, you must have a good method of load testing that simulates the conditions that will be experienced. Therefore, you should create this load test before making any changes. Run the plan against the test system and record your selected measurements so that you have something to compare to your changes during the postimplementation testing. By monitoring a system with the same counters during the performance of the original production system test script, and then monitoring the same system after a change is made, you can judge whether the changes you are examining pose a detectable threat to the production environment.

This task takes a considerable amount of analysis and can be time consuming. There are tools available on the Microsoft Developer Network (MSDN) (*http://msdn.microsoft.com*) that allow configuration of database test scripts, or you can adapt a good Profiler trace instead. You can also use a third-party tool for testing, rather than using a Transact-SQL–based process.

Release Readiness Review

The beginning of the operations group's ownership of the system begins with a release readiness review, also called a "go/no-go" meeting, which determines whether this project is ready for implementation. Although operations staff should be involved throughout the project, this is the first meeting that is run by them, rather than by the development or quality assurance teams.

The purpose of this meeting is to allow members from each team to indicate their final approval (or disapproval) and raise any issues they wish to discuss. This is the last chance to alter the implementation schedule, barring any unforeseen circumstances. Any no-go votes should be seriously considered; if no resolution can be reached by those present, the meeting should be adjourned with a no-go status until resolution is reached or the objection is overridden by senior IT staff. In any case, the objection, the reasons for it, and any risks that are brought up should be recorded for future reference.

The DBA or DSE might occasionally need to postpone or reject changes that have been requested for business or technical reasons. In either case, when this happens, the business impact of the decision (to change or not to change the system) should be evaluated and documented.

The agenda for the go/no-go meeting should include the following:

- The readiness of the release itself
- Alterations to the physical environment
- The preparedness of the operations staff and processes
- The installation plan
- The contingency plan
- Potential impacts on other systems
- Staffing and availability

Completing a Change Request Form

Once the processes for implementation have been decided on and the risks mitigated, a change request form should be filled out as described earlier in this chapter and signed by the proper people.

Implementing Change

After planning to implement a change and testing the change thoroughly in a test or staging environment, it is time to execute the well-tested plan. Be sure you have at hand the contact numbers of the on-call server room technicians, network administrators, or security administrators whose help you might need during the implementation.

Step 1: Notify Users of the Systems

All users of the system have an SLA (in some cases, an implied SLA) and must be notified in advance of the work that will occur on the system. This process should be clearly documented in the SLA to avoid confusion or omission of important groups.

Step 2: Back Up, Back Up, Back Up

The first step of any implementation must always be a backup of the current system, from the system down to the databases. Once this is complete and verified, you are ready to begin. Because the DBA group is rarely the lead on the implementation, the person leading the deployment effort should coordinate with the DBA group to either do the backups using some other method or have the DBAs themselves do the backups of the SQL Server databases. The person doing the deployment can then take the process from there.

Step 3: The Rollout

Except on the very smallest of teams, there should always be at least two DBAs on hand for an implementation. In a large implementation, you might have several DBAs involved in the deployment of the system, but you should still have a standby in the event that someone becomes ill, or in case there are related or unrelated system failures. Remember, even if another production server goes down during an implementation, every effort should be made to continue the deployment as planned; there should be processes in place to handle that failure.

Despite the best-executed plans, something truly unforeseen could occur during a production implementation. Notate your implementation script with whatever action you had to perform, documenting the difference. Do not wait until the crisis has passed to start making notes, as they could be lost or forgotten. The sequence of events and steps taken might be needed for future use, including subsequent support calls, analysis, or future implementations. Remember that meticulous accuracy is more important than anything else at this stage. Due diligence requires that even if you make a mistake, you record it. Your thoroughness now might save someone else from making the same mistake later on, and it will help the group learn as a whole.

During the deployment process, status e-mails should be sent letting the powers that be know what has and has not happened, and if the deployment plan is proceeding according to the plan, including being on schedule. There should also be a no-go point if the maintenance window cannot be achieved due to unforeseen problems. If this decision is made, the rollback plan must be put into action. Although this is rare, it can happen. The same applies for a failure: if a severe failure occurs, the rollback plan must be started. Without the rollback plan as your insurance policy, you might be faced with implementing a full disaster recovery plan, which is not a fun proposition. That could mean hours—or possibly days—of reconfiguration. For a failure or a no-go, document the reasons; these are needed for a postmortem. The problem might not be related to the database at all.

If the implementation is seemingly successful (that is, everything on the surface went smoothly), test it with the test scripts and plans used in the planning and testing phases. This is a crucial step for ensuring that the entire operation was a success. The results should be the same as those found in the testing phase. If they are not, there is a chance the change might have failed.

If the implementation is a failure—whether determined during testing or even earlier—or a success, the users who might have been inconvenienced by the downtime should be notified. If the communication is about a success, include contact information should users encounter problems.

The deployment process is not just about technical issues, but teamwork as well. Good teamwork is a vital part of the success of an implementation team, which crosses many departments in IT. It relies on the irreproachable accuracy of the information provided by team members.

Step 4: When It Is All Over

Whether the deployment process was successful or not, a few things should happen when it is complete.

- If the deployment had many sequential steps, and yours was only one, notify the next people when you are complete so that they can start their portion. Do not go home; you might still be needed.

- Send an e-mail to the implementation team and all relevant parties with a final status update, including all work done, any observations, and so on.

- If there was a failure, include the details of the failure in that e-mail.

- Once sufficient testing has been done, notify all users that the system is now ready for requests.

■ A postmortem meeting should occur, so all parties involved can learn from the process, improve the process for future production deployments (similar or not), and analyze what went wrong if there was a failure. Everything, including the project plan, the design, the arguments, the solutions, the crises, and the final outcome should be examined. Everyone involved in the process from planning to execution should be invited to the meeting. The point of this process is to learn from the events that occurred. If you have things to add, take your documentation with you to share. For the sake of the team, remember to share your positive remarks, not just the negative ones.

System and Process Standardization

Configuration and process management are subjects unto themselves. For purposes of this high availability discussion, the cornerstone of configuration management is to develop a standardized base configuration for all classes and types of servers. Although servers will need to be deployed that deviate from your standard, the standard is still useful because it sets a minimum expectation of performance, as well as a guide to where to find everything and what settings you can assume are in place. Anything that varies from the standard can then be documented with less effort. This is a simpler approach than trying to remember numerous server configurations individually. Similarly, administrative processes across groups can be derived to ensure a consistent, repeatable, and reliable experience.

Standardization can be accomplished through the establishment of technical specifications for products, working methods, and similar components to create system uniformity. Use of the standard specifications can be made mandatory for subordinate organizations. Ideally, you want to create standards for everything (although don't make that a laborious process in itself) and then simply reference the qualities of a system that diverge from the standard. This is much simpler than documenting each individual system separately.

Standardized administrative and support strategies, standardized directories, drive letters used, and hardware configuration make it possible to come closer to ideal manageability. The real advantage to having a standards-based system is that decisions can be made more reliably and more accurately based on familiar standardizations.

Documentation

Documentation has been mentioned briefly numerous times in both this chapter and in Chapter 1, but it needs to be mentioned again in its own right. Without good documentation, a data center will not be able to function smoothly. If the operator responsible for the day-to-day monitoring does not know the system configuration and its purpose, how can he or she know that there is problem if a blip occurs in Performance Monitor? Are there baseline performance benchmarks to compare against? Baselining and monitoring are discussed in Chapter 15, "Monitoring for High Availability."

The document most data centers will have is what is referred to as a *run book*. A run book is a collection of documents—from system configurations to disaster recovery plans and everything in between—that will become the primary resource for system administrators and developers alike. The run book needs to be kept up to date with any changes, and all changes should stay in the run book so anyone who comes into contact with it will understand the history. Chapter 12, "Disaster Recovery Techniques for Microsoft SQL Server," discusses run books in more detail, including how to create one.

Summary

Anything built without a solid foundation risks crumbling. Following the basic tenets of high availability is crucial for success; avoiding the common pitfalls is not easy. In fact, more basic tenets that are specific to certain scenarios and technologies are covered later in the book, and others mentioned here are expanded on as they relate to a specific technology or scenario. Concepts such as reliability, security, growth, and performance are all recurring themes throughout this book.

Proper staffing is crucial, and the company benefits most from DBAs who can act as leaders in the data center. Beyond people, a major part of a successful data center is how it is configured and managed, as well as the process of how changes flow from environment to environment. The systems, processes, and agreements put in place must be realistic and maintainable, and they must be documented. All parties involved—from executive sponsors to administrators, end users to a vendor's support engineers—must have similar expectations and know how the entire process works. Any failures or missed steps along the way could prove fatal.

These first two chapters lay the foundation for the rest of the book, which is largely technology-specific.

3

Making a High Availability Technology Choice

Now that the first two chapters have addressed at a high level the basic questions of why you need high availability and how to achieve it, it is time to delve into the world of technology. It is not enough to consider technology and high availability from a Microsoft SQL Server standpoint only—you must also consider the operating system, which is Microsoft Windows. Without Windows there is no SQL Server. This chapter helps you to make an informed decision by providing a basic understanding of the high availability technologies used throughout this book. The following technologies are discussed:

- Windows Clustering, which includes:
    - Server clusters
    - Network Load Balancing clusters
- Geographically dispersed clusters
- Microsoft SQL Server 2000, which includes:
    - Failover clustering
    - Log shipping
    - Replication
    - Backup and restore

The word *cluster* describes clustered servers, clustered indexes for databases, and more. As you can see from the preceding list, clustering is involved in many of the options discussed in this chapter. This chapter standardizes the terminology and helps you distinguish between the different types of clusters for the rest of the book.

One thing this chapter and this book will not do is to give you a decision tree and point to one right answer. Two words govern high availability solution decisions—*it depends*. High availability is not a clear-cut concept, but one that involves a lot of ambiguity.

Windows Clustering

Before addressing SQL Server high availability technologies, it is important to understand what the operating system provides, as some of the SQL Server functionality depends on its foundation—Windows.

Windows Clustering is the name that represents the umbrella of clustering technologies in the Microsoft Windows 2000 Server and Microsoft Windows Server 2003 families. Windows Clustering is a feature in the following versions of the operating system:

- Windows 2000 Advanced Server (32-bit)
- Windows 2000 Datacenter Server (32-bit)
- Windows Server 2003 Enterprise Edition (32-bit and 64-bit)
- Windows Server 2003 Datacenter Edition (32-bit and 64-bit)

Windows Clustering is comprised of two technologies: server clusters and Network Load Balancing clusters.

> **More Info**   Chapter 5, "Designing Highly Available Windows Servers," reviews in depth the planning, configuration, and administration of a highly available Windows server and how these factors relate to SQL Server high availability.

Server Clusters

A *server cluster* is Microsoft's form of clustering for the operating system that is designed for availability. It has also been referred to as Microsoft Cluster Service (MSCS) when the component itself was available as part of Microsoft Windows NT 4, Enterprise Edition. It is a collection of servers that, when configured, provide an environment for hosting highly available applications. A server cluster protects against hardware failures that could take down an individual server, operating system errors that cause system outages (for example, driver problems or conflicts), and application failures. Simply put, it protects the business functionality within certain limitations, but not necessarily the server itself.

Once a problem is detected, a cluster-aware application tries to restart the process on the current server first. (The cluster-aware application must be installed into the cluster.) If that is not possible, it automatically switches to another server in the cluster. The process of switching from one server to another in a cluster is known as a *failover*. Failovers can also happen manually, as in the case of planned maintenance on a server.

Server clustering requires a minimum of two servers; otherwise you essentially have a stand-alone system. A server cluster by itself does not really do much—applications or specific uses, such as SQL Server or file and print servers, must be configured to use the cluster to provide availability. An instance of Microsoft SQL Server 2000 installed on a node that is part of a server cluster will not failover to another node if it is not configured to use the cluster mechanics; it will act as a stand-alone SQL Server.

Important   All server cluster configurations must appear as a complete hardware solution under the cluster list on the Microsoft Hardware Compatibility List (HCL) for the operating system choice you are making. The configuration is a viewed as complete solution, not individual parts that can be put together like a jigsaw puzzle. Microsoft can support only a completely HCL-compliant cluster solution. Please consult *http://www.microsoft.com/hcl/* for more information.

The main constraint of a server cluster is the distance between redundant parts within the cluster itself. Conceptually, the limit is just a latency for synchronous operations, which is really a data consistency issue dependent on the underlying technology and its limitations (for example, in an older cluster, the limitations of Small Computer System Interface [SCSI]). During implementation, this means that any intracluster communications would be affected, because a server cluster relies on a single image view of the storage subsystem used, whether it is direct attached storage or a storage area network (SAN).

Another important aspect of any solution that has a server cluster as the basis for a back end is the compatibility of the applications that will be running on the cluster. One of the biggest misconceptions about server clusters is that because of automatic failover, they solve most availability problems. As noted in Chapter 1, "Preparing for High Availability," a solution is only as good as its weakest link. For most applications to work properly in a cluster, they should be coded to the Microsoft Clustering application programming interface (API) and become cluster-aware, allowing them to react to cluster-specific events. This means that if a problem is detected in the cluster and the process fails over to another server, the application handles the failover gracefully and has minimal or no impact on end users. More information about the Clustering API and coding cluster-aware applications appears in Chapter 5, "Designing Highly Available Windows Servers."

> **Important**   When using any prepackaged application from a vendor, such as backup software, consult the vendor to ensure that the application will run properly on your cluster.

Cluster Components

A server cluster is comprised of the following essential elements:

- **Virtual Server**   A virtual server is one of the key concepts behind a server cluster: to a client or an application, a virtual server is the combination of the network name and Internet Protocol (IP) address used for access. This network name and IP address are the same for a clustered service, no matter what node it is running on. The actual name and IP are abstracted so that end users or applications do not have to worry about what node to access. In the event of a failover, the name and IP address are moved to the new hosting node. This is one of the primary benefits of a server cluster. Two examples: When SQL Server 2000 failover clustering is installed on a cluster it acts as a virtual server, as does the base cluster.

- **Cluster Node**   A node is one of the physical servers in the cluster. With Windows Server 2003, the operating system might support more nodes than the version of SQL Server that you are using. Please review Table 3-1 and consult Chapter 6, "Microsoft SQL Server 2000 Failover Clustering," for more details.

Table 3-1   Cluster Nodes Supported Per Operating System

Operating System	Number of Nodes
Windows 2000 Advanced Server (32-bit)	2
Windows 2000 Datacenter Server (32-bit)	4
Windows Server 2003, all versions	8

- **Private Network**   The private network is also commonly referred to as "the heartbeat." It is a dedicated intracluster network that is used for the sole purpose of running processes that check to see if the cluster nodes are up and running. It detects node failure, not process failure. The checks occur at intervals known as heartbeats.

- **Public Network**   The public network is used for client or application access. The heartbeat process also occurs over the public network to detect the loss of client connectivity, and can serve as a backup for the private network.

- **Shared Cluster Disk Array**   The shared cluster disk array is a disk subsystem (either direct attached storage or a SAN) that contains a collection of disks that are directly accessible by all the nodes of the cluster. A server cluster is based on the concept of a "shared nothing" disk architecture, which means that only one node can own a given disk at any given moment. All other nodes cannot access the same disk directly. In the event that the node currently owning the disk fails, ownership of the disk transfers to another node. This configuration protects the same data stored on the disk from being written to at the same time, causing contention problems.

    Shared versus shared nothing is a topic of debate for some. A completely shared environment would require whatever clustered software is accessing the shared disk from n number of nodes to have some sort of a cluster-wide synchronization method, such as a distributed lock manager, to ensure that everything is working properly. Taking that to the SQL Server 2000 level, any given clustered instance of SQL Server has its own dedicated drive resources that cannot also be used by another SQL Server clustered instance.

- **Quorum Disk** The quorum disk is one of the disks that resides on the shared cluster disk array of the server cluster, and it serves two purposes. First, the quorum contains the master copy of the server cluster's configuration, which ensures that all nodes have the most up-to-date data. Second, it is used as a "tie-breaker" if all network communication fails between nodes. If the quorum disk fails or becomes corrupt, the server cluster shuts down and is unable to start until the quorum is recovered.

- **LooksAlive Process** LooksAlive is an application-specific health check that is different for each application. For SQL Server, this is a very lightweight check that basically says, "Are you there?"

- **IsAlive Process** The IsAlive check is another, more thorough, application-specific health check. For example, SQL Server 2000 in a cluster runs the Transact-SQL statement SELECT @@SERVERNAME to determine if the SQL Server can respond to requests. It should be noted that in the case of SQL Server, this check does not guarantee that there is not a problem in one of the databases; it just ensures that if someone wants to connect and run a query in SQL Server, they can.

> **Note** Neither IsAlive nor LooksAlive can be modified to run another query or check.

As shown in Figure 3-1, for SQL Server, the external users or applications would connect to the SQL Server virtual IP address or name. In the example, Node 1 currently owns the SQL resources, so transparent to the client request, all SQL traffic goes to Node 1. The solid line connected to the shared disk array denotes that Node 1 also owns the disk resources needed for SQL Server, and the dashed line from Node 2 to the shared disk array means that Node 2 is physically connected to the array, but has no ownership of disk resources.

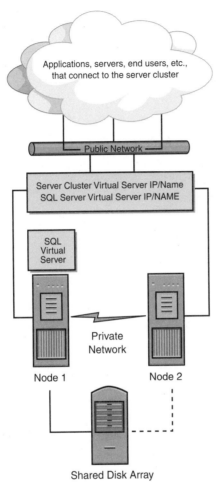

Figure 3-1   An example of a server cluster.

Cluster Concepts

Now that the basics of the cluster components have been covered from a high level, it is important to mention two important cluster concepts that are exposed when a cluster is installed and used by an administrator:

■   **Cluster Resource**   The most basic, lowest level unit of management in a server cluster. Some of the standard resource types include Dynamic Host Configuration Protocol (DHCP), File Share, Generic Application, Generic Service, IP, Network Name, Physical Disk, Print Spooler, and Windows Internet Naming Service (WINS).

- **Cluster Group**   A collection of server cluster resources that is the unit of failover. A group can only be owned by one node at any given time. A cluster group is made up of closely related resources and resembles putting a few documents about the same subject in a folder on your hard disk. For example, each SQL Server 2000 instance installed on a server cluster gets its own group.

Network Load Balancing Clusters

A Network Load Balancing cluster is a collection of individual servers configured to distribute Transmission Control Protocol/Internet Protocol (TCP/IP) and User Datagram Protocol (UDP) traffic among them according to a set of rules. Network Load Balancing creates an available, scalable solution for applications such as Internet Information Services (IIS) and Internet Security and Acceleration Server (ISA Server), but not necessarily SQL Server.

> **Important**   Unlike a server cluster, a Network Load Balancing cluster can be made up of nonspecialized complete solutions. However, the hardware must still be on the HCL.

From a SQL Server perspective, Network Load Balancing is not always the best choice to provide either scalability or availability, as it presents some challenges in the way that it operates, which differs from the transactional way in which SQL Server operates. For Network Load Balancing and SQL Server to work in, say, a load balanced and write situation, they would have to be coded to use the shared disk semantics described earlier with some sort of lock manager. Network Load Balancing, however, can be used to load balance read-only SQL Servers (such as catalog servers for a Web site), which also provides greater availability of the catalog servers in the event one of them fails. Network Load Balancing can also be used in some cases to abstract the log shipping role change and switch to another replicated SQL Server if those are used as availability technologies in your environment.

> **Important**   Administrators commonly want to combine the functionality of server clusters with Network Load Balancing to provide both availability and scalability, but that is not how the product is currently designed, as each technology has specific uses.

The following concepts are important to understanding how Network Load Balancing works:

- **Virtual Server**   Like a server cluster, a virtual server for Network Load Balancing represents the "virtualized" network name and IP address used for access. The important difference is that Network Load Balancing does not persist state in which each node knows if all the member nodes are up or not, but it does know which nodes are running. In a server cluster, every node knows about all cluster members, whether they are online or not, as state is persisted.

- **Cluster Node**   A node is one of the physical servers in the cluster, just like in a server cluster. However, each node is configured to be identical to all the other nodes in the cluster (with all of the same software and hardware) so that it does not matter which node a client is directed to. There is no concept of shared disks as there is with a server cluster. That said, for example, a Web service could be making requests to one file share, but it is not the same as the shared disk array for a server cluster. There can be up to 32 nodes in a Network Load Balancing cluster.

- **Heartbeat**   Like a server cluster, a Network Load Balancing cluster has a process for ensuring that all participating servers are up and running.

- **Convergence**   This process is used to reach consensus on what the cluster looks like. If one node joins or leaves the Network Load Balancing cluster, because all nodes in the cluster must know which servers are currently running, the convergence process occurs again. Because of this, convergence results in the high availability of services that can take advantage of Network Load Balancing because connections that were going to a now-dead node are automatically redistributed to others without manual intervention.

Figure 3-2 shows how a read-only SQL Server could be used with Network Load Balancing. The external users or applications would connect to the Network Load Balancing virtual IP address or name; however, behind the virtual IP address, things are different. Each node has its own database configuration and disk. When a client request comes in, an algorithm at each node applies the port rules and convergence results to drop or accept the request. Finally, one of the nodes services the request and sends the results back.

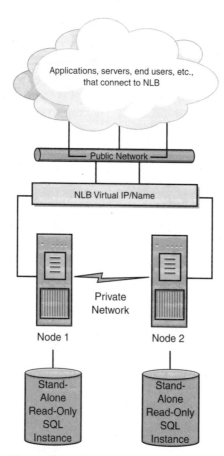

Figure 3-2   An example of a Network Load Balancing cluster.

Geographically Dispersed Clusters

A geographically dispersed cluster is no different from a standard server cluster, except that one or more nodes of the server cluster reside in another location. This type of cluster is achieved through specialized hardware, software, or a combination of both. There are still distance restrictions due to how long, say, a dark fibre network can be, but a geographically dispersed cluster removes the data center as a single point of failure. (See Chapter 4, "Disk Techniques for High Availability," for more information about a dark fibre network.) One barrier to adoption is the cost of implementation, because the network needs great bandwidth across a long distance, as well as a duplicate set of hardware, including the disk subsystem, in both locations. Technically, the secondary location does not have to completely mirror the primary location (that is, it could have fewer nodes and disks as long as it has enough processing power to handle the highest priority applications if something occurs on the primary), but the environment should mirror the production environment as closely as possible.

> **Important**   All geographically dispersed server cluster configurations must appear as a complete hardware solution under the specific geographic cluster list on the Microsoft HCL for the operating system choice you are making. The configuration is a viewed as complete solution, not individual parts that can be put together like a jigsaw puzzle. Microsoft supports only a completely HCL-compliant cluster solution. Please consult *http://www.microsoft.com/hcl/* for more information.

SQL Server 2000

Now that the technologies for the operating system have been laid out, it is time to focus on what SQL Server 2000 offers for providing availability. Each of the topics introduced in this section has its own chapter later in this book.

Failover Clustering

When you install SQL Server 2000 for use on a server cluster, this configuration is known as SQL Server 2000 failover clustering. This installation is also considered a virtual server, and is an instance of SQL Server 2000. The virtual server can either be a named instance or a default instance, but just like a stand-alone configuration, there can only be one default SQL Server 2000 instance per server cluster. A SQL Server 2000 failover cluster supports the core SQL Server functionality; Analysis Services is not cluster-aware. Chapter 10, "Designing High Availability Solutions with Microsoft SQL Server," addresses how to make Analysis Services available. To administrators and end users alike (with any exceptions noted here or in Chapter 6), a failover cluster should act, look, and feel like a stand-alone SQL Server. Each SQL Server 2000 failover cluster installation gets its own group and set of resources in the server cluster.

> **More Info**   Chapter 6 details the planning, configuration, and administration of a SQL Server 2000 failover cluster.

SQL Server 2000 Failover Clustering versus Previous SQL Server Clustering Implementations

If you are familiar with the Microsoft SQL Server 6.5 or Microsoft SQL Server 7.0 implementation of clustering, you will realize that SQL Server 2000 greatly enhances clustering functionality. In fact, with SQL Server 2000, clustering support was redesigned from the ground up. This is one of the reasons that the feature in SQL Server 2000 is called failover clustering, whereas in SQL Server 7.0, it was just called clustering.

One of the first differences with SQL Server 2000 failover clustering is the support for more than a two-node server cluster. Microsoft Windows NT 4.0 Enterprise Edition, the platform for which SQL Server 8.0 clustering was originally designed, only supported two-node clustering. SQL Server 2000 takes advantage of more nodes when they are available. With the introduction of Windows Server 2003, up to eight nodes can be supported by the operating system. As noted in Table 3-2, the 32-bit version of SQL Server is still limited to a maximum of four nodes per virtual server.

Table 3-2 SQL Server Node Support per Version

SQL Server Version	Maximum Number of Nodes
SQL Server 6.5 and 7.0	2
SQL Server 2000 (32-bit)	4
SQL Server 2000 (64-bit)	8

Instance support is the primary difference between SQL Server 2000 and earlier versions. An instance, simply put, is a separate installation of SQL Server that can run side-by-side with another SQL Server installation on the same machine. The instance can either be a default instance or a named instance. Think of a *default instance* as the way SQL Server has historically been architected. A *named instance* is just that—one that is given a name to make it distinct. SQL Server 2000 supports up to 16 instances (clustered or not), which can include 1 default and 15 named instances, or 16 named instances. Instances allow multiple SQL Server virtual servers to be installed on a cluster with ease. With SQL Server 6.5 and SQL Server 7.0 clustering, you were limited to at most two installations of SQL Server on any given server cluster.

SQL Server 6.5 and SQL Server 7.0 clustering relied on the concept of active/passive and active/active clustering. When you only have two installations of SQL Server, these concepts are easy to grasp. *Active/passive clustering* occurs when you have only two nodes, and one controls the active resources. *Active/active clustering* occurs when both nodes in the cluster have active resources (such as two SQL Servers). When instances were introduced with SQL Server 2000, these definitions proved problematic. Because the operating system and SQL Server itself can now support more than two nodes, the terms really do not fit. The new equivalent terms are *single-instance cluster* for active/passive and *multiple-instance cluster* for active/active. If you only have up to two nodes and two SQL virtual servers, active/passive and active/active might still apply, but it is better to use the new terminology. Single-instance clusters are also sometimes referred to as single active instance clusters, and multiple-instance clusters are sometimes referred to as multi-instance clusters or multiple active instance clusters.

Other enhancements with SQL Server 2000 failover clustering include the following:

■   Installing and uninstalling a SQL Server 2000 failover cluster are both now done using the SQL Server 2000 Setup program, and not through the combination of setting up your database server as a stand-alone server, then running a wizard. Clustering is part of the installation process. This also means that SQL Server 2000 failover clustering is a permanent option, and the only way to remove it is to uninstall the clustered instance of SQL Server.

■   SQL Server 2000 includes extensive support for recovering from a server node failure in the cluster, including a one-node cluster. If a node fails it can be removed, reinstalled, and rejoined to the cluster while all other nodes continue to function properly. It is then a simple operation with SQL Server 2000 Setup to add the new server back into the virtual server definition. SQL Server 6.5 and SQL Server 7.0 clustering did not have this capability, and in some cases, a severe problem could result in a complete cluster rebuild. Although, this can still happen with SQL Server 2000 in extreme cases, it can be avoided for most problems.

■   All nodes now have local copies of the SQL Server tools (including performance counters) as well as the executables, so in the event of a failover, you can administer the server from a remote system or the clustered node itself. SQL Server 6.5 and SQL Server 7.0 required that the binaries be installed on the shared cluster disk subsystem. This was a problem, because only the cluster node that performed the installation had the tools registered.

■   Each SQL Server 2000 virtual server has its own full-text resource. In previous versions of SQL Server clustering, full-text functionality was not supported. The underlying Microsoft Search service is shared among all things accessing it on the node, but if your database requires Full-Text Search it is now an option if you decide to use failover clustering.

- SQL Server 2000 failover cluster configurations can be updated by rerunning the setup program, which simplifies the configuration process.

- Database administrators can now use all of the SQL Server tools, including SQL Server Service Manager or SQL Server Enterprise Manager, to fully administer the database, including starting and stopping SQL Server. Previously some functionality, such as stopping and starting SQL Server, required using Cluster Administrator. That meant database administrators (DBAs) had to be SQL Server experts, as well as Server Cluster experts, which could cause problems if something was done in the wrong place.

- Service packs are applied directly to the SQL Server 2000 virtual server. With SQL Server 7.0, you had to uncluster the server prior to applying a service pack.

- SQL Server 2000 is now a fully cluster-aware application. This allows SQL Server 2000 to interact properly with the Cluster service, and it provides some benefits such as preventing the creation of databases on invalid logical drives.

How SQL Server Failover Clustering Works

Each node of the cluster is capable of "owning" a resource, whether it is SQL Server, a disk, and so on. The node currently owning the disk resource (whether it is a SQL Server disk, or the quorum disk), which hopefully is the designated primary owner, reserves the resource every three seconds. The point of the reservation process is to protect against physical access by another node; if a node loses the reservation, another node can now take ownership.

For example, if the node owning the instance fails due to a problem (network, disk, or something else) at second 19, the competing node detects it at the next reservation cycle. If the reservation cycle fails for the node that owned the disk resource three more times, the new node takes ownership, in this case at around second 34.

From a SQL Server perspective, the node hosting the SQL Server resource does the LooksAlive check. Remember that this does not mean that SQL Server is up and running. The IsAlive is then run, and that issues the aforementioned SELECT @@SERVERNAME. Again, this does not guarantee that the database you need can service a request, but SQL Server itself can. Should the IsAlive check fail (which means the query fails), it is retried five times. In the event all five retries fail, the SQL Server resource fails. Depending on the failover threshold configuration (discussed in Chapter 6) of the SQL Server resource, the server cluster either attempts to restart the resource on its current node or fails it over to the next preferred node that is still running (see Figure 3-3). The execution of the IsAlive tolerates a few errors, such as licensing issues or having a paused instance of SQL Server, but ultimately fails if its threshold is exceeded.

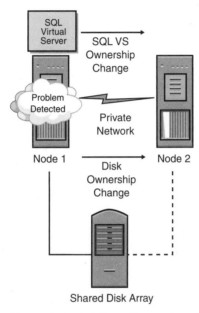

Figure 3-3   A failure detected on the node currently owning the SQL Server virtual server.

During the failover process from one node to another, the server cluster starts the SQL Server service for that instance on the new node and goes through the recovery process to start the databases. The entire switch of the SQL Server virtual server from one node to another takes a fairly short time. After the service is started and the *master* database is online, the SQL Server resource is considered to be running (see Figure 3-4). This process, on average, takes less than a minute or two. However, keep in mind the user databases will go through the normal recovery process, which means that any completed transactions in the transaction log are rolled forward, and any incomplete transactions are rolled back. The complete length of the recovery process depends on how much activity must be rolled forward or rolled back at startup, so the entire failover process takes longer than it takes to start the processes and bring up the master on the other node. This behavior is the same as a stand-alone instance of SQL Server that would be stopped and started.

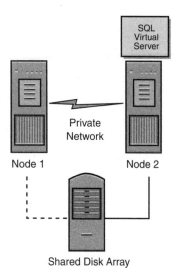

Figure 3-4 The new node after failover.

Clients and SQL Server 2000 Failover Clustering

As noted earlier, end users and applications access the SQL virtual server with either its name or IP address, not the name or IP address of the node hosting the resources. Users and applications do not need to worry about which node owns the resources. That is one of the best benefits of failover clustering—things are largely transparent to the end user. One noticeable result, depending on how the application is designed, is that during the failover process, any active connections are broken because the SQL Server is stopped and started. Therefore, whatever the user was working on when the server fails over might not be completed unless the transaction completes before the server goes down or the transaction and subsequent reconnect is handled within the application. This possibility must be taken into account in any decision to involve a cluster on the back end.

SQL Server 2000 failover clustering is always transactionally current: when the database is started on another node, it starts at the exact state it was in prior to failover. This is one of the benefits—no transactions are lost from a database, so the database is always current. Only transactions that were incomplete or issued after the failure and before SQL Server is restarted are lost, and that can be handled in the application. In fact, because the whole SQL Server instance fails over to another node, all databases and their objects (including logons, stored procedures, and so on) survive the switch intact.

Failover Clustering and Wasted Resources

This topic is dealt with in more depth in Chapter 6, but sometimes there is the notion—especially in a single-instance cluster or a multiple-node Windows Datacenter cluster with only one SQL virtual server—that unused nodes are being wasted. However, these nodes serve as an insurance policy in the event of a failure. If you start utilizing the "wasted" node for something else, what will happen in a failover? Will SQL Server have enough resources to allocate to it?

Because only one SQL Server can own a given disk resource (for more information, see Chapter 4, Chapter 5, and Chapter 6), you cannot share certain resources among clustered SQL instances. For example, if you have a drive D with 100 GB of space and need only 30 GB of it for one SQL virtual server, you cannot use any of the remaining disk space on drive D for another SQL virtual server.

Finally, because there is no load balancing with failover clustering, two SQL Servers cannot share the same underlying database because of the shared nothing mechanics of the server cluster. So you cannot, for example, use one SQL Server instance to do the reporting and another to do the inserting on the same database.

Log Shipping

Log shipping is not a new technology for SQL Server 2000; DBAs have used it for some time. *Log shipping* is the process of taking a full database backup from a specific point in time and restoring it in a special way on another server such that transaction log backups can be applied to it. Transaction logs are then made on the active server, also known as the *primary*, and then copied and applied to the waiting server. This server can be known as the *secondary* or *warm standby*. The secondary server stays in this mode until it needs to be brought online. If the switch needs to be made to the warm standby, this process is called a role change, not a failover. (Role change is described in detail in Chapter 7, "Log Shipping.")

The first released Microsoft implementation of log shipping was released in the *Microsoft BackOffice Resource Kit 4.5* (published by Microsoft Press, ISBN 0-7356-0583-1), and it was script-based. SQL Server 2000 took the log shipping functionality a step further and integrated it into the platform, but and it is available only in SQL Server 2000 Enterprise Edition and SQL Server 2000 Developer Edition (which can only be used for development purposes). Microsoft does recommend the use of the built-in functionality, as it also provides a Log Shipping Monitor to display the status of the process. Log shipping can be custom scripted for other editions of SQL Server or to accommodate other requirements, such as compression or encryption of the files being sent across the wire. Functionality like the Log Shipping Monitor would also need custom coding. Log shipping does not require any specialized hardware or solutions other than the proper version of SQL Server.

Log Shipping Transactions

Log shipping is always transactionally consistent, although there is usually some sort of latency involved. It is not considered "real time," in which each transaction is sent as soon as it occurs. With log shipping, you are only as current as:

■   The last transaction completed on the primary

■   The last transaction log backed up on the primary

■   The last transaction log copied from the primary

■   The last transaction log applied to the secondary

The log sent to the secondary is only as current as the last transaction log that is applied, so if the delta is five minutes off of the primary, your secondary should always remain five minutes behind if all is functioning properly. Analyzing these points is fairly straightforward given the previous sentence. If a transaction is completed, it is written to the transaction log. If the SQL Server experiences a failure before that transaction log is backed up, there is a chance that if the server cannot recover and read the transaction log, it will be lost, and you will only be as current as the secondary. If a transaction log is backed up but not copied over to the secondary, and either the copy process fails or the hard disk that contains that transaction log is lost, again, you are only as current on the secondary as what is available to it. If a transaction log is copied from the primary, and is still accessible to the secondary, it can be applied, so your secondary will be as current as the last transaction in the transaction log.

One benefit of log shipping is that anything that is recorded as a transaction for the database being log shipped is applied to the secondary. On the flip side, when the log shipped database is configured, only the objects found in that database exist at the secondary. Anything outside of the immediate database—logons, stored procedures used in another database, and so on—would have to be transferred using another process external to the core log shipping process.

Another use of log shipping, but not its main or intended use, is that the secondary database can potentially be used for read-only reporting-type access. The problem, however, is that to apply the transaction log, SQL Server needs exclusive access to the database, so no users can be accessing the database. If even one connection is left open, you could be putting your availability solution at risk. If the transaction logs are applied frequently, there might not be enough time between transactions to allow read-only access.

If full-text searching is required by the database that is being log shipped, you need to consider what to do in the event of a role change. Here is the crux of the issue: you cannot generate a full-text index on the secondary while the database is loading transaction logs. Even if you are backing up the full-text index and performing maintenance on it on the primary, even on the primary it will be out of sync if applied to a database that is at a later moment in time. Unless you can get to the full-text index and ensure that it is exactly at the same point as the log shipped secondary, you cannot "bolt it on" to the secondary. In that case, you will likely have to regenerate the full-text index after the database is brought online.

Clients and Log Shipping

Another consideration regarding log shipping is its affect on clients and applications. Applications do need to take various things into account, including connecting to another server, as it will have another name. Application issues relating to log shipping are detailed in Chapter 7. Because the role change is not an automatic process, you need to have a tested plan in place to perform the switch in servers. There will definitely be some sort of availability outage during the switch. Network Load Balancing might be able to help abstract the name change of the server, but it certainly does not prevent downtime. The switch time could take anywhere from seconds if all available transaction logs are applied, to much longer if they are not.

> **More Info**   Chapter 7 details the planning, configuration, and administration of log shipping.

Replication

Replication is another technology that is not new to SQL Server. Replication has been part of SQL Server since SQL Server 4.21a. There are three forms of replication, as follows:

- **Merge Replication**   Designed to allow sites to work autonomously and allow updates of data to occur in multiple places, and then have those changes rolled up to a central repository at specified intervals. Merge replication is a good choice for disconnected environments that need to update data, but is not appropriate for most availability scenarios.

- **Snapshot Replication**   Just that, a "snapshot" of where the data is at a particular moment. Because a snapshot is a complete copy of the data and there is usually quite a bit of latency between publications, it is not appropriate for availability.

- **Transactional Replication**   Allows data to be replicated to a subscriber as soon as it is modified at the publisher. Transactional replication can be bidirectional, meaning subscribers can update publishers. Because of the low latency involved with transactional replication, it is appropriate in certain cases to use for SQL Server high availability. Any further discussions in this chapter and book refer to transactional replication in the availability context.

Each form of replication shares a similar architecture. Each has a publisher, a distributor, and a subscriber. The publisher is the originator of the data or publication, which then sends it to the distributor. The distributor sends the data to be published to the appropriate subscribers. The subscriber is the "end user" of the data from a SQL Server perspective. For more information about each form of replication, consult SQL Server 2000 help files—SQL Server Books Online.

Transactional replication was not designed with availability in mind, much like using Network Load Balancing with SQL Server was not the original intention of Network Load Balancing. Replication allows the customization of articles and publications sent. So, if you need to have only a certain portion of data available, transactional replication allows you to send a smaller portion of your data elsewhere. No other SQL Server-based technology allows this customization.

Replication Issues

There are some issues to consider when using replication as your method of high availability. One of the main issues is that certain objects associated with each database or that are created do not necessarily get re-created as part of the article or publication. It is important to understand what objects replication brings over and what it does not. Another issue is that because it was not designed for transactional replication, there is really no out-of-the box solution for switching from one server to the replicated warm standby. Tasks that ensure synchronization of the proper logons, stored procedures, and so on must also now have a process devised to move them to the standby.

Transactional replication is always transactionally consistent. With replication (any form), you are only as good as the following:

- The last transaction completed on the publisher

- The last transaction or publication sent to the distributor

- The last transaction or publication applied to the subscriber

The scenarios are similar to the one detailed earlier for log shipping in terms of what the delta is between the publisher and the subscriber.

Obviously, one of the main uses of replication is that you are making data available elsewhere, whether it is reporting or another use. Therefore, you do not have to worry about accessing the secondary while it is being updated.

Full-text indexing will have to be configured against the replicated database. If you intend on possibly using the replicated database as a primary at some point, do not wait to start generating the full-text index. In addition, if only a subset of the data is replicated, and that database now needs to assume full functionality, you might not be able to use that database with the application. Different types of replication have limits on how much data is transferred in an article or publication.

Clients and Replication

Replication suffers from the same dilemmas as log shipping when it comes to clients: if a client or application expects to be connected to one server, how does it handle being changed to another server? The switch process also needs to be planned; it is not automatic. Replication does not detect the failure, other than, perhaps, showing up in the Replication Monitor as everything being out of sync. There will be downtime in the switch and the length of the downtime varies depending on the circumstances.

> **More Info**   Chapter 8, "Replication," details the planning, configuration, and administration of replication for high availability.

Backup and Restore

Backup and restore really needs no introduction. You do not have to be a DBA to understand that databases and all files related to the solution (including the operating system) need to be properly backed up, no matter what other availability methods are employed, such as failover clustering. You still need a proper backup and restore plan. The other technologies do not supplant the need to do the basics!

No matter your current situation, there is a chance that backup and restore might be the only option available. A well-planned backup and restore process can greatly increase availability. For most DBAs, this simply means that being able to restore the system quickly is a good idea in addition to whatever else you are doing to increase uptime. However, in the case of a very large database, you might need to consider a hardware-assisted solution to assist with quick restoration of the data.

It is imperative to ensure that backups are made frequently and tested to verify that the backups made are good and that you know the timings. If you have an overall availability goal as well as service level agreements (SLAs) that require certain availability requirements, you need to know if the restore will not meet the time specified in the SLA, and then possibly adjust your backup and restore strategy accordingly.

> **More Info**   Chapter 9, "Database Environment Basics for Recovery," and Chapter 10, "Implementing Backup and Restore," go into depth about the planning, configuration, and administration of the backup and restore process for high availability.

Decisions, Decisions ...

When selecting the right availability technology or technologies for your environment, trust becomes a huge issue: can your company, whether it is a small business or a global powerhouse, bet your server or solution availability, and possibly even the survival of the company, on the investment? That is a lot of pressure, but it is also one of the main reasons that this book emphasizes proper planning: the wrong decision could be costly on many levels.

The Decision Process

The decision process itself is, like achieving availability itself, deceptively simple: analyze your requirements, compare those against the technologies being evaluated, and select the technology that will provide you the best availability based on all factors. This, of course, is easier said than done.

Step 1: Analyzing Requirements

Look back at the guiding principles that came out of the questions posed in Chapter 1. Those guide the rest of the decision process, as they detail the overall availability goals for the solution. The technology should meet those goals, but there will obviously be some compromise involved. No one solution can be 100 percent perfect. The choice or choices made should meet your most important criteria. If perfection is the goal, the end implementation will never happen, and it will be costly on many fronts.

One crucial decision that comes up at this stage is the budget for the project. The amount of money you have to spend greatly affects what type of availability solution you can implement. Do not plan a solution—even down to rollout plans and support documents—only to find out you cannot afford it. As casinos tell gamblers, "Bet with your head, not over it." For example, a regional financial company provides online services 24 hours a day, including all aspects of banking (automated teller machines, bill payments, account balances, investments, and so on). Any moment of downtime could cost millions of dollars in lost transactions—an unacceptable situation on the surface. Geographically dispersed clusters seem like an ideal solution, right? They provide an automatic switch that log shipping does not, and should be transparent to end users. It also protects you from having one data center as a single point of failure.

Unfortunately, most geographically dispersed clusters, whether pure hardware or a combination of hardware and software, cost—at a bare minimum—hundreds of thousands of dollars. Realistically, the cost is probably in the millions. Add to that the cost of the network to ensure the cluster response time and overall network performance. A wide area network (WAN) of this type is very expensive to implement and requires specialized hardware as well. This combined price tag rules out even many enterprise customers. The sooner that you realize that the "ultimate" in availability might be out of your reach, the better off you will in planning a solution that will provide you with the best availability you can afford and manage. This is not to say that geographically dispersed clustering is not the solution for you—it might very well be, and it might work well. However, if you cannot afford it, it is not worth putting the company out of business and yourself out of a job just to say you achieved the ultimate in high availability.

With the cost factor out of the way, it is easier to focus on how to make the right decision for your environment—as long as you stick to the guiding principles. Other sample questions to ponder during this phase are:

- What is the skill level of the staff that will deploy, administer, and maintain the solution? Do they have any experience with the technologies being considered? Do you have the proper staff in place or do you need to hire? Is there the budget to hire more staff?

- What is the deployment time frame? Will the technology choice meet that goal?

- Do the applications using the technologies being considered work well with the technology of choice? If the technology is not compatible or does not produce the desired results, it will be a painful experience for everyone involved, making it a bad choice. Consult application vendors or developers to see what their disaster recovery scenarios include for their applications on your platform of choice.

- If you are building an application and complete solution from the ground up, do the application developers and testers have experience with the technologies, or do they need training? How long will that training take, and how will it impact the schedule?

- Can you afford to have duplicate equipment for development, testing, staging, and production environments?

- What hardware will be used? Is it new? Repurposed? Will it actually work and be a supported platform for the technology?

Step 2: Comparing Technologies

Now that you have analyzed your internal situation, it is time to evaluate the technologies. First, pick the version of Windows that meets your current and future growth needs from a memory, processor, and feature standpoint. That said, your decision might change depending on the SQL Server technologies being considered. The operating system choice is usually a fairly straightforward one, but the SQL Server choice is not. For a direct comparison of the SQL Server-based technologies, see the section "A Comparison of the SQL Server Technologies" later in this chapter. Consult other chapters in the book for more information and attend conferences, ask consultants or salespeople, ask for trial versions, and perform actual proofs of concept. Go into the actual selection process with as much knowledge as you can to make the right decision. Hopefully this book will assist in that process, but it would be naïve to think that it is the only source of information on high availability on the Microsoft platform. It is better to take your time than to make the wrong decision.

Step 3: Selecting Technology

With all of the relevant questions asked and answered, and everything thought through as much as possible, it's time to make your choice. Again, this is easier said than done, given that you have multiple technology choices available from which to decide.

A Comparison of the SQL Server Technologies

This section compares and contrasts failover clustering, log shipping, and replication. Backup and restore is woven in.

Choosing Between Log Shipping and Transactional Replication

On the surface, log shipping and transactional replication are deceptively similar. They both offer the ability to send transactions from one server to another in an automated fashion to create a warm standby. They both involve a manual switch to a secondary server, both can be used for reporting, and so on. The subtle differences ultimately become the key points.

The biggest considerations are the ones loosely described in the earlier sections about log shipping and replication:

- How many transactions are generated per hour? Will the solution be able to keep the secondary in sync quickly enough to allow low latency between the two?

- How much downtime is acceptable to the end users? Will the switch process invalidate any availability SLA you have in place?

- How much data can you realistically afford to lose in an extreme emergency? Will the solution meet your transactional requirements?

- Will the solution be too expensive from a hardware, software, or administrative standpoint?

- Do you have enough network bandwidth between the primary and secondary?

- How large are the entities (transaction log files or transactions) being sent across the wire?

- How long will it take to apply the transaction or transaction log to the secondary? Seconds? Minutes? Hours?

- What is the capacity of the secondary server? Can it handle the current production load?

- Is it a goal to eventually switch back to the original primary after a failure? If so, how will you perform this task?

The answers must be in line with your business requirements.

Transactional replication stores the transactions both at the publisher and the distributor. At the publisher, they are kept in the publication database, and if for some reason they are not published, they still exist there. If they have been replicated, they also exist in the distribution database. Should the publication or distribution databases fail, the log reader process cannot read the transactions.

Log shipping stores the transactions only in the database (and subsequently in the transaction log). Depending on what transaction log backups are available, and assuming you can still get to the transaction log on the primary server if it has been updated after the last transaction log backup, you might still be able to get the remaining transactions. This means that with log shipping, not with transactional replication, there is a higher probability of transactional recoverability.

Replication might require more server overhead than log shipping. Both log shipping and replication will have input/output (I/O) overhead, but remember that replication has replication agents doing work that consumes system resources. If you are sending over every transaction in a highly utilized online transaction processing (OLTP) database, this cannot be discounted. Log shipping has overhead, but because it is run less frequently, the overhead might be less. Log shipping and replication both use SQL Server msdb database, but neither really uses it more than the other.

Latency between the primary server and the secondary server is also a concern. Although transactional replication might have a lower latency, it also requires a synchronized backup strategy, which log shipping does not. See the topic "Strategies for Backing Up and Restoring Transactional Replication" in SQL Server Books Online for more information. When the replication option Sync With Backup is set on both the publisher and distributor to ensure that both can be restored to the same point, you will get roughly the same latency as log shipping.

For transactional replication, it is paramount that the distribution database is available, so making that SQL Server available impacts the end solution. If you are using the built-in version of log shipping found in SQL Server 2000 Enterprise Edition, the monitor needs to be made available to report status. Not having all pieces available could affect the solution. The backup and restore situation with replication comes into sharper focus if for some reason you need to restore replication for disaster recovery, because if Sync With Backup is not set, replication has to be started from scratch, which could be troublesome.

With transactional replication, there might be an issue if the publisher, distributor, and subscriber are out of sync in terms of the SQL Server version. Generally, a distributor must be of a version equal to or greater than its publishers and a publisher must be of a version equal to or greater than the subscribers. There are sometimes exceptions to the rule in terms of subscribers. Log shipping should function no matter what version of SQL Server 2000 is installed, but all SQL Servers should be at the same level to ensure compatibility and similar behavior after the role change.

Because the distribution database contains the transactions that will be sent to the warm standby, a failure of the distribution database will impact transactional recoverability if the transactions are lost, as well as ability to recover the standby after a failure. You should weigh which one is more important to your business, as log shipping will give you better transactional recoverability. In a catastrophic failure, both log shipping and replication would need to be set up again.

If using the standby as a reporting server is crucial to your business and if you are choosing only one technology, replication might be the better option. Log shipping and its requirement to have exclusive database access, combined with frequent transaction log loads, makes it less than ideal for read-only access to that particular database. However, you also have the ability to stack transaction logs and apply them later. Obviously, this puts your log shipped secondary more out of sync with higher latency, but it can be used for reporting. If disaster recovery is more important than read-only databases, log shipping definitely has the edge in this category.

The process of bringing either the replicated database or log shipped database online must be considered. Technically, the replicated database is online, but does it have all the elements to assume the production role? Does the log shipped database have all the transaction logs applied? How long does the entire process take? Is it tested? How will you notify the end users? The complexity will vary a little, but historically, it is much more defined from an availability standpoint for log shipping. Transactional replication and its lower latency might mean that a replicated standby is closer to the source for disaster recovery purposes, but the lack of processing would make log shipping a much more attractive option. You still need to weigh what is more important to your business.

Does introducing log shipping or transactional replication add more complexity because there are "moving parts" and dependencies? Be certain your availability solution cannot end up becoming a barrier to availability! Remember the maintenance of these added points of failure, too. All servers need to be well maintained. Managing and monitoring log shipping is generally easier than it is for replication.

Choosing Between Failover Clustering and Log Shipping or Replication

If you base your decision purely on the choice between automatic or manual switching to a standby server, SQL Server 2000 failover clustering wins hands down. The problems for most people considering it are the aforementioned "wasting of resources" and the interruption in service that results from the automatic switch. These two factors, coupled with the fact that the hardware is a more specialized solution (even down to driver levels), might scare some away, but they should not. In reality, although SQL Server 2000 failover clustering is a little more complex in some ways than a log shipping or replication solution, in other ways it is not. Failover clustering has "moving parts," but you do not need to worry about things like Log Shipping Monitors or making sure that the distributor is up and running to keep the process going. As long as the underlying server cluster is properly configured, there should be no issues with the failover cluster built on top of it.

Now, log shipping or replication might be considered by some "poor man's clustering" if Network Load Balancing is thrown in the mix to abstract the role change so that the back-end SQL Servers appear to act as one. In reality, however, it is not a server cluster or a failover cluster, so if you really do need the functionality provided by failover clustering, please consider it.

Using the SQL Server Availability Technology Comparison Table

Here is a guide to the terminology used in Table 3-3:

- **Standby type**   How Microsoft classifies the solution. The ratings are hot, warm, and cold. Hot represents a solution that provides excellent uptime given all of its features and considerations. Warm provides good availability. Cold is not the best, but it can be achieved. For example, backup and restore would be considered cold.

- **Failure detection**   Processes invoked by the technology can detect a failure and react to it.

- **Automatic switch to standby**   No manual intervention is required to switch to the standby.

- **Masks disk failure**   Does not mean that it completely masks a failure to a local or shared disk subsystem. It means that in the switching process, you will not encounter the same disk failure and can still recover on the standby.

- **Masks SQL process failure**   If something goes wrong in the process, the technology can handle the problem.

- **Metadata support**   The level of data definition language (DDL) support offered by the technology.

- **Transactionally consistent**   The standby server is transactionally consistent.

- **Transactionally current**   The standby server is at exactly the same point as the primary server.

- **Perceived downtime**   The time that an interruption in service might occur.

- **Client transparency**   The client will notice a problem.

- **Hardware requirements**   The technology requires specialized hardware.

- **Distance limitations**   The technology is constrained by distance.

- **Complexity**   The technology is significantly more complex than implementing a normal SQL Server-based solution.

- **Standby accessible for read-only access**   The standby server is available for reporting or other read-only functionality.

- **Performance impact**   The technology impacts overall server performance.

- **Impact to backup strategy**   A backup and restore plan needs to take into account additional complexities due to the technology.

- **Full-text support**   The technology supports Full-Text Search in a disaster recovery scenario.

Table 3-3   SQL Server Availability Technology Comparison Table

Availability Feature	Failover Clustering	Log Shipping	Transactional Replication
Standby type	Hot	Warm	Warm
Failure detection	Yes	No	No
Automatic switch to standby	Yes	No, but Network Load Balancing might help	No, but Network Load Balancing might help
Masks disk failure	No, shared disk can possibly be a single point of failure	Yes	Yes
Masks SQL process failures	Yes	Yes	Yes
Masks other process failures	Yes	No	No
Metadata support	Yes, the entire server is failed over	Yes, but only all metadata in the log shipped database; anything outside the database, no	Only selected objects
Transactionally consistent	Yes	Yes	Yes (transactional only)
Transactionally current	Yes, database in a failover is always at the point it is at the time of failure	No, only as current as the last transaction log applied	No, only as good as the last transaction applied

(continued)

Table 3-3 SQL Server Availability Technology Comparison Table

Availability Feature	Failover Clustering	Log Shipping	Transactional Replication
Perceived downtime	Usually under two minutes, plus database recovery	Time to switch servers plus any transaction logs that need to be applied	Time to switch servers
Client transparency	Yes, if referring to the server name or IP address; application must still reconnect or be made cluster aware, so there might be minimal impact	No	No
Hardware requirements	Specialized solutions	No	No
Distance limitations	Normal networking limitations	None	None (limited to network bandwidth, though)
Complexity	Potentially more	Some	More
Standby accessible for read-only access	No, only one copy of the data	Possibly, depending on transaction log load times	Yes
Performance impact	Minimal to none	Minimal: I/O and overhead of log shipping jobs	Minimal: I/O and overhead of replication agents
Impact to backup strategy	Minimal	Minimal to none, depending on if transaction logs are already backed up	Yes, because in a disaster recovery scenario, the publisher and distributor would need to be in sync
Full-text support	Yes, full-text functions normally after failover	No, full-text indexes would need to be rebuilt after database is brought online or if the database from the primary was left at the same point the secondary was brought online, you might be able to attach the indexes	Yes, but need to configure an index to be built on the standby as the transactions are inserted

What Should You Use?

The general rule of thumb is that failover clustering provides the highest availability. That statement has merit from a technology standpoint—whether or not a geographically dispersed cluster is involved—because you get an automatic process that switches resources from one computer to another without human intervention.

If you cannot afford SQL Server 2000 Enterprise Edition and the versions of Windows that support clustering, failover clustering is obviously not an option. It might be right for your situation, but if you cannot afford the solution, you need to think about alternatives.

Log shipping is a great primary or secondary solution, and it compliments failover clustering well. It is a trusted, time-tested method that is geared toward making a standby server. The issue winds up becoming the delta of time between the primary server and the secondary server. Because log shipping is not an ideal reporting solution, but a good availability solution, if reporting is needed, you could combine replication with log shipping to provide that functionality. Transactional replication might work for some, but in terms of availability, it should be considered after failover clustering or log shipping.

Again, no matter what, remember your backup and restore strategy. In a complete disaster recovery scenario, your backups might be the only remaining option.

This section outlines some basic guidelines. They will help, although ultimately additional considerations based on the technical details of each technology will help you decide which choice is the best fit for your particular environment.

Summary

Making technology decisions for high availability is not easy. Remember these two words and apply them to your environment: *it depends*. What works for one company or one solution might not be appropriate for another; there are no absolutes. Consider what each technology brings to the table in terms of strengths and weaknesses, and then match those against your needs—cost, application, administration, and so on. If possible, as an insurance policy, choose more than one method of high availability. For a complete example of designing a solution that includes cost, hardware, and technology choices, see Chapter 10.

Part II

Technology Building Blocks

4

Disk Configuration for High Availability

Disks are the heart and soul of a database system—they physically store the data accessed by the database server. From both performance and high availability standpoints, ensuring a proper disk configuration is one of, if not *the* most, important aspect of planning and configuration when it comes to the system that will run Microsoft SQL Server 2000. Even though the decisions of how many processors and how much memory you need are important, you will probably get the most from your SQL Server investment by planning and implementing the best disk subsystem for your needs.

Whenever you design a system for availability, growth, and performance, as noted in Chapter 1, "Preparing for High Availability," there is some form of trade-off involved. This chapter guides you step by step through the decision-making, planning, and implementation of disk subsystems used with SQL Server.

Quick Disk Terminology Check

This section defines a few terms that are used throughout the rest of the chapter.

- **Spindle** The physical disk itself. The term is derived from the shape of the disk inside the enclosure, which is a round platter with a head, somewhat resembling a spindle.

- **Logical Unit, LUN** This will be hardware and software vendor–dependent, but each of these terms has the same meaning—it is one physical disk or a group of disks that appear as one unit to the operating system at a physical level.

> **Important** If you want to configure more than eight LUNs, you must involve the hardware vendor in the planning and configuration. Microsoft Windows server products support up to eight buses per adapter, 128 target IDs per bus, and 254 LUNs per target ID. Adding support for more LUNs involves modifying the registry. See Chapter 5, "Designing Highly Available Microsoft Windows Servers," for more information. Also keep in mind that your registry cannot grow infinitely large.

- **Logical Disk** A logical disk is part, or all, of a volume carved out and formatted for use with Windows, and is usually represented by a drive letter. Some storage vendors use the word *containers*, which can contain multiple logical volumes that represent one logical disk to Windows. In storage vendor language, this might be referred to as a LUN, which is not how LUN is defined here.

> **Tip** Work with your hardware or storage vendor to ensure that you are both speaking the same language when it comes to your storage solution.

Capacity Planning

Numerous factors go into deciding how your disks will be configured. The first part of that decision process must be capacity planning, the art of determining exactly how much space you need. For new systems, this can range from very simple to very complex, depending on how much information you have up front. For extending existing systems, upgrading, or migrating to a new hardware or software platform, capacity planning should be easier because there should be documented history on the prior growth of that system, database, and application.

Two kinds of disk space usage must be known: raw space, and the physical number of disk drives needed for storage and to achieve the desired level of performance. Remember that figuring out how much raw space, which will then dictate how many drives you need, is based on your application's requirements of how it will be using SQL Server. The information and equations are based on these basic tenets of disk capacity planning.

> **Note**   The disk space presented by the disk controller at the LUN level and the disk space that is available to the application are not the same. All capacity planning must be based on the *actual usable* capacity as seen by Windows at the file system level, not what the storage controller thinks is being presented.

> **Important**   Remember that any physical implementation is vendor-specific because each storage vendor might use similar—but different—architectures and structures.

Raw Disk Space Needed

Conceptually, the amount of raw disk space is represented by the following equation:

Minimum Disk Space Needed = Size of Data (per database, including system databases) + Size of All Indexes (per database, including system databases)

There is a flaw in this equation, however. Calculating your disk space based on the minimum amount needed would be a mistake. You need to take into account the growth of the database over the time that the system will be in service. That would transform the equation into this:

Minimum Disk Space Needed = Size of Data (per database, including system databases) + Size of All Indexes (per database, including system databases, full-text indexes, and so on) + Planned Growth + Microsoft Distributed Transaction Coordinator (MS DTC) Logging Space + Amount of Operating Reserve + Amount Reserved for Hardware Optimization

The revised equation is much more realistic. The amount of operating reserve is the total drive space needed to handle an emergency situation.

For example, if you need to add a new column to a table, you need enough transaction log space for the entire table (possibly two times the table) because all changes are logged row by row and the table is affected in its entirety within one transaction. The amount reserved for hardware optimization is based on the disk drive performance of the inner tracks of the physical drive, which might be slower than the outer tracks (see the section "Understanding Your Hardware" later in this chapter for information on media banding and physical drive characteristics).

In this case, the amount can range from 10 to 40 percent depending on whom you ask, but the performance characteristics might be different on more modern disk drives (up to 25 percent faster on the outer tracks than the inner tracks). You can combine this reserve space with the operating system reserve in most cases. With MS DTC usage, if you have high transactional volume, the logging of MS DTC might become a bottleneck.

> **Note**   How do you actually determine the size of each database? You need to know how the applications will be using the databases—not only the user databases created specifically for the application, but system databases msdb and tempdb as well.

Application Database Usage

Each application using SQL Server has its own signature that is its distinct usage of SQL Server. Assess each application that will be utilizing one or more databases. What kind of work is it doing? Is it mainly reads? Mainly writes? A mixture? Only reads? Only writes? If the workload is a combination of reads and writes, what is the ratio of reads to writes? (Some hardware solutions can assist you in this matter to report on real read versus write statistics, as well as storage caching statistics.) If this is an existing database system, how has the usage changed over time? If this is a new system, what is the projected usage of the system? Do you anticipate changes in usage patterns? You might need to ask more questions. For a packaged application that you are not developing, ensure that your vendor can reasonably answer the questions so you can plan your hardware appropriately. If possible, get the input of other customers who have used that software as well.

For example, an accounting package might have heavy inserts, for 70 percent on average, and 30 percent reads. Because the software is doing some aggregations at the SQL Server level and bringing back intermediate result sets, it also uses tempdb heavily. The company that manufactures the accounting package recommends a minimum of 60 GB as a starting size for the database, but you can best determine how the software would be used in your environment.

These questions are vital to starting the disk configuration process because, like the guiding principles that will carry through the entire high availability process, how the database is to be used directly influences every decision made about disk configuration.

Application Schema

Knowing the schema and how data is used also helps you determine the capacity needed. Important things to track are whether it is a custom in-house application or a third-party application; usage of data that is inserted, updated, and deleted; the most frequently used tables (for reads and writes); and how much these tables grow. A database administrator (DBA) or someone else, if appropriate, should track these items on a regular basis. Tracking these items over time for new and existing systems not only provides an accurate picture of your database usage, but also helps in areas such as performance tuning (figuring out what indexes to use, avoiding hotspotting at a physical level when designing a disk subsystem). If you have been using a database for years and now need to migrate it to a new version of the database software (for example, from Microsoft SQL Server 7.0 to Microsoft SQL Server 2000), you can accurately know how to configure your disk subsystem and SQL Server file sizes only if you know the answers to the above questions.

One consideration when thinking about schemas is the use or nonuse of Unicode. Unicode data is stored as nchar, nvarchar, and ntext data types in SQL Server as opposed to char, varchar and textr. This means that Unicode data types take up twice as much storage as non-Unicode data types, effectively halving how data is actually stored at a physical level (or doubling your space requirement, depending on how you look at it). This must be taken into account when calculating how much each row will total in terms of bytes—if a row that is non-Unicode is 8000 bytes, for a Unicode row it will be 16,000 bytes.

Another consideration is fixed-length versus variable-length text columns. To be able to predict row length, and ultimately table growth over time, you should use fixed-length fields such as a char instead of a varchar. A varchar also consumes more disk space. If you are writing an application that must support international customers in different languages, you need to account for the space required for each language. Therefore, if you are writing an application that must store information in English, French, Spanish, Dutch, Japanese, and German, you need to account for up to six different versions of each column. As with many other things related to system and application designs, there are trade-offs when it comes to schema design.

For example, you have an application that accesses a table named CustomerInfo. Table 4-1 shows the table structure.

Table 4-1 **CustomerInfo Table**

Column Name	Type/Length	Column Size (in Bytes)
Customer_id	Int	8
Customer_lname	char(50)	50
Customer_fname	char(50)	50
Cust_addr1	char(75)	75
Cust_addr2	char(75)	75
Cust_city	char(30)	30
Cust_state	Int	8
Cust_province	char(40)	40
Cust_postalcode	char(15)	15
Cust_country	Int	8
Total		359

According to Table 4-1, each row inserted into the CustomerInfo table consumes 359 bytes. Assume that this is an e-commerce application, and the database is expected to grow to 500,000 customers in two years. That equates to 179,500 kilobytes, or just fewer than 180 MB for this table alone. Each entry might also include updates to child tables (such as customer profiles or customer orders). With each insert, you need to take into account all parts of the transaction. If your table has 10, 20, 50, 100, or 500 tables in it, suddenly 180 MB is only a small part of the puzzle. If you have not gathered already, things get complex very quickly when it comes to disk architecture.

> **Important** Remember to take into account columns that might also be able to contain a value of NULL, such as VARCHAR. Most column types require the same space at a physical level even if you use NULL and technically do not store data. This means that if you do not count the nullable column into your row size calculations in determining how many rows fit per page, you might cause page splits when actual data is inserted into the row.

Indexes

Indexes are integral to a schema and help queries return data faster. Take performance out of the equation for a moment: each index takes up physical space. The total sum of all indexes on a table might actually exceed or equal the size of the data. In many cases, it is smaller than the total amount of data in the table.

There are two types of indexes: clustered and nonclustered. A clustered index is one in which all the data pages are written in order, according to the values in the indexed columns. You are allowed one clustered index per table. Clustered indexes are great, but over time, due to inserts, updates, and deletions, they can become fragmented and negatively impact performance.

Indexes can help or hurt performance. UPDATE statements with corresponding WHERE clauses and the right index can speed things up immensely. However, if you are doing an update with no WHERE clause and you have several indexes, each index containing the column being updated needs to be updated.

In a similar vein, if you are inserting a row into a table, each index that contains the row has to be updated, in addition to the data actually being inserted into the table. That is a lot of disk input/output (I/O). Then there is the issue of inserting bulk data and indexes—indexes hinder any kind of bulk operation. Think about it logically—when you do one insert, you are not only updating the data page, but all indexes. Multiply that by the number of rows you are inserting, and that is a heavy I/O impact no matter how fast or optimized your disk subsystem is at the hardware level. For performing bulk inserts, indexes should be dropped and re-created after the inserting of the data in most cases.

Queries might or might not need an index. For example, if you have a lookup table with two columns, one an integer, and one a fixed length of five characters, putting indexes on the table, which might only have 100 rows, could be overkill. Not only would it take up more physical space than is necessary, but also a table scan on such a small amount of data and rows is perfectly acceptable in most cases.

> **More Info**   You also need to consider the effect of automatic statistics and their impact on indexes. See the sections "Index Statistics" and "Index Cost" in Chapter 15 of *Inside Microsoft SQL Server 2000* by Kalen Delaney (Microsoft Press, 2000, 0-7356-0998-5) for more information. SQL Server Books Online (part of SQL Server documentation) also explores indexes in much more detail than what is offered here.

Deletes, Inserts, Selects, and Updates

The code you write to delete, insert, select, and update your data is the last part of the application troika, as it contains the instructions that tell SQL Server what to do with the data. Each delete, insert, and update is a transaction. Optimizing to reduce disk I/O is not an easy task because what is written is directly related to how well designed the schema is and the indexing scheme used. The key is to return or update only the data that you need, keeping the resulting transaction as atomic as possible. Atomic transactions and queries are ones that are kept extremely short. (It is possible to write a poor transaction that is seemingly atomic, so do not be misled.) Atomicity has an impact on disk I/O, and in terms of technologies like log shipping and transactional replication, the smaller the transaction that SQL Server has to handle, the better off you are in terms of availability.

For example, a Web-based customer relationship management (CRM) program used by your sales force allows you to access your company's entire customer list and page through the entries one by one. The screen only displays 25, and at a maximum, displays up to 200. Assume the schema listed earlier for the CustomerInfo table is used. The application developer implements this functionality by issuing a SELECT * FROM CustomerInfo query with no WHERE clause; as you might have deduced, the combination of a SELECT * that pulls back all columns and no WHERE clause to narrow the result set is not recommended. The application then takes the results and displays only the top 200 customers. Here is the problem with this query: when you reach 500,000 customers, every time this functionality is called, it returns 180 MB of data to the client. If you have 500 salespeople, 100 of whom are always accessing the system at one time, that is 18,000 MB or 18 GB of data that can potentially be queried at the same time. Not only will you be thrashing your disks, but network performance will also suffer. A better optimization would be to issue the same query with a TOP 200 added so that you are only returning the maximum result set handled by the application. Another way to handle the situation is to make the *rowcount* a parameter allowing each user to customize how many rows he or she would like returned, but that would not guarantee predictability in the application.

To make matters worse, if the user wanted to do different sorts, the application developer would not utilize the 180 MB result set that was already queried: he or she issues another SELECT * FROM CustomerInfo query, this time with a sorting clause (such as ORDER BY Customer_lname ASC). Each round trip, you are thrashing disks and consuming network bandwidth when you want to do a sort! If there were any sort of action associated with the rows returned, you would now have multiple users going through the list in different directions, potentially causing deadlocks and compounding the problem. Unless the data that will be pulled back changes, the application should be able to handle the sort of the data for display without another round trip. If you need to pull back different data, using a WHERE clause combined with the aforementioned TOP also helps disk I/O, especially if you have the proper indexing scheme, as you can go directly to the data you are looking for.

Transact-SQL statements that use the locking hints in SQL Server, such as HOLDLOCK, NOLOCK, and so on can either help or hinder SQL Server performance and availability. You should not use locking hints because the query processor of SQL Server in most cases chooses the right locking scheme behind the scenes as its default behavior. For example, a user of the same CRM application updates a row into the CustomerInfo table. The developer, with the best of intentions, wants to ensure that no one else can update the record at the same time, so naively he or she adds the XLOCK hint to the UPDATE statement. Adding XLOCK forces the transaction to have an exclusive lock on the Customer-Info table. This means that no other SELECT, INSERT, UPDATE, or DELETE statements can access the table, backing up requests for SQL Server, backing up disk resources, and causing a perceived unavailability problem in the application because the users cannot do their work. Thus one seemingly small decision can affect not only many people, but also various resources on the server.

> **More Info**   For more information on locks, see Chapters 14 and 15 of *Inside Microsoft SQL Server 2000*, by Kalen Delaney (Microsoft Press, 2000, 0-7356-0998-5).

Understanding Physical Disk Performance

If you are using a database now, or are testing one that is going into production, you need to capture statistics about what is going on at the physical and logical layers from a performance perspective under no load, light load, medium load, and heavy load scenarios. You might be set with raw disk capacity in terms of storage space, but do you already have a performance bottleneck that might only get worse on a new system configured in the same way?

For Microsoft Windows 2000 Server and Microsoft Windows Server 2003, disk performance counters are permanently enabled. If, for some reason, they are not currently configured in Performance Monitor (they should appear as the LogicalDisk and PhysicalDisk categories), execute DISKPERF –Y to enable the disk performance counters at the next system restart. Obviously, this causes a potential availability problem if a restart is required immediately. For more information about the different options with DISKPERF, execute DISKPERF /? at a command prompt. Having the disk performance counters turned on adds approximately 10 percent of overhead to your system.

Once the disk performance counters are enabled, you can begin capturing information to profile your disk usage. There are two types of disk statistics to consider:

- **Logical**   A logical disk performance counter relates to what the operating system and application uses, which is usually represented by a drive letter, such as D.

■   **Physical**   A physical disk performance counter relates to what is going on at the hardware layer.

The most important statistics are the physical counters, although the logical ones could help in some environments. It really depends on how your disk subsystem is configured and what is using each physical and logical disk. More on logical and physical disks is covered in the section "Pre-Windows Disk Configuration" later in this chapter.

The performance counters described in Table 4-2 should provide you with a wealth of information about your disk subsystem.

Table 4-2 Performance Counters

Category	Counter	Purpose	How to Interpret
Physical Disk	% Disk Time— track for each physical disk used	Percentage of the elapsed time that the selected physical disk drive has spent servicing read and write requests.	This number should be less than 100 percent. However, if you are seeing sustained high utilization of the physical disk, it might either be close to being overutilized, or should be tracked according to its mean time between failures (MTBF). For further follow-up or information, % Disk Read Time and % Disk Write Time can be tracked.
Physical Disk	Avg. Disk Queue Length— track for each physical disk used	The average number of requests (both reads and writes) that were waiting for access to the disk during the sample interval.	Realistically, you want the number to be 0. However, 1 is acceptable, 2 could indicate a problem, and above 2 is definitely a problem. However, keep in mind that this is relative—there might not be a problem if the queuing is not sustained, but was captured in one interval (say, one reading of 3), or if it is sustained. Remember that the number should not be divided by the number of spindles that make up a LUN. Queuing relates to the single worker thread handling the physical volume and therefore still represents a bottleneck. Follow-up or additional information can be captured with Avg. Disk Read Queue Length, Avg. Disk Write Queue Length, and Current Disk Queue Length for more isolation.

Table 4-2 Performance Counters   *(continued)*

Category	Counter	Purpose	How to Interpret
Physical Disk	Avg. Disk sec/ Read	The average time (in seconds) it takes a read of data to occur from the disk.	This can be used to help detect latency problems on disk arrays, especially when combined with the total number of updates and the aggregate number of indexes.
Physical Disk	Avg. Disk sec/ Write	The average time (in seconds) it takes a write of data to occur from the disk.	This can be used to help detect latency problems on disk arrays, especially when combined with the total number of updates and the aggregate number of indexes.
Physical Disk	Disk Bytes/sec —track for each physical disk used	The total amount of data (in bytes) at a sample point that both reads and writes are transferred to and from the disk.	This number should fit the throughput that you need. See "Pre-Windows Disk Configuration" for more details. For more information or follow-up, Disk Read Bytes/sec and Disk Write Bytes/sec can further isolate performance. The average, and not actual value, can also be tracked in addition to or instead of this counter (Avg. Disk Bytes/Read, Avg. Disk Bytes/ Transfer, Avg. Disk Bytes/Write).
Physical Disk	Disk Transfers/ sec—track for each physical disk used	The sum of all read and write operations to the physical disk.	For more information or follow-up, Disk Reads/sec and Disk Writes/sec further isolate performance.
Physical Disk	Avg. Disk sec/ Transfer	The time (in seconds) on average it takes to service a read or write to the disk.	Sustained numbers mean that the disks might not be optimally configured. For follow-up or more isolation, use Avg. Disk sec/Read and Avg. Disk sec/Write.
Physical Disk	Split IO/sec	The rate (in seconds) at which I/Os were split due to a large request or something of that nature.	This might indicate that the physical disk is fragmented and is currently not optimized.

(continued)

Table 4-2 Performance Counters   *(continued)*

Category	Counter	Purpose	How to Interpret
LogicalDisk	% Free Space— track for each logical disk used	The amount of free space available for use.	This should be an acceptable number for your organization. Note that with NTFS, there is something called the master file table (MFT). There is at least one entry in the MFT for each file on an NTFS volume, including the MFT itself. Utilities that defragment NTFS volumes generally cannot handle MFT entries, and because MFT fragmentation can affect performance, NTFS reserves space for MFT to keep it as contiguous as possible. With Windows 2000 and Windows Server 2003, use Disk Defragmenter to analyze the NTFS drive and view the report that details MFT usage. Remember to take MFT into your free space account. Also keep in mind that database disks rarely get extremely fragmented because file creation does not happen as often (unless you are expanding frequently or using the SQL disks for other purposes).
	Logical Disk Free Megabytes	The amount of free space on the logical drive, measured in megabytes.	As with % Free Space, this should be at an acceptable level.

Some of the counters in Table 4-2, such as Avg. Disk sec/Transfer, have equivalents in the LogicalDisk category. It is a good idea to further isolate and gather performance statistics to track numbers for each logical disk used by SQL Server to help explain some of the numbers that occur on the PhysicalDisk counters.

Using SQL Server to Assist with Disk Capacity Planning

SQL Server can also help you understand what is happening with your disk usage. SQL Server has a function named fn_virtualfilestats that provides I/O information about all of the files (data, log, index) that make up an individual database. fn_virtualfilestats requires the number of the database you are looking for statistics about, which can be gathered by the following query:

```
SELECT * FROM master..sysdatabases
```

Or you could use the following:

```
sp_helpdb
```

To see the actual names of the files used in your database, execute the following query:

```
SELECT * FROM databasename..sysfiles
```

Finally, to get the statistics for all files for a specified database, execute a query using fn_virtualfilestats. It takes two parameters: the database ID, which is the first number, and the file number. If you want to return all files, use -1 for the second parameter. This example retrieves the results for all files used with pubs, as shown in Figure 4-1.

	DbId	FileId	TimeStamp	NumberReads	NumberWrites	BytesRead	BytesWritten	IoStallMS
1	5	1	12053732	12	1	98304	8192	830
2	5	2	12053732	7	3	151552	91648	541

`select * from ::fn_virtualfilestats(5,-1)`

Figure 4-1   The results of a query designed to show the I/O statistics for all files comprising the pubs database.

If you take the data returned from the IOStallMS column and divide by the sum of NumberReads and NumberWrites (IOStallMS/[NumberReads+NumberWrites]), the result determines if you have a log bottleneck.

Types of Disk Subsystems

There are three main types of disk subsystems you need to understand when putting together a SQL Server solution: Direct-Attached Storage (DAS), Network-Attached Storage, and storage area networks (SANs).

Direct-Attached Storage

Direct-Attached Storage (DAS) is the traditional SCSI bus architecture. There are quite a few variations of SCSI, and describing them all is beyond the scope of this chapter. With DAS, you have a disk or set of disks dedicated to one host, or in the case of a failover cluster, potentially available to the nodes. SCSI has some inherent cabling issues, such as distance limitations, and adding a new disk with DAS can cause an availability outage. One of the biggest problems with DAS is that when it is used with a server cluster, you have to turn all caching off, so you take a potential performance hit because the redundant array of independent disks (RAID) controllers are located in each node. However, this can vary with each individual hardware implementation. If the node's SQL Server resources fail to the other node and there are uncommitted transactions in the cache of the local controller, assuming that node is not cycled and you fail the resources back at some point, you then potentially corrupt your data when the original node sees the disks again and flushes its cache.

Keep in mind that if the material in the cache is not something that needs to be written to the log (such as an insert, update, or delete), it might not matter. SQL Server automatically rolls back any unfinished transactions in a failover.

Network-Attached Storage

Network-Attached Storage devices are fairly new to the storage arena. These devices are function-focused file servers that enable administrators to deploy and manage a large amount of disk storage in a single device. Network-Attached Storage behaves like any other kind of server—it integrates into a standard IP-based network to communicate with other clients and servers. Some storage vendors present Network-Attached Storage as a DAS device. Network-Attached Storage is usually used for file-based storage, but it can be used with SQL Server if it meets all of your performance, availability, and other goals. Besides generic Network-Attached Storage devices, there are also Windows-powered Network-Attached Storage devices based on Windows 2000 that are optimized and preconfigured for file storage. Before purchasing a Network-Attached Storage–based SQL Server storage solution, consider the following:

- If you do not use a Windows Hardware Quality Labs (WHQL) certified Network-Attached Storage, it might not meet the I/O guarantees for a transactional database, although it might work with your SQL Server solution. Should there be data corruption due to use of a non-WHQL certified Network-Attached Storage, Microsoft will not support the data-related issues and instead will refer you to the Network-Attached Storage vendor for support. Check with your vendor about compatibility of the device for use with SQL Server and database systems.

- If the Network-Attached Storage device offers support for snapshot backup using split-mirror (with or without copy-on-write), the Network-Attached Storage device must support the SQL Server Virtual Device Interface (VDI) for backups. The vendor-supplied Network-Attached Storage utilities and third-party software should also support the VDI if this functionality is needed. If the VDI is not supported, availability could be impacted (SQL Server would need to be stopped so that the mirror could be split) or the SQL Server databases could become corrupt (by splitting the mirror without allowing SQL Server to cleanly flush pending writes and leaving the databases in a consistent state for backup).

■   Make sure that your network bandwidth can handle the traffic that will be generated by SQL Server to and from the Network-Attached Storage devices. Consider a dedicated network that will not impact any other network traffic.

■   SQL Server 2000 failover clustering is currently not a supported configuration with Network-Attached Storage as the disk subsystem. SQL Server 2000 currently only supports stand-alone instances for use with Network-Attached Storage.

■   For a normal non-Network-Attached Storage–based SQL Server installation, if the network or a network card malfunctions, it is probably not a catastrophic failure because SQL Server and its disk subsystem are properly working. On a clustered SQL Server installation, a network or a network card malfunction can result in a SQL Server restart and possible failover of the service. This implication does not apply because Network-Attached Storage use is not supported with virtual servers. Because Network-Attached Storage solutions are based on the network and network card being available, you must guarantee 100 percent uptime for the network and network card to avoid any data problems, data corruption, or data loss.

■   If you are using RAID, make sure that the Network-Attached Storage device supports the level of RAID that will give you the performance and availability that you require.

■   When deploying Network-Attached Storage for a transactional database, contact the Network-Attached Storage vendor to ensure that the device is properly configured and tuned for use with a database.

Performance Considerations

Prior to making any storage purchase decisions, you need to determine the required disk throughput, disk capacity, and necessary processor power. If you are considering a Network-Attached Storage solution, these additional requirements need to be taken into account:

■   Network-Attached Storage performance is dependent on the Internet Protocol (IP) stack, the network interface card, other networking components, and the network itself. If Network-Attached Storage is used as the data store for SQL Server, all database I/O is processed by the network stack instead of the disk subsystem (as it would be in DAS) and is limited by the network's bandwidth.

■ Because processor utilization can increase with database load, only databases with a smaller load should be used with Network-Attached Storage. However, if a high-speed switched network interconnect is used between your SQL Server and Network-Attached Storage device, such as the Virtual Interface Architecture (VIA), processor utilization and network latency can be reduced for every SQL Server I/O. If you have a multiprocessor system, you need multiple network cards, and vice versa: if you have multiple network cards, you need multiple processors, otherwise you might see unbalanced processor loads, especially in a high-bandwidth network or Network-Attached Storage environment.

■ Most networks are configured at 10 or 100 megabits (Mb). This means that Network-Attached Storage performance might be significantly less than that of DAS or SANs, which are optimized for high disk transfer rates.

■ If many Network-Attached Storage devices are placed on a shared network, they might consume a large portion of network bandwidth. This has a significant impact not only on SQL Server, but also on anything else accessing the network.

Using Network-Attached Storage as a Data Store with SQL Server

SQL Server is not configured by default to support the creation and usage of a data store on a network file share, either those located on a standard server or a Network-Attached Storage device. In the case of Network-Attached Storage, data corruption could occur due to network interruptions if the process that ensures database consistency issues a write that cannot be committed to the disks of the Network-Attached Storage device.

To enable support for network file shares, trace flag 1807 must be enabled. This trace flag bypasses the check to see if the location for the use and creation of the database file is on a network share. Use Query Analyzer, select the master database, and execute the following command:

```
DBCC TRACEON(1807)
```

The successful result of this command should be as follows:

```
DBCC Execution Completed. If DBCC Printed Error Messages, Contact Your
System Administrator.
```

It is now possible to use a mapped drive or a Universal Naming Convention (UNC) path (that is, *servername**sharename*) with SQL Server 2000. If trace flag 1807 is not enabled prior to using a Network-Attached Storage device with SQL Server, you will encounter one of the following errors:

- 5105 (Device Activation Error)
- 5110 (File *'file_name'* Is On A Network Device Not Supported For Database Files).

> **Warning**   Although the preceding section illustrates how SQL Server can be configured to use Network-Attached Storage for its data store, remember that the usage is currently limited to a stand-alone SQL Server installation. A clustered SQL Server installation is not supported using Network-Attached Storage. Consult *http://support.microsoft.com* to see if this changes in the future.

Storage Area Networks

SANs are a logical evolution of DAS, and they fix many of the issues, such as the caching problem, associated with DAS. The purpose of a SAN is to give you flexibility, scalability, availability, reliability, security, and device sharing. SANs cache work at the physical level on the disk of sectors, tracks, and cylinders.

SQL Server itself technically does not care what protocol you use to access your SAN, but your choice impacts performance. SCSI and Fibre Channel have been mentioned, but there is also the VIA protocol, traditional IP, Ethernet, and Gigabit Ethernet. Fibre Channel, which does have some low-level SCSI still embedded, is strongly recommended. It is the most effective at carrying block-type data from storage to the computer writing or reading data. It also delivers predictable performance under higher loads than traditional Ethernet loads. Most important, Fibre Channel is extremely reliable.

> **More Info**   Remember to separate the transport from the actual protocol. For example, iSCSI, Fibre Channel, and VIA are transports. Typically the block transfer protocol on top is SCSI. So, for example, iSCSI is SCSI over IP. Fibre Channel fabrics are SCSI over Fibre Channel, and so on.

The speed of your SAN is largely related to its architecture, which has a host bus adapter that is in each server accessing the SAN, controllers for the disk, switches, and finally, the disks themselves. Each manufacturer implements SANs a bit differently, although the overall concepts are the same, so it is important to work with your hardware vendor to ensure you understand what you are implementing.

From a security standpoint, with a SAN, you can do things like zoning and masking, although your SAN vendor must support these features. Zoning occurs when you set up the SAN so that systems can be isolated from one another, and this feature is very useful for clustering. Masking allows you to hide LUNs from certain systems. Cluster nodes can be in the same or different, overlapping zones that are configured with masking.

Because SANs support a wide range of operating systems and servers, a company might purchase a large SAN for use with many different servers or types of workload. Although it is good that you have a SAN, you need to realize the implications of this. Because all systems attached to the system have different workloads and the SAN only has one cache, you will be sharing the cache among multiple systems. If, for example, you also have an Exchange server on your SAN that is heavily utilizing the cache, this could impact the performance of your SQL Server.

Also consider how the other operating systems or applications interface with the SAN at a base level—if another Windows server or cluster issues a bus reset as it comes online (say, after a reboot of a node), will it affect your current Windows server or cluster with SQL Server that is running with no problems? These are things you should know prior to putting the SAN into production.

You might also be sharing spindles between different servers on a SAN depending on how the vendor implemented its disk technology. What this means is that one physical disk might be carved up into multiple chunks. For example, a 36-GB disk might be divided into four equal 9-GB partitions at a physical level that Windows and SQL Server would never even see; they only see the LUN. You must recognize if your hardware does this and plan accordingly.

> **More Info**   For a good reference on SANs, read the book *Building SANs with Brocade Fabric Switches* by Chris Beauchamp (Syngress Publishing, 2001, 1-9289-9430-X).

What Disk Technology to Use

With so many choices available to you, what should you choose? Simply put, choose what makes sense for your business from many standpoints: administration, management, performance, growth, cost, and so on. This is not like other decisions you will make for your high availability solution, but it might be one of the most important *technology* decisions you make with regard to SQL Server. When considering cost versus performance, features, and so on, look at the long-term investment of your hardware purchase. Spending $100,000 on a basic SAN might seem excessive when compared to a $10,000 traditional DAS solution, but if your company is making millions of dollars per month, and downtime will affect profitability, over time, that SAN investment gets cheaper. The initial cost outlay is usually a barrier, however.

As you might have gathered, Network-Attached Storage is currently not the best solution when you want to configure SQL Server. From an availability standpoint, your network is one large single point of failure, and the possibility of data corruption due to network interruption decreases your availability if you need to restore from a backup.

That leaves DAS and SAN. At this point the main issues will be cost, supportability, and ease of expansion and administration. DAS is usually SCSI-based and it is much cheaper, but it is less flexible, and because you cannot, for example, use the write cache (read is just fine), it might not be ideal for your high availability usage of SQL Server. SANs are the way to go if you can afford a solution that fits your needs. The ease of configuration and expansion as well as flexibility are key points to think about when looking at SANs.

Although they are not mentioned directly, there is always the option (in a nonclustered system) to use separate disks internal to a system, whether they are SCSI or Integrated Device Electronics (IDE). Some internal SCSI disks also support RAID, which is described in more detail in the section "A RAID Primer" later in this chapter.

Server Clusters, Failover Clustering, and Disks

There are two types of storage I/O technologies supported in server clusters: parallel SCSI and Fibre Channel. For both Windows 2000 and Windows Server 2003, support is provided for SCSI interconnects and Fibre Channel arbitrated loops for two nodes only.

> **Important**   For larger cluster configurations (more than two nodes), you need to use a switched Fibre Channel (fabric/fiber-optic, not copper) environment.

If you are implementing SCSI, the following considerations must be taken into account:

- It is only supported in Windows 2000 Advanced Server or Windows Server 2003 up to two-nodes.

- SCSI adaptors and storage solutions need to be certified.

- SCSI cards that are hosting the interconnect should have different SCSI IDs, normally 6 and 7. Ensure device access requirements are in line with SCSI IDs and priorities.

- SCSI adaptor BIOS should be disabled.

- If devices are daisy-chained, ensure that both ends of the shared bus are terminated.

- Use physical terminating devices and do not use controller-based or device-based termination.

- SCSI hubs are not supported.

- Avoid the use of connector converters (for example, 68-pin to 50-pin).

- Avoid combining multiple device types (single ended and differential, and so on).

If you are implementing Fibre Channel, the following considerations must be taken into account:

- Fibre Channel Arbitrated Loops (FC-AL) support up to two nodes.

- Fibre Channel Fabric (FC-SW) support all higher combinations.

- Components and configuration need to be in the Microsoft Hardware Compatibility List (HCL).

- You can use a multicluster environment.

- Fault-tolerant drivers and components also need to be certified.

- Virtualization engines need to be certified.

When you really think about it, clusters are networked storage configurations because of how clusters are set up. They are dependent on a shared storage infrastructure. SCSI-based commands are embedded in fiber at a low level. For example, clustering uses device reservations and bus resets, which can potentially be disruptive on a SAN. Systems coming and going also lead to potential disruptions. This behavior might change with Windows Server 2003 and SANs, as the Cluster service issues a command to break a reservation and the port driver can do a targeted or device reset for disks on Fibre Channel (not SCSI). The targeted resets require that the host bus adapter (HBA) drivers provided by the vendor for the SAN support this feature. If a targeted reset fails, the traditional entire buswide SCSI reset is performed. Clusters identify the logical volumes through disk signatures (as well as partition offset and partition length), which is why using and maintaining disk signatures is crucial.

Clusters have a disk arbitration process (sometimes known as the challenge/defense protocol), or the process to reserve or "own" a disk. With Microsoft Windows NT 4.0 Enterprise Edition, the process was as follows: for a node to reserve a disk, it used the SCSI protocol RESERVE (issued to gain control of a device; lost if a buswide reset is issued), RELEASE (freed a SCSI device for another host bus adapter to use), and RESET (bus reset) commands. The server cluster uses the semaphore on the disk drive to represent the SCSI-level reservation status in software; SCSI-III persistent reservations are not used. The current owner reissues disk reservations and renews the lease every 3 seconds on the semaphore. All other nodes, or challengers, try to reserve the drive as well. Before Windows Server 2003, the underlying SCSI port did a bus reset, which affected all targets and LUNs. With the new StorPort driver stack of Windows Server 2003, instead of the behavior just described, a targeted LUN reset occurs. After that, a wait happens for approximately 7 to 15 seconds (3 seconds for renewal plus 2 seconds bus settle time, repeated three times to give the current owner a chance to renew). If the reservation is still clear, the former owner loses the lease and the challenger issues a RESERVE to acquire disk ownership and lease on the semaphore.

With Windows 2000 and Windows Server 2003, the arbitration process is a bit different. Arbitration is done by reading and writing hidden sectors on the shared cluster disk using a mutual exclusion algorithm by Leslie Lamport. Despite this change, the Windows NT 4.0 reserve and reset process formerly used for arbitration still occurs with Windows 2000 and Windows Server 2003. However, the process is now used only for protecting the disk against stray I/Os, not for arbitration.

More Info   For more information on Leslie Lamport, including some of his writings, go to *http://research.microsoft.com/users/lamport/*. The paper containing the fast mutual exclusion algorithm can be found at *http://research.microsoft.com/users/lamport/pubs/pubs.html#fast-mutex.*

As of Windows 2000 Service Pack 2 or later (including Windows Server 2003), Microsoft has a new multipath I/O (MPIO) driver stack against which vendors can code new drivers. The new driver stack enables targeted resets using device and LUN reset (that is, you do not have to reset the whole bus) so that things like failover are improved. Consult with your hardware vendor to see if their driver supports the new MPIO stack.

> **Warning** MPIO is not shipped as part of the operating system. It is a feature provided to vendors by Microsoft to customize their specific hardware and then use. That means that out of the box, Windows does not provide multipath support.

When using a SAN with a server cluster, make sure you take the following into consideration:

- Ensure that the SAN configurations are in the Microsoft HCL (multi-cluster section).

- When configuring your storage, the following must be implemented:

  - **Zoning** Zoning allows users to sandbox the logical volumes to be used by a cluster. Any interactions between nodes and storage volumes are isolated to the zone, and other members of the SAN are not affected by the same. This feature can be implemented at the controller or switch level and it is important that users have this implemented before installing clustering. Zoning can be implemented in hardware or firmware on controllers or using software on hosts. For clusters, hardware-based zoning is recommended, as there can be a uniform implementation of access policy that cannot be disrupted or compromised by a node failure or a failure of the software component.

  - **LUN masking** This feature allows users to express a specific relationship between a LUN and a host at the controller level. In theory, no other host should be able to see that LUN or manipulate it in any way. However, various implementations differ in functionality; as such, one cannot assume that LUN masking will always work. Therefore, it cannot be used *instead of* zoning. You can combine zoning and masking, however, to meet some specific configuration requirements. LUN masking can be done using hardware or software, and as with zoning, a hardware-based solution is recommended. If you use software-based masking, the software should be closely attached to storage. Software involved with the presentation of the storage to Windows needs to be certified. If you cannot guarantee the stability of the software, do not implement it.

❏   **Firmware and driver versions**   Some vendors implement specific functionality in drivers and firmware and users should pay close attention to what firmware and driver combinations are compatible with the installation they are running. This is valid not only when building a SAN and attaching a host to it, but also over the entire life span of the system (hosts and SAN components). Pay careful attention to issues arising out of applying service packs or vendor-specific patches and upgrades.

> **Warning**   If you are going to be attaching multiple clusters to a single SAN, the SAN must appear on the both the cluster and the multicluster lists of the HCL. The storage subsystem must be configured (down to the driver level, fabric, and HBA) as described on the HCL. Switches are the only component not currently certified by Microsoft. You should secure guarantees in writing from your storage vendor before implementing the switch fabric technologies.

> **Tip**   Adding a disk to a cluster can cause some downtime, and that amount of downtime is directly related to how much you can prepare for it. If you have the disk space, create some spare, formatted LUNs available to the cluster if you need to use them. This is covered in more depth in Chapter 5, "Designing Highly Available Microsoft Windows Servers."

Pre-Windows Disk Configuration

Now that you understand how to calculate disk capacity from a SQL Server perspective, it is time to put that knowledge into planning and action. Disks require configuration before they can be presented to Windows and, ultimately, SQL Server. A few tasks must be performed prior to configuring a disk in Windows to allow SQL Server to use it.

Number of Spindles Needed

How many disks do you need to get the performance you desire and the space you need? Calculate the number of spindles (actual disks) based on the application data you have gathered or should have available to you.

> **Important**   Remember when figuring out the number of spindles needed to take into account how many will make up a LUN. Some hardware vendors allow storage to be expanded only by a certain number of drives at a time, so if you need to add one disk, you might actually need to add six. Also, just because your storage vendor supports a certain number of spindles per LUN, it does not mean you should actually use that many disks. Each vendor has its own optimal configuration, and you should work with the vendor to determine that configuration.

Step 1—Amount of Data Being Returned

This is the easiest of the calculations. For this, you need to know the following:

- The number of concurrent users

- The amount of data each user is returning

- The time interval used by the user

Assume you have 250 concurrent users. Each needs to simultaneously bring back 0.5 MB of data in less than one second. This means that in total, you must be able to support constantly bringing back 125 MB of data from your disk subsystem in less than a second, every second, to get the performance you desire.

Step 2—Individual Drive Throughput

It is time to calculate the throughput of a single physical drive. You must know the following information:

- Maximum I/Os supported for the physical drive in its desired configuration (that is, RAID level, sector size, and stripe size are factors).

- Ratio of 8k page reads to 64k readaheads for the operations. You might not know this information, but it is ultimately useful. You can use the numbers shown here as a rough estimate if you do not know. Each drive is rated at a certain number of I/Os that the hardware manufacturer should be able to provide.

Continuing from step 1, assuming 80 percent 8k page reads and 20 percent 64k readaheads, and knowing that the drive can support 100 I/Os per second:

$$(80 \times 8) + (20 \times 64) = 1.6 \text{ MB/second throughput on the individual drive}$$

> **Note**   Individual drive throughput might or might not be as important with SANs as it is with DAS. It depends. Because high-end storage subsystems might have lots of cache space, physical performance can be optimized, compensated for, or masked by the architecture of the solution. This does not mean you should buy lower speed 5400 rpm speed disks. It just means you should understand the physical characteristics of your disk subsystem.

Step 3—Calculating Number of Spindles

Now that you have the amount of data being returned and the throughput of the individual drive, you can calculate the number of drives needed. The formula is:

Number of Spindles = Data Returned/Drive Throughput

Continuing the example started in step 1, 125/1.6 = 78 spindles. Realistically, not many companies buy 78 disks just to achieve optimum performance for your data. This does not even take into account space for indexes, logs, and so on. More important, this does not even take into account the type of RAID you will use. This is just performance, so you can see where trade-offs come into play.

Understanding Disk Drives

Disks are physical hardware, and understanding their benefits and limitations will help you during the planning process. Each manufacturer's hardware is different, so sometimes it is hard to perform a comparison, but when it comes to implementation, understanding the disk technology you are employing enhances your ability to administer disks and make them available.

Here are some key points to consider:

- How fast are the disks that will be fitted in the enclosure? This is measured in rpm, and in most cases, faster is better because it translates directly into faster seek and transfer times. However, many fast-spinning drives generate heat and greater vibration, which translates into planning at a datacenter level (that is, when you buy hardware, make sure it has proper cooling; with lots of systems that spin lots of drives in one physical location, you need sufficient cooling).

■   What is the rated MTBF for the drives? Knowing what the average life span of a drive is helps mitigate any risks that might arise from a disk failure. If you put an entire disk solution in place with drives, remember that they all have the same MBTF, which is affected by their individual usage. This might or might not be a factor for your environment, but it is worth mentioning.

■   Does the disk solution support hot-swappable drives? If it does not, what is the procedure to fix the drive array with a disk failure? If one disk drive fails, you do not want to affect your availability by having to power down your entire system just to add a new drive in. Taking your service level agreements (SLAs) into account, you can easily fail to meet them if you do not ask your hardware vendor this type of question up front.

Understanding Your Hardware

When you venture into physical design of a disk subsystem, you must understand how the servers you bought contribute to performance, and how the disk drives themselves work.

Hard disks are platters with a head that reads and writes the data, and then sends it across some protocol such as SCSI or Fibre Channel. No two drives are the same, and some are faster than others. Even drives rated at the same speed might perform differently in different circumstances. One important concept with modern hard disk drives is media banding, which occurs when the drive's head progresses from the outside track closer into the center of the drive, and data delivery rates drop. When you architect for performance, you need to understand exactly *where* on the physical platters your data could be sitting and how physical placement on the disk affects how fast your disk returns the data to you. Things like media banding are relevant today, but as storage moves toward virtualization, it might not be as important. Storage virtualization is basically the decoupling of the logical representation from the physical implementation. It allows users to present a logical storage infrastructure to operating systems and applications that is independent of how and where the physical storage is located. This will definitely change any planning that you would make, should you employ virtualization.

> **Note**   Your choice of a storage vendor will govern the architecture implemented, ranging from small and fast to large and slower, or anything in between. Individual drive characteristics might not be a choice, as the vendor solution is optimized for their use of disks.

Once you get past the drives, look at the physical architecture of your system. Historically, as you move farther away in the signal chain from the processor, bandwidth decreases, which is shown in Figure 4-2. If you have a 800-MHz processor with 512 MB of PC133 SDRAM, talking over a 300 MHz bus that has a SCSI controller that can deliver up to 40 MB per second, and finally to a single drive that can sustain 15 MB per second, you have a pyramid with its smallest point, or tip, at the disk drive. Changing that picture a bit, changing one or more components of the system, or ensuring, say, a faster front side bus, might actually result in better performance. For example, does your solution need multiple SCSI controllers to fill your existing bus, or just a fatter, higher MHz 64-bit bus?

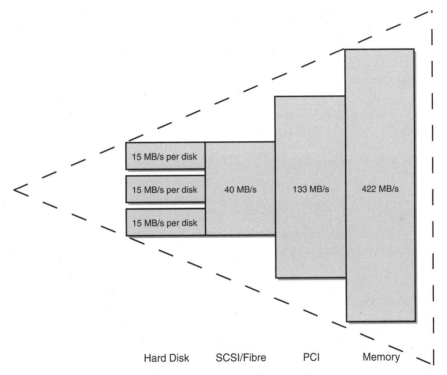

Figure 4-2   Traditional system bandwidth pyramid.

Next, break it down to your choice of hardware: what does each component bring to the table, and how can it possibly hinder you from a performance or availability standpoint? Very few people actually take the time to understand their hardware to this level, but in the availability and performance arenas, you must.

Understanding How SQL Server Interacts with Disks

SQL Server has three types of disk I/O: random, readahead, and sequential. Random I/O is the 8k reads from a page, whether it is data or index. An example of a random I/O is a query with a WHERE clause. Readahead I/O issues 64k reads, and this maps to table and index scans. Table and index scans might be advantageous because the I/O cost of retrieving 64k when contiguously placed on the disk is close to that of retrieving 8k when paying the disk "seek" time between the next 8k. The final type of I/O, sequential I/O, is what the transaction log uses. Basically, you want the head to never pick up from the disk and just have it write to the log in a continuous stream. If the head has to pick up and go elsewhere, and then go back to the next position in the virtual log file, your writes to the log are slower, so reducing or eliminating latency for logs allows log records to be written faster. When SQL Server writes to a disk, it writes at the 8k page level (data or index). One of the main reasons SQL Server writes 8k pages is that these are database engine pages, not memory pages. 8k is a memory-address page boundary aligned requirement to use the high-speed I/O employed by SQL Server.

It is extremely important to consider the page size of 8k when designing schemas and indexes. Will all data from one row fit on a single page? Can multiple rows fit on a page? What will happen if you are inserting or updating data and you need to do a page split, either in data, or more to the point, in an index? Avoid page splits if at all possible because a page split causes another I/O operation that is just as expensive as a full 8k write. Keep this in mind with Unicode, as noted earlier, because it has slightly different storage characteristics.

Types of SQL Server Systems

Online transaction processing (OLTP) systems are heavy-duty read/write systems such as e-commerce systems. There are more random reads and writes with OLTP systems, and a safe assumption is at least 100 I/Os per second. The disk controller and cache should be matched to the ratio of reads and writes (see the next section, "Understanding Disk Cache"). For an OLTP system, it is potentially better to have a larger number of smaller drives to achieve better performance. One large disk (or LUN) over a smaller amount of disks might not result in the performance you want. To optimize the log, you might want to consider a dedicated controller set to 100 percent write as long as the transaction log is on a dedicated disk.

> **Caution**   Do not attempt such a configuration unless you are certain that you are only using the write cache; otherwise you might encounter data corruption.

OLTP systems can quickly become log bound if your application performs many very small inserts, updates, and deletes in rapid succession (and you will see hotspotting on the log files if this is the case), so if you focus on the number of commits per second, ensure that the disk containing the log can handle this.

> **Tip**   Consider analyzing your percentage of reads versus your percentage of writes. If you have more reads than writes, you might want more indexes, stripes with more spindles, and more RAM. If you have more writes than you do reads, large stripes and RAM will not help as much as more spindles and individual LUNs to allow the spindles to write without contention with other write I/O requests. Write cache can also help, but make sure you are completely covered when using the write cache for RDBMS files in general, and specifically, your log.

Planning for data warehouses is different than planning for OLTP systems. Data warehouses are largely based on sequential reads, so plan for at least 150 I/Os per second per drive due to index or table scans. The controller and cache should be set to heavy read. Put your data and indexes across many drives, and because tempdb will probably be heavily used, you should consider putting it on a separate LUN. Do not try to be a hero for object placement, because the query performance profile will change over time with use, addition of different data, new functionality, and so on. Achieving maximum performance would include having a dedicated performance and maintenance staff, but if that is not possible, design for maximizing I/O bandwidth to all disks and ensure proper indexes. Try to make the top 80 percent of your queries perform at optimal levels, and realize that 20 percent will be the outliers. You probably will not be able to have 100 percent of your queries perform optimally—choose the most used and most important, and then rank them on that basis. Log throughput is not as important, as data can be loaded in bulk-logged recovery mode, but it is still important for recoverability.

Understanding Disk Cache

Taking technology out of the picture for a second, you need to understand the ratio of reads to writes in your individual application to be able to set the disk cache at the hardware level if possible (that is, you cannot do it if you are on a cluster and are using SCSI). If you have a 60 percent read, 40 percent write application, you could configure your cache to that ratio if your hardware supports this type of configuration. However, if you have more than one application or even multiple devices, say, attached to a SAN, optimizing your disk cache is nearly impossible if you have multiple applications sharing a LUN. Many SANs cache at the LUN level, but if they do not, your cache is shared among all LUNs, and you will only be able to do the best you can. This might also force you to have separate disk subsystems for different systems or types of systems to increase performance.

A RAID Primer

No discussion about availability and disks would omit a discussion on RAID. Over the years, RAID has stood for different things, but from a definition standpoint, it is the method of grouping your disks into one logical unit. This grouping of disks is called various things depending on your hardware vendor: logical unit, LUN, volume, or partition. A RAID type is referred to as a RAID level. Different RAID levels offer varying amounts of performance and availability, and each one has a different minimum number of physical disk drives required to implement it. There are many levels of RAID, and each manufacturer might even have its own variation on some of them, but the most popular forms of RAID are introduced here.

> **Important**   Not all vendors support all the choices or options listed here for RAID, and some might even force you into a single, optimized method for their storage platform. Understand what you are purchasing.

Striping

Disk striping, or RAID 0, creates what is known as a striped set of disks. With RAID 0, data is read simultaneously from blocks on each drive. Because you only get one copy of the data with RAID 0, there is no added overhead of additional writes as with many of the more advanced forms of RAID. Read and write performance might be increased because operations are spread out over multiple physical disks. I/O can happen independently and simultaneously. RAID 0 spreads data across multiple drives, which means that one drive lost makes the entire stripe unusable. Therefore, for availability, RAID 0 by itself is not a good choice because it leaves you exposed without protection of your data. RAID 0 is bad for data or logs, but might be a good solution for storing online backups made by SQL Server before they are copied to tape. However, this is a potential risk, as you would need to ensure whatever process copies the backup to another location works, because losing a disk would mean losing your backup.

Mirroring

Disk mirroring, or RAID 1, is simple: a mirrored set of disks is grouped together. The same data is simultaneously written to both drives, and in the event of one drive failure, the other disk can service requests (see Figure 4-3). Some vendors support more than two disks in a mirror set, which can result in something like a triple or quadruple mirror. Read performance is improved with RAID 1, as there are two copies of the data to read from (the first serving disk completes the I/O to the file system), and unlike RAID 0, you have protection in the event of a drive failure. RAID 1 alone does have some high availability uses, which are detailed in the section "File Placement and Protection" later in this chapter. The disadvantage of mirroring is that it requires twice as many disks for implementation.

> **Note**   RAID 1 is the most recommended form of RAID for SQL Server logs, providing you always maintain enough disk space for your log and its growth on the mirror.

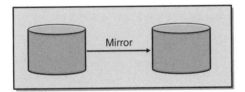

Figure 4-3   Mirroring.

Striped Mirrors

Striped mirrors are a hybrid of disks that are first mirrored with RAID 1, and then all mirrors are striped with RAID 0, as shown in Figure 4-4. Striped mirrors offer the best availability of the options presented in this chapter, as they can tolerate a drive failure easily and provides good fault tolerance. You could lose up to half of your disks without a problem, but losing the two disks constituting a mirror pair renders the entire stripe unreadable. Assuming no problems, you also have the ability to read from each mirror. When a failed disk is replaced, the surviving disk in the mirrored pair can often regenerate it, assuming the hardware supports this feature. Striped mirrors require a minimum of four drives to implement and can be very costly because the number of disks needed is doubled (due to mirroring). Striped mirrors are the most common recommendation for configuring disks for SQL Server.

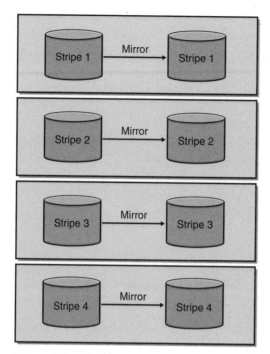

Figure 4-4 Striped mirrors.

Mirrored Stripes

Mirrored stripes are similar to striped mirrors, except the disks are first striped with RAID 0, and then each stripe is mirrored with RAID 1 (see Figure 4-5). This offers the second best availability of the RAID options covered in this chapter. You can tolerate the loss of one drive in each stripe set, as that renders that stripe set unusable. Your risk for failure goes up significantly once you encounter one drive failure. Mirrored stripes require a minimum of four drives to implement, and this solution is very costly, as you usually need at least two times the number of drives to get the physical space you need.

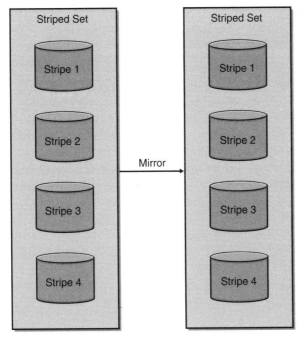

Figure 4-5 Mirrored stripes.

> **Note** Striped mirrors and mirrored stripes often confuse people, and manufacturers might call them RAID 10, RAID 0+1, RAID 1+1, RAID 01, and other terms. Work with your manufacturer to understand which one they actually implement for their disk subsystems.

Striping with Parity

Striping with parity, shown in Figure 4-6, is also known as RAID 5, but it is parity that is not contained on one dedicated drive (that would be RAID 3); it is written across all of the disks and takes up the equivalent of one drive. RAID 5 is probably the most popular RAID level, as it is often the most cost effective in terms of maximizing drives for space.

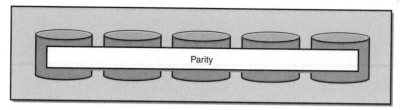

Figure 4-6   Striping with parity, also known as RAID 5.

From an availability standpoint, RAID 5 is not the best—you can only tolerate the loss of one drive. When you lose a drive, your performance suffers, and once you lose more than one drive, your LUN no longer functions. RAID 5 uses the equivalent of one drive for storing a parity bit, which is written across all disks (hence only being able to lose one drive). RAID 5 also has slower write speeds, and so would not be appropriate for, say, a heavily used OLTP system. That said, many fast physical disks might mitigate (or mask) some RAID 5 performance issues. Caching capabilities of storage subsystems might also mitigate this so that it is no longer a point of consideration.

In a situation with unlimited financial and disk resources, striped mirrors give you better performance and reliability. In a limited disk scenario (for example, having only 12 or 16 disks), RAID 5 might be a faster or better implementation than striped mirrors. Of course, that would need to be evaluated.

A physical disk controller (hardware, not software) has two channels. Striped mirrors and mirrored stripes require both to mirror. RAID 5 could use two truly separate LUNs to separate out log and data, and you could access each individually, potentially increasing performance. If you have more than one disk controller and implement striped mirrors or mirrored stripes, you could get the same effect.

Assume you have 12 disks. With striped mirrors or mirrored stripes, you would only have six disks worth of space available because your storage is effectively halved. Even if the hardware can support simultaneous reads (that is, reading from both or all disks in the mirrored pair if you have more than two mirrors), you cannot have simultaneous writes from the application perspective because at a physical level, the hardware is performing simultaneous writes to maintain the mirror. Therefore, in some cases, RAID 5 with a smaller number of disks might perform better for some types of work.

Parity is a simple concept to grasp. Each physical disk has data (in megabytes or gigabytes), which then breaks down into smaller segments, ultimately represented by zeroes or ones. Picture a stripe, of say, 8 and you get the following:

1 0 1 0 0 0 1 1 (also known as A3 in hexadecimal)

Parity is simply the even or odd bit. For even parity, the parity bit would be 0 because if you sum the preceding numbers, you get four, and if you divide by two, there is no remainder.

Now that you understand the basics of parity, what does it buy you? Assume you lose the third disk, which would now make the example look like this: 1 0 x 0 0 0 1 1. If you then sum these numbers and divide by two, you now have odd parity. Therefore, you know you are missing a drive that must have contained a 1 to make the parity check.

Hardware RAID versus Software RAID

Beyond the different types of RAID, there are two implementation forms: hardware-based and software-based. Hardware-based RAID is obviously implemented at a physical level, whereas software-based RAID is done after you start using the operating system. It is always optimal to have RAID done at a physical level.

> **Warning**   Software RAID is not supported for a clustered system. You must use hardware RAID. Software RAID is an option with a third-party product such as Veritas Volume Manager but at that point, the third-party vendor would become the primary support contact for any disk problems.

Remote Mirroring

For high availability, nothing can really beat a solution that allows you to geographically separate disks and maintain, say, two SQL Servers easily. This is more often than not a hardware-assisted solution. Remote mirroring is really the replication of storage data to a remote location. From a SQL Server perspective, the disk replication should be transactional based (as SQL Server is). If replication is not based on a SQL Server transaction, the third-party hardware or software should have a process (not unlike a two-phase commit) that ensures that the disk block has been received and applied, and if not, you are still maintaining consistency for SQL Server. If you are considering remote mirroring, ask yourself these questions:

- Which disk volumes do you want to replicate or mirror?

- What are the plans for placing the remote storage online?

- What are the plans for migrating operations to and from the backup site?

■   What medium are you going to use for your disk replication? Distance will dictate this, and might include choices such as IP, Fibre Channel over specific configurations, and Enterprise Systems Connection.

■   What is the potential risk for such a complex hardware implementation?

Torn pages are a concern with remote disk mirroring. SQL Server stores data in 8k pages, and a disk typically guarantees writes of whole 512-byte sectors. A SQL Server data page is 16 of these sectors, and a disk cannot guarantee that each of the 16 sectors will always be written (for example, in the case of a power failure). If an error happens during a page write, resulting in a partially written page, that is known as a *torn page*. Work with your storage vendor to learn how they have planned to avoid or handle torn pages with your SQL Server implementation.

Storage Composition

Each storage subsystem has a certain physical design with a high but limited number of disk slots. These are divided across multiple internal SCSI buses and driving hardware (processors, caches, and so forth), often in a redundant setup. If we now construct, for instance, a RAID 5 set but the same internal SCSI bus drives two spindles, that would be a bad choice for two reasons:

■   A failure on that internal bus would fail both disks and therefore fail the entire RAID 5 set on a single event. The same is true for two halves of a mirror, and it also applies to other redundant constructs of a storage subsystem.

■   Because RAID 5 uses striping, driving all spindles concurrently, two spindles on the same internal bus would need to wait on each other because only one device at a time on a single bus can be commanded. There is little waiting, as internally this happens asynchronously, but it still represents two consecutive operations that could have been one across all spindles at the same time, as is the intention of striping.

For these reasons, among others, some vendors do not offer these choices and abstract that to a pure choice in volume sizes, doing everything else automatically according to best available method given a particular storage solution design.

Types of Disks and File Systems in Windows

Windows supports three kinds of disks: basic, dynamic, and mount points.

- A *basic disk* is the simplest form of disk: it is a physical disk (whether a LUN on a SAN or a single disk physically attached to the system) that can be formatted for use by the operating system. A basic disk is given a drive letter, of which there is a limitation of 26.

- A *dynamic disk* provides more functionality than a basic disk. It allows you to have one volume that spans multiple physical disks. Dynamic disks are supported by both Windows 2000 and Windows Server 2003.

- A *mount point* is a drive that can be mounted to get around the basic 26-drive letter limitation. For example, you could create a drive that is designated as F:\SQLData, but maps to a local drive or a drive on a disk array attached to the server.

> **Caution**   Only basic disks are supported for a server cluster using the 32-bit versions of Windows and SQL Server 2000 failover clustering. Basic disks are also supported under all 64-bit versions of Windows. Mount points are supported by all versions of Windows Server 2003 for a base server cluster, but only the 64-bit version of SQL Server supports mount points for use with failover clustering. Dynamic disks are not supported natively by the operating system for a server cluster under any version of Windows, and a third-party tool such as Veritas Volume Manager can be used. However, at that point, the third-party vendor would become the primary support contact for any disk problems.

Windows supports the file allocation table (FAT) file system, FAT32, and the NTFS file system. Each version of Windows can possibly update the version of the particular file system, so it is important to ensure that would not have any adverse affects in an upgrade process. For performance and security reasons, you should use NTFS.

> **Important**   Only NTFS is supported for server clusters. FAT and FAT32 cannot be used to format the disks.

> **Tip** Keep in mind when that using Windows 2000 and Windows Server 2003, the 32-bit versions have a maximum limitation of 2 TB per LUN with NTFS. 64-bit versions remove this limitation, so if you are building large warehouses, you should consider 64-bit versions.

> **Warning** Do not enable compression on any file system that will be used with SQL Server data or log files; this is not supported in either stand-alone or clustered systems. For a clustered SQL Server, an encrypted file system is not currently supported. Windows Server 2003 clusters at the operating system level do support an encrypted file system. For updates, please consult *http://support.microsoft.com*.

Formatting the Disks

How you format your disks affects the performance of your disks used for SQL Server data. Disk subsystems optimized for a file server or for Exchange are not optimized for SQL Server. As discussed in the earlier section "Understanding How SQL Server Interacts with Disks," if your file system is not designed for SQL Server, you might not be able to get maximum performance. Whether using Computer Management or the command line format, set the NTFS block size appropriately (see Figure 4-7); 64K is recommended, and with 64-bit systems, this can even be set higher. If going beyond 64K, try it first on a test system. For SAN-based systems, make sure you work with your hardware vendor to ensure you are using the optimal stripe size settings for the type of RAID you employ.

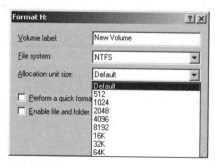

Figure 4-7 Block size in Computer Management.

> **Important**   Make sure that you work closely with your preferred hardware vendor to ensure that the disks configured for your database are exactly the way you want them to be configured and that they are not optimized for other types of disk use. It is important to get the configuration documented for verification. In addition, if a problem occurs, you should have a guarantee from the vendor that the disks were configured properly. It can also help Microsoft Product Support Services or a third-party vendor assist you in the troubleshooting of any disk problems.

File Placement and Protection

Another crucial factor in database availability and performance is where you place the data, log, and index files used by SQL Server, and what level of RAID you employ for performance and availability. This is another difficult piece in the disk puzzle, because it goes hand-in-hand with designing your storage at the physical hardware level. You cannot do one without the other. Especially at this stage, what you do not know about your application will hurt you. The physical implementation of your logical design, not unlike turning a logical schema into actual column names and data types, is a difficult process. They are both closely tied together, so one cannot be done in isolation from the other. For example, the logical design at some level has to take into account the physical characteristics of any proposed disk subsystem.

> **Note**   In a failover cluster, all system databases are placed on the shared disk array. No databases are local to either node, otherwise a failover would be impossible.

On the other hand, the SQL Server 2000 binaries for both clustered and nonclustered systems are installed to local, internal drives in the system itself. This is a change from SQL Server 7.0. As in a cluster, you needed to put the binaries on the shared cluster disk. You should standardize where on each server SQL Server will be installed so that any DBA or administrator will know where SQL Server resides. In a clustered system, these binaries must exist in the same location.

System Databases and Full-Text Indexes

For file placement of the system databases, it is easier to give general recommendations for both clustered and nonclustered systems. The only difference for a failover cluster versus a stand-alone SQL Server is that the system databases must all reside on the shared disk array in a cluster—they cannot be local to a server node. The following are the two main system databases for which you need to be concerned about file placement:

■ **Tempdb** This system database is at the top of the list. Tempdb is often forgotten in the configuration equation, but can be a pivotal linchpin in the success of your SQL Server implementation because it serves as the scratch pad for the system. Tempdb is used to store all temporary tables (the ones that have a # prefix) and temporary stored procedures, and it is also used by queries for things like joins (which can create temporary work tables) and sorts. Tempdb is re-created every time SQL Server is restarted, so it is not a database that needs to factor into a backup and restore strategy. Tempdb, because it is write-intensive, would be better off placed on a RAID 1 LUN of its own if it is heavily used. RAID 5 might not buy you much with tempdb unless you could either give tempdb its own control channel or more working spindles. Combining tempdb with user databases is not a good idea if each individual database is heavily used.

> **Tip** Remember, tempdb also has a log file. Although it is rare, there are extreme cases in which it is possible to cause the performance problems for the tempdb log with enough transactional load. This would then require you to move this log to a separate disk or disk stripe in the same way you would for user data. Again, do not configure tempdb this way unless you have to.

■ **Distribution** The distribution database is created when replication is installed. With merge and snapshot replication, the distribution database only stores status. However, with transactional replication, it is much more heavily used and must factor into any planning and performance. Hotspotting can potentially occur with RAID 5 if your disks are not quick enough to handle a heavy transactional volume with replication because of the overhead incurred to calculate and write the parity bit, so a striped mirror or mirrored stripe would probably help the distribution database. If your distribution database is located on the same server as your publication database and you have performance problems, you might try moving the distribution functionality to another server before you alter the disk subsystem.

Full-text indexes are also I/O intensive. In a cluster, these also obviously need to be on the shared disk array. In a nonclustered environment, you should not put the full-text index on the same drive or LUN as your log or data. Unless you have numerous spindles, your write performance suffers with RAID 5, so use some other form of RAID to increase your write and read performance.

Database backups are covered in depth in Chapter 9, "Backup and Restore," but they should be taken into account at the time of disk configuration. It might be cheaper and quicker to back up to disk, but if you are placing backups onto disk, or doing your primary backup to disk first, you need to account for that in your performance and storage requirements. You do not want to be performing a backup to a database and placing its resulting file on the same LUN or disk as the existing data file, as that reduces both your disk performance and available space.

For the system databases (master, model, tempdb, and so on), there is generally much less I/O than there is in a user database. Make sure that you protect them with at least RAID 1 for recovery and availability. Msdb is very important because it contains some settings that would be harder to restore without a good backup or having it available. Master is also important, but it can be rebuilt to an initial state with the REBUILDM command-line utility. You would still need a backup with your settings to restore over that, but there is no corresponding REBUILDM-like tool for msdb.

User Databases

Where to place the user databases is always the million-dollar question, with no one-size-fits-all answer. Like all of high availability, it depends, based on all of the factors presented in this chapter.

Databases, the Quorum, and Failover Clustering

As noted in Chapter 3, "An Introduction to Microsoft High Availability Technologies," only one instance of SQL Server can access a given LUN (which might even have multiple logical drive letters configured on it), so it cannot be shared among instances. Similarly, the quorum, which is used by a server cluster (but not a majority node set server cluster—for more information, see Chapter 5), must be on its own disk because the base cluster resources need this disk. The minimum size recommendation for the quorum is 500 MB, and it might be larger if you keep the default configuration for the clustered MS DTC, which logs to the quorum disk. Again, MS DTC configuration is covered in Chapter 5. All of these factors affect any placement of databases and files in the cluster, so it must be planned for up front.

Files and Filegroups

One of the biggest questions is when to use files and filegroups. Each database for SQL Server 2000 has a primary data file, and others, known as secondary data files, can also be used. In addition to the data files, there are files used for the transaction log. The primary data file has an extension of .mdf, secondary data files have an extension of .ndf, and log files have an extension of .ldf. Filegroups are exactly what they sound like: a group of files, but they are files that are grouped together. You cannot have files or filegroups used by more than one database. If you create a database named MyDatabase, only that database can use its corresponding .mdf and .ldf files.

Although there is a potential performance benefit to using multiple files and filegroups, the main reason you would consider implementing files and filegroups would be for easier administration. First and foremost, when you use multiple files for a database, whether log or data, they are filled proportionally. If you add a new file into the filegroup, it might show heavy I/O until it catches up with the other files. Second, files and filegroups allow you to deal with smaller portions of your database when doing maintenance, such as backups and restores, making maintenance windows easier to deal with. The success of files and filegroups is not to split up I/O bandwidth but to combine I/O bandwidth (that is, placing a file on each disk stripe for each filegroup). Scan density is king. SQL Server 2000 bases the degree of parallelism on the system load at the time the query execution plan is built. Readahead is based on the size of the buffer pool and the overall capacity of the I/O subsystem, so the number of files in a filegroup does not influence this.

However, as with any technology, there are always catches. Probably the biggest one for files and filegroups is that some maintenance within SQL Server 2000, such as DBCC INDEXDEFRAG, only works on a per-file basis. If you have an index that spans multiple files, you might encounter some fragmentation. DBCC DBREINDEX spans multiple files, but that is a trade-off for the potential performance impact and possible blocking due to employing it.

> **Caution** Do not use files and filegroups just for the sake of using them. If your database is small enough to easily be backed up and restored by your current strategy, files and filegroups might complicate things for you from an administrative perspective. In this case, if you decide to employ files and filegroups, it would generally be a performance improvement decision, which is not the usual case for implementing them—it is usually an administrative decision.

Database File Size

Once database file placement is worked out, one final step in the database configuration must be determined: the size of the files used for each user database, as well as tempdb. Again, what you do not know at this stage can hurt you when you move into production.

In versions of SQL Server prior to SQL Server 7.0, if you wanted to expand your database, you would have to do it by adding another segment. When you ran out of segments, you were out of luck. SQL Server 7.0 introduced the automatic growth functionality for a database, which allows a database to grow on the fly. This is a great feature, but it should be used with care, because if you accept the defaults, which are 10 percent growth and a file size of 1 MB (see Figure 4-8), you might be constantly chunking out to disk while the database is trying to continually expand as it is used.

Figure 4-8 The GUI for setting growth at database creation.

As the database grows, 10 percent growth might be sufficient, but in an initial, small database, this generally won't fit your data curve. That creates a performance and potential availability problem because a large portion of your disk I/O is dedicated to expanding your disks, not just SQL Server usage. You can alter the growth properties of a database through Enterprise Manager, or use the ALTER DATABASE Transact-SQL command with the SIZE, MAXSIZE, UNLIMITED, or FILEGROWTH options. You should not set the file growth to UNLIMITED, as it allows the file chosen to grow until the disk is full. Some might want to set a maximum file size as well. If you do use the automatic growth, set a reasonable size, either by a percentage or physical size on disk, so that the database does not have to constantly grow.

> **Tip**   Do not set the system databases to autogrow without good reason. Extra space in the system databases (with some exceptions, such as using transactional replication heavily in msdb where it stores history as well as the transactions) is generally not needed unless you are doing some sort of version upgrade or installing a service pack, and this would be detailed in the information supplied with the software you are upgrading to. Pick a size you are comfortable with when SQL Server is first installed.

- **User databases**   What you probably care about most are the databases for your applications, whether third party or custom. The initial size of your database files should cover how much data you expect to have in the database for a time period of your determination plus some reasonable amount of growth.

- **Tempdb**   Provides important functionality to SQL Server—especially for queries—so its size must be properly set. Do you know if your applications use tempdb heavily? If not, find out. If tempdb is continually expanding to meet your needs, you will always experience disk contention for tempdb, and if that file is placed in the same location as your data or log files, it has a domino effect on performance. Especially if you consolidate onto fewer SQL Servers, knowing how each application uses tempdb helps you determine the size of tempdb (it needs to accommodate all workloads), and also helps you determine if the workloads will actually work well together.

> **Important**   You can always add more space to tempdb as needed. You can also take away space, but keep in mind that you cannot reduce the size of tempdb below the size at which you initially configured it when starting the SQL Server service without stopping and restarting SQL Server.

You can use SQL Server's alerting capabilities to warn you when the file size for your database equals, exceeds, or falls below a certain size, as shown in Figure 4-9. This is a great way to notify you that there might be an upcoming problem, and if you have set a hard maximum size, you can take action, or let the alert take an action, such as issuing an ALTER DATABASE statement. See Chapter 14, "Administrative Tasks to Increase Availability," or Chapter 15, "Monitoring for High Availability," for more information.

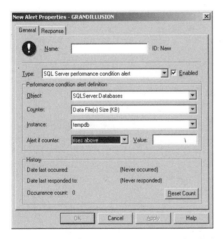

Figure 4-9   Configuring an alert for file size.

Shrinking Databases and Files

You can also decrease the size of your database and database files if, for example, you created them too large and have not experienced the growth you planned for. Like automatic growth, this should be done with care, as it might cause excessive disk I/O that will affect performance and possibly availability. To access the functionality in Enterprise Manager, right-click on a database, select All Tasks, and then select Shrink Database (see Figure 4-10).

Figure 4-10   Shrinking a database in Enterprise Manager.

To shrink a database using Transact-SQL, use the DBCC SHRINKDATABASE command. DBCC SHRINKDATABASE shrinks all data and log files for a specified database. If you only want to shrink a particular data or log file, you can issue a DBCC SHRINKFILE command. Whether you shrink the entire database or just one file, it shrinks to the specified amount of free space you designate. You can also set the AUTO_SHRINK property ON or OFF for the database. If set to ON, this property periodically shrinks the database.

Configuration Example

This section walks you through an example disk configuration. The goal is to understand the complexity of designing a disk array for a failover cluster that needs to take into account growth, performance, availability, and cost.

> **On the CD**   A sample configuration worksheet can be found on the CD-ROM that accompanies this book. The file name is Disk_Configuration_Worksheet.doc, and it can be used to hypothesize the following scenarios or serve as a reference for the environment that you put together to become a part of your run book.

The Scenario

An application is going to be upgraded to use SQL Server 2000. Currently, it is on a stand-alone machine running SQL Server 7.0 with all disks local. For a primary form of availability, you have decided to use failover clustering, which means the disk array needs to be upgraded to one on the cluster-specific HCL (including new controllers if needed) and needs some careful consideration to be optimized for the new disk usage patterns.

Unfortunately, without DBA involvement, management has already purchased the hardware, and you are constrained by the following rules:

■   The array has already been purchased and has the capacity to hold 16 disks.

■   12 disks have been purchased, and unless necessary, no more will be bought. You would need to justify the extra disks.

■   Each disk is 36 GB with a speed of 10,000 rpm.

■   The array can be configured so that two disks are online spares.

■   The array is configured to talk over one channel, so splitting the array into, say, two disks of eight that might use more than one channel, is impossible.

■   Remember the location for tempdb and the quorum in the configuration.

■   Two years' worth of growth should be factored in.

> **Important**   Outside the context of this example, be aware that having no DBA involvement in the hardware decision making is not recommended. All DBAs should be involved with hardware procurement because these decisions affect not only your servers, but your job as well. You would much rather have people praise you for the performance and availability of a system than ask you why it is down or how long it takes to run a query ("I kick off my query before lunch because it takes too long, and the results are there when I get back").

As shown in Table 4-3, this application uses three databases:

■   **Sales**   This database is currently 50 GB, and has historically grown approximately 33 percent per year. This database uses tempdb heavily.

- **Billing** This database is currently 150 GB and has seen growth of about 25 percent per year.

- **Contacts** This database is currently 500 MB in size and grows roughly 10 percent per month.

Table 4-3 **Databases Used by Sample Application**

Database Name	Size at End of Year 1 (in GB)	Size at End of Year 2 (in GB)
Sales	66.5	88.5
Billing	187.5	234.5
Contacts	1.5	4.5
Raw Space Totals	255.5	327.5

Assuming a 90:10 data-to-transaction log ratio, Table 4-4 shows the breakdown of file sizes to complement Table 4-3.

Table 4-4 **Breakdown of File Sizes**

Database Name	Size at End of Year 1 (in GB)	Size at End of Year 2 (in GB)
Sales	59.85 data/6.65 log	79.65 data/8.85 log
Billing	168.75 data/18.75 log	211.05 data/23.45 log
Contacts	1.35 data/0.15 log	4.05 data/0.45 log
Raw Space Totals	229.95 data/25.55 log	294.75 data/32.75 log

Table 4-5 shows the total amount of raw drive space available.

Table 4-5 **Available Raw Drive Space**

Number of Drives	Raw Space (in GB)
12	432
13	468
14	504
15	540
16	576

Sample Drive Configurations

There are more possible configurations, but the following four samples should give you a good idea of how challenging it is to configure a drive array. These examples all assume no use of files and filegroups. For your own edification, you might want to take these samples and try to think about how files and filegroups can be used with these configurations, and how they would change because of them.

None of the samples uses RAID 1+0/10/0+1. There are not enough drives to use that RAID level given the projected growth. None of these samples takes into account the archiving of data, either.

Sample 1

This sample (shown in Table 4-6) also adheres to the 12-drive limit. Quorum and tempdb each get their own RAID 1 LUN, and all of the data and logs are placed on a single RAID 5 LUN, meaning you will have a huge availability problem if the RAID 5 LUN fails. Notice that the total of 252 GB is not enough space for two years' worth of growth, given the projections. The company has to buy more disks. No online spares means the company would have to stock drives in the event of drive failures.

Table 4-6   Sample 1

Drive	LUN	RAID	LUN Size (in GB)	Purpose
1	1	1	36	Quorum
2	1			
3	2	1	36	Tempdb
4	2			
5	3	5	252	All data, logs
6	3			
7	3			
8	3			
9	3			
10	3			
11	3			
12	3			
13				
14				
15				
16				

Sample 2

This sample (shown in Table 4-7) also adheres to the 12-drive limit. The quorum and logs each get their own RAID 1 LUN (fixing the availability problem of Sample 1), and all of the data and tempdb are placed on a single RAID 5 LUN. Again, 252 GB is not enough space for two years' worth of growth, given the projections. If the RAID 5 partition fails, you lose all of your databases, but you do have access to your logs in this case. You will have a serious performance problem because tempdb is on the same LUN as all of your data. Once more, the company has to buy more disks. No online spares means the company would have to stock drives in the event of drive failures.

Table 4-7 Sample 2

Drive	LUN	RAID	LUN Size (in GB)	Purpose
1	1	1	36	Quorum
2	1			
3	2	1	36	All logs
4	2			
5	3	5	252	All data, tempdb
6	3			
7	3			
8	3			
9	3			
10	3			
11	3			
12	3			
13				
14				
15				
16				

Sample 3

Now that you know 12 disks are clearly not enough, there is a decision to buy two more disks. This time (Table 4-8), with 14 disks, you decide to split tempdb onto its own RAID 1 set to increase performance. You are still short on data growth space for two years' worth of growth. As with Sample 2, your logs are split out, so you do have increased availability, but because all your logs are on one RAID 1 set, you will not get the maximum performance from your logs.

You still need more drives. No online spares means the company would have to stock drives in the event of drive failure.

Table 4-8   Sample 3

Drive	LUN	RAID	LUN Size (in GB)	Purpose
1	1	1	36	Quorum
2	1			
3	2	1	36	All logs
4	2			
5	3	5	252	All data
6	3			
7	3			
8	3			
9	3			
10	3			
11	3			
12	3			
13	4	1	36	Tempdb
14	4			
15				
16				

Sample 4

The decision to max out the drive array at 16 disks is made. This configuration (Table 4-9) gives the proper amount of drive space, but you could not add online spares even if you wanted to.

Table 4-9   Sample 4

Drive	LUN	RAID	LUN Size (in GB)	Purpose
1	1	1	36	Quorum
2	1			
3	2	1	36	All logs
4	2			
5	3	5	324	All data
6	3			

(continued)

Table 4-9 Sample 4 *(continued)*

Drive	LUN	RAID	LUN Size (in GB)	Purpose
7	3			
8	3			
9	3			
10	3			
11	3			
12	3			
13	3			
14	3			
15	4	1	36	Tempdb
16	4			

Sample 5

This sample (Table 4-10) shows you from a maximum performance and space standpoint how you could potentially configure a disk subsystem if you have enough drives. This does not address files and filegroups, manageability, and hotspotting, which would come from knowing your data—this just handles space and base performance from a 10,000-foot view.

Table 4-10 Sample 5

Drive	LUN	RAID	LUN Size (in GB)	Purpose
1	1	1	36	Quorum
2	1			
3	2	1	36	Billing log
4	2			
5	3	1	36	Contacts log
6	3			
7	4	1	36	Sales log
8	4			
9	5	Striped mirrors	216	Billing data
10	5			
11	5			
12	5			
13	5			

(continued)

Table 4-10 Sample 5 *(continued)*

Drive	LUN	RAID	LUN Size (in GB)	Purpose
14	5			
15	5			
16	5			
17	5			
18	5			
19	5			
20	5			
21	6	Striped mirrors	108	Sales data
22	6			
23	6			
24	6			
25	6			
26	6			
27	7	1	36	Contacts
28	7			
29	8	1	36	Tempdb
30	8			

Summary

Proper disk configuration ensures that your SQL Server implementations are highly available and deliver the performance that you need from your disk subsystem. Planning can prevent future problems due to growth, performance, or disk availability. It is sometimes better to buy enough disk storage space—that is, the physical enclosure space—up front than it is to buy all of your disks at once. If your disk solution supports dynamic or easier growth, you can maximize your hardware investment, as you have planned for all of your growth but can expand when you need it. Using multiple controllers to support different types of reads and writes might be optimal, but it is expensive. Whatever you buy and implement affects every other aspect of your SQL Server and application solution.

5

Designing Highly Available Microsoft Windows Servers

Chapter 4, "Disk Configuration for High Availability," covered one of the main pieces of the foundation: your disk subsystem. This chapter helps to complete that foundation by providing information about configuring the true software base for Microsoft SQL Server: the operating system. This chapter covers both Microsoft Windows 2000 Server and Microsoft Windows Server 2003.

General Windows Configuration for SQL Servers

Before delving into the specific high availability options for the base operating system, there are some basic ideas you need to think about before you install the bits.

Choosing a Version of Windows

Choosing an operating system for SQL Server is no longer as clear-cut as it used to be. The operating system you choose affects the performance you get as your requirements grow. The need to make systems last longer these days makes your operating system choice that much more important.

Your operating system choice should match your SQL Server needs for processor and memory. Table 5-1 outlines the memory and processor support for editions of Windows 2000 Server and Windows Server 2003.

> **Note**   Windows Server 2003 Web Edition is not recommended for use with SQL Server 2000.

Table 5-1   Memory and Processors Supported per Operating System

Operating System	Memory Configuration	Processors
Windows 2000 Server (32-bit)	4 GB; 128-MB minimum; 256-MB minimum recommended	Up to 4; 133 MHz or higher, Pentium-compatible
Windows 2000 Advanced Server (32-bit)	8 GB; 128-MB minimum; 256-MB minimum recommended	Up to 8; 133 MHz or higher, Pentium-compatible
Windows 2000 Data-center Server	32 GB; 256-MB minimum	Up to 32; Pentium III Xeon or higher required
Windows Server 2003 Standard Edition (32-bit)	4 GB; 128-MB minimum; 256-MB minimum recommended	Up to 4; 133 MHz or higher, Pentium-compatible; 550 MHz or higher recommended
Windows Server 2003 Enterprise Edition (32-bit)	32 GB; 128-MB minimum; 256-MB minimum recommended	Up to 8; 133 MHz or higher, Pentium-compatible; 733 MHz or higher recommended
Windows Server 2003 Enterprise Edition (64-bit)	64 GB; 128-MB minimum; 256-MB minimum recommended	Up to 8; 733 MHz or higher, supported 64-bit processors; 733 MHz or higher recommended
Windows Server 2003 Datacenter Edition (32-bit)	64 GB; 512-MB minimum; 1-GB minimum recommended	Up to 64 (minimum of 8); 400 MHz or higher, Pentium-compatible; 733 MHz or higher recommended
Windows Server 2003 Datacenter Edition (64-bit)	512 GB; 512-MB minimum; 1-GB minimum recommended	Up to 64 (minimum of 8); 733 MHz or higher, supported 64-bit processors; 733 MHz or higher recommended

> **Note**   Windows Datacenter licenses allow you to run as many instances of Datacenter as you have physical processors through hardware or virtual partitioning. If you think you will ever need to use more than eight processors, a Datacenter version is your only choice, and the price premium is not that great when compared to the overall cost of an eight-processor system. Make sure you work with your preferred original equipment manufacturer to purchase expandable hardware or modular systems to prevent inadvertently being unable to expand the system at some later time.

32-Bit Versus 64-Bit

As you have already seen, Windows Server 2003 (in both Enterprise and Datacenter editions) can be found in both 32- and 64-bit versions. Cosmetically, all versions of Windows Server 2003 look and feel the same, but they are not the same inside because of the different architecture of the 64-bit chips.

What does this mean to you, the SQL Server consumer? There are two main areas that immediately come to mind: processor and memory. From a processor standpoint, even though a 64-bit chip might have double the amount of address bits and might be faster in terms of clock speed than the current Pentium-class machines, that does not guarantee you double the performance. A 64-bit machine should perform better than its 32-bit counterpart, as long as the application was coded to work with the 64-bit version of Windows Server 2003 and the 64-bit version of Microsoft SQL Server 2000. As with most applications, you should test against the 64-bit version of SQL Server 2000 to see what performance gains might be garnered from implementing this chip.

> **Important**   The 64-bit operating system requires a 64-bit version of SQL Server—you cannot install the 32-bit version of SQL Server on the 64-bit editions of Windows Server 2003.

From a SQL Server perspective, the main benefit of going to 64-bit is how memory is handled: all memory is dynamic under 64-bit, and you can address more than 4 GB of memory without setting any special options in your Boot.ini file. Under 32-bit operating systems, this is not the case. Under 32-bit operating systems, any addressable memory above 4 GB can be accessed only after configuration switches are placed in a system file, and then the application must be coded to recognize that additional amount of memory (which is why you turn on Address Windowing Extensions [AWE] support within SQL Server).

> **More Info**   Chapter 14, "Administrative Tasks to Increase Availability," covers SQL Server 2000 and memory usage in greater detail in the section "Memory Management for SQL Server 2000," as it is an aspect of SQL Server administration and configuration that affects all installations.
>
> For SQL Server 2000, when you install the 64-bit edition, you do not get all features and utilities that come with the 32-bit version. For a complete list, see the topic "Differences Between 64-bit and 32-bit Releases (64-bit)" in the 64-bit SQL Server Books Online.
>
> For information on options, especially tools, that might not be available to you under 64-bit operating systems, see the topic "Features unavailable on 64-bit versions of the Windows Server 2003 family" in TechNet at *http://www.microsoft.com/technet/treeview/ default.asp?url=/technet/prodtechnol/windowsserver2003/proddocs/ entserver/unsupported64BitFeatures.asp* or in your Windows Server 2003 documentation. If anything on this list is crucial for your environment to run on the same server as SQL Server 2000, you might not be able to use the 64-bit version of Windows Server 2003. For example, at launch time, the .NET Framework is not yet available under 64-bit.
>
> Also, consult the Windows Catalog at *http://www.microsoft.com/ windows/catalog/server2* for information on 64-bit applications.

Versions of SQL Server and Windows Server 2003

For those considering upgrading or doing a new installation of a 32-bit edition of Windows Server 2003, you can only use SQL Server 2000 RTM or Release A with SQL Server 2000 Service Pack 3 or later applied immediately after installing the base SQL Server 2000 software.

> **Important**   If you are upgrading your operating system, you must install SQL Server 2000 Service Pack 3 or later on all of the instances that will run in your server cluster or on the stand-alone server prior to upgrading the operating system.

Windows Server 2003 does not support any other versions of SQL Server—including Microsoft SQL Server 6.5, Microsoft SQL Server 7.0, and SQL Server 2000 with SQL Server 2000 Service Pack 2 or earlier. You will see the warning shown in Figure 5-1 pop up prior to the installation of SQL Server 2000. During an upgrade, you will see a message similar to that shown in Figure 5-2.

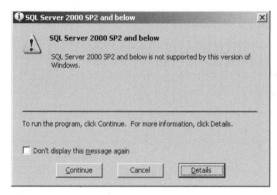

Figure 5-1   SQL Server 2000 warning prior to installation.

Figure 5-2 Warning during the upgrade process.

Disk Requirements for Windows

For an operating system configuration that will support applications, you need to configure your disks properly. This involves proper capacity planning, as well as configuring components like the page file and making sure the operating system can see the disks and access them without errors.

Whether you are implementing a server cluster or not, your system disk must be configured properly. It should be of sufficient size to accommodate all of the program files (and other files) you might place on it, the operating system, and potentially the page file. You might even want to make it part of a RAID stripe set to ensure you have redundancy in the event of a disk failure.

> **More Info** For information on configuring your page file, see the section "Page File Size and Location" in Chapter 14, "Administrative Tasks for High Availability."

With both Windows 2000 Server and Windows Server 2003, you also have the option to boot from a storage area network (SAN). The storage vendor must support this configuration; otherwise, do not attempt this because you might invalidate your support contract. If you encounter problems booting your Windows system, the storage vendor should be the first point of contact for support. You should take into account the following issues if you want to boot from a SAN, but talk to your storage vendor to get a complete list.

- Fibre Channel–Arbitrated Loop (FC–AL) is not supported if you want to boot from a SAN. The SAN must be in a switched environment or directly connected to the servers.

- The server must get exclusive access to the disk it will be booting from. No other server should be able to access or see the bootable logical unit (LUN). This means that you need to use zoning, masking, or a combination of the two.

- Redundancy can ensure that your system will always be able to see the system disk. This means that using multipathing and multiple host bus adapters (HBAs) will help greatly. However, ensure that the multipath software is on the Microsoft Hardware Compatibility List (HCL) or in the Windows Catalog for your solution.

- In a clustered scenario, the SAN needs to be on the multicluster device list if the individual nodes will be booting from a SAN.

- For Windows Server 2003, the HBA driver must be a Storport driver, which is new to Windows Server 2003. The manufacturer must code the driver to this.

- Booting from a SAN might limit your scalability and recoverability options by putting all of your eggs in one proverbial basket. For example, if you have a two-node cluster and have the shared cluster disks as well as the boot partitions on the SAN, if you lose the SAN, you literally lose everything.

- You need to ensure there will not be any I/O performance issues, especially if it is a cluster, because all disk I/O will be going through the same channels to get to the disks.

If you are implementing a server cluster, you might need to take into account the quorum disk, a disk resource for Microsoft Distributed Transaction Coordinator (MS DTC), as well as any application data (such as SQL Server data and log files).

> **Tip**   For security, you can encrypt your file system. This is fully supported with a server cluster only on Windows Server 2003. To do this, you must enable Kerberos, and all cluster node computer accounts and the cluster server service account must be trusted.

Security

The security of any server that runs SQL Server should be of paramount concern in your planning and, ultimately, your deployment of that server. You should not put any features on your server that you will not need, and you should uninstall ones you are not using. For example, if you are not using the Web-based query features of SQL Server 2000, you should not configure—or at least you should disable—Internet Information Services (IIS) so that it does not consume resources and you will not have anyone trying to access your server.

To assess your security, you can use the Microsoft Baseline Security Analyzer, which is located at *http://www.microsoft.com/technet/treeview/default.asp?url=/technet/security/tools/Tools/MBSAhome.asp*. You can download this free utility and run it on your systems to scan for potential vulnerabilities.

> **More Info**   Security is a topic that can obviously constitute a book (or books) of its own. Use the information provided in this book as a primer and then do more research on your own. See Chapter 2, "The Basics of Achieving High Availability," for information on how to think about security in a high availability environment, as well as Chapter 14 for some SQL Server–specific topics. For an excellent resource on configuring secure applications, including securing your operating system, consult the Microsoft Press book *Designing Secure Web-Based Applications for Microsoft Windows 2000*. Although this was written for Windows 2000 Server, its usage can certainly be applied to Windows Server 2003. For information on securing your Windows servers, this link for Windows has many links to security-related documents: *http://www.microsoft.com/technet/treeview/default.asp?url=/technet/security/prodtech/windows/secwin2k/default.asp*
>
> Here you can find such topics as Windows Security, Best Practices, Tools and Checklists, and more.

Terminal Server

Remember to consider how people will eventually access the server in a production environment. One way to do this is to configure Terminal Services, whereby people can log into your server remotely and do what they need to without physical access to the server. However, if you are going to be employing Terminal Services on a server cluster under Windows 2000 Server, there are a few points you need to consider:

- In the event you fail over to another node, all of the information held at the local node is lost, including the Remote Desktop Connection from the client computer. Although Terminal Services and a server cluster can coexist, they are blind to each other.

- Terminal Services must be installed only in Remote Administration mode on a cluster node.

- Remote Administration mode only allows up to two connections.

- Using Disk Management, you might see the following behavior:

  - If you change a drive letter, the change might not be reflected immediately.

  - If you create or remove a partition, if you view its properties you will see either the label of the partition is not accurate or the partition is claiming it is only 0 bytes.

- If a failover occurs, you might not be able to access a shared cluster disk, or a question mark might be displayed.

> **Tip**   To solve the display issues, log out and log back into Terminal server.

Under Windows Server 2003, you should use Remote Desktop Administration to access the nodes. You should not install Terminal Services directly on your cluster nodes when using it with SQL Server 2000 failover clustering.

Windows Server 2003 Enhancements

Any administrator will want to be aware of some new features of Windows Server 2003. These features are described next.

Server Roles

The concept of a server role, which allows your installation to be more geared to a specific use, is new to Windows Server 2003. Server roles that are configured are displayed in Manage Your Server, as shown in Figure 5-3. By default, no server roles are configured when Windows Server 2003 is installed.

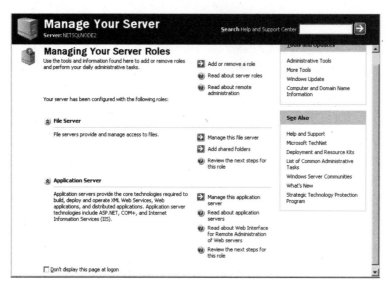

Figure 5-3 Manage Your Server application.

> **More Info** For more information on server roles in Windows Server 2003, see the documentation that comes with the operating system.

Unless you have a specific need to enable server roles (such as Application Server if you need IIS for some SQL Server features you might be using), you should disable all roles not in use to ensure not only a proper configuration but also to remove any unnecessary components that could cause a security risk to the SQL Server. To disable the roles, follow these steps:

1. Log on as someone with administrative privileges to the local server.

2. If Don't Display This Page At Logon has not been selected in the past, the Manage Your Server application appears (as in Figure 5-3). If this screen does not appear, select Start, then Manage Your Server, or under Start, Administrative Tools, select Manage Your Server. Select the Add Or Remove A Role option.

   If you want to bypass the Manage Your Server screen, select Start, Administrative Tools, and then Configure Your Server Wizard. When you select Add Or Remove A Role, this is where you are directed.

3. In the Welcome To The Configure Your Server Wizard page, shown in Figure 5-4, click Next.

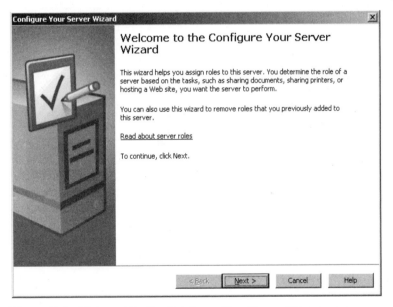

Figure 5-4   Welcome To The Configure Your Server Wizard page.

4. In the Preliminary Steps page, shown in Figure 5-5, click Next. The wizard gathers information about your Windows Server 2003 configuration.

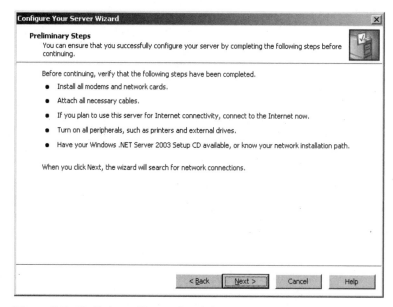

Figure 5-5   Preliminary Steps wizard page.

5.   In the Server Role wizard page, shown in Figure 5-6, all of the server roles that are configured are designated with a Yes next to the name of the server role. To select a server role to remove, select it and click Next.

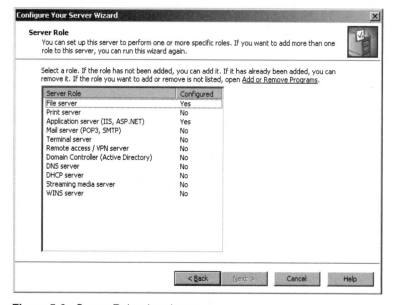

Figure 5-6   Server Role wizard page.

6.   In the Role Removal Confirmation wizard page, shown in Figure 5-7, make sure that the Summary reflects the operations you would like to perform. When ready, select the Remove The *<name of role>* Role check box and click Next.

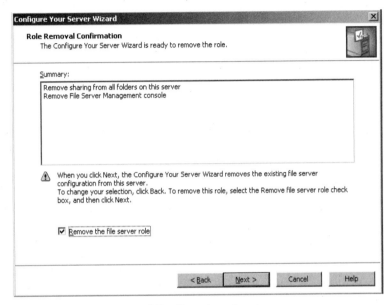

Figure 5-7   Role Removal Confirmation wizard page.

7.   Once the role is removed, a final wizard page confirms the removal, as shown in Figure 5-8. Click Finish to close the Configure Your Server Wizard.

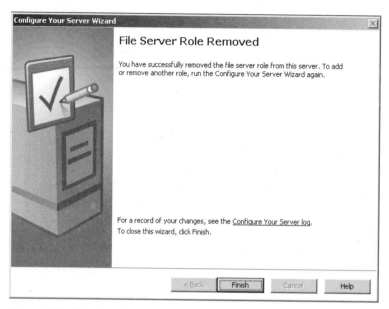

Figure 5-8 Final confirming wizard page.

8.   Repeat this process for all unnecessary server roles.

> **Tip** In your Windows Server 2003 installation directory, there is a directory called Debug. This directory contains a file called Configure Your Server.log that stores any changes made to Windows server roles. There are other log files in the Debug directory that you might also want to audit from time to time.

Shutdown

When you shut down or restart a Windows Server 2003 server, you are asked what you want to do (log off the user, shut down, or restart), as shown in Figure 5-9. You must now select the reason you are stopping or restarting your Windows server in the Option drop-down list, and you must enter a Comment. These will show up in Event Viewer, as shown in Figure 5-10. From a high availability and a security standpoint, these help you assess what has been done on the server. This provides you with an audit trail that can be analyzed later to improve processes and procedures and indicate where more training is needed or how you need to change how you do your work. It might seem annoying for administrators who are used to just shutting down or restarting your servers, but it helps force process into your organizations.

> **Important**   It cannot be said enough: technology is only a small portion of the answer to availability. The largest portion of all possible downtime is related to how you deal with process, procedure, and people.

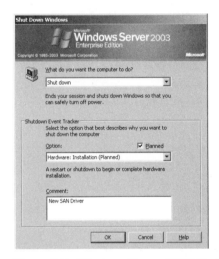

Figure 5-9   Windows Server 2003 Shut Down Windows dialog box.

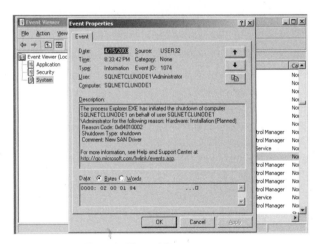

Figure 5-10   Entry in Event Viewer.

If you experienced an unexpected shutdown, when Windows Server 2003 restarts, it prompts you to enter what happened, as shown in Figure 5-11. The entry also appears in Event Viewer.

Figure 5-11   Shutdown Event Tracker.

High Availability Options for Windows

Whether you are configuring Windows 2000 Server or Windows Server 2003, you are referring to different forms of Windows Clustering. With any version of a stand-alone Windows server—unless you employ RAID for the system disks—clustering or using third-party offerings is the only way to ensure that another server will start to perform the work if the server and its applications fail. Even if you configure a duplicate server with the same software and operating system options, you would need a process to switch to that server. This is where a server cluster and Network Load Balancing might be able to assist you in increasing availability to your Windows installation.

Windows Reliability Features

In addition to clustering, there are other availability and reliability features built into Windows that are better covered in other documents. Here is a list of topics you can use to research more information.

Windows 2000 Server
The following were introduced with Windows 2000 Server to increase availability and reliability:

- Reboots minimized for some configuration tasks
- Slipstreaming of service packs and chaining of hotfixes
- Application failure recovery with IIS restart and out of process application protection
- Safe mode boot
- System Recovery Console

Windows Server 2003
The following were introduced with Windows Server 2003 to increase availability and reliability:

- Tools to measure and audit, including the already mentioned Shutdown Tracker, enhanced logging, and system tracing
- The overall hardware and software installation has been improved, including:
  - Driver install improvements
  - Driver rollback
  - New driver preference using .inf files
  - Hotplug Peripheral Component Interconnect (PCI)
  - Side-by-side assembly install
  - Hot add RAM
  - Signature support
- Volume Shadow Copy (VSS) Backups and enhanced backup and defragment APIs
- Fault tolerance system support through things like machine check architecture for 64-bit, multipath I/O and Load Balancing and Failover (LBFO)
- Better recovery through processes like autosystem recovery, last known good enhancements, up to an eight-node server cluster, geographically dispersed clusters, Majority Node Set (MNS) clusters, process cycling for IIS out-of-proc applications, COM+ object recycling, and service restarts

■   Maintenance tasks have also been improved, such as hot patch operating system hotfixes, no reboot hotfixes, and update improvements

■   Testing and qualification

❑   Driver Verifier and App Verifier

❑   Device, system, and domain controller Hardware Compatibility Tests (HCTs) and qualifications improved

❑   Certification improvements

■   Services "decomposed"

More Info   For basic information about server clusters and Network Load Balancing, see "Windows Clustering" in Chapter 3, "An Introduction to Microsoft High Availability Technologies."

Important   You cannot combine a server cluster and Network Load Balancing on the same physical hardware. They can coexist on the same network or domain, but they cannot be configured to run together on Windows installation.

Server Clusters

Server clusters are the pure availability form of Windows Clustering, and they form the basis for a SQL Server 2000 failover cluster. If you do not configure it properly, your failover cluster installation could be built on a bed of quicksand.

> **More Info**   For more information on server clusters, you can go to the Cluster Technologies Community Center, located at *http://www.microsoft.com/windowsserver2003/community/centers/clustering/default.asp*. This site covers Microsoft Windows NT 4.0, Windows 2000 Server, and Windows Server 2003. If you want direct access to white papers in the Community Center, they can be found at *http://www.microsoft.com/windowsserver2003/community/centers/clustering/more_resources.asp#MSCS*. There are many best practices papers, such as for security, which might cover topics that are not mentioned in this chapter.

Planning a Server Cluster

Planning your server cluster is in many ways more important than the implementation itself: most issues that eventually crop up with a server cluster configuration stem from a missed configuration point.

> **On the CD**   To assist you in your planning, use the document Server_Cluster_Configuration_Worksheet.doc.

Types of Server Clusters

Starting with Windows Server 2003, there are two types of server clusters: a standard server cluster, which is the same technology that can be found in Windows 2000 Server, and a new type called a majority node set (MNS) cluster. Both utilize many of the same semantics behind the scenes and behave similarly, but there are a few main differences.

The first difference is the quorum resource. The quorum not only contains the definitive and up-to-date server cluster configuration, but it also is used in the event a "split-brain" scenario occurs. A split-brain scenario can happen if two or more nodes in your server cluster lose all public and private network connectivity. At that point, you might have different "partitions" of your server cluster. The node owning the quorum resource gains ownership of all clustered resources, and the other nodes not seen by the partition that can use the quorum are evicted.

Both types require a quorum, but the mechanism is different. For a standard server cluster, this disk is accessed by one server at a time and is on the shared disk array. Under an MNS cluster, this is not a disk at all—nothing is shared. This is only found on an MNS cluster under Windows Server 2003. The quorum is actually found on your system disk in %SystemRoot%\Cluster\ QoN.%ResourceGUID%$\%ResourceGUID%$\MSCS. This directory and its contents should not be modified in any way. The other nodes access the quorum through a share named \\%NodeName%\%ResourceGUID%$ created with local access. Again, because all nodes of the cluster use this share, do not modify permissions with the share name, the Administrators group, or the Cluster Service account itself.

> **Tip** If you are implementing an MNS cluster, you should use RAID on your system disks to ensure the availability of your quorum. Do not use Integrated Device Electronics (IDE) disks.

> **Note** If the node owning the resources is still up and it is, say, the first node in the cluster, the cluster might appear to function until a reboot of that node. If all of the other nodes are still unavailable, the MNS cluster will not start and you might have to force the quorum. When nodes go offline, you might see a message pop up, alerting you that a delayed write to Crs.log failed.

SQL Server supports both types of server clusters. If you use an MNS cluster, you have the immediate benefit of not worrying about one more shared disk taking up a drive letter. It also gives you another possible geographic solution, assuming your hardware vendor certifies the solution. You are also protecting yourself from physical quorum disk failures bringing down the cluster. However, because losing the wrong number of nodes causes the entire solution to go down, it might not be a good choice. Table 5-2 shows the number of node failures tolerated. If your vendor builds a geographic solution based on MNS clusters, it might be a good thing, but for a local SQL Server cluster, you might be better off implementing a standard server cluster. You must weigh your options.

Table 5-2   Numbers of Nodes and Failure Tolerance in a Majority Node Set Cluster

Nodes	Maximum Node Failures Tolerated
1	0
2	0
3	1
4	1
5	2
6	2
7	3
8	3

> **More Info**   For more information on MNS clusters, see the white paper "Server Clusters: Majority Node Set Quorum" at *http:// www.microsoft.com/technet/treeview/default.asp?url=/technet/ prodtechnol/windowsserver2003/deploy/confeat/majnode.asp.*

Disk Subsystem

For up to a two-node Windows 2000 Advanced Server and Windows Server 2003 Enterprise Edition 32-bit server cluster, the shared disk subsystem can be either SCSI or fibre-based. For anything more than two nodes, all Datacenter editions, and all 64-bit editions, you must use fibre.

Cluster Service Account

The service account used to administer your server cluster does not need to be a domain administrator. In fact, you should not make the cluster administrator a domain administrator because that is an escalation of privileges. Because the cluster administrator account needs to be able to log into SQL Server, you could expose yourself if someone maliciously impersonated that account. The Cluster Service account must be a domain account that is a member of the local Administrators group on each node. During the installation of the server cluster, the account is configured with the proper rights, but if you ever need to manually re-create the account on each node, here are the privileges required:

- Act As Part Of The Operating System

- Back Up Files And Directories

- Increase Quotas

- Increase Scheduling Priority

- Load And Unload Device Drivers

- Lock Pages In Memory

- Log On As A Service

- Restore Files And Directories

Of this list, only Lock Pages In Memory, Log On As A Service, and Act As Part Of The Operating System are not granted when you place an account in the Administrators group on a server. As part of that group, the account also inherits the rights of Manage Auditing And Security Log, Debug Programs, and Impersonate A Client After Authentication (Windows Server 2003 only). Even if you restrict these privileges to other administrators, these rights must be granted to the Cluster Service account.

> **Tip**   If you have multiple clusters, you might want to use the same service account for each to ease administration.

> **Tip**   In some companies, security administrators lock down the rights that an account can use on a server. Without the listed privileges, your server clusters will not work. Work with your security or network administrators to ensure that the service accounts used for the server cluster and for SQL Server have the rights they need.

Server Clusters, the Hardware Compatibility List, and the Windows Catalog

Whether you are implementing a standard server cluster or an MNS cluster under Windows Server 2003, your solution must be on the Hardware Compatibility List (HCL), and going forward in the Windows Catalog. The HCL can be found at *http://www.microsoft.com/hwdq/hcl*, and the Windows Catalog for server products can be found at *http://www.microsoft.com/windows/catalog/ server2/default.aspx?subID=22*. Remember that the *entire* solution must be on the HCL—server nodes, network cards, the SAN or direct attached storage (DAS) device, driver versions, and so on.

In the Windows Catalog, there are two subcategories that you need to check under the main Cluster Solutions category: Cluster Solution and Geographically Dispersed Cluster Solution. In the HCL, the categories that you need to check are Cluster, Cluster/DataCenter 2-Node, Cluster/DataCenter 4-Node, Cluster/Geographic (2-Node Advanced Server), Cluster/Geographic (2-Node Datacenter Server), Cluster/Geographic (4-Node Datacenter Server), and Cluster/ Multi-Cluster Device. There are other cluster-related categories on the HCL, but they are for vendors only.

What is the purpose of these lists? The goal is to ensure that you have a known good platform for your server cluster solutions. Because you are combining multiple products (including drivers) to work with Windows, they need to work well together. The validation process involves low-level device tests of both the storage and the network as well as higher-level stress tests of the cluster under extreme conditions, such as many failures or heavy load. The Windows operating system has specific requirements of the hardware, particularly in a server cluster environment where data disks are physically connected to and visible to all the nodes in the cluster. Configurations that have not passed the server cluster test process are not guaranteed to operate correctly. Because disks are visible to multiple nodes, this can lead to corruption of application data or instability where the connection to the disks is not reliable.

Note   Vendors must submit their solutions for testing; Microsoft does not dictate which components they can use. With Windows Server 2003, there is a new qualification process called the Enterprise Qualification Process. The difference you will notice is that the lists displayed in the HCL or the Windows Catalog point back to the vendor's own Web sites, so it is up to the vendor to make sure the information is accurate.

Should you choose to ignore the HCL or Windows Catalog and put a non-compliant cluster into your production environment, your solution will technically be considered unsupported. Microsoft Product Support Services (PSS) will assist you as best they can, but they might not be able to resolve your issues because your solution is nonstandard. If you do buy a supported solution, what does "supported" mean? Because Microsoft cannot debug or support software from third-party vendors, or support and troubleshoot complex hardware issues alone, who supports what?

Microsoft supports qualified configurations, along with the vendors where appropriate, to provide root cause analysis. There are some deviations allowed, which are detailed in Table 5-3. When necessary, Microsoft escalates any issues found in the Windows operating system through the Windows escalation process. This process is used to ensure that any required hotfixes for the Windows operating system are provided to the customer. Microsoft supports and troubleshoots the Windows operating system and the server cluster components to determine the root cause. Part of that process might involve disabling non-Microsoft products in an effort to isolate issues to specific components or reduce the number of variables, but only if it does not impact the environment. For example, it would be possible to disable quota management software, but disabling storage multipath software would require infrastructure changes in the SAN; even worse, disabling volume management software might mean that the data is no longer available to applications.

If the analysis points toward non-Microsoft components in the configuration, the customer must work with Microsoft to engage the appropriate vendor within the context of agreements between the customer and the vendor. Microsoft does not provide a support path to vendors, so it is important that all components in the system are covered by appropriate service agreements between the customer and the third-party vendors.

Table 5-3 Supported Deviations from Windows Catalog

Component	Server Model	Deviations Allowed
Server model	Model number	Number of processors
		Memory size (unless it is lower than what is required for Windows)
		Number of network cards (but there must be at least two physically separate network cards)
		Processor speed (can be different up to 500 MHz only)
Host bus adapter (Fibre Channel only)	Driver version (miniport or full port)	See note
	Firmware version	
Multipath software (MPIO)	Driver version	See note
Storage controller	Firmware version	See note

Table 5-3   Supported Deviations from Windows Catalog

Component	Server Model	Deviations Allowed
Multisite interconnect for geographically dispersed clusters	Network technology (Dense Wavelength Division Multiplexing [DWDM], Asynchronous Transfer Mode [ATM], and so on)	No deviations allowed Latency between sites must be less than 500 ms round trip
	Switch type and firmware version	
Geographically dispersed cluster software components	Driver version Software version	No deviations allowed

Note   Third-party vendors might update versions of the drivers and firmware that deviate from the Windows Catalog and HCL listings. These can be qualified for your server clusters, but a major version change for any component requires the vendor to submit the solution for requalification, which will subsequently be listed separately. A minor version change does not require a resubmission of the clustered solution, but your vendor must provide a statement listing what combinations are supported. A vendor typically tests a specific combination of driver version, HBA firmware, multipath software version, and controller version to make up the solution.

Because complete vendor-qualified combinations are the only supported solutions, you cannot mix and match versions. The same rules apply for hotfixes and service packs released by Microsoft. A qualification for Windows 2000 Server implies all service packs and hotfixes, but vendors might not have tested their components against the latest service packs or with the hotfixes. Vendors should provide a statement indicating whether different combinations are supported and tested.

If you plan on connecting multiple servers (either other cluster nodes or stand-alone servers) on a single SAN, you also need to consult the Cluster/Multi-Cluster Device list of the HCL. Although there are many SANs out there, not all are certified for use with a server cluster, and not all can support multiple devices without interrupting others in the chain.

Under no circumstances can you mix and match components from various clusters or lists to make up your cluster solution. Consider the following examples:

- The following would not be a supported solution: Node 1 from vendor A listed under one of the System/Server categories on the HCL (or even listed as a node under the Cluster category), node 2 from vendor B listed under one of the System/Server categories on the HCL (or even listed as a node under the Cluster category), a Fibre Channel card from the Storage/FibreChannel Adapter (Large Memory Category), and a SAN from the Cluster/Multi-Cluster Device.

- If you use two servers that are on the Cluster list, but you take a different fibre controller from the Cluster/FibreChannel Adapter list (that is, change the base configuration of the cluster solution listed on the Cluster list), and use a SAN that is not on the HCL at all, this would be an unsupported cluster.

- You implement a Unisys ES-7000 as a one-node cluster because you want to use 16 processors for one Windows installation and plan on adding in the other node later. You then could not, say, go get another type of server and throw it into the cluster as a second node. Assuming your ES-7000 and disk array are part of what would be on the HCL as one of the Cluster categories, you could either add more processors to your ES-7000 and then carve out another server that way because it is a partitionable server, or buy another ES-7000.

More Info   The following are helpful Knowledge Base articles, located at *http://support.microsoft.com/*, about the Microsoft support policy for server clusters:

- 309395: "The Microsoft Support Policy for Server Clusters and the Hardware Compatibility List"

- 304415: "Support for Multiple Clusters Attached to the Same SAN Device"

- 327831: "Support for a Single Server Cluster That Is Attached to Multiple Storage Area Networks (SANs)"

- 280743: "Windows Clustering and Geographically Separate Sites"

- 327518: "The Microsoft Support Policy for a SQL Server Failover Cluster"

Certified Cluster Applications

If you use Windows 2000 Server Advanced Server and Windows Server 2003 Enterprise Edition, you are not required to check that the applications you are running on your cluster are certified to work in a cluster. With all Datacenter Editions, the opposite is true: the application must be certified for use with Windows Datacenter. Applications that earn the Certified for Windows logo are listed in the Windows Catalog, and you can also consult Veritest's Web site (*http://cert.veritest.com/CfWreports/server/*).

Ports, Firewalls, Remote Procedure Calls, and Server Clusters

Server clusters can work with firewalls, but you need to understand what ports you need to open. A server cluster uses User Datagram Protocol (UDP) port 3343 for the intracluster, or heartbeat, communication. Because this is a known port that is registered with the Internet Assigned Numbers Authority (IANA), you need to ensure that you cannot encounter a denial of service type of attack that can interfere with and potentially stop your server cluster.

A server cluster is dependent on remote procedure calls (RPCs) and the services that support them. You must ensure that the RPC service is always up and running on your cluster nodes.

More Info   For more information on ports, firewalls, and RPCs, reference the following resources:

- Knowledge Base article 154596: "Configure RPC Dynamic Port Allocation to Work with Firewall"

- Knowledge Base article 258469: "Cluster Service May Not Start After Restricting IP Ports for RPC"

- Knowledge Base article 300083: "Restrict TCP/IP Ports on Windows 2000"

- Knowledge Base article 318432: "BUG: Cannot Connect to a Clustered Named Instance Through a Firewall"

- "TCP and User Datagram Protocol Port Assignments" (from the *Windows 2000 Server Resource Kit*)

- On Microsoft TechNet, search for "TCP and UDP Port Assignments."

Geographically Dispersed Clusters

If you want to physically separate your cluster nodes to provide protection from site failure, you need a certified geographic cluster solution on the HCL or in the Windows Catalog. You cannot take two or more nodes, separate them, and implement a server cluster. That configuration is completely unsupported.

Antivirus Programs, Server Clusters, and SQL Server

In the past few years, use of antivirus software on computers has increased dramatically. In many environments, this software is installed as a de facto standard on all production servers. In a clustered environment and with SQL Server, antivirus requirements should be evaluated because antivirus programs are typically not cluster-aware, meaning they are not aware of how disks work in a clustered environment. The software might interfere with cluster operations. The server running SQL Server itself, unless it is, say, hosting a Web server or files for a solution, should technically have no need for virus scanning because the database-related .mdf, .ndf, and .ldf files are always managed by SQL Server and are not like a Microsoft Word or other text file that could be handled by an arbitrary application, or contain executable code or macros.

If you do need to place antivirus software on your server clusters, use the program's filters to exclude the \Mscs directory on the quorum for a standard server cluster. For SQL Server, use the filter to exclude all data and log directories on the shared disk array. If you do not filter the SQL Server files out, you might have problems on failover. You might also want to filter the \Msdtc directory used by MS DTC.

For example, consider a situation in which you encounter a failover and there is no filter. When the shared disks are recognized by another node, the virus scanner scans them, preventing the failover from completing and SQL Server from recovering. If your databases are very large, the problem will be worse.

> **More Info** See Knowledge Base article 250355, "Antivirus Software May Cause Problems with Cluster Services," at *http://support.microsoft.com*.

Server Clusters, Domains, and Networking

Network requirements are a source of contention among some people considering a server cluster. These requirements are often misunderstood. No clustered solution can work without domain connectivity. If you cannot guarantee that the nodes will have domain access, do not attempt to implement a server cluster.

Network Configuration

The following are the requirements for configuring your network cards for use with a server cluster:

■ To configure a server cluster you will need the following dedicated IP addresses: one IP address for each node on the public network, one IP address for each node on the private network, one IP address for the server cluster itself, and at least one IP address for each SQL Server 2000 instance that will be installed.

■ All cluster nodes must have domain connectivity. There is no way to implement a server cluster without it. If your cluster is going to be in a demilitarized zone (DMZ), you must have a domain controller in the DMZ or open a hole to your corporate network for the clusters.

■ All cluster nodes must be members of the same domain.

■ The domain the nodes belong to must meet the following standards:

   ❏ There must be redundant domain controllers.

   ❏ There must be at least two domain controllers configured as global catalog servers.

   ❏ If you are using Domain Name System (DNS), there must be redundant DNS servers.

   ❏ DNS servers must support dynamic updates.

   ❏ If the domain controllers are the DNS servers, they should each point to themselves for primary DNS resolution and to others for secondary resolution.

■ You should not configure your cluster nodes as domain controllers; instead, you should have dedicated domain controllers. If you do configure your nodes in any combination of a primary and backup domain controller, it could have direct implications for any SQL Server environment, as noted in Knowledge Base articles 298570, "BUG: Virtual SQL Server 2000 Installations May Fail if Installed to Windows 2000 Domain Controllers," and 281662, "Windows 2000 and Windows Server 2003 Cluster Nodes As Domain Controllers." In general, you should not install SQL Server 2000 on a domain controller.

- Windows Server 2003 does not require NetBIOS, so you can disable NetBIOS support. However, you need to know the implications of doing this and ensure that nothing else you have running on your cluster needs NetBIOS name resolution. This includes Cluster Administrator, which uses NetBIOS to enumerate the clusters in the domain, meaning you cannot use the browse functionality. By default, NetBIOS is enabled, but you can disable it on each IP resource's properties.

- Use two (or more) completely independent networks that connect the two servers and can fail independently of each other to ensure that you have no single points of failure. This means that the public and private networks must have separate paths (including switches, routers, and hubs) and physically independent hardware. If you are using a multiport network card to serve both the private and public networks, it does not meet the stated requirement.

- Each individual network used for a server cluster must be configured as a subnet that is distinct and different from the other cluster networks. For example, you could use 172.10.x.x and 172.20.x.x, both of which have subnet masks of 255.255.0.0. You should use separate subnets for the networks due to the implications of multiple adapters on the same network, as noted in Knowledge Base article 175767, "Expected Behavior of Multiple Adapters on Same Network."

- If desired, you can use a crossover cable to connect your cluster nodes for intracluster communications. Using a regular network is recommended.

- If you are implementing a geographically dispersed cluster, the nodes can be on different physical networks. The private and public networks, on the other hand, must appear to the cluster as a single, nonrouted LAN using something like a VLAN.

- Round-trip time between cluster nodes for the heartbeat must be less than 500 ms for all types of server clusters, local or geographic.

Network Card Configuration

To configure your network cards for use in a server cluster, address the following public network and private network configuration points.

Public Network Configuration   Consider the following points when configuring your public network dedicated for cluster communications:

- The speed of the network card should match the maximum speed of the network card and its underlying network. This must be set the same on each public adapter. Do not set auto detect.

- You cannot enable Network Load Balancing on the same server or network card used for a server cluster.

- Both a primary and secondary DNS must be configured.

- Static IP addresses are strongly recommended. Do not use Dynamic Host Configuration Protocol (DHCP).

- The public network should be configured for all cluster communications to have redundancy for your private network. Because that is a requirement of a server cluster, it is the recommended implementation method.

Private Network (Heartbeat) Configuration   Consider the following when configuring your private network dedicated for cluster communications:

- The speed of the network card should match the maximum speed of the network card and its underlying network. This must be set the same on each private adapter. Do not set auto detect.

- Do not set a default gateway.

- Disable NetBIOS. This can be found on the WINS tab of the Advanced Properties dialog box for the network card.

- Only TCP/IP should be enabled. No other protocol or service (such as Network Load Balancing or sharing) should be checked in the properties of the network card.

- Although network teaming cards are supported in a server cluster, using them for the private network cards used for internal communication only in the cluster is not supported.

- For private network redundancy, set the publicly faced network to handle both private and public traffic.

- For a private network, the valid blocks of IP addresses are as follows:

  ❏   10.0.0.0

  ❏   172.16.0.0

  ❏   192.168.0.0

- You can use a crossover cable, but a regular network is recommended. If you use a crossover cable between the cluster nodes, you must still use static IP addresses.

- If you are using a crossover cable with Windows 2000, add the following registry key to each node:

```
HKEY_LOCAL_MACHINE\System\CurrentControlSet\Services\Tcpip\Parameters
Value Name: DisableDHCPMediaSense
Data Type: REG_DWORD
Data: 1
```

  This disables the TCP/IP stack destruction feature of Media Sense.

Warning   Do not modify the registry entry for Media Sense on Windows Server 2003 clusters.

- Disable autosensing or automatic detection of the speed of the network. This could cause problems on the private network.

- The speed of the network card should match the maximum speed of the network card and its underlying network. This must be set the same on each private adapter. Setting this to 10 MB/sec and half duplex should provide sufficient bandwidth.

Implementing a Server Cluster

Whether you are implementing a standard server cluster or an MNS cluster, you will have to handle some preconfiguration and postconfiguration tasks in addition to installing the cluster itself.

Preconfiguration Tasks

Before you install your server cluster, you must perform some tasks to make sure you are prepared.

> **On the CD**   Use the document Server_Cluster_Pre-Installation_ Checklist.doc to ensure that you are ready to install your server cluster. Also take this time to fill out the worksheet Node_Configuration_Worksheet.doc for each node's configuration.

Configuring Network Cards   Configure your network cards per the recommendations given earlier.

Network Cards Used on the Public Network   To configure a network card for use on a public network, follow these steps:

1. From your desktop, right-click My Network Places, and select Properties. Under Windows Server 2003, you might need to enable the Classic Start menu view from the Properties menu on the taskbar to see this.

2. In the Network And Dial-up Connections (Windows 2000 Server) or Network Connections (Windows Server 2003) window, select the network card. Rename this to something recognizable and usable, such as Public Network, by selecting it, right-clicking, and selecting Rename. This is the same value on all nodes.

3. Select the Public Network network card, right-click, and select Properties.

4. Select Internet Protocol (TCP/IP) and click Properties. Set the static IP address of the card to a valid IP address on the externally facing network. This address is different for each node of the server cluster. These addresses will all be on the same subnet, but a different subnet from the private network. Click OK.

5. Make sure the Subnet mask is correct.

6. Enter your default gateway.

7. Enter your primary and secondary DNS servers.

8. Click OK to return to the Public Network Properties dialog box. Click Configure.

9. In the Properties dialog box for the network card, select the Advanced tab, shown in Figure 5-12.

10. For the External PHY property, set the value for the correct network speed. You set this to be the same on each node. Click OK.

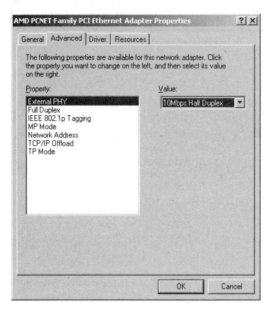

Figure 5-12 The Advanced tab of the Properties dialog box for a network card.

11. Click OK to close the Public Network properties dialog box.

Network Cards Used on the Private Network   To configure a network card for use on a private network, follow these steps:

1. From your desktop, right-click My Network Places, and select Properties. Under Windows Server 2003, you might need to enable the Classic Start menu view from the Properties menu of the taskbar to see this.

2. In the Network And Dial-up Connections (Windows 2000 Server) or Network Connections (Windows Server 2003) window, select the network card. This network card is located only on the private network on the approved subnets. Rename this to something recognizable and usable, such as Private Network, by selecting it, right-clicking, and selecting Rename. This is the same value on all nodes.

3. Select the Private Network network card, right-click, and select Properties.

4. Make sure that Client For Microsoft Networks, Network Load Balancing, File And Printer Sharing For Microsoft Networks, and any other options are not selected, as shown in Figure 5-13.

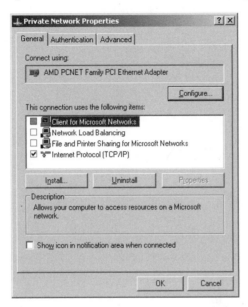

Figure 5-13   The General tab of the Properties dialog box for a network card.

5. Select Internet Protocol (TCP/IP) and click Properties. Set the static IP address of the card to a valid IP address on the externally facing network. This address is different for each node of the server cluster, and must be in the proper class. These addresses will all be on the same subnet, but a different subnet from the public network. Click OK.

6. Make sure the subnet mask is correct.

7. Do not enter a default gateway.

8. Do not enter any DNS servers.

9. Click Advanced.

10. Select the WINS tab of the Advanced TCP/IP Settings dialog box, shown in Figure 5-14, and select Disable NetBIOS Over TCP/IP if you are not on an MNS cluster. Click OK.

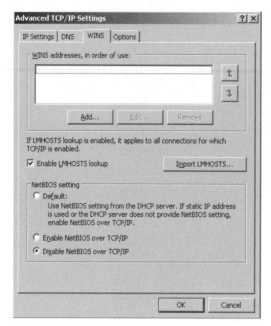

Figure 5-14   The WINS tab of the Advanced TCP/IP Settings dialog box.

11. Click OK to return to the Private Network Properties dialog box. Click Configure.

12. Click Advanced. In the Properties dialog box for the network card, select the Advanced tab.

13. For the External PHY property, as shown in Figure 5-12, set the value for the correct network speed. Set this to be the same on each node. Click OK.

14. Click OK to close the Private Network Properties dialog box.

15. If you are on a Windows 2000 server, add the following registry key and its associated values only if you are using a crossover cable:

```
HKEY_LOCAL_MACHINE\System\CurrentControlSet\Services\Tcpip\
Parameters
Value Name: DisableDHCPMediaSense
Data Type: REG_DWORD
Data: 1
```

> **Warning**   Do not perform this step if you are using Windows Server 2003.

16. Repeat this procedure for each node in the server cluster and for each private network.

Changing Network Priority   You need to configure your networks so that they have the right priority and one will not impede the other. At the server level, the public networks should have the priority. You can configure the network by following these steps:

1. On your desktop, right-click My Network Places and select Properties. If you are using Windows Server 2003, you might need to enable the Classic Start menu view from the Properties menu on the taskbar to see this.

2. From the Advanced menu, select Advanced to open the Advanced Settings dialog box, shown in Figure 5-15.

3. All public, or externally faced, networks should have priority over the private ones. If this is not the case, set the proper order and click OK. If you have multiple networks, set them in the proper order. This order is the same on all nodes.

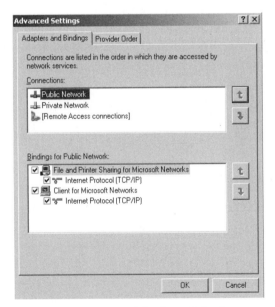

Figure 5-15   Advanced Settings dialog box.

4. Close the Network Connections (Windows Server 2003) or Network And Dial-Up Connections (Windows Server 2000) window.

5. Repeat this procedure for each node of the cluster.

Verifying Your Network Connectivity   To verify that the private and public networks are communicating properly prior to installing your server cluster, perform the following steps. It is imperative to know the IP address for each network adapter in the cluster, as well as for the IP cluster itself.

Verifying Connectivity and Name Resolution from a Server Node   This method shows how to check both IP connectivity and name resolution at the server level.

1.   On a node, from the Start menu, click Run, and then type **cmd** in the text box. Click OK.

2.   Type **ping *ipaddress*** where *ipaddress* is the IP address of another node in your server cluster configuration. This must be done for both the public and private networks. Repeat for every other node, including the node you are on.

3.   Type **ping *servername*** where *servername* is the name of another node in your server cluster configuration. Repeat for every other node, including the node you are on.

4.   Repeat Steps 1–3 on each node.

Verifying Connectivity and Name Resolution from a Client or Other Server   This method shows how to check both IP connectivity and name resolution at the client or other servers that will access the server cluster.

1.   On a client computer, from the Start menu, click Run, and then type **cmd** in the text box. Click OK.

2.   Type **ping *ipaddress*** where *ipaddress* is the public IP address of one of the nodes in your server cluster configuration. If there is more than one public IP address, you must repeat this step.

3.   Type **ping *servername*** where *servername* is the name of one of the nodes in your server cluster configuration.

4.   Repeat Steps 2 and 3 for each node.

Creating the Shared Disks   Prior to installing your server cluster, you should also configure all disks that will be used in the cluster up front to minimize downtime later should you need to add a disk. Mountpoints do not get you around the main drive letter limitation, but they give you the ability to add a disk without a drive letter to an existing disk without interrupting the availability of a resource such as SQL Server.

Important   When configuring your server clusters, always configure the first node and the shared disks before you power on the other nodes and allow the operating system to start. You do not want more than one node to access the shared disk array prior to the first node being configured.

Also, for 64-bit editions of Windows Server 2003, the shared cluster disks must not only be basic disks, but they must be partitioned as master boot record (MBR) and not GUID partition table (GPT) disks.

More Info   For more information on using mountpoints with SQL Server 2000, see Chapter 6, "Microsoft SQL Server 2000 Failover Clustering."

Creating Basic Disks   To create a basic disk, follow these steps:

1. Start Computer Management from the Administration Tools menu.

2. Select Disk Management.

3. Select the disk you want to use, right-click, and select New Partition.

4. Click Next in the Welcome To The New Partition Wizard page.

5. In the Select Partition Type wizard page, classify this as either a primary partition or an extended partition. Click Next.

6. In the Specify Partition Size wizard page, enter the size (in megabytes) of the partition. You do not have to use the entire disk, but if you do not, all partitions created are presented as one disk to a server cluster. Click Next.

7. In the Assign Drive Letter Or Path wizard page, select a drive letter from the Assign The Following Drive Letter drop-down list. Click Next.

8. In the Format Partition wizard page, select NTFS from the File System drop-down list, define the Allocation Unit Size (which should be 64K for SQL Server disks that will contain data), and specify a name for the Volume. Click Next.

9. If the disk is not a basic disk (which is the default under Windows Server 2003), convert it to a basic disk.

Creating a Volume Mountpoint   To create a volume mountpoint, follow these steps:

1. Start Cluster Administrator and pause all nodes of the cluster.

> **Important**   You will experience a brief bit of downtime when configuring the mountpoint, but it will not be as bad as adding a new disk.

2. Start Computer Management from the Administration Tools menu.

3. Select Disk Management.

4. Select the disk you want to use, right-click, and select New Partition.

5. Click Next in the Welcome To The New Partition Wizard page.

6. In the Select Partition Type wizard page, classify this as either a primary partition or an extended partition. Click Next.

7. In the Specify Partition Size wizard page, enter the size (in megabytes) of the partition. You do not have to use the entire disk, but if you do not, all partitions created are presented as one disk to a server cluster. Click Next.

8. In the Assign Drive Letter Or Path wizard page, do not assign a drive letter. Click Next.

9. In the Format Partition wizard page, select NTFS from the File System drop-down list, define the Allocation Unit Size (which should be 64K for SQL Server disks that will contain data), and specify a name for the Volume. Click Next.

10. If the disk is not a basic disk (which is the default under Windows Server 2003), convert it to a basic disk.

11. On the disk you want to use as the root of your mountpoint, create a blank folder.

12. In the Disk Management window, select the new volume that you created, right-click, and select Change Drive Letter And Paths. Click Add.

13. In the Add Drive Letter Or Path dialog box, select the Mount In The Following Empty NTFS Folder option, and select the folder created in Step 11 (or you can also do it here). Click OK. The change will be reflected in the Change Drive Letter And Path dialog box.

14. Click OK. Close the Computer Management console.

> **Note**   Steps 15 and 16 refer to specific cluster steps to be done after your server cluster is configured, and they are listed here for completeness.

15. Using Cluster Administrator, in the resource group with the disk that has the root folder, create a new disk resource (see the section "Adding a New Disk" later in this chapter). During the process, you must add the dependency of the root disk to the disk that will serve as a mountpoint.

16. Unpause all nodes in Cluster Administrator and test failover for the new disk resource.

> **Important**   Do not create a mountpoint on a drive that is not part of the shared disk array. Also, do not use the quorum disk or the disk for MS DTC. You can use mountpoints to expand these drives, however.

Installing the Server Cluster

Once you have completed the preconfiguration tasks, you are ready to install the server cluster. The process under Windows 2000 Server differs from the process under Windows Server 2003.

Under Windows 2000 Server, you have two options to configure the server cluster: using the Cluster Service Configuration Wizard or the command line. Under Windows Server 2003, you have three options to configure your server cluster: through the GUI, using the command line, and an unattended installation.

> **On the CD**   For instructions on configuring a server cluster, see the document Server_Cluster_Installation_Instructions.doc.

Important   When configuring your server clusters, always configure the first node before powering on the other nodes and allowing the operating system to start. A Windows 2000 server cluster is dependent on the IIS Common Files being installed on each node during the operating system installation, or later adding the components through Add/Remove Windows Components. Do not attempt to copy these DLLs from another server into the right locations, as having the DLLs alone is not enough. For informational purposes only, here is a list of the DLLs installed as part of the IIS Common Files:

%systemroot%\Admwprox.dll
%systemroot%\Adsiis.dll
%systemroot%\Exstrace.dll
%systemroot%\Iisclex4.dll

%systemroot%\Iisext.dll
%systemroot%\Iismap.dll

%systemroot%\IisRtl.dll
%systemroot%\Inetsloc.dll
%systemroot%\Infoadmn.dll
%systemroot%\Wamregps.dll
%systemroot%\System32\Inetsrv\Coadmin.dll
%systemroot%\System32\Inetsrv\Isatq.dll
%systemroot%\System32\Inetsrv\Iisui.dll
%systemroot%\System32\Inetsrv\Logui.ocx

Postconfiguration Tasks

Once you have installed your server cluster, there are a few things that you must do prior to installing any applications like SQL Server.

On the CD   For a useful checklist to use when performing these tasks and for auditing capabilities, use the document Server_Cluster_Post-Installation_Checklist.doc.

Important   There are some post-Windows 2000 Service Pack 3 hot-fixes that you should apply to your nodes that are important for server clusters. As of the writing of this book, the following list is accurate. Please check to see if there are any additional hotfixes for Windows 2000 or any for Windows Server 2003 before you configure your server clusters.

Information about the hotfixes can be found in the following Knowledge Base articles:

- 325040: "Windows 2000: Drive Letter Changes After You Restart Your Computer"

- 323233: "Clusres.dll Does Not Make File System Dismount When IsAlive Fails"

- 307939: "Disks Discovered Without the Cluster Service Running Are Not Protected"

- 815616: "Clustered Disk Drive Letter Unexpectedly Changes"

- 326891: "The Clusdisk.sys Driver Does Not Permit Disks to Be Removed by Plug and Play"

There is one other fix that should not be applied unless you have spoken with the storage hardware vendor for your SAN or shared disk array and he or she indicates that the fix is valid and required. You can find more information about this in the following Knowledge Base article:

- 332023: "Slow Disk Performance When Write Caching Is Enabled"

Configuring Network Priorities   Besides setting the network priorities at the server level, you need to do it in Cluster Administrator for the cluster. In the cluster, the private network is the ruler. Follow these steps to configure network priorities:

1. Start Cluster Administrator. Select the name of the cluster, right-click, and select Properties, or you can select Properties from the File menu.

2. Select the Network Priority tab, shown in Figure 5-16. Make sure that the private heartbeat network has priority over any public network. If you have multiple private and public networks, set the appropriate order.

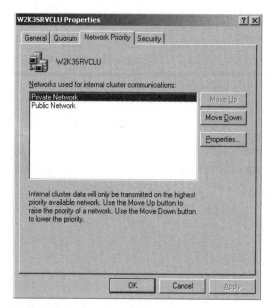

Figure 5-16   Network Priority tab.

3.   Click OK. Close Cluster Administrator.

Enabling Kerberos   If you are going to be using Kerberos with your cluster, ensure that the Cluster Service account has the appropriate permissions. Then perform the following steps:

1.   Start Cluster Administrator.

2.   Select the Groups tab, and select the Cluster Group resource group. In the right pane, select *Cluster Name*, right-click, and select Take Offline.

3.   Once *Cluster Name* is offline, right-click it and select Properties.

4.   On the Parameters tab, select the Enable Kerberos Authentication check box, and click OK.

5.   Bring online.

Changing the Size of the Cluster Log   The cluster log size defaults to 8 MB, which is not very big. If the cluster log becomes full, the Cluster Service over-writes the first half of the log with the second half. In that case, you can only guarantee that half of your cluster log is valid. To prevent this situation, you must create a system environment variable named ClusterlogSize, following these steps. You should make this value great enough to ensure validity of the cluster log in your environment.

> **More Info**   For more information, consult Knowledge Base article 168801, "How to Turn On Cluster Logging in Microsoft Cluster Server."

1. From Control Panel, select System (or right-click My Computer).

2. Select the Advanced tab, and click Environment Variables.

3. In the Environment Variables dialog box under System Variables, click New.

4. In the New System Variables dialog box, type **ClusterlogSize** for the Variable Name, and for Variable Value, enter **ClusterlogSize=x**, where *x* is the size in MB.

5. Click OK. The new environment variable will be displayed.

6. Click OK two more times to exit.

7. Reboot the cluster nodes one by one so that the change takes effect. Verify that the Cluster.log file is the appropriate size after the final reboot.

Configuring MS DTC   Microsoft Distributed Transaction Coordinator (MS DTC) is used by SQL Server and other applications. For a SQL virtual server to use MS DTC, it must also be clustered. Its configuration will vary depending on your needs. You cannot use a remote MS DTC; you must configure an MS DTC resource for your server cluster.

> **Note**   MS DTC is shared for all resources in the cluster. If you are implementing multiple SQL Server instances, they will all use the same MS DTC resource.

MS DTC does require disk space; in general, the size used should be roughly 500 MB. However, some applications might have specific requirements. For example, Microsoft Operations Manager recommends a minimum MS DTC size of 512 MB. You obviously need to consider this in your overall disk subsystem planning.

Creating MS DTC on Windows 2000 Server   Under Windows 2000 Server, there are two schools of thought when it comes to designing a server cluster when MS DTC is used:

■   Use the default configuration, which configures MS DTC to use the quorum drive. This is the most popular and most often recommended solution for use with SQL Server. If MS DTC is going to utilize the quorum, be sure there is enough room for the cluster files. You should also set the MS DTC resource so that it does not affect the group in the event of a failure.

■   Plan in advance and create a separate cluster disk dedicated to MS DTC. This might reduce contention on the quorum drive if MS DTC is being used in the cluster, but it might also mean that not enough drives will be available for the SQL Server instances. It also involves a few more steps in configuring the cluster. For example, a clustered Microsoft BizTalk Server configuration requires that MS DTC be placed on a separate drive and in a separate cluster group.

For a default installation of MS DTC using the quorum, perform the following steps:

1.   From the Start menu, choose Run, and type **comclust.exe**.

2.   Repeat this on each cluster node.

If you want to create MS DTC in its own group, or you need to move it after creating it in the default location, follow the steps given next. Do not place it in the group with SQL Server or make it dependent on any of its resources. You should create a new group (or use an existing one with an unused disk) with its own dedicated IP address, network name, and disk for MS DTC, move the DTC resource into the new group, and add the network name and the disk resource as dependencies of the MS DTC resource.

> **Important**   Make sure no users or applications are connected to your cluster while you are performing this procedure.

1.   Start Cluster Administrator. Select the group that has the dedicated disk you will use for MS DTC and rename the group appropriately.

2. If you already have a clustered MS DTC in a group (such as the one containing the quorum), delete the existing MS DTC resource. If you have not yet configured MS DTC, you can skip this step.

3. From the File menu, select New, and then Resource (or right-click the group and select the same options). In the New Resource dialog box, in the Name box, type an appropriate name, such as **MS DTC IP Address**; in the Resource Type drop-down list, select IP Address. In the Group drop-down list, make sure the right group is selected. Click Next.

4. In the Possible Owner dialog box, all nodes of the cluster should appear as possible owners. If they do not, add the nodes and then click Next.

5. In the Dependencies dialog box, select the disk resource in the group you selected from the Available Resources, and then click Add. The disk resource appears in the Resource Dependencies list. Click Next.

6. In the TCP/IP Address Parameters dialog box, enter the TCP/IP information. In the Address text box, enter the static IP address that will be used with MS DTC. In the Subnet Mask text box, enter the IP subnet if it is not automatically chosen for you. In the Network To Use text box, select the public cluster network you want to use. Click Finish.

7. You will see a message confirming that the IP address is successfully configured.

8. In the Cluster Administrator window, the newly created resource appears in the right pane.

9. From the File menu, select New, and then Resource (or right-click the group and select the same options). In the New Resource dialog box, in the Name text box, type an appropriate name such as **MS DTC Network Name**. In the Resource Type drop-down list, select Network Name. In the Group drop-down list, make sure the proper group is selected. Click Next.

10. In the Possible Owner dialog box, all nodes of the cluster should appear as possible owners. If they do not, add the nodes, and click Next.

11. In the Dependencies dialog box, the MS DTC IP address resource you configured previously appears in the Available Resources list. Select the resource, and then click Add. The resource appears in the Resource Dependencies list. Click Next.

12. In the Network Name Parameters dialog box, type **MSDTC**, and then click Finish.

13. You will see a message confirming that the Network Name resource is successfully configured.

14. In the Cluster Administrator window, the newly created resource appears in the right pane.

15. From the File menu, select New, and then Resource (or right-click the group and select the same options). In the New Resource dialog box, in the Name text box, type an appropriate name such as **MS DTC**. In the Resource Type drop-down list, select Distributed Transaction Coordinator. In the Group drop-down list, make sure the proper group is selected. Click Next.

16. In the Possible Owner dialog box, all nodes of the cluster should appear as possible owners. If they do not, add the nodes, and click Next.

17. In the Dependencies dialog box, the MS DTC IP address and network name resources you configured previously appear in the Available Resources list. Select both, and then click Add. The resource appears in the Resource Dependencies list. Click Next.

18. In the Network Name Parameters dialog box, type **MSDTC**, and then click Finish.

19. You will see a message confirming that the Distributed Transaction Coordinator resource is successfully configured.

20. In the Cluster Administrator window, the newly created resource appears in the right pane.

21. On each node, rerun Comclust.exe.

22. On the node that currently owns the MS DTC disk resource, you must reset the log. At a command prompt, type **msdtc -resetlog.**

23. To start the new resources, which are all offline, right-click each one, and then click Bring Online.

Creating MS DTC on Windows Server 2003   With Windows Server 2003, the process is completely different, and it is not unlike the second process detailed under Windows 2000 Server. You can no longer run Comclust.exe. You must now manually create an IP address, network name, and Distributed Transaction Coordinator resource, following these steps:

> **Important**   When configuring MS DTC, do not use the group containing a disk with the quorum or any of the ones planned for use with SQL Server.

1. Start Cluster Administrator. Select the group that has the dedicated disk you will use for MS DTC and rename the group appropriately.

2. From the File menu, select New, and then Resource (or right-click the group and select the same options). In the New Resource dialog box, in the Name text box, type an appropriate name, such as **MS DTC IP Address**. In the Resource Type drop-down list, select IP Address. In the Group drop-down list, make sure the right group is selected. Click Next.

3. In the Possible Owner dialog box, all nodes of the cluster should appear as possible owners. If they do not, add the nodes, and click Next.

4. In the Dependencies dialog box, select the disk resource in the group you selected from the Available Resources, and then click Add. The disk resource appears in the Resource Dependencies list. Click Next.

5. In the TCP/IP Address Parameters dialog box, enter the TCP/IP information. In the Address text box, enter the static IP address that will be used with MS DTC. In the Subnet Mask text box, enter the IP subnet if it is not automatically chosen for you. In the Network To Use list box, select the public cluster network you want to use. Click Finish.

6. You will see a message confirming that the IP address is successfully configured.

7. In the Cluster Administrator window, the newly created resource appears in the right pane.

8. From the File menu, select New, and then Resource (or right-click the group and select the same options). In the New Resource dialog box, in the Name text box, type an appropriate name such as **MS DTC Network Name**. In the Resource Type drop-down list, select Network Name. In the Group drop-down list, make sure the proper group is selected. Click Next.

9. In the Possible Owner dialog box, all nodes of the cluster should appear as possible owners. If they do not, add the nodes, and click Next.

10. In the Dependencies dialog box, the MS DTC IP address resource you configured previously appears in the Available Resources list. Select the resource, and then click Add. The resource appears in the Resource Dependencies list. Click Next.

11. In the Network Name Parameters dialog box, type **MSDTC**, and then click Finish.

12. You will see a message confirming that the Network Name resource is successfully configured.

13. In the Cluster Administrator window, the newly created resource appears in the right pane.

14. From the File menu, select New, and then Resource (or right-click the group and select the same options). In the New Resource dialog box, in the Name text box, type an appropriate name such as **MS DTC**. In the Resource Type drop-down list, select Distributed Trans-action Coordinator. In the Group drop-down list, make sure the proper group is selected. Click Next.

15. In the Possible Owner dialog box, all nodes of the cluster should appear as possible owners. If they do not, add the nodes, and click Next.

16. In the Dependencies dialog box, the MS DTC IP address and net-work name resources you configured previously appear in the Avail-able Resources list. Select both, and then click Add. The resource appears in the Resource Dependencies list. Click Next.

17. In the Network Name Parameters dialog box, type an appropriate name such as **MS DTC**, and then click Finish.

18. You will see a message confirming that the Distributed Transaction Coordinator resource is successfully configured.

19. In the Cluster Administrator window, the newly created resource appears in the right pane.

20. To start the new resources, which are all offline, right-click each one, and then click Bring Online.

Verifying Your Server Cluster Installation

Once you have configured your base server cluster, you need to test it to ensure that it is configured and working properly.

Verifying Connectivity and Name Resolution   To verify that the private and public networks are communicating properly, perform the following steps. It is imperative to know the IP address for each network adapter in the cluster, as well as for the IP cluster itself.

1. On a node, from the Start menu, click Run, and then type **cmd** in the text box. Click OK.

2. Type **ping *serverclusteripaddress*** where *serverclusteripaddress* is the IP address for the server cluster you just configured.

3. Type **ping *serverclustername*** where *serverclustername* is the network name for the server cluster you just configured.

4. Repeat Steps 2 and 3 for each node.

5. Repeat Steps 2 and 3 for representative servers or client machines that will need access to the server cluster.

Failover Validation   You need to ensure that all nodes can own the cluster resource groups that were created. To do this, follow these steps:

1. Start Cluster Administrator.

2. Verify that all nodes configured for the failover cluster appear in the bottom of the left pane of Cluster Administrator.

3. For each cluster group, make sure it can be failed over and back from all nodes in the server. To do this, right-click the group, and select Move. If the server cluster has more than two nodes, you must also select the destination node. This change will be reflected in Cluster Administrator.

Server Cluster Administration

Whether you are implementing a standard server cluster or an MNS cluster, you still need to take care of some administrative tasks. Most administration is done either in Cluster Administrator or using the command-line cluster tool.

Changing Domains

Should you ever need to change the domain of your server cluster, perform the following steps. Changing domains will affect your availability.

1. Create the Cluster Service account in the new domain, as well as any other necessary logins such as the SQL Server service account.

2. On the current cluster, change the startup type for the Cluster Service to Manual on each node.

3. Make sure no users are connected to your clustered applications such as SQL Server. Shut down your applications properly.

4. Stop the Cluster Service on each node.

5. Shut down all nodes except one.

6. Change the domain of the node.

7. Add the Cluster Service account and any other necessary users with their appropriate rights.

8. Start the Cluster Service.

9. Verify that the cluster is functioning properly.

10. Repeat Steps 6 to 9 for each node.

11. Reset the startup for the Cluster Service to Automatic on each node.

12. Follow the instructions in Chapter 6 for changing domains for SQL Server.

Changing a Node's IP Address or Name

You cannot change the name of a node without uninstalling and reconfiguring the server cluster. However, you can change the underlying IP addresses of the network cards by following these steps:

Warning   Do not do this unless your servers need to change subnets.

1. Change the IP addresses of the network adapters on one node. This might require the computer to be rebooted.

2. Start Cluster Administrator on the node whose IP addresses changed and connect to ".". Cluster Administrator might display the following error message because it attempts to connect to the last cluster it administered:

   ```
   A connection to the cluster at cluster name could not be opened. This
   may be caused by the Cluster Service on node cluster name not being
   started. Would you like Cluster Administrator to attempt to start the
   Cluster Service on node cluster name?
   ```

3. Select the proper IP Address resource to open its properties, and double-click it.

4. On the Parameters tab in the IP Address Resource Properties dialog box, make sure that the Network To Use box contains the new network as the network to use.

5. Fail all groups over to the functional (which is the node whose IP address you changed).

6. Change the IP addresses for the network adapters on all other nodes, and reboot them. On reboot, when all nodes agree on the subnets, the old networks disappear and the new networks are created.

7. Rename the networks appropriately.

Changing Service Accounts and Passwords

Should you ever need to change the domain of your server cluster, follow the guidelines in this section.

> **On the CD**   Included is a small utility named Update_Pwd.exe, which is found in Update_Pwd.zip along with the corresponding instruction document Update_Pwd_Readme.doc. This can be used on both clustered and nonclustered servers to change the password of a service while minimizing downtime. Do not use this for the SQL Server services, because they have their own documented procedure elsewhere in this book. Also, if this is Windows Server 2003 and a server cluster, use the command-line tool Cluster.exe to change the password, as described later.

Windows 2000 Server

Under Windows 2000 Server, changing the service account or password for a service account causes an availability outage for your cluster. Follow these steps:

1. Make sure that no users are accessing the applications in the cluster.

2. Gracefully stop the SQL Server virtual servers with the SQL Server tools.

3. Under Administrative Tools, launch the Services tool.

4. Stop the Cluster Service.

5. Once Cluster Service is stopped, double-click it to open its properties.

6. Select the Log On tab.

7. Change the account and/or password for the Cluster Service.

8. Click OK.

9. Start Cluster Service.

10. Although you might not encounter issues if everything seems to be working, while things are down, you should rerun SQL Server Setup from the node owning the SQL Server resource. Follow the instructions found in Chapter 6 in the section "Adding or Removing a Cluster Node from the Virtual Server Definition and Adding, Changing, or Updating a TCP/IP Address." Click Next for all options, but when you reach this step, enter the new account information. This ensures that the instance is associated with the right account and password.

11. Repeat Step 10 for each clustered instance of SQL Server.

12. Bring the SQL virtual servers online.

Windows Server 2003

With Windows Server 2003, you can change your service account and its password as an online operation. You can change the base cluster password on the fly, but you still need to take into account Steps 10 and 11 from the Windows 2000 Server instructions for SQL Server virtual servers. Change passwords through the command-line cluster tool with the /changepassword switch, as shown in Figure 5-17. You must then use one or both of these switches:

■   /skipdc to change the password only on the cluster nodes themselves. If you do not specify /skipdc, it changes the password at the domain level. This is useful if you already changed the password at the network level if you need to do a password update that was not completed on all nodes.

■   /force will force the password to be changed on all accessible nodes, even if they are down, joining, or in an unknown cluster state.

You can also use /verbose to see all output or /quiet to see no output other than errors.

So a full example might look like this:

```
Cluster /cluster:clustername /changepassword:newpassword,oldpassword /force
/verbose
```

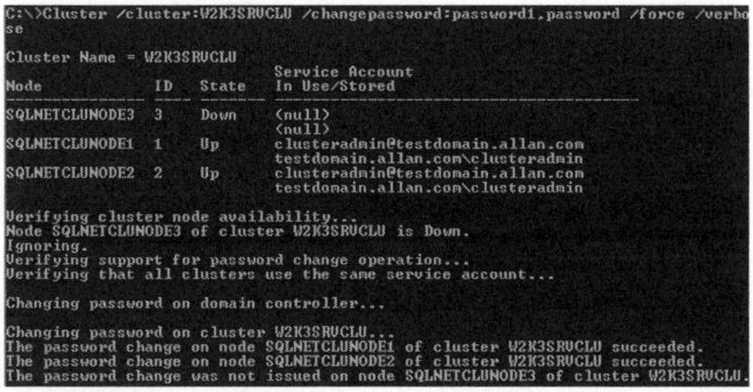

Figure 5-17   Using Cluster.exe to change the service account password under Windows Server 2003.

Disk Management

At some point, you might need to expand your disk capacity. There are two ways to go about that: expanding the disks you have if there is space that has not been allocated, or physically adding a new LUN to present to Windows.

Adding a New Disk

If you need to physically add a new disk to the server cluster, follow the steps below.

> **Important**   If you are using a Windows 2000–based server cluster that has Service Pack 2 or earlier, you need to shut down all nodes but one while performing the next steps. The disk is not automatically recognized even if you can create it dynamically using a SAN. For Windows 2000 with Service Pack 3 or later and the hotfix from Knowledge Base article 326891 (listed earlier), you can add the disks to Windows without restarting the nodes as long as the SAN supports it. There are two other ways to add a disk without rebooting the node with the active resources (such as rebooting a node with no resources to recognize the LUN or using Cluster.exe to force it in even though the GUI for Cluster Administrator does not recognize it, but it requires getting some hexadecimal values for the disk signature), but applying the hotfix is the recommended way.

1. Create the new LUN on the SAN or DAS. Check with your storage vendor to see if this is an online operation, or one for which you need to shut down your cluster nodes, and then act appropriately.

2. Once the LUN is added at the disk level, if you need to, restart your nodes. If this is a Windows 2000–based cluster with Service Pack 2 or earlier, only power up one node.

3. Start the Computer Management console.

4. Select Disk Management. The new disk should appear. Prepare it as instructed in the section "Creating the Shared Disks."

5. Close the Computer Management console.

6. Start Cluster Administrator.

7. From the File menu, select New, and then Resource (or right-click the group and select the same options). In the New Resource dialog box, in the Name text box, type an appropriate name such as **Disk M:**. In the Resource Type drop-down list, select Physical Disk. In the Group drop-down list, make sure the proper group is selected. Click Next.

8. In the Possible Owner dialog box, all nodes of the cluster should appear as possible owners. If they do not, add the nodes, and click Next.

9. In the Dependencies dialog box, the MS DTC IP address resource you configured previously appears in the Available Resources list. Select the resource, and then click Add. The resource appears in the Resource Dependencies list. Click Next.

10. In the Disk Parameters dialog box, select the new partition in the Disk drop-down list, and then click Finish.

11. You will see a message confirming that the new disk resource is successfully configured.

12. In the Cluster Administrator window, the newly created resource appears in the right pane. Bring the resource online by selecting it, right-clicking it, and selecting Bring Online.

Using DISKPART to Expand Disk Capacity

If you have the capacity on your cluster disk, but have not used all of it (that is, you did not format all of your disk), you can use Diskpart.exe to easily expand without affecting availability. This tool is built into Windows Server 2003 and is available for download for Windows 2000 Server at *http://www.microsoft.com/ windows2000/techinfo/reskit/tools/new/diskpart-o.asp*. It is also available in the *Windows 2000 Resource Kit*. DISKPART is also a very useful utility to display information about your disks without having to use the Disk Management console.

> **Note**   Make sure your disk subsystem manufacturer supports the use of DISKPART to expand your disk capacity before you use it.

Follow these steps to use DISKPART to expand the size of your disks:

1. Open a command window and type **diskpart**. You are now running the utility, as shown in Figure 5-18.

Figure 5-18   Starting DISKPART.

2.   Use the list disk command to show the available disks and their respective numbers. When you see the disk that contains the volume you want to modify, type **select disk *n***, where *n* is the number of the disk. An example is shown in Figure 5-19.

Figure 5-19   Selecting a disk to modify.

3.   Use the LIST VOLUME command to show the available volumes and their respective numbers. When you see the volume you want to modify, type **select volume *n***, where *n* is the number of the disk. An example is shown in Figure 5-20.

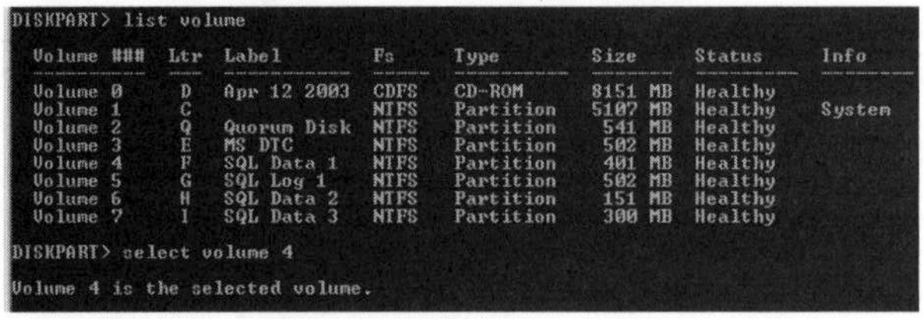

Figure 5-20   Selecting a volume.

> **Tip** You can use Computer Management's Disk Management functionality to assist you in determining which disk and volume you want to use.

4. Expand the disk capacity by typing the command **extend disk=*n* size=*n***, as shown in Figure 5-21.

```
DISKPART> list disk

  Disk ###  Status      Size     Free     Dyn  Gpt
  --------  ----------  -------  -------  ---  ---
  Disk 0    Online      5114 MB  8033 KB
  Disk 1    Online       548 MB  7168 KB
  Disk 2    Online       503 MB  1024 KB
* Disk 3    Online       504 MB   103 MB
  Disk 4    Online       503 MB  1024 KB
  Disk 5    Online       504 MB    53 MB
  Disk 6    Online       504 MB   504 MB

DISKPART> extend disk=3 size=10

DiskPart successfully extended the volume.
```

Figure 5-21 Extending the capacity.

5. To verify that the disk has been expanded, you can view it using DISKPART itself with the LIST DISK command (see Figure 5-22), Computer Management's Disk Management functionality, Windows Explorer, or your application (such as SQL Server's Enterprise Manager).

```
DISKPART> list disk

  Disk ###  Status      Size     Free     Dyn  Gpt
  --------  ----------  -------  -------  ---  ---
  Disk 0    Online      5114 MB  8033 KB
  Disk 1    Online       548 MB  7168 KB
  Disk 2    Online       503 MB  1024 KB
* Disk 3    Online       504 MB    93 MB
  Disk 4    Online       503 MB  1024 KB
  Disk 5    Online       504 MB    53 MB
  Disk 6    Online       504 MB   504 MB
```

Figure 5-22 Expanded disk verification.

> **Tip** You can also create a script for DISKPART to use instead of entering the commands one by one. Create a text file with your commands, and from a command line, execute the following statement:
>
> `diskpart /s` *`nameofscript.txt`* `>` *`output.txt`*
>
> where *nameofscript.txt* is your command file, and *output.txt* is the filename (and location) of the file you want to store the results of the action.

Forcing Quorum for an MNS Cluster

If you need to allow the MNS cluster to continue to function even if a particular node does not own the quorum, you need to manually force the quorum. However, you should not do this unless it is necessary. A good example of an instance in which to force the quorum is if you are using a geographically dispersed cluster and you lose communications with the primary site or experience a failure. Obviously in an MNS cluster, the secondary nodes fail because you no longer have a majority of nodes available. However, to get back up and running, you force the quorum by following these steps:

> **More Info**   You can also use the /forcequorum switch of Cluster.exe as described in the Windows Server 2003 documentation topic "Force-quorum command," but it is recommended that you follow the steps listed here.

> **Caution**   Do not change your cluster configuration while the cluster is operating in this interim state. For example, do not add or remove nodes or install or modify applications running in the cluster. Changing the cluster configuration in this state might result in application data inconsistencies if the other nodes come back online.

1. Start Cluster Administrator.

2. Stop the Cluster Service on all remaining nodes.

3. Open the Registry Editor with Regedt32.exe.

4. Under   HKEY_LOCAL_MACHINE\SYSTEM\CurrentControlSet\Services\ClusSvc\Parameters, create a string value called ForceQuorum.

5. Set the value of ForceQuorum to a comma-separated list of the names of the nodes that are to be part of the quorum set. If you have a four-node MNS cluster, and Node1 and Node2 are the nodes still available, the values should be Node3 and Node4.

> **Important**   If you do not list all the nodes stopped in Step 2 in the ForceQuorum key, then you must either power off the nodes not listed or physically disconnect them from the network before starting the Cluster Service on the remaining nodes.

6.   Start the Cluster Service on the remaining nodes.

> **Note**   When you force quorum in an MNS cluster, you might see an error message indicating that the Cluster Service failed to start. Ignore the message, because the Cluster Service will continue its startup processes after the end of the startup timeout period for Service Control Manager.

Network Load Balancing

Network Load Balancing clusters are a feature of all versions of Windows 2000 Server and Windows Server 2003. This section details the specific configuration used as a role change or switch process for highly available SQL Servers or Analysis Servers, which might be different from how other programs utilize Network Load Balancing.

> **More Info**   For a basic look at Network Load Balancing, read Chapter 3. You can also find much more information on Network Load Balancing at the Cluster Technologies Community Center at *http://www.microsoft.com/windowsserver2003/community/centers/clustering/default.asp.* This site covers Windows NT 4.0, Windows 2000 Server, and Windows Server 2003. If you want direct access to white papers in the Community Center, they can be found at *http://www.microsoft.com/windowsserver2003/community/centers/clustering/more_resources.asp#NLB.*

General Network Load Balancing Best Practices

This section describes some best practices and necessary information you need to know about Network Load Balancing:

- You can have up to 32 nodes in a Network Load Balancing cluster.

- There is the potential that Network Load Balancing can flood the ports with network traffic if you have a heavily used implementation. You must monitor this carefully. Windows Server 2003 introduces Internet Group Membership Protocol (IGMP) support, which limits flooding to only the ports used that have Network Load Balancing nodes. This allows non–Network Load Balancing nodes to not be affected by Network Load Balancing traffic. All other computers and servers can see the Network Load Balancing clusters, but no longer need to worry about the extra traffic.

- Setting multicast increases the traffic generated by Network Load Balancing. Use unicast mode instead.

- Network Load Balancing can be implemented over VLANs. This might also help segment the network traffic generated by Network Load Balancing to reduce flooding.

- Network Load Balancing can work with one or two network cards. Two are not required, but you might want to consider two network cards if you are using unicast, because each node will have the same IP address, making them look identical from a network perspective.

- All nodes need to be set to the same mode: unicast or multicast.

- You can mix Windows 2000 Server and Windows Server 2003 servers in a Network Load Balancing cluster. However, if you are mixing versions, you might not be able to use things like IGMP support, which is a new feature of Windows Server 2003.

- You can only bind Network Load Balancing to multiple network cards in Windows Server 2003. This is not possible in Windows 2000 Server.

- Network Load Balancing does not support Windows Internet Name Service (WINS) resolution.

- Network Load Balancing does not support dynamic DNS. You will have to add the name of the Network Load Balancing cluster to any DNS server if you are using name resolution.

- If you are using remote administration of Network Load Balancing, UDP ports 1717 and 2504 are used. You should use Network Load Balancing Manager, and not a remote WLBS command, in Windows Server 2003.

- You will need dedicated IP addresses for each node as well as for the Network Load Balancing cluster itself.

- All nodes need to be in the same subnet.

- All clients and servers accessing the Network Load Balancing cluster need to be in the same subnet.

- You can use fault-tolerant network adapters (sometimes known as NIC teaming) with Network Load Balancing. For support information, consult Knowledge Base article 278431, "INFO: Using NIC Teaming Adapters with Network Load Balancing May Cause Network Problems."

Implementing Network Load Balancing for SQL Server–Based Architectures

There are two scenarios in which you can employ Network Load Balancing with your SQL Servers. One is for load balancing read-only (no writes from applications or clients at all) databases; the other is using it as the front mechanism hiding a server name change in a disaster recovery scenario for log shipping, Analysis Services, or replication.

> **On the CD**   For a worksheet to fill in for your Network Load Balancing cluster configuration, see NLB_Cluster_Configuration_Worksheet.doc.

> **More Info**   If you want to do an unattended install of Network Load Balancing, it is possible under Windows Server 2003. See the white paper at *http://www.microsoft.com/technet/treeview/default.asp?url=/technet/prodtechnol/windowsserver2003/deploy/confeat/nlbclust.asp* for details.

Configuring the Network Cards

To configure your network cards, follow these steps:

1. Log on to the server as someone with administrator privileges who can configure Network Load Balancing.

2. Right-click My Network Places, and select Properties.

3. In the Network Connections window, select the network card that you wish to assign Network Load Balancing to. This should be on an externally facing network. You should also rename this network card to something such as Public Network. This can be done by selecting it, right-clicking, and selecting Rename. For the other network card, you should rename it something like Private Network to designate that it is the dedicated network between the servers participating in Network Load Balancing.

4. Select the Public Network network card, right-click it, and select Properties.

5. Select Internet Protocol (TCP/IP) and click Properties. Set the static IP address of the card to a valid IP address on the externally facing network. Click OK.

6. Click OK to close the Properties dialog box for the public network.

7. In the Network And Dial-Up Connections window, select the private network, right-click it, and select Properties.

8. Select Internet Protocol (TCP/IP) and click Properties. Set the static IP address of the card to a valid IP address (such as 10.0.0.1) on the internal-only network. Click OK.

9. Click OK to close the Properties dialog box for the private network.

10. Repeat this process for all nodes in the Network Load Balancing cluster.

Configuring Network Load Balancing for Use with SQL Server

To use Network Load Balancing with SQL Server, you must adhere to all of the following guidelines:

- Two network cards must be installed in each computer. One of these cards must be dedicated to a private network that is not routable from the public network, similar to that of a server cluster.

- Network Load Balancing is installed on only the externally facing adapter.

- TCP/IP is the only network protocol present on the cluster adapter. Do not add any other protocols (such as IPX) to this adapter.

- Only unicast is supported. If only one network adapter is used, no intercluster communications can occur.

- For a switch situation (not read-only load balanced SQL Servers), all hosts are set to not start automatically. This ensures that, in the event of a switch, the nodes are not available. You must manually start Network Load Balancing.

- In dual-homed configurations, network adapters are nonroutable to each other.

On the CD   For instructions on configuring Network Load Balancing for use when facilitating a server change for log shipping, replication, and Analysis Services, see the file Installing_NLB_For_A_Server_ Switch.doc. For instructions on configuring Network Load Balancing for load balancing read-only SQL Servers, see the file Installing_NLB_For_ Read_Only_SQL_Servers.doc.

Starting Network Load Balancing on the Primary   With Windows 2000 Server, to start Network Load Balancing on the first node, open a command window and type **wlbs start**, as shown in Figure 5-23. If this is a read-only load balanced use of SQL Server, execute this on each node.

```
C:\>wlbs start
WLBS Cluster Control Utility V2.3. (c) 1997-99 Microsoft Corporation
Cluster operations started.
```

Figure 5-23   Starting NLB under Windows 2000 Server.

Under Windows Server 2003, select the node in Network Load Balancing Manager, right-click the node, select Control Host, and then select Start. You can also accomplish this by selecting the Host menu, Control Host, and then Start. Once started, Network Load Balancing Manager should look like Figure 5-24.

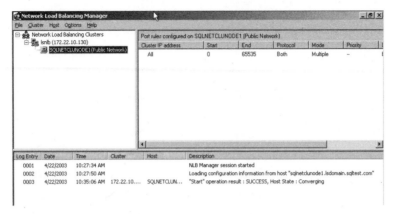

Figure 5-24   Starting NLB under Windows Server 2003.

Verifying a Network Load Balancing Cluster

Once you install your configuration, you need to verify it is working properly.

Switch Method   To verify a Network Load Balancing cluster using the switch method, follow these steps:

1. In the command window on each node, type **wlbs display** for Windows 2000 Server. You should see a message about your current Network Load Balancing parameters. If this is Windows Server 2003, you should also see a message reflecting the fact that Network Load Balancing has been started in Network Load Balancing Manager.

2. Type the command **ping *w.x.y.z*** where *w.x.y.z* is the IP address of your Network Load Balancing cluster. This should be successful. Repeat this step from client machines, other servers, and other nodes to ensure connectivity.

3. If you are resolving by name, type the command **ping *nlbname*** where *nlbname* is the name of your Network Load Balancing server. This should be successful. Repeat this step from client machines, other servers, and other nodes to ensure connectivity. Only perform this step if you have manually added your NLB cluster to DNS.

4. On your first node's SQL Server, create a database with one table and one column with a unique value.

5. On the other nodes, repeat Step 4 but add another unique value to the instance on that server and use the same name to create the database.

6. Open Query Analyzer from anywhere. When connecting to the SQL Server, use the Network Load Balancing cluster name or the Network Load Balancing cluster IP address.

7. Query for the unique record. Currently, it should get that value from the first node.

8. In the command window for the first node, type the command **wlbs drainstop** using Windows 2000 Server, or using Windows Server 2003, select the node, right-click it, and select Control Host, and then Drainstop. This clears all connections to that node.

9. To verify that the process is done, type **wlbs query** in Windows 2000 Server or look at the status window in Network Load Balancing Manager to ensure that everything is okay with Network Load Balancing.

10. In the command window of the next node, type **wlbs start** under Windows 2000 or use Network Load Balancing Manager under Windows Server 2003 to start Network Load Balancing on the new node.

11. Reissue your query to see that the unique value of the second node is displayed.

12. Repeat Steps 6–11 for each subsequent node.

Read-Only SQL Servers   To verify a Network Load Balancing cluster for a read-only SQL Server, follow these steps:

1. In the command window on each node, type **wlbs display**. You should see a message about your current Network Load Balancing parameters. If this is Windows Server 2003, use Network Load Balancing Manager to check the status and parameters for Network Load Balancing.

2. Type the command **ping *w.x.y.z*** where *w.x.y.z* is the IP address of your Network Load Balancing cluster. This should be successful. Repeat this step from client machines, other servers, and other nodes to ensure connectivity.

3. If you are resolving by name, type the command **ping *nlbname*** where *nlbname* is the name of your Network Load Balancing server. This should be successful. Repeat this step from client machines, other servers, and other nodes to ensure connectivity.

4. On your first node's SQL Server, create a database with one table and one column with a unique value.

5. On the other nodes, repeat Step 4 but add another unique value to the instance on that server and use the same name to create the database.

6. Open Query Analyzer from anywhere. When connecting to the SQL Server, use the Network Load Balancing name or the Network Load Balancing IP address.

7. Query for one of the unique records.

8. Reissue your query to see that the unique value of another node is displayed. With enough refreshes, you should eventually see all unique values.

9. Repeat Steps 6–8 for each subsequent node.

Adding a Network Load Balancing Cluster to DNS

Once your Network Load Balancing cluster is installed, there are a few remaining tasks to perform. You need to add your Network Load Balancing cluster name manually to DNS. Depending on your DNS vendor, this procedure will vary. After you configure your Network Load Balancing cluster, you must manually update DNS to resolve the cluster name. Network Load Balancing does not utilize dynamic DNS updates when it is configured. You might also need to add it to the reverse lookup zone of your DNS as well.

Configuring Logging for Network Load Balancing Manager

When you are using Network Load Balancing Manager, you can log all commands issued to a log file. This creates a permanent record of all Network Load Balancing commands issued. To configure this option, perform the following steps:

1. Start Network Load Balancing Manager.

2. From the Options menu, select Log Settings.

3. In the Log Settings dialog box, shown in Figure 5-25, select the Enable Logging check box. In the Log Filename text box, enter the name and path of the log file. If you do not specify a path name, the file is created in the C:\Documents and Settings*username* directory, where the *username* is the name of the person currently logged into the server. Click OK.

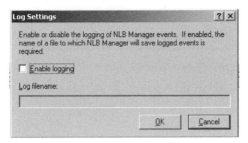

Figure 5-25   Log Settings dialog box.

Uninstalling Network Load Balancing

Under Windows Server 2003, in Network Load Balancing Manager, select the cluster name in the upper left pane. From the Cluster menu, select Delete, or right-click the cluster name and select Delete. You are then asked if you want to remove Network Load Balancing from all nodes, as shown in Figure 5-26. Click Yes.

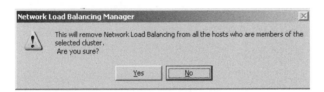

Figure 5-26   Removing NLB confirmation.

When you are finished, the log entries in Network Load Balancing Manager should appear similar to the ones shown in Figure 5-27.

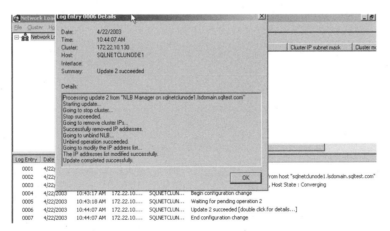

Figure 5-27   Network Load Balancing Manager after removing Network Load Balancing.

Summary

Configuring your Windows servers to be reliable, available, and scalable to form a strong base for SQL Server is not impossible. Although some of the recommendations in this chapter are specific to SQL Server, many are not, and the best practices can be applied to any Windows server. It is crucial to get this step of your entire high availability solution correct and verified; otherwise, you will be placing your SQL Server instances on a questionable foundation.

Part III

Microsoft SQL Server Technology

6

Microsoft SQL Server 2000 Failover Clustering

Once you have installed your server cluster as described in Chapter 5, "Designing Highly Available Microsoft Windows Servers," you can proceed to install and configure your SQL Server virtual servers. This chapter walks you through the planning, implementation, configuration, and administration of a Microsoft SQL Server 2000 failover cluster.

> **More Info**   For a basic understanding of failover clustering, including resources for each SQL Server 2000 virtual server, read Chapter 3, "Making a High Availability Technology Choice."

Planning for Failover Clustering

The most important step of installing your failover cluster is planning. Most flawed installations or problems stem from points missed during this phase of implementation. The main things you need to plan for are the network and disk resources, advanced security, service accounts, applications connecting to the cluster, and the use of any shared resources.

> **On the CD** To assist you in your planning, use the document Failover_Clustering_Configuration_Worksheet.doc.

Versions of Windows Supported

To install a SQL Server virtual server on a server cluster, you must be using one of the following: Windows 2000 Advanced Server, Windows 2000 Datacenter Server, Windows Server 2003 Enterprise Edition (32- or 64-bit), or Windows Server 2003 Datacenter Edition (32- or 64-bit). If you are implementing on a 64-bit edition, you must use the 64-bit version of SQL Server 2000. If you are installing on one of the 32-bit versions of Windows Server 2003, follow these rules:

- If you have the SQL Server 2000 RTM or SQL Server Release A media, you must install SQL Server 2000 Service Pack 3 or later immediately after installing your SQL Server 2000 failover cluster. If you are using SQL Server 2000 Service Pack 2 or earlier (including RTM), those versions are not supported under Windows Server 2003.

- If you are upgrading your existing Windows 2000 or Windows NT 4.0 Enterprise Edition clusters to Windows Server 2003 already configured with SQL Server 2000 failover clustering, you must install SQL Server 2000 Service Pack 3. Install the service pack to all SQL Server 2000 instances immediately prior to upgrading your operating system. If you are installing SQL Server 2000 under Windows Server 2003, you must immediately apply SQL Server 2000 Service Pack 3 or later. During the upgrade process, a message is displayed as another warning. If you have not applied the appropriate SQL Server 2000 service pack by the time you see this warning, cancel the installation process and apply it. To see these warnings, see Figures 5-1 and 5-2 in Chapter 5.

Number of SQL Server 2000 Instances per Server Cluster

As a quick reminder from Chapter 3, remember that a SQL Server 2000 failover cluster is built on top of a server cluster, and that a clustered instance of SQL Server 2000 is also known as a SQL Server virtual server because it has an associated IP address and network name in the server cluster. On a server cluster, as with a stand-alone server, you can install up to 16 clustered instances of SQL Server 2000 per server cluster. This is the same for both 32- and 64-bit versions of SQL Server. The 16-instance limitation is the tested limit; in theory you can have more. The 16 instances can be made up of 1 default instance and 15 named instances or 16 named instances. You can also combine local instances on a node and clustered instances of SQL Server, but it is not recommended. On a server cluster, you are limited only by the available resources—namely disk, processor, networking, shared resources, and number of nodes.

> **Note**   Remember, you can only have one default instance per server cluster.

Name of the SQL Server Virtual Server

If you are going to have multiple instances, each SQL Server failover cluster's name must be unique within a domain, whether it is a default or a named instance.

> **Important**   The SQL Server 2000 virtual server name cannot be the same as the name of any of the nodes or the name of the server cluster itself, so its behavior is not the same as that of a stand-alone server that assumes the name of its underlying server. This point is often misunderstood.

For a server cluster with two nodes, PO8ServerA and PO8ServerB, Table 6-1 shows valid and invalid *virtual_server_name\instance_name* names for your SQL Server virtual servers.

Table 6-1 Virtual Server Names on a Single Server Cluster

Proposed SQL Server Virtual Server Name	Valid or Not Valid
PO8	Valid. This installs a SQL Server virtual server named PO8 on the server cluster; there is no instance name, therefore this installs a default instance.
PO8\INS1	Not valid because there is already a virtual server named PO8. A virtual server can have only one instance with that name.
PO8a\INS1	Valid. This would configure a second SQL Server virtual server.
PO8a\PO8a	Valid, but not recommended due to the probable confusion between (virtual) server name and instance name.
PO8a\INS2	Not valid because there is already an instance with a virtual server name of PO8a.
PO8b\INS1	Not valid because there is already a named instance of INS1 assigned to PO8a.
PO8b\PO8b	Valid, but again, not recommended due to the probable confusion between server and instance names.

Number of Nodes

The number of nodes available to failover clustering is directly tied to the version of SQL Server as well as the operating system that you have chosen to install, as listed in Table 6-2.

Table 6-2 Number of Nodes Available

Operating System	Maximum Number of Nodes in a SQL Server 2000 Failover Cluster
Windows 2000 Advanced Server	2
Windows 2000 Datacenter Server, Windows Server 2003 Datacenter and Enterprise Editions (32-bit)	4
Windows Server 2003 Datacenter and Enterprise Editions (64-bit)	8

Although the 32-bit versions of Windows Server 2003 Enterprise Edition and Windows Server 2003 Datacenter Edition support up to eight nodes at the operating system level, SQL Server 2000 32-bit can only support up to four nodes due to the way the installer was originally coded. SQL Server 2000 64-bit supports up to eight nodes because the installer was rewritten specifically for the 64-bit version. Some might see supporting only four nodes as a limitation in the 32-bit version of SQL Server 2000 under Windows Server 2003, but you do get two more nodes out of the box than you did with Windows 2000 Advanced Server, making Windows Server 2003 Enterprise Edition a more attractive option than Windows 2000 Datacenter Server (and there is also the additional memory supported by Windows Server 2003 Enterprise Edition).

Having more than two nodes allows you to configure an $N + 1$ or an $N + I$ scenario. These scenarios are not unlike log shipping, where you have one or more nodes waiting for resources to fail to them. For example, if you have a three-node cluster, you could be hosting instances on both nodes 1 and 2, and in the event of a failover, you can set your clustered instance so that the third node will be the primary failover node for both instances. This makes balancing resources in the event of a failover much easier than it was under Windows 2000 Advanced Server, which limits you to a maximum of two nodes. The $N + 1$ scenario is demonstrated in Figures 6-1 and 6-2.

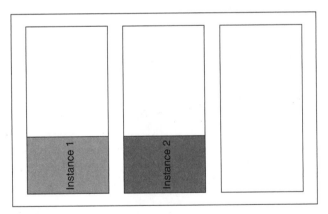

Figure 6-1 $N + 1$ prior to failover.

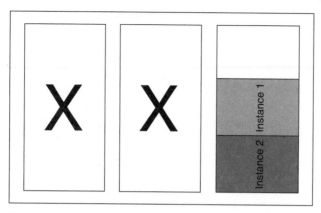

Figure 6-2 *N* + 1 after two node failures.

In an *N* + I scenario (note that it is *I*, and not a *1*), you would have more than one node serving purely as failover nodes. The *N* + I scenario is more easily facilitated with 64-bit SQL Server 2000 because you have up to eight nodes available to you.

Disks

Configuring your disks properly is arguably the single most important aspect of failover clustering. Each clustered instance must have dedicated resources assigned to it. Two SQL Server virtual servers in the same server cluster cannot share disk resources. It is a 1:1 ratio for disks to SQL Server instance. In this case, a disk is defined as what is presented to the operating system. If you have one disk at the operating system, but you carve out multiple drive letters or partitions on it, it is considered one disk even though there are multiple drive letters. For example, you create a 50-GB logical unit (LUN) on your storage area network (SAN). When you configure it in Windows, you give it two 25-GB partitions with the letters I and J, respectively. When you install failover clustering, that LUN appears as one drive to SQL Server. This means that if you need to have more than one instance of SQL Server in a cluster, even if you configure two logical drive letters on one LUN, only one instance can use it. This is illustrated in Figure 6-3.

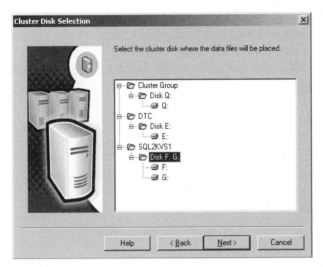

Figure 6-3   One LUN with two drive letters as seen by SQL Server Setup.

Consider this configuration example: you have two clustered instances of SQL Server, A and B. You also have five disk resources dedicated to the cluster, two of which are already used by the quorum (Q) and MS DTC (E), and drive letters A, C, and D are taken with your floppy drive, internal hard drive, and DVD-ROM drive, respectively. That leaves 18 available drive letters. Now, of the three disk resources left (F, G, and H), you need to make sure each SQL Server instance can use what it needs. Each instance needs at least one drive letter associated with it, so that takes care of drives F and G, leaving only drive H. As you can see, the number of drive letters available to you (a maximum of 26 but, realistically, probably around 22) severely limits the number of instances and drive resources that can be used by SQL Server in a clustered environment.

More Info   See Chapter 4, "Disk Configurations for High Availability" for detailed information on disks and SQL Server 2000. The section "Configuration Example" has an example of a clustered implementation of SQL Server.

Basic disks are supported for use with failover clustering. Mounted drives, sometimes known as *mountpoints*, are supported for clustering in Windows Server 2003 only, and can be used with a SQL Server 2000 failover cluster. This should help you if you run out of drive letters to configure, because the mounted drive you add to the cluster does not need to be assigned a drive letter. To achieve this, create a blank directory on a disk used by the SQL Server virtual server (such as E:\SQLMountData) and then associate the newly mounted drive with that directory in Disk Management, add the mounted drive to the resource group with SQL Server, and add the new Physical Disk clustered resource as a dependency of the drive you created the blank directory on. Do not add the mounted drive as a dependency of SQL Server.

Although this will let you use different disks in your cluster without making it a direct dependency of SQL Server, there is seemingly no way to control how the mounted drive uses the directory that is part of the mountpoint. If you create a mountpoint that references a disk used for other things and your disk becomes full, you have created additional problems for yourself.

Warning   If you decide to use mountpoints, make sure the mounted drive is located only on the shared disk array and is never a local (that is, system) disk that only exists in one of the nodes. Only use disks on the shared drive array, as everything comprising the mountpoint would need to be available to SQL Server after the failover. For information on creating a mountpoint, see "Creating a Mountpoint" in Chapter 5.

Dynamic disks provide features that basic disks do not, such as the ability to create volumes that span multiple disks (spanned and striped volumes), and the ability to create fault-tolerant volumes (mirrored and RAID 5 volumes). Dynamic disks are not supported natively in the operating system for clustering. If you choose to use dynamic disks, you have to use a third-party program such as Veritas Volume Manager, and the third-party vendor will be the first point of contact for any disk issues.

IP Addresses, Ports, and Network Card Usage

For each SQL Server virtual server, you need at least one dedicated IP address. During the installation process, this is bound to one of the public networks of the server cluster, which means it is, in essence, also bound to a physical network card. SQL Server 2000 supports assigning multiple IP addresses to one instance. To do this, you must have separate network cards and public networks to be able to assign another IP address. You do not want to share IP addresses on one network or network card, because that affects the availability of all SQL Server IP addresses if the network card or cluster network goes down. If you have more than one instance per server cluster, you need separate network cards for each instance to ensure availability.

During the installation of a SQL Server virtual server, as with a stand-alone instance, a port number is dynamically assigned. The first instance is usually assigned port 1433, and the rest are randomly picked during setup. Pick static port numbers prior to installing your SQL Server virtual servers and change them to the ports you want after installation. If you do not assign ports postinstallation, when the SQL Server resources fail over to another node, it might not grab the same port number because it might not be available or because a dynamic one might be assigned. For predictability alone, you should assign the port numbers. This is very important if you have machines with older versions of Microsoft Data Access Components (MDAC) that need to have the port number of SQL Server specified.

Applications and Failover Clustering

Before you implement failover clustering, check to see that the applications accessing the virtual server can handle a failover of your SQL Server instance, much as you would with any other availability technology. If your application does not behave well in a failover, it could cause other problems for your end users. For example, remember that during the failover process, SQL Server goes through a stop on one node, and the resources are started again on another node automatically. However, suppose your application persists an Open Database Connectivity (ODBC) connection to SQL Server that is dropped during the failover. Because the application developers did not take this into account in their design, the Web server needs to be restarted, which affects other applications as well.

■   Failover might not be transparent to end users. You do not have to worry about a change in server name because the SQL Server virtual server keeps the same name and IP address in a failover. However, you do need to ensure that the application can reconnect again after a failover. You have to either code a cluster-aware application (which is preferred, but not necessary) or code retry logic into your applications. SQL Server 2000 applications (such as Query Analyzer) are cluster-aware, which is why they handle failovers gracefully.

> **More Info**   For more information on coding cluster-aware applications, see Knowledge Base article 273673, "INF: SQL Virtual Server Client Connections Must Be Controlled by Clients," at *http://support.microsoft.com*, as well as the information about the clustering API (which is part of the Platforms Software Development Kit) in Microsoft Developer Network at *http://msdn.microsoft.com*.

- Make sure your application has "friendly" error messages to handle the failover.

- During the startup process, any transactions that are incomplete will be rolled back. However, if the application tolerates the failover, during the switch to another server, if your application allows more transactions to be submitted, those new transactions might be lost if you do not employ some mechanism to capture them. You can do something locally at the client (such as using a cookie on a Web-based application) or use middleware (such as Microsoft BizTalk Server) to queue transactions until SQL Server is available.

- Because the transaction log is applied during the restart of SQL Server, a long-running transaction that failed will need to be rolled back, which could take some time. If possible, ensure that your transactions are fairly small so that your recovery time will be minimal. Commit in logical units of work.

- Set timeout values in the application effectively to close connections gracefully or perform some other appropriate response, such as a friendly message, so that the user experience is positive. The end user should never have to be concerned with what is happening on the back end.

Third-Party Applications, File Shares, Dependencies, and SQL Server 2000 Failover Clustering

Beyond adding disks as dependencies of the SQL Server resource so that SQL Server can use them, you should not make any other application or clustered resource a dependency of any of the SQL Server resources. The reason for this is simple: once you make something a dependency, the resource that you added the dependency to cannot come online if that other resource fails (for whatever reason). So if you have a perfectly working SQL Server virtual server, but a dependency that it really did not need (say an application or a file share) fails, it takes down your SQL Server. There are other reasons not to configure resources like file shares or other applications as a dependency: you could experience increased failover time due to the additional resource needing to be online, added disk I/O (in the case of a file share), driver issues, controller or network issues, SAN or disk array reconfiguration, DNS issues, bad policies, registry corruption, and permissions that could affect any cluster resource.

> **Tip**   If you need to make a resource dependent on a SQL resource, it would be better to use SQL Server Agent than SQL Server. Although SQL Server Agent is vital to SQL Server, if it goes down, it does not affect normal SQL Server usage for client applications.

A good example is a piece of third-party backup software that is supposedly cluster-aware, but winds up being a generic cluster application that makes itself dependent on the disk resources of SQL Server so that it can back up your data. The problem is that the backup software has now installed a few resources in your SQL Server resource group that it is dependent on. If this is the case and you must use this software, make sure that the Do Not Affect The Group check box is selected on the Properties tab of the added third-party generic resource to ensure that if that resource fails, it does not take your SQL Server disks offline. That in turn would take your SQL Server instance offline and cause a failover. Another example is that if you are not using the SQL Server Fulltext resource, you can also clear the Do Not Affect The Group check box to ensure that if an underlying Microsoft Search problem occurs, it does not affect your SQL Server.

Hardware-Assisted Backups and SQL Server 2000 Failover Clustering

It is important to ensure that if you are employing a hardware-assisted backup, sometimes known as a snapshot/split-mirror, the backup software is coded not only to the SQL Server 2000 Virtual Device Interface (VDI) mentioned earlier, but also when adding the mirror back into your RAID set, that the disk signatures will not be altered. A cluster depends on disk signatures remaining the same.

Service Accounts and SQL Server 2000 Failover Clustering

There are a few Windows-level accounts that need to be configured prior to installing both the server cluster and the SQL Server 2000 virtual server.

■ The account already used to configure the server cluster, as described in Chapter 5. This is a valid domain account with the proper rights on each node. This account is also used during the installation of the SQL Server virtual server.

■ At least one domain account must be created to administer the SQL Server and the SQL Server Agent. This can be two separate accounts, and does not need to be, nor should it be, a domain administrator, but a valid domain account is required. If you make the SQL administrator account(s) a domain administrator, you will be giving that user escalated privileges he or she does not need. If desired, it can be the same as the account for the server cluster, but you should not use the same account as the server cluster administrator.

❏ You do not have to put the SQL Server and SQL Server Agent accounts in the Administrators group on each node for Windows 2000 Server or Windows Server 2003. If you were installing on Windows NT 4.0 Enterprise Edition you *would* need to.

❏ The SQL service accounts are automatically assigned the rights listed in Table 6-3 during setup. If you ever need to manually re-create the login, you need to assign it these privileges.

Table 6-3   SQL Server Service Account Privileges Needed

Act as part of the operating system
Bypass traverse checking
Increase quotas
Lock pages in memory
Log on as a batch job
Log on as a service
Replace a process level token

❏ The service account for the Cluster Service must have the right to log in to SQL Server. If you accept the default, the account [NT Authority\System] must have login rights to SQL Server so that the SQL Server resource DLL can run the IsAlive query against SQL Server.

Warning   Keep in mind that any corporate policy that requires the changing of an account's password (such as having to change it every 90 days) could affect your virtual server's availability because you need to periodically reconfigure each SQL Server 2000 virtual server, including stopping and restarting it for the change to take effect. You must take this into account when planning the amount of availability your environment needs and balancing it with corporate security.

Important   You must use SQL Server Enterprise Manager if you need to change the accounts associated with the SQL Server virtual server (SQL Server or SQL Server Agent). This changes the service password on all the nodes and grants the necessary permissions to the chosen user account. If SQL Server Enterprise Manager is not used to change passwords, and the Windows-based Services tool is used to modify the underlying service instead, you might not be able to start SQL Server after a shutdown or a failover, and things such as Full-Text Search might not function properly. See "Changing SQL Server Service Accounts" later in this chapter; also refer to Chapter 14, "Administrative Tasks to Increase Availability" under "Security" for more information.

Memory

It is important to remember that how you configure your memory directly influences your failover times and your ability to have multiple instances in a cluster (assuming at some point that all instances need to coexist on one node simultaneously). If you are using large amounts of memory, that memory needs to be available on the failover node. So if you have a two-node cluster, each currently configured with 8 GB of memory as well as two instances of SQL Server (one with 5 GB of memory and the other with 7 GB), 7 + 5 does not equal 8; it equals 12. If they both happen to run on the same node, one will probably be able to get the memory it needs and the other will not. You need to adjust the amount of memory your instances are using so that, in a failover scenario, you do not starve one instance or possibly have it not start up after failover.

> **More Info**   Detailed coverage of setting memory for all types of SQL Server 2000 instances, including clustered ones, is in Chapter 14.

Coexistence with Stand-Alone Instances and Other Versions of SQL Server

Although you can install local instances of SQL Server 2000 on each node of your server cluster, or have a local instance of Microsoft SQL Server 7.0 configured as a local (nonclustered) default instance (meaning all of your clustered instances are named instances of SQL Server 2000), this is not recommended. You cannot have any other version of SQL Server clustering (such as 6.5 or 7.0) configured and running on the same machine (and active) at the same time as a SQL Server 2000 failover cluster. Because of instance support, you can have multiple clustered instances of SQL Server 2000 in the server cluster.

Analysis Services and Failover Clustering

Microsoft SQL Server 2000 Analysis Services is not cluster-aware. This means that it cannot be configured for use in a cluster and made available in the way that SQL Server 2000 can. To make Analysis Services available, you have two options: you can use Network Load Balancing, which was discussed in Chapter 5, or you can use a server cluster and install Analysis Services as a generic resource in the server cluster. The following are some caveats regarding use of Analysis Services on a server cluster:

- Registry replication synchronizes the memory settings for Analysis Services, which might be a problem if the two nodes in the cluster have different amounts of RAM.

- Although it is possible to administer and query Analysis Services by using the name of the currently active node on the cluster, you should not do this. You must perform all administration and querying using the cluster server name.

- Analysis Manager registers Analysis Services by using the machine name of the node. You must remove this server registration and then register the cluster server name.

- Analysis Manager stores all server registrations in the registry. Registry replication synchronizes the registered servers on the two nodes of the cluster. Therefore, you must perform any new server registrations in Analysis Manager on the currently active node of the cluster.

> **More Info**   For full instructions on how to install Analysis Services in a server cluster, refer to Knowledge Base article 308023, "HOW TO: Cluster SQL Server 2000 Analysis Services in Windows 2000," which you will find at *http://support.microsoft.com*.

SQL Mail and Failover Clustering

If you intend to use SQL Mail with a SQL Server 2000 virtual server, be aware that it might or might not work. The underlying MAPI protocol that is used is not cluster-aware. You need to configure each node with the same MAPI profile, such as the Microsoft Outlook profile. If you change the password or account used for your SQL Server virtual server, you also need to update the Mail profile in the Control Panel on each node. With the 64-bit edition of SQL Server 2000, SQL Mail is not available at all. You can use SQL Server Agent Mail remotely configured by SQL Server Enterprise Manager as long as the client connecting uses SQL Server 2000 Service Pack 3 or later.

> **More Info**   For more information on SQL Mail and failover clustering, refer to Knowledge Base articles 298723, "BUG: SQL Mail Not Fully Supported for Use in Conjunction with Cluster Virtual SQL Servers," and 263556, "INF: How to Configure SQL Mail," at *http://support.microsoft.com*. For more information on configuring mail capabilities with 64-bit SQL Server 2000, see the section "SQL Mail" under the topic "Differences Between 64-bit and 32-bit Releases (64-bit)" in the 64-bit edition of SQL Server Books Online.

Exchange and SQL Server on the Same Cluster

You should not place Microsoft Exchange Server and SQL Server on the same cluster. First and foremost, both are mission-critical applications. You do not want to have one starve the resources of the other, especially under Windows 2000 Advanced Server. There are also some potential conflicts in things like memory models and versions of MDAC or versions of the Microsoft Search functionality. If you choose to implement both on the same server cluster and encounter problems, Microsoft Product Support Services (PSS) will assist you to the best of their abilities, but their recommendation might be to remove one of them from the server cluster if the issue cannot be resolved. It would be best to deploy separate clusters for SQL Server and Exchange.

> **Tip** If both SQL Server and Exchange must exist on the same cluster, install Exchange first and then install SQL Server 2000. There are certain shared resources, such as the underlying Microsoft Search service. Modifications to one application could negatively affect the other.

Cluster Group Configuration for Failover Clustering

Your SQL Server 2000 failover cluster should resemble the following when it is configured:

- The Cluster Group resource group contains the Cluster IP address, cluster name, and quorum disk in one group.

- Microsoft Distributed Transaction Coordinator (MS DTC) should be configured as described in Chapter 5. This is version-dependent.

- Each SQL Server virtual server needs its own dedicated group, which will contain the SQL Server IP Address, SQL Server Network Name, SQL Server, SQL Server Agent, and SQL Server Fulltext resources. Two instances cannot share the same group. See Figure 6-4 to see the resources that exist after a base SQL Server virtual server installation.

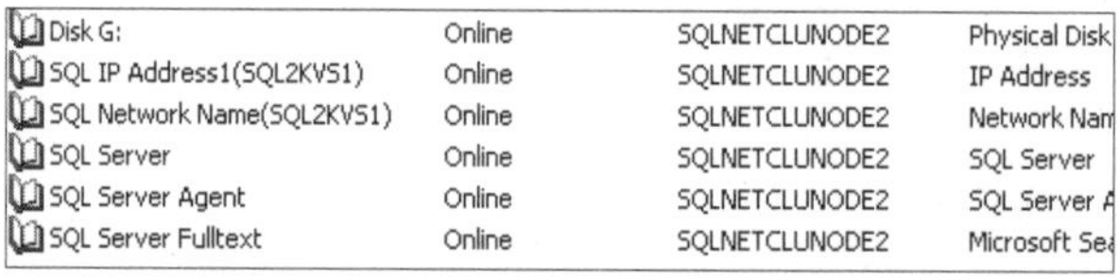

Disk G:	Online	SQLNETCLUNODE2	Physical Disk
SQL IP Address1(SQL2KVS1)	Online	SQLNETCLUNODE2	IP Address
SQL Network Name(SQL2KVS1)	Online	SQLNETCLUNODE2	Network Nam
SQL Server	Online	SQLNETCLUNODE2	SQL Server
SQL Server Agent	Online	SQLNETCLUNODE2	SQL Server A
SQL Server Fulltext	Online	SQLNETCLUNODE2	Microsoft Se

Figure 6-4 Resource configuration in Cluster Administrator.

Implementing SQL Server 2000 Failover Clustering

This section describes the implementation considerations when you configure a failover cluster.

> **On the CD** Use the document Failover_Clustering_Pre-Installation_ Checklist.doc to assist in your installation to ensure that you are ready to install failover clustering.

Prerequisites

Prior to installing SQL Server 2000, make sure there are no errors in Event Viewer that could prevent a successful cluster installation. Verify that only the services necessary for the operating system are running. Any other services should be stopped because they could interfere with the installation process. These services include Simple Network Management Protocol (SNMP), the World Wide Web Publishing service, and vendor-specific programs. The easiest way to start and stop multiple services is to create two batch files: one that contains multiple net stop commands and one that contains the corresponding net start commands.

Installation Order

This section provides the installation order for various versions of Windows and SQL Server 2000.

Windows 2000 Advanced Server and Windows 2000 Datacenter Server

Install Windows 2000 Advanced Server and Windows 2000 Datacenter Server in this order:

1.   Install Windows 2000 Advanced Server (the vendor installs Windows 2000 Datacenter Server).

2.   Install any necessary Windows 2000 service packs or hot fixes.

3.   Install Microsoft Internet Explorer 5 Update (if necessary).

4.   Create the necessary domain user accounts.

5.   Complete any server cluster preinstallation tasks required, as described in Chapter 5.

6.   Create the server cluster.

7.   Create the clustered MS DTC.

8.   Complete any server cluster postinstallation tasks required, as described in Chapter 5.

9.   Stop unnecessary services, such as Internet Information Services (IIS) or Simple Mail Transfer Protocol (SMTP). This will vary on a case-by-case basis, and although it is not required, it is recommended.

10.   Rename the cluster group with the disk to be added during the failover cluster installation.

11.   Install SQL Server 2000.

12.   Install the latest SQL Server 2000 service pack, as well as any hot fixes.

Windows Server 2003 Enterprise Edition and Windows Server 2003 Datacenter Edition

This is the order for installing Windows Server 2003 Enterprise Edition and Windows Server 2003 Datacenter Edition:

1. Install Windows Server 2003 Enterprise Edition (the vendor installs Windows Server 2003 Datacenter Edition).

2. Install any necessary Windows Server 2003 service packs or hot fixes.

3. Create the necessary domain user accounts.

4. Complete any server cluster preinstallation tasks required, as described in Chapter 5.

5. Create the server cluster.

6. Create the clustered MS DTC.

7. Complete any server cluster postinstallation tasks required, as described in Chapter 5.

8. Stop unnecessary services such as IIS. Although this is not required, it is recommended.

9. Rename the cluster group with the disk to be added during the failover cluster installation.

10. Install SQL Server 2000. SQL Server 2000 Release A is recommended.

11. Install SQL Server 2000 Service Pack 3 or later. SQL Server 2000 Service Pack 2 and earlier versions are not supported under Windows Server 2003.

12. Install any necessary SQL Server 2000 hot fixes.

> **Warning** If you attempt to set up a SQL Server virtual server on a server cluster where you select the default of having all nodes as part of the virtual server definition for SQL Server and the computer name of the primary domain controller is more than 14 or 15 characters, you might encounter an access violation. This commonly occurs when the cluster nodes are set up as domain controllers. For any updates to this, see Knowledge Base article 289828, "PRB: SQL Server Setup in a Cluster Environment Encounters an Access Violation If You Have a Long Computer Name," at *http://support.microsoft.com*.

Installing a SQL Server Virtual Server

Installing a failover cluster is very similar to the process of installing a stand-alone SQL Server 2000 instance.

> **On the CD**   Full installation instructions for a failover cluster can be found in the document Failover_Clustering_Install_Instructions.doc.

Postinstallation Tasks

This section highlights some best practices when implementing a SQL Server 2000 failover cluster.

> **On the CD**   Use the document Failover_Clustering_Post-Installation_Checklist.doc to assist in your installation.

Configuring Antivirus Software

If there is no reason to put antivirus software on the cluster nodes dedicated to SQL Server, very secure, and without file shares on it, do not install the software. If your corporate security policy dictates that antivirus software must be configured on all servers, you must set the filtering of the antivirus program to exclude the scanning of all SQL Server drives that contain data and log files. You do not want the scanner on another node in the event of a failover to detect the drive and prevent SQL Server from starting because the virus scanner is now scanning your database and log files. Also remember, as noted in Chapter 5, to exclude the \MSCS directory on the quorum if you are using a disk-based quorum.

Adding Drives for SQL Server Use

During SQL Server setup, you can choose only one drive letter out of your available cluster drives. To be able to use additional drives, you must add them as dependencies to the SQL Server resource.

> **Important**   Plan ahead and add all drives that will be used by SQL
> Server when you configure your server cluster, and then your failover
> cluster. If you do not do this, because the process to add a drive letter
> for SQL Server use involves taking the SQL Server resource offline,
> you will have an availability outage if you do not plan your capacity
> properly. Also, the shared disks must be recognized by Cluster Admin-
> istrator to be seen by SQL Server.

1. Start Cluster Administrator.

2. Fail all disk resources that will be added to the SQL Server virtual server
    to the same node that currently owns the SQL Server resources.

3. Drag and drop the additional disk resources to the folder containing
    the SQL Server resources to move them. A message will be dis-
    played, similar to the one shown in Figure 6-5.

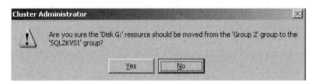

Figure 6-5   Cluster Administrator confirmation message.

4. In the Move Resources dialog box, shown in Figure 6-6, click Yes.

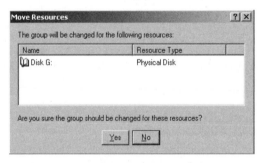

Figure 6-6   Move Resources dialog box.

5. Take the SQL Server resource offline by right-clicking it and selecting
    Bring Offline. Or, you can use SQL Server Service Manager and stop
    SQL Server. Both methods are supported.

6. Right-click the SQL Server resource and then click Properties.

7. In the Properties dialog box, click the Dependencies tab, and then click Modify.

8. In the Modify Dependencies dialog box, shown in Figure 6-7, the available resources for the cluster appear in the Available Resources list. Select the drives to add, click the arrow to move the resource to the Dependencies list, and then click OK.

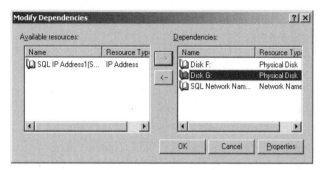

Figure 6-7   Modify Dependencies dialog box.

9. To verify that the resource is now a dependency, in the Properties dialog box click the Dependencies tab, shown in Figure 6-8.

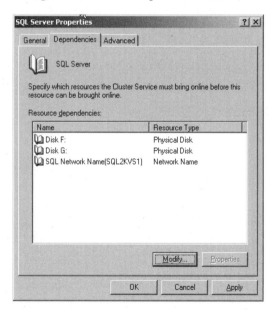

Figure 6-8   Verify the new dependency in the SQL Server Properties dialog box.

10. Bring the SQL Server resource online when complete. Also restart SQL Server Agent and SQL Server Fulltext if necessary.

Verifying the Drive Configuration To ensure all of your drives are added to SQL Server properly, you can do two things:

1. Execute the following Transact-SQL query:

   ```
   select * from ::fn_servershareddrives()
   ```

   The output, shown in Figure 6-9, should reflect all of the drives SQL Server can use.

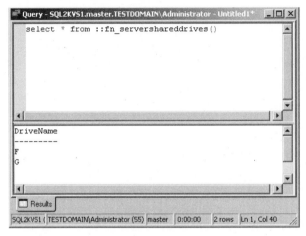

Figure 6-9 Output of the fn_servershareddrives function.

2. Open SQL Server Enterprise Manager, and try to create a new database. All drives should be available for use, as shown in Figure 6-10.

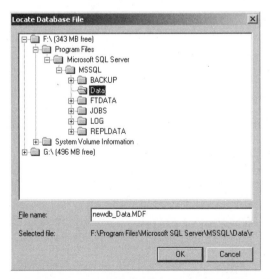

Figure 6-10 Drive letter available in SQL Server Enterprise Manager.

Disabling Unnecessary Services

If you have not done so already, disable any Windows services that SQL Server does not use and are not needed for core operating system functionality.

Assigning a Static Port Number

For each IP address, you should use a static port number to ensure that the port is always the same in a failover. To change the port number associated with each IP address of your instance, follow these steps:

1. Start Server Network Utility (SQL Server Server Network Utility) from the SQL Server menu group.

2. From the server drop-down list, in the Instances group, select the instance to modify. Under Enabled Protocols, select TCP/IP. Click Properties, as shown in Figure 6-11.

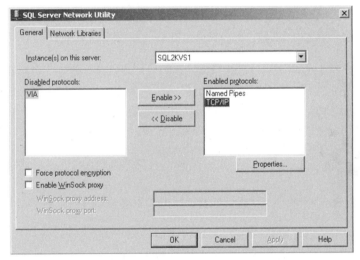

Figure 6-11   General tab of the SQL Server Network Utility dialog box.

3. In the next dialog box, enter a number for the port, as shown in Figure 6-12. Click OK.

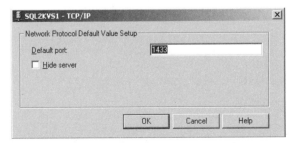

Figure 6-12   Changing the port number.

4. Click OK.

5. Repeat Steps 2 to 4 to change any other IP ports associated with the instance.

6. Click OK when finished. The message in Figure 6-13 is displayed. Click OK.

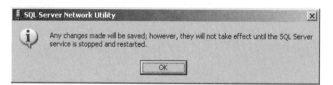

Figure 6-13   Information confirmation message.

7. Stop and restart SQL Server virtual server for the port changes to take effect.

Enabling Advanced Security

If you need to use IPSec, Kerberos, or Secure Sockets Layer (SSL) with your failover cluster as part of your overall security, it is definitely possible. It takes proper planning, so read the following information carefully.

IPSec   IPSec, although it technically can work in a clustered environment, is not really designed for that, so you might want to evaluate the effectiveness of IPSec in your cluster scenario. The underlying issue is that in a failover, the Internet Key Exchange Security Associations are not moved from one node to another. Also, by default, the Security Association Idle Timer times out in 5 minutes. This means that after a failover, applications or users accessing the cluster cannot reconnect until at least 5 minutes after all cluster resources are up after the failover. Your application, should you choose to use IPSec, has to tolerate these problems.

> **More Info**   For any changes to this, see Knowledge Base article 306677, "IPSec Is Not Designed for Failover."

Kerberos   Kerberos is supported on a server cluster and subsequently failover clustering under both Windows 2000 (with Windows 2000 Service Pack 3 or later) and Windows Server 2003. To see the steps to configure Kerberos on a Windows 2000 post–Service Pack 3 server, read Knowledge Base article 235529, "Kerberos Support on Windows 2000–Based Server Clusters."

> **More Info**   For more information on Kerberos and Windows, you can also read the following white papers: *http://www.microsoft.com/windows2000/techinfo/howitworks/security/kerberos.asp* and *http://www.microsoft.com/windows2000/techinfo/howitworks/security/kerbint.asp*. Knowledge Base article 248758, "Information About the Windows 2000 Kerberos Implementation," includes additional information.

SSL Certificates   SSL certificates are fully supported on all versions of Windows 2000 and Windows Server 2003 clustering. To use SSL encryption on a SQL Server 2000 cluster, a certificate must be issued to the Virtual SQL Server Name.

> **More Info**   Review Knowledge Base article 283794, "Problems Using Certificate with Virtual Name in Clustered SQL Servers."
>
> For full instructions on how to enable SSL certificates for use with SQL Server, see Knowledge Base articles 276553, "HOW TO: Enable SSL Encryption for SQL Server 2000 with Certificate Server," and 316898, "HOW TO: Enable SSL Encryption for SQL Server 2000 with Microsoft Management Console." There is also a Microsoft Support Webcast at *http://support.microsoft.com/default.aspx?scid=/servicedesks/webcasts/wc042302/wcblurb042302.asp* that might also prove useful in configuring SSL certificates for your SQL Server instances.

> **Warning**   If the process of configuring your certificates somehow goes awry, you might have to reinstall your failover cluster. To prevent this, back up all databases and nodes (Windows-level backup) prior to configuring SSL certificates for SQL Server.

Configuring SQL Server Resources

Once your failover cluster is installed, you might need to modify some of the parameters associated with the SQL Server resources. These include setting a preferred owner if you have more than two nodes, as well as your failover and failback policies.

Setting Preferred Owners   When you use more than two nodes in a failover cluster, it is important to consider which node should own the SQL Server processes in the event of a failover. The potential owners are configured with SQL Server Setup. With up to four nodes available under 32-bit and eight under 64-bit, there should be an order that makes logical sense for the production environment. You should set the failover preferences for the group containing all the resources for the instance of SQL Server (not only on the virtual server) to ensure that all resources properly fail over to the same node. For example, in an $N + 1$ configuration, each group would have the idle node second in the list of preferred owners. This means that if any of the nodes failed, the resources on that node would move to the idle node. To set preferred owners, follow these steps:

1.   Start Cluster Administrator. Right-click the group containing the SQL Server 2000 virtual server, and then click Properties.

2.   On the General tab, the Preferred Owners list box displays all cluster nodes that can potentially own the processes in that group, and the current order in which they would fail over. To change the order, click Modify.

3.   In the Modify Preferred Owners dialog box, shown in Figure 6-14, make any changes to the preferred failover order. All nodes currently configured as potential owners appear in the right pane in the order of failover preference. For example, there are four nodes in a cluster: Dennis, James, Tommy, and Chuck. All four nodes of the cluster can be potential owners, and the order of failover if Dennis goes down is set to be James, then Tommy, and finally Chuck if both James and Tommy are unavailable.

> **Important**   Do not use this procedure to add nodes to the SQL Server virtual server definition. You must use SQL Server Setup as described later in the section "Adding or Removing a Cluster Node from the Virtual Server Definition and Adding, Changing, or Updating a TCP/IP Address."

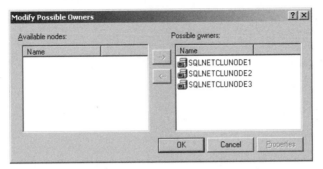

Figure 6-14   Modify Preferred Owners dialog box.

Failing Back to the Preferred Owner, Thresholds, and Other Parameters   You need to determine how you want your resources to behave in the aftermath of a failover—do you want them to automatically fail back to the preferred owner once it comes online? How many times do you want to try to start the resources on the current node before allowing it to fail over to another server?

Resource Group Failback   All resources fail over to another node at the group level. In the event of a failover, the cluster group containing the SQL Server resources can be configured to fail back to the primary node when and if it becomes available again. By default, the Prevent Failback option is not selected because usually there is no problem with continuing on the secondary node when you have properly planned all of your resources. This setting provides an opportunity to analyze and repair the problem on the failed node. If you need to move the resources, you can do it manually later. You should not change this setting, but if you need to, here is how:

1.   Start Cluster Administrator. Right-click the group containing the SQL Server 2000 virtual server, and then click Properties.

2.   In the Properties dialog box, click the Failback tab, shown in Figure 6-15.

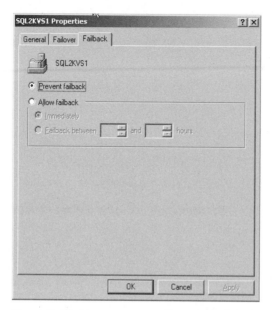

Figure 6-15   Resource group Properties Failback tab.

3.   To prevent an automatic failback, select Prevent Failback. To allow automatic failback, select Allow Failback, and then one of the following options:

❑   **Immediately**   This means that the moment Windows Clustering detects that the preferred cluster node is online, it fails back any resources. This is not advisable because it could disrupt clients and applications, especially at peak times in the business day.

❑   **Failback Between N And N1 Hours**   This option allows a controlled failback to a preferred node (if it is online) during a certain period. The hours are set using numbers from 0 through 23.

Configuring Resource Parameters   Failovers can also be controlled in terms of a threshold, meaning that after a certain point, a resource is not able to fail over to another node. There are two levels of thresholds: resource and cluster. Depending on how the resource is configured, it can affect the group failing over to another node. To configure resource parameters, follow these steps:

1.   Start Cluster Administrator. Select the proper group containing the SQL Server 2000 virtual server, then right-click the resource to alter, and click Properties.

2. In the Properties dialog box, click the Advanced tab, shown in Figure 6-16.

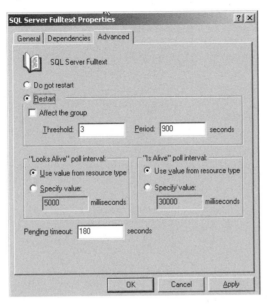

Figure 6-16 Advanced tab of the Properties dialog box for a cluster resource.

3. Select Do Not Restart if the Cluster Service should not attempt to restart or allow the resource to fail. By default, Restart is selected. If Restart is selected, configure the restart policy:

❑ **Affect The Group** To prevent the failure of the selected resource from causing the SQL Server group to fail over after the specified number of retries (Threshold) has occurred, you should clear the Affect The Group check box.

❑ **Threshold** This is the number of times the Cluster Service will try to restart the resource, and Period is the amount of time (in seconds) between retries. For example, if Threshold is set to 0, and the Affect The Group check box is selected, on detection of a failure the entire group with the resource is failed over to another node. Do not modify Threshold unless you are directed to by Microsoft PSS.

> **Tip**   If you are not using a resource, such as the clustered
> full-text resource for each SQL Server virtual server, clear the
> Affect The Group check box. Do not change the Affect The
> Group status of data or log disks, the SQL Server IP address
> or network name, or SQL Server Agent and SQL Server itself.

4.   Do not *ever* modify the Looks Alive Poll Interval and Is Alive Poll
      Interval settings. These settings are configured to be optimal for the
      specific application, which in this case, is SQL Server.

5.   Do not modify Pending Timeout. The value, represented in seconds,
      is the amount of time the resource in either the Offline Pending or
      Online Pending states has to resolve its status before the Cluster Ser-
      vice puts the resource in either Offline or Failed status.

6.   Click OK.

Cluster Group Thresholds   Not unlike a resource's thresholds, you can configure
thresholds at a group level to tell the server cluster how many times to try to
restart the group on one node before attempting to fail the group over to
another node in the server cluster.

1.   Start Cluster Administrator. Right-click the group containing the SQL
      Server 2000 virtual server, and then click Properties.

2.   In the Properties dialog box, click the Failover tab, shown in
      Figure 6-17.

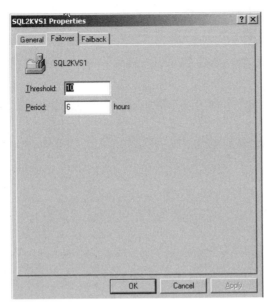

Figure 6-17   Failover tab for a cluster group.

To configure the failover policy, in the Threshold box, enter the number of times the group is allowed to fail over within a set span of hours. In the Period box, enter the set span of hours. For example, if Threshold is set to 10 and Period is set to 6, the Cluster Service fails the group over a maximum of 10 times in a 6-hour period. At the 11th failover in that 6-hour period, the server cluster leaves the group offline. This affects only resources that were failed over; therefore, if the SQL Server resource failed 11 times, it would be left offline, but the IP could be left online.

Verifying Your Failover Cluster Installation

Once you have configured your virtual server, you need to test it to ensure that it is configured and working properly.

> **On the CD**   For test plans you can use in your environment, see the document Failover_Clustering_Test_Plan.xls.

Verifying Connectivity and Name Resolution

To verify that the private and public networks are communicating properly, perform the following procedures. You must know the IP address for each network adapter in the cluster, as well as for the IP cluster.

Verifying Connectivity and Name Resolution from a Server Node

You need to verify that each node can access the SQL Server resources. The most basic test is to check for name and IP connectivity by following these steps:

1. On a node, on the Start menu, click Run, and then type **cmd** in the text box. Click OK.

2. Type **ping *ipaddress*** where ***ipaddress*** is the IP address for the SQL Server virtual server.

3. Repeat for all IP addresses the SQL Server virtual server is configured to use.

4. Type **ping *sqlnetworkname*** where ***sqlnetworkname*** is the name of the SQL Server virtual server.

5. Repeat this test on each node.

Verifying Connectivity and Name Resolution from a Client

Clients must also be able to recognize the virtual SQL Server. Wait a few minutes, as it might take some time to register with DNS.

1. On a client computer, on the Start menu, click Run, and then type **cmd** in the text box. Click OK.

2. Repeat Steps 2, 3, and 4 from the previous section.

Validating Failover

Finally, perform a failover of all SQL Server virtual servers to all nodes of the server cluster to ensure that all resources fail over and restart on each node without problems and without affecting any other groups.

1. Start Cluster Administrator.

2. Right-click a group containing the SQL Server resources you are testing (for example, SQL Server Ins1), and then click Move. If you have more than two nodes, select the node to move the group to. The group selected and its resources are then moved to its preferred failover node. This change is reflected in Cluster Administrator.

3. On that node, start Windows Explorer and verify that you can access the drives with no errors.

Verifying the SQL Server Service Account and Node Participation

For SQL Server to be able to manage its resources and perform correctly, the service account must be part of the cluster access control list (ACL). To ensure that this is configured properly, execute the following in a SQL Query Analyzer window:

```
select * from ::fn_virtualservernodes()
```

The output, as shown in Figure 6-18, should reflect the nodes configured. If there is no output, ensure the account SQL Server is running under is part of the cluster ACL. This query can also be used to verify which nodes are part of the SQL Server virtual server definition.

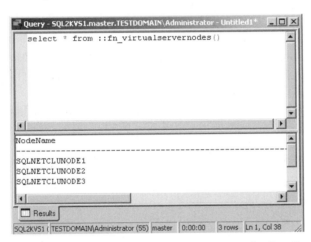

Figure 6-18   Output of the fn_virtualservernodes function.

> **Tip**   You can also use fn_virtualservernodes and fn_servershareddrives in your normal administration and reporting for your failover cluster to see its definition.

Verifying the Application with Failover

Once you verify that the base failover clustering functionality is working, configure your user application databases. You must then verify that your application will behave properly during a failover.

> **On the CD** A test plan for verifying an application can be found in Failover_Clustering_Test_Plan.xls.

Administering SQL Server Virtual Servers

There are four places you can administer your SQL Server 2000 virtual server. It is important to understand the similarities and differences among them so you use the right tool.

■ **SQL Server tools, especially SQL Server Enterprise Manager** SQL Server Enterprise Manager and the other SQL Server tools should be used to administer the database. All changing of accounts and passwords associated with SQL Server and SQL Server Agent will be changed in Enterprise Manager, and if a port number needs to be changed, use the SQL Server Server Network Utility. Use the other SQL Server tools as you would for a nonclustered instance.

■ **SQL Server Setup** To uninstall the virtual server, to add or remove the nodes participating in the failover cluster, or to change or add IP addresses to the failover cluster, use SQL Server Setup.

■ **Cluster Administrator** This tool is an operating system-level tool located in Administrative Tools. Prior to SQL Server 2000, most configuration changes to SQL Server clustering were done in Cluster Administrator. With SQL Server 2000, however, use Cluster Administrator only where it is outlined in this chapter to ensure proper use with SQL Server 2000 failover clustering. Do not use Cluster Administrator to add nodes to the resource definitions or to modify IP addresses.

■ **The command-line cluster utility** The cluster command-line tool is basically the operating system command-line interface for most functionality within Cluster Administrator. As with Cluster Administrator, use it only when necessary.

> **Warning**   Do not use the Windows 2000 Datacenter application Process Control to modify SQL Server virtual server configurations. Process Control is not a cluster-aware application, and in the event of a failover, the virtual server modified on one node does not carry over the process control constraints from the failed node automatically. Use SQL Server Enterprise Manager and the other SQL Server–supplied tools to modify the SQL Server virtual server configuration. This is documented in Knowledge Base article 296382, "Windows Datacenter Server Process Control Service Is Not Cluster Aware."

> **More Info**   Certain topics for SQL Server administration for a failover cluster are not covered here because they are covered elsewhere. For memory management, see Chapter 14. For rebuilding the master database, see Chapter 12, "Disaster Recovery Techniques for Microsoft SQL Server." For service packs and failover clustering, see Chapter 13, "Highly Available Upgrades."

Ensuring a Virtual Server Will Not Fail Due to Other Service Failures

To prevent the failure of specific services from causing the SQL Server group to fail over, configure those services properly using Cluster Administrator. See Step 4 of the "Cluster Group Thresholds" section earlier in this chapter for instructions. For example, if SQL Server Full-Text Search functionality, which is represented as the SQL Server Fulltext resource, is not used as part of your solution, you should ensure that the Affect The Group check box is cleared in the Properties dialog box for the resource.

Adding or Removing a Cluster Node from the Virtual Server Definition and Adding, Changing, or Updating a TCP/IP Address

Another feature of SQL Server 2000 failover clustering is the ability to add or remove a cluster node from a SQL Server virtual server definition. Adding nodes to the existing SQL Server virtual server definition performs all the necessary operations on the new nodes (including installing binaries, system components, and creating services) and performs the necessary modifications to the cluster configuration.

> **Warning**   Never modify an IP address for a SQL Server virtual server in Cluster Administrator. You will break its definition. If a network or system administrator accidentally does this, change it back to the old IP address and then perform the steps outlined next.

1. Insert the SQL Server 2000 Enterprise Edition compact disc in your CD-ROM drive. Select Install SQL Server 2000 Components.

2. Click Install SQL Server 2000 Components, click Install Database Server, and then click Next.

3. In the Computer Name dialog box, select Virtual Server, and enter the name of an existing clustered instance of SQL Server 2000.

4. In the Installation Selection dialog box, shown in Figure 6-19, select Advanced Options, and then click Next.

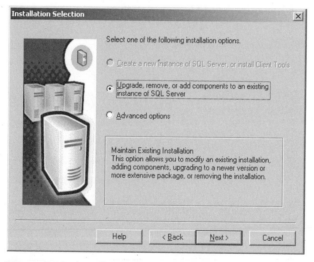

Figure 6-19   Installation Selection dialog box.

5. In the Advanced Options dialog box, shown in Figure 6-20, select Maintain A Virtual Server For Failover Clustering, and then click Next.

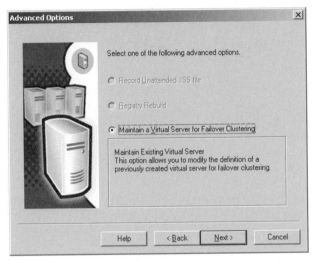

Figure 6-20   Advanced Options dialog box.

6. In the Failover Clustering dialog box, shown in Figure 6-21, a TCP/IP address can be added to or removed from the selected instance of SQL Server 2000.

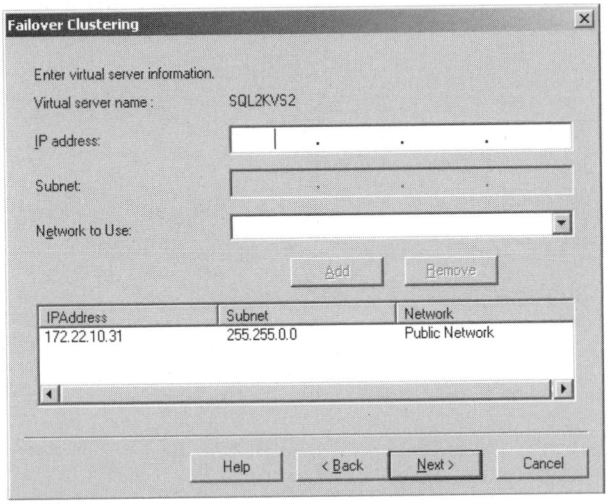

Figure 6-21   Failover Clustering dialog box.

7. To remove a TCP/IP address, select the address, and click Remove.

> **Important**   An instance of SQL Server 2000 in a failover cluster requires a TCP/IP address to function. Only remove a TCP/IP address if more than one exists and if this does not affect users or applications accessing SQL Server.

8. To add a TCP/IP address, enter the new TCP/IP address in the IP Address text box, select the network to use, and then click Add. The new IP address appears after the existing IP address. Click Next.

9. In the Cluster Management dialog box, shown in Figure 6-22, select the appropriate nodes to add or remove from the cluster, and then click Next when you are finished.

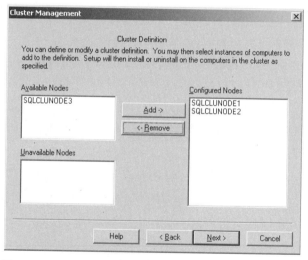

Figure 6-22   Cluster Management dialog box.

10. In the Remote Information dialog box, shown in Figure 6-23, enter the user name and password for the domain administrator account used for the clustered instance of SQL Server 2000, and then click Next.

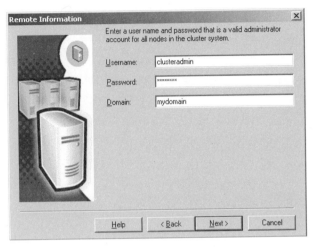

Figure 6-23   Remote Information dialog box.

11. When the process is complete, click Finish. Verify that the changes you wanted to take place are there.

Renaming a SQL Server 2000 Virtual Server

Renaming a SQL Server 2000 virtual server is neither possible nor supported. The only way to rename a SQL Server virtual server is to uninstall it and reinstall with the new name.

Uninstalling a SQL Server Virtual Server

If you need to remove your failover cluster installation, perform the following steps:

1. Insert the SQL Server 2000 Enterprise Edition compact disc in your CD-ROM drive. Select Install SQL Server 2000 Components.

2. Click Install SQL Server 2000 Components, click Install Database Server, and then click Next.

3. In the Computer Name dialog box, select Virtual Server, and enter the name of an existing clustered instance of SQL Server 2000.

4. In the Installation Selection dialog box, select Upgrade, Remove, Or Add Components To An Existing Instance Of SQL Server as shown in Figure 6-19, and then click Next.

5. In the Instance Name dialog box, click Next if this is the default instance, or enter the name of your named instance in the Instance Name text box. Click Next.

6. In the Existing Installation dialog box, shown in Figure 6-24, the only option that should be available and selected is Uninstall Your Existing Installation. Click Next. The uninstall process will now begin.

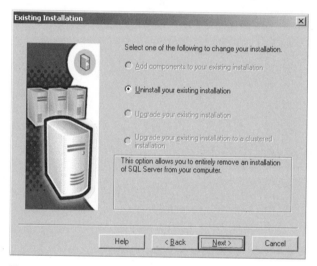

Figure 6-24   Existing Installation dialog box.

7. When complete, you should see a message like the one shown in Figure 6-25, acknowledging that the instance has been uninstalled from the cluster. Click OK.

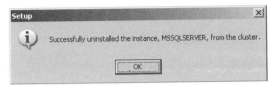

Figure 6-25   Information message confirming successful uninstall.

8. In the Setup Complete dialog box, click Finish. You might need to reboot the nodes of the cluster listed. An example is shown in Figure 6-26.

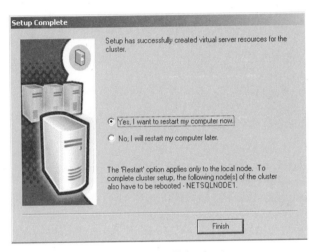

Figure 6-26   Setup Complete dialog box.

Manually Removing Failover Clustering

Sometimes you might not be able to cleanly uninstall your SQL Server 2000 failover cluster as described in the previous section. Although in some cases where it seemed to uninstall cleanly, if you try to reinstall a virtual server, you might see a message such as "A previous program installation created pending file operations on the installation machine. You must restart the computer before running setup." A reboot should clear this problem because there are only pending file operations that will get cleared on a reboot.

However, if this is not your problem, you can manually remove your failover clustering implementation, but you should only perform the following tasks with extreme caution.

Warning   You might have databases that you want to save in their present state. You might also want to save changes that were made to the system databases. If either of these is the case, before you follow these steps, make sure that you have a known good backup of the data or that you save a copy of all the data and log files in a folder other than the MSSQL folder, because you must delete the MSSQL folder. The files you must save include these database files that SQL Server 2000 installs:

Distmdl.*
Master.*
Mastlog.*
Model.*
Modellog.*
Msdbdata.*
Msdblog.*
Northwnd.* (optional install)
Pubs.*
Pubs_log.*
Tempdb.*
Templog.*

You should also do the following:

Verify that no other cluster resources have dependencies on SQL Server, if SQL Server 2000 is clustered.

Stop SQL Server, because active connections can prevent the uninstall process from completing successfully.

Close all SQL Server 2000 Client or Administration tools on other nodes.

Log on to the server with an account that has administrator privileges for SQL Server 2000.

Caution   Do not modify the registry without making a full system backup. If you damage your registry, your node might become unusable, forcing you to reinstall everything.

Depending on the nature of your problem, use the steps that apply to your environment. These steps are intended to get the system to a state where you can perform a successful installation so that you can then remove the SQL Server 2000 installation that is being recovered.

1. Follow the steps in the previous section "Uninstalling a SQL Server Virtual Server" to attempt to remove SQL Server cleanly.

2. Run Regedt32, and then locate this registry key: HKEY_LOCAL_-MACHINE\SOFTWARE\Microsoft\Windows\CurrentVersion\Uninstall. Under the Uninstall key, locate the product code for the instance of SQL Server 2000 that you are trying to remove. On the taskbar, click Start, and then click Run. In the Run dialog box, copy and paste, or type, this command:

```
%systemroot%\IsUninst.exe -f"C:\Program Files\Microsoft
SQLServer\MSSQL$Server1\Uninst.is" -c"C:\Program Files\Microsoft
SQLServer\MSSQL$Server1\sqlsun.dll" -Mssql.miff i=I1
```

> **Note**   Your path names might be different. Make sure your paths match your installation.

This should run the SQL Server 2000 uninstall program and uninstall your instance. If this does not work, continue on to Step 3.

3. Locate the Data folder for your installation, and then rename it if you have to save the data. Otherwise, delete the Data folder. Keep the Data folder so that you have a file backup of the databases in their .mdf and .ldf format available and so that you can possibly use sp_attach_db at a later time.

> **Tip**   If your master and other system databases are still valid and you renamed the folder it was in, see Chapter 12 for instructions on how to restore them (assuming you reinstall with an instance of the same name).

Manually Removing Clustered Instances of SQL Server

Follow these steps to manually remove clustered instances of SQL Server.

1. Locate, and then delete *x*:\Program Files\Microsoft SQL Server\ MSSQL\Binn or *x*:\Program Files\Microsoft SQL Server\ MSSQL$*InstanceName*\Binn folder on each node.

2. Locate, and then delete these registry keys:

   ❏ HKEY_LOCAL_MACHINE\SOFTWARE\Microsoft\MSSQLServer

   ❏ HKEY_LOCAL_MACHINE\SYSTEM\CurrentControlSet\Services\MSSQLSERVER

   ❏ HKEY_LOCAL_MACHINE\SYSTEM\CurrentControlSet\Services\SQLSERVERAGENT

   ❏ HKEY_LOCAL_MACHINE\SYSTEM\CurrentControlSet\Services\MSSQLServerADHelper

   If you are deleting named instances, you would also look for:

   ❏ HKEY_LOCAL_MACHINE\SYSTEM\CurrentControlSet\Services\MSSQL$InstanceName

   ❏ HKEY_LOCAL_MACHINE\SYSTEM\CurrentControlSet\Services\SQLAgent$InstanceName

   ❏ HKEY_LOCAL_MACHINE\SYSTEM\CurrentControlSet\Services\MSSQLServerADHelper$InstanceName

3. Manually delete any clustered resources that still remain in Cluster Administrator. Do not remove anything except SQL Server resources. Leave disk resources intact.

4. Reinstall SQL Server 2000 and use the same name, paths, and IP address as before.

5. Run Setup for the installation, and use the steps found in the section "Uninstalling a SQL Server Virtual Server" earlier to uninstall the instance.

> **Note**   You need to reinstall and uninstall to ensure that you cleanly delete entries from the registry. Steps 1 and 2 allow you to get to the point to do that.

6.   Repeat this procedure for all instances that need to be removed.

7.   If you need to remove SQL Server Full-Text Search, locate and then delete these registry keys:

   ❏   HKEY_LOCAL_MACHINE\SOFTWARE\Microsoft\Search

   ❏   HKEY_LOCAL_MACHINE\SYSTEM\CurrentControlSet\Services\MSFTPSVC

   ❏   HKEY_LOCAL_MACHINE\SYSTEM\CurrentControlSet\Services\MSSCNTRS

   ❏   HKEY_LOCAL_MACHINE\SYSTEM\CurrentControlSet\Services\MSSEARCH

   ❏   HKEY_LOCAL_MACHINE\SYSTEM\CurrentControlSet\Services\MSSGATHERER

   ❏   HKEY_LOCAL_MACHINE\SYSTEM\CurrentControlSet\Services\MSSGTHRSVC

   ❏   HKEY_LOCAL_MACHINE\SYSTEM\CurrentControlSet\Services\MSSINDEX

> **Warning**   Do not remove any Microsoft Search components if they are in use by other applications. You should also back up your Full-Text indexes as well.

Because the removal process did not complete previously, if you are concerned about being able to remove an instance in the future, you can use the steps found in the section "Uninstalling a SQL Server Virtual Server" earlier to verify that you have resolved all the issues that can cause a recurrence of this problem. You do not have to perform the task just to make sure that this particular removal completed; it only checks whether the automatic removal process is working. If this fails, you must continue to investigate to determine and resolve the cause of the failure.

> **Note**   In some cases, the folder *x:*\Program Files\Microsoft SQL Server\80 might not be deleted with this process, and you must manually delete the folder.

If, on the reinstall, you still get the pending files message after a reboot, the files that were going to be removed are marked as read-only. To check this, follow these steps:

1. Find the registry key HKEY_LOCAL_MACHINE\SYSTEM\ CurrentControlSet\Control\SessionManager\PendingFileRename- Operations.

2. Make a note of the filenames.

3. Verify that those files do not have the read-only attribute set.

4. Restart the server again.

Changing SQL Server Service Accounts

To change SQL Server service accounts on a SQL Server virtual server, you must use SQL Server Enterprise Manager. This is done in two places because SQL Server and SQL Server Agent have separate accounts. Changing each account means that SQL Server and SQL Server Agent need to be restarted.

SQL Server Service Account

To change the SQL Server service account, follow these steps:

1. In SQL Server Enterprise Manager, select the virtual server name, right-click it, and select Properties.

2. On the Security tab, as shown in Figure 6-27, enter the name of the new domain account in the This Account text box with the syntax *DOMAINNAME\username*, and then enter the password in the Password text box. Click OK.

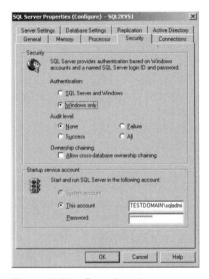

Figure 6-27   Security tab.

3. A warning similar to the one in Figure 6-28 is displayed. Click OK.

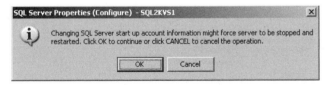

Figure 6-28   Configuration warning message.

SQL Server Agent Service Account

To change the SQL Server Agent service account, follow these steps:

1. In SQL Server Enterprise Manager, open the Management tree, right-click SQL Server Agent, and select Properties.

2. In the SQL Server Agent Properties dialog box, shown in Figure 6-29, enter the name of the new domain account in the This Account text box with the syntax *DOMAINNAME\username*, and enter the password in the Password text box. Click OK.

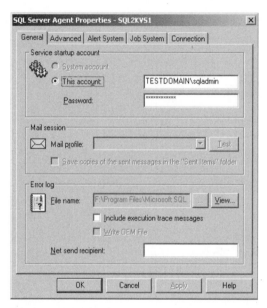

Figure 6-29   SQL Server Agent Service Properties dialog box.

3. A warning similar to the one in Figure 6-30 is displayed. Click OK.

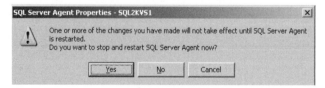

Figure 6-30   Restart Server message.

Changing Domains

If you ever need to change domains for your failover clustering installation, perform the following steps. This assumes you have moved the main server cluster to the new domain already. If you have not, follow the instructions for doing so in Chapter 5.

1. Follow the steps found under "Adding or Removing a Cluster Node from the Virtual Server Definition and Adding, Changing, or Updating a TCP/IP Address." In Step 10 of that procedure, enter the new Cluster Service account information. Do not modify anything else.

2. Start Cluster Administrator.

3. Verify the properties for each SQL Server IP Address resource.

4. Delete any resource that is configured for the old IP addresses only.

5. Run Regedt32.

> **Warning**   If you use Registry Editor incorrectly, you could cause serious problems that might require you to reinstall your operating system. Microsoft cannot guarantee that you can solve problems that result from using Registry Editor incorrectly. Use Registry Editor at your own risk.

6. For a default instance, find HKEY_LOCAL_MACHINE\SOFTWARE\Microsoft\MSSQLServer\Cluster, and for a named instance find HKEY_LOCAL_MACHINE\SOFTWARE\Microsoft\Microsoft SQL Server*Instance Name*\Cluster, where *Instance Name* is the name of the instance being modified.

7. Modify the ClusterIPAddr value to only contain the current valid IP address for the SQL Server virtual server.

8. Repeat step 7 for any IP addresses configured for the SQL Server virtual server.

9. While your failover cluster is offline, use the Services tool to change the virtual SQL Server's startup accounts for SQL Server and SQL Server Agent to the new domain account for SQL Server and SQL Server Agent.

> **Note**   This is about the only time you will use the Services tool to change the service account associated with the SQL Server virtual server.

10. Bring the SQL Server virtual server and its resources online.

11. Start SQL Server Enterprise Manager and change the service account passwords as described in the section "Changing SQL Server Service Accounts." This sends the change to all other nodes.

Troubleshooting SQL Server 2000 Failover Clusters

Troubleshooting SQL Server 2000 in a failover cluster configuration is not always the same as diagnosing problems on a stand-alone server. Because the configuration is a bit more complex, you need to diagnose in a specific order. Before that, however, you must understand the barriers that can exist when implementing failover clustering.

Barriers for Failover Clustering

Microsoft PSS has identified these barriers as the leading culprits for failover clustering problems:

1. Lack of planning. One of the problems is that a missed configuration step can lead to significant problems in production. If your server cluster is unstable, your failover cluster will be, too, and possibly vice versa. For example, is the driver for your SAN the right version? Take the time to plan your installations properly using the tools presented throughout this book.

2. Failure to comply with the Hardware Compatibility List (HCL) requirements. SQL Server failover clustering is only supported on HCL or Windows Catalog–certified systems as described in Chapter 5.

3. Not understanding the technology. There might be a lack of understanding about why clustering is being used, what it provides, and what it does not provide. This can lead to dissatisfaction with the platform, even though it is performing as designed. Please take the time to review Chapter 3 to understand the basics of clustering.

4. Internal politics. If the customer has one group for SQL Server, another for networking, and yet another for system work, the groups must be able to work together, understand the technical issues (such as the need for domain accounts and dedicated IP addresses), and understand how they must interact both on a technical level and on a political level. Internal "turf wars" are a common problem and can prove to be a significant barrier to availability. Teamwork is crucial.

5. Failure to troubleshoot high availability technology systematically. Provided nothing has changed in the application environment, you have to troubleshoot the technology in layers—consistently.

6. Lack of technology-aware diagnostics. How you diagnose a system depends on the technology involved. This is no different with SQL Server high availability systems. For example, make sure that if you are using a cluster, your diagnostic systems are cluster-aware.

7. Building cluster awareness and understanding into applications. SQL Server developers need to build in cluster awareness to make the end-user experience seamless. For example, if your database takes n minutes to go through failover and recovery, how does your application respond during those n minutes? This can be controlled by building awareness of the failover process into your application for any high availability technology approach, not just for clustering.

8. Securing SQL Server access with use of an SSL certificate, which is covered earlier in this chapter. If this is applied wrong, you might need to completely reinstall or recover your failover cluster.

Support for Failover Clustering

When you are working with PSS to solve a problem, make sure that you fulfill all requests for information—especially when supporting a cluster. PSS can gather and send subsets of clustering information to different specialists for concurrent analysis, as long as you supply this information. Your level of cooperation and communication in interacting with PSS affects the time it takes to resolve your issue.

Most SQL Server cluster issues (more than 75 percent) have nothing to do with SQL Server, and therefore cannot be solved by sending log information in isolation. Proper resolution of a case requires proactive communication. This involves keeping accurate records of changes and times of changes (deliberate alterations or observed fluctuations). Track configurations. Keep complete notes of all error messages received or observed rather than recording generic comments, such as "Installation failed." Communicate any actions you took and their results, as well as anything you suspect and why, or anything that is happening simultaneously. For example, detail the following:

■ Was a file in use? If so, identify which file you could not update.

■ Was a share missing?

■ Did the user have permission?

■ Was there a hardware problem detected? Fix the errors constantly being reported in the Setupapi.log file so PSS can use that as a resource to see if there are system file-protection issues being encountered.

Once you have involved PSS, refrain from making any changes to the system without confirming them with PSS. This is a simple extra step that can facilitate resolution. It can prevent additional problems from arising (for example, if your plan has known issues).

The Troubleshooting Process

Roughly 70 to 80 percent of all SQL Server virtual server problems are not SQL Server–based. They have to do with base cluster issues at the operating system or a hardware failure, driver issue, and so on. Always troubleshoot in the following bottom-up order, as this uncovers the layers of problems. Never assume that SQL Server is your issue until you discover that it is. If you troubleshoot in a different order than that listed here, you might have success, but experience has proven that following this exact sequence uncovers your problems with greater certainty:

1. Hardware issues

2. Base Windows issues

3. Networking issues

4. Security issues (such as permissions)

5. Server cluster or other base clustering issues

6. SQL Server issues

Where to Look for Problems

Check the operating system's Event Viewer at the application, system, and security logs. Sometimes the problem is apparent, such as a disk or network card failure, or relevant error messages from the operating system or SQL Server might appear. Next, check the relevant log files. The SQL Server installation log files are located under %windir%, and the cluster logs are located where the system variable %clusterlog% is set (generally \\Windowsinstalldir\Cluster). These are the files:

- **Setup.log**   Log for the local binaries setup portion of a SQL Server installation.

- **Sqlstp*n*.log**   The log for the SQL Server Setup, where *n* is the number of the setup attempts.

- **Sqlsp*n*.log**   The log for SQL Server Service Pack Setup, where *n* is the number of the setup attempts.

- **Sqlclstr.log**   The log for the clustered instances of SQL Server.

- **Cluster.log**   The main cluster log file.

Microsoft Product Support Reporting Tool

If you call PSS, there is a good chance they will want you to run the Microsoft Product Support (MPS) Reporting Tool. The MPS Reporting Tool gathers detailed information regarding a system's current configuration in a nondestructive way. The reporting tool does not make any registry changes or modifications to the operating system. The data that is collected will assist the Microsoft Support Professionals with fault isolation. When used with a cluster, this tool should be executed on all nodes that are part of the SQL Server failover cluster definition.

In addition to the information the tool gathers, you will be asked to provide information specific to your installation that PSS cannot gather manually. When the tool finishes, a text document appears on your screen with details of the requested information.

> **On the CD**   A version of the MPS Reporting tool is included with this book in MPSRPT_2002_SQLv6f.zip. Test it on your systems, both clustered and nonclustered, and you can also store this information in your run book. PSS might have a later version that they will ask you to use if you open a support case.

Common Troubleshooting Issues

This section presents some of the common issues and solutions when implementing failover clustering.

Installation Problems   When the installation process attempts to install the SQL Server binaries on the other nodes, it fails (possibly with a failed logon request error). When installing on the remote nodes, the SQL Server Setup program is actually run on each of the nodes. If you install from a network share, ensure that all nodes have connectivity to the share without having to specify a network password. (For example, you should be able to view \\sharecomputer\sharepath without specifying credentials.) If you are installing from a compact disc on a particular node, make sure that the drive is actually shared and that the other cluster nodes are configured to communicate properly. This includes making sure that the proper accounts exist on each node and that the other nodes are set up for Windows Authentication. Mapping a drive letter, even if it is the same on all nodes, does not work because the installation process accesses the UNC path of the share.

After installing and rebooting the server, the SQL Server install does not seem to complete. Sometimes file renames (for example, MDAC files) are blocked at startup due to locks on files in use during startup. Therefore, if the file remains read-only, the installation process never completes.

Connectivity   Windows Clustering loses connectivity to the SQL Server virtual server. This could be because the process used to perform the IsAlive check is run in the context of the Windows Clustering service account. This account must have sysadmin rights in SQL Server. If you encounter problems with this, check all logins and cross-reference them with the cluster logs to see if there is an IsAlive check.

Note   If you removed Builtin\Administrators from SQL Server, you have to manually add the Cluster Service account to the Sysadmin group of SQL Server so it can run IsAlive.

After installation of a new SQL Server virtual server, clients cannot connect to the server, especially when using graphical user interface (GUI) tools. Sometimes a successful manual connection using a command-line tool (for example, the bcp or osql utilities) must be initiated first. This sometimes occurs when the virtual server is not yet registered in Windows Internet Name Server (WINS). If your installation was a named instance, you have to verify that your clients are using a minimum of MDAC 2.6.

Full-Text Search Setup

In some cases, Setup might fail because the Full-Text Search resource type does not exist. The resource is called Microsoft Search Service. If this is the case, you might have to manually create the type to get the installation to complete next time. To create the resource, go to a command prompt and execute

```
cd %windir%\cluster
regsvr32 gathercl.dll
```

It is helpful to register this file on all nodes. You can then rerun Setup.

Disaster Recovery for Failover Clustering

As you know, things can and do happen to your cluster. You have to be prepared to handle these situations when they arise. Whether it is a corrupt disk, failed disk, or bad node, the more you know up front, the more effectively you can deal with the problem. The following sections present some scenarios that you should consider when attempting to restore your server clusters that have SQL Server virtual servers on them.

> **Note**   Although some scenarios might apply to other clustered applications such as Microsoft Exchange, each application has its own exact set of steps to restore. The steps outlined here are for SQL Server 2000 only.

> **Tip**   If you are using Windows 2000, the *Microsoft Windows 2000 Server Resource Kit* (Microsoft Press, ISBN 1-57231-8058) includes a few tools you might find useful:
>
> 1. Under \Apps\Clustool, there is a tool named Clusrest.exe. It might assist you in the restoration of your quorum log to a live quorum. This can also be downloaded from *http://www.microsoft.com/ windows2000/techinfo/reskit/tools/existing/clusrest-o.asp.*
>
> 2. Dumpcfg.exe can be useful for backing up and restoring disk signatures, which are crucial for the health of a server cluster.
>
> 3. Clustool.exe can be useful for backing up and restoring parts of your server cluster configuration. Please note that things like the cluster IP address, the cluster name, and the quorum disk are *not* restored with this.
>
> Read more information on each of these tools before deploying them in your environment to see if they will be useful to you.
>
> Windows 2003 Server Resource Kit tools are available from the *Microsoft Windows Server 2003 Deployment Kit: A Microsoft Resource Kit* (Microsoft Press, ISBN 0-7356-1486-5) or from *http:// www.microsoft.com/windowsserver2003/techinfo/reskit/ resourcekit.msp.*

Scenario 1: Quorum Disk Failure

In this scenario, all of the cluster nodes themselves are apparently fine, but the Cluster Service cannot start on any node because the quorum resource cannot be brought online. This issue will appear in the Event Log. To resolve this issue you have two options:

■ **Option 1**   Replace the quorum disk if the drive itself has failed or reformat the quorum disk if the physical drive has not failed. Use an Authoritative Restore, if you have one, to bring up one node.

■ **Option 2**   Follow these steps:

a.   Open a Command window on one node.

b.   Enter the following command: **cluster -fixquorum**
This starts the Cluster Service, knowing that the quorum cannot be brought online. The -fixquorum command does not fix any data

for you. It allows you to choose an alternate quorum resource (assuming you have one available to use; you could always try Local-Quorum). By setting a new quorum, new quorum log files are created on the quorum but the registry checkpoint files are not restored because the old quorum is not available. For the checkpoint files, use the instructions for Scenario 4.

> **Tip**   There is a tool in the *Windows 2000 Resource Kit*, ClusterRecovery, that can help in this scenario.

Scenario 2: Cluster Database Corruption on a Node

This happens if a node cannot join the cluster and entries in the cluster log indicate a corrupted hive. You have three possible options (only perform one):

- **Option 1**   Do a Non-Authoritative Restore on this node and have it join the cluster.

- **Option 2**   Copy the latest checkpoint (ChkXXX.tmp) file from the quorum disk and overwrite the file %windir%\Cluster\Clusdb on the affected node and restart the service.

- **Option 3**   Perform the following steps:

    a.   Stop the service on a working cluster node. Unload the cluster hive using Regedt32.

    b.   Copy the file %windir%\Cluster\Clusdb from the working node to %windir%\Cluster\Clusdb on the affected node, and restart the Cluster Service on all nodes.

Scenario 3: Quorum Corruption

If no nodes can join the cluster, a node cannot start the Cluster Service, and Event Viewer indicates a corrupt quorum log, you can do the following: Start the Cluster Service from a command line using the -resetquorumlog switch of Cluster.exe. If all of the resources start successfully and there do not seem to be any lingering issues, you do not need to do anything else. You reset the quorum and created new quorum log files on the quorum disk. However, the registry checkpoint files are not restored because the old quorum is not available. You need to follow the steps in Scenario 4 to restore those.

If using -resetquorumlog does not work, restore using an Authoritative Restore on one node and restart the Cluster Service to form the cluster. Use a Non-Authoritative Restore on all other nodes.

Scenario 4: Checkpoint Files Lost or Corrupt

In the event a registry checkpoint file cannot be found or loaded due to corruption, resources might not have the most up-to-date information in the registry when they are brought online. The impact depends on the resource. In some cases, a resource might fail to come online. In other cases, configuration changes that were made might be lost. If a checkpoint file is missing, this is not logged to Event Viewer's event log, but it is in the cluster log. If you see this is an issue, use the ClusterRecovery tool mentioned earlier to re-create the resource checkpoint files. However, do it only for the resources that cannot start, not all checkpoint files. You will create more problems if you do that.

If that does not solve the problem, perform an Authoritative Restore on one cluster node and restart the Cluster Service to form the cluster. Use a Non-Authoritative Restore on other nodes.

Scenario 5: Cluster Node Failure

In this case, assume that the quorum disk is functioning and the cluster database is intact. In these procedures, you might have to evict cluster nodes from your definition because they might be damaged.

> **Warning**   Never evict the node from the cluster in Cluster Administrator before removing it from the SQL Server virtual server definition using SQL Server Setup. You might encounter issues that require a complete reinstall.

Single Node Failure

Because the other nodes and the cluster itself are up and running, you can concentrate only on the failed node. Because the quorum is intact, you can perform a Non-Authoritative Restore, which should work with either the system state backup or a local backup. The end result is that the cluster database on the damaged node is not restored; you can then have that node rejoin the cluster.

Once it joins the server cluster, it synchronizes the cluster database with the most recent copy available. The exact steps are as follows:

1. Verify that all functionality that was owned by the failed server has started on another node.

2. Run SQL Server Setup and evict the failed node from the SQL Server virtual server definition as described in the section "Adding or Removing a Cluster Node from the Virtual Server Definition and Adding, Changing, or Updating a TCP/IP Address" earlier in this chapter. You might see messages similar to the ones shown in Figures 6-31, 6-32, and 6-33 during the process.

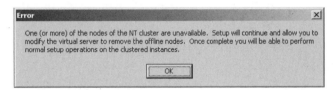

Figure 6-31   Error message 1.

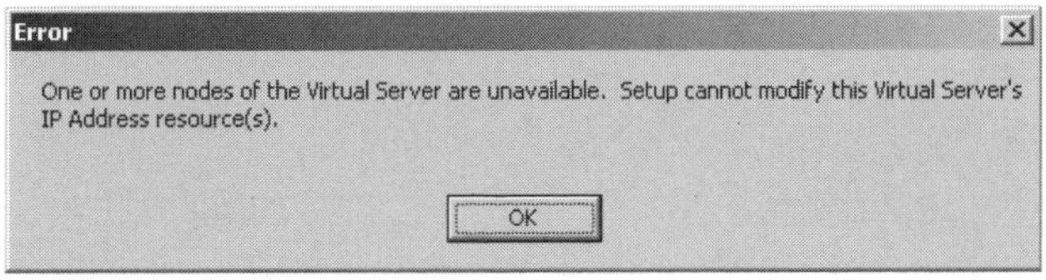

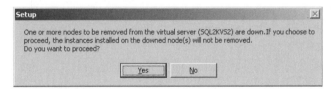

Figure 6-32   Error message 2.

Figure 6-33   Error message 3.

3. Verify that the node has been removed by issuing the following query:

```
SELECT * FROM ::fn_virtalservernodes()
```

4. Evict the node itself from Cluster Administrator. To do this:

    ❑   In the left-hand pane of Cluster Administrator, select the node to evict, right-click it, and select Stop Cluster Service if it is still running the Cluster Service. If not, skip this step.

    ❑   Once that node has indicated that the service is stopped (a red circle with a white X should appear next to it, as shown in Figure 6-34), right-click it and select Evict Node.

    ⊞ 🖳 SQLNETCLUNODE2

    Figure 6-34   Stopped cluster node.

5. Rebuild or restore the failed node (whichever procedure is most appropriate for your environment).

6. Rejoin the node to the server cluster.

7. Run SQL Server Setup and rejoin the SQL Server virtual server definition.

8. Reinstall the SQL Server 2000 service pack on the previously damaged node only, as detailed in Chapter 13.

9. Test failover to the node. This causes an availability outage, but it is the only way to ensure everything is working properly.

Multiple Node Failure

As long as you have one node functioning in the cluster, perform the steps found in the preceding section on each of the failed nodes.

All Nodes Failed

This is the worst-case scenario: your entire cluster is down. At this point, if none of the nodes can start, you are looking at using your backups. Use a Non-Authoritative Restore on one node. If the quorum disk is fine, the node should be able to form the cluster with the current state on the quorum disk. Then run a Non-Authoritative Restore on all other nodes.

If that does not work, restore an Authoritative backup on one node and use a Non-Authoritative Restore for all other nodes.

Scenario 6: A Cluster Disk Is Corrupt or Nonfunctional

If a disk fails and resources are dependent on it, the resource will not start. This could be due to corruption or some other problem. If the disk itself comes online and is recognized by the operating system, perform a restore from a backup on that disk. If the disk does have corruption, replace the physical disk and perform a Non-Authoritative Restore on one node. Then restore the data to the disk. Instead of that procedure, you could use ClusterRecovery to replace an existing physical disk resource without having to do a system state restore, and then you could restore the data on the disk.

If You Do Not Have Backups

At this point, if you have walked through the preceding six scenarios and you could not recover due to the fact you did not have proper backups, you can try the things listed in the following sections, but there is no guarantee that you can avoid a complete reinstall.

Problems on One or More Cluster Nodes

If the cluster database is intact and the quorum disk is fine, follow the steps in Scenario 5. If you lose all nodes and do not have backups, you have to do a complete reinstall from the ground up knowing that you might have lost all of your SQL Server data.

Bad Quorum Disk, Intact Cluster Nodes

Use Option 2 from Scenario 1 to employ the -fixquorum flag option of the cluster command.

Corrupt Cluster Database on One Node

You can try to copy the latest checkpoint (ChkXXX.tmp) file from the quorum disk and overwrite the file %windir%\Cluster\Clusdb on the affected node and restart the cluster service. Or you might want to try the following:

1. Stop the service on another node. Unload the cluster hive using Regedt32.

2. Load the registry hive on the affected node.

3. Copy the file %windir%\Cluster\Clusdb from one of the running nodes in the cluster to %windir%\Cluster\Clusdb on the affected node and restart the Cluster Service on all nodes.

Corrupt Quorum

Use the steps found in Scenario 3 to use `-resetquorum`.

Corrupt or Missing Checkpoint Files

Follow the instructions in Scenario 4 to use the ClusterRecovery tool.

Corrupt or Bad Cluster Disk

If the disk has been forcefully dismounted, you might need to run chkdsk to bring the disk online. The Cluster Service runs chkdsk automatically when the disk is brought online. Windows Server 2003 preserves a chkdsk log so that you can see what state the disk is in and what issues were found.

> **Important**   If the application data on the disk is corrupted or deleted and you do not have a backup, there is no way to recover the data.

Summary

You should now have a thorough understanding of how to configure a SQL Server 2000 failover cluster. Chapter 5 showed you how to plan, implement, and maintain a base server cluster, and this chapter addressed the SQL Server 2000 aspect of clustering. Although clustering involves a lot of preparation work, it can also provide you with some of the best availability for your databases. Do not skip some of this planning, as it will impact you in production. If you ever need to troubleshoot or perform maintenance, refer back to these chapters. Although to end users a cluster is like a stand-alone server—it should appear no different—from an administrative standpoint, you must do some things differently to ensure that you do not invalidate your configuration.

7

Log Shipping

As noted in Chapter 3, "Making a High Availability Technology Choice," log shipping is a tried-and-true method for achieving high availability for a Microsoft SQL Server database. There are two types of log shipping: you can code your own or you can use the log shipping functionality provided with the Developer or Enterprise editions of Microsoft SQL Server 2000 (depending on whether you are working in a development or production environment, respectively). This chapter describes how to plan for, configure, and administer a log shipping solution for SQL Server.

> **More Info**   For a refresher on the basic concepts and terminology of log shipping, review Chapter 3, "Making a High Availability Technology Choice."

Uses of Log Shipping

Log shipping has a variety of uses, most of which are related to availability, as follows:

- **Primary or additional form of availability for SQL Server**   This is the "no-brainer" use of log shipping. You can use log shipping without any other technology for SQL Server high availability as a primary method of availability for your SQL Servers (for example, if you cannot afford or are not able to use failover clustering as a primary method) or in more of a disaster recovery role as a secondary form of availability (for example, to ensure that a failover cluster, which is local, is protected if the data center is damaged and you need to switch to a remote site).

- **Planned downtime**   Planned downtime on the primary database (such as to apply a SQL Server service pack) can be longer than what you can normally tolerate. Instead of waiting for the primary server to become available while waiting for maintenance to complete, you can increase availability by switching to the secondary server. Doing so means that you are promoting the secondary server to be the new primary database accessed by applications and clients.

- **Upgrading or migrating SQL Server**   Whether you are upgrading from Microsoft SQL Server 7.0 or going from SQL Server 2000 to another instance of SQL Server 2000, log shipping can facilitate highly available upgrades or migrations.

> **More Info**   To see how to log ship from SQL Server 7.0 to SQL Server 2000, see the section "Configuring Log Shipping from SQL Server 7.0 to SQL Server 2000" later in this chapter.

- **A database for read-only access**   This scenario applies only in limited cases. Although it is not a high availability use of log shipping, it is possible to use the secondary database for read-only reporting purposes as transaction logs are being applied at scheduled intervals. Using the log shipped database for read-only access is not recommended if your primary goal is high availability and you are generating and applying transaction logs on a very frequent basis; use another method. If you want to use your log shipped database for read-only access, be aware of the following:

  ❑   When restoring the database that will have the transaction logs applied to it, you must restore it with the STANDBY option.

  ❑   Because SQL Server requires exclusive access to apply transaction logs to the database, no users can be accessing the now read-only copy of the database during the transaction log restore. As noted earlier, you can configure the database not to kill the connections to the database, but that means you have to manually kill the connections, adding administrative overhead.

This also means that, no matter what, the users cannot have continuous access to the database for read-only use; they will be interrupted at regular intervals.

❑   You must ensure that users have the proper user names, logons, and permissions configured to access the secondary.

❑   Set the copy and load times appropriately, which means longer intervals between copies and loads of the transaction logs, to allow users sufficient time to use the secondary for reporting queries. This could cause transaction logs to queue, thereby lengthening the time to bring the secondary online as a new primary in a disaster recovery scenario.

❑   Secure the secondary in the same way you secure the primary for read-only access.

❑   If you disabled the guest account on the secondary before configuring log shipping and you want to use it for read-only purposes, you might cause a failure when logging into the secondary server to access the read-only database.

> **More Info**   See Knowledge Base article 315523, "PRB: Removal of Guest Account May Cause Handled exception Access Violation in SQL Server," and article 303722, "HOW TO: Grant Access to SQL Logins on a Standby Database When 'quest' User Is Disabled," to see how to enable a database restored with STANDBY to be accessed for read-only purposes. Knowledge Base articles can be found at *http://support.microsoft.com*.

Basic Considerations for All Forms of Log Shipping

With log shipping, whether you use the SQL Server 2000 Enterprise Edition functionality or code your own, there are some common points you must think about prior to configuring your log shipping solution.

> **More Info**   Many of the concepts and rules that apply to configuring log shipping are similar or the same as those for upgrading or migrating to SQL Server 2000. For more information, see Chapter 13, "Highly Available Microsoft SQL Server Upgrades."

Ask the Right Questions

Before you even think about implementing log shipping, you must determine the answers to certain questions. Without the answers, you cannot accurately plan and set up log shipping from both an availability and performance perspective.

Business Questions

Perhaps the most important questions to ask are not the technical ones but the ones related to *why* you are implementing log shipping and *what the cost* to the business will be.

- **How many transactions are generated per hour?**   Although transactions from an application or business standpoint are ultimately represented as one or many different SQL Server transactions, you need to understand the volume of the business that is planned or occurring and translate that into SQL Server usage. For example, if each business transaction inserts data into three tables, that is a 1:3 ratio from business to SQL Server transactions. Multiply that number by the number of users over time, and you have your total transactions per hour. The eventual number of transactions should account for all work done, not just one type.

- **How much downtime is acceptable to end users?**   Nearly every business can tolerate some downtime, it is just a matter of how much. Although there is no set number, the measurement is usually in minutes or, at most, hours. This number guides how frequently transaction logs are backed up, copied, and applied. Remember to take any existing service level agreements (SLA) into account when figuring out acceptable downtime, modify them as necessary, or put new ones in place that reflect the current state of the business.

- **How much data or how many transactions can be lost?**   Like the downtime question, most businesses are quick to respond, "We cannot lose any data or transactions." The reality, as with downtime, is that some losses can be tolerated; it is just a matter of how many.

You will always be transactionally consistent as of the last transaction log applied to the secondary, but you might not be as current as the primary. Again, this number is usually measured in minutes or, at most, hours. The usual comfort level of lost data is anywhere from five minutes to about an hour for most businesses. Remember to take any SLA (new or existing) into account when figuring out acceptable loss of data.

■   **How much money is allocated to the project?**   Although money is not the top linchpin, because log shipping is essentially an easier solution to conceptually understand, if, say, your network is too slow or your secondary is not at the same capacity as your primary, will you need to revamp things and if so, is that possible? You do not want to attempt to implement anything—including something as simple as log shipping—if you cannot handle it financially.

Technical Questions

After you understand the nontechnical issues and potential barriers, you can then consider the technical issues and barriers.

■   **How large are the transaction log files generated?**   The size of the transaction logs generated is a crucial bit of information because it directly impacts your network as well as the time to copy and apply the transaction log. If you are consistently generating transaction logs in the 1 GB range (plus or minus), what will the effect be on a slower network? It certainly will not be good, especially if that network, which might only be 100 megabit, is shared with all other traffic and is already heavily used.

■   **What is your network topology and speed?**   Your network can quickly become a barrier to availability in a log shipping solution if your network cannot handle the file sizes generated by the transaction log backup, as evidenced by the previous item.

■   **How long does it take to copy the transaction log file?**   In conjunction with the previous two points, knowing how long it takes to copy the transaction log impacts how you configure your log shipping solution. This measurement is closely related to how fast the transaction logs can be made and then sent across the wire. For example, if it takes you two minutes to back up your transaction log, you should not be attempting copies every minute. That makes no sense. If it takes another two minutes to copy, that number influences how often you can then apply the transaction log.

- **How long does it take to apply each transaction log file?**   This number saves you in a disaster recovery scenario. If you know definitively it will take you, say, two minutes to apply your transaction logs (on average; some might be longer, some might be shorter) and you have 10 of them queued up, that means that, at the very earliest, your standby server could be brought online to the latest data available in about 20 minutes.

- **What is the capacity and configuration of your secondary server?**   Ideally, the capacity of your secondary server should be equal to that of the primary if you want things to run with the same horsepower.

- **Will you switch back to the primary if you perform a role change to a secondary server?**   As with failover clustering, once you have switched to another server, will you incur the availability hit again once the old primary is back in a state where it can assume its original role? If you have the proper capacity on the secondary, this should not be an issue.

- **Do you have domain connectivity?**   Log shipping only requires that all servers be able to connect to each other. However, some log shipping solutions might require domain connectivity. If you do not have domain connectivity and it is a requirement (such as to use Windows Authentication), this could be a potential barrier for some solutions involving log shipping.

- **Will any maintenance interfere with log shipping?**   Certain administrative tasks for SQL Server interfere with the ability for SQL Server to generate transaction logs. How often will you run such maintenance to ensure your secondary is as current as it needs to be? Or will you not run it at all?

- **How long will transaction logs be kept? Will they be archived?**   The transaction logs should be kept in accordance with an overall corporate archival scheme for your backups. Such a policy must be agreed on and set before implementing log shipping, as it will affect the planning stage.

- **Is replication configured on the primary database?**   If you are looking to combine log shipping and replication on a database, you need to take some considerations into account. For example, if you are looking to use log shipping to protect the publisher, you need to be able to rename the secondary SQL Server instance—something that is not possible with failover clustering.

> **More Info**   For more information on log shipping and replication, see "Log Shipping and Replication" in Chapter 8, "Replication."

How Current Do You Need To Be?

To briefly revisit a point mentioned in Chapter 3, log shipping inherently involves some amount of latency; it is not real time. Transactions are only applied to the secondary after they are backed up, copied, and restored from the transaction log. With log shipping, you are only as current as:

■   The last transaction completed on the primary

■   The last transaction log backed up on the primary

■   The last transaction log copied from the primary

■   The last transaction log applied to the secondary

The log shipping secondary is only as current as the last transaction log that is applied, so if the delta is five minutes off of the primary, your secondary should always remain five minutes behind if all is functioning properly. Analyzing these points is fairly straightforward.

■   If the SQL Server experiences a failure before that transaction log is backed up, there is a chance that if the server cannot recover and read the transaction log, it will be lost, and you will only be as current as the secondary.

■   If a transaction log is backed up but not copied over to the secondary and either the copy process fails or the hard disk that contains that transaction log is lost, again, you are only as current on the secondary as what is available to it.

■   If a transaction log is copied from the primary and is still accessible to the secondary, it can be applied, so your secondary will be as current as the last transaction in the transaction log.

Secondary Server Capacity and Configuration

As mentioned briefly earlier, the capacity and configuration of your secondary is crucial for the success of any log shipping solution. If you underpower your secondary server, end users will notice the performance difference. The point of switching servers is to provide, at a minimum, the same quality or level of service you provided before.

Log Shipping More Than One Database to One Secondary

One of the nice features of log shipping is that you can, as long as you have the capacity, use one instance as a standby for multiple databases. This takes two assumptions into account: that you have the capacity to handle the additional workload in the event that all databases would need to be servicing end users at once (not unlike planning failover clustering to ensure that multiple instances do not affect each other in a failover), and that there are no conflicts or security issues in doing so. Some common issues related to log shipping more than one database to a single secondary include the following:

- **Master and msdb databases**   Because you cannot have multiple msdb and master databases, it is not possible to restore master or msdb databases from a different server with a different name. Any differences need to be manually reconciled.

- **Logins**   You cannot have duplicate login names at the SQL Server level. Also, if you do configure more than one database that genuinely uses the same login, but the user has different security privileges that might compromise another database, that is not a wise choice.

- **Capacity**   Do you have enough horsepower to run all the databases should they all become active?

- **Objects**   Do you have any duplicate objects (such as jobs, alerts, and so on) that will conflict with those of other databases? If so, you need to resolve these types of issues prior to configuration.

> **More Info**   Log shipping more than one database to a single standby is not unlike server consolidation. For more information on SQL Server consolidation and upgrades, consult Chapter 13.

Disk Space, Retention, and Archiving

It is very important to plan the disk capacity needed for implementing log shipping. You must know how large your transaction log file sizes are and how much disk capacity you have, and then coordinate those two factors with your corporate archival scheme. During the configuration of the built-in feature of SQL Server 2000, you can configure a retention period for the transaction log files, so it must be known from the start.

> **More Info**   For more information on retention and archiving of backup files, see the topic "Backup Retention" in Chapter 10, "Implementing Backup and Restore."

Full-Text Searching and Log Shipping

If the primary database utilizes full-text searching, you must consider how you will handle anything relating to full-text after the role change. The issues are pretty straightforward:

■   Full-text indexes are built as data is inserted into a database. In the event of a catastrophic failure, you cannot even consider moving the index on the primary server to the secondary because it is not available. Even if the primary server were available, what is the state of your secondary database? Is it in the same exact spot, and can you ensure that no changes were made prior to the role change? If the role change is planned and you know the two databases are in exactly the same consistent place, you might be able to copy the full-text index to the secondary. This scenario of a planned role change would also require the following:

  ❑   The two databases are loaded with the same database identifier (DBID) as the primary.

  ❑   The catalog must be re-created on the secondary server at least once before the database is loaded in STANDBY or NORECOVERY states. This is required because the MSSearch service places catalog-specific information in the registry when the catalog is rebuilt and repopulated.

  ❑   Catalog files must be copied only after the MSSearch service is stopped on both machines.

  ❑   Catalog files must be copied each time the catalog is repopulated or updated and as often as possible when using Change Tracking.

❑   Copying the registry entries mentioned earlier might make the MSSearch service unusable, so they should not be modified.

The steps to do this are listed below. The only steps that you would need to perform (once you establish the backup of the database and the DBID) when using Change Tracking are Steps 4, 5, and 6. These should be performed as often as possible because all the changes made to the full-text catalogs are in files in the FTDATA folder. To roll these changes to the secondary server in log shipping, you need to copy these files over to the secondary machine at regular intervals.

> **Important**   Stopping and starting MSSearch could cause an availability problem from an application perspective and cause perceived unavailability or downtime of your application. Do this with caution after making the proper risk assessment of your business.

1.   Create and populate the full-text catalog on the primary machine.

2.   Back up the primary database.

3.   Restore the primary database on the secondary server. The DBID has to be the same. Follow the procedure in Knowledge Base article 240867, "INF: How to Move, Copy, and Back Up Full-Text Catalog Folders and Files," to restore a database with the same DBID.

4.   Stop the MSSearch service on both the primary and secondary servers.

5.   Copy the SQL*xxxxxxyyyyy* folder under FTDATA over to the location on the secondary server.

6.   Restart the MSSearch service.

7.   Re-create and repopulate the catalogs on the secondary database.

8.   Restore the database backup using the STANDBY option and a .tuf file extension.

9.   Run the wizard and select the existing database restored in Step 7.

10.   Select the appropriate settings for log shipping.

11.   Create a scheduled job to stop MSSearch, copy the catalog files from the FTDATA folder over to the secondary machine, and restart the MSSearch service.

- You cannot take a copy of an older full-text index and apply it to a database that is out of sync with that copy. Although it might seem to work for a while, you will eventually encounter problems. This is not supported or recommended.

- You cannot build a full-text index on a database that is in NORECOVERY or STANDBY mode, which is required for the transaction logs to be applied. You thus have to start building the index after the database is brought online after the role change. This means some features of the application will not be functioning (which might prove unacceptable) and, depending on the size of the index, it could take quite some time to generate.

> **More Info**   The Microsoft Support Knowledge Base article 240867, "How to Move, Copy, and Back Up Full-Text Catalog Folders and Files," details the process of how to move, copy, and back up full-text files to another server. This article can be found at *http://support.microsoft.com.*

Recovery Models and Log Shipping

Log shipping requires that the databases participating in log shipping be in either Full or Bulk-Logged recovery models. By default, all databases are configured with Full recovery, as that is the default behavior of the model database. Recovery models were first introduced in SQL Server 2000, and there is no real equivalent of this feature in prior versions of SQL Server. Simple recovery does not allow you to make transaction log backups, and therefore does not let you use log shipping because it will break the log sequence number (LSN) chain. When you apply transaction logs, the process checks to see that the first LSN in the new backup file comes sequentially after the last LSN applied. A SQL Server 2000 error in LSNs during the transaction log applications should look similar to this:

```
Server: Msg 4305, Level 16, State 1, Line 2
The log in this backup set begins at LSN 6000000007200001, which is too late to
apply to the database. An earlier log backup that includes LSN 6000000005000001
can be restored.
Server: Msg 3013, Level 16, State 1, Line 2
RESTORE LOG is terminating abnormally.
```

This is the SQL Server 7.0 error:

```
Server: Msg 4305, Level 16, State 1, Line 2
This backup set cannot be restored because the database has not been rolled for
ward far enough. You must first restore all earlier logs before restoring this
log.
Server: Msg 3013, Level 16, State 1, Line 2
Backup or restore operation terminating abnormally.
```

With all versions of SQL Server prior to SQL Server 2000, if you did anything such as a Transact-SQL BULK INSERT or a nonlogged operation or if you set the Truncate Log On Checkpoint option (which is no longer valid in SQL Server 2000), you would invalidate regular transaction log backups. First and foremost, with Truncate Log On Checkpoint, it is what it says: when a checkpoint happens, the log is truncated and not backed up. Database administrators (DBAs) frequently like to turn this on without thinking about the recoverability of SQL Server.

From a log shipping perspective, there is no apparent difference between Full or Bulk-Logged but there are some differences that affect performance. If you are using Bulk-Logged, the transaction logs contain information added or modified since the transaction log backup. In addition, the transaction log contains the data pages modified by any bulk operations (such as BULK INSERT or BCP) since the last backup. This means that you will have potentially larger file sizes that need to be backed up, copied, and restored if you are doing bulk operations. This definitely impacts your time to copy if you have limited network bandwidth. Consider the following example: if you do a bulk load of data on a single processor server that runs at 3 MB per second and takes 10 minutes, that means you may have generated 1800 MB (or 1.8 GB) of changed data pages!

With Full, you still have the same issue as Bulk-Logged with large file sizes. However, one of the benefits of Full is that the data rate will be reduced to nearly match your network. Even though you are technically moving a bit more information across the network in total (Bulk-Logged and Full are about the same file size; Bulk-Logged gathers the data directly from the data file instead of indirectly from the transaction log as redo log records), the secondary server does not lag far behind because the primary is being loaded much more slowly due to the logging of all inserted data. If you have a server with eight processors, it stands to reason that if the load rate is eight times, it affects the time for logs.

> **Caution**   If you configure log shipping and then switch the recovery model to Simple at any point after it is up and running, you invalidate log shipping. An example of when this could occur is if you were doing a bulk insert and wanted to minimize your log file size and not have a record of the page changes. The same would also apply if someone— even briefly, whether accidentally or on purpose—switched the recovery model to Simple and immediately changed it back.

> **More Info**   For more information on recovery models, see Chapter 10, "Implementing Backup and Restore."

Network Bandwidth

Network bandwidth is a potential barrier to successful log shipping implementation. The three main issues associated with network bandwidth were listed in the earlier section, "Technical Questions." They are:

- How large are the transaction log files generated?

- What is your network topology and speed?

- How long does it take to copy the transaction log file?

Although log shipping is arguably the easiest SQL Server–based high availability method to configure, it can crush a network if your transaction log backup files are huge. That will eventually affect the delta of time for which the primary and secondary are out of sync. Coupled with that, you also need reliable network connections between the participating servers. Intermittent network problems will not increase your availability when it comes to log shipping; they can only hurt it.

> **Tip** If you are sending large transaction logs on a regular basis, you should configure a separate and dedicated network card as well as a private network (such as a 10.x.x.x network) for sending transaction logs between the primary and secondary servers. This ensures that user traffic will not be affected. You might also want to consider a faster network (such as Gigabit Ethernet) to ensure that your recoverability happens much more quickly.

Logins and Other Objects

Log shipping only captures anything in the initial database backup (including users, but not their corresponding server-level login) as well as any transactions captured in subsequent transaction logs. That leaves any other objects that reside outside the database or are not captured as part of the transaction log to be dealt with.

> **Tip** As far as objects go, outside of Data Transformation Services (DTS) packages, you should really be placing any objects related to the database *in* the database itself. Unless there is a logical reason to put the objects outside the database, you will create problems when you are trying to synchronize a secondary server to become a warm standby. If such objects exist, they should be recorded and placed in any document related to the solution. If possible, script the objects and have those scripts available.

Stored Procedures, Extended Stored Procedures, Functions, and More

As just noted, things such as stored procedures should be created in the database itself. Because the creation of a normal stored procedure is captured in the transaction log, it will automatically be created at the secondary. If you have anything residing outside the database, such as in msdb, you need to manually create all of these objects on the secondary server to ensure a successful role change.

Logins

There are two levels of logins that you need to take into account:

- **Server level**   These are the top-level users referenced by the user in a database. These reside in the syslogins system table.

- **Database level**   These are the users that a connection uses to access the database.

If you do not take both types into account, you could end up with a situation in which you have orphaned users in your database and application-related problems accessing the database after the role change process.

> **More Info**   The section "Step 3: Post-Wizard Configuration Tasks" later in this chapter details one way to configure the transfer of your logins and users.

DTS Packages

To move DTS packages to another SQL Server, the easiest method is probably to save the package to a file and manually copy and add it to the secondary. There is no automated way to perform this task.

> **Caution**   Make sure that the DTS package is compatible with the version of SQL Server that is the destination. If, for example, functionality or the format of the file is changed due to a fix in a service pack (as it did between SQL Server 7.0 Service Pack 1 and SQL Server 7.0 Service Pack 2), if the other server cannot either handle the functionality or it will be broken on the standby, you need to resolve those issues prior to bringing that secondary online as a primary. Similarly, you might need to fix settings (such as source server names or destination server names) within the DTS package to match the new server. Do not assume that it works unmodified.
>
> Also, the DTS functionality does not exist if your source or destination servers are 64-bit SQL Server 2000 instances. You have to create DTS packages under 32-bit and run them from a 32-bit instance of SQL Server against a 64-bit instance.

Clients, Applications, and Log Shipping

One of the most important considerations for using log shipping is planning for how you will redirect end users and applications to the new server. Unlike failover clustering, where the switch to another physical server is abstracted to an end user or application, a change to another server in most cases is not abstracted. That means the systems and applications accessing SQL Server must tolerate such a change. Like failover clustering, there will be some downtime involved.

Coding Your Application for Log Shipping

The following are some tips for application developers when coding for a solution that will eventually include log shipping:

- Heed the earlier warning about object placement. If developers create objects outside of the database, the IT staff should be notified and it should be well documented so that this can be accounted for in disaster recovery planning.

- Make all transactions as small, or atomic, as possible. Atomic queries might increase performance and reduce some resource contention (such as I/O), but in the recovery process and application of transaction logs they could ensure that things go more quickly.

> **Note**   This is not to say that longer running transactions are not appropriate, and you should not take one logical transaction and break it up for the sake of making it smaller. Small transactions usually minimize lock contention. I/O will be close to the same as a longer transaction because you are essentially doing the same work, just broken up into smaller chunks. A long running transaction, if it is interrupted (that is, canceled), could require a long undo operation, and it might also prevent log truncation.

- Similarly, when queries are written, if they cross databases, how will that work after a role change? Can the queries tolerate two databases residing on different servers?

- With SQL Server 2000, the worry of nonlogged operations does not exist because page changes and such are tracked with Bulk-Logged or Full recovery models (either is required for log shipping). However, those types of operations will impact the log size, so the use of those types of operations should still be taken into account to some degree.

■ Ensure all objects related to the log-shipped database are uniquely named. This prevents problems in the event that multiple databases are log shipped to a single secondary.

■ Do not code your application for a specific SQL Server service pack level, because if your secondary is not the same as your primary, you might encounter issues in a role change.

■ Do not hard-code server names and IP addresses into applications. This ensures that you could never name the server anything other than what it is in the application, and, for example, if you are using failover clustering for both your primary and secondary, you are unable to rename the server. Make applications flexible to handle a server name change.

■ Use fully qualified names for each object to ensure that you are always referencing the correct object. This not only helps your performance, it helps clarify things when you might have more than one database on a SQL Server with the same object name.

■ Code retry logic in your application to attempt a failed transaction again. If this is not possible, at a bare minimum you should post graceful error messages to give your end users a positive experience.

■ One way to mitigate lost transactions in the event of a failure is to use some form of middleware—such as Microsoft Transaction Server, Microsoft BizTalk, Microsoft Message Queue, or Microsoft Distributed Transaction Coordinator—to queue the transactions. This needs to be integrated into your application and overall solution should you choose to do this.

■ If you are using the SQL-DMO transfer operation in your code, it truncates the transaction log, thus breaking log shipping.

More Info   For updates or workarounds, see Knowledge Base article 316213, "FIX: SQLDMO Transfer Operation Truncates Transaction Log of Destination Database."

■   Similarly, if you are using the Copy Objects task of DTS in any of your packages, it might break log shipping because it switches the recovery mode to Simple for the database in its operations.

> **More Info** For updates or workarounds, see Knowledge Base article 308267, "FIX: DTS Copy Objects Task (DMO) Breaks Transaction Log Backup Chain By Switching Recovery Mode to Simple During Transfer."

Role Change

Performing the role change from a SQL Server perspective is straightforward, but redirecting clients is not, so you can have the least impact on applications and end users. As in failover clustering, not only is there an interruption in service, you are also switching to a completely different server. You have a few options available to you to assist in the role change:

■   As mentioned earlier, code a mechanism into the application to set the SQL Server.

■   Code your application to use Open Database Connectivity (ODBC), and all you would need to do is change the server that the ODBC Data Source Name (DSN) is pointing to. With this solution, you would still have the interruption, but the connection string would always be the same.

■   You can also use Network Load Balancing to abstract the server switch during the role change. This is one of the few uses for which Network Load Balancing works well with SQL Server.

The goal is to pick a manageable solution that will incur the least downtime.

> **More Info** For more information on configuring Network Load Balancing for use with log shipping, see Chapter 5, "Designing Highly Available Microsoft Windows Servers."

Security

As with any technology, with log shipping there are security considerations you must consider up front that influence how you will plan and deploy a solution. Because all security changes (such as GRANT statements) are in the transaction log, they are applied automatically to the secondary server once log shipping is configured and working properly.

> **More Info**   For additional information or changes to what is written in this section, please reference Knowledge Base article 321247, "HOW TO: Configure Security for Log Shipping," which can be found at *http://support.microsoft.com.*

SQL Server Startup Account

If the server hosting your SQL Server 2000 instance is part of a domain, and not a workgroup, you should use a domain account to start the SQL Server services. A domain account is absolutely required for certain features, such as failover clustering. If this is a nonclustered instance, you can use a local network account or the Local System account.

■ A local network account is one that is created on the server, but it is not the Local System account. This would be used if you are using pass-through security. This means that all SQL Servers participating in log shipping must use the same network account, privileges, and passwords created locally on the server. You are bypassing traditional network security when a SQL Server process requests resources from another SQL Server.

■ Various processes on the server use a Local System account, also known as LocalSystem. SQL Server can also potentially use it, but modifying it in any way could have consequences outside of SQL Server. LocalSystem cannot be used for network pass-through security because the LocalSystem account's password should be different on each server.

> **More Info**   For more information, see the topic "Setting Up Windows Service Accounts" in SQL Server Books Online.

Securing the Transfer of Logins

Because the transfer of logins using the built-in functionality requires a bulk copy out of the syslogins table, this file should be contained in a secure directory. Files generated by the bcp utility are in plaintext and not encoded in any way.

Securing the Backup Share

You also need to secure the directories that contain your transaction log backups. The files created by SQL Server are not encrypted in any way. The network share should be secured so that all servers participating in log shipping should be able to access it.

Log Shipping Across Domains

You can log ship a database across domains. To do this, you should set up two-way trusts between the domains involved in log shipping. This is done through the Active Directory Domains and Trusts tool located in the Start menu in the Administrative Tools folder, as shown in Figure 7-1. If it is not there, it can be started from *%systemroot%*\System32\Domain.msc. If you cannot establish trusts, you can use pass-through security, which involves the use of the local network account. This cannot be done on a clustered instance of SQL Server.

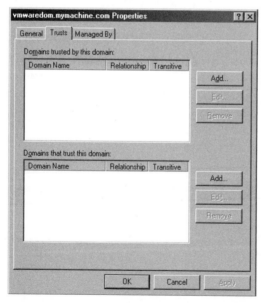

Figure 7-1   The Active Directory Domains and Trusts tool of Windows 2000.

Authentication for Log Shipping

Microsoft recommends you use Windows Authentication for the SQL Servers participating in log shipping. If you use mixed mode security, with the built-in functionality, a login with the name of log_shipping_monitor_probe will be created if it does not already exist.

Log Shipping and Database Backups

Will log shipping break if you still implement your daily, weekly, monthly, or other full or differential backup scheme? No. Log shipping can coexist peacefully with any full or differential backup on a database. However, if you are performing a full or differential backup, you cannot do a scheduled transaction log backup during the backup process; it will occur at the next possible scheduled time after the full or differential backup is complete. This means that the transaction log might grow while the full backup takes place (depending on your database usage). On a small database, this should be fairly insignificant, but on a very large database this is not trivial. It means that the log will take longer to copy and apply. It also means that the secondary server will be further out of sync than it is while log shipping is not happening. You need to take this into account in your planning.

The only way a full or differential backup will affect log shipping is if, in some way, you truncate the transaction log prior to doing an actual log backup. A good example is if your transaction log is growing quickly and you want to reclaim disk space by using a BACKUP LOG *databasename* NO_LOG or switch to Simple recovery.

On the other hand, if you have an existing transaction log backup plan for a database, log shipping will be affected by that plan. Although Microsoft cannot stop you from setting up multiple transaction log backup jobs for one database (you can only do one per database with the Database Maintenance Plan Wizard; when you code your own using Transact-SQL syntax, however, you can technically do an infinite amount), you need to take into account *each* transaction log and how it will be applied to a secondary server. For example, your senior DBA already has a custom SQL Server Agent Job that backs up the transaction log for the database named MyDatabase every 15 minutes. Another DBA then decides to configure log shipping using the Database Maintenance Plan Wizard with a transaction log backup frequency of 10 minutes.

■   **Problem 1**   Log shipping knows nothing about the existing transaction log backup plan.

- **Problem 2** You now have two conflicting transaction log back-ups happening. Assuming log shipping is configured correctly, you will more than likely see the aforementioned 4,305 errors almost immediately.

- **Problem 3** Not only does log shipping not know about the existing job, but you have two different schedules. What is the actual required frequency for the database in question? You need to decide on one and then modify the Database Maintenance Plan with the right interval, and you need to delete or disable the custom job.

As you can see by this example, which assumes using the built-in functionality of SQL Server 2000, you can easily create a problem without realizing it right away. The same would be true for any custom solution. Before you configure log shipping, make sure there will be no conflicts in terms of existing backup plans.

If you have some "intrusive" maintenance that prevents the creation of a transaction log backup, you will not get a transaction log backup until these tasks are completed. These tasks more often than not require exclusive access to the database or something similar. A good example of maintenance that will prevent a transaction log backup is the aforementioned full backup as well as a database restore. These maintenance tasks and how to deal with more intrusive maintenance are discussed in more detail in Chapter 14, "Administrative Tasks to Increase Availability."

> **Note** In terms of the transaction log backup itself, all committed and uncommitted work is sent as part of the transaction log. If you have a long-running transaction that fails midway through its execution and you need to bring the secondary server online, it needs to go through the rollback process of the transaction in the role change process. This affects your recovery time.

> **More Info** For more information on backups, see Chapters 9, "Database Environment for Discovery," and 10. To mitigate the creation of false errors by intrusive maintenance, see the section "Intrusive Maintenance" in Chapter 14.

Service Packs and Log Shipping

SQL Server 2000 service packs can be applied to instances that have log shipping with the following caveats, as documented in the Readme file (this was taken from SQL Server 2000 Service Pack 3).

> **More Info**   For more information on SQL Server 2000 service packs and log shipping, see Chapter 13.

If Service Pack 3 Setup detects user databases or filegroups that are not writable, it:

- Applies the Service Pack 3 replication updates to all writable user databases.
- Writes a list of the nonwritable databases to the Setup log, which is located at %windir%\Sqlsp.log.
- Displays the following warning message:

  ```
  Setup has detected one or more databases and filegroups which are not
  writable.
  ```

This means that you might need to rerun the SQL Server 2000 service pack once the secondary server's database has been recovered so that it is at the same level as the rest of the server.

> **Caution**   Do not apply any SQL Server 2000 service pack prior to Service Pack 2 on a log shipped server. Service Pack 1 would not apply successfully on a server that had databases that could not be written to.

Files, Filegroups, and Transaction Logs

If you want to add a file to an existing filegroup and you are performing regular transaction log backups (as you would with log shipping), you break the restore of the transaction log. This occurs only if the specific path to the file does not exist on the secondary or if the target file already exists. If the file system structure is the same on the secondary, this should not be a problem. There is a two-step fix for the problem scenario:

1.   The restore process is now expecting the secondary to have the same physical structure as the primary. Chances are you are seeing this error message:

```
[Microsoft SQL-DMO (ODBC SQLState: 42000)] Error 5105:
[Microsoft][ODBC SQL Server Driver][SQL Server]Device activation
error. The physical file name 'C:\Program Files\Microsoft SQL
Server\MSSQL$SQL2K1\data\lsdb_data2.NDF' may be incorrect.
[Microsoft][ODBC SQL Server Driver][SQL Server]File 'lsdb_data2' can
not be created. Use WITH MOVE to specify a usable physical file name.
[Microsoft][ODBC SQL Server
```

To solve this problem, restore the next transaction log manually including the WITH MOVE syntax. Then log shipping should continue without any more problems, unless you add another file. Here is an example of the RESTORE ... WITH MOVE statement:

```
RESTORE LOG LOGSHIPDB FROM DISK ='path for the transaction log backup
file'
WITH MOVE 'Logical name of the new data file'
TO 'physical name of the new data file (where you want the file to be
created on the destination server)',
NORECOVERY
-- Or use STANDBY instead of NORECOVERY
```

2.   If you are using the built-in functionality of SQL Server 2000, you might need to see if the load_all column of the table log_shipping_plan_databases is set to 0 and then check the last_loaded_file column. It should be set to the transaction log file you loaded manually. If it is not, manually update the last_loaded_file column. If load_all is set to 1, all should be fine.

Custom Log Shipping Versus Microsoft's Implementation

One of the decisions you need to make is whether or not you will use Microsoft's implementation or code your own. Both have specific uses and advantages. Whether you are using a custom configuration or the built-in feature, you can log ship between all versions of SQL Server 2000 because the file formats and on-disk structures are the same. If an incompatibility that would not allow you to log ship from one version to another is introduced in a SQL Server service pack or some other hotfix, this will be documented. This section details the technological considerations. If your constraints are somewhat cost-based (that is, you might not be able to afford or do not need the functionality of SQL Server 2000 Enterprise Edition), you must code your own solution. The technical reasons for coding your own log shipping usually boil down to the following three points for most IT shops:

- You need to use an alternate protocol such as File Transfer Protocol (FTP) to send the transaction log backups to other servers. Microsoft's implementation uses a simple copy.

- You need to compress the transaction log backups that are made. The built-in solution does not involve compression at all, and it cannot be incorporated. A third-party product such as SQL LiteSpeed or PKZIP is needed. In some cases, this might shorten the time it takes to copy and possibly apply the transaction log.

- You want a fully scriptable configuration process. Although the Microsoft implementation is built on stored procedures, you cannot set it up using stored procedures. You must use the Database Maintenance Plan Wizard.

> **More Info**   For more information on coding a custom log shipping solution, see the section "Creating a Custom Coded Log Shipping Solution" later in this chapter.

Configuring and Administering the Built-In Functionality Using SQL Server 2000 Enterprise Edition

Microsoft recommends that whenever possible, you should use the log shipping functionality provided by SQL Server 2000 Enterprise Edition (or Developer Edition if you are in a development or testing environment). This feature is not present in any other edition of SQL Server 2000; if you want to use log shipping with another edition, you need to code your own solution. This section walks you through the components of what you get when using the built-in log shipping, how to configure it, and how to administer the solution. Figure 7-2 illustrates the workflow of the log shipping feature found in SQL Server 2000 Enterprise Edition.

> **Important**   For the primary server that is the source of the data as
> well as any secondary server that will have the transaction logs
> applied to it, you must use SQL Server 2000 Enterprise Edition or
> SQL Server 2000 Developer Edition. However, Developer Edition can-
> not be used in a production environment.

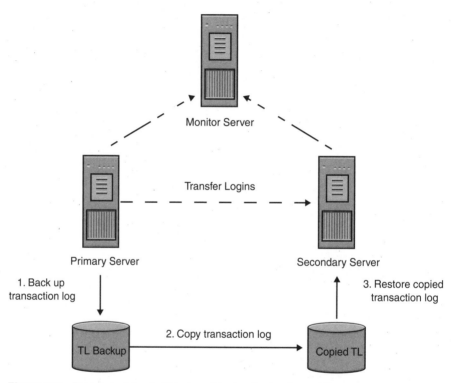

Figure 7-2   Diagram of the built-in log shipping feature's workflow.

Log Shipping Components

The built-in log shipping functionality is comprised of a database maintenance
plan, stored procedures, SQL Server Agent jobs, and tables in msdb. There
might be differences between the primary, secondary (or secondaries), and the
Log Shipping Monitor about which objects exist and which edition of SQL
Server is used.

> **Caution** The stored procedures, tables, and jobs used by log shipping are listed here for informational purposes only. Just because they exist does not mean you should or can use them, as they are used by SQLMAINT behind the scenes. What you can use is detailed later in this section.

Stored Procedures

The following list of stored procedures includes all stored procedures that are used by log shipping. Most are located in msdb, and some are in master.

- sp_add_log_shipping_database
- sp_add_log_shipping_monitor_jobs
- sp_add_log_shipping_plan
- sp_add_log_shipping_plan_database
- sp_add_log_shipping_primary
- sp_add_log_shipping_secondary
- sp_can_tlog_be_applied
- sp_change_monitor_role
- sp_change_primary_role
- so_change_secondary_role
- sp_create_log_shipping_monitor_account
- sp_define_log_shipping_monitor
- sp_delete_log_shipping_database
- sp_delete_log_shipping_monitor_info
- sp_delete_log_shipping_monitor_jobs
- sp_delete_log_shipping_plan
- sp_delete_log_shipping_plan_database
- sp_delete_log_shipping_primary
- sp_delete_log_shipping_secondary

- sp_get_log_shipping_monitor_info
- sp_log_shipping_get_date_from_file
- sp_log_shipping_in_sync
- sp_log_shipping_monitor_backup
- sp_log_shipping_monitor_restore
- sp_remove_log_shipping_monitor
- sp_remove_log_shipping_monitor_account
- sp_resolve_logins
- sp_update_log_shipping_monitor_info
- sp_update_log_shipping_plan
- sp_update_log_shipping_plan_database

Tables

Table 7-1 shows the tables used only for log shipping and which server has them populated. The tables are located in msdb.

> **Note** If the monitor is configured on SQL Server 2000 Standard Edition, the only log-shipping-specific tables that will exist are log_shipping_primaries and log_shipping_secondaries.

Table 7-1 Table Usage for Log Shipping

Table	Primary	Secondary	Monitor
log_shipping_databases	Used	Not used (unless this is also a primary)	Not used (unless this is also a secondary)
log_shipping_monitor	Used	Used	Not used (unless this is also a secondary)
log_shipping_plan_databases	Not used (unless this is also a secondary)	Used	Not used (unless this is also a secondary)

Table 7-1   Table Usage for Log Shipping

Table	Primary	Secondary	Monitor
log_shipping_plan_history	Not used (unless this is also a secondary)	Used	Not used (unless this is also a secondary)
log_shipping_plans	Not used (unless this is also a secondary)	Used	Not used (unless this is also a secondary)
log_shipping_primaries	Not used (unless this is also a monitor)	Not used (unless this is also a monitor)	Used
log_shipping_secondaries	Not used (unless this is also a monitor)	Not used (unless this is also a monitor)	Used
log_shipping_databases	Used	Not used (unless this is also a primary)	Not used

Jobs

The following SQL Server Agent job exists on the primary for each database being log shipped:

■ **Transaction Log Backup Job for DB Maintenance Plan '*database maintenance plan name*'**   This is a job created as part of the database maintenance plan to back up the transaction log of the primary database on a scheduled basis. It also exists on the secondary if you select the Allow Database To Assume Primary Role option during configuration.

The following SQL Server Agent jobs exist on the secondary for each database being log shipped:

■ **Log shipping copy for *SQLSERVERPRIMARYSERVERNAME. databasename_logshipping***   This job exists on the primary server and copies the transaction log files from the primary.

■ **Log shipping Restore *SQLSERVERPRIMARYSERVERNAME. databasename_logshipping***   This job exists on the secondary server and restores the transaction logs.

The following SQL Server Agent jobs exist on the monitor server for each database being log shipped:

- Log Shipping Alert Job—Backup
- Log Shipping Alert Job—Restore

Log Shipping Monitor

One of the best reasons to use the functionality provided with SQL Server is the Log Shipping Monitor, which provides status about the log shipping process through Enterprise Manager. It is located on a server designated by the person configuring log shipping.

> **Note**   Although the primary and secondary servers for log shipping require SQL Server 2000 Enterprise Edition or Developer Edition, the Log Shipping Monitor can be placed on any version of SQL Server 2000, including SQL Server 2000 Standard Edition. You can use one Log Shipping Monitor to monitor multiple log shipping pairs, so if you have a dedicated server as recommended here, you do not need to worry about configuring a separate Log Shipping Monitor for each pair. However, keep in mind that you need to ensure that the Log Shipping Monitor itself is available or that you know how to move it.

Configuring Log Shipping

This section takes you through the process of configuring log shipping with SQL Server 2000 Enterprise Edition.

> **On the CD**   Use the file SQL_Server_2000_Log_Shipping_Worksheet.doc when planning your installation. This document corresponds to Table 7-2. There is also a checklist to use to verify all preconfiguration tasks in the file Preconfiguration_Log_Shipping_Checklist.doc.

Step 1: Restoring the Initial Backup on the Secondary

Although you can use the Database Maintenance Plan Wizard to do the initial backup, copy, and restore of the databases for log shipping, you should do each of these outside of the wizard. The main reason for this procedure is that the way log shipping is coded, it uses your default backup drive (which is usually C$) for the backup. Therefore, if you are trying to initialize a large database, you could run out of space on your drive, causing the operation to fail. Because this is not detected immediately, you could waste time if you get an error two hours into a backup operation. That said, if your database is small to medium sized and you know you have plenty of hard disk room, the wizard might work for you, although it is still probably better to do it on your own.

There is also a known issue with the Database Maintenance Plan Wizard such that even if you select the NORECOVERY mode during the install and have the wizard perform your backup, copy, and restore, the database is restored with STANDBY. However the database is switched to NORECOVERY mode after the application of the first transaction log backup. Therefore, if you need your database to start out with NORECOVERY (even though it will be corrected once logs are applied), the only way to do this is to restore the database manually.

If you do not restore the database with STANDBY or NORECOVERY, you will see an error similar to the following:

```
Error on loading file c:\backups\Log_Source_tlog_200010090015.TRN : [Microsoft
SQL-DMO (ODBC SQLState: 42000)] Error 4306: [Microsoft][ODBC SQL Server
Driver][SQL Server]The preceding restore operation did not specify WITH
NORECOVERY or WITH STANDBY. Restart the restore sequence, specifying WITH
NORECOVERY or WITH STANDBY for all but the final step. [Microsoft][ODBC SQL
Server Driver][SQL Server]Backup or restore operation terminating abnormally.
```

One reason for this is that sometimes mistakenly the database might have been placed within a database that is already recovered, or active, into read-only mode. Read-only mode of an active database is just that; you cannot apply a transaction log to the database. Visually, this appears similar to the way a database restored with STANDBY appears in Enterprise Manager (see Figure 7-3). To see if your database is set to read-only, look at the Options tab in the Properties dialog box for the specific database, as shown in Figure 7-4.

Figure 7-3 How a database that is restored with the STANDBY option appears in Enterprise Manager.

Figure 7-4 The Options tab for a database.

Caution Please ensure that you are applying the proper database backup to the secondary server. For example, if you apply the wrong point-in-time full backup file, you will not be able to restore transaction logs. A sample error message follows:

```
[Microsoft SQL-DMO (ODBC SQLState: 42000)]
Error 4305: [Microsoft][ODBC SQL Server Driver][SQL Server]The log in
this backup set begins at LSN 7000000026200001, which is too late to
apply to the database. An earlier log backup that includes LSN
6000000015100001 can be restored. [Microsoft][ODBC SQL Server
Driver][SQL Server]RESTORE LOG is terminating abnormally.
```

Step 2: Running the Database Maintenance Plan Wizard

Once the point-in-time full backup is restored, you can run the Database Maintenance Plan Wizard. Table 7-2 lists all the parameters associated with configuring log shipping using the Database Maintenance Plan Wizard.

On the CD For complete installation instructions using the Database Maintenance Plan Wizard, see the file Configuring_Log_Shipping.doc.

Table 7-2   Log Shipping Parameters and Recommended Values

Parameter	Server Affected	Value or Recommendation
Back up database as part of the maintenance plan	Primary	By default, this is selected in the Specify The Database Backup Plan dialog box. It creates a SQL Server Agent job named DB Backup Job for DB Maintenance Plan '*Configured Plan Name*'. You might not have to select this option if a backup plan already exists for the database or you are just configuring log shipping and not an overall Database Maintenance Plan.
Primary server name	Primary	Name of the primary server.
Secondary server names	Secondary	Names of the secondary servers to log ship.
Database to log ship (on primary)	Primary	This is the database from which the transaction log files will be generated.
Directory to store the backup file	Primary	This can be an explicit path (such as C:\Tranlogs) or a Universal Naming Convention (UNC) file path. This directory is used by the primary to back up transaction logs, and although it can be located on the primary, it might be smarter from a high availability perspective to place it elsewhere. Some might make this the same as Network share name for backup directory.
Create a subdirectory under the UNC for each database	Primary	Set this to Yes, as it avoids confusion and makes it easier to find files if you have configured log shipping for more than one database.
Delete transaction log files older than a certain time period	Primary	The value you choose for this parameter depends on how long you need to keep older backup files. Prior to deletion, back these files up to a medium that can be stored offsite for archival purposes.
Backup file extension (default is .trn)	All	Leave as .trn.
Network share name for backup directory	Primary and secondary	This directory, usually a UNC name, needs to be accessible by both the primary and the secondary. This is where the transaction logs are accessed from the secondary. This is basically the same directory as Directory to store backup file, but with a share associated with it.

(continued)

Table 7-2   Log Shipping Parameters and Recommended Values *(continued)*

Parameter	Server Affected	Value or Recommendation
Transaction log destination directory (should be a valid UNC on secondary server)	Secondary	As with Directory to store the backup file, this can be an explicit path (such as C:\Tranlogs) or a UNC file path. This directory is used to copy the transaction logs from the network share to this location on the secondary.
Create and initialize new database	Secondary	Choose No and do the initial backup, copy, and restore yourself.
Database load state	Secondary	Set to No Recovery if you want to just apply transaction logs for high availability, or to Standby if you want to make it a read-only reporting server.
Terminate user connections in database	Secondary	Set to Yes only if Standby is selected for Database load state and you are using the secondary for read-only purposes. If No is selected and you have selected Standby, you have to set up a job to terminate the connections, otherwise the logs will never be applied. The syntax is as follows:

```
ALTER DATABASE databasename
  SET SINGLE_USER
  WITH ROLLBACK IMMEDIATE
```

If you are using your log-shipped database for reporting, you must reset it to allow users to have access after the transaction log is applied with the following:

```
ALTER DATABASE databasename SET
MULTI_USER
```

Parameter	Server Affected	Value or Recommendation
Allow database to assume primary role	Secondary	Set this to Yes to allow the secondary to become the primary. Set the Transaction log backup directory to the same one as Directory to store backup file if it was not located on the primary or set it to the same as Directory to store backup file as you did on the original primary.
Perform a full backup (if not using an existing database)	Primary	No.

Table 7-2   Log Shipping Parameters and Recommended Values (*continued*)

Parameter	Server Affected	Value or Recommendation
Use most recent backup file (if not using an existing database)	Primary	No.
Transaction log backup schedule (default is every 15 minutes)	Primary	This should be set to a lower number for higher volume sites and smaller files. If you set this to a larger number, the files might be large and your standby will not be as close in time to the primary.
Copy/load frequency (default is 15 minutes)	Primary/ secondary	The smaller the number, the closer match the log shipping pair will be. If you are using the secondary as a reporting server, use a higher value, as the user sessions would otherwise have to be terminated more frequently.
Load delay (default is 0 minutes)	Secondary	This is the amount of time the load process waits after the copy process is complete to restore the transaction log. The smaller the number, the closer match the log shipping pair will be. However, if the transaction log files are large, you might need to adjust this to allow time for the file to copy. If you are using the secondary as a reporting server, you might want to set this higher to stack the log files and allow users to do reporting. The default of 0 means that the transaction log will be loaded immediately.
File retention period		The default value is 24 hours. Configure this to match your corporate archival scheme.
Backup alert threshold		If the backups are large, adjust this number accordingly so you do not get false errors. The rule of thumb is to set this to three times the frequency of the backup job.
Out of sync alert threshold		Same as the backup alert threshold. If the file takes 15 minutes to copy because it is 3 GB and takes 45 minutes to apply, set this number accordingly; an hour or even two might be appropriate in this case. The rule of thumb is to set this to three times the amount of the slowest copy and restore job (if you are doing multiple secondaries).

(*continued*)

Table 7-2 Log Shipping Parameters and Recommended Values *(continued)*

Parameter	Server Affected	Value or Recommendation
Log Shipping Monitor server	N/A	This should be on a completely separate server than either the primary or secondary server.
Authentication mode for monitor server	Monitor	Set to Microsoft Windows, if possible, but if you change the password for the account that the SQL Server runs under, you must change it on all servers defined in log shipping only if all SQL Servers are starting under the same Windows account.
		If you choose SQL Server, it creates the log_shipping_monitor_probe user, for which you enter a password. Do not set this to a blank password.
Generate a report	Primary	This is optional, and you would need to configure a directory to hold the reports and configure how long to retain the reports or whether to e-mail them using SQL Mail.
Limit number of history entries in the sysdbmaintplan_history table		Log shipping is verbose. This can enlarge your table quickly if you generate frequent transaction logs. Adjust accordingly. Also, ensure that if you allow unlimited growth, msdb is set to autogrow. To clear out the entries, you need to execute the `sp_delete_backuphistory` stored procedure.
		Also, log shipping puts entries in the Application Event Log, so that might need to be backed up and cleared out from time to time.

> **Warning** There is a known issue documented in Knowledge Base article 311801, "BUG: Error 3154 Reported in Log Shipping Restore Job Sporadically." If you configure log shipping for more than one database, back up all databases to the same share, and the transaction logs only differ by _tlog in name, this causes failures on the RESTORE job on the secondary. To fix the problem, you need to ensure each database gets its own directory for backups. See the article for any other relevant information.

Step 3: Post-Wizard Configuration Tasks

After you configure log shipping with the Database Maintenance Plan Wizard, your configuration is not complete. There are a few remaining tasks that must be performed. The four tasks involve the following:

- Creating the DTS package for transferring database users to the secondary.

- Creating a job to regularly bcp out syslogins for the system-level logins.
  Remember, as discussed earlier, there are two levels of logins that you need to worry about. All database logins are linked to some system-level login. Without the ability to properly synchronize them, you create what are known as orphans, and after the role change the users will be unable to connect to the database. An orphan happens because each database user does not have a corresponding server-level login in SQL Server.

- Creating jobs to eventually run the stored procedures to perform the role change.

- Modifying `sp_resolve_logins`.

In the event of a problem, you do not want to be worried about syntax. These steps remove that worry. If you do not want to make each procedure a SQL Server Agent job, you can also create the scripts for each server based on the information provided here, and then put them in a well-known place to have them ready for execution.

Task 1: Configure Transfer Logins Task DTS Package   In this exercise, you create the DTS package that transfers any database users from the primary to the secondary.

> **Note**   Remember, DTS does not exist for 64-bit editions of SQL Server 2000. You must create DTS packages on a 32-bit instance to run against your 64-bit instances.

1. In Enterprise Manager, expand the Data Transformation Services control tree.

2. Right-click Local Packages and choose New Package from the shortcut menu.

3. In the DTS Package window, go to the Task menu and select Transfer Logins Task.

4. In the Transfer Logins Properties dialog box, click the Source tab. In the Source Server text box, enter the name of the primary server. Select Use Windows Authentication.

5. On the Destination tab, select the name of the secondary server. Select Use Windows Authentication.

6. On the Logins tab, select Logins For Selected Databases and then select the database that is being log shipped.

7. Click OK.

8. In the DTS Package window, go to the Package menu and choose Save As.

9. In the Package Name text box, type **Copy *DBTOLOGSHIP* Users** or another name that makes sense. In the Server drop-down list box, select the name of the primary server. Select Use Windows Authentication.

10. Click OK.

11. Close the DTS Package window.

12. In the Local Packages window, right-click Copy DBTOLOGSHIP Users and click Schedule Package.

13. Schedule the package to run as often as required.

14. Modify the job Copy DBTOLOGSHIP Users by changing the owner to the name of the owner of the primary database.

> **Warning**   If you are transferring large numbers of logins with the transfer logins task, it could be slow. Check Knowledge Base article 311351, "BUG: Transfer Login Task Is Slow with a Large Number of Logins," for updates.

Task 2: Set Up a Job to bcp out SYSLOGINS   In this task, you create a new job on the primary server to back up the syslogins table.

1. In Enterprise Manager, expand the Management control tree on the primary server.

2. Expand SQL Server Agent.

3. Right-click the Jobs icon and select New Job.

4. On the General tab, in the Name text box, type **Backup SYSLOGINS** or another name that makes sense to you. Set the owner to a user who has privileges to access the system tables.

5. On the Steps tab, click New.

6. In the New Job Step dialog box, click the General tab. In the Step Name text box, type **BCP Out** or something that makes sense.

7. In the Type drop-down list box, select Operating System Command (CmdExec).

8. In the Command text box, type the following command:

```
BCP master..syslogins out pathforfile\syslogins.dat /N /S
name_of_current_primary_server /U sa /P sa_password
```

   ❏ *Pathforfile* is the path where the file will be created. This should be the same location where the transaction logs are copied because it is accessible by both servers. It also eliminates the problem of one server being a single point of failure.

   ❏ *Syslogins.dat* is the file containing the login information. You can name this anything you want.

9. Click OK.

10. On the Schedules tab, create a new schedule called Transfer Syslogins. Schedule this job to run as often as required. It should also be synchronized to some degree with the job to DTS out the database logins.

11. Click OK to close the New Job Properties dialog box.

Task 3: Configure the Role Change SQL Server Agent Jobs for Manual Execution

In this exercise, you create the jobs on the proper servers that will contain the stored procedures used in the role-change process.

Subtask A: Create a Job to Demote the Primary   On the primary server, create a SQL Server Agent job named Change Primary Role. Set the owner to the owner of the database or one that has the appropriate privileges. This job executes the sp_change_primary_role stored procedure, which has the following options:

- **@db_name** This parameter is the name of the primary database currently being log shipped. The value is enclosed in single quotes.

- **@backup_log** This parameter tells SQL Server to back up the transaction log once more before changing the state of the database. This is set to either 0, which tells SQL Server not to make a final transaction log backup, or 1, which instructs SQL Server to make a final transaction backup. The default is 1.

- **@terminate** This parameter tells SQL Server to immediately roll back any active transactions and puts the database in single-user mode for the duration of this stored procedure execution. This is set to either 0, which tells SQL Server not to roll back any pending transactions, or 1, which instructs SQL Server to do an immediate rollback of transactions and put the database in single-user mode. The default is 0.

- **@final_state** This parameter sets the final state of the primary database after the stored procedure is run. The values that can be configured are 1, which leaves the database in recovery mode (available for writes and reads, but no longer the primary); 2, which leaves the database in no recovery mode (maps to the NORECOVERY function of the RESTORE statement) and allows the database to accept transaction logs but not be available for read-only access; and 3, which leaves the database in standby mode (maps to the NORECOVERY function of the RESTORE statement) and allows the database to accept transaction logs and also makes it available for read-only access. The default is 1, and if you want to eventually use the database again as a secondary in log shipping, you should set it to 2 or 3.

- **@access_level** This parameter sets the accessibility of the primary database after the stored procedure is run. The values that can be configured are 1, which leaves the database accessible for multiple users; 2, which allows access only by restricted users (maps to the RESTRICTED_USER function of the RESTORE statement) and is used only when *@final_state* is set to 1 and you want only members of db_owner, dbcreator, or sysadmin roles to have access; and 3, allowing only one user to access the database. The default value, if not specified, is 1.

The following is an example for this stored procedure with all of the parameters. If you do not put this in the job step, you must use msdb.dbo prior to sp_change_primary_role. If this is in a job step, you do not need msdb.dbo prior to sp_change_primary_role.

```
EXEC msdb.dbo.sp_change_primary_role @db_name = 'mylogshipdb',
```

```
@backup_log = 1,
@terminate = 0,
@final_state = 2,
@access_level = 1
```

Here are the full steps to create the job:

1. In Enterprise Manager, expand the Management control tree on the primary server.

2. Expand SQL Server Agent.

3. Right-click the Jobs icon and select New Job.

4. On the General tab, in the Name text box, type a name that is easily understood, such as **Run sp_change_primary_role**. Set the owner to the owner of the primary database.

5. On the Steps tab, click New.

6. In the New Job Step dialog box, click the General tab. In the Step Name text box, enter a name that makes sense to you.

7. In the Type drop-down list box, select Transact-SQL Script (TSQL).

8. Enter the syntax for the stored procedure (such as the example just shown).

9. Click OK.

10. Do not create a schedule for the job on the Schedules tab. You want to execute this job only on demand.

11. Click OK to close the New Job Properties dialog box.

Subtask B: Create a Job to Promote the Secondary   On each secondary server, create a SQL Server Agent job named Change Secondary Role. Set the owner of the job to the owner of the database or one who has the appropriate permissions. Further define the job to have one Transact-SQL step named `Run sp_change_secondary_role` and to use the database msdb. Do not schedule this, but allow it to be executed on demand. This step executes the `sp_change_secondary_role` stored procedure, which has the following options:

■ *@db_name*   This parameter is the name of the secondary database that will be promoted to the primary. The value is enclosed in single quotes.

■ *@do_load*   This parameter forces all remaining transaction logs that are pending to be copied and restored prior to recovering the database. This is set to either 0, which tells SQL Server to force the copy and restore, or 1, which tells it to make a final transaction backup. The default is 1.

- **@force_load** This parameter forces SQL Server to restore the pending transaction logs. This only works if *@do_load* is set to 1. This is set to either 0, which tells SQL Server not to force a restore, or 1, which tells SQL Server to force the restore. The default is 1.

- **@final_state** This parameter sets the final state of the primary database after the stored procedure is run. The values that can be configured are 1, which leaves the database in recovery mode (available for writes and reads, but no longer the primary); 2, which leaves the database in no recovery mode (maps to the NORECOVERY function of the RESTORE statement) and allows the database to accept transaction logs but not be available for read-only access; and 3, which leaves the database in standby mode (maps to the NORECOVERY function of the RESTORE statement) and allows the database to accept transaction logs and be available for read-only access. The default is 1, and it would make no sense to set it to 2 or 3 if this is to be the new active database.

- **@access_level** This parameter sets the accessibility of the primary database after the stored procedure is run. The values that can be configured are 1, which leaves the database accessible for multiple users; 2, which allows access only by restricted users (maps to the RESTRICTED_USER function of the RESTORE statement) and is used only when *@final_state* is set to 1 and you only want members of db_owner, dbcreator, or sysadmin roles to have access; and 3, allowing only one user to access the database. The default value if not specified is 1, and it would make no sense to set it to 2 or 3 because this will be the new primary.

- **@terminate** This parameter tells SQL Server to immediately roll back any active transactions and puts the database in single-user mode for the duration of this stored procedure execution. This is set to either 0, which tells SQL Server not to roll back any pending transactions, or 1, which makes it perform an immediate rollback of transactions and put the database in single-user mode. The default is 1.

- **@keep_replication** This parameter specifies that if replication was in use on the original primary, the settings will be preserved when restoring any pending transaction logs. This option is ignored if you do not set *@do_load* to 1. The default is 0.

> **Caution** If you do not set *@do_load* to 1 and *@keep_replication* to 1, you will lose all your replication settings when the database is recovered after the last transaction log loads.

- **@stopat** This parameter sets the accessibility of the primary database after the stored procedure is run. This option is ignored if you do not set *@do_load* to 1. The default value is NULL.

The following is an example for this stored procedure with all of the parameters. If you do not put this in the job step, you must use msdb.dbo prior to sp_change_primary_role. If this is in a job step, you do not need msdb.dbo prior to sp_change_primary_role.

```
EXEC msdb.dbo.sp_change_secondary_role @db_name = 'mylogshipdb',
@do_load = 1,
@force_load = 1,
@final_state = 1,
@access_level = 1
@terminate = 1
@keep_replication = 1
@stopat = NULL
```

Follow the steps listed under Subtask A to create the SQL Server Agent job, renaming appropriately and inserting the proper syntax for this stored procedure.

Subtask C: Create a Job to Resolve the Logins On the secondary server, create a SQL Server Agent job, which should be executed by someone with sysadmin privileges to execute sp_resolve_logins and to use the database master. This stored procedure has the following variables:

- **@dest_db** This parameter is the name of the database where logins will be synchronized. The value is enclosed in single quotes.

- **@dest_path** This parameter is the location of the BCP file you have been creating. The value is enclosed in single quotes.

- **@filename** This parameter is the exact file name that you have been creating.

The following is an example for this stored procedure with all of the parameters. If you do not put this in the job step, you must use master.dbo prior to `sp_resolve_logins`. If this is in a job step, you do not need master.dbo prior to `sp_resolve_logins`.

```
EXEC master.dbo.sp_resolve_logins @dest_db = 'mylogshipdb',
@dest_path = 'h:\mydirectory\',
@dest_filename = 'syslogins.dat'
```

Follow the steps listed under Subtask A to create the SQL Server Agent job, renaming appropriately and inserting the proper syntax for this stored procedure.

Subtask D: Create a Job to Change Primaries at the Log Shipping Monitor On the server containing the Log Shipping Monitor, create a SQL Server Agent job, which should be executed by someone with sysadmin privileges to execute `sp_change_monitor_role` and to use the database msdb. This stored procedure has the following variables:

■ *@primary_server* This parameter is the name of the original primary server. The value is enclosed in single quotes.

■ *@secondary_server* This parameter is the name of the secondary server that was converted to the new primary server. The value is enclosed in single quotes.

■ *@database* This parameter is the name of the database promoted to the new primary. The value is enclosed in single quotes.

■ *@new_source* This parameter is the path where the new primary will be putting its transaction logs. The value is enclosed in single quotes.

The following is an example for this stored procedure with all of the parameters. If you do not put this in the job step, you must use msdb.dbo prior to `sp_resolve_logins`. If this is in a job step, you do not need msdb.dbo prior to `sp_resolve_logins`.

```
EXEC sp_change_monitor_role @primary_server = 'primarysrv',
@secondary_server = 'secondarysrv'
@database = 'mylogshipdb',
@new_source = '\\newprisrv1\tlogs\'
```

Follow the steps listed under Subtask A to create the SQL Server Agent job, renaming appropriately and inserting the proper syntax for this stored procedure.

Step 4: Verifying and Testing the Log Shipping Pair

The easiest way to verify that the process is working properly is to open the Log Shipping Monitor after the process has had some time to do some copies and restores on the secondary. It is located on the Management tab of Enterprise Manager on the server you designated during configuration.

> **More Info**   For more information on the Log Shipping Monitor, see the section "Administering Log Shipping" later in this chapter.

Before this goes into production, you should also test the role-change process. This means you might have to reconfigure the log shipping pair (if you do not set the secondary to also become the primary at some point, and so on), but you can also have confidence that everything you have set up is correct. For a disaster recovery drill, it is absolutely crucial that you have this down pat.

> **On the CD**   For a test plan to test the log shipping role-change process, see the file Log_Shipping_Test_Plan.xls. There is also a checklist to easily verify all postconfiguration tasks in the file Postconfiguration_Log_Shipping_Checklist.doc.

Task 4: Modify sp_resolve_logins   As documented in Knowledge Base article 310882, "BUG: sp_resolve_logins Stored Procedure Fails If Executed During Log Shipping Role Change," there is a known issue with the `sp_resolve_logins` stored procedure that requires a manual fix. This stored procedure exists in the master database. Here's the problem. The code currently contains

```
SELECT *
INTO #sysloginstemp
FROM syslogins
WHERE sid = 0x00
```

which is incorrect. This incorrectly uses the syslogins table because it does not qualify it. The new statement should be manually corrected to this:

```
SELECT *
 INTO #sysloginstemp
 FROM master.dbo.syslogins
 WHERE sid = 0x00
```

> **Tip**   Back up your system databases before performing a modification to a system-stored procedure such as this one.

Troubleshooting Log Shipping

There are some steps that you can follow to troubleshoot an installation that is not behaving as expected:

- Make sure the SQL Server Agent is started on the primary and the secondary.

- Make sure you have no other transaction log backup jobs or processes configured or running for the database.

- Make sure that no operations (such as changing the database back to simple recovery model) are breaking or have broken the LSN chain.

- If you are only seeing *first_file_000000000000.trn* in the Log Shipping Monitor, it could mean one of a few things:

  - You have not given log shipping enough time to complete a full cycle.

  - The secondary has no rights or just cannot access the share that was configured during installation.

  - If *last_file_loaded* and *last_file_copied* still reflect *first_file_000000000000.trn*, even if the copy is occurring, the tables driving the GUI might not be getting updated. *Last_file_loaded* and *last_file_copied* are driven by msdb.dbo.log_shipping_secondaries, and *last_backup_file* is driven by msdb.dbo.log_shipping_primaries. This usually happens when you have configured log shipping to use Windows Authentication only and the SQL Server Agent service startup account of the primary or secondary does not have enough privileges to update the table on the monitor. It also could be an indication that the *primary_server_name* column of log_shipping_primaries or the *secondary_server_name* column of log_shipping_secondaries does not reflect the proper names. If it turns out to be a permissions problem, grant the UPDATE and SELECT rights for the appropriate account. If it is the server name issue, update the tables appropriately.

■   If you upgraded from SQL Server 2000 Standard Edition to Enterprise Edition and could not configure log shipping because the components seem to be missing (you will most likely see Errors 208 and 2812), run the file Instls.sql, which is found in the Install directory of the SQL Server 2000 Enterprise Edition installation CD.

> **Warning**   If you have access to the Enterprise Edition CD, do not run this script on any other version of SQL Server. It is not supported.

■   Make sure that you applied the right point-in-time backup and that nothing could have broken the LSN chain. Fixes for those errors more than likely will involve a full reconfiguration of log shipping, which means you must remove the current install first. The error messages for these types of root causes were detailed earlier in this chapter.

> **Note**   If you need to reconfigure log shipping, you will have to delete the current configuration and also possibly remove the Database Maintenance Plan that was created. This is documented later in the section "Removing Log Shipping." If for some reason you are still having problems, you might have to manually check each log shipping table in msdb and delete the offending rows.

Administering Log Shipping

After configuring log shipping, you need to understand how to administer log shipping, including how to monitor the process.

Removing Log Shipping

Use the following steps to remove log shipping from a Database Maintenance Plan:

1.   Open the Database Maintenance Plan for the database on the primary server.

2.   Select the Log Shipping tab and click Remove Log Shipping.

3.   You are prompted with the question, "Are you sure you want to remove log shipping?" as shown in Figure 7-5. Answer Yes or No, and SQL Server will do your bidding.

Figure 7-5   Removing log shipping from a Database Maintenance Plan.

> **Caution**   If you choose Yes, you remove all pairs participating in log shipping. If you have multiple secondaries and only want to remove one, follow the instructions in the next section, "Deleting a Secondary"

Deleting a Secondary

If you choose this option, you delete only one of the secondaries if multiple secondary servers are configured. The following are the steps to delete a single secondary from the log shipping definition:

1.   Open the Database Maintenance Plan for the database on the primary server.

2.   Click the Log Shipping tab and click Remove Log Shipping.

3.   You are prompted with the question "Are you sure you want to remove log shipping?" as shown in Figure 7-6. Answer Yes, and SQL Server will remove the secondary. The only confirmation you receive is that the secondary no longer appears in the Database Maintenance Plan.

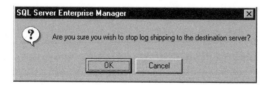

Figure 7-6   Removing a secondary from a Database Maintenance Plan.

> **Caution**   If you have only one secondary, performing this operation would be the same as clicking Remove Log Shipping, as shown in the previous section. You would need to reconfigure log shipping from scratch.

Monitoring Log Shipping

To view information about log shipping, you have five options:

■ **Log Shipping Monitor**   The Log Shipping Monitor is the first place you should look to see the status of the log shipping process for the log shipping pair. It is located on the Management tab of Enterprise Manager on the server you designated during configuration. Figure 7-7 shows what the Log Shipping Monitor displays in Enterprise Manager.

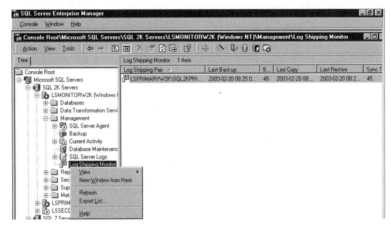

Figure 7-7   The basic Log Shipping Monitor.

If you select a log shipping pair in the right-hand pane of the Log Shipping Monitor and double-click it, you bring up more information about the pair, as shown in Figure 7-8. The Status tab of the Log Shipping Monitor is the most important one from a monitoring stand-point—it tells you the last file backed up on the primary, the last file copied, and the last file applied, with the appropriate time deltas. The other two tabs are discussed in the section "Changing Log Shipping Parameters After Configuration" later in this chapter.

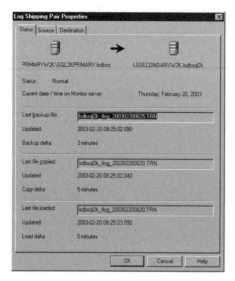

Figure 7-8   Detailed status information from the Log Shipping Monitor.

Important   The Log Shipping Monitor is not automatically refreshed. You must refresh it each time you want to see the updated status of log shipping, as shown in the left-hand pane of Figure 7-7.

- **SQL Server Agent jobs history**   Each SQL Server Agent job related to log shipping contains a status history, like any other normal job. This is a good place to look when trying to determine why things are failing.

- **Event Viewer**   Log shipping status is also logged to the Application Log of the Windows Event Viewer.

Warning   If you do frequent transaction log backups, this could fill up your Event Viewer quickly and cause alerts to go off unnecessarily in a monitoring center. Figure 7-9 shows the message that will pop up on your server. Please monitor your Event Viewer and maintain it as necessary.

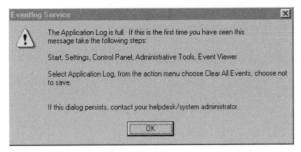

Figure 7-9   An error message indicating that the Event Viewer is full.

■ **Database Maintenance Plan on the primary**   The Database Maintenance Plan contains all of the information about the log shipping
configuration. Database Maintenance Plans are located under the Management control tree of Enterprise Manager. There are two tabs to be
concerned with: Log Shipping and Transaction Log Backup. An example of the Log Shipping tab is shown in Figure 7-10.

Figure 7-10   Log Shipping tab of a Database Maintenance Plan.

■ **Querying the log shipping tables**   You can also code your own
queries against the tables listed earlier (Table 7-1) to create your own
monitoring scheme.

Changing Log Shipping Parameters After Configuration

You can change the parameters for log shipping postinstallation. Parameters are not centralized in one place to be changed.

Database Maintenance Plan The Database Maintenance Plan is generally the first place you would go to tweak parameters for log shipping.

Log Shipping Tab When you select the Log Shipping tab in the Destination Server Information window (see Figure 7-10), select the secondary you would like to modify and then click Edit. You are presented with three tabs: General, Initialize, and Thresholds.

■ **General tab** The General tab, shown in Figure 7-11, allows you to tweak a few options: where the transaction logs are copied to on the secondary and if the secondary will be able to assume the role of the primary.

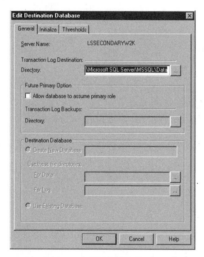

Figure 7-11 General tab of a Log Shipping secondary in a Database Maintenance Plan.

■ **Initialize tab** The Initialize tab, shown in Figure 7-12, allows you to tweak the state of the secondary database after the transaction log loads, if the log shipping process will automatically terminate the users in the database, and the copy and load frequencies.

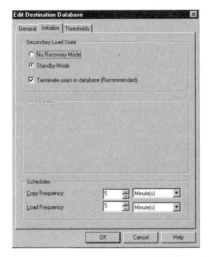

Figure 7-12   Initialize tab of a Log Shipping secondary in a Database
Maintenance Plan.

- **Thresholds tab**   The Thresholds tab, shown in Figure 7-13, is
  important. It controls when SQL Server alerts you if you are too far
  out of sync as well as the load delay, file retention, and history retention. You have to update the number for the Out Of Sync Threshold
  if you change your transaction log frequency. If you feel the number
  is too high or too low for your environment, change it.

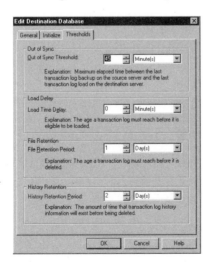

Figure 7-13   Thresholds tab of a Log Shipping secondary in a Database
Maintenance Plan.

Transaction Log Backup Tab If you want to change anything relating to the transaction log backup scheme you must do it in the Transaction Log Backup tab, as shown in Figure 7-14. The parameters you can tweak are also shown in Figure 7-14.

> **Important** Changing any values here affects all secondary servers. Also, you might need to tweak the Out Of Sync Threshold value if you change the frequency of the transaction log backups.

Figure 7-14 Transaction Log Backup tab of a Database Maintenance Plan.

> **Note** There is no way to change the backup network share using the Enterprise Manager GUI once you have log shipping configured. This must be done using one of the two following methods:
>
> 1. If the new destination folder lives on the same server as the old folder, remove the old share and rename the new share to the old share's name.
>
> 2. If the new destination folder is on a different computer, which is the more likely scenario, run the query listed here to update the location. You should back up msdb prior to executing the query.
>
> ```
> UPDATE msdb.dbo.log_shipping_plans
> SET source_dir = '\\new_computer_name\new_sharename'
> WHERE source_dir = '\\old_computer_name\old_sharename'
> ```

Log Shipping Monitor   The Log Shipping Monitor is also used to change some parameters associated with log shipping. The two tabs you use are Source and Destination.

Source Tab   The Source tab, shown in Figure 7-15, allows you to control various settings for when you want to be notified about when backups fail.

> **Tip**   If you are performing intrusive maintenance regularly, or even once, on the primary, configure the day and times under Suppress Alert Generation Between. For example, if you do a full index rebuild every Sunday night between midnight and 3 A.M., set that time. That way, those monitoring it will not see false errors.

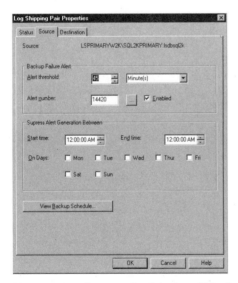

Figure 7-15   Source tab of the Log Shipping Monitor.

Destination Tab   The Destination tab, shown in Figure 7-16, allows you to control settings in terms of when you want to be notified about how out of sync the secondary is.

Figure 7-16 Destination tab of the Log Shipping Monitor.

> **Tip** Both the primary server and the secondary servers must be registered in the Enterprise Manager where the monitor instance is registered. If this is not the case, you will not be able to tweak the parameters just listed. See Figures 7-17 and 7-18 for the error messages you would see.

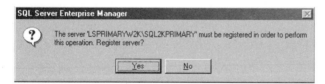

Figure 7-17 Error message if the primary is not registered in Enterprise Manager.

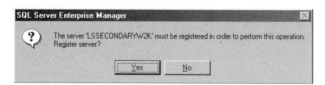

Figure 7-18 Error message if the secondary is not registered in Enterprise Manager.

Moving the Log Shipping Monitor

Moving the Log Shipping Monitor functionality to another SQL Server 2000 instance is not documented elsewhere. You would need to do this if the server containing the Log Shipping Monitor fails or you want to move it to another server.

> **Tip**   Because you need to get information from the current Log Shipping Monitor to re-create another one, you should gather the information directly after configuring log shipping.

Step 1: Configure the New Log Shipping Monitor   You need to insert information into the database so that the Log Shipping Monitor knows about the primary. Repeat this for the primary in each log shipping pair by following these steps:

1. Get the information needed to populate the Log Shipping Monitor. On the current monitor server, run the following query:

```
SELECT primary_id, primary_server_name, primary_database_name,
maintenance_plan_id, backup_threshold, threshold_alert,
threshold_alert_enabled, planned_outage_start_time,
planned_outage_end_time, planned_outage_weekday_mask
FROM msdb.dbo.log_shipping_primaries
WHERE primary_database_name = 'mydbname'
```

> **On the CD**   This query, saved as a Transact-SQL script, is on the CD for you to use. The file name is Monitor_Primary_Info.sql.

2. Run the stored procedure sp_add_log_shipping_primary on the new Monitor server, which uses the information from the preceding query. An example is shown here:

```
EXEC msdb.dbo.sp_add_log_shipping_primary
@primary_server_name = 'MyPrimaryServer',
@primary_database_name = 'logshipdb',
@maintenance_plan_id = '9B4E380E-11D2-41FC-9BA5-A8EB040A3DEF',
@backup_threshold = 15,
```

```
@threshold_alert = 14420,
@threshold_alert_enabled = 1,
@planned_outage_start_time = 0,
@planned_outage_end_time = 0,
@planned_outage_weekday_mask = 0
```

Conversely, you could also insert the information directly into the msdb.dbo.log_shipping_primaries table on the Log Shipping Monitor.

You now need to insert information into the database so that the Log Shipping Monitor knows about the secondary. Repeat this for each secondary in each log shipping pair using the following steps:

1. Get the information needed to populate the Log Shipping Monitor. On the monitor server, run the following query:

```
SELECT primary_id, secondary_server_name, secondary_database_name,
secondary_plan_id, copy_enabled, load_enabled, out_of_sync_threshold,
threshold_alert, threshold_alert_enabled, planned_outage_start_time,
planned_outage_end_time, planned_outage_weekday_mask
FROM msdb.dbo.log_shipping_secondaries
WHERE secondary_database_name = 'mysecondarydbname'
```

> **On the CD**   This query, saved as a Transact-SQL script, is on the CD for you to use. The file name is Monitor_Secondary_Info.sql.

2. Run the stored procedure sp_add_log_shipping_secondary, which uses the information from the preceding query. An example is shown here:

```
EXEC msdb.dbo.sp_add_log_shipping_secondary
@primary_id = 1,
@secondary_server_name = 'MySecondaryServer',
@secondary_database_name = 'logshipdb',
@secondary_plan_id = 'B5C330FF-1081-4FCB-83D0-955DDFB56BA5',
@copy_enabled = 1,
@load_enabled = 1,
@out_of_sync_threshold = 15,
@threshold_alert = 14421,
@threshold_alert_enabled = 1,
@planned_outage_start_time = 0,
@planned_outage_end_time = 0,
@planned_outage_weekday_mask = 0,
@allow_role_change = 0
```

Important   Make sure that the value for @primary_id matches the one inserted into the log_shipping_primaries table, as it is an automatically generated value. If you do not, you will get a message similar to this:

```
Server: Msg 14262, Level 16, State 1, Procedure sp_add_log_
shipping_secondary, Line 20
The specified primary_id ('msdb.dbo.log_shipping_primaries') does not
exist.
```

Example Transact-SQL to get the new primary_id from the inserted row on the new monitor is:

```
select primary_id
from log_shipping_primaries
where maintenance_plan_id = 'CE6960C2-F51F-4585-B79B-172E35AF8B4B'
```

Conversely, you could also insert the information directly into the msdb.dbo.log_shipping_secondaries table on the Log Shipping Monitor.

3.   Create the jobs and alerts that are necessary for the Log Shipping Monitor. The easiest way to do this is to script out the current alerts configured on the current monitor and then modify them as necessary.

Step 2: Update the *log_shipping_monitor* Table   On the primary server and all secondary servers that will be using the new Log Shipping Monitor, execute the following Transact-SQL on each server to change the monitor defined in the *log_shipping_monitor* table:

```
EXEC msdb.dbo.sp_define_log_shipping_monitor
@monitor_name = 'GRANDILLUSION',
@logon_type = 1,
-- Use a @logon_type of 2 for SQL Server authentication that is using the
log_shipping_monitor_probe user
--@password = 'password'
--Only use the @password if @logon_type = 2
@delete_existing = 1
```

On the original monitor server, also execute the following. Do not do this on the new monitor server.

```
delete from log_shipping_primaries where primary_id = n
delete from log_shipping_secondaries where primary_id = n
```

where *n* is the original primary_id. You must also delete the alert jobs from the old Log Shipping Monitor.

> **Note**   In some cases, the existing Log Shipping Monitor will still exist, but it will no longer be updated. All updates should now be done at the newly defined Log Shipping Monitor. Use Step 3 (below) to verify this.

Step 3: Verify the New Log Shipping Monitor   To verify that the newly configured Log Shipping Monitor has been set up properly, check for the following:

■   The Log Shipping Monitor should now display the information for all log shipping pairs defined in Step 2.

■   Wait for some time to ensure that all log shipping pairs are now functioning properly and in sync, or in sync according to the delta that you set.

■   Check the status of all the SQL Server Agent jobs on the server hosting the Log Shipping Monitor; no errors should be found.

Step 4: Delete Old Monitor History and Entries   There are now system tables that have orphaned rows or old rows. You can delete the relevant rows from the tables if you want. The tables can include the following:

■   *msdb.dbo.log_shipping_plan_history*

■   *msdb.dbo.sysdbmaintplan_databases*

■   *msdb.dbo.sysdbmaintplan_history*

■   *msdb.dbo.sysdbmaintplan_jobs*

■   *msdb.dbo.sysdbmaintplans*

■   *msdb.dbo.sysjobs*

■   *msdb.dbo.sysjobschedules*

- *msdb.dbo.backupfile*

- *msdb.dbo.backupmediafamily*

- *msdb.dbo.restorefile*

- *msdb.dbo.restorefilegroup*

- *msdb.dbo.restorehistory*

- *msdb.dbo.backupset*

- *msdb.dbo.backupmediaset*

> **Caution**   Do not delete data from system tables without thinking first. Chances are you should qualify by using a WHERE clause so as not to delete more than you want to.

Adding Additional Secondaries

Adding another secondary database to the Database Maintenance Plan is simple. Keep in mind that it utilizes the same transaction log backup schedule; you cannot customize it for each secondary. However, you can customize certain variables, such as how often you copy and load the transaction log.

To add a new secondary, click Add on the Log Shipping tab of the Database Maintenance Plan. You are then presented with three tabs—General, Initialize, and Thresholds—that are basically the same as the ones you use when editing an existing secondary. These are shown in Figures 7-19, 7-20, and 7-21. The parameters are also basically the same as those you use when configuring a secondary in the wizard. When you are finished, click OK. The only confirmation you see is that the new secondary has been added to the Database Maintenance Plan.

To verify that things are working properly, refresh the Log Shipping Monitor. The new pair is then displayed. Wait until one cycle is finished and see that the monitor reflects that the secondary is receiving and applying the transaction logs.

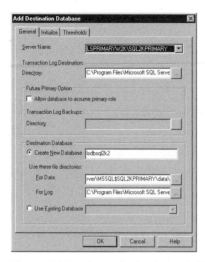

Figure 7-19   General tab when adding a new secondary.

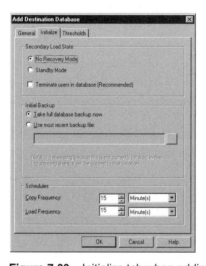

Figure 7-20   Initialize tab when adding a new secondary.

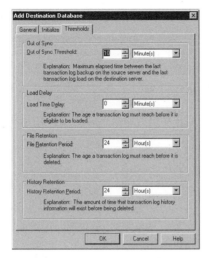

Figure 7-21   Thresholds tab when adding a new secondary.

Role Changes

A role change is the process of promoting the current secondary to the new primary. This process might or might not include the demotion of the current primary, depending on its availability and status. There are different types of role changes and drivers for each type that influence the process.

Types of Role Changes

The two types of role changes are simple: planned and unplanned.

■   A planned role change is exactly what it sounds like—you will have planned downtime. This is the easiest one when you know you will be doing something like performing the role change due to maintenance on the primary because it is the easiest to plan for.

■   An unplanned role change is the most common scenario for log shipping. This is when a problem occurs on the primary and you need to switch to the secondary.

Performing a Role Change

The following steps show how to switch the roles of the primary and the secondary servers.

> **Tip**   Before you proceed to the next step, where appropriate check the job history of each stored procedure run, which will tell you if it was a success or a failure.

1.   Notify any users or anyone who needs to know that there will be an interruption of service. How you do this and who you notify should be defined in your SLA.

2.   If there is a catastrophic failure (triggering an unplanned role change) on the primary server, skip directly to Step 5. This also means that you will not be able to back up the tail of the log and therefore will be a larger delta of time off of the primary. If the primary server is still available and there are connections into the current primary database, allow them to complete but do not allow new transactions. Make sure that a final transaction log backup is made and copied in this case.

3.   Before proceeding, you might want to consider putting the primary database (if it is still available) into single-user mode once activity winds down to ensure no other transactions or connections interfere with the role change process. This can be done using Enterprise Manager or Transact-SQL in the ALTER DATABASE command. If the primary database is not available or you set the *@terminate* option of `sp_change_primary_role` to 1, this is not necessary.

4.   On the primary server, execute the SQL Server Agent job you configured to run `sp_change_primary_role`.

5.   On the secondary server, execute the SQL Server Agent job you configured to run `sp_change_secondary_role`.

6.   On the secondary server, execute the SQL Server Agent job you configured to run `sp_resolve_logins`.

> **Warning**   `sp_resolve_logins` only resolves typical SQL Server logins. If you have remote logins configured on the primary, they need to be manually re-created on the secondary. Also, if you do not configure the Transfer Logins Task DTS package and the bcp of the syslogins table to be run, execution of `sp_resolve_logins` will fail.

> **More Info**   Running `sp_resolve_logins` is not necessary if you use the methods provided in Knowledge Base article 303722.

7. On the server containing the Log Shipping Monitor, execute the SQL Server Agent job you configured to run `sp_change_monitor_role`.

8. If you need to rerun a service pack to upgrade the promoted database on the secondary, do it now.

9. Test to ensure that the new primary server functions properly, and then redirect client applications to the new server using your technology of choice.

   ❑ If it is ODBC, change the server name (and subsequent entries) for the proper ODBC data source name (DSN). The tool Data Sources (ODBC) is located in the Start menu under Administrative Tools. Figure 7-22 shows the screen where you would select the new server.

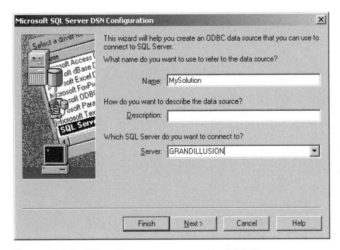

Figure 7-22   Changing server names in ODBC.

   ❑ If you are using Network Load Balancing under Windows 2000, execute the following in a command window. It ensures that all traffic will be redirected to the new primary server.

```
WLBS drainstop NLB_cluster_name:primary_server_name /PASSW
password_for_NLB_cluster
```

❏ If you are using Windows Server 2003, use Network Load Balancing Manager to issue the drainstop.

❏ Make sure Network Load Balancing is now started on the new Network Load Balancing cluster node using either wlbs on Windows 2000 or Network Load Balancing Manager under Windows Server 2003.

> **More Info**   For more information on Network Load Balancing, see Chapter 5.

❏ If you are using any other method, such as a custom switch in an application, make sure it is done to point users and applications to the new primary.

10. Notify end users and others that the database is now ready for use and provide them with contact information should any problems be encountered after the role change.

11. If you selected the Allow Database To Assume Primary Role option during the configuration of log shipping, configure it properly and start the appropriate SQL Server Agent job to start log shipping again.

> **Important**   The Allow Database To Assume Primary Role option only sets up the proper maintenance plan on the secondary to start performing the transaction log backups. You need to add all secondaries and enable the jobs to start the log shipping process again once you have promoted the database on the secondary.

> **Tip**   As noted earlier, the SQL Server Agent jobs make life easier in a role change. If you have these scripted, run the scripts in the order listed previously. Do not under any circumstances allow your DBA staff to enter syntax at the time of a failure. This only raises tensions and leaves room for errors and other failures.

Switching Back to the Original Primary

If you want to switch back to the original primary server, you have two options. However, make sure you need to go back to the primary server. If you are up and running on the secondary with no problems, is it worth causing another interruption in service, especially if you have SLAs that will be affected? You have the following options:

- You can initiate the process from the start from the new primary to the old primary. Specifically, do a new backup of the current primary, apply it to the old primary, configure log shipping from the primary to what would be the new secondary, and finally pick a point in time to do a manual role change. Because you will probably want the server to assume the secondary role again, you should leave the database in NORECOVERY or STANDBY mode.

- If you selected the Allow Database To Assume Primary Role option during the configuration of log shipping, the appropriate Database Maintenance Plans and SQL Server Agent jobs should have been created for you. You would just need to add secondary databases and create the transfer login tasks and the role-change procedures on the proper servers with the correct syntax reflecting the new roles of each server. If you left the primary database in NORECOVERY or STANDBY mode and the last transaction log from the original was applied to the secondary before it was brought online *and* no other transactions occurred in the primary database, you should now be able to reverse the process because the two databases were left in the same state.

Creating a Custom Coded Log Shipping Solution

If you have determined that coding your own log shipping solution is the best way to implement log shipping in your environment, all the considerations apply as they do to the built-in feature, but you need to create everything manually that is already included with SQL Server 2000 Enterprise Edition. This includes the following:

- A process to restore the point-in-time full backup to the secondary server.

- A process to back up, copy, and restore the transaction logs. Sometimes the easiest way to create transaction log backups is to use the Database Maintenance Plan Wizard because it creates unique file names for the transaction log backups without requiring you to code your own logic.

- A process to change the roles of the servers. This will be custom for each solution.

- A process to transfer users and logins. If your version of SQL Server has the stored procedure sp_resolve_logins in the master database, you should be able to use the same process as detailed for the built-in feature (using the DTS transfer logins task and bcping out the syslogins table) in the role change to synchronize logins. Otherwise, follow the information found in the section "Transferring Logins, Users, and Other Objects to the Standby" in Chapter 14.

- Monitoring functionality (if it is desired to see the status other than in, say, SQL Server Agent jobs).

- Testing procedures to verify that everything is working properly.

- Custom alerts and notifications.

> **On the CD** For an example of a custom log shipping solution you can use or extend that also includes compression, see the file Custom_Log_Shipping.zip, which contains all the relevant Transact-SQL scripts and documentation. The scripts do not configure any additional functionality such as dealing with logins. The scripts do cover the backing up, copying, and applying of the transaction logs, as well as the monitoring of the process.

Log Shipping From SQL Server 7.0 to SQL Server 2000

It is possible to manually configure log shipping from SQL Server 7.0 to SQL Server 2000. The best use of this is to facilitate an upgrade from SQL Server 7.0 to SQL Server 2000 where you need to minimize the amount of downtime in the server switch. There are some constraints for doing this, though, namely the following:

- SQL Server 7.0 must be configured with at least SQL Server 7.0 Service Pack 2.

- The pending upgrade option must be set on SQL Server 7.0. This is a database-level option that will only affect the database that it is configured on. Setting pending upgrade means that indexes cannot be created and statistics cannot be generated. Therefore, you should not allow log shipping to occur for a lengthy period of time, as it will affect performance of the SQL Server 7.0 database.

- Because recovery models are new to SQL Server 2000, truncate log on checkpoint and select into/bulk copy cannot be set as options on the SQL Server 7.0 databases.

- When restoring the database under SQL Server 2000, you must use NORECOVERY only. STANDBY is not supported when an upgrade is required.

- Replication cannot be configured between the server running SQL Server 7.0 and the SQL Server 2000 instance if log shipping is going to be used. If you are currently replicating using these servers, you have to script your configuration and unconfigure replication.

- As with custom log shipping, there is no monitoring functionality for log shipping between SQL Server 7.0 and SQL Server 2000. You have to code your own.

> **Note**   Transaction logs for SQL Server 2000 are not backward-compatible. Therefore, it is not possible to apply transaction logs (or full backups for that matter) generated on SQL Server 2000 to a SQL Server 7.0 installation.

Configuring Log Shipping from SQL Server 7.0 to SQL Server 2000

The following steps show how to configure log shipping between SQL Server 7.0 Service Pack 2 or later and SQL Server 2000.

1. Install and configure an instance of SQL Server 2000.

2. Perform full backups for all databases on SQL Server 7.0.

3. Restore the database that will be log shipped on your SQL Server 2000 instance using NORECOVERY. Here is example syntax:

```
RESTORE DATABASE mydb
FROM DISK = 'C:\mydbbackup.bak'
WITH NORECOVERY
```

If requiring a new location:

```
RESTORE DATABASE mydb
FROM DISK = 'C:\mydbbackup.bak'
WITH NORECOVERY
MOVE 'data file' TO
'x:\newlocation\dbdatafile.mdf',
MOVE 'log file' TO
'x:\newlocation\dblogfile.ldf'
```

4. Make sure that truncate log on checkpoint and select into/bulk copy are not selected as options for the database being log shipped from SQL Server 7.0.

5. Create a location for the transaction logs to be stored.

6. Execute the following command using Transact-SQL: sp_dboption 'database name', 'pending upgrade', 'TRUE', where the database name is the name of the database that will be log shipped to SQL Server 2000.

7. Using the Database Maintenance Plan Wizard, back up your transaction logs on a regularly scheduled basis. Use the directory created.

> **Warning**   If this is an actual SQL Server 7.0 to SQL Server 2000 upgrade and not just a way of creating a test database or something similar, stop all traffic and users from accessing the database at this point to ensure that if you have a problem, the database is in the state it was prior to the switch to SQL Server 2000. You will then have no data loss should you need to go back to SQL Server 7.0.

8. Manually apply each transaction log generated. The following is example syntax:

```
RESTORE LOG mydb
FROM mydb_log1
WITH NORECOVERY
```

9. When it is time to restore the final transaction log, the syntax is slightly different. You now bring the database online and make it available for use. Here is sample syntax:

```
RESTORE LOG mydb
FROM mydb_finallog
WITH RECOVERY
```

10. Ensure that all users, objects, and other items not brought over as part of the transaction logs exist under SQL Server 2000.

11. If necessary, redirect any applications to the new SQL Server 2000 database. Test all applications against the new database on SQL Server 2000 to ensure that everything functions as it did under SQL Server 7.0. If this is an upgrade, do not allow end users to access the new server if it has not been verified.

12. If you need to use the SQL Server 7.0 installation again, disable the pending upgrade option with the following Transact-SQL statement:

```
sp_dboption 'database name', 'pending upgrade', 'FALSE'
```

Summary

Log shipping is an extremely flexible and compelling option as a primary or secondary method of availability with SQL Server. It is a proven solution with a good track record. From an implementation and cost perspective, log shipping provides one of the best methods of protection for your databases. It overcomes the distance limitations that are inherent in most clustered solutions, and it is based on standard SQL Server processes like SQL Server Agent jobs, DTS, and backup and restore. As with any high availability technology, it comes with its caveats, and it is not the best solution for all environments.

l

8

Replication

Replication is a popular feature of SQL Server because it allows you to make copies of your data and keep them synchronized with a standardized process that can be automatic or manual. How does replication fit into the high availability picture? This chapter discusses the two ways to think about replication: using replication to make your databases available and making your replication architecture available.

Using Replication to Make a Database Available

As noted in Chapter 3, "Making a High Availability Technology Choice," although transactional replication or merge replication can be used to make a database available, they would be third on the list of Microsoft SQL Server technology choices. For the purposes of high availability, if you had to choose one form of replication, it would be transactional because it has the lowest latency from Publisher to Subscriber. Remember that you can only use replication for high availability in certain scenarios and with certain considerations.

The best (and most likely) scenario is one in which you need to make a copy of all your data for read-only reporting purposes, which is something log shipping cannot do well. In the event of a disaster, with the proper objects and users added, you might also be able to use the replicated data for your application. If you generate this copy of the database by transactional replication, also unlike log shipping, your latency can perhaps be seconds instead of minutes. This section details what you need to know to plan for implementing replication for availability purposes.

The other likely scenario is the need to make a synchronized copy of a subset of your data, which is also not possible using log shipping. Log shipping, like clustering, provides a solution for your entire database—you cannot log ship a single table or a subset of a table.

Choosing a Replication Model for Availability

As noted already, you more than likely will employ transactional replication for high availability uses. Depending on the situation, more than one form of replication might provide some sort of benefit for you.

Merge Replication

Merge replication is useful when the following criteria are met:

- Multiple Subscribers have to update data at various times. Those changes are sent back to the Publisher and finally to other Subscribers. An example of this is near-real-time inventory updates for a chain of stores. This would allow each individual store to query other stores for an out-of-stock item. As long as the employee knew there was a bit of latency (for example, updated every half hour), he or she could call the other store to check. All of this would ensure customer satisfaction and maybe a sale.

- Site autonomy is critical. As with the previous inventory example, each individual store needs to have data specific to that location, but also needs some shared corporate data (such as product numbers and prices).

- Merge replication provides a rich framework for conflict resolution for updating Subscribers. You can either use the conflict resolution provided by SQL Server or code your own custom solution. As a general rule, conflicts should be infrequent. The data should not be very complex if you are allowing Subscribers to update data, because it means a more complex conflict resolution. Remember, data ownership is at the heart of all conflicts.

> **Note**   There might be certain instances in which merge replication can have a lower latency than transactional replication. It depends on the distributor and distribution database as well as the size of transactions.

Snapshot Replication

Snapshot replication is unlikely to be useful as a means of providing high availability, but a short description is provided here for completeness. Snapshot replication can be used when the following criteria are met:

■   The amount of data you are replicating is not large, and is read-only.

■   The data being replicated does not change often. Snapshot replication is useful if changes to the data are substantial, but infrequent. For example, if you batch update catalog data and you affect most of the database, it is more efficient to generate and deliver a complete snapshot than replicate individual rows. If you want to compare this to any other SQL Server–based technology, you can think about backup and restore. A snapshot is a point-in-time picture of your data, just like a backup is a point-in-time picture of your data. How current the Subscriber will be is dependent on the frequency of the snapshots you generate and apply.

■   New data does not have to be distributed immediately because out-of-date data is still usable. This also infers that latency would be acceptable in this case because Subscribers do not need up-to-the-minute updates. A good example of this type of data is census information, which is updated every 10 years in the United States.

■   Subscriber sites are often disconnected, as when they are located all around the world. Again, this implies that a high latency tolerance exists, especially if your network connection is slow and possibly unreliable.

Transactional Replication

Transactional replication is useful when the following criteria are met:

■   Low latency for change delivery to the Subscriber is required. In this case, you are looking for things like real-time reporting that will give you accurate information that is much more current than merge or snapshot replication can provide.

■   In terms of transactional consistency, with transactional replication, all the changes associated with a transaction executed at the Publisher are guaranteed to be delivered to the Subscriber together and in the same order. Merge replication, on the other hand, achieves data convergence using row-by-row reconciliation and does not guarantee that all the changes associated with a transaction will be delivered in the same synchronization session.

- You need high throughput and low data latency. Merge replication can run frequently, as can log shipping, but it is measured in minutes and not seconds. With transactional replication, depending on the volume of transactions, you need good network connectivity and guarantees that the links between your sites will be available. The larger the distance between sites, the more you need to plan your architecture properly.

- Your application cannot tolerate changes to the database schema.

Switch Methods and Logins

If you are going to use replication to create a warm standby, it is like log shipping: You can use Network Load Balancing to abstract the name change, or you can change the name of the instance if it is possible to match the name of the original Publisher.

More problematic, however, is ensuring that the logins needed for use at the Subscriber exist so that the warm standby can function as the Publisher. Part of the problem here, too, is that all data might not be at the Subscriber, so can you really use the Subscriber as a new database?

Replication and Database Schemas

In using replication, your schema design is very important because it dictates if you can use replication or not. If you are considering replication, you need to think about it long before you even implement your solution. It starts with the design phase.

Primary Keys

With transactional and merge replication, all published tables must contain a declared primary key. Merge replication requires that for any tables that have foreign keys, the referenced table should also be in the publication. You are ensuring data integrity at the Subscriber. You therefore need to design your schema properly to include proper primary and foreign keys.

Only transactional replication requires an explicitly declared primary key on a published table. Furthermore, merge replication does not require all referenced tables to be in the publication.

Some packaged applications do not support the modification of your database schema, in particular primary keys and foreign keys. Do not implement replication without asking your third-party software vendor if this invalidates their application support.

Uniqueidentifier Columns and Merge Replication

If your replicated table does not contain a column with a uniqueidentifier data type, SQL Server adds one when the publication is generated. This is used to identify a row so that it can be reconciled if it is updated elsewhere.

Different forms of replication support different row sizes and numbers of columns that can be replicated. With snapshot or transactional replication, a table being replicated can support up to 255 columns and a maximum row size of 8000 bytes in the publication. A table used by merge replication can have up to 246 columns and a maximum row size of 6000 bytes to allow 2000 bytes for the overhead of conflict resolution. If the row size is greater than 6000 bytes, conflict-tracking metadata may be truncated. Think back to Chapter 4, "Disk Techniques for High Availability," where you learned how to calculate a table's row size. Using this, you will know enough about your schema to help you configure replication. Do not assume that you will be able to send every column in your table to a Subscriber if you want to send the entire table and you exceed the 6000- or 8000-byte limit for each row.

Schema Changes, Data Definition Language, and Replication

One major difference from log shipping is that not all changes tracked in the transaction log are sent over as part of replication in any model.

> **Important** If you update replicated objects beyond their initial publication, it is not straightforward to send these as part of replication.

More important, your schema cannot be very flexible. If you make constant changes to your database structure, it might be hard to maintain a replication solution. The only things you can do schema-wise are add a column to a publication or delete a column from a publication using Enterprise Manager or using sp_repladdcolumn and sp_dropreplcolumn directly. Considering that adding and dropping a column are the most common schema changes people make on their tables, this satisfies most requirements.

Text and Image Fields

If you are replicating these columns as parts of your publications, consult the SQL Server Books Online topics "Planning for Transactional Replication" and "Planning for Merge Replication." One of the biggest differences between transactional replication and merge replication is that with merge, WRITETEXT and

UPDATETEXT are not supported. You must perform an explicit UPDATE on the column as described in the steps later in this section.

With transactional replication or snapshot replication, you can send text or image data types, but if you are using the immediate updating or queued updating options, changes made at the Subscriber to data replicated with text or image data types is not supported. If these are read-only subscriptions, replicating text and image data types as part of transaction or snapshot replication is supported.

If you are using UPDATETEXT or WRITETEXT to update text and image columns when publishing those columns using transactional replication, the text pointer should be retrieved within the same transaction as the UPDATE-TEXT or WRITETEXT operation with read repeatability. For example, do not retrieve the text pointer in one transaction and then use it in another. It might have moved and become invalid.

In addition, when you obtain the text pointer, you should not perform any operations that can alter the location of the text pointed to by the text pointer (such as updating the primary key) before executing the UPDATETEXT or WRITETEXT statements.

This is the recommended way of using UPDATETEXT and WRITETEXT operations with data to be replicated:

1. Begin the transaction.

2. Obtain the text pointer with read repeatable isolation.

3. Use the text pointer in the UPDATETEXT or WRITETEXT operation.

4. Commit the transaction.

```
DECLARE @textpointer binary(16)

WRITETEXT MyTable.MyColumn @textpointer 'Sample Text'

-- Dummy update to fire the trigger that will update metadata and ensure the
-- update gets propagated to other Subscribers. If you set the value to
-- itself, there is no change.

UPDATE MyTable

SET MyColumn = MyColumn

WHERE ID = '1'
```

Integer Columns

In your current schema, if you are using automatically generated integer columns as identity columns or as columns to help partition data, you might have to use the NOT FOR REPLICATION constraint in your schema.

> **Note**   NOT FOR REPLICATION can only be implemented using Transact-SQL and not through Enterprise Manager. NOT FOR REPLICATION is an option of ALTER TABLE, ALTER TRIGGER, CREATE TABLE, and CREATE TRIGGER.

Note that with transactional replication, the identity property is not propagated by default to a read-only Subscriber. If you are using data types with the identity property, consider these carefully when setting up replication for warm standby to ensure that your application works correctly after failover to the warm standby database. In this case, there are two options: Choose another technology to create the warm standby server, or manually manage the identity property at the Subscriber as described in the "Replication Data Considerations" section in SQL Server Books Online.

Timestamp Columns

You can replicate timestamp columns with merge replication or transactional replication with queued updating, but note that the column is replicated and the value is regenerated at the Subscriber. Therefore, you do not get the value that is at the Publisher. Generally, this does not create a problem for an application. Timestamps are not specifically representative of clock time, but are instead increasing numbers based in part on the ID of the database in which the timestamp column exists. As a result, these columns have unique context only within the database in which they are generated.

Timestamps are most commonly used to perform optimistic concurrency control where a preread timestamp value on a row is compared to the current value just before issuing an update on the row. If the timestamps differ, you know another user updated the row. The application can then choose to prevent the update or take other appropriate action. Replicating the actual originating value of a timestamp column from one location to another is, in many cases, not highly useful, so the replication subsystem masks this column out of the propagated update and allows each site to calculate a unique timestamp value for each row that is appropriate to its database context. This helps ensure consistency in most common timestamp uses (for example, optimistic locking), regardless of whether an update arrived at a given replica as part of a replicated transaction or directly from a user application. If you do want to replicate time-stamp columns and keep values the same, you might have to store it in another way and perform a conversion. If you want to include time-based data, consider the use of a datetime data type instead of a timestamp.

If you are using timestamp data type columns in your database and employing snapshot or transactional replication with read-only Subscribers or those that allow immediate updating, the literal values are replicated but the data type of the column at the Subscriber is changed to a binary(8). This might cause problems if you want to use the Subscriber later in a failure scenario. For example, a data type difference at the Subscriber means that any application behavior that is expecting a timestamp will not function if the secondary is used for updating. If the secondary is for read-only reporting or for read-only access in a disaster recovery scenario while the primary is being repaired, the data type change might not matter.

Server Collations and Case Sensitivity

If you are replicating between SQL Servers with different character sets, no translation of data and data types occurs between Publisher and Subscriber. You therefore need to ensure that all servers in your replication topology have the same code page and sort order. If you do not ensure that all of the Subscribers match the Publisher in this regard, you might experience different results from your queries. If such a scenario exists, you might not want to use that Subscriber as a potential secondary.

Highly Available Replication Architecture

There are three words that should apply to any replication architecture: *keep it simple*. The more complex it is, the more difficult it is to maintain over the long term. In the event of a disaster (see the later section, "Disaster Recovery with a Replicated Environment"), the simpler the topology, the easier it should be to recover. You should also test the normal operation of replication and simulate an actual switch to the replicated secondary, and, if applicable, a switch back to the original Publisher, prior to rolling out your replication architecture in a production environment.

The three obvious components that you are looking to protect are the Publisher, Distributor, and Subscriber. Of these three, the first two—the Publisher and Distributor—are the most important to protect. Without the Publisher, you have no source. Without the Distributor, you do not have anything to push the data. It is as simple as that.

> **Note**   Remember that if you are deploying merge or bidirectional transactional replication, you will need some sort of conflict resolution to ensure that there will always be a "winner" if more than one update of the same bit of data is generated. Merge replication has conflict resolution built in, and transactional replication needs custom resolvers. For more information, see the topic "Implementing Non-partitioned, Bidirectional Transactional Replication" and the whole topic "Merge Replication Conflict Detection and Resolution" in the updated SQL Server Books Online. They describe more factors you need to take into account in any disaster recovery scenario.

Replication Agents

Before you can plan for your architecture you must understand which replication agents, the underlying components that initiate different actions of replication, are used by the different methods of replication (see Table 8-1).

> **Warning**   Do not modify any replication objects—tables, triggers, stored procedures, and so on—that are created on your Publisher, Distributor, or Subscriber. Doing so makes your solution unsupported.

Table 8-1   Agents Per Model of Replication

	Snapshot	Merge	Transactional
Snapshot Agent	Yes	Yes	Yes
Distribution Agent	Yes	No	Yes
Log Reader Agent	No	No	Yes
Merge Agent	No	Yes	No
Queue Reader Agent	No	No	Yes

Snapshot Agent

The Snapshot Agent is used with all models of replication. It prepares schema and initial data files of published tables and stored procedures, stores the snapshot files, and inserts information about initial synchronization in the distribution database. The Snapshot Agent typically runs at the Distributor.

There is one Snapshot Agent per publication. When you create a snapshot of data, there are physical files, or objects, associated with it, and it differs with the model of replication, as shown in Table 8-2. These objects vary in number depending on your replication configuration's publication and articles; there is no exact formula to calculate it. You can only get the exact count by testing. All forms of replication imply that a snapshot initiates them.

Once you create the initial snapshot, you should consider backing up the snapshot files if you want to use them to initiate replication again. You can either back up the snapshot folder itself or allow another execution of the snapshot agent to generate another snapshot. As part of a disaster recovery plan, you can use the old or the new snapshot files (depending on your strategy) for the publication prior to creating a new subscription or reinitializing an existing one.

Note   Triggers configured with replication are AFTER triggers and behave as normal AFTER triggers. The `sp_trigger_order` stored procedure is not run by the configuration of replication.

Table 8-2   File Types Associated with Replication

	Merge	Snapshot or Transactional
Conflict tables (.cft)	Yes	No
Constraints (.idx)	No	Yes
Constraints and indexes (.dri)	Yes	Yes
Data (.bcp)	Yes	Yes
Schema (.sch)	Yes	Yes
System table data (.sys)	Yes	No
Triggers (.trg)	Yes	No

Distribution Agent

The Distribution Agent is used with snapshot replication and transactional replication. It moves snapshot files and incremental changes held in the distribution database to Subscribers. The Distribution Agent typically runs at the Distributor for push subscriptions and at the Subscriber for pull subscriptions.

Log Reader Agent

The Log Reader Agent is used with transactional replication. It moves transactions marked for replication from the transaction log on the Publisher to the distribution database. Each database marked for transactional replication has one Log Reader Agent that runs on the Distributor and connects to the Publisher.

Merge Agent

The Merge Agent is used only with merge replication. It applies the initial snapshot at the Subscriber. It then moves and reconciles incremental data changes that occurred after the initial snapshot was created. Each merge subscription has its own Merge Agent that connects to and updates both Publisher and Subscriber. The Merge Agent typically runs at the Distributor for push subscriptions and at the Subscriber for pull subscriptions.

Queue Reader Agent

The Queue Reader Agent is used with snapshot or transactional replication when you select the Queued Updating Subscribers option. It moves transactions and reconciles those incremental changes from a Subscriber with those at the Publisher as needed. There is one Queue Reader Agent per published database and the Queue Reader Agent typically runs at the Distributor regardless of whether push or pull subscriptions are employed.

> **Note**   In the end, what is important is where the agents run and consume resources.

Scenario 1: Separate Publisher and Distributor

When you use transactional replication, you should not put the Publisher and Distributor on the same server, which is otherwise known as a Local Distributor (see Figure 8-1).

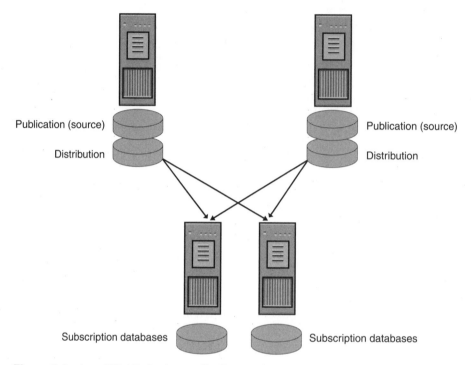

Figure 8-1   Local Distributor in a replication topology.

It is better to separate the Publisher and Distributor and create what is known as a Remote Distributor (see Figure 8-2). In fact, you can have more than one Distributor, but a Publisher can only talk to one Distributor. Multiple Publishers can share the same Distributor.

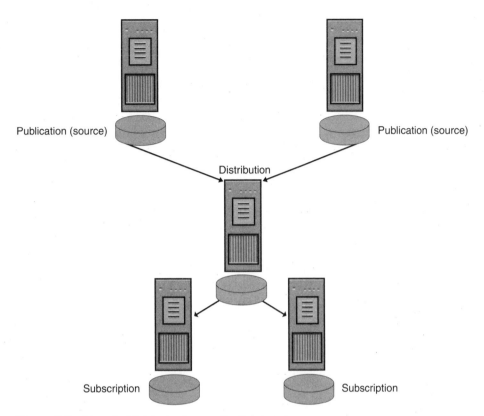

Figure 8-2   Remote Distributor in a replication topology.

Using a Remote Distributor has the following benefits:

■   It can improve performance because it offloads work performed by the Replication Agents from the primary computer.

■   It allows for the smoothest possible upgrade paths. SQL Server replication is designed to support replication among servers of differing versions. This can be an advantage because you can upgrade one computer at a time, redirecting client connections to a replica during the upgrade process. Users achieve an aggregate data-access availability that might not be possible in a nonreplicated scenario. You can also do this with merge and transactional replication with queued updating even if the Publisher and Distributor are on the same machine, but the best scenario is if they are separated.

- One SQL Server with both Publisher and Distributor roles is removed as a single point of failure. Although the Publisher and Distributors can still potentially be single points of failure, you are not creating a bigger problem with them on the same server.

- In a disaster recovery scenario, you might only be dealing with one server and one piece of functionality, not multiple problems. This approach helps to minimize single points of failure, and is a compelling reason to use a Remote Distributor.

Scenario 2: Using a Republisher

This scenario is not dissimilar to using a Remote Distributor. You still have a Publisher and a Distributor, but you then take a Subscriber and have it publish the data out to other servers. That Subscriber is then known as a Republisher, or a Publishing Subscriber (see Figure 8-3). In this case, the Republisher would act as its own Distributor, or you could even set up another one. This scenario would benefit you if your company has sites around the world. Because of network issues, it is easier and more cost-effective to have more local resources generating data to Subscribers. This also increases the availability of your solution so that even if the original Publisher or Distributor goes down, if there are changes to be propagated out to other Subscribers that are still in the Republisher, they will still get to the other Subscribers.

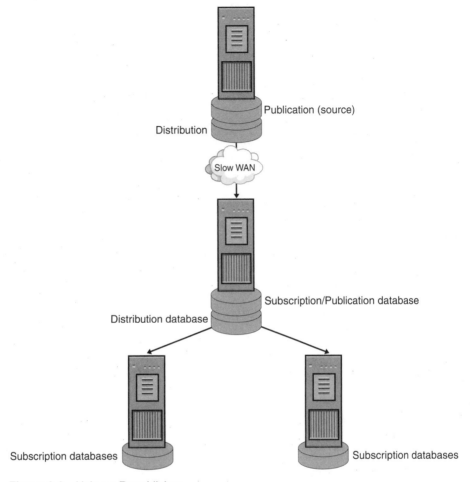

Figure 8-3 Using a Republisher.

> **Note** The Republisher is really a hierarchy of servers, and not something you use to employ bidirectional transactional replication.

SQL Server Service Packs and Replication

SQL Server service packs will definitely make an impact on your replication implementation. If you apply them wrongly, you might need to reinitialize your replicated environment or use the disaster recovery procedures detailed here. See the section "Applying a SQL Server 2000 Service Pack" in Chapter 13, "Highly Available Upgrades," for more information on replication and SQL Server service packs. The order in which you apply the service pack to your servers participating in replication matters. First, you must update the Distributor; then comes the Publisher; and finally the Subscriber.

You can also use replication to help keep your database available during a service pack install, much like you can use log shipping. Switch to the standby, and allow updates to happen on the standby assuming that it can function as the primary in every way it needs to. Once the service pack is done on the Publisher, switch back and upgrade the Subscriber. This is only applicable after the Distributor upgrade, which might even be the same server as the Publisher.

Planning Disk Capacity for Replication

Replication makes an impact on your planning for your disk capacity (in addition to anything outlined in Chapter 4 and the rest of the book), which is an obvious concern for any highly available environment. You do not want to run out of disk space before you even implement your solution. Table 8-3 walks through the requirements for each model of replication.

Table 8-3   Disk Requirements for Replication

Model of Replication	Impact on Transaction Log	Disk Space Needed
Merge	Database and its log file will have a small amount of growth when updates to a published table are made because the change tracking meta data results in additional inserts, updates, or deletes to system tables during the execution of user transactions. Changes are tracked in the database itself, not in the log, so there is no impact on backup strategy of replication frequency as it relates to truncating the transaction log.	Review SQL Server Books Online for a description of the change tracking tables created by merge replication in a user database. The maximum size of data columns is rarely used, but row-tracked tables can incur up to 249 bytes of change tracking overhead and column-tracked tables can incur up to 2048 bytes per changed row. Remember, only changed rows get a meta data entry; rows that are never updated do not result in change meta data accumulation. Also, the merge agent takes care of trimming aged meta data out of these system tables based on the publication retention period. The distribution database does not store tracked changes and instead only stores history and error information, which is also trimmed periodically based on the publication retention period.

(continued)

Table 8-3   Disk Requirements for Replication   *(continued)*

Model of Replication	Impact on Transaction Log	Disk Space Needed
Snapshot	Not a concern from a replication standpoint because the Subscriber gets everything in the primary.	A snapshot generates files in the filing system representing the schema and data for all published objects. The Snapshot Agent typically BCPs (bulk copies) data out from the Publisher to a file in a SQL Server binary format. Further reduction in disk impact can be achieved by setting a publication property such that the files generated by the snapshot are compressed in a .cab file. The ultimate disk impact then varies depending on the number of objects published, the amount of data published, and the use of compression in generating the snapshot files. In general, if you have a large database, the file system storage requirements will be large. The distribution database itself will store relatively little and will include a few bytes of control data directing the subsequent forwarding of the snapshot files to the Subscribers and a small amount of history and error information reflecting the execution of the Snapshot Agent.

Table 8-3   Disk Requirements for Replication *(continued)*

Model of Replication	Impact on Transaction Log	Disk Space Needed
Transactional	Transactional changes are tracked in the transaction log of the publishing database. The Log Reader Agent moves transactions from the publishing database's transaction log to the distribution database where they are queued for subsequent distribution to Subscribers. The transaction log cannot be truncated beyond the last transaction processed by the Log Reader Agent so additional log growth can incur when replication is employed. To minimize the potential growth of the publishing database log, run the Log Reader Agent continuously.	Disk space is an obvious concern because the Distributor is now storing copies of the transactions generated at the publishing database until they can be distributed to all Subscribers. The transaction log is a concern because on the database being replicated, transactions might not be flushed until they are put into the distribution database. So you need to set your data and log portions appropriately for your database and the distribution database.

> **Important**   No matter what model of replication you use, you should not use the Simple Recovery model for your databases. For more information on recovery models, consult Chapter 9, "Database Environment Basics for Recovery," and Chapter 10, "Implementing Backup and Restore."

Disaster Recovery with a Replicated Environment

In the event of a problem with a SQL Server solution using replication, you need to know how to recover. If this is a temporary outage, as when you are applying an update (like a hotfix) to each one, then there really is no problem. You need to assess why the servers are unavailable before you reinitialize snapshots or restore servers from backups.

> **Tip** No matter what model of replication you employ or what architecture you decide on, always script out your replication installations once they are configured and working properly.

To script your replication on an instance of SQL Server, select the Replication folder in Enterprise Manager, and right-click it. Select the Generate SQL Script option. You then see the dialog box shown in Figure 8-4. This should be done on each participating server. Place these scripts in a safe place that is documented in your run book for use in any disaster recovery scenario or ease of recreating in a test environment.

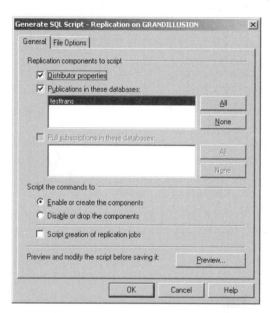

Figure 8-4 Generating SQL Script For Replication dialog box.

Backing Up Replication Databases

Your backup and restore strategy is crucial when you deploy replication. To recover from a disaster, you must back up the databases used in replication. The strategy changes depending on your replication model. If you are using transactional replication with log shipping, it impacts everything. See the later section "Log Shipping and Replication" for more information.

A comprehensive backup and restore plan for replication must include the Publisher, Distributor, and Subscriber, as well as SQL Server system databases. Good backups are crucial for disaster recovery. You have to test and stress every aspect of the replication environment; otherwise you have no test, meaning you really do not have a replicated environment you can feel confident about. Whatever your eventual plan, its complexity will match that of your replication topology.

> **Note**   This topic is not covered in Chapters 9 or 10, as it is specific to replication and its dependencies. Remember to take this into account when reading Chapters 9 and 10, as this obviously affects an overall backup and restore plan.

Publisher

The Publisher is arguably the most important part of your replication, as it is the source of your data for Subscribers. You should be doing full backups on the publication database, as well as backing up msdb and master databases, because they are integral to the success of replication. Besides full backups, you should also perform differential or transaction log backups and periodically generate SQL scripts from the Publisher database. Here are some common things that influence your Publisher backups; each bullet point represents a change to the Publisher:

- Creating new publications
- Altering any publication property including filtering
- Adding articles to an existing publication
- Performing a publication-wide reinitialization of subscriptions
- Altering any published table using a replication schema change
- Performing on-demand script replication
- Cleaning up merge meta data (running `sp_mergecleanupmetadata`)
- Changing any article property, including changing the selected article resolver
- Dropping any publications
- Dropping any articles
- Disabling replication

For snapshot replication, you only need to back up the publication database when changes are made to publications (adding, deleting, or modifying them). With merge replication, because the data can potentially reside anywhere, your backup scheme might or might not be more flexible. You have other ways of synchronizing your data, because Global Subscribers can be used to catch a restored Publisher and include previously merged changes that were not part of the backup.

Distributor

The Distributor is equally as important as the Publisher, as it pushes the data out to the Subscribers. With merge replication, the Distributor does not push data, but it does store history and information. A backup plan for a distribution database must include backing up the distribution database along with master and msdb. Realistically, a recovery strategy would include full as well as transaction log or differential backups because the distribution database can grow large, depending on your model of replication. Here are some common things that influence your Distributor backups; each changes the distributor database:

■ Creating or modifying replication agent profiles

■ Modifying replication agent profile parameters

■ Changing the replication agent properties (including schedules) for any push subscriptions

For snapshot replication, you need to synchronize the backup of this database with the Publisher. That means you need at least two SQL Server Agent jobs executed in parallel. You might also want to run the Distribution Cleanup Task to shorten your backup time and remove unused data from the distribution database prior to backing it up. While you are backing up these databases, do not add new publications or subscriptions.

Using the Sync with Backup Option with Transactional Replication Publisher and Distributor

The sync with backup option affects how often transactional replication sends transactions to the Distributor. This option should always be used when configuring transactional replication, because it is the only way to ensure that the distribution and publication databases can be recovered to the same point in time. The only way you can get to a point in time without using sync with backup is to stop all updates, perform a backup of both the Publisher and Distributor while no activity is occurring, and then allow activity again. Sync with backup is not an option for any other model of replication, nor is it available if your Publisher is another version of SQL Server (such as Microsoft SQL Server 7.0). To set this option, use the following syntax:

```
sp_replicationdboption 'publication_db', 'sync with backup', 'true'
```

This restricts the Log Reader Agent from sending any transactions at the Publisher to the Distributor's distribution database until they have been backed up. Although this creates a bit of latency that will be as frequent as your transaction log backups are made, it ensures that the Distributor will never get ahead of any Subscriber and both will be perfectly in sync. The last backup for the Publisher and Distributor can then be restored with identical transactions. On the distribution database, sync with backup prevents transactions that have not been backed up at the Distributor from being removed from the transaction log of the Publisher until the Distributor has been backed up. Your latency for transactional replication is dependent on the volume of transactions, the time it takes to complete the transaction log backup, and the frequency of the backup.

If you use this option, you need to back up the publication database and distribution databases (usually you would back up the transaction log or make differential backups) frequently because the frequency of backups determines the latency with which replication delivers changes to Subscribers.

If you try to restore the Publisher without setting sync with backup, your Publisher and Subscriber might be out of sync.

> **Tip**   If you want to see what transactions might not have yet been propagated to the distribution database, run DBCC OPENTRAN, and look for Oldest Distributed and Oldest Non-Distributed transactions. If these parameters exist, you are more than likely out of sync.

Subscriber

For a Subscriber, you should back up the subscription database. If you are using pull subscriptions, you should also back up msdb and master (if you are not doing so already) for replication purposes.

When using merge replication or transactional replication, restoration of a qualified Subscriber backup allows replication to continue normally. A non-qualified backup requires a reinitialization of the subscription after the backup is restored. For a merge backup to be qualified, it must be a backup from within the meta data cleanup interval. For a transactional replication backup to be a qualified backup, the publication must have the immediate_sync property set to true and the backup must be taken within the transaction retention period of the Distributor.

Note When setting the transaction retention period or meta data retention periods, you must consider the space and performance trade-offs.

To set the transaction retention period, follow these steps:

1. Select the Replication folder in SQL Server Enterprise Manager or a database participating in replication, and right-click it. Select the Configure Publishing, Subscribers, And Distribution … option.

2. When the Publisher And Distributor Properties dialog box appears (shown in Figure 8-5), make sure the Distributor tab is selected.

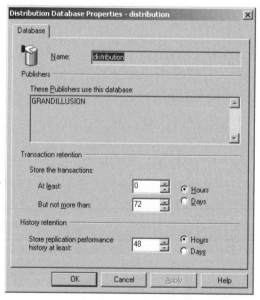

Figure 8-5 Publisher And Distributor Properties dialog box.

3. Select the correct distribution database, and click Properties.

4. Modify the transaction retention setting to the period for which you want to have a transaction stored in the distribution database. Remember that this has an impact on the size of your database, but it also ensures recoverability.

> **Note** If you want to modify the retention of the history of your replication, you can also do that here.

5. Click OK when you are done. Click Apply, and finally click OK to close the Publisher And Distributor Properties dialog box.

6. Modify any scheduled SQL Agent backup jobs configured on the database that are used to back it up so that you can recover from this scenario.

If you configure this, it guarantees that when you restore a Subscriber's database, all the transactions necessary for the Subscriber to catch up will still be available in the distribution database. After you restore the Subscriber, the Distribution Agent delivers any transactions the Subscriber is missing.

To set the merge meta data retention period, execute this stored procedure on the publication database:

```
sp_changepublication @publication= 'publication_name', @property=
'retention', @value=n
```

where n is number of hours, value for the retention property.

System Databases

Msdb contains all of the job definitions for the replication agents. With transactional replication, if you are using pull subscriptions, you have to back up this database on the Distributor and Subscriber if you add or drop a subscription or make any changes to the replication agent. If you are using Data Transformation Services (DTS) packages as part of transactional replication, you also need to back up msdb. Otherwise, you have to ensure that the DTS packages are saved to the file system and easily restorable. Here are some common actions that influence your msdb backups in relation to replication:

■   Enabling or disabling replication

■   Adding or dropping a distribution database (at the Distributor)

- Enabling or disabling a database for publishing (at the Publisher)
- Creating or modifying replication agent profiles (at the Distributor)
- Modifying any replication agent profile parameters (at the Distributor)
- Changing the replication agent properties (including schedules) for any push subscriptions (at the Distributor)
- Changing the replication agent properties (including schedules) for any pull subscriptions (at the Subscriber)

Each time you add a new Subscriber, the sysservers table is updated in master, so you have to back up master on your servers after you add a new Publisher or Subscriber. Here are some common actions that influence your master backups in relation to replication:

- Enabling or disabling replication
- Adding or dropping a distribution database (at the Distributor)
- Enabling or disabling a database for publishing (at the Publisher)
- Adding the first or dropping the last publication in any database (at the Publisher)
- Adding the first or dropping the last subscription in any database (at the Subscriber)
- Enabling or disabling a Publisher at a Distribution Publisher (at the Publisher and Distributor)
- Enabling or disabling a Subscriber at a Distribution Publisher (at the Subscriber and Distributor)

> **Important**   Remember that you cannot restore system databases onto another SQL Server instance if it has another name.

Disaster Recovery Restore Scenarios

Table 8-4 lists scenarios that you must consider if you ever need to restore your replication solution.

Table 8-4 Replication Disaster Recovery Scenarios

Scenario	Publisher	Distributor	Subscriber
1	Up	Up	Down
2	Up	Down	Up
3	Up	Down	Down
4	Down	Up	Up
5	Down	Up	Down
6	Down	Down	Up
7	Down	Down	Down

Scenario 1

Scenario 1 is the least problematic in terms of overall replication availability. Although users accessing the data from the Subscriber are affected, the processes driving replication are still intact. This does become a problem, however, is if this database also publishes data elsewhere. This underscores the point that the more complex your replication configuration, the more it affects any disaster recovery planning that involves replication.

When you restore the Subscriber database to the last good backup, assuming the database backup is made after replication was configured and contains the replication tables, you might not have to reinitialize the subscription. If possible, the subscription resynchronizes the data without requiring a reinitialization; however, you need to reinitialize the subscription if the data required to bring the Subscriber up to date has been cleaned up.

> **Note** This scenario obviously works with merge and transactional replication. Snapshot replication is a complete snapshot of your data (there is no way to do a "differential" snapshot like a differential backup), so modifying your replication settings if you are sending out all of your data each time makes no sense.

Scenarios 2 and 4

If you are using transactional replication and specify sync with backup on both the Publisher and Distributor, you can restore the Publisher or Distributor to the same point. If you are using merge replication and want to restore a Publisher, you have a few options. You could reinitialize all subscriptions with the restored publication database, but you might lose data at a Subscriber that was updated. You could also synchronize the Publisher with another database so it is fully in sync. If you choose the latter option, you must synchronize with a Subscriber that has a global subscription. If you use a Subscriber with anonymous subscriptions, it will not have enough meta data to apply the changes to the production database.

Scenario 3

If you lose both the Distributor and the Subscriber databases at the same time, the procedures outlined for Scenario 1 and Scenario 2 apply in most cases. Merge replication and queued are exceptions.

Scenario 5

If you lose both the publication and the subscription database at the same time, the procedures outlined for Scenarios 1 and 3 apply.

Scenario 6

This can happen if the Distributor is local (that is, the Publisher and Distributor are running on the same server). In this case, the Publisher and Distributor databases can be restored as outlined in Scenarios 2 and 4.

Scenario 7

This is the absolute worst-case scenario, in which every participating server is down for something other than a temporary reason. However, if the servers are genuinely damaged (for example, the datacenter burned down), you will be relying on the restore steps outlined for Scenarios 1, 2, and 4 to get your replication environment up and running again.

Log Shipping and Replication

Log shipping and replication can coexist, and in some cases, log shipping can be used to protect replication. However, you need to understand how these two features work together and the caveats of implementing them on the same databases.

> **Important**   You cannot use a log shipped secondary's database as part of an active replication environment (such as a Republisher or a Distributor) because it is in STANDBY or NORECOVERY. You can only use the database once it is fully recovered.

Both transactional and merge replication interoperate with log shipping. The main reason to use log shipping with replication in a highly available environment is to provide protection in the event of a Publisher failure. The secondary server can assume the Publisher's role if you meet all conditions, including the renaming of the server. If you cannot rename the server, you have to reinitialize all subscriptions.

> **Important**   If you use SQL Server 7.0 (with Service Pack 2) as your source, you cannot enable log shipping to work with a database that has replication.

Transactional Replication and Log Shipping

If the Publisher fails, you can use log shipping to protect it. This can only be configured between Microsoft SQL Server 2000 instances only; you cannot combine log shipping and replication if SQL Server 7.0 is the source. There are two modes that enable transactional replication to work with log shipping: synchronous and semisynchronous.

Synchronous Mode

Synchronous mode means that you are going to synchronize the various replication agents with your Publisher and Distributor backups using the Publisher and Distributor sync with backup options. The primary benefit of using synchronous mode is that in the event of a role change, your new Publisher (the old secondary) is completely synchronized with the backups. You do not have to worry about the Publisher, Distributor, and Subscriber being out of sync as long as the backups are completely applied after the restore. Note, however, that the restored Publisher will be missing any of the transactions that were not present in the backup.

> **Tip**   If you want to see what transactions might not have yet been propagated to the distribution database, run DBCC OPENTRAN, and look for Oldest Distributed and Oldest Non-Distributed transactions. If these parameters exist, you more than likely are out of sync.

Semisynchronous Mode

If your business needs dictate that the latency of synchronous mode is unacceptable, you can use semisynchronous mode instead. After a restore when using semisynchronous mode, the Publisher and the Subscribers are possibly out of sync because transactions that were on the old primary or Publisher might not have been backed up, sent, and applied to the warm standby. Despite this problem, you can get replication up and running after a role change. Once you perform the role change and the additional steps provided in the later section "Performing a Role Change Involving Replication," you must also run the `sp_replrestart` stored procedure. Once you run `sp_replrestart`, change the profile of the Distribution Agent to SkipError or set `-SkipError` on the command line at run time to ensure that transactions that exist at the Subscriber but not the Publisher can be reapplied to the Publisher.

`-SkipError` is required because the Publisher and Subscriber might be out of sync after issuing the `sp_replrestart` because the Publisher backup does not match the Subscriber state. If you do not specify `-SkipError`, additional failures could occur during replication. For example, if the Publisher has a row that the Subscriber does not yet have, then an update or delete to that row could cause a "not found" failure when replicated to a Subscriber. If the Publisher is missing a row that the Subscriber has, then an insert of a row with the same key could cause a "duplicate" failure when replicated to the Subscriber. Once the Publisher has been completely synchronized with the Subscribers again, you can disable the `-SkipError` option.

Merge Replication and Log Shipping

Like transactional replication, merge replication can use log shipping to protect the Publisher. You have two options for using merge replication with log shipping: semisynchronous mode and alternate synchronization partners.

Semisynchronous Mode

This is similar to the semisynchronous mode of transactional replication: your Publishers and Subscribers might be out of sync. If this is the case, you have only two real options. You can reinitialize the Subscribers to the new Publisher immediately after it is recovered, but this could cause data loss. The other option is to synchronize the Publisher with a Subscriber that has newer data.

Alternate Synchronization Partners

Subscribers of merge replication are able to use other servers besides the Publisher to synchronize their data. If the Publisher is down for some reason (planned or unplanned, including a log shipping role change), replication can continue uninterrupted. There are different methods of setting up alternate synchronization partners for named and unnamed subscriptions, and you can use Windows Synchronization Manager, Enterprise Manager, or the SQL Server merge replication ActiveX control to select your alternate synchronization partner. For a named subscription, you have to enable the Subscriber at the designated alternate synchronization partner and also create a subscription that is the same as the one on the current Publisher. If it is an unnamed subscription, set the alternate synchronization partner on the publication itself.

> **More Info**   For more information on alternate synchronization partners and how to enable them, see the topics "Alternate Synchronization Partners," "How Alternate Synchronization Partners Work," and "Optimizing Synchronization" in SQL Server Books Online.

Performing a Role Change Involving Replication

If you plan to use the secondary database after it is restored as a new primary (regardless of the model), you need to ensure that the *@keep_replication* option of the sp_change_secondary_role is set to 1 if you are using the functionality of Microsoft SQL Server 2000 Enterprise Edition. You also have to set the *@do_load* option to 1 as well; otherwise setting *@keep_replication* has no impact. If you do not set these parameters, all replication settings are erased when the database is recovered. If this is a custom implementation of log shipping, you need to set the WITH KEEP_REPLICATION option of the RESTORE LOG (or RESTORE DATABASE) functionality. Using WITH KEEP_REPLICATION is not possible with databases restored with NORECOVERY, so if you are using replication, make sure you restore your database with STANDBY.

> **More Info**   To see the exact steps for performing a log shipping role change, see the section "Performing a Role Change" in Chapter 7, "Log Shipping."

In addition to the normal role change process, there are a few additional steps that you need to add after the database is recovered:

1. If you recover a database from secondary status to be the active database servicing requests, you do not need to reapply a SQL Server 2000 service pack unless there are meta data changes that would affect the database in question (as noted earlier). This would be clearly documented in the documentation that ships as part of the update. An exception to this rule occurs if you are using replication and use the KEEP_REPLICATION option when bringing the database online. Once the database is fully recovered, before opening it up to users and applications, run the `sp_vupgrade_replication` stored procedure to upgrade the replication meta data. If you do not do this, the replication meta data for that database will be out of sync. If running `sp_vupgrade_replication` is not necessary, it should be noted in the accompanying documentation.

2. You have to rename the secondary server to be the same as the original primary. This affects you in a few ways. First and foremost, you cannot use a clustered instance of SQL Server 2000 as your primary or secondary, as you cannot rename them. Second, if you want to eventually perform a role change back to the original primary, you cannot have two servers of the same name in the same domain.

> **Tip**   You can mitigate this using Network Load Balancing like you would to abstract the role change. That way anything connecting to the underlying SQL Server would only have to know about the name to connect to, which is the Network Load Balancing cluster. Again, this is a very specific use of Network Load Balancing with SQL Server and is not meant for load balancing. See the section "Implementing Network Load Balancing for SQL Server–Based Architectures" in Chapter 5, "Designing Highly Available Microsoft Windows Servers," for information on setting up this solution.

Summary

Replication can be used to enable high availability through data redundancy by storing your application data in more than one database. When deploying replication to solve problems other than high availability, you should still consider the impact of a failure on the replicated system and plan accordingly by combining a sound backup strategy and replication retention periods. There is no easy solution when it comes to replication and high availability, but combining replication with the other technologies covered in this book can make your environment more highly available.

9

Database Environment Basics for Recovery

Whether you implement failover clustering, log shipping, replication, or a combination of these, they cannot supplant a solid backup and recovery plan. Things can—and will—go wrong. Even a well-planned highly available system is subject to user error, administrative error, procedural failure, or a catastrophic hardware failure. Creating, testing, and maintaining a database environment in which little to no data is lost and downtime is entirely avoided in a disaster is no trivial task. Because backup and restore are important, required parts of any disaster recovery plan, your backup and restore strategy should minimize both data loss and downtime. This chapter gives you the basic understanding to be able to proceed to Chapter 10, "Implementing Backup and Restore," where you learn how to implement a backup and restore plan in your environment.

Fundamentals

No matter what size the database or the availability requirements, restore is always an option. In some cases, such as in the event of accidental data modifications or deletions, it is the only option that lets you restore the database to the state it was in before the modification. But what does it mean to have a backup and restore strategy focused on high availability?

To be focused on high availability you must be focused on whether or not the system is accessible and, if it is not, on how long it will be down. A successful disaster recovery plan lets you recover your database within your company's defined acceptable amount of downtime and data loss. If downtime must be kept to an absolute minimum, the key requirement for your backup strategy is recovery speed. How do you make your recovery fast? Are there database and server settings that can impact the recovery of your database? What options must be determined as part of your strategy? There are many possible backup and restore strategies, each of which offers different levels of trade-offs between hardware costs, administrative complexity, potential work loss exposure (data loss in the event of a failure), performance during the backup, performance of batch operations or maintenance operations, as well as day-to-day performance of user operations around the clock. Finally, the options that you choose to employ could also have effects on the transaction log in terms of active size, backup size, and whether log backups are negatively affected during other operations.

For example, did you know that log backups are paused while a full backup is running? Do you know the impact of pausing log backups on other features that depend on frequent log backups, such as log shipping? Do you know what else could go wrong if the log backup does not occur? The decisions you make here are truly critical to the overall success of your recovery plan. But where do you start?

Technology Last

First, you must know the barriers for which backup and restore will be the solution. This helps you determine where you are at risk. Second, you must know your environment. Knowing your data; the database structures; how the data is being used; changes made to database settings throughout the day, week, or month; and the acceptable amount of downtime and data loss (which could vary at different times of day) is important. You must be familiar with user, administrative, and batch processes so that you are aware of all that could fail and what was happening at the time of the failure. This information will help you estimate how much time is acceptable for repair and recovery, which in turn helps to dictate your hardware choices. Third, you must have a recovery-oriented plan that fully aligns with the process of database recovery and the restoration phases.

Using these key facts, you can decide among the backup types available and come up with the best strategy for your environment. Only after you fully understand each one of these factors should you determine which backup strategy is best. Unfortunately, administrators commonly define backup strategies by learning only the backup technologies available without considering recovery. This is exactly the wrong approach; instead, you should consider technology last and recovery first. If you do not have a recovery-oriented plan, you will more than likely suffer data loss and significant downtime.

Understanding Your Backup and Restore Barriers

Whether you are recovering from accidental data deletion, hardware failure, natural disaster, or other unplanned incident, you will want your recovery to be well thought out. There are really two categories of barriers that are likely to be overcome with your backup and restore strategy: hardware failure and application or user error.

Hardware Failure

You should not use backups to recover from hardware failure as a common practice, as it is likely your system already has hardware redundancy in place. Whether you are trying to set up a highly available server or just a production database server, you should always start by using some form of disk redundancy, such as RAID. In Chapter 4, "Disk Configuration for High Availability," you looked at many disk considerations for the foundation of your database, and it is likely you have chosen some form of mirroring, striped mirrors, or striping with parity. However, what if you lose an entire RAID array? What if a single disk is lost in a RAID 5 set and the administrator replaces the wrong disk during the hot swap to replace the failed disk? In the case of hardware failure, you might choose to minimize downtime by bringing a secondary or standby server online; however, you will need to recover the failed primary. Often, this is done with backups.

User Error

You might think that your job would be great if there were no users or even other DBAs or system administrators. Quite frankly, no human intervention of any sort would be preferable for most! If you could create a database and then *never* use it, it would be much easier to manage. Nevertheless, if users can modify data, inevitably someone at some time will modify something incorrectly. Similarly, if system administrators have direct access to the production server, they have the ability to directly change your production data. In Chapter 14, "Administrative Tasks to Increase Availability," you will look at the administrative processes that should be in place to maintain and secure a highly available system, but even with extensive preparations, accidents will happen. In fact, accidental damage is the most difficult from which to recover and it can spread much further than just an incorrectly dropped table. Application, user, and process error could occur almost anywhere. Examples include the following scenarios:

- Administrators or database owners (DBOs) dropping a table incorrectly because they are connected to their production and development databases all day long—within the same tools.

- Users accidentally modifying the wrong data because they have direct base table permission to INSERT, UPDATE, and DELETE, and although they normally remember a WHERE clause, they forget to highlight it when executing their query.

- Batch processes accidentally dropping the wrong database because the script performs a drop and re-create of the database. It is the first time the script is being run on that server, where a different database—named the same as the other database but supporting different functionality—already exists.

- Batch processes accidentally creating objects or making changes to the wrong database because the initial database creation fails due to a path error or a not enough disk space error. With little or no error handling in the script, it continues to run incorrectly in the wrong database. All of the script's objects end up in the connected user's default database, which in this case is set to the master database.

All of these scenarios are possible, and these few examples are really only the tip of the iceberg. More important than the original failure is the recovery process that follows. Incorrect data modifications are the most difficult to recover from because the longer any problem is left unmanaged, the more likely you are to lose data. Additionally, the longer you wait, the more difficult it is to recover the data from the still potentially changing database.

How quickly do your users come running down the hall or pick up the phone to tell you about their accidental data deletion? Does the DBA immediately refer to the disaster recovery plan when he or she makes a mistake, or does he or she try to troubleshoot the problem, possibly compounding it? What is the best plan of recovery and, more important, how can you prevent some of these mistakes from happening in the first place?

Minimizing Human Error

To make a system both secure and highly available, you need to have administrative change control as well as maintenance processes in place to minimize direct access to production databases. There is a common question asked by DBAs: Is there a way that SQL Server system administrators can be prevented from dropping tables? This sometimes garners the answer, "Get new system administrators." All kidding aside, this can and does happen. This problem is so common that many system administrators have learned quite a few tricks, and the next several paragraphs include a few ideas—not specific to backup and restore—picked up from them along the way.

To prevent tables from being incorrectly dropped, consider schema-bound views using declarative referential integrity (DRI), which makes inadvertently dropping a table more difficult. However, DRI prevents a dropped table only when the table is being referenced with a foreign key constraint. A sales table, for example, often references other tables, but other tables do not always reference it. So how can you prevent an accidental table drop? Consider using a schema-bound view. If a view is created with SCHEMABINDING, then the table's structure cannot be altered (for all columns listed in the view), and the table cannot be dropped (unless the view is dropped first).

> **More Info**   For details on how to create schema-bound views in Microsoft SQL Server, see Instant DocID#22073 on the *SQL Server Magazine* Web site at *http://www.sqlmag.com*. This article does not require a subscription.

To prevent data from being incorrectly modified, consider eliminating all direct access to the base tables. Often having applications designed to manipulate the data are best; however, users might then require direct ad hoc access to your data. Is it really necessary? This requirement usually indicates that the users are not getting the information they need and the developers gave up. Regardless, creating boundaries within the ad hoc environment is better than complete chaos that is marked by bad queries, poor performance, and unhappy users. Instead of granting direct access (SELECT, INSERT, UPDATE, and DELETE) to the base tables, create views, stored procedures, and functions to handle the data access. Using these objects, you can add error handling, trap unwanted change, manage data redundancy, and generally prevent accidental modifications where a WHERE clause has been left off inadvertently.

If this seems like a lot of work, you might be surprised at the secondary benefits. Typically when users write ad hoc queries, performance suffers because of mistakes in writing Transact-SQL. Users who do not write a lot of Transact-SQL code are prone to writing poorly performing code. You can optimize objects through the development and quality assurance testing of the views, procedures, and functions, providing a better outcome for everyone.

Finally, to prevent mistakes in batch processing, consider error handling and a scheduled code review with all key personnel. The code review allows other experienced DBAs to determine if anything could interfere with what they are responsible for. Additionally, another set of eyes to review the batch could prevent something that might otherwise be a problem with running the batch in the existing environment. This need not be a line-by-line code review (although it could be), but it should at least explain the general principles behind the script's execution. Give special attention to all components of the script that drop or modify already existing data, objects, or databases. If the script includes proper error handling, the time for the code review could be reduced.

As a trick in batch processing, consider using RAISERROR. There is a special value for the state parameter of RAISERROR that might help by forcing the termination of a complex script and preventing further execution when the script is processing incorrectly. Raising an error with a state of 127 causes the script to stop processing, and this can be especially helpful when the script might end up processing in the wrong database. However, setting the state value does not always appear to terminate the session. Applications such as SQL Server Query Analyzer might automatically reconnect when a connection is broken. To fully realize the benefit of the state option, you need to use a tool such as Osql.exe, which does not reconnect automatically after the connection is terminated.

> **More Info**   For details on some of the benefits of using RAISERROR in your Transact-SQL statements, see Instant DocID#22980 on the Web at *http://www.sqlmag.com*. This article does not require a subscription.

However, be aware that nothing is guaranteed. Even if you prevent many errors using these techniques, the database probably will still need to be recovered after some form of human or application error.

Symptoms and Recovery

Recovering a database after hardware failures or incorrect data modifications can be quite complex, as there are numerous elements that can fail. Even more numerous are the options for recovery. The failure might be isolated to one disk, one RAID array, one table, a group of tables, or only part of the data. Remember, to create a strategy for high availability you want to recover as fast as possible. If the damage is isolated, can your restore and recovery be isolated? Possibly, if you plan for it.

Backup

Before creating your backup strategy, there are a few key facts to know about how SQL Server works with regard to backup and recovery. First and foremost, there is no need for a traditional backup window. Backups can occur concurrently with other operations and while users are online actively changing the data. Backups have very little impact on the existing workload, as they do not rely on reading the active data (this is discussed in detail later). Additionally, backups run as fast as the hardware allows and they are self-tuning.

With this in mind, you might wonder why you cannot just perform backups constantly, and when one completes, begin another. There are many reasons why this might or might not be a good idea, and this is what this chapter is about: knowing the basics before you implement your backup and restore plan. More important, are you familiar with the technology? Are you aware that some backups conflict with some administrative operations? For example, when performing a full database backup, you can neither change the database's file and filegroup structure (either manually or through autogrow options) nor back up the transaction log. These limitations might prove significant as you review possible backup strategies.

Understanding Database Structures

Every database has a data portion and a log portion. When you define the database you must create a log—whether you want one or not—and you cannot turn logging off. In fact, SQL Server creates a transaction log file for you if one is not specified. When the size of the log is not specified, the default size varies between the syntax and the Enterprise Manager dialogs so it is important to explicitly state the size (the Create Database dialog uses a default of 1 MB for the transaction log and the CREATE DATABASE syntax defaults to 25 percent of the total size of the data portion; neither is usually appropriate). However, sizing the transaction log is not easy, as there are numerous factors on which the log size is based. One of the most important is related to backup.

> **Warning**   Do not use file system compression with SQL Server data files, as it is not supported. When SQL Server writes to the transaction log, it needs to guarantee sector-aligned writes. When using compressed volumes, SQL Server loses the ability to guarantee exact placement of data within a sector (a sector is 512 bytes, and SQL Server writes in 8 KB blocks). Putting SQL Server data files on compressed volumes has resulted in lost data. For more information, review Microsoft Knowledge Base article 231347, "INF: SQL Server Databases Not Supported on Compressed Volumes," found at *http://support.microsoft.com.*

Understanding the Write-Ahead Log

When modifications are written to the database, SQL Server goes through a series of steps to ensure consistency and recovery. To ensure consistency, SQL Server takes the necessary locks; to ensure recovery, SQL Server writes information to the transaction log portion of the database. A simplified version of the process is described in the following steps and text. Although this version is simplified, it will give you a good understanding of how the log is defined as a write-ahead log and why it is important for both SQL Server and manual recovery.

1. A user submits a single data modification statement—for example, an update. This update will affect five rows out of the one million rows within that table. This is considered an implicit transaction as all five rows need to be modified or the transaction will not be complete.

2. SQL Server begins the modification by taking update locks on all of the rows required (there are other locks at the page level, table level, and database level; however, for this example, they are not significant). An update lock is an interesting lock that represents someone who has the intent to modify but has not yet modified the row. SQL Server can proceed to perform the changes only after all update locks on all rows involved take place. Although the rows have only the update lock (as SQL Server is repeating Step 3 for each row), rows with an update lock are accessible to readers, allowing better concurrency.

3. Modifying the data actually occurs in a number of steps. For each row, SQL Server follows this process:

   a. It obtains the exclusive lock, which is sometimes referred to as X. To perform the actual data modification, SQL Server must guarantee that no one else can see this data (that is, no one can access this "dirty" and uncommitted data). To do so, a stricter lock is required (an exclusive lock). The exclusive lock specifies that only *this* transaction can access this data exclusively until the transaction no longer needs it (once the transaction is committed).

   b. SQL Server modifies the row (performs the modification as defined by the modification statement).

   c. It logs the modification to the transaction log (which for this modification might solely be in memory at this point). However, once all of the rows have been modified, the next step is to commit this transaction and make it recoverable.

4. Once all of the modifications have been performed, the transaction is ready to commit. The process of committing the changes also occurs in a number of steps:

   a. SQL Server writes the changes to the transaction log on disk (this might have already happened, but if any of the log pages on which this transaction resides are still in memory, they are written at this point).

   b. It releases the locks.

   c. It notifies the client that the modifications are complete. The user receives the "5 Rows Affected" message.

This information is interesting, because it shows that there is a time when information about a transaction is only in memory (Step 3) and another time when it is both in memory and its log changes are on disk (Step 4). When does the data make it to the data portion of the database? A separate process synchronizes changes from memory to their appropriate locations on disk. This process, called a *checkpoint*, really exists to synchronize *all* dirty pages with their appropriate location on disk, regardless of the state of the transaction (this is one of the reasons a log page might have already been written to disk before Step 4). Log pages are always written ahead of data pages, and in many cases it might be minutes ahead. A checkpoint is a batch operation (not to be confused with a bulk operation) that allows modified pages to be written to disk quickly in batches rather than as they occur. How long does it wait? That is dependent on SQL Server, and even though you can change this, it is not recommended.

More Info If you are interested in learning more about this configuration option, check out the Recovery Interval setting in SQL Server Books Online and in the Microsoft Knowledge Base.

The checkpoint process is batched to minimize thrashing to disk, as some data pages might change due to numerous transactions over a short period of time. Instead of writing those pages to disk as they occur, the checkpoint batches them, minimizing the writes to disk. However, to guarantee a user that his or her transaction is in the database, even if there is a power failure (remember, the user has received the "5 Rows Affected" message), SQL Server writes transaction log information at the commit of a transaction. This allows the transaction log activity to be predominantly sequential writes and the data portion (except at checkpoint) to be more random reads (yes, some users read large sequential amounts of data, but with numerous users it is more random).

In summary, this is why the transaction log is called a write-ahead log. The log information is written to disk on the commit of a transaction ahead of the data. The data is written later during a checkpoint. To improve performance, you can always place the transaction log portion of your database on a dedicated disk. This can improve performance, and it is also important for recovery because it allows you to set different options for the drives on which these files are located. So how does this apply to backup and restore in terms of recovery?

For databases to recover from incidents like power failure, transactional information must be available. The transaction log provides this set of instructions, which can be used in recovery. The instructions contain what has changed within your database, and this always gets you from one version of the data to another, not unlike how driving directions get you from one location to another. Have you ever wanted to tell someone how to get somewhere? When you are talking to them you always start with a point of reference. For example, starting at X, you take Y to Z, and so on. The same is true for the transaction log. All transaction log entries act as instructions based on how the data looked at the time. To use those instructions, the system must have the data in the same state as it was in at the time, or the instructions will not make sense.

There are really two purposes for the transaction log. Automatic Recovery is SQL Server's primary use for the transaction log. Automatic Recovery occurs each time SQL Server is started to ensure transactional consistency. If transactions were being processed when the server was stopped, SQL Server can recover those changes by accessing the log when the server restarts. This ensures that only committed transactions are within the database and uncommitted transactions are rolled back. SQL Server recovers system databases and then user databases at startup. Automatic Recovery first reads the log and goes through a phase called redo (roll forward). During this phase, the transaction log is read to find all of the changes and perform them, loading the information into the cache. Once redo is finished, SQL Server performs the undo phase. During this phase, SQL Server rolls back any changes that do not have a corresponding commit. If the server was shut down properly this should process very quickly; however, if the server suffered a power failure or improper shutdown, Automatic Recovery might take significantly longer.

During Automatic Recovery, SQL Server needs to see the instructions about the changes that are kept in the transaction log if they have not yet made it into the data portion of the database on disk. Remember, at Step 4 (above), the transaction is partially on disk and partially in memory. Specifically, the instructions about the change are in the transaction log on disk and the result of the data changes is in the data portion of the database in memory. Once the transaction log has been read and all steps have been processed through redo and undo, the last step of Automatic Recovery is performing a checkpoint. This synchronizes memory to disk to ensure that all changes processed by Automatic Recovery are on disk and would not need to be processed again if the server were to suffer another power failure. Once recovery completes, SQL Server makes the database available.

Once the checkpoint process synchronizes that information to disk, SQL Server no longer needs the information for Automatic Recovery. In fact, SQL Server even allows you to set an option to clear the information if you choose to. However, this is where the secondary benefit of having the transaction log can be seen: manual recovery. You might need to perform manual recovery if the database is damaged.

> **Important**   Although secondary to SQL Server, the advantage of being able to do a manual recovery is the most important reason to keep the transaction log and not let SQL Server clear it.

This is another reason the transaction log should be created on a physical disk that is separate from the data portion of the database. By keeping these instructions in the transaction log, you can set up a process to capture these changes later, potentially even when the data portion of the database has been damaged. To capture these changes, you perform transaction log backups. In the event of a failure that renders the database inaccessible or corrupts the data in the database (due to application or human error), having the transaction log backed up gives you something external to the corrupted database from which you can recover, potentially even up to the time (or just prior to the time) at which the database became corrupt. In fact, you can perform backups of the transaction log at periodic intervals. Each one will act as a set of directions to get you from one point to another. The more frequently you capture these instructions, the closer and closer you can get without directly accessing the original data.

In total, a complete sequence of log backups can get you from various starting points up to the time of a failure, especially if you have the final set of instructions. Once you have captured these instructions, SQL Server removes the inactive instructions (instructions from transactions still being processed cannot be removed) from the transaction log portion of the database. This helps to maintain the overall size of the transaction log. Second, by frequently capturing these instructions, you create smaller backups. In turn, these smaller transaction log backups can be performed with little impact on users. Because the transaction log is critical to recovery, you should make an effort to make it as efficient as possible.

Optimizing the Performance of the Transaction Log

The log portion of the database should have exactly one file (maximum number of total files—both data and log—is 32,767); there is rarely a need for more than one transaction log because you will not see any performance benefits. More than one transaction log could be useful only if your log needs to span multiple volumes. If you have more than one file based on capacity alone, you should consider increasing the frequency of transaction log backups so that a buildup of instructions does not occur. Also, consider using hardware RAID to handle the increased need for capacity over having multiple log files. Increasing the frequency of log backups not only minimizes the need for a large transaction log, it also minimizes your potential data loss exposure.

Because the transaction log is critical in most recovery scenarios, it is also important to make sure that the drive on which the transaction log resides is also on some form of RAID. RAID 1 mirroring is acceptable if the transaction log is not overly active. For extremely active transaction logs where disk activity queues or where performance is not optimal, consider using a combination of mirroring and striping (preferably striped mirrors) for the transaction log. This might mean giving a significant amount of disk space to a relatively small amount of information, but therein lies the trade-off of disk space versus performance (and possibly availability).

Even if the transaction log is only one physical file, as recommended, SQL Server maintains that file internally as multiple virtual log files (VLFs). At the creation of a database, the transaction log is divided into multiple VLFs. SQL Server determines the size of the VLFs, which is not generally interesting to the typical administrator. However, you should be concerned with how many VLFs get created because you do not want to create fragmentation and noncontiguous log access. If the transaction log size was properly estimated during capacity planning and the database was set up with the appropriate size when it was created, the number of VLFs will be optimized for the size of the file. If the file was properly created at the correct size it will have very few VLFs.

For example, a 1-GB transaction log will have only eight VLFs. Again, having an optimal number of VLFs is based on the file being initially created at (and not autogrowing to) 1 GB. If the file is added at only 100 MB and grows to 1 GB, you end up with significantly more VLFs; in fact, at least one VLF for each autogrowth. With a transaction log that grows automatically by 10 percent, starting the transaction log at 100 MB and growing it to 1 GB would create roughly 25 VLFs instead of 8. (In some cases you might see hundreds of VLFs when autogrow is growing by a smaller amount, more frequently.) Having more than the necessary number of VLFs adds overhead both in terms of backup performance and transaction log performance (logging).

To minimize the number of VLFs, you need to define the transaction log size appropriately (or at least reasonably) at creation. For the databases where files are set to autogrow, you can also minimize the number of VLFs by setting the autogrowth size to a reasonable fixed number of megabytes (the default is 10 percent, but this requires calculation, as it might not be enough). Additionally, transactions processing at the time of autogrowth are paused (or blocked) and might time-out based on your client settings. Instead, actively monitoring your transaction logs, performing frequent transaction log backups, and minimizing long-running transactions gives you a more appropriate number of VLFs and better performance.

To see the number of VLFs your database's log file has, execute DBCC LOGINFO.

> **Caution**   DBCC LOGINFO is an undocumented READ ONLY command that displays information about the transaction log. There is no guarantee that it will work as defined here in future releases.

For the purpose of this discussion, all you are interested in is the number of rows—this indicates the number of VLFs. If you have more than 16 VLFs, you should consider trying to consolidate them. The best way to do this is to clear the transaction log with a regular transaction log backup (if being performed), then shrink the transaction log with a DBCC command and then finally, manually set the size to the more appropriate size through one execution of ALTER DATABASE (instead of numerous autogrowths).

In Microsoft SQL Server 2000, shrinking the transaction log *should* occur easily by performing a regular transaction log backup and then using DBCC SHRINKFILE (*logfilename*, TRUNCATEONLY) to shrink the transaction log to the smallest possible size. Immediately following the SHRINKFILE, execute ALTER DATABASE, and increase the transaction log's size as appropriate. Make sure to set the maximum size to a finite value instead of allowing it to be unlimited. Additionally, you should make sure to monitor the log size and create both jobs and alerts to regularly manage the transaction log.

Understanding Continuity of the Transaction Log

Even though recommended recovery strategies are discussed later, along with how the different backups work, it is important to make sure that you completely understand the importance of maintaining continuity of the transaction log. The database's transaction log contains instructions and a transaction log backup allows those changes to be recorded in another location (a backup device). When a transaction log is backed up, SQL Server can clear much of what was backed up because it no longer needs the information for Automatic Recovery. Due to this clearing (or truncation), transaction log backups are usually instructions only since the last log backup (there is an option that allows you to back up a transaction log and not clear it; however, this is not the default and it is typically used only in special circumstances). Other backups do not affect the transaction log; only transaction log backups manage the transaction log.

Take the following example in which full database backups are represented as F_1 and F_2 and 20 transaction log backups are shown as l_1 through l_{20}. Consider the group of backups, starting with each of the full database backups, as a recovery set. One recovery set begins with F_2 and the previous begins with F_1.

$$\mathbf{F_1}\ l_1\ l_2\ l_3\ l_4\ l_5\ l_6\ l_7\ l_8\ l_9\ l_{10}\ l_{11}\ l_{12}\ \mathbf{F_2}\ l_{13}\ l_{14}\ l_{15}\ l_{16}\ l_{17}\ l_{18}\ l_{19}\ l_{20}$$

This example shows a total of 22 backups. With these two recovery sets you have created multiple recovery paths. The optimal recovery path would be to recover with the last full database backup and then apply all of the remaining transaction log backups.

$$\mathbf{F_2}\ l_{13}\ l_{14}\ l_{15}\ l_{16}\ l_{17}\ l_{18}\ l_{19}\ l_{20}$$

What if the full database backup F_2 were bad? Do you have any other options? Yes, you do. This is the beauty of the design of both the transaction log and transaction log backups. If the full database backup at F_2 is bad, you can recover using the F_1 full database backup instead. At F_1 you can apply the entire series of transaction log backups in sequence and still recover up to transaction log l_{20}. If recovery from F_1 was desired, the restore sequence would be as follows:

$$\mathbf{F_1}\ l_1\ l_2\ l_3\ l_4\ l_5\ l_6\ l_7\ l_8\ l_9\ l_{10}\ l_{11}\ l_{12}\ \quad l_{13}\ l_{14}\ l_{15}\ l_{16}\ l_{17}\ l_{18}\ l_{19}\ l_{20}$$

In fact, even if the full database backup F1 was bad, you could go back to the previous full database backup—assuming it is still available and all of the transaction log backups are accessible—and you could still roll forward to the last transaction log backup at l_{20}.

Many interesting observations stem from this example. As transaction log backups are performed, SQL Server completes the backup by essentially clearing (truncating) what was backed up (with the exception of that which is still active). Transaction log backups have a very specific sequence to them and you must perform recovery using *all* transaction logs. Each and every transaction log must be applied in sequence; if one is not available, the recovery process cannot move forward. More important, even when other backups are performed, they do not affect the continuity of the transaction log. The full database backup performed at F_2 can be skipped as though it had not occurred, and recovery can occur seamlessly by beginning with the full database backup F_1 and then restoring all of the transaction logs from l_1 through l_{20}.

You can learn numerous lessons from this discussion. First and foremost, transaction log backups are the most critical backups to have in a recovery scenario. If a transaction log backup is damaged, the last successfully loaded transaction log will be the final transaction log backup to which you can recover. In fact, you might even consider creating multiple copies of your transaction log backups or mirroring them to multiple backup devices. That said, with certain backup hardware you might be able to back up transaction logs to multiple devices simultaneously. In Figure 9-1, a single transaction log backup is written to four tapes.

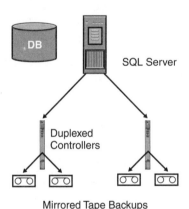

SQL Server

Duplexed
Controllers

Mirrored Tape Backups

Figure 9-1   Duplexed and mirrored transaction logs.

It is also important that you keep more than one set of backups on hand. Before you discard a recovery set's starting point (that is, before you discard a full database backup), you should test the recovery set you are keeping. To ensure comprehensive recovery of a database during a restore you must have a *complete* sequence of all transaction logs up to the time of the failure or the point in time to which you want to recover. Having all of these logs gives you continuity. Anything that breaks the continuity of the log causes that to be the last log you can apply.

Other operations could affect the continuity of the transaction log, but they are not recommended when you want to recover from the transaction log. In fact, in a production transaction-processing database, the only operation that should ever truncate a transaction log is a transaction log backup. When this is true and you maintain transaction log continuity, you have added redundancy to your backup strategy.

What If the Transaction Log Fills?

Nothing is certain, and even with precautions the transaction log could still fill. This might not seem like it could be problematic but it is very important to realize that a full transaction log translates to downtime. When the transaction log is full, the database stops all modifications, and any transactions pending at the time the log fills are rolled back. Additionally, new modifications are not allowed. By most definitions this is downtime. The database is available, but only for read operations. No new modifications are allowed until space is made available. The correct—and simple—response to the full transaction log is to perform a backup of the transaction log so that SQL Server can clear the inactive portion of the transaction log (something that occurs as part of a transaction log backup).

In previous releases of SQL Server, a special command was used in this scenario, but it was mainly because of how previous versions were designed. When the transaction log filled, there was no room for SQL Server to mark (or log) the fact that the transaction log was being backed up. Because of this, transaction log backups were not allowed when the transaction log filled. The special clause WITH NO_LOG had to be added to the BACKUP LOG command to clear the log without backing it up. In Microsoft SQL Server 7.0, this was fixed and BACKUP LOG now works for most transaction logs, even when they are full.

For those of you experienced with previous releases, this might come as quite a shock, but this reaction—to flush the transaction log when it fills—is not only the *wrong* response, it should be avoided! If you flush the log, you are doing something worse than just throwing it away: you are breaking the continuity of the transaction log. In fact, in SQL Server 7.0 or SQL Server 2000, the BACKUP LOG with the NO_LOG option is really no longer necessary; it has become synonymous with BACKUP LOG WITH TRUNCATE_ONLY. You should never need either of these commands in a properly maintained database.

However, because so many people have this improper response to a transaction log filling, which is usually automated with a SQL Server Agent job, a trace flag was added. Trace flag 3231 makes *both* of these backup commands benign. You can turn on a trace flag in multiple ways. First, you can set it as a startup parameter. The easiest way to do this is through the Enterprise Manager. Right-click your server and choose Properties. In the General Tab, click Startup Parameters. In the Startup Parameters tab, enter **-T3231** in the Parameter text box and then click Add. This will be set the next time you restart SQL Server. If you want to turn off the trace flag permanently you can remove the startup parameter. If you want to turn off the trace flag temporarily you can just execute DBCC TRACEOFF(3231). This statement turns the trace flag off until you turn it back on with DBCC TRACEON(3231) or until you restart your server (if it still remains a startup parameter).

Trace flag 3231 protects the continuity of the transaction log from common and inappropriate reactions to a full transaction log. In fact, with this trace flag turned on neither of the following commands

```
BACKUP LOG dbname WITH NO_LOG
```

```
BACKUP LOG dbname WITH TRUNCATE_ONLY
```

does anything in databases where the recovery model is set to Full or Bulk-Logged. In fact, these commands are so unnecessary that the trace flag makes them behave as if the BACKUP LOG WITH ... commands execute successfully (so that automated batches do not fail), but both commands are turned into a no operation (NO-OP). With this trace flag turned on, you can ensure that the continuity is never broken by an improperly executed backup log command, minimizing the potential for human error. However, the transaction log will still be full and you still have to take the appropriate actions to resolve this.

> **Caution**   Even if the continuity of the transaction log is broken, there are cases where subsequent log backups do not generate an error and are allowed. Even if a warning message is produced, it is likely to go unnoticed if transaction log backups occur through scheduled operations that continue automatically.

Unfortunately, there are rare cases when backing up the log might not be possible. Even then you still have options. If a normal transaction log backup does not work or it is going to take too much time (therefore causing downtime; remember, the database is unavailable until space is available), there are two options. The best of them would be to add space to the size of the trans-action log. There are three ways to do this: allow autogrowth, manually increase the size, or add another file to the transaction log. The easiest way is to allow the transaction log to increase through autogrowth, but make sure to set a predetermined maximum size so it does not use all disk space, and always monitor it (especially with Administrative Alerts). If the transaction log still fills, then you need to reevaluate the maximum and manually increase the size while setting a new maximum size. If the maximum is unlimited and you are out of disk space, temporarily adding another file to the log to get back up and run-ning quickly is the best choice (and can often be the fastest, especially when the size of the file being added is significantly smaller than the current size of the transaction log). If you add a file, you should remove it once the transaction log has been backed up properly. To remove this file you can use DBCC SHRINKFILE with the EMPTYFILE option; this causes SQL Server to stop using this file for transaction log extent allocations. Once the file is properly emptied, it can be removed with the ALTER DATABASE REMOVE file option.

The other option, which is never recommended if recoverability or avail-ability is a goal, is to flush the information that is currently in the transaction log. You should always remove the inactive entries from the transaction log with a transaction log backup. If you choose to clear the log and not back it up (maybe because nothing else is working, as you have no free space and no additional disks on which you can create another file and seemingly nothing else to do), then you will have broken the continuity of the transaction log and need to create a backup that does not require transaction log backups—either a full database backup, a differential database backup, or a complete set of file or filegroup backups (a new recovery set).

It is very important that you create a backup after the continuity of the transaction log is broken. If your database becomes corrupt before you have a chance to create a new recovery set, a disaster would possibly cause a loss of data. Without a new recovery set, the backups you have can only restore up to the last successful transaction log backup performed before the continuity of the log was broken. Every transaction log backup performed after the continu-ity of the log was broken is useless. Having a new full database backup or dif-ferential database backup allows you to get your system back up and running, which is the most important thing. However, you have lost the ability to go back to the previous recovery set and move beyond where the continuity of the log has been broken (with the exception of differential backups) and move for-ward. At this point, you have lost some redundancy in your backup strategy and it is even more important that this backup is protected and tested. This is an important point when reviewing the pros and cons of various backup strategies!

Important   Remember, although SQL Server provides functionality to truncate (clear) the transaction log and it is very easy to do, clearing the transaction log significantly compromises your available options during recovery. If you do truncate the transaction log, immediately perform the correct backups to create a new recovery set. Simply put, you must follow this operation with a full or differential database backup, or a complete set of full or differential file or filegroup backups.

Breaking the Continuity of the Transaction Log

In well-maintained databases, meaning those that have a well-planned backup and restore strategy and effective log monitoring, and databases for which capacity planning and testing have defined an appropriately sized transaction log, operations that clear the transaction log—other than normal log backups—should never occur. In fact, it is critical to understand what operations should not be performed. The following operations break the continuity of the log:

- Clearing the log with

  - BACKUP LOG *dbname* WITH TRUNCATE_ONLY

  - BACKUP LOG *dbname* WITH NO_LOG

- Changing the recovery model to Simple

- Discarding a transaction log backup (by overwriting it or deleting the file)

- Having a transaction log backup become corrupt

All but the last operation are controllable. Corruption of a transaction backup log is hard to control, but performing transaction log backups to hard disk is usually safer than using tape, as tapes have a higher rate of error. Mirroring the backup device (either disk or tape) where the transaction log backups are written can significantly reduce the chance of corruption. Finally, there are additional backup types that can also minimize the reliance on a significant number of transaction log backups in sequence (that is, differential). In fact, there are numerous precautions you can take when managing backups of the transaction log.

Properly Managing the Transaction Log

Proper maintenance of the transaction log is, obviously, critical to keeping the database up and running. Additionally, proper management keeps the transaction log size smaller and eliminates the need for emergency operations that could compromise your recovery. Performing more frequent log backups is the best way to minimize the potential for data loss. However, there are a few key things that could make backups of the transaction log more difficult. It is very important that you understand how the transaction log works and how a transaction log backup works. Even if transaction log backups are set to occur frequently, you might not see the full benefit of performing them frequently unless the system is designed to support frequent transaction log backups. Simply put, SQL Server can only clear inactive transactions that have completed from the transaction log. To optimize the transaction log backup process it clears everything up to the first open transaction in the log. To keep the actively processing portion of the transaction log small, you should perform transaction log backups frequently and clear the inactive portion of the log. Some operations could prevent the transaction log from being cleared. For example, SQL Server 2000 (as well as SQL Server 7.0) never backs up any of the transaction log more than once even if a long-running transaction is active through multiple log backups, so the long transaction prevents log truncation and reuse, but does not affect anything else. All of this means you should avoid certain operations that create a significant amount of log activity or those that keep the active portion of the log active, such as the following:

- Avoid long-running transactions. Consider breaking the large transactions into more manageable chunks, and consider partitioning some of your larger tables to minimize the impact to the log during table management operations such as index rebuilds (if required). Instead of performing a single update statement against the entire set, break it into smaller batches. For example, instead of changing the entire year's sales, change them month by month, day by day, or hour by hour.

- Avoid spreading a transaction over multiple batches. If there is user interaction and the user does not interact because he or she is distracted, the transaction is considered active in the transaction log until it completes. When SQL Server backs up a transaction log it clears only the inactive portion of the log. If you suspect that a user has long-running and open transactions there are a few procedures you can use to monitor these situations: sp_who2 and DBCC OPENTRAN.

Make sure that your transaction log is sized for all operations, especially those that might occur during the hours of a full database backup. Why? If the transaction log fills while a full database backup is being performed, you cannot back up, clear, or increase the size of the transaction log until the backup completes, meaning your database is unavailable until then. This is the case unless you try to cancel the backup, and that might not be possible—nor is it generally a good idea, as you need to restart it again later. All of these concepts come together as you understand the process of how full database backups and transaction log backups work. However, there are still other factors—database settings.

Initial Database Settings and Recovery Models

When you create a database you always begin with a copy of the model database. All database settings are inherited from the model database at creation. The recovery model is probably the most critical setting with regard to backup and recovery, and it has different default values depending on the version of SQL Server you have installed. However, with respect to high availability, the only versions of SQL Server you are likely to be using are Enterprise or Developer editions (possibly Standard, but quite a few high-availability-related features require Enterprise Edition). The engine edition of these versions returns either Enterprise or Standard.

> **Note**   If you are interested in seeing the engine edition setting, you can use the SERVERPROPERTY function. Use the following query to see which engine edition you are running:
>
> ```
> SELECT SERVERPROPERTY('EngineEdition')
> ```
>
> There are only three possible return values for SQL Server 2000: 1 for the Personal and Desktop Engines editions, 2 for the Standard edition, and 3 for the Enterprise, Enterprise Evaluation, and Developer editions.

> **Note**   The default setting for the recovery model of the model database is Full recovery model if you are using the Enterprise (or Standard) edition. Use the following query to see the recovery model setting of the model database:
>
> ```
> SELECT DATABASEPROPERTYEX('model', 'Recovery')
> ```
>
> Make sure to use DATABASEPROPERTYEX and *not* DATABASEPROPERTY. DATABASEPROPERTYEX is the appropriate function in SQL Server 2000 that includes all of the *extended* properties not available in SQL Server 7.0.

The concept of a recovery model is new to SQL Server 2000 and the logging that is performed for numerous commands is not like any other release of SQL Server. More important, even though the name of one of the new recovery models (Bulk-Logged) sounds similar to a previous database option (SELECT INTO/Bulk Copy), this recovery model does not behave exactly the same in terms of logging and recovery. You must make sure that you completely understand the recovery models or you might be surprised by some of their effects on performance, the size of the active log, the size of the backed up log (as it differs from the size of the active log), and potential work loss exposure.

Understanding Recovery Model Settings by Default

If you worked with SQL Server releases prior to SQL Server 7.0, it is likely you have seen a full transaction log. In earlier releases the transaction log was not set to autogrow, nor did it clear by default. Because of the importance of transaction log continuity, the only operation you should use to clear the transaction log is a transaction log backup. However, the behavior of the transaction log when a database is first created might surprise you. When a database is created, by default, the transaction log runs in a mode that clears the transaction log after checkpoint until you begin your recovery strategy with your first full database backup or file/filegroup backup.

After the first backup is performed in SQL Server 2000, the behavior of your log is solely dependent on the setting for your database recovery model. In SQL Server 7.0, logging was controlled by database options (Trunc. Log On Chkpt. and SELECT INTO/Bulk Copy) and the statements and tools you executed (for example, SELECT INTO and *bcp*). In fact, prior to SQL Server 2000, the ability to completely and accurately know the state of the current transaction log was hampered. Even worse, it was during recovery that people would realize how these options and operations affected them (not realizing that they had an impact on recovery operations). Often it was too late for adequate recovery, and data loss occurred. Recovery models were introduced to simplify recovery planning and tie together the importance of the log with certain activities. In SQL Server 2000, the logging of all operations is dependent on the setting for recovery model.

Understanding Log Behavior on Initial Database Creation

In SQL Server 7.0 and later versions (including SQL Server 2000), the transaction log is in a pseudo truncate log on checkpoint mode until you perform a backup. The database option will not show as being set, and in SQL Server 2000, this behavior occurs regardless of your recovery model setting. After the creation of a database the log is set to clear on checkpoint because a transaction log backup (if you were able to back it up, which you are not) would be useless. Think back to the basics of a transaction log: it is a log or report, per se, of what has occurred within your database. This report always gets you from one point to another, almost as detailed directions to a location would. However, you always have to have a starting point of reference. The same is true for a transaction log: it always gets you from one defined point to another. If a transaction log backup were allowed after creating a database, what would be the starting point in recovery? To which backup would you apply that log? Would it be the creation of a new database? Could you create a database, at any time, and ensure that it will *always* be the same as the original database? The answer is no. If there have been any changes to the model database, then the newly created database would inherit those changes, rendering the log backup useless because you have directions from a different starting point. Instead of leaving this vulnerability, SQL Server does not allow a log backup until you have created a starting point for recovery to which a log backup would make sense. For recovery there are really two options as starting points: a full database backup or a file or filegroup backup.

To fully understand what happens to the transaction log on the creation of a database, think through this simple scenario while reviewing the recommended performance monitor counters.

> **On the CD**   The code for this log behavior example can be found in the script file Default_Log_Behavior.sql.

1.   Create a test database. For this exercise you can name the database anything you want; for this example, the name TestDB is used.

```
CREATE DATABASE TestDB
```

2.   Create a table. This is just a simple table that allows you to add rows quickly:

```
CREATE TABLE dbo.TestTable

col1      int          identity(100,10),

col2      datetime     DEFAULT current_timestamp,

col3      datetime     DEFAULT getdate(),

col4      char(30)     DEFAULT user_name(),

col5      char(30)     DEFAULT user_name(),

col6      char(80)     DEFAULT 'This is a wide column created to
                       simulate data and therefore create log space.' )
```

3. Verify that the recovery model of the new TestDB database is set to Full.

```
SELECT DATABASEPROPERTYEX('TestDB', 'Recovery')
```

4. Start the System Monitor and add the Percent Log Used counter for the instance of TestDB (see Figure 9-2). The Percent Log Used counter is under the Performance Object of SQLServer:Databases.

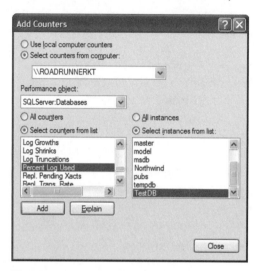

Figure 9-2   Percent Log Used counter.

5. Leave System Monitor running and create log activity with the following WHILE loop. Once you start running this infinite loop it continues to add rows to the database (autogrowing the data portion) until you manually stop the execution.

```
WHILE 1=1

INSERT dbo.TestTable DEFAULT VALUES
```

6. Return to the System Monitor and watch the log increase and then drop while the overall size of the log does not grow (see Figure 9-3). Add the Log File Size to the Performance Monitor as well. You should see that the Log File Size does not change even with all of the log activity.

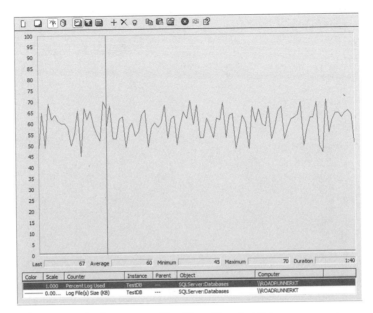

Figure 9-3 Performance of log file with autogrow.

7. Make sure you stop the WHILE loop relatively quickly; otherwise, you could fill your hard drive though database autogrowth. Remember, the database files are set to grow automatically by default.

8. Next, create a database backup using Transact-SQL. This simulates the beginning of your recovery strategy:

```
BACKUP DATABASE TestDB TO DISK = N'C:\TestDB.bak'
```

9. Run the WHILE loop again and then return to the Performance Monitor. This time you will see the Percent Log Used stay at the top of the graph, indicating that the log is almost full. You will also see that it dips, but only by roughly 10 percent, because of the automatic growth that is occurring. You will also notice that the size of the log is increasing quickly (see Figure 9-4).

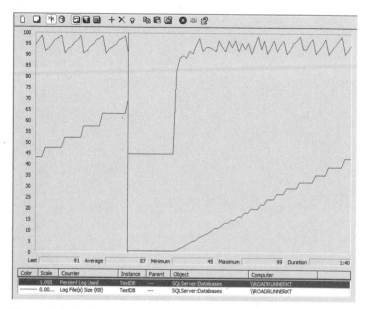

Figure 9-4 Performance of log after recovery plan is started using backup.

10. Finally, make sure that you stop the loop, delete the backup, and drop the TestDB database.

Recovery Models

There are three recovery models in SQL Server 2000: Full, Bulk-Logged, and Simple. Because there is a lot of confusion about the different recovery models, it is critical to eliminate the common misunderstandings associated with recovery models. To do this well, you should understand what the recovery models are not. Recovery models are completely new for SQL Server 2000. There are *some* similarities to former (prior to SQL Server 2000) database options, but there is no direct correlation between recovery models and previous database options. Unfortunately, this has not stopped the common comparisons between the new database recovery models and the old database options SELECT INTO/ Bulk Copy and Trunc. Log On Chkpt. Table 9-1 shows the database options as they are usually compared. However, for completeness they are listed in terms of what they are not.

Table 9-1   SQL Server 2000 Recovery Models

SQL Server 2000 Recovery Model	Common Incorrect Comparisons with the Database Options SELECT INTO/Bulk Copy and Trunc. Log On Chkpt.
Full	Not the same as if neither option is set. Some operations take longer and require more log space.
Bulk-Logged	Not the same as having the select into/bulk copy option set—although there is still similar performance, the recovery has changed.
Simple	Not exactly the same as having both options set (this is the closest, however).

Truthfully, there are many resemblances between the database options and the new recovery models, but they are mostly superficial. The Full recovery model logs information in a new way. For some commands, this has never been done within SQL Server before SQL Server 2000. You might have learned this the hard way, as batch operations are likely to take more time and more log space than they did in previous releases because, for some operations, this new style of logging is more extensive.

The Bulk-Logged recovery model is also new. From a performance perspective, you can compare it to having the SELECT INTO/Bulk Copy option. However, the performance similarities exist for different reasons, as the logging has changed. In previous releases the performance gains occurred because the operations were run in a "nonlogged" state (they really were not nonlogged, as you could have still filled the transaction log; for the purposes of this discussion nonlogged means that the operation was not recoverable from information in the log). In releases before SQL Server 2000, SQL Server required these database options. Under certain circumstances the operations would run faster due to less log activity. Unfortunately, when bulk operations were performed with SELECT INTO/Bulk Copy set to true, the operation would break the continuity of the log, subsequently requiring a full database or differential database backup on completion from which you could recover. When you added the cost of the full database backup or the differential database backup to the batch operation's time, it was no longer very "fast."

In contrast, the operations run quickly in SQL Server 2000 but for different reasons: the way in which they are logged and the way in which SQL Server allows log backups on their completion. With SQL Server 2000 it is more appropriate to refer to these operations as minimally logged instead of nonlogged.

Do not be fooled, however; the performance gains of minimally logging certain operations come at a price. There is some potential for work loss if you are running the Bulk-Logged recovery model and you have performed a Bulk-Logged operation at the time of a disaster. However, if the database is accessible on completion of the bulk operation, a transaction log backup is all you need to fully recover the batch operations (this was not true before SQL Server 2000). Finally, the Simple recovery model is most like the old Trunc. Log On Chkpt. option with which the log is cleared at checkpoint, meaning that SQL Server has enough information from which committed transactions are guaranteed even after an unintended shutdown (for example, a power failure). However, because the log is cleared periodically, no log backups can occur; this eliminates manual recovery options involving the log including up-to-the-minute recovery and point-in-time recovery.

Where are the similarities between the recovery models? What should your expectations be at the time of a disaster? Using the Simple or Bulk-Logged recovery models, bulk operations should yield the same performance. However, transaction log backups are possible in the Bulk-Logged recovery model and the transaction log will not be cleared when a checkpoint occurs. You can perform transaction log backups—with the exception that the "tail" of the transaction log is not accessible after a bulk operation has been performed—to manage the transaction log size, and compared to the Full recovery model it should stay relatively small. However, the savings are only realized while the database is actively processing. The transaction log backup is significantly larger when backed up and it can only be backed up when the data portion of the database is accessible. The size of the transaction log backup should be similar in size to a transaction log backup performed when the database is in Full recovery model. However, whether or not a transaction log backup can be performed is not in question when you are running in Full recovery model. In the Full recovery model, the actual transaction log and the transaction log backup are both large. This allows you to back it up even when the database is not accessible. This is what allows the "full" range of recovery options for the Full recovery model.

Understanding the Purpose of Recovery Models

To fully understand the purpose of the recovery models, you must always speak in terms of how much and until what point data can be recovered as well as how efficiently database operations will perform. The primary focus is on what can be recovered, how it can be recovered, and what options are allowed. Before you can understand the key recovery model concepts, you must also understand the importance of the transaction log and two key concepts regarding the transaction log: how to achieve continuity (covered earlier) and how to access the "tail" of the log.

The "Tail" of the Log and Recovery Models

The transaction log is a series of instructions from the last time the transaction log was cleared (preferably when it was last backed up). If all transaction log backups are available and the current log is available then you are said to have continuity of the transaction log up-to-the-minute. What if the database is not available? If you backed up the transaction log at 3 P.M. and the database is damaged at 3:45 P.M., you have to determine up to what point data can be recovered. When a database becomes unavailable because of file corruption, disk failure, controller failure, or other situation, one of the first steps you should try to perform is a backup of the "tail" of the log. The tail of the log is the transaction log backup of all changes from the time of the last log backup until the time when the database became damaged or suspect. The tail of the log cannot be accessed if the log portion of the database is damaged. Additionally, the tail of the log cannot be accessed if the database is in Bulk-Logged recovery model and a bulk operation has occurred. If the tail of the transaction log is available, up-to-the-minute recovery is possible. Because of this, choosing the right recovery model is critical to your overall recovery strategy.

Choosing the Right Recovery Model

Generally speaking, most database recovery scenarios rely on the accessibility of the transaction log. The setting of the recovery model dictates whether or not the log is accessible and the performance impact logging has during certain operations. With SQL Server 2000, DBAs can trade performance for recovery options. Fortunately, it is completely up to the DBA and it is significantly simpler than it was in previous releases. However, in high-end databases where every transaction is critical and downtime must be at an absolute minimum, an understanding of the recovery models is required. As each recovery model is defined, keep in mind the key reasons for the addition of recovery models to SQL Server 2000:

- To better tie together the idea of the transaction log and recovery. In past releases, developers and new DBAs often learned about the transaction log after it filled. Once it filled, they also seemed to learn (very quickly) how to clear the log (that is to use the Trunc. Log On Chkpt. option), but they did not seem to learn about disaster recovery until a disaster. This happened because the option did not make it obvious that the log was needed for recovery. Now the options are database specific and their title (Recovery Model) makes it more apparent.

- To centrally and more appropriately define potential work loss exposure. DBAs should always have control over what operations are to be recoverable. In previous releases it was a complex combination of database options, user operations, and other factors that determined a database's ability to recover.

- To allow database administrators the ability to choose from among a variety of trade-offs between transaction log management, system and data recovery, and operational and batch performance for some of the more expensive operations.

- To minimize the complexity of knowing whether or not an operation can be performed. For example, SELECT INTO can be used to create a permanent table in any recovery model and no longer requires a database option. The logging of the SELECT INTO operation is determined by the database's recovery model.

- To no longer break the continuity of the log for batch processes and bulk operations, yet still allow the operations to perform optimally with only a transaction log backup required on their completion.

- To simplify SQL Server's logging logic. When an operation was logged, earlier versions of SQL Server had to evaluate numerous criteria to determine the correct logging. In SQL Server 2000, all statements are logged based on the recovery model; it is no longer statement specific (although the performance gains are only for a select number of specific statements).

- To determine whether or not up-to-the-minute recovery is required.

Full Recovery Model   The Full recovery model requires SQL Server to log every operation in full. This means that every operation will have rows written to the transaction log that allow the database to be recovered to any point in time and with no work loss exposure in the event of a database failure where the log is still accessible. This is based on a solid backup strategy, but if you are running in the Full recovery model, you have the most options available to you. It is also the best model to be in at the time of a failure (if data is changing—read-only databases have a few other options).

In the Full recovery model, no operations run with minimal logging. In fact, some operations might not perform as they did in SQL Server 7.0. This is a common source of misunderstanding, especially for people upgrading from SQL Server 7.0 to SQL Server 2000. Batch operations, which performed minimally logged operations (for example, building or rebuilding indexes), require more log space and take longer in SQL Server 2000 than they did in SQL Server 7.0. If you want to run in a minimally logged mode, you can change your recovery model to Bulk-Logged; however, there are some important trade-offs of which you should be aware.

Who Should Use the Full Recovery Model?   The Full recovery model is the only recovery model that has no work loss exposure as long as the continuity of the log is not broken and the transaction log is accessible at the time of failure. Therefore, if your databases are processing transactions at all times and every transaction should be recoverable, this is the only recovery model you should consider. The Full recovery model is the one that can provide all recovery options, and it also has the least potential for data loss. Both point-in-time recovery and up-to-the-minute recovery are possible only when the database recovery model is set to Full.

Bulk-Logged Recovery Model   The Bulk-Logged recovery model allows certain operations to run more efficiently than the Full recovery model because it minimally logs certain operations. Instead of logging every operation fully, the Bulk-Logged recovery model only logs the extents modified during the operation. This keeps the active log small and might allow you to have a smaller defined transaction log size than the Full recovery model. To be able to recover the operation, the transaction log should be backed up immediately on the completion of any Bulk-Logged operation, and this is true for any of the recovery models.

When the transaction log is backed up in this mode there are two steps. First—and this is the big difference for the Bulk-Logged model—SQL Server backs up all of the extents modified by the bulk operations performed (the specific commands defined by "bulk" are listed later). Second, the transaction log is backed up as it would be during a log backup in the Full recovery model. This is similar in concept to how a differential backup works, but the extents backed up are only those changed by the bulk operation. This allows some operations to occur quickly and with minimal logging (only a bitmap is maintained through the operation), but your recovery options are limited. First, if you have performed a bulk operation, this transaction log backup does not allow point-in-time recovery during a restore. Second, if the data portion of the database is not accessible (because, for example, the disks failed), a transaction log backup is not possible after a bulk operation has occurred and you are running in Bulk-Logged recovery model. The following bulk operations are minimally logged in this recovery model:

- Index creation or rebuilds

- Bulk loading of data (fast load) including (but not limited to) BULK INSERT, Data Transformation Services (DTS) Bulk Load, and *bcp*

- SELECT INTO when creating permanent tables

- WRITETEXT and UPDATETEXT for binary large object (BLOB) manipulation

Technically, you can still have point-in-time and up-to-the-minute recovery when running in Bulk-Logged recovery model, but this is possible only when bulk logged operations have not occurred since the last transaction log backup. However, this can create confusion and the process is error-prone. Instead of running in Bulk-Logged recovery model all the time, change between recovery models as part of your batch processes. If you are in control of the recovery models, you can force transaction log backups to occur at the most appropriate times, minimizing the potential for data loss.

It is important that you perform log backups immediately after a batch operation to ensure that everything is recoverable. Consider this timeline:

- 12:00 A.M.—Transaction log backup occurs (transaction log backups occur hourly).

- 12:10 A.M.—Batch operation begins.

- 12:20 A.M.—Batch operation completes.

- 12:47 A.M.—Database becomes suspect due to drive failure.

- 12:50 A.M.—You become aware of the suspect database. You attempt to access the tail of the transaction log, but you receive the following errors:

```
Server: Msg 4216, Level 16, State 1, Line 1
Minimally logged operations cannot be backed up when the database is
unavailable.
Server: Msg 3013, Level 16, State 1, Line 1
BACKUP LOG is terminating abnormally.
```

> **On the CD**   If you would like to see this process and log backup failure, use the script Cannot_Backup_Tail_After_Bulk_Operation.sql to test.

At 12:50 A.M., all you can do is restore the database and the logs up until 12:00 A.M. If you had backed up the log at 12:20 A.M., your database would not have been in a bulk logged state (regardless of the recovery model setting to Bulk-Logged). You can back up the tail of the transaction log when you are running in Bulk-Logged recovery model only if no bulk operations have occurred. By backing up the transaction log immediately after a bulk operation you are in effect resetting the bulk logged state such that transaction log backups can be performed without requiring access to the data portion of the database. If the database had not been in a bulk logged state at 12:50, then you would have been able to get the tail of the transaction log. If the tail of the log had been accessible, you would have up-to-the-minute recovery and no data loss. Instead you have lost *all* activity since 12:00 A.M.

To take these concepts further, look at another scenario. What if the database were to become corrupt at 12:15 A.M. in the middle of the batch operation? You know that the tail of the transaction log is not accessible because you are in the process of a bulk operation in the Bulk-Logged recovery model. However, your data loss is everything past 12:00 A.M. You certainly could have prevented some—and possibly all—of this data loss. Performing a transaction log backup at 12:10 A.M. when the database was accessible (right before the bulk operation began) would have at least brought you up to 12:10 A.M., the moment prior to the bulk operation. If the bulk operation were the only operation occurring from 12:10 A.M. to 12:15 A.M. (when the database became corrupt), the transaction log backup could be used to bring the database up to 12:10 A.M. Once recovered to 12:10 A.M., the bulk operation could be executed again to bring the database up to the time of the failure and continue it moving forward.

It is critical to back up your transaction log both immediately before performing batch operations and immediately after performing a batch operation. Both minimize the overall potential for data loss in the event of a failure. Remember that if the database is set to the Bulk-Logged recovery model *and* you have performed a bulk operation, you cannot backup the tail of the log even if the transaction log file is accessible. If you have not performed a bulk operation, you can back up the log. For this reason, some people might consider always running in the Bulk-Logged recovery model. However, this can be dangerous because you are no longer entirely in control of the recovery. Bulk operations are not necessarily limited to only DBAs or system administrators. Anyone who owns a table can create or rebuild indexes of their tables, anyone with Create Table permissions can use SELECT INTO to create a permanent table, and anyone who has access to text data can manipulate it with WRITE-TEXT and UPDATETEXT. Because of this, it is very important to know and limit when operations are logged fully or minimally. If you are responsible for data recovery and your environment cannot afford data loss, the only way to minimize data loss is by running in the Full recovery model and controlling changes to the Bulk-Logged recovery model. Only when the Bulk-Logged recovery model is appropriate should you switch. In some environments it might not even be possible to switch. The best practice, if you determine that it is acceptable to periodically change to the Bulk-Logged recovery model, is to change within batch processes. This practice ensures that the window of potential work loss is limited to only appropriate times of day.

Who Should Use the Bulk-Logged Recovery Model?   If your databases are not processing transactions around the clock or if you are willing to have work loss exposure to achieve better performance of your batch operations, you might consider a temporary change to the Bulk-Logged recovery model. However, even if you decide that this is acceptable, you should change to Bulk-Logged during the batch operation (preceding the switch with a log backup) and then change back when the operation is complete (following the switch with another log backup). Again, these operations only protect data and minimize the potential window for data loss. For batch processes, an example is given to completely detail the process to optimally change recovery models in the section "Changing Between Recovery Models" later in this chapter.

Also, as a secondary consideration, depending on the length of the bulk operation, you might consider trying to break down large or complex batch operations that might cause the transaction log to grow excessively large. In fact, to minimize the potential for data loss (because you cannot back up the tail of the log if the database becomes suspect), you might perform log backups during the batch process and between some of the steps of the bulk operations. Breaking down any very large or complex operations and performing log backups between the larger steps allow more recovery options.

Simple Recovery Model   The Simple recovery model logs data as if the database were in the Bulk-Logged recovery model; however, the log is periodically cleared. Instead of keeping all of the log information until a transaction log backup is performed, SQL Server clears the log information from the transaction log as the data is synchronized from memory to its appropriate location on disk (at checkpoint). Because the data no longer resides solely in memory (for the data portion of the database) there is no need for the information to be stored in the transaction log for automatic recovery (remember, this is SQL Server's primary reason to have a transaction log). However, if the transaction log is periodically cleared, transaction log backups are not possible.

The Simple recovery model is the easiest recovery model to use, as the log is cleared periodically and automatically. In the Simple recovery model, administration is simple because no transaction log maintenance is required (the transaction log is maintained through log truncation when a checkpoint occurs). In fact, only two backup types are possible: full database backups and differential database backups. However, this simplified administration comes at the expense of significant work loss if the database becomes suspect. In fact, you can recover only up to your last full database backup or your last differential database backup.

Who Should Use the Simple Recovery Model?   If your databases are periodically built as copies of data from other transaction processing systems and can be rebuilt if necessary, you might consider the Simple recovery model with a full database backup on completion of the database build. The Simple recovery model is common for predominantly read-only or development and test databases for which up-to-the-minute recovery is not necessary and data loss is not critical to the success of the business.

Choosing the Right Recovery Model: An Example Test Case   To show a quick overview of the effects on the database's transaction log size (meaning the amount of space required to "log" the operation), the size of the transaction log backup, and the speed of the operation, a simple test was performed using a very specific operation: SELECT INTO (see Table 9-2). SELECT INTO creates a new table called TestTable based on a table called a charge table from another database. The charge table has 800,000 rows and the data is roughly 40 MB in size.

Table 9-2   SELECT INTO Operation

Database Recovery Model	Duration (Seconds)	Database Transaction Log Size	Transaction Log Backup Size
Simple	8.5	< 4 MB	Not allowed
Bulk-Logged	8.5	< 4 MB	~40 MB
Full	14	~40 MB	~40 MB

The interesting observations come from the fact that Simple and Bulk-Logged seem to have the same performance and the same active log size. However, recovery models do not affect all operations. In the second test a single update is performed against all 800,000 rows in TestTable. This caused the transaction log for all three databases to grow significantly to handle the modification and there was no difference in the operation's duration or the size of the transaction log (where a transaction log backup is permitted).

Table 9-3   UPDATE Operation

Database Recovery Model	Duration (Seconds)	Database Transaction Log Size	Transaction Log Backup Size
Simple	18	230 MB	Not allowed
Bulk-Logged	18	230 MB	~54 MB
Full	18	230 MB	~54 MB

From an interpretation of Tables 9-2 and 9-3, you might think that the best recovery model to use is the Bulk-Logged recovery model, because it seems to allow transaction log backups and because the operations affected by recovery models run faster. However, you are missing a key element, because the transaction log is not always available for a transaction log backup when running the Bulk-Logged recovery model. If the device on which the data resides is not available when a transaction log backup is attempted, then a transaction log backup cannot be performed, resulting in data loss. Up-to-the-minute recovery is not always possible with the Bulk-Logged recovery model. Getting familiar with the different recovery models and their trade-offs is very important for production databases, as the recovery model can affect speed, logging, and recovery.

> **On the CD**   The code for these two operations and tests can be found in script file Recovery_Model_Log_Sizes.sql. The code for this script might need numerous alterations to run on your test server. Be sure to carefully read all comments.

Changing Between Recovery Models

Generally, you will choose a recovery model and stick with it. However, in some cases you might want to switch between two recovery models and then switch back. For example, some databases run in Full recovery model most of the time and switch to Bulk-Logged during bulk loading or batch processing. As long as you realize the potential work loss exposure if your database were to become suspect and you have decided it is acceptable, then changing between the recovery models is reasonable. There are six possible combinations as shown in Table 9-4, but only two are common. In fact, the recovery model is usually only changed for certain operations and then returned after the operation completes. However, changes to the simple recovery model should be performed with caution, as this change breaks the continuity of the transaction log.

Table 9-4   **Changing Recovery Models and Impact on Backups**

		FROM		
		Simple	**Bulk-Logged**	**Full**
TO	**Simple**	N/A	Nothing required. A transaction log backup is recommended before the switch.	Nothing required. A transaction log backup is recommended before the switch.
	Bulk-Logged	New recovery set required; full database or differential database backup or a complete file or filegroup backup must be performed.	N/A	Nothing required. A transaction log backup is recommended before the switch.
	Full	New recovery set required; full database or differential database backup or a complete file or filegroup backup must be performed.	Nothing required. A transaction log backup is recommended after the switch.	N/A

The most common changes occur from the Full recovery model to the Bulk-Logged recovery model and then back to the Full recovery model again. In fact, the most common strategy actually includes steps to minimize the window of potential data loss by performing the recovery model changes and the transaction log backups as part of the batch process. The following is a high-level overview of the steps that should be performed when switching between full and Bulk-Logged recovery models.

> **On the CD**   If you would like to see sample code, including various optional parameters to each of these commands, use the script DB_Alter_For_Batch_Operation.sql.

- Database is currently in the Full recovery model.

- As part of the bulk operation's batch process, perform a transaction log backup immediately before changing to the Bulk-Logged recovery model.

- Change the recovery model to Bulk-Logged using the ALTER DATABASE command:

```
ALTER DATABASE SET RECOVERY BULK_LOGGED
```

- Perform your bulk operations, data loads, index builds or rebuilds, and so on.

- Change the recovery model back to Full again using the ALTER DATABASE command:

```
ALTER DATABASE SET RECOVERY FULL
```

- Immediately after the change, perform a transaction log backup.

By performing a transaction log backup before as well as after the bulk operation, you ensure that the window for potential data loss is significantly reduced. As long as the transaction log backup occurs, you have something from which you can recover during manual recovery. However, you cannot back up the tail of the log if the database were to become damaged during the bulk operation. If there are any user transactions that are not recoverable by rerunning your bulk operation, you should remain in the Full recovery model instead of changing to the Bulk-Logged recovery model. You will lose these transactions if the database becomes inaccessible.

Recovery models have an obvious and significant impact on the available recovery options. Knowing how the environment is defined and actively choosing your recovery model is the first step in a complete and effective recovery strategy. In the next section you will combine your understanding of recovery models with each backup type to determine the specific database requirements necessary to support your downtime and data loss specifications.

Backup Types

You always plan your backup strategy based on your desired recovery abilities. A recovery-oriented strategy is always best. For example, if you want up-to-the-minute recovery you must use the Full recovery model. How do you actually achieve an up-to-the-minute recovery? Which backups are critical and in what order? What could go wrong? Are there operations, settings, or user actions that could negatively affect the database recovery? In this section, all of the backup types are discussed, and more important, the common combinations that yield effective strategies to offer the most options for recovery are debated. Some plans even include redundancy within the backup strategy (yes, a backup plan in the backup plan!).

SQL Server 2000 (as well as SQL Server 7.0) offers seven different backup types: full database backups, transaction log backups, differential database backups, full file backups, full filegroup backups, differential file backups, and differential filegroup backups. Each one of these is often called something similar in other documentation and articles, and even the authors of this book have probably used multiple terms. For consistency and clarity in this chapter, only the terms listed in Table 9-5 are used. However, when you read other documentation you might see slightly different names used for each of these backup types.

Table 9-5   Backup Naming Conventions

Naming Conventions Used in This Chapter	Naming Conventions Commonly Used Elsewhere or Important Notes About Usage
Full database backup	Database—complete, complete database, full database, database backup
Differential database backup	Database—differential, differential backup
Transaction log backup	Log backup, tranlog backup, T-log backup, transaction backup
Full file backup	File backups
Differential file backup	File differentials
Full filegroup backup	Filegroup backups
Differential filegroup backup	Filegroup differentials
Full file/filegroup backups	Applies to both full file backups and full filegroup backups
Differential file/filegroup backups	Applies to both differential file backups and differential filegroup backups
File/filegroup backups	Applies to all types of file/filegroup backups: full file/filegroup backups and differential file/filegroup backups
Full backups	Applies to all three: full database backups, full file backups, and full filegroup backups
Differential backups	Applies to all three: differential database backups, differential file backups, and differential filegroup backups

Full Database Backups

A full database backup is the most complete backup you can create. Because it is the easiest recovery strategy to manage, it is the foundation for the most commonly used recovery strategy. Although full database backups are complete, they are often not used alone. Typically full database backups are used in conjunction with other transaction log backups and differential database backups.

> **Tip**   A full database backup is the most common backup type used to define the starting point of a recovery strategy, but it is not the only starting point. In fact, it is not even necessary that you ever perform a full database backup. There are really two starting points for your recovery process: full database backups or file/filegroup backups.

A full database backup is complete in that everything necessary to access the data of that database—even the database structure—is backed up and the information about the backup (what was backed up, when it was backed up, what the database structure looks like, and what type of backup it is) can be easily queried from backup devices. On the restore, you do not need to create the database prior to restoring a full database backup; instead you can let the restore create and even move the database files to other locations. When a full backup is performed it is optimized to back up only pages (rather extents) that contain data, so the size of a backup is the size of the database minus the unallocated space. When a full database backup is performed, the image created in the backup is an image of the database at the backup's completion.

How Do Full Database Backups Work?   SQL Server needs a way to access data quickly to generate an image of the database while users are actively processing and create a backup that can restore a transactionally consistent database to the way it looked on the completion of a backup. This process is quite logical. Figure 9-5 shows a graphical representation of the logical sequence of steps for the full database backup process.

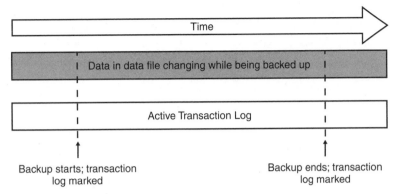

Figure 9-5   Full backups do not block active transactions.

The logical sequence of steps is as follows:

1. The first step is to perform a database checkpoint. Remember, the purpose of a checkpoint is to write all dirty pages to disk. A dirty page is one that has changed since it was brought into memory, regardless of the state of the transaction that modified it. The checkpoint is performed to batch the writes to disk and simplify Automatic Recovery, the process that SQL Server goes through on startup to make sure that each database is transactionally consistent. By performing a checkpoint, SQL Server guarantees that what is in the data portion of the database is as close to current as possible, even if the transactions are still processing.

2. Mark the transaction log. A marker is put into the transaction log to define where the backup began. This is used later in the backup process.

3. Read from data files. In this step SQL Server reads the image of data from the data files. Even while active users are processing, SQL Server continues to use only the pages that are already on disk, even if they are not logically consistent with the processing transactions. This does not seem like it would work, but it does! The result of this phase is considered a logically inconsistent (often called fuzzy) set of pages.

4. Again, mark the transaction log. This marker defines where the backup completed.

5. Back up the interesting part of the transaction log. By using the two markers created by Steps 2 and 4 and some additional information about the earliest transaction in the log (if it is earlier than the first marker), SQL Server is able to get directions for how to update the logically inconsistent image of data that has been backed up (although this only needs to be used during a restore). The transaction log backup that is performed is not a typical log backup, per se. The log is only backed up. The log is not cleared (this is the default setting for a transaction log backup). In fact, a full database backup does not touch nor does it break the continuity of the transaction log.

The end result of this sequence is that active transactions *never* wait and are not negatively impacted by a full database backup. It is true that the system will see a heavier I/O load, but if the backup devices and database files are well balanced and placed properly, the impact of the full database backup on actively processing users is minimal.

If full database backups are so optimal, why not perform them constantly? It might seem logical to begin another full database backup once one completes. This, in fact, is not typically a good idea.

> **Note** Certain storage-assisted strategies exist and can successfully perform full backups in a rolling fashion. This is even recommended for some situations. However, without storage-assisted backups, rolling full database backup after full database backup is not recommended.

Why? Full database backups conflict with other operations. In fact, while a full database backup is running there are other operations that will be paused until it completes. This can cause a few negative side effects. The operations and side effects with which full database backup conflicts are as follows:

■ **Transaction log backups** The effects of this can be quite serious. Remember, SQL Server backs up the transaction log as part of a full backup to make the full backup transactionally consistent during restore. To back up the transaction log, the transaction log needs to be accessible and complete, meaning that SQL Server must have access to all log activity that has occurred throughout the entire full backup. For the log to be accessible, it cannot have been cleared. If there are other operations that depend on the transaction log (for example, log shipping), log shipping will be paused until the full database backup completes. If your full database backup takes 6 hours to run, your secondary site could be 6 hours behind. Is 6 hours of data loss acceptable if you were to have site failure and lose the primary? Using full database backups as the base for your database backup strategy might not be best! There are other options.

■   **Alternatives**   Any operation that changes the database structure:

- ❏   No autogrow
- ❏   No manual growth with ALTER DATABASE
- ❏   No autoshrink
- ❏   No manual database shrinks with DBCC SHRINKDATABASE
- ❏   No manual database file shrinks with DBCC SHRINKFILE

A secondary problem related to the transaction log filling, the effect on the database once the transaction log is full is that no modifications are allowed until space is available in the transaction log. However, when a full database backup is already being performed, no operations can run to clear the transaction until the full database backup has finished. Neither the data portion nor the log portion is allowed to grow during a full database backup. It is not as critical that the data portion cannot autogrow, as this should be relatively unlikely with proper capacity planning. However, if you decide to use full database backups as the base for your backup strategy, make sure you have an adequately sized transaction log—as large as necessary to hold the transactions that occur over the entire time you perform full database backups. Because most database backups are performed at "off" hours during which activity is minimal, this might not present a problem for you. However, if a full database backup is performed for some other purpose (during regular or heavy-use business hours) it could present a problem.

> **Tip**   Not allowing autoshrink or manual shrinks of the database should not present a problem, as these are rarely used. Autoshrink is not a typical option for production servers; it is an option more appropriate to scaled-down SQL Server databases.

Speaking of very large databases (VLDBs), does your VLDB have a large portion of data that is predominantly read-only? Do you really need complete backups of that data very often? VLDB presents additional concerns with the strategies based on full database backups. As various strategies are discussed, you will see other alternatives to frequent full database backups that are helpful for VLDBs, possibly allowing a strategy that works without ever performing a full database backup.

Transaction Log Backups

For high availability, transaction log backups are the most important type of backup. They are a critical component to any backup strategy that desires up-to-the-minute or point-in-time recovery. The more frequent your log backups are, the more likely you will have a successful recovery with minimal data loss (see Figure 9-6). A transaction log backup provides a way to capture the changes that have occurred since the last transaction log backup. Additionally, when transaction log backups occur, SQL Server clears the inactive portion of the transaction log; this helps free space within the transaction log and removes the instructions so that recovery is possible.

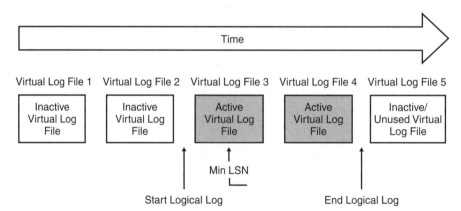

Figure 9-6 Frequent log backups minimize potential data loss.

> **Note** Clearing the log does not necessarily clear the entire log. If you review the percent log used within the System Monitor, you might never see the percent log used value for the transaction log (even immediately after a backup) drop to zero. This is based on how the transaction log backups work and is not likely a concern.

How Do Transaction Log Backups Work?   Take, for example, a 100-MB transaction log divided into five VLFs (for details on VLFs review the earlier section "Understanding Database Structures"). Log activity starts at the beginning of the log and at the current time activity is midway through the fourth VLF. There is an open transaction that began in the third VLF and that is marked as the minimum log sequence number (min LSN). You have just requested a transaction log backup.

SQL Server reviews the log to determine where it is active versus where it is inactive. VLFs that do not contain any active transactions are inactive, but used VLFs. SQL Server then backs up all VLFs and clears those that are inactive. At the time of the backup, at least one VLF is always active. Depending on the size of the VLFs and the size of the open transactions, you might not be able to clear anything from your transaction log. To ensure optimal transaction log backups and optimal performance for log-related operations, it is important to make sure that you have small, efficient transactions. In fact, if you have large batch operations you might consider one of two options:

■ Use the Bulk-Logged recovery model (if the work loss exposure is acceptable and the operation has performance and logging advantages when running in the Bulk-Logged recovery model).

■ Break the batch operations into smaller, more manageable chunks, if possible, and perform log backups as part of the batch operation.

If all transactions and operations are relatively small, this allows more effective management of the transaction log, keeping it small and easily recoverable.

The Effects of Recovery Models on the Transaction Log   Effects on the transaction log made by the recovery model are evident in many areas: performance, active log size versus transaction log backup size, and whether or not log backups are allowed. In the simple recovery model, transaction log backups are not allowed. In the Bulk-Logged recovery model the active log is much smaller than the transaction log backup because SQL Server uses a bitmap to keep track of changed extents during bulk operations. This keeps the active log size small, but causes the transaction log backup size to be as large as a transaction log backup performed in a database running with the Full recovery model. For databases running in the Full recovery model, the transaction log backup should be close to the size of the current transaction log space used. To estimate the size of the transaction log backup, use DBCC SQLPERF (logspace) or directly query the master.dbo.sysperfinfo table. For example, to see the "used" size of the transaction log for a database in the Full recovery model, use the following query prior to performing a backup:

```
SELECT * FROM master.dbo.sysperfinfo
WHERE object_name = 'SQLServer:Databases'
AND counter_name = 'Log File(s) Used Size (KB)'
AND instance_name = 'YourDatabaseName'
```

This query is not helpful for estimating the size of the transaction log backup for a database running in the Bulk-Logged recovery model. This cannot be estimated and the transaction log backup could be as large as the database if there has been a significant amount of Bulk-Logged activity. Make sure to test transaction log backup sizes during testing and development and be sure to plan for (in terms of backup device location) much larger transaction log backups than the database's transaction log size.

> **More Info**   Using sysperfinfo for monitoring will be covered in Chapter 15, "Monitoring for High Availability."

Differential Database Backups

A new feature introduced with SQL Server 7.0, differential database backups specifically minimize backup and recovery time. Differential database backups reduce recovery time by allowing databases with somewhat isolated activity to have only the changed extents backed up. When a differential backup is performed, SQL Server goes through the same process as a full database backup. However, the backup focuses on only the extents that were changed since the last full database backup. Differential backups can be performed in any database at any time, *even after* the continuity of the transaction log has been broken. However, a differential backup—as does a full database backup—pauses transaction log backups until it has completed. Instead of requiring a full database backup, a differential database backup allows you a faster way to back up your database and protect your recovery process, not relying so heavily on transaction log backups or complete backups of the entire database.

The recovery of a database using differential database backups is similar to applying the sequence of log backups that occurred over the same period of time. However, it is significantly faster. For all work that has been committed prior to the start of the differential database backup, there are completed images of those pages, even if a page was changed multiple times. The differential database backup is almost like a "mini" full database backup, but of only those extents that have changed. After the extents are restored, the transaction log of activity that occurred while the differential database backup was being performed is applied. As with the full database backup, the differential database backup restores a transactionally consistent image of the database as it looked at the completion of the differential database backup instead of at the beginning. This results in a faster recovery sequence than if using only transaction log backups. Instead of applying all of the individual changes that led up to a specific point in time, the differential database backup already includes the end result of all of the changes. Differential backups can be a key element of any backup strategy focused on high availability, as recovery time must be optimized.

Should every database use the differential backup strategy? Differential database backups are best in cases in which activity is somewhat isolated or in which the database has a large amount of relatively static data. If almost every page changes within your database during the expected time between the differential backups or if you have the ability to perform full database backups frequently because there are no negative issues associated with costs (for example, backup media costs, administrative costs, and recovery costs in terms of the operations that are paused), then performing full database backups instead of differential database backups can lead to an even shorter recovery time because fewer backups need to be restored. Differential database backups have the same conflicts with changes in database structures or transaction log backups as do full database backups.

How Differential Database Backups Work   To keep track of which extents have changed within the database, there is an internal bitmap within each file. Every time the information within the file is backed up completely, as with a full database backup, the bitmap is reset. This is very efficient because only one bit is used per extent. Therefore one 8-K page maps to approximately 4 GB of data. Even in larger files, there is only one bitmap per 4 GB and they are a doubly linked list starting with the first.

> **Note**   The bitmap is new to SQL Server 2000. When a differential database backup was performed, SQL Server 7.0 would scan the entire database, reviewing the header of every page to see if it had been modified since the last full database backup. This was extremely inefficient when the backup was performed, but had no effect on the restore. The restore was as efficient as it is in SQL Server 2000. SQL Server 7.0 was optimized only for restore. SQL Server 2000 is optimized for both backup and restore.

A differential database backup is therefore very similar to a full database backup, except that it is only the extents that have changed; therefore the backup is usually significantly smaller. However, because the bitmap is only reset when the file is completely backed up—as with a full database backup— the size of the differential database backups might approach the size of a full database backup over time or if an operation is performed that affects most of the pages of the database.

> **Note**   There are some caveats to this if you combine full database backups and differential database backups with full file/filegroup backups and differential file/filegroup backups. The differential bitmap, which is file based, gets reset anytime the full database or the full file/filegroup is backed up. Therefore, if they are combined, you can end up with a significantly slower backup to determine the differential. However, combining file, filegroup, and full backups for the same database is uncommon and therefore not recommended.

Even if you choose to add differential database backups to your recovery strategy, it is important that you also continue to periodically perform full database backups as part of a complete backup strategy. By performing full database backups you will reset the bitmap and have a more recent backup (this is sometimes good because of poor media quality).

Full File/Filegroup Backups

Both full file backups and full filegroup backups work in the same way that a full database backup works in terms of the data that is backed up. However, full file/filegroup backups do not back up the transaction log as part of the backup. Instead, you are required to back up the transaction log separately to make the full file/filegroup backup consistent at the time of restore. This means two things: you must be using either the Full or Bulk-Logged recovery model and log backups are never paused. This is one of the best choices for systems using log shipping or systems with large databases. It is excellent for log shipping because log backups will never have significant delays due to full database backups. It is also ideal for VLDBs because you can set different frequencies for the different files (and usually different types of data) within your database. If your VLDB has a large portion of read-only data that only needs to be backed up monthly, then you can back up the file or files in which that data resides only monthly.

Why should some implement their backups based on file/filegroup strategies and others not consider it? The reason is simple: implementing a file/filegroup backup strategy adds a significant amount of administrative complexity. You must design your database with file and filegroup strategies in mind, and restoring the proper combination of backups is also more challenging.

Differential File/Filegroup Backups

Both differential file backups and differential filegroup backups work in the same way that a differential database backup works. When the differential file or filegroup backup is performed, all of the extents that changed since the last full file or filegroup backup, respectively, will be backed up. The file-based bitmap is reset each time a full file backup or a full filegroup backup is performed. This is the only part about these that can be tricky. If you were to perform a full filegroup backup and then a differential filegroup backup, the differential filegroup backup would include only those extents that have changed, and it would use the bitmap to do so. If you start combining differential filegroup backups with differential file backups with differential database backups, the bitmaps might get reset. If the bitmap is reset, SQL Server needs to walk the entire database to ensure that all extents are properly backed up. This does not impact the restore, but it will be a less efficient backup. If you choose a file/filegroup-based backup strategy, you should be consistent with the levels at which you perform differential backups. This ensures not only a speedy restore, but also an efficient backup.

> **Tip**   It is important to realize that even when filegroups are used for read-only activity, SQL Server 2000 requires that transaction log backups be applied during recovery to make the file or filegroup consistent, even when no data has changed. It is important to perform file/filegroup differential backups on the file/filegroups that are logically read-only. During the restore, you can use the last full file/filegroup backup, the last file/filegroup differential backup, and all of the transaction logs from there. The differential backups will be effectively empty, but it significantly reduces the number of transaction logs that must be applied and therefore reduces the amount of time it takes to recover.

Summary

This chapter provides you with the foundation you need as you start to understand backup and restore better. You must know how SQL Server works behind the scenes if you are to put together a backup and restore plan that fits the needs of your company. That means knowing what is possible, when it can happen, and what you should do if something does not go as planned. Without this understanding, you will have a hard time putting together a cohesive disaster recovery plan.

10

Implementing Backup and Restore

Chapter 9, "Database Environment Basics for Recovery," provided the foundation to help you prepare your backup and restore strategy. This chapter guides you through that process.

Creating an Effective Backup Strategy

On many production servers, the backup and restore strategy is to perform only periodic (such as weekly) full database backups with transaction log backups between the full database backups (with a frequency of, say, every two hours). Some companies add occasional differential database backups (for example, nightly except on the day when full backups occur). The basic strategy of performing full database backups and transaction log backups is adequate to minimize data loss.

However, if you want to achieve high availability, you can minimize downtime by restoring a differential database backup instead of all of the logs over the same period. Restoring a differential backup is significantly faster because it contains extents that contain the completed results of *all* modifications that have occurred without having to read them from the log. In some cases, however, the size of the differential backup might approach the size of a full backup. If this is your scenario, then you are better off performing a full database backup so that you have less to restore (just the full backup and the appropriate transaction logs). Regardless of whether or not you add differential database backups to your strategy, you must use a full backup as the starting point for a restore.

If you have a very large database (VLDB), which is usually measured in hundreds of gigabytes or even terabytes, you must consider how long your VLDB takes to back up. More important, you also have to consider the time it will take to restore the database. Are these times acceptable based on your business requirements?

> **Tip**   Always use recovery-oriented planning when determining your backup strategy, no matter what size your databases are. Do not base your strategy on how long your backups take to run; base it on how long it will take to recover from a data-loss event. Unless your strategy uses storage-assisted backups such as split-mirror, a restore that incorporates a full database backup as part of the strategy is likely to take a long time, possibly multiple hours or even days depending on the size of your database. Even if a time span of hours or days of downtime is acceptable (if so, chances are this book is meaningless to you), how much data can you afford to lose? What is your site redundancy strategy? Do you use log shipping or copy all your log backups to a secondary site?

Microsoft SQL Server temporarily prevents certain operations such as a transaction log backup while a full database backup or a differential database backup is running. You could encounter a significant amount of data loss if you had site failure during the full or differential database backup. This scenario might sound unlikely, but when your full database backup time is measured in hours, your work loss exposure and risk for data loss increase dramatically. If your database backup takes eight hours to perform, your secondary site could be as much as eight hours behind at the time of a failure. This situation could result in eight hours of data loss if the backup was not complete or had not copied to the secondary location. Losing eight hours of data is unacceptable in most cases.

What if you could allow transaction log backups to occur while you were performing a different type of backup? Then it would be possible to continue to send transaction log backups to the secondary site even while your large backups are occurring. You might choose not to perform a full database backup regularly if you back up transaction logs on a frequent basis. (Every minute or two is a common frequency for minimizing data loss. However, you are limited by the speed of your systems as well as your workload if you try to perform transaction log backups that frequently; it might not be possible.) By using a file/filegroup backup strategy, you can completely avoid performing a full database backup, and log backups will never be paused. This strategy allows a secondary site to always be as close as possible to the primary site and minimizes the potential data loss.

Some basic backup and restore strategies have few restrictions. A full database backup has no real restrictions; it can be performed anytime. However, the more advanced file and filegroup backup strategies have some basic requirements you need to understand. Primarily, you must perform transaction log backups, a crucial component of restore, on a regular basis. When you perform transaction log backups, you minimize the risk of data loss and take advantage of features such as decreased total downtime in the event of isolated failure by using file/filegroup strategies. To be able to perform transaction log backups, first you must set the database recovery model to either Full or Bulk-Logged. If you set the recovery model to Simple, you cannot back up the transaction log, and you will not be able to use the file/filegroup backup strategy.

> **Important**   Transaction log backups are required for recovery if you use a file/filegroup backup strategy.

One optional configuration decision you can make for your databases is that when you are creating your database objects, place them strategically within the database itself. In most databases and especially in a VLDB, your data will likely vary in the way it is used. For example, some data will be predominantly read-only and some will be predominantly read/write. In some tables, new rows might be read/write to accommodate frequent inserts, whereas old rows (historical data used mainly for analysis) would be read-only. For other tables, the distribution might vary based on corporate policy. For example, if price changes to products in a catalog are infrequent, price information would be predominantly read-only until price increases were periodically propagated as changes to the database.

After reviewing the overall use of your data, you can determine table use and strategically place read-only tables (or tables with isolated or batch modifications) in their own filegroup and read/write tables on another. Then you not only save time during a restore, but you also save money and time during backups. Although the read-only portion of your database might be large, it does not need to be backed up as often as the read/write portion.

> **Note**   There are two important factors to be aware of:
>
> 1.   Even though a filegroup is read-only, you still have to restore all the log files until the end of the transaction log backup files. See the topic "How to restore files and file-groups (Transact-SQL)" in SQL Server Books Online.
>
> 2.   You can back up all the filegroups immediately followed by a transaction log backup and get the equivalent of a full database backup. In this case, you have all the data in one backup set and will need only to restore log backups after that point. The strategy of using file backups to allow for continuous frequent log backups is therefore not as cumbersome as it might seem. You restore the main data backup, then all the log backups they have taken while the data backup was in progress. However, be aware that the first log backup to restore after the data backup might have been taken *before* the data backup.

Additionally, partitioning your larger tables to split read activity from write activity can improve maintenance performance. Operations such as rebuilding an index take less time on physically smaller tables. For example, consider a typical sales table that holds the online sales information for a large company. Sales for the current month are read and write (which requires frequent index maintenance). In contrast, sales from the previous month or quarter are read-only because they are now used only for analysis, meaning maintenance occurs only once a month when the data is moved to the read-only portion of the database.

For tables with different usages, consider using separate filegroups for each type of data. For example, creating four separate filegroups—one for read-only data, one for read/write data, one for text and image data, and one for extremely large tables—can help when you are determining your backup strategies. Not only will you reduce maintenance times for each of the smaller tables (in other words, data partitions), but you will also add numerous backup and, especially, restore strategy options that can reduce downtime and backup costs.

> **Important**   Do not partition databases into multiple files or filegroups in a production environment without first testing to see if you will actually benefit from implementing files and filegroups. Although there are good arguments for moving things into their own files and filegroups, as noted earlier, doing this can ultimately add to your administrative overhead and, in turn, maintenance. The maintenance might run more quickly in some cases, but you might have more tasks to perform and more objects and tasks to manage. Ultimately, you will be making some trade-off. You want to create an entire SQL Server solution—including a backup and restore strategy—that you can maintain and perform day in and day out.

Finally, remember to back up all of your operating system files, application files, registry entries, and so on. In most cases, it is faster to restore the base state of your servers than it is to install again from scratch from CDs or DVDs. Although a database administrator (DBA) is not usually responsible for backing up these files, a DBA must coordinate with those people who are responsible for doing this to ensure that their systems are fully protected.

Backup Retention

Before you can devise a backup strategy, take into account your company's archival scheme, if one exists. An archival strategy is also known as a *retention period* for your backup files. A retention period involves the following:

- How long you will keep a backup, whether it is a SQL Server database, the operating system, or any other application data. The amount of time a file is retained is usually dictated by a corporate policy, but is also governed by cost, space, and other logistics.

- How long you will keep media active in the backup mix, otherwise known as *rotation*. Using the same tape repeatedly is not the proper strategy because you are just overwriting your backups onto the same tape or disk without being able to go back to an older backup should that backup process fail. Media also fails, which is another reason for rotation. Do not let your media be a huge point of failure. Along with rotating your media, label each tape or disk with the contents and backup date so you are not playing the "Guess the Proper Backup Tape" game in a potential disaster recovery or restore situation.

- The location of backup storage. Whether it is on a tape or disk, the media the backups are stored on take up physical room. Do you store the media on site? off site? If your corporate disaster recovery strategy states that you must be able to go back a week, it might make sense to keep a week (or even two) on site, but anything older than that should be stored in a secure, climate-controlled off-site facility. Also, you might be at risk if your datacenter is damaged and it not only housed your systems, but your complete corporate archive of backup tapes as well. Remember that backup tapes take up physical storage space and have a cost associated with them, so you might not be able to keep every backup since the inception of your company. Many companies implement an archival and rotation schedule of somewhere between 30 days and 90 days, unless they are regulated by some external auditing agency or specific industry rules (for example, a financial company) and are mandated to retain large amounts of archived backups.

- Off-site location access. If you store your backups at an off-site location, you need to have physical access to the location at all hours, so choose your storage facility wisely.

> **On the CD**   Use the file SQL_DB_Backup_Info.xls to record your backup strategy. It has two main tabs that you can copy and modify. One is for an entire instance of SQL Server so you can record the databases, and one is per application. This strategy allows you to have two views to understand the scope of your backup strategy better.

Devising a Backup Strategy to Create an Optimal Recovery Strategy

The most effective backup approach combines two strategies: one strategy is based on full database backups (the full database–based backup strategy), and the other is based on file/filegroup backups (the file-based backup strategy). Both strategies can use differential backups, but all strategies involve the use of transaction log backups.

The Full Database–Based Backup Strategy

This strategy is the most common strategy. It is generally based on backup types that have been available since the introduction of SQL Server, yet if the environment is right it might also utilize one of the newer backup types to improve recovery time. This strategy is easier to administer than the file-based backup strategy and offers up-to-the-minute recovery and point-in-time recovery. You can change between the Full and Bulk-Logged recovery models without breaking the continuity of the log. Remember to also review the recommended practices for batch processing, because using the Bulk-Logged recovery model will significantly reduce the work-loss exposure created during the changes in recovery models.

The typical strategy consists of automated backups of these types:

- Full database backups

- Differential database backups

- Transaction log backups

Their frequency is dictated by your database but usually follows something like this:

- Full database backups weekly (although less frequent full backups are an option, as these might be quite large and expensive to manage).

- Differential database backups nightly (except on the night of the full database backup).

- Transaction log backups—consistent and automated, as well as two special cases. The frequency dictates the potential work-loss exposure in terms of minutes and the transaction log size. The smaller the interval, the smaller the log will be, which is, of course, dependent on database activity.

   ❏ **Automated**   Hourly, every 30 minutes, every 5 minutes, every 1 minute, and so on.

   ❏ **Special Case 1 (Proactive)**   When the transaction log "percent log used" reaches a higher than normal level, back it up proactively before it fills up.

   ❏ **Special Case 2 (Reactive)**   When the transaction log fills up, back it up.

Consider the following example using full and transaction log backups, as well as differentials, because performing full database backups weekly leads to a large number of logs being created hourly. In a week, if you performed a transaction log backup every hour, you would have nearly 170 transaction log backups ($24 \times 7 = 168$, but because you perform one full backup, no transaction logs are generated during the process).

Restoring all of these transaction logs from transaction log backups takes time and is cumbersome. You want a streamlined process, not one in which you need to write close to 180 Transact-SQL statements. So although it takes significantly less time than the original modification took to apply all of the operations in the transaction logs, it could still take a lot of time to implement (again, no computations, no functions, just data is applied—but for every log row). Instead of having to build a version of a database by reapplying changes row by row, you can get to a specific point in time much more quickly by using a differential backup.

In this scenario full database backups are represented as F_1 and F_2, differential database backups are represented as D_1, D_2, D_3, and D_4, and 20 transaction log backups are shown as l_1 through l_{20}. At point in time x you decide to recover the database.

> **Note** In this example, only automated backups are used to describe recovery. When disaster recovery using backups is discussed, you will learn how (and when) to access a final backup, which includes the changes since the database was taken offline. In this case a 28th backup would be necessary. This backup is called the *tail* of the transaction log and it provides up-to-the-minute recovery. This part of your recovery process is the most important, and the procedure has not yet been discussed. However, all of the sample scripts include the code for backing up the 28th backup—backing up the tail of the log.

F_1 l_1 l_2 l_3 D_1 l_4 l_5 l_6 D_2 l_7 l_8 l_9 D_3 l_{10} l_{11} l_{12} F_2 l_{13} l_{14} l_{15} D_1 l_{16} l_{17} l_{18} D_2 l_{19} l_{20} x

This example shows a total of 27 backups. With this backup strategy, you have *multiple* potential recovery paths and more efficient recovery. The most optimal recovery path is to use the last full database backup, the last differential backup *after* that full database backup, and then all of the transaction log backups after the differential backup to restore the database up-to-the-minute when it is possible.

$$\mathbf{F_2} \qquad\qquad\qquad\qquad \mathbf{D_2}\, l_{19}\, l_{20}$$

This strategy is optimal because you can recover all of the activity that occurred between the full database backup at F_2 and the differential backup at D_2 with only a single restore. This restore is a copy of how the pages looked at the point in time when the differential backup was made, and it includes all changes since the full backup. Remember, each differential database backup includes all changes since the last full backup. Each differential could get larger and larger, so you will still want to periodically perform a full database backup. However, differentials offer the ability to perform a potentially smaller backup (maybe a fraction of the entire database) more frequently and not burden the system by performing full database backups. But what if the last differential backup was bad? Do you have any other options? You could use the differential backup prior to that as shown here:

$$\mathbf{F_2} \qquad\qquad \mathbf{D_1}\, l_{16}\, l_{17}\, l_{18} \qquad l_{19}\, l_{20}$$

If that differential backup were bad as well, then you could use *only* the transaction logs and still recover:

$$\mathbf{F_2}\, l_{13}\, l_{14}\, l_{15} \qquad l_{16}\, l_{17}\, l_{18} \qquad l_{19}\, l_{20}$$

If the last full database backup were bad, you have other options. If the backup at F_2 is bad, go back to F_1. However, when you go back to a previous full database backup, you must remember that the only differentials you can apply are those that apply to that version of the full database backup. For the full database backup performed at F_1 you can apply any differentials performed after that full backup (not another) and before the next full database backup (F_2 in this case). If F_1 were required for the restore then the *most* optimal restore sequence starting with F1 would be the following:

$$\mathbf{F_1} \qquad\qquad\qquad \mathbf{D_3}l_{10}\, l_{11}\, l_{12} \qquad l_{13}\, l_{14}\, l_{15} \qquad l_{16}\, l_{17}\, l_{18} \qquad l_{19}\, l_{20}$$

You could then repeat the same process described previously and return to an earlier differential if the differential database backup D_3 were bad. A complete list of all of your remaining options follows:

$$\mathbf{F_1} \qquad\quad \mathbf{D_2}\, l_7\, l_8\, l_9 \qquad l_{10}\, l_{11}\, l_{12} \qquad l_{13}\, l_{14}\, l_{15} \qquad l_{16}\, l_{17}\, l_{18} \qquad l_{19}\, l_{20}$$

$$\mathbf{F_1} \qquad \mathbf{D_1}l_4\, l_5\, l_6 \qquad l_7\, l_8\, l_9 \qquad l_{10}\, l_{11}\, l_{12} \qquad l_{13}\, l_{14}\, l_{15} \qquad l_{16}\, l_{17}\, l_{18} \qquad l_{19}\, l_{20}$$

$$\mathbf{F_1}\, l_1\, l_2\, l_3 \qquad l_4\, l_5\, l_6 \qquad l_7\, l_8\, l_9 \qquad l_{10}\, l_{11}\, l_{12} \qquad l_{13}\, l_{14}\, l_{15} \qquad l_{16}\, l_{17}\, l_{18} \qquad l_{19}\, l_{20}$$

In fact, even if this full database backup at F_1 were bad, you could return to the previous full database backup, assuming you kept it, and still roll forward to the last transaction log backup. Or you could return to the previous full database backup—or the one before that, or the one before that—*as long as you have the entire sequence of log backups to apply.*

> **Tip**   Never truncate the transaction log; it breaks the log backup sequence.

Case Study: A Differential Rotation Schedule and Cost Analysis

As part of an overall cost savings analysis, a company determines that by implementing a differential backup strategy its backup needs can be covered completely and the company can save money at the same time by implementing a differential backup strategy. Because transaction log backups are critical, the company decides that transaction log backups should be performed to disk. Additionally, it augments the backup strategy with a log shipping site at a remote location. The current full database backup strategy costs $44,380 annually. The breakdown of the costs associated with it is as follows:

- **Tape costs**   Each Linear Tape-Open (LTO) tape costs $70, and each full database backup requires 3 LTO tapes. Full database backups are performed daily, requiring 21 LTO tapes per week. Tapes are reused every 12 weeks (allowing the company to keep each month of history and then reuse after roughly 3 months). Proactively, tapes are cycled out after 24 weeks, allowing an archive off site of roughly 6 months. The total cost per year is $35,280. (All price quotations in this book are in U.S. dollars.)

- **Labor costs**   A typical operator who is paid $50 an hour takes half an hour a day to locate; mount, dismount, label, and file each backup. Each week this process requires a total of 3.5 hours, and this specific task takes a total of 182 hours per year. The total labor cost per year is $9,100.

However, the database is over 1 terabyte (TB) and only 2 percent of the data changes daily. If 1 TB of data can fit on 3 tapes, several database differential backups can easily fit on the same tapes. In fact, numerous differentials can even fit on a single tape. The first day the backup will be 20 GB (the total backup space needed 20 GB); the second day it will be 40 GB (if appended, the total backup space needed is 60 GB); the third day it will be 60 GB (again, if appended, the total backup space needed is 120 GB); the fourth day it will be 80 GB (if appended, the total backup space needed is 200 GB); and so on.

Effectively, you could fit an entire week's worth of differential database backups on one set of tapes; however, the decision is made to rotate tapes after three differential database backups and store them on only a single tape (instead of using a stripe set). This strategy yields a significant savings in both tape media and operational costs for a total of $10,350 annually. The breakdown of the costs associated with it is as follows:

- **Tape costs**   Instead of performing full database backups daily, a full database backup is performed once per week and still requires 3 LTO tapes. Differential database backups are performed six nights per week; however, only three differential database backups are stored on each backup set. Because the size is expected to be less than 120 GB, only a single tape is used to store the differential database backups. The archiving process does not change, but instead of requiring 21 LTO tapes per week, this process requires only 5. The rotational practices are the same. The total cost per year is $8,400.

- **Labor costs**   A typical operator who is paid $50 per hour takes .5 hours per day to locate, mount, dismount, label, and file each full database backup. Each week, this new process requires a total of 45 minutes. A total of 39 hours per year is spent on this specific task. The total labor cost per year is $1,950.

The total saving for using differential backups is $34,030 ($44,380 − $10,350). The differential database backup saves 75 percent of the cost of the full database strategy. Additionally, because the differential database backs up only a maximum of 12 percent of the database (2 percent per day over the six days until a full database backup), the type of backup affects the production workload significantly less than the full database backup. Furthermore, the transaction logs are paused for a far shorter period of time, keeping the log shipping secondary more up to date.

> **Note**   This example shows the cost savings of using different backup strategies. Not all databases can benefit in this way. Carefully weigh your needs and resources against your required recovery times and database type.

The File-Based Backup Strategy

This strategy was introduced and possible in Microsoft SQL Server 7.0, but there were limitations using SQL Server 7.0 that made it less robust than the implementation in SQL Server 2000. The most significant difference is that in SQL Server 7.0, files could not be backed up individually if they were part of a filegroup or if there were data dependencies within other filegroups. If they were, SQL Server required that *all* files or filegroups be backed up at the same time. In SQL Server 2000, you can back up any file or filegroup at any time, with the only restriction being that your database be in the Full or Bulk-Logged recovery model (which all production databases should be running in anyway).

The typical strategy consists of automated backups of these types:

- Full file/filegroup backups
- Differential file/filegroup backups
- Transaction log backups

> **Note** Many applications that tend to get very large are usually vendor-neutral. As such, they do not usually support database proprietary extensions such as filegroups, even though they are transparent to the application. So before you start breaking up the database, make sure your software vendor will support you if you implement this file structure.

In the file-based backup strategy, you can completely customize the frequency and granularity of the backups—a huge benefit for VLDB—in which different portions of the data have different uses. You should customize the granularity based on the way the data is distributed within the database (such as targeting specific types of data to specific locations within a database). Moreover, you should determine the frequency of each backup based on the type of data that that is stored there.

Determining which type of user data should go into your filegroups requires some strategizing. As a simple start, the Primary filegroup should contain only the system tables, and you need only one transaction log file. As discussed earlier, you need only one transaction log file because frequent log backups minimize the space required to hold the changes, and you do *not* gain performance when you have more than one transaction log. For example, if your transaction log is backed up every minute, the size of the transaction log is the size to hold one minute's worth of log entries.

> **Note**   Long-running transactions might require a larger log. Make sure you have tested the sizing of your transaction log against all of the types of activities that must occur within your database.

You should store user-defined data in nonprimary filegroups. In general, you should rarely split individual tables and their indexes into separate filegroups. However, you might consider this approach if you have a single large table that you want to place directly into a filegroup for better scan performance and more backup options. Remember, do not implement it without testing properly.

> **Tip**   You cannot restore filegroup backups to another location without restoring the entire database. However, if you are using a full database backup, you can restore filegroups by using the WITH PARTIAL option on a restore. This approach is beneficial when recovering from user error. When recovering from hardware failure, and recovering in place, restoring a filegroup from a filegroup backup is faster than restoring from a full database backup. For more information, see the topic "Partial Database Restore Operations" in SQL Server Books Online.

Here are a few recommendations for filegroup usage:

- **Read-only tables**   A great benefit if the VLDB has a large portion of read-only data. For this portion of the database, you can significantly decrease the frequency of full filegroup backups and then only perform occasional filegroup differential backups. If the recovery plan includes only recovering the damaged file or filegroup and not an entire database, frequent file differential backups will minimize the cost of rolling the database forward.

- **Read-write tables**   Can often make up the smaller percentage in VLDBs, yet still be critical to the database. The read-write tables need more frequent backups, yet they are only a minor fraction of the total size of the database. By placing them in their own filegroups, you can then set the frequency of backup of that filegroup.

- **Text or image data**   Often in VLDBs, binary large objects (BLOBs) can take up a large amount of read-only space. As with read-only tables, you can benefit greatly by backing these up less frequently if all in the filegroup are read-only or with differentials if little changes.

- **Large tables**   Benefits are few if you want to have better control over the frequency of the large table backups. If you choose to put a table into its own filegroup, file-based backups help only in being able to choose a different granularity of backup. For example, you might back up less frequently because of so few modifications. Unfortunately, you cannot perform a partial database restore from file and filegroup backups unless you are restoring because of hardware or file corruption. When an isolated failure occurs, SQL Server allows the recovery to include only the affected part of the database in place.

  Once the file or filegroup has been restored, transaction log backups can be used to bring that file up to the point in time when the database became suspect. If you are trying to recover from an accidentally dropped table and return a part of the database to an earlier point in time, then this approach has *no* benefits. However, you can restore the *entire* database to an alternate location and then choose a more manual recovery process to bring an earlier version of the table into the database.

In fact, the file-based backup strategy provides some key benefits because it is so flexible, yet it is also complex in design, administration, and recovery. The most important part is making sure you back up every file at some point. You must achieve a complete backup set similar to what the full database backup provides (all data files must have been backed up) so that you can re-create the database structure completely, if necessary (for example, if you need to recover the database from the ground up). You can create this backup set (from which you can build the database framework, if needed) by either backing up the files individually, backing up the filegroups individually, or backing up some combination of the two—as long as *all* files are backed up at some point.

What Both Strategies Do Well

Both strategies use differential backups as well as transaction log backups, which provides some significant benefits, such as the following:

- **Up-to-the-minute recovery**   If the log is accessible and no Bulk-Logged operations have occurred since the last log backup, you will be able to back up the tail of the transaction log.

- **Built-in redundancy**   If a full backup (file/filegroup or database) is damaged because of inaccessible media or for some other reason, you can use the previous full (file/filegroup or database) backup. Similarly, if a differential (file/filegroup or database) backup is damaged because of inaccessible media or for some other reason, you can use the previous differential (file/filegroup or database) backup.

The Pros and Cons of the Full Database–Based Backup Strategy

Although this strategy is the most common, you must be aware of its pros and cons. Better to know now your potential for downtime, data loss, or both during planning rather than at the time of a disaster!

The pros include the following:

- Administration is simple.

- When you combine it with other strategies (such as log shipping), this strategy is especially good at achieving minimal downtime and data loss in the event of a failure.

- You can perform partial restores of the database to another location (which can be helpful in some recovery strategies).

The cons include the following:

- Log backups are paused during the full backup (which can affect some of the other strategies, such as log shipping).

- Log backups are paused during the differential backup. (Although this process should take less time than the full database backup, it can also affect other strategies.)

- Significant data loss could occur if a disaster were to strike during a long-running full backup.

- Full database backups can be quite large, and repetitively backing up predominantly read-only data is a waste of time and resources (disk or tape).

The Pros and Cons of the File-Based Backup Strategy

Although this strategy is not widely used, you should consider it if you have a VLDB. This strategy requires design techniques that focus on physical placement of objects to best use the strategy. However, any database can use some of the basic principles of this strategy by having multiple files. This strategy is best for situations in which log shipping is used and recovery is being optimized for hardware failure. If human error is the main purpose for choosing this strategy, you must be aware of the restrictions!

The pros include the following:

- You can back up portions of the database on a more granular level and at different intervals.

- You can perform log backups without delay or interruption to other dependent technologies (such as log shipping).

- You can restore a portion of the database more quickly in the event of an isolated hardware failure.

The cons include the following:

- Administration is complex.

- You cannot perform partial restores of the database to another location. Only the full database–based backup strategy allows you to perform partial database restores from full database backups. The database must use a structural design that supports files and filegroups; then on restore, the full database backup must be read to find the file/filegroup that is being restored. However, using a log shipping secondary that has a load delay can resolve this problem, especially in a VLDB where loading the database—even partially—can be extremely time-consuming. This recovery option can be important in disasters involving human error.

Implementing Your Backup Strategy

To properly create an effective strategy, there are numerous issues you must consider. For example, how are you going to execute your backup? To what storage medium are you going to back up your databases? Where are you going to store your backups? Conversely, can you find the necessary backups during a restore? Now that you think you have a strategy, it is time to figure out backup options, syntax, recommendations, and requirements.

Options for Performing a Backup

There are several ways to create backups: Transact-SQL syntax executed real time within SQL Server Query Analyzer; Transact-SQL syntax that has been automated through SQL Server Agent jobs and alerts; the Database Maintenance Plan Wizard; SQL-DMO; or any custom applications or third-party tools where you can access SQL Server. Although all are acceptable options, there are some basic recommendations for each option's usage.

There are numerous options related to how backups are written to backup devices. Backups can be performed to a new device (a new file or tape) for each backup, or a backup device can be used multiple times by either appending subsequent backups, keeping different backups on the same device, or overwriting the backups on the same device, keeping only the most recent backup. Many utilities that help to create automated backups use a new file for each backup. In this case, the filenames for the backups typically are created using the date and timestamp of when the backup was performed. For example, using the Database Maintenance Plan Wizard to create full database backups or transaction log backups, the filename has the following format:

dbname_backuptype_YYYYMMDDHHMM.bak.

Although this naming convention is helpful for finding backups by filename, it does not necessarily scale well. In fact, using the Database Maintenance Plan Wizard for small databases is acceptable, but for larger and more complex configurations where a variety of backup types are desired, it is likely you will create your backup strategy a bit more manually.

Typically, administrators automate the backup to disk through the day, and then have some type of nightly backup operation that picks up all of the backup files at the operating system level and backs them up to tape. The main reason for this is speed. Typically it is faster to back up and restore files from disk than tape because you avoid the long mechanical process of positioning the tape and rewinding. Transaction log backups are commonly automated using SQL Server Agent jobs that run at fixed points in time.

Creating a Backup Device

When you perform a backup, there are two ways you can specify the destination. You can either physically reference the output device (tape or disk) at the time of the backup, or you can make a logical reference to it by creating a backup device. Making a logical reference to the location by creating a backup device eliminates later problems with backup scripts. By abstracting the name from your scripts, you can update the hardware or devices and just update the logical definition.

For example, by backing up to a device with the logical name *Tape-Backup*, you do not rely on the physical tape unit to stay the same. If the underlying tape units change from \\.\tape0 to \\.\tape12, only the logical definition needs to be updated, not all of the individual backup scripts and jobs. The same is true for backups directly to a hard disk. If a drive is starting to become full and you decide to place backups on a new drive, then you can change the device without changing all of your backup scripts. During the restore process you need only to have the backups themselves. You can restore them from any location even if that is not the location to which you backed up the database.

You can create backup devices by using the `sp_addumpdevice` system stored procedure or using SQL Server Enterprise Manager. (Expand Management, right-click Backup, and select New Backup Device.) When you use the `sp_addumpdevice` stored procedure, remember that no paths or filenames are verified for access or even existence. This point is important because verification does not occur until you later attempt to back up to this device, which is when you would see errors causing the backup to fail. Make sure all of your paths and filenames are verified at the time of creation, and if the device is an over-the-network backup, you should also verify the path for appropriate permissions.

When using a network device using a Universal Naming Convention (UNC) name (*servername**sharename**pathname**filename*.ext), SQL Server must have the appropriate permissions to use the device. If you execute a backup command through Transact-SQL syntax (for example, in SQL Server Query Analyzer), then the command will be executed by the underlying MSSQLServer service. If you execute a backup as part of a job, then the backup will be performed by the SQLServer Agent service. You must verify that the domain accounts under which these two services are started have the appropriate write permissions to create and write files to the UNC device.

You can view the list of existing backup devices by using the `sp_helpdevice` system procedure or by reviewing the list in SQL Server Enterprise Manager under Management, Backup. When you perform a backup, you specify the device (or devices) to which the backup should be performed, and SQL Server writes to the location as defined by the device. A simple example of using a backup device follows:

```
BACKUP DATABASE DatabaseName TO DeviceName
```

Caution   When you use Transact-SQL or SQL Server Enterprise Manager to remove a backup device, the default behavior is to leave the files intact and *not* delete them. This approach has advantages and disadvantages. It is advantageous if you truly want to remove only the logical reference to the device. In fact, you can immediately create a new logical device name (for example, with a new name) that points to the same file if you want. Creating backup devices does not affect the physical file.

The disadvantage is that you will leave a (potentially large) backup file on disk. If you want to delete the file when you drop the device, you must specify the DELFILE option.

Special Backup Device: NUL

In addition to creating permanent or temporary devices, there is an output device called NUL. NUL is an operating system "device" that acknowledges a write operation without actually writing the data anywhere.

> **Note**   This is not a typo; the device is spelled *NUL*, not *NULL*.

NUL is used in special cases to test the read side of the backup process; however, the backup is not saved. Instead the backup is processed as if it were a regular backup but the write portion of the backup is never actually done. There are a few interesting uses for this device:

- Testing backup size
- Testing backup scripts
- Testing the impact of a backup on your disk subsystem and throughput

Using the NUL device in code is performed the same way as the use of any device physically defined at backup. The following full database backup command uses the NUL device to test the size and impact of the backup:

```
BACKUP DATABASE Inventory TO DISK = 'NUL'

go
```

The result will be similar to the following:

```
Processed 17888 pages for database 'Inventory', file 'InventoryData' on file 1.

Processed 1 pages for database 'Inventory', file 'InventoryLog' on file 1.

BACKUP DATABASE successfully processed 17889 pages in 5.872 seconds (24.955 MB/
sec).
```

From this output, you can determine the size of your backup. SQL Server does not need to back up every page of the database; instead, it needs to back up only allocated extents. The size of a backup is therefore the size of the database minus the free space. How large is that? In the previous example, a full database backup was performed to the NUL device. The backup showed that a total of 17,889 pages were processed. At 8 KB per page, the backup size would be about 146.5 MB. This information is helpful to know if you need to estimate storage because of space restrictions or if you are backing up to disk to copy the backup device(s) to CD or DVD.

As an alternative, you could use the `sp_spaceused` system procedure or run a system table query to get the same number that `sp_spaceused` produces. However, of the two, using a system table query is easier to add to programmatic scripts, batches, and so on. To get an estimate of the space usage for a database, use the following query:

```
SELECT sum(reserved)*8/1024 -- Estimate in MB

FROM sysindexes

WHERE indid IN (0, 1, 255)
```

Unfortunately, both `sp_spaceused` and this system table query might not be as accurate as you need them to be sometimes. To get a more accurate value you can run `sp_spaceused @updateusage = 'true'` and the information will be more accurately gathered by scanning the entire database; however, this can create quite a burden on the system.

Finally, there are some technical notes to be aware of when using the NUL device. Performing a backup to NUL will indicate that the backup strategy has begun—even though nothing exists from which you could recover. This situation requires you to manage the transaction log if you are not already doing so. You must always perform another real full database backup after backing up to the NUL device because you will need a proper full database backup from which you could recover. Differential database backups performed after a backup to the NUL device cannot be applied to a previous full database backup; in fact, only the transaction log backups are useful. Performing *any* full database backup—even with the NUL device—resets the differential bitmap. Because this backup to NUL performs exactly the same steps as a regular full database backup without the actual capture, you should use this option only in test or development scenarios when you are truly looking to evaluate the performance impact of the read side of backup on your disk subsystem.

> **Important**   Transaction log backups to NUL will break the log sequence chain.

Parallel Striped Backup

To improve performance, you can use multiple backup devices in parallel to create a striped backup set. The biggest benefit of creating a striped set is that you can back up to as many as 64 independent devices at a time. If you have two drives to which you would like to store backups, then you might be able to cut the backup time in half (depending on system configuration). Realize, however, that the benefits of parallel striped backup are really only achieved when the devices are different physical devices. Backing up to multiple backup devices on the same physical disk is probably not beneficial at all unless you need the files to be of a certain size. For example, you might back up to three files on one physical disk to ensure that the three files are small enough to individually burn to a certain media type, such as a 680-MB CD-R. You can then later restore directly from the CDs. If you had backed up to one large file and then split it across multiple CDs, you would need to put the file back together on disk before commencing with the restore process.

> **Note**   Backing up to multiple files on a device does not give you any performance improvements. You will actually have worse performance than if you were backing up to one file on that device.

Additionally, if you have multiple devices that you would like to act as one, consider creating a RAID 0 array and then using that as your backup location. Creating a parallel striped backup has the same configuration as a RAID 0 array. There is zero redundancy, and only performance gains because to successfully restore from a parallel striped backup, you must have *all* devices at the time of the restore. This is not true of tape devices, but it also means that you need all of the tapes to perform your restore; each media family is processed before another one can be used. Handling media families that span multiple tapes is not an easy task.

When you back up to multiple devices in parallel to a hard drive, for example three devices, approximately one-third of the database will be placed on each of the three devices. For tape, an algorithm is used where a faster tape can consume more of the data. If one device or file is not accessible at the time of recovery, the two remaining devices are essentially useless.

The following example shows a full database backup of the Inventory database to three devices: InventoryBackup1, InventoryBackup2, and InventoryBackup3.

```
BACKUP DATABASE [Inventory]

TO [InventoryBackup1], [InventoryBackup2], [InventoryBackup3]
```

If the file or tape on which InventoryBackup2 resides were to become damaged, then the complete backup would be unusable. You cannot recover *any* data from the two remaining devices (InventoryBackup1 and InventoryBackup3) without also having the data from InventoryBackup2.

When creating a parallel striped backup, you must have good naming conventions. If recovery were necessary, you would want to be able to find all components of your backups as quickly as possible. In fact, in addition to naming the individual backup devices, you can name the media set. Creating a media set name makes finding backups a lot easier because each device shows the media set name and description. Without the name and description, the only identifier you will have is a globally unique identifier (GUID) that SQL Server places into the backup device's header at the time of media set creation (which is a good secondary check, but it is harder to read and harder to work with). Therefore, you should always use a media set name and description, and you must set them with the very first backup. When performing the first backup (or later if you want to break up a media set or change the use of a device), you can add the FORMAT option to define the device's use.

> **Caution**   If any information is currently on the devices, it will be overwritten and useless. Use the FORMAT option only when necessary.

Using the same example as before, the syntax changes to the following when you add a media set name and description:

```
BACKUP DATABASE [Inventory]

TO [InventoryBackup1], [InventoryBackup2], [InventoryBackup3]

WITH FORMAT, MEDIANAME = N'InventoryStripeSet',

MEDIADESCRIPTION = N'3 Devices = InventoryBackup1-3'
```

If you decide to use parallel striped backup to disk devices, you must make sure that each independent device has enough space to handle the appropriate portion of the database. Remember that files of filegroups do not always fill evenly. If one of the devices runs out of space, the backup will terminate.

Multifile Backups

After you have created a backup device or backup devices in a media set, you might want to save multiple backups to the same device(s). In fact, if you use the syntax to back up to a device without specifying any options other than the database and the devices to which you would like to back up, SQL Server automatically appends the new backup to the backup device. This has both advantages and disadvantages. If you back up the same database to a backup device three times over the course of a week, for example, and then you need to restore your last backup, you would probably do this:

On Monday, you execute the following:

```
BACKUP DATABASE [Inventory]

TO [InventoryBackup1], [InventoryBackup2], [InventoryBackup3]
```

On Wednesday, you execute the following:

```
BACKUP DATABASE [Inventory]

TO [InventoryBackup1], [InventoryBackup2], [InventoryBackup3]
```

On Friday, you execute the following:

```
BACKUP DATABASE [Inventory]

TO [InventoryBackup1], [InventoryBackup2], [InventoryBackup3]
```

The following Monday, you decide you want to restore the Inventory database to its state at the Friday backup, so you execute the following:

```
RESTORE DATABASE [Inventory]

FROM [InventoryBackup1], [InventoryBackup2], [InventoryBackup3]
```

And you restore Monday's backup, not Friday's. This mistake is one of the most common user errors when using multifile backups. To restore the appropriate backup, you must specify the backup based on position within the multifile backup device(s). To see the list of backups performed to a backup device(s), you can use the RESTORE HEADERONLY command, which has the following syntax:

```
RESTORE HEADERONLY FROM [InventoryBackup1]
```

This lists all of the backups (in this case, three rows) that have been performed to this device or these devices. You need to specify only one device because SQL Server can access the header from any of the devices of a parallel striped media set. After you list the header, you can use the position column to determine which backup must be restored. In this case the position is 3, so the restore command would use the following:

```
RESTORE DATABASE [Inventory]

FROM [InventoryBackup1], [InventoryBackup2], [InventoryBackup3]

WITH FILE = 3
```

If you would like to overwrite the contents of backup devices while backing up, you can do so by using the INIT option instead of appending. Because appending (NOINIT) is the default, you must specify when you want to overwrite. INIT only works when you are overwriting a media set with exactly the same format (which means the same number of backup devices) and when the backup set does not have a required retention period. If you want to break up a media set, which is changing the number of backup devices, you must use WITH FORMAT. If the backup set has a required retention period and you want to INIT the devices before the retention period has been met, you can tell SQL Server to SKIP the backup device headers.

Useful Backup Options

Although many backup options are offered, not all are available for each individual backup method (for example, the password options are not available through SQL Server Enterprise Manager). For more details, spend some time testing and working with your own server. The options are as follows:

Defining a media set   Use the following:

```
[[,] FORMAT | NOFORMAT]

[[,] MEDIADESCRIPTION = {'text' | @text_variable}]

[[,] MEDIANAME = {media_name | @media_name_variable}]

[[,] MEDIAPASSWORD = {mediapassword | @mediapassword_variable}]
```

Format implies INIT and SKIP. FORMAT can be used to break up a striped media set; however, use caution because FORMAT renders all devices unusable. Every media set should have a descriptive name as well as a description that details the number and name of the devices that make up the media set. If a password is used on the backup, a media set password will need to be supplied for every restore. Good naming conventions can save time and minimize errors in disaster recovery.

Defining an individual backup   Use the following:

```
[[,] NAME = {backup_set_name | @backup_set_name_var}]

[[,] DESCRIPTION = {'text' | @text_variable}]

[[,] PASSWORD = {password | @password_variable}]
```

Every backup should have a name and a description. If you have issues with the physical security of your backups or backup media, consider using a password. This password is for the individual backup, *not* the media set. Good naming conventions can save time and minimize errors in disaster recovery.

Manipulating the media or backup device   Use the following:

```
[[,] INIT | NOINIT]

[[,] NOSKIP | SKIP]

[[,] EXPIREDATE = {date | @date_var}

| RETAINDAYS = {days | @days_var}]

[[,] STATS [= percentage]]
```

INIT initializes backup devices only when they are in the correct structure. INIT does not allow the backup to proceed if the backup device was previously used in a media set and has not been reformatted. You must use FORMAT to break up the media set. NOINIT is the default, meaning that every backup is automatically appended to the backup devices. EXPIREDATE and RETAINDAYS set the backup retention period. EXPIREDATE is the date when a backup can use INIT—to the same device—without error. RETAINDAYS is similar, except the retention period is set as the number of days that must pass before the backup can be overwritten with INIT. Neither option invalidates the backup or prevents it from being restored once the time has expired. These options are effectively retention settings, not expiration dates.

> **Important**   All bets are off and all expiration options are discarded if FORMAT is used or if SKIP is used. If you use FORMAT, it implies the use of SKIP.

The STATS option defines when progress messages are returned from a backup. Using WITH STATS when performing backups manually, as well as when automating backups, provides a mechanism to see the progress of a backup.

Working with tape devices   Use the following:

```
[[,] NOREWIND | REWIND]
[[,] NOUNLOAD | UNLOAD]
[[,] RESTART]
```

NOREWIND is important to use if you plan to perform automated multifile backups to tape. However, it is not essential. Specifying NOREWIND allows SQL Server to leave the tape heads in position to perform (and append) the next tape backup where the previous one left off. Therefore, you save time when backing up (or restoring from) tape. NOREWIND implies NOUNLOAD. However, if only NOUNLOAD is specified, the tape will still rewind. This can be useful if you want to backup and then immediately restore. Finally, if a power failure were to occur during the backup, you could use RESTART to resume the backup at the point at which it failed.

> **Important**   NOREWIND holds the tape device locked, so other applications cannot use it.

Third-Party Backup and Restore Tools and SQL Server

Some third-party hardware and tools, such as enterprise backup software or storage area network (SAN) devices, can back up your file systems and databases as well. This might simplify management in an organization because all backup-related work is standardized, bypassing learning syntax for each product you run. However, it is still helpful to know the syntax because it is essentially what is issued behind the scenes for whatever technology you employ.

Nevertheless, you must understand that a "normal" backup tool cannot just back up an active SQL Server database file. SQL Server must be accessed properly so that when the software starts a backup, SQL Server believes and responds as if a native backup is occurring. Otherwise, you might damage your databases, obtaining an inconsistent set of database files on restore. To enable SQL Server to believe a native backup is happening, device drivers and software must utilize the SQL Server Virtual Backup Device (VDI) API. You must check with your preferred software or hardware vendor prior to implementing or purchasing a solution to ensure that it not only works properly with your servers running SQL Server instances, but also supports the VDI. Similarly, if your system administrators use a program already for performing backups and now want to use it to back up your live SQL Server databases, verify that it is capable of doing so.

If you intend to use a third-party program that does not support the SQL Server VDI, one of the best options to integrate it into your SQL Server backup strategy is to have a SQL Server Agent job back up the database to a specified disk, and then have the program back up the SQL Server–generated file. Other variations on this theme obviously exist, but this example illustrates that you can leverage your existing backup solution even if it cannot back up your SQL Server databases directly. If the program does support the VDI, you might want to use it to manage your entire backup strategy. Mixing SQL Server Agent jobs or manual backups might interfere with your packaged solution. You should choose one strategy and stick to it.

> **More Info**   For information on the SQL Server 2000 VDI, go to *http://www.microsoft.com/sql/downloads/virtualbackup.asp*.

Storage Assisted Backups

Your storage vendor might provide technologies that greatly enhance your ability to back up and restore large amounts of data quickly, especially in a SAN environment. SQL Server 2000 supports these technologies through extensions to the VDI previously mentioned. Relative to SQL Server, a storage assisted backup is usually referred to as a split-mirror backup.

> **Note**   Although SQL Server 2000 supports these hardware-based backups through the VDI, the technology itself is not built into SQL Server. Check with your storage vendor to see whether any storage assisted backup options are available to you.

Split-Mirror Basics, Pros, and Cons   A *split mirror* is pretty much what it sounds like: You take one of your RAID mirrors and "separate" it from the others. You can combine a storage assisted backup with conventional database backups to accomplish rolling your database forward to the point of failure or to an arbitrary point in time—or both. Like any other type of database backup, the history is stored in msdb if the application writes backup history there. The utility provided by the storage or backup vendor might automatically determine the files that comprise the database and determine which volumes to capture. In other cases, you might have to supply a list of volumes to the utility.

In terms of usage, a split-mirror backup is applicable to media-failure scenarios as well as application-error or user-error scenarios. From a high availability perspective, split-mirror backups are beneficial because the process is usually measured in seconds, and not minutes, hours, or even days. Imagine trying to back up a petabyte of information using another method—on any database platform for that matter—in a matter of seconds. The same principle is applicable on a restore; what you gain in speed might be worth the additional cost of the solution.

Another good use of a split-mirror backup is to initialize a log shipping secondary. If you have a large database, again, you need to weigh the risks and rewards. But if you need to initialize a 1 TB database as your base database for log shipping, virtually no other method can perform the task more quickly because using a form of a "normal" restore, at some point, no matter how much you tweak disk I/O and such, you are still trying to restore 1 TB of data. Along the same lines, if you need to initialize a test or development database housing your large production VLDB, as with the log shipping secondary, there are very few ways to restore a large database easily.

Pros   Split-mirror backups can virtually eliminate the time it takes to accomplish the backup itself as well as the data copy phase of a restore, which is the most time-consuming aspect. The exact benefits depend on the vendor's implementation. If the production disks are reconciled with the clone in the background, the restore itself is almost instantaneous. So from both a SQL Server and high availability standpoint, this is probably the biggest advantage. The database needs only to be rolled forward to the target time and recovered. It is then available for updates while the disks are reconciled in the background. And because backups are performed on a separate mirror that is already in sync at the time of the split, you get the benefit of no I/O hit for reading the data and then writing to a file. Therefore, you reduce the impact of the entire backup process on a live production system.

Cons   Ultimately, the biggest drawback of implementing a split-mirror solution is the cost. These solutions are usually out of the price range of most small and midsized companies, and even some large companies. The biggest cost is obviously the number of disks. If your disk solution already has, say, 48 disks, with two stripes of 24, you need to add another 24 for a total of 72. Assuming for the sake of this example that each disk costs US$1,000 because of its large capacity and high speed, that is US$72,000 in just physical disks alone. Then you need to consider the enclosures, the racks to house them, all cabling, proper cooling, and so on—you get the idea.

Furthermore, you need to ensure that your staff is properly trained in the use of split mirrors. Unlike a normal SQL Server backup in which you are dumping a file to a disk or tape, this is a specialized solution. Even if you have the money, do not implement a backup solution that you cannot manage.

Unlike a normal backup to disk, split mirrors really have no concept of versioning. Once you split the mirror, and then remirror, that backup you made by doing the original split is gone unless you backed it up to tape or disk elsewhere. You will therefore need to manage your backups more carefully if nothing else is employed. Other caveats specific to each process are outlined next.

Using a Split Mirror for Database Backups   If you employ split mirrors, a backup is accomplished by physically splitting one mirror away from the others at the disk level. This mirror contains a copy of the data at the time of the split. This mirror can be referred to by different names depending on the storage vendor. Some names are *clone, snapshot,* or *business-continuance volume* (BCV). The mirror, together with the small amount of descriptive data created by SQL Server, is the backup.

The benefit of splitting one mirror off is that it is a fast operation. SQL Server briefly stops all writes to the database while the split is initiated and completed so that you will not have torn pages in your database. This process should usually be measured in seconds and is vendor-dependent in terms of timings and implementation. The availability of the database should not be affected except for the brief stop to ensure consistency. If you have a VLDB, a split mirror might be the only way to achieve some of your service level agreements (SLAs) if you cannot use a traditional backup and restore scenario that is outlined in this chapter.

> **Important**   Use a minimum of a three-way mirror to ensure that your production disk subsystem will still be highly available. Using only two mirrors leaves you exposed if you encounter a disk failure. Work with your storage vendor to ensure that your configuration is optimal for both SQL Server and the hardware level for using an advanced technology such as a split mirror.

Remirroring the Disk Stripe   To use the disk stripe that was split, you must remirror it with the active disk mirrors to update it. During the remirroring process, the stripe data is copied from the active mirror(s) at a low level to synchronize it; the process is not handled by SQL Server. Your database is completely available for use during this process. However, especially on large databases, your other mirrors will be active, so you might see some sort of performance impact on your database because the stripe remirroring will be reading from the other disk stripes. Some storage vendors can perform the reconciliation by copying only what has changed, and others will synchronize everything. Many will allow you to prioritize the remirroring against being able to run your daily workload on the same set of disks.

> **Warning**   If you are employing a split mirror in conjunction with SQL Server 2000 failover clustering, when the remirroring process occurs, you must guarantee that the disk signatures will not be altered. If they are altered, you can damage your cluster. Talk to your hardware vendor, because this mistake could be painfully expensive.
>
> Also, do not confuse a split mirror with a geographically dispersed cluster. Geographically dispersed cluster solutions employ a special form of mirroring technology to ensure that the SANs in each location are kept in sync and are used for different purposes.

Using a Split Mirror to Restore Databases   Performing a restore with a split mirror is similar to a remirror, but the actual data copy process flows the other way. The mirror is the master and the production volumes are synchronized with it. As part of the restore, the backup utility gives SQL Server the proper description of the backup being restored, as well as the appropriate restore options, such as NORECOVERY. The database might be rolled forward using conventional differential, file-differential, transaction log backups, or all three after main file is restored.

Ideally, the data is presented to SQL Server immediately, and the reconciliation occurs in the background. In this case, the restore occurs in a matter of seconds, and the database can be recovered and made available immediately. This functionality is the primary benefit of implementing a split mirror.

Planning Considerations for Split Mirroring   When you want to implement a split-mirror backup solution for SQL Server, consider the following:

- A backup can be restored only once. Restoring a split-mirror backup converts that backup into a database. After that, the backup no longer exists. If you need to maintain a backup, you would either need another mirror or you need to back up the mirror that was split to a media such as tape before restoring it in SQL Server.

- The time it takes to complete remirroring limits the frequency of backups. Remirroring can take significant time for large databases, even if done incrementally. Although the database is available, this time limits the frequency of your database or file backups. As with conventional backups, this limitation increases the amount of roll-forward required after a failure.

■ Performance of your databases might be affected by the remirroring process for the obvious reasons already stated. You must account for this in your planning, and you should work with your storage vendor to understand the impact on your systems so you have realistic expectations.

■ Once you remirror, you no longer have a backup of your database. Consequently, you must somehow maintain some sort of backup solution to account for this. Two options available to you are backing up the mirror to another medium before remirroring (which might take some time, but it will not leave you exposed) or adding an additional mirror that will be split off right before the other is remirrored (which gives you two mirrors that you can roll in and out, and you are still protected as long as you have at least two active mirrors).

■ On one volume, do not store data and log files from different databases. If you do, you will not be able to back up or restore the databases independently. Restoring one database will corrupt the other, which means your mirror to database ratio is 1:1.

Windows Server 2003 Volume Shadow Copy Service and SQL Server 2000

A new feature of Windows Server 2003 is the Volume Shadow Copy Service (VSS). It is a volume-oriented, snapshot-based backup. Windows Server 2003 also ships with something known as the SQLWriter, which is the back-end component of VSS that interacts with SQL Server. Under Windows, the writer is displayed as MSDEWriter. This can be verified by executing a VSSADMIN LIST WRITERS command in a command window.

SQLWriter is a VDI-based application that utilizes the VDI's BACKUP WITH SNAPSHOT support. Because of the SQLWriter, you can use VSS with SQL Server 2000 to perform full backups. All recovery models are supported, and NORECOVERY allows you to roll the database forward. Differential, transaction log, and file backups are not supported with VSS. However, full database backups made with VSS can be combined with any other native backup strategy (such as transaction log backups or a third-party tool and so on) to handle the rolling forward after the VSS backup is restored to your instance.

> **Important**   For user databases, you can restore them to a live SQL Server instance, but for system databases (master, model, and msdb), you have to stop SQL Server to restore the VSS backup. VSS is fully supported in a server cluster.

> **Note**   Due to the timing of the release of Windows Server 2003 and the writing of this book, there is not a lot of information available on implementing VSS with SQL Server 2000. Check *http://www.microsoft.com* for updated information.

Executing the Full Database–Based Backup Strategy Using Transact-SQL

You can execute backups in many ways, but ultimately it all boils down to the syntax of the command being executed. Whether you use SQL Server Enterprise Manager to set up the backup or type it in yourself, it is just a command. This brief section shows examples of how to use the syntax to create your backup.

> **On the CD**   There is a script included, Full_Database_Based_ Backup_Strategy.sql, which is an example of a full database backup and restore and is detailed in this section.

Executing a Full Database Backup

When using the full database–based backup strategy, you always use a full backup to create the recovery set. This backup will be the first one used during the restore. To create a full database backup, you must use the BACKUP DATABASE command and all of the appropriate options. In the following example, a full database backup will be performed to three devices in parallel. The backup set will have a defined media set name, description, and password to protect the media set, a password to protect this specific backup, and the backup will be performed to tape devices so that the next backup can immediately append. Additionally, this backup will be set to prevent INIT for seven days and it will return the status of the backup every 10 percent backed up. The syntax for this command is:

```
BACKUP DATABASE [Inventory]

TO [InventoryBackup1], [InventoryBackup2], [InventoryBackup3] WITH FORMAT,

MEDIANAME = N'InventoryStripeSet',

MEDIADESCRIPTION = N'3 Devices = InventoryBackup1-3',
```

```
MEDIAPASSWORD = N'InventoryStripeSetPassword',

RETAINDAYS = 7,

NAME = N'InventoryBackup',

DESCRIPTION = N'Full Database Backup of Inventory',

PASSWORD = N'InventoryBackupFullDBPassword',

NOREWIND, STATS = 10
```

Executing a Transaction Log Backup

As the most important type of backup to perform, transaction log backups are critical to maintaining an optimal database size and allowing the full spectrum of recovery options. Transaction log backups—like all others—should be automated. In fact, to make a system highly available you will automate all of these backups to run at a consistent and frequent interval. Transaction log backups are the most frequent. In the upcoming section "Simplifying and Automating Backups," you will automate three different situations that trigger a transaction log backup to occur.

To create the transaction log backup you use a very similar command (BACKUP LOG) with many of the same options as BACKUP DATABASE used. To perform against the same three devices that the full database backup used, you submit the media set password. The media set password is required for *all* commands that need to access this media set. Without the password you will receive the error "Access is denied due to a password failure." To create an individual backup password for the transaction log backup, to leave the tape ready for another backup, and to return stats to know the status of the transaction log backup, use the command listed next.

> **Note**   Using a password is not mandatory. In the big picture, although it will secure the backup in SQL Server, it only prevents access by SQL Server tools. A disk-based backup is more exposed than one on tape.

```
BACKUP LOG [Inventory]

TO [InventoryBackup1], [InventoryBackup2], [InventoryBackup3] WITH NOINIT,

MEDIAPASSWORD = N'InventoryStripeSetPassword',

NAME = N'InventoryTLogBackup',

DESCRIPTION = N'Transaction Log Backup of Inventory',
```

```
PASSWORD = N'InventoryBackupTlogPassword',

NOREWIND, STATS = 10
```

Executing a Differential Database Backup

Executing a differential database backup is actually exactly the same as executing a full database backup, except that you back up only the extents that have changed. You use the same command with one additional clause added: WITH DIFFERENTIAL. Following the same command as the full database backup (removing the media set definition parameters because they are necessary only on the first backup)—including STATS for progress and this time telling SQL Server to rewind and unload (unload implies rewind) the tape—use the following syntax:

```
BACKUP DATABASE [Inventory]

TO [InventoryBackup1], [InventoryBackup2], [InventoryBackup3]

WITH DIFFERENTIAL, NOINIT,

MEDIAPASSWORD = N'InventoryStripeSetPassword',

NAME = N'InventoryDiffBackup',

DESCRIPTION = N'Differential Database Backup of Inventory',

PASSWORD = N'InventoryBackupDiffPassword',

UNLOAD, STATS = 10
```

Executing the File-Based Backup Strategy Using Transact-SQL

The commands for executing the file-based backup strategy are exactly the same for all parameters immediately after the TO portion of the BACKUP command, including the device list, media set information, tape option, password protection, and retention options. The file-based strategy differs *before* the TO clause. To perform file-based and filegroup-based backups, specify the database you are backing up with the BACKUP DATABASE command. Before you state the devices, you must specifically state the subset of the database you want based on the file (or files), the filegroup (or filegroups), or both.

When using the file-based backup strategy, you must create a complete set of all files by backing each file up individually, or by backing up groups of files as defined by your database's filegroups. During the restore process, you always start with the file or filegroup backups and then roll forward using other backup types. To create file or filegroup backups, you must use the BACKUP DATABASE command and specify the files, filegroups, or both that you want backed up in this backup set.

On the CD To create the File_Based_Backup_DB sample database and all the backups shown in the case study diagram shown in Figure 10-1, run the File_Based_Backup_Strategy.sql script, which you will find on the CD that accompanies this book. You can execute this script in its entirety, but you should work your way through the script, slowly reviewing the syntax to fully understand the backup strategy. For best understanding, review the syntax descriptions from this section prior to execution.

The example uses seven database files: a primary file (.mdf), three nonprimary data files in a filegroup named RWFG (used for read-write data), two files in a filegroup named ROFG (used for read-only data), and one transaction log file. After creating the FileBasedBackupDB database, the script modifies data between each of the backups. The FileBasedBackupDB figure shows the backup types from left to right in this sequence (the number corresponds to the number along the timeline).

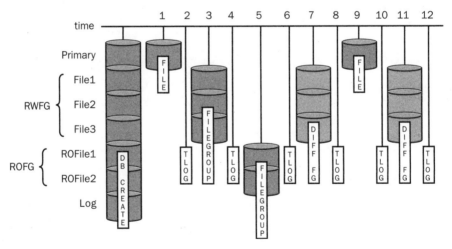

Figure 10-1 File-based backups offering significant flexibility.

1. Full file backup of the primary file
2. Transaction log backup
3. Full filegroup backup of the RWFG filegroup
4. Transaction log backup

5. Full filegroup backup of the ROFG filegroup

6. Transaction log backup

7. Differential filegroup backup of the RWFG filegroup

8. Transaction log backup

9. Full file backup of the primary file

10. Transaction log backup

11. Differential filegroup backup of the RWFG filegroup

12. Transaction log backup

Using the example shown for FileBasedBackupStrategy.sql, the first backup is a file backup of the primary file named FileBasedBackupDBPrimary. Because all of the options for tape backup, media set names, descriptions, and passwords are the same, the syntax is kept to a minimum. The syntax for the file backup at point in time 1 is as follows:

```
BACKUP DATABASE [FileBasedBackupDB]

File = N'FileBasedBackupDBPrimary'

TO [FileBasedBackupDev]

WITH NAME = N'FileBasedBackupDB Backup',

DESCRIPTION = N'File = FileBasedBackupDBPrimary', INIT
```

Transaction log backups are an integral part of the file and filegroup strategy because they ensure transactional integrity of a backup when it is restored. Transaction log backups can use the same device or devices as the database backups when necessary. In the script, a transaction log backup occurs at every even position: 2, 4, 6, 8, 10, and 12. Each transaction log backup uses the exact same syntax:

```
BACKUP LOG [FileBasedBackupDB]

TO [FileBasedBackupDev]

WITH NAME = N'FileBasedBackupDB Backup',

DESCRIPTION = N'Transaction Log', NOINIT
```

The next backup type, shown in position 3, is a filegroup backup. The RWFG filegroup backup is performed with the following syntax:

```
BACKUP DATABASE [FileBasedBackupDB]

FILEGROUP = N'RWFG'
```

```
TO [FileBasedBackupDev]

WITH NAME = N'FileBasedBackupDB Backup',

DESCRIPTION = N'FileGroup = RWFG', NOINIT
```

In the backup shown in position 5, the ROFG filegroup is backed up with the following syntax:

```
BACKUP DATABASE [FileBasedBackupDB]

FILEGROUP = N'ROFG'

TO [FileBasedBackupDev]

WITH NAME = N'FileBasedBackupDB Backup',

DESCRIPTION = N'FileGroup = ROFG', NOINIT
```

In the backup at positions 7 and 11, a filegroup differential is chosen for the RWFG. To perform a differential backup, the syntax is exactly the same as a file or filegroup backup, with the addition of the WITH DIFFERENTIAL clause. The syntax for the RWFG filegroup differential backup is as follows:

```
BACKUP DATABASE [FileBasedBackupDB]

FILEGROUP = N'RWFG'

TO [FileBasedBackupDev] WITH DIFFERENTIAL, NOINIT,

NAME = N'FileBasedBackupDB Backup',

DESCRIPTION = N'FileGroup DIFFERENTIAL = RWFG'
```

The syntax for the file-based strategy is just as straightforward as the syntax for backing up databases using the full database–based strategy. The complexities with this strategy are not in the backup, but instead in the recovery process.

> **Caution**   You must perform significant testing so that all possible recovery paths are implemented properly. If even one file is missing, the database cannot be recovered from backups.

Simplifying and Automating Backups

The Transact-SQL syntax is not overly complex once you get a feel for it. However, creating a backup plan is hardly about syntax. To create an optimal strategy, you must have a recovery-oriented plan that is well tested and well defined—and most important—automated. Backups should never be handled manually because they will be more prone to human error or might even be forgotten. To ensure optimal recovery, implement a consistent and automated plan to handle backups. One of the easiest ways to perform this task is by creating automated jobs using the SQL Server Agent.

For each backup type you choose, you should implement a job to automate that backup type at the necessary frequency. As a simple first step, you can use SQL Server Enterprise Manager to help you create an automated backup schedule for your full database backup. To create a full database backup that runs weekly, right-click your database, select Tasks, and then select Backup Database. Select all of the options you want, as if you were actually going to perform the backup. *Before* you click OK, however, select the Schedule check box, as shown in Figure 10-2.

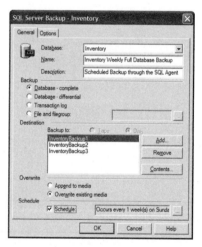

Figure 10-2 The SQL Server Backup - Inventory dialog box to simplify creating a scheduled backup.

You can set the schedule now by clicking the ellipses (...) button, or you can set it later, after the job is created. Instead of performing the backup, SQL Server creates a job with the chosen schedule when you click OK. The backup is not performed; only the job is created as long as you have the Schedule check box selected. Once created, you can add additional steps such as sending e-mail regarding the completion or failure of the backup and modifying additional properties about your backup.

To demonstrate the simplicity of setting up jobs using the SQL Server Enterprise Manager backup user interface, the following example creates a backup of the transaction log that will be automated to run every 10 minutes. The time interval you choose depends on several criteria:

- **Database activity**   If the database is predominantly read activity, the transaction log does not need to be backed up as frequently.

- **Data loss potential**   If all activity needs to be captured to minimize the likelihood of data loss if a failure occurs, more frequent log backups should be performed. Especially when you have a secondary site, the frequency of your log backups determines the maximum amount of data loss you could incur if you had a site failure.

- **Transaction log size**   To keep the transaction log size to a minimum, increase the frequency of backups.

Because it is a time-based backup, some transaction log backups will be larger (such as those made during working hours) and some will be smaller (such as those made during off hours when less work is being performed). To check the percentage of the log currently used, run the DBCC SQLP-ERF(LOGSPACE) command. This command shows you percentages used and free for all transaction logs on your SQL Server instance:

```
DBCC SQLPERF(LOGSPACE)
```

To automate the transaction log backup for the Inventory database, as shown in the previous examples, right-click your database, choose All Tasks, and select Backup Database. On the General Tab (shown in Figure 10-2), enter a name, description, and all of the backup properties.

Once you have set the options, click ... (ellipses) to set the schedule for the transaction log backups. The Edit Schedule dialog box opens, as shown in Figure 10-3.

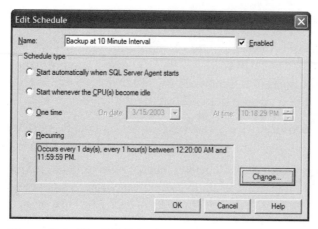

Figure 10-3   The Edit Schedule dialog box to define backup frequency.

Once the schedule has a name, select Recurring. On this tab, shown in Figure 10-4, you can set the exact frequency of your backups. Once you create the job, you can create multiple schedules for the execution of the job: for example, weekly full backups, the second Wednesday of every month, or the first or second weekend day of the month. Make sure you investigate all of the possibilities in these dialog boxes. The smallest granularity is 1 minute.

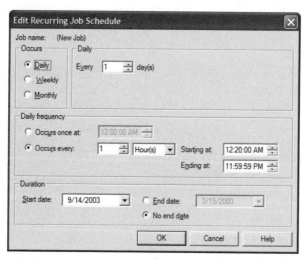

Figure 10-4   The Edit Recurring Job Schedule dialog box to provide numerous scheduling possibilities.

Once you have set all of the options, click OK to create the scheduled job. To review the job, modify its properties so you can modify the job if you want.

(For example, you cannot set the media set name or password within this dialog box.) All jobs are executed by SQL Server Agent, which should be set to Auto-start. In SQL Server Enterprise Manager, expand Management, click SQL Server Agent, Jobs, and then double-click the Inventory Transaction Log Backup job. Here, you can set properties for completion notifications (whether successful or failed) by using SQL Mail—using e-mail, e-mail-based paging, or the NET SEND command. You can add additional steps to the backup job, and you can build complex jobs that include custom external executables or other applications.

For the job in this example, the execution occurs only at the scheduled time. With something fairly frequent, you might think that everything is covered. Unfortunately, some transaction-log-related events could occur that could cause you downtime, for example, if a long-running transaction occurred and filled the log. When the transaction log fills, all activity is stopped. Luckily, this problem is relatively simple to fix: back up the transaction log to free up some space. In this case, you want the transaction log backup job to execute at an unscheduled time, on the log full error (error 9002 – "The log file for database *dbname* is full. Back up the transaction log for the database to free up some log space.").

This process might seem complex, yet it is extremely easy using an alert. In addition to supporting regularly scheduled jobs, the SQL Server Agent also has alerts. An alert is a reaction to an event that has occurred in SQL Server. Errors of a higher severity—those written to the Windows Event Viewer's Application Log—are errors on which you can define an alert. In fact, you can even create your own user-defined errors that are logged.

To set up the alert to perform a transaction log backup when the Inventory database's transaction log is full, use SQL Server Enterprise Manager. Expand Management, select SQL Server Agent, select Alerts, right-click Alerts, and select New Alert. In the New Alert Properties dialog box shown in Figure 10-5, type the name of the alert and select the kind of event that should trigger it—error 9002. Also, be sure to select the database in which this error should be triggered. (Yes, you must set up an alert for each of your production databases.)

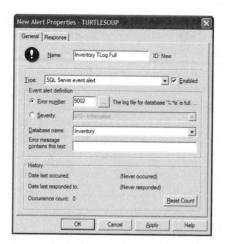

Figure 10-5 The New Alert Properties dialog box to trigger transaction log backups when the transaction log is full.

The Response tab of the New Alert Properties dialog box is important for two reasons: here, you set the job to execute as the response and define how long it will take for SQL Server to respond. More specifically, setting the delay between responses is the most important option to set appropriately. When an error occurs, SQL Server must have time to see the error and respond to it. SQL Server reacts quickly to the error being raised, yet the response might take minutes to run. If a transaction log backup takes roughly 4.5 minutes to execute, setting the delay between responses to 4 minutes and 30 seconds minimizes the number of times this alert is fired. SQL Server fires another alert only if another log full message is issued after the 4 minutes and 30 seconds have passed.

What if you think your system is well automated, but when the log fills, you have downtime? You can set a transaction log backup to occur just before the log fills, preventing the transactions from failing. Not only can you create alerts to react to SQL Server errors, but you can create alerts to react to performance monitor counters, such as Percent Log Used. In the next error, you create the same response but this time, the setup for the alert is a bit different. Again, select New and then Alert from the SQL Server Agent node of the Management folder Enterprise Manager. In the New Alert Properties dialog box, shown in Figure 10-6, change the default type from SQL Server Event Alert to SQL Server Performance Condition Alert. The options to define the alert change, allowing you to set the exact conditions under which the response should be triggered.

Figure 10-6   The New Alert Properties dialog box set to trigger transaction log backups when the transaction log is 85 percent full.

After you create this job and define the two alerts, this database is less likely to go down because of log full errors. Make sure you monitor long-running transactions and get a sense of what could potentially cause the log to fill. The end result is that the Inventory Transaction Log Backup Properties dialog box (Figure 10-7) shows three schedules: the recurring job schedule, the SQL Server event alert, and the SQL Server performance condition.

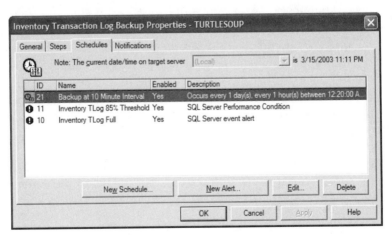

Figure 10-7   Inventory Transaction Log Backup schedules.

Creating a Production SQL Server Agent Backup Job

Creating a production SQL Server Agent backup job is deceptively simple.

> **On the CD**   A diagram with the flow of an automated SQL Server Agent job that runs a full database backup nightly can be found in Agent_Backup_Job.pdf.

The specific details for each of the seven steps found in the Visio diagram are provided here.

> **Note**   Please note that you can use your preferred method for alerts, such as SQL Server's built-in alerts, but using operating system shell commands or other tools might present a security risk to your environment. This example shows other tools to demonstrate how you can integrate them into your SQL Server workflow.

1. Disable the Transaction Log Backup. Because full database backups pause transaction log backups, the first step within this automated job disables the transaction log backup that normally runs every 10 minutes. You do not need to disable the job, but this simplifies errors created by the transaction log backup job not succeeding. As soon as the full database backup completes, the transaction log backup job will be re-enabled. From the msdb database, the transaction log backup is disabled using the sp_update_job system stored procedure:

    ```
    sp_update_job @job_name= N'Transaction Log Backup...', @enabled= 0
    ```

2. Execute a full database backup. This backup uses three LTO tapes for backing up this VLDB in parallel. The syntax of the command is:

    ```
    BACKUP DATABASE Inventory

    TO LTO1, LTO2, LTO3

    WITH FORMAT, UNLOAD, STATS = 2
    ```

    Step 2 uses the Advanced tab to determine the next step (see Figure 10-8). If there is success, then go to Step 3. If there is a failure, then go to Step 4. Additionally, the output of the backup stats will be directed to a file using the Output File box to generate information that is used as part of the backup status e-mail.

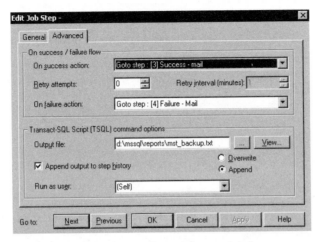

Figure 10-8   SQL Server Agent job step detail.

3.   On success, e-mail operations that all is OK—additionally, page the on-call support person to let him or her know the backup completed successfully. For this job a custom SMTP-based e-mail application is used to e-mail the text of the backup output. The operating system command executed is:

```
d:\batchjobs\common\SMTP.exe "operations_email"

"LTO backup complete"

"Please check file:\\server\d$\mssql\reports\backup.txt"
```

If the mail was sent OK, go to Step 5; otherwise run Step 4.

4.   On failure, e-mail operations that the backup failed and needs imme-diate attention. The on-call support staff is also paged to let them know a failure occurred.

```
d:\batchjobs\common\SMTP.exe "alert"

"URGENT: backup failed"

"Please call operations & check

file:\\server\d$\mssql\reports\backup.txt"
```

5. Page the on-call analyst and let him or her know that the backup succeeded. The command also used a special application created for their paging application:

```
d:\batchjobs\common\cpage.exe oncall "LTO Backup Completed"
```

6. Page the on-call analyst and let him or her know that the backup failed:

```
d:\batchjobs\common\cpage.exe oncall "LTO backup failed!"
```

7. Either way, re-enable the transaction log backup. From the msdb database, the transaction log backup is disabled using the sp_update_job system stored procedure:

```
sp_update_job @job_name= N'Transaction Log Backup...', @enabled= 1
```

The details of the steps as seen in the SQL Server Agent are shown in Figure 10-9.

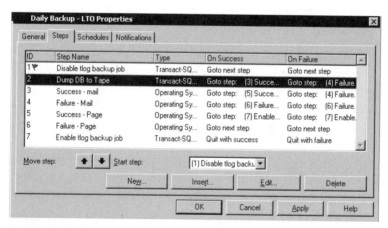

Figure 10-9 SQL Server Agent backup job.

Checking the Completion of a Backup

When a backup job is being run using SQL Server Agent, it is tough to see how complete the job is as it is running because there is no graphic representation. However, if you use the STATS option with the BACKUP command, you can see the percentage completed using the DBCC OUTPUTBUFFER command against the session performing the backup. The percentage complete is shown in the right-hand column of the output.

To see the percentage completed you must first know the system process ID (SPID) of the backup process. To get the SPID of the backup use the following query:

```
SELECT DISTINCT(spid)

FROM master.dbo.sysprocesses (nolock)

WHERE cmd LIKE 'BACKUP%'
```

Output:

```
spid

------

742
```

Next, use the DBCC OUTPUTBUFFER command with the backup process' SPID:

```
DBCC OUTPUTBUFFER(742)
```

When reviewing the output, the far right column shows the character values for the hexadecimal output. This is where you can see the last percentage returned by the job. The following is an example output showing that the backup is at 3 percent:

```
Output Buffer

---------------------------------------------------------------------

00000000 04 00 00 5d 02 e6 03 00 79 01 00 00 00 ab 44 00 ...].µ..y....½D.

00000010 8b 0c 00 00 01 00 14 00 33 00 20 00 70 00 65 00 ï.......3. .p.e.

00000020 72 00 63 00 65 00 6e 00 74 00 20 00 62 00 61 00 r.c.e.n.t. .b.a.

00000030 63 00 6b 00 65 00 64 00 20 00 75 00 70 00 2e 00 c.k.e.d. .u.p...
```

Verifying Backups

Once you have performed your backups and likely automated them, it is critical that you periodically test that your process and strategy is occurring. These verification procedures *do not* guarantee that a restore will be successful, but they do guarantee that you have the backups you are expecting to have.

> **Warning**   There is only *one* way to truly test your backup strategy—perform periodic and *complete* restore testing on a test system.

In the interim, there are four ways you can verify your backups:

- **Using RESTORE LABELONLY** To view information about the backup media set and the retention period, use RESTORE LABELONLY. If you have used good naming conventions then you should easily be able to see if devices belong to the same media set. Otherwise, you will need to review the MediaFamilyID, which is a GUID, to make sure you have all devices in the parallel striped backup. To see the device label use:

```
RESTORE LABELONLY FROM BackupDevice
```

- **Using RESTORE HEADERONLY** To view information about the backups that exist on a multifile backup, use the RESTORE HEADERONLY command. This command works against a single device—even when the device is part of a parallel striped media set. If the device is part of a media set, all devices in that media set will return exactly the same information. This command lists numerous pieces of useful information, and the most useful are the BackupType and the Position columns as shown in Table 10-1.

Table 10-1   Example Output

BackupName	BackupType ...	Position ...	BackupSize ...	BackupStartDate ...
FileBasedBackupDB	1	1	1843200	2003-03-16 22:00:00.000
FileBasedBackupDB	2	2	1195008	2003-03-16 22:10:00.000
FileBasedBackupDB	2	3	1712128	2003-03-16 22:20:00.000
FileBasedBackupDB	5	4	2243584	2003-03-16 22:30:00.000
FileBasedBackupDB	2	5	139264	2003-03-16 22:40:00.000
FileBasedBackupDB	2	6	2246656	2003-03-16 22:50:00.000
FileBasedBackupDB	5	7	2243584	2003-03-16 23:00:00.000
FileBasedBackupDB	2	8	1843200	2003-03-16 23:10:00.000
FileBasedBackupDB	2	9	2178048	2003-03-16 23:20:00.000

Table 10-1   Example Output

BackupName	BackupType ...	Position ...	BackupSize ...	BackupStartDate ...
FileBasedBack-upDB	2	10	3284992	2003-03-16 23:30:00.000
FileBasedBack-upDB	2	11	2245632	2003-03-16 23:40:00.000

The BackupType column can have one of the following values:

❑   1 = Full Database Backup

❑   2 = Transaction Log Backup

❑   4 = File or Filegroup Backup

❑   5 = Database Differential Backup

❑   6 = File or Filegroup Differential Backup

The Position column refers to the number of backups performed against this device (or media set). During a restore, this is the most important column to understand for multifile backups. If the wrong restore is performed, this could lead to additional downtime and frustration. The syntax to view the header information is:

```
RESTORE HEADERONLY FROM BackupDevice
```

■   **Using RESTORE FILELISTONLY**   To view the files affected by each backup, use the RESTORE FILELISTONLY command. This is most useful when you have received a backup device from someone and you are unsure of the exact name, path, and size of the files required by the database. Because a database's structure cannot be changed during a restore, knowing the complete file list can save you time. By reviewing this information, you will be able to determine how you can restore the database and what the exact location of the files must be. If any of the paths are not available because database devices are damaged, the restore command can use WITH MOVE during the restore to place the database files on new drives. The syntax to view the file list from a backup is:

```
RESTORE FILELISTONLY FROM BackupDevice WITH FILE = 6
```

> **Note**   You must state the correct position of the backup on a multifile backup; otherwise, you will return the file list for the first backup (FILE = 1).

When you restore a database, be sure the correct underlying directory paths exist *before* you start. The following is an example of the output:

```
LogicalName PhysicalName          Type FileGroupName Size  MaxSize
------------------------------------------------------------------
CreditData  F:\data\CreditData.MDF  D  PRIMARY  69795840 104857600
CreditLog   H:\log\CreditLog.LDF    L  NULL     47185920 52428800
```

By reviewing the PhysicalName and Size columns, you can determine whether you have the proper location available and enough space to perform the restore.

■ **Using RESTORE VERIFYONLY**   To verify the backup device files to ensure that they are complete (if in a parallel striped backup) and readable, use RESTORE VERIFYONLY. This *does not guarantee* a future successful restore. However, it is very easy to perform and always a good idea to check. The syntax for verifying the backup device or media set requires that all devices (if parallel striped backup) are supplied. To verify that your backup is readable use:

```
RESTORE VERIFYONLY

FROM BackupDevice1, BackupDevice2, BackupDevice3
```

Implementing an Effective Backup Strategy: In Summary

Here's a summary of what you must to do implement an effective backup strategy:

1. Determine the acceptable amount of downtime, if any.

2. Determine the acceptable amount of data loss, if any.

3. Determine the priority of other operations such as bulk operations and log shipping.

4. Determine your recovery model—static or changing for batch operations.

5. Design your database using filegroups, if necessary.

6. Consider various strategies, determining which pros and cons are appropriate to your database environment.

7. Perform scenario-based studies based on the risks you have assessed to see if your strategy works.

8. Implement it in a test environment.

9. Test it.

To really put the backup strategy to the test you need to determine if you can recover to the point in time of the failure with little to no data loss within your defined downtime interval. In the next section you will get a better understanding of how to react quickly and effectively to help minimize the overall downtime you will suffer due to each type of failure.

Database Recovery

The first step in recovering any database is determining precisely what has been damaged. In the event of a hardware failure, it is likely the database is marked as suspect. In the event of human errors (such as dropping a table), the database might still be accessible. What do you do? Your first step should be to access the disaster recovery plan and follow it meticulously, but for this section, only the actual process is addressed. You have all of the background and you know the technology, but to really create the best strategy, you must start thinking in terms of recovery time. To create a recovery-oriented strategy for a highly available system, you must remember speed is of the utmost importance. To make the recovery process as fast as possible you must be able to execute your recovery strategy with precision. This recovery strategy should be well documented and well tested; in fact, it should be scripted or automated in some other way if at all possible.

Recovery strategies will differ for user error versus hardware-related disasters. However, there are similarities in the strategies. Whenever a disaster occurs, your first question should be whether you can access the *tail* of the transaction log. In the event of *any* failure, the tail of the transaction log should be your primary concern. Before you start verifying backups and before you start recovery, *always* check to see if the tail of the transaction log is accessible. If the tail of the transaction log is accessible, then up-to-the-minute recovery is possible. Up-to-the-minute recovery ensures that all committed transactions up to the time of the failure can be recovered (if desired). This backup might not be used (or desired) because of the type of error. If the disaster is based on some form of human error, then you might end up returning to an earlier version of the database altogether, disregarding the tail of the transaction log.

Accessing the tail of the transaction log depends on two factors: physical access to the files and the recovery model state. The tail of the transaction log will be accessible if the physical devices on which the transaction log resides are accessible and the files are not corrupt. Additionally, the transaction log will only be accessible if you are in Full recovery model or in Bulk-Logged recovery model if you have not performed a Bulk-Logged operation since the last transaction log backup. Once it is determined that the tail of the log is accessible, then you should back up the transaction log and add it to your complete set of backups. Once you have backed up the tail of the transaction log, you need to recover your database.

Tip   Are you sure hardware failure is responsible for your problem? Whenever a database is marked suspect and signs of damaged disks are visible (such as Event Viewer's System Log messages pointing to a disk failure), try resetting the status of the database. This simple trick is worth the few minutes it takes—especially if it works. It requires that you stop and restart SQL Server. However, if it succeeds, this might be all you have to do to recover. Sometimes, the database gets improperly marked suspect and only a status change is necessary. In this case, resetting the database status (using `sp_resetstatus`) and then restarting SQL Server might be the only recovery step you need. If the database is still marked suspect after restarting SQL Server, maybe only a file is corrupt. This will mark the beginning of your restore.

Do not perform this procedure if you are not sure what you are doing. You would be better off seeking the help of a support professional, if necessary, than potentially damaging your installation further.

The next step is to back up the tail of the log. To back up the tail of the log, SQL Server requires special syntax. Everything about the transaction log backup is the same—the devices to which you plan to back up, the options you want to specify, and so on—with one notable exception. To back up the tail of the transaction log, you must specify the NO_TRUNCATE clause. This can just be added to the end of the BACKUP LOG command. For example, to back up the tail of the transaction log for the Inventory database using the same devices, media set password, and options presented earlier in "Executing the Full Database–Based Backup Strategy Using Transact-SQL," the syntax only changes slightly:

```
BACKUP LOG [Inventory]

TO [InventoryBackup1], [InventoryBackup2], [InventoryBackup3] WITH NOINIT,

MEDIAPASSWORD = N'InventoryStripeSetPassword',

NAME = N'InventoryTLogBackup',

DESCRIPTION = N'Transaction Log Backup of Inventory',

PASSWORD = N'InventoryBackupTAILPassword',

NOREWIND, STATS = 10,

NO_TRUNCATE
```

Once you have backed up the tail of the log, you can start to investigate further what type of damage has occurred and what the logical course of action is. If the damage is user error, the next step is to determine whether or not users should still be allowed within the database. If not, then restrict the database access to database owners only. Next, you need to investigate the extent of the damage: rows, tables, files, filegroups, entire databases, and so on. Each one will potentially have a different recovery path. Next, regardless of type of failure, you need to determine where you are going to perform the restore—in place, on the same server, or to a different server. Each option has different requirements that should be well thought out. Begin to verify your backups, ensuring that you have a complete set based on the strategy you have chosen. Additionally, you should be thinking about (and have documented already) contingencies. Finally, start your restore.

What is the actual process of recovery? How does a database recover? What are some of the critical options to understand when recovering a database? What are the phases of restore and recovery? Can they be altered, sped up, or skipped? After answers to all of these questions are understood, numerous recovery scenarios are covered to help you create the best recovery plan for your environment.

Phases of Recovery

When a database backup is used to recover a database, there are actually four phases each backup can go through: the file creation or initialization phase, the copy media phase, the redo phase, and finally the undo phase.

File Creation

The file creation phase is only performed when the file or files of the database being restored do not already exist in the appropriate size or location. The location can be changed during restore (RESTORE WITH MOVE) but the size cannot. If the database was defined at a total size for data of 10 GB, yet the backup yielded only a 300 MB full database backup because the database does not currently have a lot of data, it does not matter. The database created during the restore *must completely resemble the database structure as it was backed up.* The structure for all files and filegroups cannot be changed during restore. If you are restoring in place or if a subset of files is damaged, be sure *not* to drop the database. If the files are already there, you can save time during the restore. Because speed is the key to recovery in high availability, this is the first step to improving the restore performance. Even if the database is suspect and one or more of the files are damaged, you can still restore that database in place, replacing the files that are damaged (specifying their new location using RESTORE WITH MOVE).

Media Copy

The second phase that a restore goes through is the media copy phase. During this phase, only faster hardware can help. SQL Server reads the pages from the backup, determines their page location (from the page header), and writes the pages to their appropriate location on disk. Even if the pages are logically inconsistent (see "How Full Database Backups Work" in Chapter 9), this phase is uninterested. The sole purpose of this phase is to copy from the backup medium as fast as possible.

Again, focusing on speed, there are a few options. If you performed your backup to a parallel striped media set then your restore is also performed in parallel. If your database files being recovered are on faster RAID arrays, this can improve the copy phase (that is, striped mirror or mirrored stripes are faster than RAID 5; however, you will need to know how your hardware behaves, including things like the write cache, and so on).

Finally, maybe you can restore less. In the case of isolated corruption for a database that uses multiple files or filegroups, you can restore just the files or filegroups that are damaged.

> **Tip** When a database has isolated failures, you can restore the files or filegroups by restoring from a full database backup or a file or filegroup backup. However, when restoring files from a file or filegroup backup, the restore can take substantially less time as the backup is smaller and only contains the necessary data.

Redo and Undo

The two final phases a backup goes through during restore relate to the transactions that must be applied. This occurs in almost every type of backup with the exception of file/filegroup restores (the transaction log is not backed up during these backups). Because all other backups include some portion of the transaction log or are solely transaction log backups, the restore must use the transaction log to recover what is not already in the database. To do this there are two phases of log analysis: redo and undo.

During the redo phase, SQL Server reviews the log to apply any transactions not already in the database. Because some of the transactions might not have committed by the time the backup completed the final phase, undo must be performed. However, the undo phase is actually determined by the RESTORE command's recovery completion state. If more backups are to be restored, then there is no reason to undo. Undo is only performed for the final restore, which is the restore that is meant to bring the database online for users. Determining when to recover the database is based on the recovery completion state specified during the restore.

Recovery Completion States

When each backup is restored, a recovery completion state *must* be defined. The recovery completion state defines the state in which the database will be when that particular backup is restored. More specifically, because each backup is an image of the database as it looked when the backup completed, SQL Server must determine the fate of the transactions that were pending when the backup completed. With each option you accomplish something different—for different purposes. The recovery completion states are RECOVERY, NO-RECOVERY, and STANDBY.

RECOVERY   The RECOVERY completion state indicates that all four phases of the restore should be performed, including undo. When the undo phase is performed with the RECOVERY completion state, no additional backups can be applied. The RECOVERY option should *not* be specified on any backup except the very last one. However, RECOVERY is the default when no recovery completion state is specified. If a database is recovered too early (meaning that you still have backups to apply) then you will need to restart the restore sequence with the first backup. The opposite is not true. If you accidentally use NO-RECOVERY on the very last backup, you can still recover the database easily and quickly. To recover the database without restoring any backups use this syntax:

```
RESTORE DATABASE DatabaseName WITH RECOVERY
```

> **Important** Never use the RECOVERY option unless you are absolutely certain that you have no other backups to restore. Recovering a database too early will cause a significant delay while you go through your restore process again.

NORECOVERY The NORECOVERY completion state is not the default for SQL Server, but in reality, you should be using it all the time. When a series of backups must be restored, each backup should be restored with NORECOVERY. This option tells SQL Server that the undo phase can be skipped because the next step will be to perform another restore. However, this phase does not allow anyone, including system administrators, to access the database. This option leaves the database nonoperational but able to restore additional backups. NORECOVERY is not the default, but it is always safer to err on the side of NORECOVERY. Perform every restore with NORECOVERY and when you are absolutely certain that you just applied the very last transaction log (usually the tail of the transaction log), recover the database using the RECOVERY option.

STANDBY The STANDBY recovery completion state is a special combination of the two. With this recovery completion state specified, SQL Server performs undo yet keeps the transactional information that was undone in a file that can be used when the next log is applied. If another transaction log is to be applied you might wonder how this differs from NORECOVERY. In fact, it even sounds as though it has more overhead in saving the information so that you can just re-apply it when the next backup is restored. If all you are planning to do is immediately apply another restore, then you are right; this is more overhead. However, the STANDBY recovery completion state offers the ability to use the database for read activity in between the restores. This allows you to verify the state of the data between restores. This is extremely useful if you are trying to determine when data became damaged. Additionally, this allows you to create a secondary copy of the database that can be used for read activity until the next restore must be performed. Log shipping allows this option for recovery; however, when backups are restored, users cannot be using the database.

> **More Info** For more information on log shipping and the use of NORECOVERY and STANDBY, see Chapter 7, "Log Shipping."

Useful RESTORE Options

In learning about parallel striped backup and multifile backup, we covered numerous options. Now that these backups have been performed, how do you read from them appropriately so that you optimally restore the correct backups? Additionally, what happens if you performed a parallel striped backup to six tape devices and one of the tape devices stopped working? Can you restore the six tapes from five devices?

- **Accessing a media set**   If a media set password was specified, all backups accessing this media set must supply the correct password. Without the password, the media set is useless. This precaution secures your backups, but remember, someone needs to know the password in a disaster recovery scenario.

  ```
  [[,] MEDIAPASSWORD = {mediapassword}
  ```

- **Accessing an individual backup**   As with the media set password, any backup that has a password defined needs to have the password specified to access the individual backup. Even if you know the backup password you will not be able to access it without the media set password.

  ```
  [[,] PASSWORD = {password | @password_variable}]
  ```

- **Reading the media or backup device**   When backups are performed, the default SQL Server 2000 behavior is to append backups to the existing media set or to a device. If you want, you can specify WITH INIT to overwrite the backup device. However, if you choose multifile backup, multiple backups will reside on the same backup device. When restoring from multifile backups, you must always be sure to restore the correct backup based on its position on the backup device. If you do not specify the exact backup to restore by position, you will restore the first backup performed to the media set or device. This backup will always be the oldest one and possibly not the backup you want. To examine the list of all backups on a device (even when part of a media set), use the RESTORE HEADERONLY command. To restore a specific backup, you must specify FILE = # on the restore command. The pound sign (#) corresponds to the Position column shown in the header information of the multifile backup set.

  ```
  [[,] FILE [= FileByPosition]]
  ```

> **Important** Always verify the backups that exist on your media set before you restore. Look specifically at the header information and each backup's position number *before* restoring. Make sure you are familiar with the backup type, date, version, and so on. For more information, see the section "Verifying Backups" earlier in this chapter.

- **Restore statistics** The STATS option defines when progress messages will be returned from a restore. Using WITH STATS when performing restores helps you determine the status of the restore. More important, though, you should have a rough estimate of how long the restore usually takes.

```
[[,] STATS [= percentage]]
```

- **Tape-only options** NOREWIND is important if you have multiple backups to restore from the same tape. You can use RESTART if a power failure occurs during the restore. Instead of restarting from the beginning, you can execute the RESTORE with RESTART, and SQL Server resumes the restore where it left off. Finally, with tape devices, unlike disk devices, SQL Server allows you to restore from fewer than you backed up to. However, all backups must be restored before the database will become accessible. With tape devices solely, specify the devices you have and continue to restore the database until all tapes have been restored.

```
[[,] NOREWIND | REWIND]
[[,] NOUNLOAD | UNLOAD]
[[,] RESTART]
```

Disaster Recovery with Backup and Restore

Database recovery can occur in one of many ways and often depends on the type of damage sustained. When a database has become corrupt due to hardware failure, the problem is ironically easier to handle because there are fewer options. This is not to say that the problem is less severe at all. When a database is suspect or corrupt, then either no users can get into the database and all activity has ceased, or users are receiving data errors and the database is rendered corrupt. Because the damage is localized, it is most likely you will recover in place after the damaged devices have been replaced. Optionally, you might recover almost immediately if you have other devices to which the damaged files can be moved during the restore. Regardless, the recovery options are well defined.

Conversely, if the damage has occurred due to human error, the database is likely still accessible. Should it be? How soon after the damage occurred did you find out about it? How are you going to begin your recovery? Are you going to recover the whole database to an earlier point in time, or are you going to recover the database to an alternate location and manually merge the data back into the production database? Managing a disaster after human error is the more difficult problem from which to recover.

Recovering from Hardware Failure: In Place and Up to the Minute

To perform database recovery in place (that is, replacing the existing—and damaged—database), you will need to make sure that there is a place for all files required for this database. To see the list of files for a database, you can use RESTORE FILELISTONLY. This tells you the number of and location for all files in the database. If drives are damaged and no space exists on other drives (which are large enough for the file), then the database cannot be restored until damaged devices are replaced. If devices are damaged, yet other drives have plenty of space, the restore can "move" the files from their damaged location to a new location during the restore.

Recovering In Place and Up to the Minute with Full Database–Based Backup Strategy   If you are running with the full database–based backup strategy the recovery process is straightforward. The process consists of these steps:

- Back up the "tail" of the transaction log.

- Repair the damaged devices or locate another acceptable device to which the files can be restored.

- Verify your backups.

- Restore the most recent full database backup.

- Restore the last differential database backup (if you are using differentials).

- Restore the transaction log backups—including the tail.

- Recover the database (optionally you could recover the database on the last transaction log backup restored).

The following example describes a database corruption situation, and then explains how to recover. In this example, multifile backups are performed to a single device.

First the background:

■   Your database is using the Full recovery model.

■   The DBA makes:

❏   A full backup every Sunday night at 10 P.M.

❏   Differential backups Monday through Saturday at 10 P.M.

❏   Transaction log backups every 15 minutes during the day. They are multifile to one log backup device on disk.

■   You get a page from operations saying that an error of severity 24 has occurred and users are unable to access certain data. Reviewing the error log, you see the following:

```
2003-01-24 23:00:26.54 spid618 Error: 823, Severity: 24, State: 2

2003-01-24 23:00:26.54 spid618 I/O error (bad page ID) detected
during read at offset 0x000009f407c000 in file
'F:\mssql\DATA\DATA3.NDF'..
```

■   You run a DBCC CHECKDB that shows that there are allocation errors. Further investigation shows that the SAN firmware is not the latest revision.

■   You decide you need to restore the database to the last clean state at about 11 P.M.

Now for the recovery plan:

1.   You update your firmware to the current revision levels supported if it is necessary.

> **Warning**   Make sure that this revision, especially if on a cluster, is supported for your solution. Applying firmware for the sake of updating it can lead to more problems than it can solve. Only perform this if necessary.

2.   Reformat the disk and ensure no errors.

3.   The Sunday night full database backup needs to be restored with the NORECOVERY option. The syntax for this command is:

```
RESTORE DATABASE Payroll

FROM PayrollFullBackupDevice WITH NORECOVERY
```

4.   The Friday night differential backup from 10 P.M. needs to be restored with the NORECOVERY option.

```
RESTORE DATABASE Payroll
FROM PayrollDifferentialBackupDevice
WITH FILE=5, NORECOVERY
```

5.   All transaction logs from 10 P.M. to 11 P.M. need to be restored with the NORECOVERY option.

```
RESTORE LOG Payroll

FROM PayrollLogBackupDevice WITH FILE=88, NORECOVERY

RESTORE LOG Payroll

FROM PayrollLogBackupDevice WITH FILE=89, NORECOVERY

RESTORE LOG Payroll

FROM PayrollLogBackupDevice WITH FILE=90, NORECOVERY

RESTORE LOG Payroll

FROM PayrollLogBackupDevice WITH FILE=91, NORECOVERY
```

6.   For the last transaction log, recover the database using the RECOVERY syntax.

```
RESTORE LOG Payroll

FROM PayrollLogBackupDevice WITH FILE=92, RECOVERY
```

> **Note**   The DBA only has to restore the transaction logs *after* the last differential because the differential is the cumulative of all changes since the last full backup. Thus, the DBA does not have to apply the transaction logs prior to the differential.

Although this scenario provides a simple mechanism for restoring a database up to the time of the failure, it requires the entire database to be restored. If your database was designed using multiple files and filegroups, you can restore the damaged files or filegroups more efficiently from a full database backup using the same syntax shown in the file-based recovery scenario.

Recovering In Place and Up to the Minute with the File-Based Backup Strategy

If you are running with the file-based backup strategy, the recovery process is more complex but is likely to be faster in the case of isolated hardware failure. With the full database–based backup strategy the easiest option is to recover the entire database and roll forward using other backups. The restore of the full database backup could take a significant amount of time. If you have a database designed using multiple files and filegroups, then you can restore only the damaged files. Better yet, if you have chosen to backup the individual files and filegroups then the recovery process is more granular as well. In place, you can restore *only* the damaged files and filegroups, restore the differentials for the files and filegroups restored, and then (and only then) apply the *correct sequence* of transaction log backups to get up to the minute. Of this entire process, finding the correct sequence of transaction log backups to apply is the most challenging stage. Above all, it requires an understanding of how to read backup history information from backup devices or preferably from msdb backup history tables.

Using the database backups showing the file-based backup case study earlier in this chapter in the section "Executing the File-Based Backup Strategy Using Transact-SQL," what happens if there is a disk failure on the file c:\Program Files\Microsoft SQL Server\MSSQL\Data\FileBasedBackupDBRWFile2.NDF? If this file is not accessible, SQL Server marks the database as suspect, as shown in Figure 10-10.

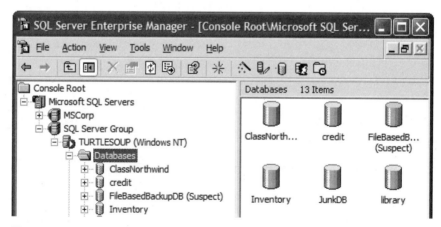

Figure 10-10   FileBasedBackupDB: A suspect database.

The entire database is inaccessible, so how can you determine the exact cause of error? Review the SQL Server error log, which can be found as a text file in the LOG directory. Additionally, you can find these messages in the Application Log of Event Viewer. Or, if SQL Server Enterprise Manager is accessible, you can obtain the graphical version of the error log. In the error log, you should be able to find a data file error for the damaged file, as shown in Figure 10-11.

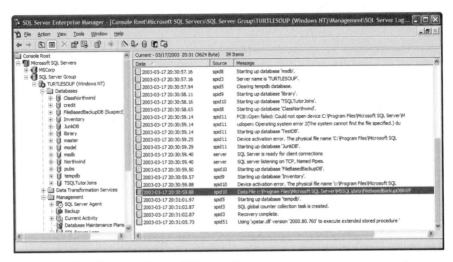

Figure 10-11   FileBasedBackupDB: Data file error.

By double-clicking on the error you can see even more details, as shown in Figure 10-12.

Figure 10-12   FileBasedBackupDB: Specific file error.

At this point, you know exactly what is damaged. You have file- and file-group-based backups, so the recovery process can be performed with just the damaged files. The recovery process always begins with a backup of the tail of the transaction log. In this case, you execute:

```
BACKUP LOG [FileBasedBackupDB]

TO [FileBasedBackupDev]

WITH NAME = 'FileBasedBackupDB Backup',

DESCRIPTION = 'FINAL Transaction Log (Tail up-to-minute)', NOINIT, NO_TRUNCATE
```

> **On the CD**   To perform the recovery as described, first create the File_Based_Backup_DB sample database and all the backups shown in the earlier case study diagram. All of this setup can be found in the File_Based_Backup_Strategy.sql script on the companion CD. The recovery process beginning with the backup of the tail of the transaction log can be found in the File_Based_Backup_Strategy-Restore_InPlace_UpToTheMinute_Isolated_Corruption.sql script. Review the syntax descriptions from this section prior to execution for best understanding.

Once the tail of the transaction log is backed up you have the set of back-ups shown in Figure 10-13.

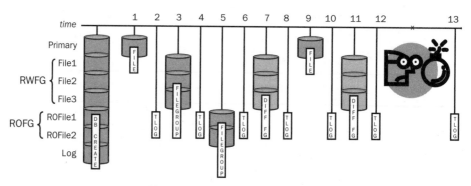

Figure 10-13   File corruption of RWFile2 between points in time 12 and 13.

Because only RWFile2 is damaged, only that file needs to be recovered. To recover this file you need to first find the last "full" version of this file backed up. At point in time 3, the entire filegroup was backed up. This is your starting point for this restore. Beginning with the filegroup backup at position 3, you can restore just this damaged file using:

```
RESTORE DATABASE FileBasedBackupDB

FILE = 'FileBasedBackupDBRWFile2'

FROM [FileBasedBackupDev]

WITH FILE = 3, NORECOVERY
```

To move this file to a forward point in time, use the last differential for this file, which was performed at point in time 11. To recover just this file from this differential, the syntax is exactly the same with the exception of pointing SQL Server to the correct differential backup. To recover the differential at position 11 use:

```
RESTORE DATABASE FileBasedBackupDB

FILE = 'FileBasedBackupDBRWFile2'

FROM [FileBasedBackupDev]

WITH FILE = 11, NORECOVERY
```

Finally, transaction logs need to be applied. This is the most challenging part about recovering from file and filegroup backups. Because transaction log backups can occur concurrently, multiple transaction log backups could "overlap" with a file- or filegroup-based backup. To restore the correct transaction logs you must determine the minimum effective log sequence number (LSN). In other words, you must review the earliest point that needs to be restored. In this case, because it was isolated failure, there is only one file affected. The last restore was for point in time 11. Review the backup history with the following query:

```
SELECT Backup_Start_Date, [Name], [Description],

First_LSN, Last_LSN, Backup_Finish_Date

FROM msdb.dbo.backupset AS s

 JOIN msdb.dbo.backupmediafamily AS m

 ON s.media_set_id = m.media_set_id

WHERE database_name = 'FileBasedBackupDB'

ORDER BY 1 ASC
```

The output returned for all of the backups (the backup number refers to the backup as shown by the case study) for just the First_LSN and Last_LSN columns is shown in Table 10-2.

Table 10-2 Output Returned for All of the Backups

Backup	First_LSN	Last_LSN
1	13000000163000001	13000000163300001
2	13000000163000001	14000000057900001
3	14000000267300001	14000000268200001
4	14000000057900001	15000000159400001
5	16000000049400001	16000000050100001
6	15000000159400001	19000000112100001
7	19000000319000002	19000000319200001
8	19000000112100001	20000000210000001
9	21000000098500001	21000000098700001
10	20000000210000001	21000000304900001
11	22000000192900002	22000000193100001
12	21000000304900001	24000000030800001
13	24000000030800001	26000000141800001

Reviewing the First_LSN column for backup set number 11, you can see that the minimum LSN is 22000000192900002. To determine the appropriate transaction log to restore, you must find the *first* transaction log that includes this LSN. Review only transaction log backups by adding AND type = 'L', as well as adding the appropriate value for the First_LSN. The value of Last_LSN should be less than or equal to the First_LSN of the next backup set, which is greater than the value for Last_LSN of the existing backup set. If you follow this rule and add these to a WHERE clause in the SELECT statement shown earlier, you can determine the proper transaction log to restore. Below is an example:

```
WHERE database_name = 'FileBasedBackupDB'

AND type = 'L' AND First_LSN <= 22000000192900002

AND Last_LSN >= 22000000192900002
```

Once executed, it becomes clear that the backup you will restore is the backup at position 12 (in this case the backup is after the last differential;

although this is likely, it is not guaranteed). The good news is that if you accidentally restore a transaction log that is too early (for example, the transaction log backup at position 10), SQL Server generates this error message:

```
Server: Msg 4326, Level 16, State 1, Line 16
```

The log in this backup set terminates at LSN 21000000305600001, which is too early to apply to the database. A more recent log backup that includes LSN 22000000193600002 can be restored.

```
Server: Msg 3013, Level 16, State 1, Line 16
```

RESTORE LOG is terminating abnormally.

Along the same lines, if you restore a transaction log that is too late then SQL Server also gives a comparable message:

```
Server: Msg 4305, Level 16, State 1, Line 1
```

The log in this backup set begins at LSN 24000000031500001, which is too late to apply to the database. An earlier log backup that includes LSN 22000000193600002 can be restored.

```
Server: Msg 3013, Level 16, State 1, Line 1
```

RESTORE LOG is terminating abnormally.

Executing NORECOVERY only with file 12 leaves the transaction log at position 12. To restore the last set of transaction logs and recover the database, you complete the restore with the last two transaction log restores:

```
RESTORE LOG FileBasedBackupDB

FROM [FileBasedBackupDev]

WITH FILE = 12, NORECOVERY

RESTORE LOG FileBasedBackupDB

FROM [FileBasedBackupDev]

WITH FILE = 13, RECOVERY
```

Once the database is restored with RECOVERY then no additional restores can be performed. Additionally, users are allowed back into the database.

Additional Recovery Examples

The following examples assume that you are restoring to the same database you backed up from, or you have also restored the master database prior to starting the restore. The reason for this is that the user IDs will not be in sync if you restore to a different server than the one users were created on.

For more information on synchronizing users, see the topic "Transferring Logins, Users, and Other Objects Between Instances" in Chapter 14, "Administrative Tasks to Increase Availability."

Point-In-Time Recovery

There are times when it is not necessary to recover a complete log. In fact, you might not want to because the complete transaction log has information in it that you do not want applied to the database. A good example of this is that someone accidentally forgot to provide a WHERE clause on a DELETE statement and wiped out a critical table.

If you know what time the person deleted the rows from the table, you can recover all the way up to the moment *before* it happened. SQL Server provides this functionality using the STOPAT syntax. In the following situation, this part of RESTORE is explored:

- Your database is using the Full recovery model.

- The DBA makes a full backup every day of his development database at 11 A.M.

- The DBA makes transaction log backups every 15 minutes during the day. They are multifile to one log backup device on disk.

- A developer was testing some code before lunch at 11:50 A.M., but forgot to fully qualify the DELETE statement with a WHERE clause to restrict the rows deleted. When the code is run, the production payroll table is affected.

- You were paged at 12:15 P.M. when the development team realized the error and let the contact know that the table needed to be recovered and about what time it occurred.

Recovery Plan   Follow the steps in this order:

1. The full database backup needs to be restored with the NORECOVERY option.

2. All transaction logs up to 11:45 A.M. need to be restored with the NORECOVERY option.

3. For the last transaction log, you need to use the STOPAT and RECOVERY syntax. This tells SQL Server to stop at the moment before the table was deleted and recover the database so users can log in.

4. The database can now be opened for users.

The following is the script for this scenario:

```
-- restore the full backup made at 11AM

restore database dev_db from full_backup with norecovery

go



-- restore the 11:15AM log backup

restore database dev_db from log_backup with file=1, norecovery

go



-- restore the 11:30AM log backup

restore log dev_db from log_backup with file=2, norecovery

go



-- restore the 11:45AM log backup

restore log dev_db from log_backup with file=3, norecovery

go



-- restore the noon backup, but STOP recovery at 11:49AM, just before
-- the table was deleted at 11:50AM

restore log dev_db from log_backup with file=4, recovery, STOPAT = 'Jan 28, 2003
11:49:00.000 AM'

go
```

Moving Data on a RESTORE

There are times when you are restoring a database that you need to move the data to a new location. Common examples of this include the following:

- Someone gives you a database from a different system that has different disk drive mappings or directory paths. An example of this is that you need to refresh a test database from a copy of production.

- For performance reasons you need to move the data files among the disk drives. For example, you built a new SAN and want to take advantage of the new LUN slicing the hardware engineers configured for you.

- If you rebuild disk drives or want to move data files around for better performance, you can restore the database to the new disks.

SQL Server provides the MOVE syntax for this purpose. You need to know the logical names of the files you are going to move. To get this information, run the command RESTORE FILELISTONLY against the backup. This lists the logical names. After that, you only need to do a restore and provide the new target locations.

In the following example, a production database is to be restored to a test server from an LTO array. The database has 12 data files and one log file. Due to the size of the database, you want to monitor the progress, so you have added the STATS syntax to show the percentage complete.

```
-- Examine the logical and physical locations on the backup

restore filelistonly from LT01, LT02, LT03, LT04

go



-- First, create the new directories on the file system so we can

-- RESTORE to them.



-- Now, restore the database as you normally would, except

-- specify to SQL Server the new locations for the data devices
```

```
restore database test_db

from LTO1, LTO2, LTO3, LTO4

with

move 'data1' to 'H:\mssql\DATA\DATA1.MDF',

move 'data2' to 'I:\mssql\DATA\DATA2.NDF',

move 'data3' to 'J:\mssql\DATA\DATA3.NDF',

move 'log1' to 'U:\mssql\LOG\LOG1.LDF',

recovery, stats=1
```

Collected Wisdom and Good Ideas for Backup and Restore

The following list is an accumulation of experiences that are really not documented in one place, but all belong together in a proper review of backups and restores.

- Make sure that you label each tape appropriately with information such as what is on it, date and time, and so on.

- Tapes go bad. They are a mechanical device and also magnetically sensitive. Both are causes of failure. Plan for this. Buy extra tapes and be aware of the possible contingencies within your chosen backup strategy.

- Try to avoid putting too much data on a tape. SQL Server allows you to append multiple backups on a tape as space permits. The problem is if all your backups are on one tape and that tape goes bad, you lose all your backups. Spread your risk. Use multiple rotations.

- Cycle your tapes appropriately. Do not keep backing up databases to the same tapes repeatedly. This wears down the tape mechanism, and you might get confused about what is exactly on the tape.

- Store your tapes properly. Label them. Keep them in their cases. Recovery time is extended if you do not know what is on each tape.

- Consider multiple copies of your backups and rotate one copy to an off-site location. For a small shop, this can mean keeping a copy in a bank safe deposit box. For a large shop, there are sites that specialize in off-site data storage. Remember, a bank safe deposit box is only open during banking hours—a dedicated off-site provider is open 24/7. Additionally, make sure all critical parties are on the list to retrieve the tapes. Just like anything, you get what you pay for.

- Many companies have rotations that go into permanent off-site storage due to government regulations. However, in 10 years, will the tape media that you have off-site be restorable? Technology changes very fast. That QIC40 tape from 1992 is pretty useless today if you do not have a QIC40 tape drive and the accompanying software. Plan for this. This is where backing up to disk and then to tape is better.

> **Tip** SQL Server will not always support restoring backups from one version of SQL Server to another (such as restoring SQL Server 6.5 backups to a SQL Server 2000 instance), so if you need to keep backups for some time, you might want to consider periodically restoring them, upgrading the database to the newer version, and then backing it up.

- If you have to restore at a remote location, make sure that location has the same tape drives you do. If you have LTO technology, but the remote site has DLT, you needlessly waste time. This needs to be planned for.

- Know what versions of software you are running. Older versions of SQL Server can be incompatible with current ones. The physical characteristics of SQL Server storage changed from SQL Server 6.5 to SQL Server 7.0. Have xp_msver, @@version, and SQLDIAG information stored with your backups.

- Have copies of your binaries stored off site, too. This should include the operating system, SQL Server, and the associated license keys, too.

- At a minimum, make regular backups of the master and msdb databases in addition to your user database.

- Backups do not validate the data they are backing up. Run DBCC CHECKDB as part of a regular maintenance plan. Remember, you can back up corruption.

> **Tip** You might want to restore the backup and perform DBCC CHECKDB to bolster your confidence in your backup strategy and the backups itself.

- Automate as much of your backup strategy as possible. Human intervention causes many frequent problems. Use the SQL Server Agent and possibly the Database Maintenance Wizard to simplify automation if it is appropriate.

- Review the backup logs. This sounds obvious, but many people just change the tapes without bothering to see if the backup even ran. For example, a backup might have aborted due to a faulty tape drive.

- You are only as safe as the last good backup you restored. Tapes can and do go bad. No one can guarantee the quality of a backup until it has been restored. As such, restore from your backups frequently to test their validity and the process you have in place for recovery. Tape vendors generally specify how long their products will hold information. Written specifications often indicate many years. However, do not rely on the published media life numbers. The more use, the more wear on the tape.

Backing Up the Operating System

The bulk of this chapter has detailed how to back up and restore your SQL Server databases. However, for a complete backup and restore plan, which directly impacts your disaster recovery plan, you also need to back up Windows. In many cases, restoring backups is easier than rebuilding the system from scratch. With Windows, you have different backup options available to you, which are listed here:

- An Authoritative System Restore (ASR) backup, which includes cluster configuration, registry entries, boot files, system files (in other words, DLLs), and so on. This data is known as *System State data*.

> **Tip**   To perform an Authoritative RESTORE, a System State backup is required. In a cluster, if you perform an ASR on one node, you should perform a Non-Authoritative RESTORE on the other cluster nodes. A Windows 2000 ASR restores the cluster configuration to %Systemroot%\Cluster\Cluster_backup, which still needs to be fed into the registry using the command-line tool CLUSREST.

- A Local Backup, which contains all files and binaries for the individual server that the backup is executed on.

To back up your operating system and its associated files, you can use a third-party tool or you can use the built-in tool that ships with all versions of Microsoft Windows 2000 and Microsoft Windows Server 2003: Backup. To access the Backup tool, use the Start menu and go to the Accessories folder under System Tools. You can also launch Windows Backup if you run Ntbackup.exe from a command prompt, and you can also run it with command-line switches as well. It is flexible to meet the needs of your company. Figure 10-14 displays the main Backup window.

> **Important**   If you are going to use a third-party backup tool, make sure it supports what you need it to, especially features like ASR backups.

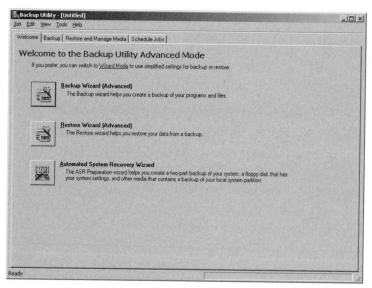

Figure 10-14   Windows Backup.

You should back up your systems prior to and after you make any changes (such as service packs or hotfixes), and periodically in between. As long as the snapshot of your system is accurate, you do not need to back up all system files every night. You are concerned about the changes because unless you are using the server as a file system (which you should not be), the only files that will probably change are the SQL Server backup files. You should have a process to back up the SQL Server backup files after they are generated.

> **Tip**   Do not try to back up the active database files for SQL Server with a normal backup tool such as Backup. As mentioned earlier in the section "Third-Party Backup and Restore Tools and SQL Server," the backup program must support the SQL Server VDI. You can use the backup program to back up SQL Server backup files generated and placed on the file system.

Using Backup

Backup is a fairly straightforward utility to use. This section provides a basic overview of how it works.

Creating a Backup

To create a backup using the Backup tool, follow these steps:

1. Click the Backup tab, which is where you will create your backups that you can subsequently schedule. You can choose to back up whatever folders and files you want, including System State data, or you could just back up only System State data. Figure 10-15 shows an example of checking only System State.

Figure 10-15   Selecting System State.

2. At the bottom of the Backup tab, enter the name and location of the backup file. By default, a backup using Backup has the .bkf extension. Click Start Backup.

3. The Backup Job Information dialog displays as shown in Figure 10-16. Here you can schedule the backup, choose other relevant options (such as appending or overwriting the existing data), and so on.

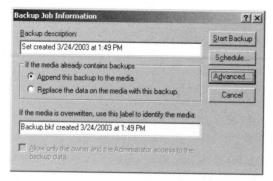

Figure 10-16 Backup job information.

If you click Advanced, you will see the Advanced Backup Options dialog box, as shown in Figure 10-17. The most important information here is the backup type; it tells the program which type of backup to perform. Click OK to close this dialog box, and then click Start Backup in the Backup Job Information dialog box to back up your choices.

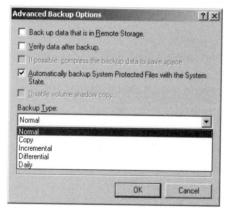

Figure 10-17 The Advanced Backup Options dialog box.

4.   When finished, you should see a dialog box similar to the one in Figure 10-18. Click Close.

> **Tip** Alternatively, you can use the Backup Wizard (Advanced) or Automated System Recovery Wizard on the Welcome tab to help you generate the proper backups.

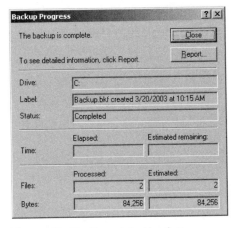

Figure 10-18   Completed backup.

Restoring a Backup

To restore a backup using the Backup tool, follow these steps:

1. Select the Restore And Manage Media tab in the Backup tool.

2. In the left pane, select the backup you want to restore as shown in Figure 10-19.

3. At the bottom of the tab, select the location to which you want to restore the files, and click Start Restore.

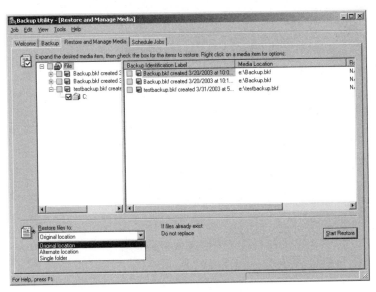

Figure 10-19   Restore And Manage Media tab.

4. In the Confirm Restore dialog box shown in Figure 10-20, you can click OK to start, or if you want to modify advanced options prior to starting, click Advanced, and the dialog box shown in Figure 10-21 is displayed.

Figure 10-20   Confirm Restore dialog box.

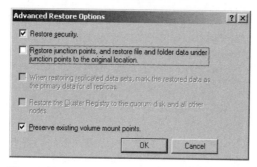

Figure 10-21   Advanced Restore Options dialog box.

5. When finished, you should see a dialog box similar to the one in Figure 10-22. Click Close.

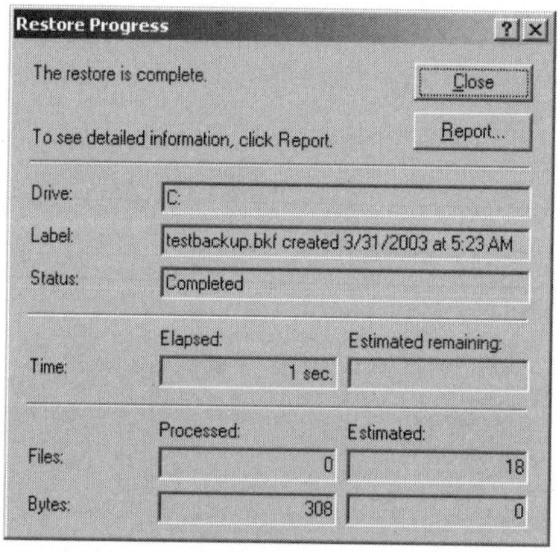

Figure 10-22   Completed restore.

> **Tip**   Alternatively, you can use the Restore Wizard (Advanced) on the Welcome tab to assist you in the restore process.

Backing Up and Restoring Clustered Environments

As you might have already guessed, backing up a server cluster is not exactly the same as backing up and restoring a stand-alone server. You have other dependencies, namely the cluster database and the registry settings for clustering.

> **More Info**   For more information on the objects listed in this section, consult Chapter 5, "Designing Highly Available Microsoft Windows Servers."

Backing Up a Standard Server Cluster

In terms of backing up the necessary components to perform an eventual restore, you need to understand how backup programs interact with clustering. If you choose to only back up the system state data (as seen in Figure 10-15), only the quorum disk and the system state data will be backed up—nothing else. A backup that contains this information has the following:

- **\Mscs\Chkxxxx.tmp**   These are the cluster database snapshot files.

> **Tip**   If there is more than one of these files, you might have had some problems on your cluster, and should evaluate before backing up potential corruptions.

- **\Mscs\Quolog.log**   The cluster log file.
- **\Mscs\<GUID of resource>**   The registry checkpoint files for the .cpt resource (identified by GUID).

- **\Mscs\\<GUID of resource>**   The crypto checkpoint files for the .cpr resource (identified by GUID).

- **\Mscs\Clusbackup.dat**   A read-only, hidden file that is 0 bytes in size, and is the backup completion marker file.

> **Important**   When you elect to back up the system state data, the local node's cluster registry hive, also known as clusdb (\Mscs\Chkxxx.tmp is a binary copy of clusdb), is not backed up because the quorum, which is the master, is backed up. Because the file is open and locked, you might see some errors such as "Completed with Skipped Files" and "Examining the NTBackup log, both Clusdb and Clusdb.log failed to be backed up." You can ignore these errors because \Mscs on the quorum drive has been backed up.

> **Important**   Back up the system state data only on the node that owns the quorum; otherwise you will encounter errors. Also, you need to back up the quorum's system state data only once because it will take care of the entire cluster. Do not move the quorum resource to each node when backing up system state data.

After you have backed up the system state data, you should back up each individual node's files, software, and system state data. Remember that each node of the server cluster that does not own the quorum drive in a standard server cluster will not back up anything on the quorum drive.

> **Note**   If you understand the technology behind a server cluster, you might conclude that you hardly ever need a backup because there are always at least three copies on the cluster at any given time. However, to full cluster-aware applications such as SQL Server, checkpoints are important, and you might want to use tools specifically designed for this and other purposes such as CLUSTOOL and CLUSDIAG. At the time of the launch of Windows Server 2003, CLUSDIAG was only available for that version, but will be released for Windows 2000 at a later date.

Third-Party Backup Software and SQL Server 2000 Failover Clustering

Ensure that when you evaluate enterprise-class third-party backup software, it works properly in a cluster and is truly cluster-aware. As discussed in Chapter 6, "Microsoft SQL Server 2000 Failover Clustering," you do not want resources to depend on any SQL Server resources that do not need to be there. Some third-party backup packages technically "work" in a cluster; however, to be able to operate, they add their own resources into your SQL Server virtual server's resource group and make them dependencies of the disks with the data and log files. This is otherwise known as a generic application in a server cluster.

> **Warning**   If you must implement backup software that is not fully cluster-aware on your cluster that must have dependencies placed on SQL Server resources, you must check to see that the Do Not Affect The Group option is selected on the Properties tab of the added third-party generic resources. After configuring this option, if that resource fails, it will not take your SQL Server disks offline, which will in turn take your SQL Server instance offline and cause a failover that you did not want. Some third-party programs also do not contain any logic to handle clustered situations and simply restart all of that day's backup jobs from scratch after a failover. Because you do not want to restart all backup jobs, you might also want to disable the Restart option on the Properties tab in addition to selecting Do Not Affect The Group."

Summary

The message is simple: you cannot talk about high availability without talking about backup and restore. You do not have a backup until you have done a restore. Simple principles are often overlooked and undervalued. You cannot have a highly available environment without significant risk assessment. Some risks—some of the most challenging from which you will need to recover—can be recovered only through a solid backup and recovery plan. This chapter discussed backup types, effective recovery strategies, benefits and complexities for each strategy, and how best to perform each backup strategy. To ensure an efficient recovery, you must understand the environment settings and database structures that are most conducive to the availability you are trying to achieve. For each backup type you must understand the downtime potential as well as the costs and the effects on actively processing users, in terms of both performance as well as log activity. After thorough testing, you should have a solid strategy that minimizes downtime as well as data loss.

Part IV

Putting the Pieces of the Puzzle Together

11

Real-World High Availability Solutions

Now that you have learned about high availability technologies, you need to understand how to put the pieces of the puzzle together. This chapter walks you through a real-world example and identifies the decision points and how you would need to confront the challenges. This exercise addresses mainly the technology aspect; the people and process aspect is covered, but is better handled by other examples in this book. The chapter concludes with a case study of Microsoft.com and details of how they achieve high availability.

The Scenario

Your company is starting to plan for a new, custom-built application to support its sales field in North America and Europe. Other global sales territories will be incorporated in later versions. The application will be a sales management tool with other capabilities, such as reporting. The people in the field will be able to access and modify the data from a traditional client/server–based application when they are on the corporate network, and they will be able to view reports from a Web page.

The database portion of the solution must satisfy two main goals that, in the actual solution, can be hosted on more than two physical servers. These goals are to establish:

- A central repository of data
- A reporting server that is updated with five-minute-delayed feeds from the central repository

The company is striving for an availability goal of 99.99%, or fewer than 52 minutes of downtime, for the systems involved with this application. That decision is based on the fact that the systems must service people worldwide, and it factors in all planned downtime (application upgrades, service packs, server upgrades, hardware upgrades, and so on) in addition to unplanned downtime. The solution must be available and scalable and will be in a production capacity for a minimum of two years.

> **Note**   For the sake of this exercise, assume all other parts of the solution, such as domain controllers and Web servers, are accounted for in the overall availability plan but are not factored into cost. In your environments, you have to take into account every last detail of your solution. Also, for this exercise, assume that you have a preferred hardware vendor.

Conditions and Constraints

You have a maximum budget of $500,000 for all database-related hardware. The hardware should take into account at least two to three years' worth of system growth. The growth for the database in that time frame is predicted to be approximately 700 GB, with an 80/20 ratio of data to log. No capacity planning numbers for processor or memory usage exist to help you plan your hardware purchase because the information has not been tracked. You need to make an educated guess. The company, starting with this database solution, will institute policies for monitoring to facilitate capacity planning.

Software licensing and software support come out of a different budget, and are not factors in this exercise. Components such as cabling and racks are also outside the scope of this exercise, but in the real world you need to consider these factors as well.

> **Note**   Keep in mind that this scenario is heavily focused on the SQL Server side of things and not on the application or the rest of the infrastructure, including the aforementioned cabling, racks, and other forms of hardware and software that will comprise the entire solution. For a full real-world solution, those would all be part of the planning process.

The company has decided that hardware can be purchased only from the options listed in the Excel spreadsheet HW_Cost.xls on the "Hardware Base Costs" tab.

The Planning Process

Step 1: Breaking Down the Requirements

The bullet points below indicate how you should approach a set of requirements. Do not try to define technology solutions at this stage. As database administrators (DBAs) or system engineers, which many of you reading this book probably are, your natural tendency is to lead with technology. Your goal, however, first and foremost, is to *understand* the requirements before attaching any technology. Any risks that are drawn up at this stage do not necessarily need answers; they will be answered in time as you move through the process.

Here is what you know so far:

- There will be a minimum of two databases: one for reporting and one for your main data. The main data will be OLTP, and the reporting data will be read-only with regular data loading.

- Near-real-time reporting looks to be an absolute requirement.

- With 700 GB of total disk space needed, following the 80/20 split, there will be 560 GB of data and 140 GB of log. However, that really means 1120 GB of data and 280 GB of log because you have at least two systems hosting copies of the data.

- You will have both directly connected and Internet-based users, therefore you will need at least two different security models for the solution.

- Because the one system is mainly writes and the other is mainly reads with write updates every few minutes, their disk characteristics are similar.

Here are some questions you must answer:

- You have two security models: authenticating users through the Web and directly in the application. Will they be handled the same way in the code?

- How will the database logic be implemented—are you using direct code or stored procedures? This affects your memory requirements.

- What is your network bandwidth? Can it handle whatever mechanism you employ for synchronizing the databases?

- What type of staffing will be required? What type of expertise is needed, and is it already in-house?

- What are the service level agreements (SLAs) beyond the general four nines? Is it four nines from 5 A.M. to 9 P.M. Eastern Standard Time since you cover both North America and Europe? What are the standard support contracts for your company?

- Do you need to create a warm standby in addition to the reporting server? Is it possible to make them the same?

At the same time, draw up a list of initial risks:

- How will the disks be protected?

- Are there any barriers to adopting a technology such as failover clustering?

- Where should the servers be placed for ultimate availability?

- Will $500,000 be enough? Will trade-offs need to be made?

- What is the business impact of downtime?

- Are there proper monitoring systems in place to handle the new systems?

- What type of maintenance will be needed, and how will it interface with current plans for other systems?

- How many Web servers are needed, and do you set up a demilitarized zone (DMZ) environment? Where will each server be placed? (This is outside the database scope, but in an overall project, you need to consider this.)

- How will you load test the system? How will you test it in general? Will there be the same equipment to develop and test on? If not, what is the risk from a production standpoint? What is the budget for doing a load test (including dedicated systems and software), and will it be done in-house or externally?

Step 2: Considering Technologies

With enough basic information in hand, you can take the known factors, questions, and risks and turn them into technology decision points. This must be done *before* you look at purchasing hardware. One of the biggest mistakes that many people or companies make, even without capacity planning information, is to purchase hardware based on a recent system put into production or some basic corporate standard. On paper, whatever the chief purchasing officer buys might seem as if it has the capacity you need, but does it really?

Tackling the database synchronization issue, you have a few choices available to you:

- **Log shipping**   This would solve both the reporting and availability and standby issues, but with frequent transaction loads, you really could not use it for reporting.

- **Replication**   This would solve the reporting problem, but does the data you need to send fit in the row size limits for replication? If not, that would rule out replication. You would need to consult the developers and development DBAs for these numbers. What method would you choose? If you chose replication, how would you construct your replication architecture?

- **Data Transformation Services (DTS) packages**   Creating a DTS package is definitely possible, but how would you monitor such a solution and ensure that it is working? What logic would you put into it? How would it impact the OLTP database? Do your developers have the expertise to code it? Would it affect the development timeline?

From the main OLTP database standpoint, how frequently is data changing? That is, are there many inserts, updates, and deletes occurring or is your data changing by only a small percentage? This impacts your maintenance plans and whether you implement log shipping or replication. How will you protect this database? Failover clustering seems like a logical choice because of automatic failover, but it might be overkill depending on the rest of the solution, or you might not be able to afford it. Remember that cost always lurks in the shadows.

As a first stab, you decide to use failover clustering for protecting the main OLTP database and the distributor—they will be housed in one instance, transactional replication to populate the reporting server, and log shipping for protecting the entire solution in the event of a whole site failure. Using log shipping means that you not only have another data center but also that you are taking the risk that the log shipped database will serve as both the reporting database and the OLTP database. That might impact performance and would need to be tested.

You also decide to implement this entire solution on Microsoft Windows Server 2003 because it will provide the longest supportability and you know the system will stay in production for at least two years.

Step 3: Designing the Architecture

There are a few phases to designing your architecture: designing the hardware and then dealing with people and processes.

> **Note**   Because people and processes are extremely important in your design, they are covered extensively and in much detail in other chapters. They are also presented at a high level in this chapter, and all considerations are reviewed.

Designing the Hardware

First, examine your disk requirements. On the primary OLTP system, you decide that it will serve as both the Publisher and the Distributor. You need to plan for the OLTP database, a distribution database, msdb usage, transaction logs, MS DTC, and a quorum disk, as shown in Table 11-1. You are looking at more than 700 GB of disk space for each copy of the data.

Table 11-1   Planning the Disk Subsystem

Requirement	Disk Space Planned	Separate LUN
Publisher/main database—data portion	600 GB	Yes
Publisher/main database—log portion	200 GB	Yes
Distributor	50 GB	Yes
MS DTC	1 GB	Yes
Quorum	1 GB	Yes

Notice that extra space was allocated to all databases. This allows for some extra room should the estimates provided actually turn out to be lower than what is needed or for additional growth.

Now it is time to address the problem of how to deal with the reporting server and warm standby. Should you use the warm standby as a replication primary? No, because you have clustering in place. It will be used purely for high availability, so you need 800 GB of disk space to match the primary. On the replicated server, you need the 800 GB as well. It is beginning to look as if you will incur a large cost by purchasing enough disk space to host the three copies of the data.

Next, examine your memory requirements. Because you can expand memory as time goes on (although that will incur some downtime), you decide to reduce costs and start with 4 GB of memory and then see how the application behaves before you expand to 8 GB. The /3GB boot.ini switch (described in Chapter 14, "Administrative Tasks to Increase Availability") will be used, allowing SQL Server to use up to 3 GB of total memory, leaving 1 GB for the operating system. The same is true for processor power—you will start with four processors, but you will buy the fastest available to give you the longest system life. You should also specify that each system be the same brand and, if possible, the same model for ease of management and maintenance.

People and Processes

At this point, start thinking about how you will monitor, maintain, and administer these systems in a production environment. Choosing the technologies involved will dictate how you staff the project from a development and operational standpoint as well as what expertise is needed. If you do not have the expertise in-house, you will need to hire or train people. Along the same lines, is the architecture decided on actually viable for your environment? Will lack of expertise impede its adoption? Is it too complex? Will it meet all growth, performance, availability, reliability, and scalability goals? How will that affect SLAs? Do SLAs need to be rewritten? What backup schemes and other maintenance will need to be revised? Is there monitoring in place? If so, how can it be leveraged? If not, what is needed?

Step 4: Choosing Hardware and Costs

Although it does not matter in what order you configure the systems, this example starts with the cluster. Disks will more than likely represent your greatest cost. Do you go with larger, slower disks or smaller, faster disks? Start by looking at the number of disks needed for an optimal deployment.

> **Note**   The next section goes into depth on cost and disk configuration. Although the amount of detail might be painful, it is necessary.

Server Cluster

- **Quorum disk**   Two dedicated disks (must be the same size as all other disks, even though you are using a small portion).

- **MS DTC**   Same as the quorum requirements.

- **Publisher/main data**   At 600 GB, in terms of raw space, that is 17 36-GB disks or 9 72-GB disks. However, that is raw space only; Windows needs a bit more for formatting. Pad that by at least one drive, meaning 18 and 10, respectively. Now, if you implement RAID 5, add another disk for parity, which translates into 19 and 11, and if you do mirrored stripes or striped mirrors, double the disk amounts to 36 and 20. Now triple these numbers because you have the data on three separate systems.

- **Publisher/main log**   At 200 GB, this is approximately six 36-GB disks and three 72-GB disks in terms of raw space. Again, add another disk for Windows formatting, making it seven or four. You do need to mirror your log disk, so double the number, making it 14 or 8.

- **Distributor (data and log)**   At 50 GB, you could satisfy this with two 36-GB disks or one 72-GB disk. With RAID 5, that is three or two disks, and if you mirror and stripe, four disks (as that is the minimum for mirroring and striping, otherwise it is just mirroring).

- **System databases**   This means mainly msdb and tempdb. Here, plan on at least the same space as the Distributor. Remember, however, that tempdb usage will vary. Because you do not have any testing numbers, you are guessing about the usage you need.

Now you must configure your cluster based on the numbers you determined. Because there is only one main cluster system on your pick list, it makes your decision a bit easier.

- You already decided to use the best processor. This will be a two-node cluster. That translates into the 900-MHz model at $81,200 per node (all dollar amounts given are in U.S. currency) or $162,400 for the two cluster nodes alone. You might have to rethink the decision to cluster, as this represents 32.5 percent of your entire budget.

- You need two network cards for each node and, at $250 per card, that is $1,000. You are now up to $163,400.

- You will use two controller cards per disk enclosure at $5,000 each. Combined with the disk enclosure, which holds 12 disks, each will be $17,000. The cost of the entire disk subsystem will be added in later.

- One host bus adapter (HBA) is already included, and you will not have redundant disk paths. This is an availability risk, but you are trying to keep your costs down, and you determine that having only one card combined with clustering is an acceptable risk for this solution.

- You need a fibre hub for your disks, which is $3,000, bringing your new total to $166,400.

> **On the CD**   For your disk situation, the math can be found on the CD in the file HW_Cost.xls on the Cluster Disk Costs tab.

- As you can see in the file on the CD, HW_Cost.xls, there are many permutations of how you can configure the disk subsystem, with the cheapest being around $94,000 and the most expensive at $140,000. These costs include the number of disk enclosures and controller cards for the enclosures. Assume you will use the option on line 52—all 72-GB disks, with RAID 5 used for the Distributor and the system disks, but some form of striping and mirroring for the OLTP system. You are making the trade-off on Distributor write performance and system disks to save cost here and put more into your main OLTP database. This will give you decent speed, large disks, and a smaller amount of disk enclosures. The cost is $115,800, which brings you to a total cost for the cluster of $282,200. That is 56.4 percent of your overall budget.

> **Tip**   Remember, in a real-world situation outside of this book example, take into account the cost of racks and other infrastructure-related items such as determining if you have enough room in the data center to house them or the proper cooling system for the large number of disks and the heat they will generate.

Reporting Server and Log Shipped Secondary

Because you use racks in your data center, only stand-alone system option number two is valid. That translates into the following:

- $45,000 for the base system that comes with 2 GB of memory

- $3,400 to add another 2 GB of memory

- $1,600 for the fibre adapter (HBA) for the server

- $1,200 for the fibre hub

- $7,000 for the fibre switch

- $3,500 for the extra warranty

This calculates to a base cost of $61,700. Add an additional $250 for the log shipped secondary, as you want to use a private network to send the transaction logs, bringing the cost to $61,950 for that system. Those two elements added to the cluster now cost $123,900 for a new total of $406,100. Next comes the disk configuration for the two systems, which can be found on the Rack System – Non Cluster tab of the Excel spreadsheet. Remember that you will have separate storage area networks (SANs) for each system, which means that you need separate controllers, hubs, and so on. You could use the same SAN, but that would be an availability risk. The cost of the hub and switch was already factored into the price of the systems. Again, the decision is made to use 72-GB disks with mirroring and striping on the data and RAID 5 for the system databases. The cost per system is $93,600, for a total of $187,200. You are now at $593,300, nearly $100,000 over your budget. Because you are over budget, there is no way you can even consider buying test systems without rethinking things because this solution is not viable.

Rethinking the Strategy

Because the reporting server is in the same data center as the cluster, you can utilize the same SAN (assuming it is on the multicluster list). That would take the server price down to $50,000 for that system (including 4 GB of memory and a fibre adapter). That would put the cluster node costs at $164,400–$50,000 for the replication server and $61,950 for the log shipped server. Combining the disk space for the SAN choosing the same option (which can be found on the One SAN – Cluster and Repl tab of the Excel spreadsheet) costs $224,400, and the disk for the log shipped server is $93,600. All of this totals $594,350, which means you still have a cost problem. You now decide to switch to an all RAID 5–based disk solution on the cluster/replication SAN, using 36-GB 10,000 rpm disks, which costs $168,200. That will reduce the total to $538,150, which is better but still over budget. You decide to go with a RAID 5 data solution for log shipping, which brings the SAN cost down to $61,200, reducing the overall cost to $505,750. You are exposed here because you are filling all 36 slots with used disks, leaving no room for hot spares.

Although you are still over budget, you go to management to explain the trade-offs you had to make and to get approval for the additional $5,750, which, over the life of the system, works out to be just under $240 per month for the two years. Although you have what seems to be a winning design, management questions the need for the log shipping server and says that if they approve any additional money to go over budget, it should be used for a testing system. This puts your availability in a disaster recovery scenario in jeopardy.

You need to factor in the disk enclosure space. Because you need to use the 36-GB 10,000 rpm disks, that is $11,400 for the disks. Because you are using 82 slots and each enclosure has 12 slots, you must add two more disk enclosures for a total of $34,000. That brings the system cost back up to $539,750. If the log shipped system ever becomes the primary, you will need to do backups on that as well. You will need to use 36-GB disks, which will cost $10,925 with RAID 5. Because you have filled up the slots on the three disk enclosures, you will need another two, which adds up to $26,400. Adding this $37,325 to the total, you are now at $577,075.

At this point, you have the following problems:

- You are over budget.

- You have no test system.

- There is not a lot of backup room for every database as it grows, reducing the amount of retention you can have on the active system. You have not budgeted disk space or cost for dedicated backup drives, which is a big problem.

- You have what you consider nonoptimal disk configurations for your data (log is fine because it is using RAID 1), possibly exposing you to availability and performance problems.

- You have no hot spares for disks.

Unfortunately, there is no good solution without significantly increasing budget. If you eliminate the log shipped server, which dramatically puts you in harm's way in a disaster recovery scenario, you can subtract $160,475, bringing you under budget for the system as it is configured. However, you might lose $160,475 or more in revenue and leads if the system goes down. Will saving money on test systems further increase your risk for potential problems in production?

At this point, you need to make some hard decisions. What is most important to the core solution? Obviously the main OLTP system is required. Up for debate are replication and log shipping as well as the reporting functionality as a whole. If you eliminate the replicated reporting server, go back to using mirrors and stripes for the main production system and allow reporting to take place on it. This would result in $164,400 for the nodes and using 36.4-GB 15,000 rpm disks and a form of mirroring and striping for the data. You decide to use faster, smaller disks to get a performance benefit because you will have more users accessing the system. You no longer need a distribution database, so you need the items shown in Table 11-2.

Table 11-2   New Server Configuration

Function	# of Disks	Cost
Quorum RAID 1	2	$2,000
MS DTC RAID 1	2	$2,000
System databases RAID 5	3	$3,000
OLTP data	36	$36,000
OLTP log	14	$14000
Backups	40	$40,000
Total	97	$97,000

Taking into account the nine disk enclosures at $17,000 per unit, that is a cost of $153,000 for a total disk subsystem price of $250,000. The cluster will now cost $414,400. However, because you are adding load to the system, you add another 4 GB ($8,500) of memory per node, bringing the total cost to $431,400. This solution should satisfy your main concerns about the reporting and main OLTP capabilities. The one question here is your use of tempdb. If it is heavily used, you will need more or separate disks, but you now have the drive space for it, not to mention the room for hot spares, so you have also increased your expandability and availability.

You now have $68,600 left in your budget. This is not enough money for either a test system or a log shipped secondary for disaster recovery. At this point, you need to look at the following options:

■ Request the additional $91,875 for the log shipped secondary to cover yourself if something catastrophic happens, sacrificing the test system, although the log shipped secondary is not to the same specifications as the production system.

- Request the additional $91,875 for the test system to cover yourself if something catastrophic happens, sacrificing the log shipped secondary. Although this test system is not to the same specifications as the production cluster, it would be better than having no test system at all.

- Request another $431,400 for a proper test system, no matter what decision you make about the log shipped secondary. This ensures that your production and development environments will be equal. If this is done, the entire solution will cost $1,000,000 or double the original budget.

- Document your exposures and hope for the best.

The reality is that the last point—documenting your risks—is most likely to be the case, and the remaining $68,600 will go into other aspects such as cost overruns in development. The money might not be spent, but multiple people weighing the risk or reward of doing so will make that decision.

Exercise Summary

As you can tell, designing a technology solution to meet all of your requirements optimally is by no means straightforward or easy. You will win some battles and lose others. In the end, there is no absolutely correct architecture because trade-offs will have to be made for one reason or another. In this case, you sacrificed a whole testing environment and disaster recovery site, but you got basically the architecture you needed from a production standpoint. Not having a proper test system could introduce risk into your production system because you will not know how it will behave under load, meaning you do not know what to monitor (among other things). Not having the disaster recovery system leaves you greatly exposed from an availability standpoint. Throughout this book, the ability to test for load is highlighted as a crucial factor.

In terms of your disk subsystem, you did not really sacrifice disk performance in going from the larger disks to the smaller ones. Most people prefer smaller, faster disks. The problem you now face is that you intended to use some combination of mirroring and striping but only did so on your OLTP data, exposing your system databases to a potential availability problem or tempdb performance problem. Not having the testing environment hardware is starting to come into play. Because of the sheer number of disks (97) now involved in your solution, you need to stock spare drives to be used at a moment's notice. Your risk exposure on the OLTP disks is less than, say, your system databases, but if enough drives fail, an entire LUN could fail. You could experience the impact of making trade-offs.

Unfortunately, cost always has to be addressed in the trade-off mix of cost, performance, growth, and availability. It is not easy to achieve all of those while staying at or under budget. In fact, most people do not have a $500,000 budget for just the database portion of the hardware; the budget might be for all servers or (worse) the budget might be even smaller! This example was designed to show you how difficult it is with a lot of money, let alone a smaller budget. People tend to suggest "ideal" architectures, start to design maintenance plans and applications, and then find that the business cannot afford their "awesome" solution, so they have to go back to the beginning and plan everything…again. Not only did you waste the days, weeks, or months already put into the project, but your project end date probably did not change. That means that you will have less time to deliver. In this example, you saw very quickly that the desire for performance, growth, availability, and scalability did not fit your budget.

Remember to do checks, both real and in your head, during the entire process. Some questions you can ask are listed below; there will be more that are project specific. Hold regular meetings to make sure everyone is in agreement that the solution is right.

- Does the architecture seem sound? What are the potential flaws?

- Is the solution you designed supportable or is it too complex? Is it flexible and scalable? Or is it too rigid, and will it be outdated within the proposed life span of the hardware?

- Does the solution meet the availability requirement? Are there any risks or points of exposure?

- Does the solution fit the budget, or does there need to be some compromise? If so, where would you make trade-offs? Consider questions like these:

    - Where would you place the most memory or processors?

    - Are you valuing performance over availability?

- Do you design a base level of hardware first and build from there?

- Did you consider special requirements such as the quorum disk or domain connectivity if you are using a cluster?

Case Study: Microsoft.com

Microsoft.com is one of the world's most visited Web sites. Because it is the company's portal to the world, Microsoft maintains multiple versions of the Web site in different languages, all of which are available 24 hours a day, 7 days a week. This is the goal for most companies, but how does Microsoft achieve it?

Background Information

The operations side of Microsoft.com employs many of the principles and best practices in this book, with obvious tweaks for their own environment. To give you a better understanding of the topology that Microsoft.com employs, as of the writing of this book they have 930 servers (of all types—SQL Server, domain controllers, IIS servers, and more), and might have as many as 1500 in the next 18 months. The SQL Servers used by Microsoft.com currently house approximately 1100 databases. Microsoft.com has a dedicated monitoring group for all servers (including SQL Server) that is staffed around the clock to ensure that any problems that occur can be detected quickly. Microsoft.com also has redundant data centers in the United States that host all versions of Microsoft.com, including localized versions for international customers. Downloads, such as service packs for Microsoft products, are the only things hosted outside of these data centers because it is more cost-effective to use global caching vendors, because the files are closer to you, and the download is as quick as possible, no matter where you are.

With an enterprise of this magnitude, you imagine that a small army deploys, maintains, administers, and monitors these servers. That could not be further from the truth. As of the writing of this book, Microsoft.com employs 53 full-time employees, only nine of whom are DBAs. Having nine DBAs translates to an average of slightly more than 120 databases per person. For most, that seems like a massive amount of responsibility. Microsoft.com achieves this streamlining through effective team cross-training and coordination. No one, including the Group Operations Manager for Microsoft.com, carries a pager. This makes a bold statement.

Each component hosted on Microsoft.com, including all of the databases, has ownership with responsibilities attached to it. DBAs, as advocated in this book, are involved early on in the process, including system design, capacity planning for hardware purchasing, database design, code reviews, and availability architecture. If something goes wrong, they are called directly. There is no middle escalation point. It is therefore in the best interest of the database or application owner to get it right the first time, every time, because if there is a problem, the owner is called directly, no matter what time of day or night. The person responsible for each section must write a troubleshooting guide that is provided to the 24/7 monitoring staff. The goal is to design systems that are reliable, available, scalable, and easily maintainable out of the gate.

Microsoft.com stresses that no matter how good your monitoring system, you must monitor the monitor. How do you know the monitor is available? If it goes down, how do you recover quickly so that you are up and running to respond to other alerts? Microsoft.com uses an in-house, custom monitoring tool that consolidates everything under one interface.

Microsoft.com also uses prerelease and beta versions of Microsoft software in production. This is a proving ground for many Microsoft technologies because it is a high-volume Web site that needs to be scalable and available. This is one of the keys to success—although you are supporting current and past platforms, you also need to look forward. The experiments might not always work out as you had hoped, but the lessons learned can always be applied elsewhere. For Microsoft.com, employing prerelease software has not affected its overall availability.

In terms of technology, Microsoft.com uses failover clustering for some systems because clustering offers failover to prevent downtime when performing some routine maintenance. They employ other technologies—for example, Network Load Balancing coupled with log shipping—where the cost of implementing a cluster did not make sense or was overkill. They also use high-quality components and hardware designs including fibre, redundant power supplies, and error-correcting memory. They then match that to a quality over the software architecture design.

For the workers at Microsoft.com, availability goals are a point of personal pride in addition to the 24/7 SLA. The goal is to be the most highly available site on the Web as well as one of the largest. That presents particular challenges; for example, how do you maintain availability when you need to take the back-end database down for routine maintenance, upgrades, and so on?

Planning and Development

One of the most important policies implemented at Microsoft.com is that each project has not only its owners but also a process that covers the lifecycle of the project. The group operations manager and his counterpart have formal project reviews once a week. These must be polished presentations, not unlike a business review. If they feel that the team is not ready, they do not let them proceed. Microsoft.com is too critical to risk, and application designs must be virtually bulletproof when they are released.

Another important aspect of the availability of Microsoft.com is the development of troubleshooting guides for the monitoring staff to use prior to production rollout. These troubleshooting guides must be well written, because if the problem cannot be solved by using the guide, the person responsible for it will have a call escalated to them. If the proper procedures are clearly defined, the phone does not ring. Additionally, operations guides, maintenance plans, and monitoring solutions are designed at this stage. The application itself is designed with a monitoring method. Either it maps to existing tools or you build a new component that interfaces with the existing tools. Many developers historically do not design with implementation in mind, including monitoring, but at Microsoft.com it is a way of life.

> **On the CD**   A sample project checklist in outline format used by Microsoft.com is in the file MSCOM_Project_Checklist.doc. The checklist includes all phases of the lifecycle and the development, deployment, and testing efforts as well as management involvement through project or program managers.

How Microsoft.com Achieves High Availability in Production

There are two basic rules that allow Microsoft.com to achieve high availability in their production environment:

1. Once the application is deployed and monitoring is in place, leave it alone as much as possible.

2. Once the application is in production, it is all about process.

These are two very simple tenets, but they are very hard for most companies to achieve. Achieving scalable, reliable, available systems is a combination of good people, good processes, and good architecture. Once an application makes it into production, it is no longer subject to change on a frequent basis (due to schema changes, new code updates, new versions every month, and so on). The goal is stability. To achieve stability, Microsoft.com restricts access to the servers. If you do not need to physically log into the server, you are not permitted to do so. Monitoring and other administration tools are there for a good reason.

Microsoft.com's Barriers to Availability

Microsoft.com deals with the classic barriers that everyone needs to contend with: network configuration, hardware configuration, software configuration, and service availability. Running SQL Server adds three main considerations to the mix:

- Determining the availability of the database to the application. If the database is down, how does the application respond?

- General database design issues that could lead to availability issues.

- Challenges presented by highly utilized OLTP systems. You want to ensure that they are not a single point of failure, so redundancy is built in. But how do you synchronize standby servers to ensure no loss of transactional consistency?

In terms of what would be considered "normal" problems related to SQL Server, the top three issues that Microsoft.com encounters, listed here, will probably sound familiar to most of you.

1. **Hotfixes and Service Packs** Hotfixes and service packs are an obvious availability concern. When you cycle a server, you cause an availability outage. Microsoft.com is lucky enough to have a dedicated test lab to determine what each hotfix or service pack will do to the behavior of their applications. The advantage of being Microsoft.com is that they have a unique relationship with the SQL Server development team. As soon as a hotfix or service pack is in development, the Web group works with the SQL Server development team and has access to new builds. Although this might seem like an advantage—and it is—it is only marginal. They still need to roll out the fixes and patches like everyone else, taking into account their availability.

2. **Service account password changing** Any time a service account is changed, you might need to stop and start your SQL Servers (including clustered servers).

3. **Ensuring code that will be deployed is written properly** Developers, by nature, are not usually production DBAs. They do not always understand that what they write has a direct impact on everything—disk I/O, memory, locking and blocking, and so on. Microsoft.com does not have any dedicated developers on their operations staff, but for Microsoft.com as a whole, there is another

dedicated team of more than 60 developers to augment the operations group. Because of thorough reviews throughout the project lifecycle, DBAs and other people responsible for the operational side can ensure that the code they are ultimately going to roll out in production meets their standards. It is not meant to be an adversarial relationship; if someone, for example, uses recursive cursors, it is not enough to tell a developer "Do not do that." The DBAs at Microsoft.com document the reasons why it is not optimal and communicate that to the developer. In the end, it is about synergy.

Outside of the usual realm of these problems, Microsoft.com has a problem not everyone faces: because they represent Microsoft and Microsoft.com is on the Internet 24 hours a day, they are frequently subject to attacks and hackers. Remember, one of the most important aspects of availability for a public system is security. Microsoft.com has a dedicated person for SQL Server security as well as a counterpart for Internet Information Services. Although this is not possible in every environment, if security is important to you, you should assess the need to dedicate a resource to this important task. One of the reasons Microsoft.com is so successful is that their monitoring group knows what to look for and can detect problems.

Microsoft.com is a good example of how you can achieve high availability purely with Microsoft-based technologies.

Summary

Designing a highly available SQL Server–based solution takes careful planning, and planning is based on knowledge. You need to ask the right questions. Any missed step up front can lead to problems in production. Although the example in this chapter focuses largely on technology, you need to build in the people and processes to manage the solution you devise. As shown in the Microsoft.com case study, it is quite possible to build an architecture that is reliable, available, scalable, and manageable purely on the Microsoft platform. You do not need an army to be up and running 24 hours a day if you have the proper designs and planning in place from the beginning. That means that all parties who will be responsible for the system, from developers to DBAs to system architects to those who rely on the system, are on the same page and communicating throughout the entire process. Your corporate culture might not be easy to change, but start small and improve your processes over time. You will be surprised at how much difference the little things make. In the end, perhaps the most important consideration is to understand your barriers, whether they are people, processes, or technology. You must have a definitive list prior to planning, otherwise you could develop and design fully redundant, highly available, fault-tolerant systems that still can't tolerate the type of outage you encounter. Your list will help you ensure that you do not miss the mark.

12

Disaster Recovery Techniques for Microsoft SQL Server

You can make individual parts of a system fault tolerant. You can design in redundancy for the systems, making the solution highly available. But what happens when a catastrophe strikes and your fault-tolerant, redundant, highly available systems do not weather the proverbial storm? This is where disaster recovery comes into play.

Many will argue that high availability and disaster recovery are not related, and some incorrectly mistake high availability for disaster recovery. The truth is that high availability planning must include the entire scope of what it takes to keep an application, business, or other enterprise up and running. Technology that makes your solutions fault tolerant, such as failover clustering, might not be sufficient for your disaster recovery needs. For example, although a technology like log shipping can be employed as a primary method of availability, it can also be used in a disaster recovery scenario. People and processes are crucial to all aspects of high availability, and they also form the backbone of most aspects of disaster recovery. This chapter guides you through planning and preparation for disaster recovery, as well as what you can do from a SQL Server perspective to recover your systems.

Planning for Disaster Recovery

There is no easy or "add on" solution to disaster recovery needs. Disaster recovery planning does not start late in the cycle; it starts from the first day of any project, when you are first assessing risk. Contrary to popular belief, each disaster recovery plan is unique, even for the same technology, because companies are different and their tolerances are different. When you seriously plan for disaster recovery and have your "local" high availability story well defined, two overriding questions govern the rest of the discussion:

- What are our site disaster risks, and which ones are acceptable?

- What are our dependencies from the hardware layer right on through to the end user applications?

> **Important**   This book is mainly focused on SQL Server, but disaster recovery encompasses all aspects of a particular solution or system, from people to Microsoft Windows and everything in between. No stone can be left unturned in putting together a disaster recovery plan.

Run Book

There are several benefits to keeping historical records of your environment, including every change made to your servers. The first is, obviously, to help you rebuild it in the event of a disaster. For this reason a complete document, sometimes known as a *run book*, is crucial to disaster recovery planning and execution. A run book can contain a subset of the configuration information or a very high level of detail, depending on what suits your needs. The run book should also include contact information, disaster recovery plans, and so on.

The run book can be referred to on a daily basis for an easy way to get information about a system. If you keep contact and related system information in it, it can also help you identify systems that send or receive data from your systems and the people who need to be contacted in emergencies (or those who might be willing to answer some questions if, for example, you're researching elusive performance problems).

A run book does not have to be an actual printed book, although you should be sure to print several copies on a regular basis. One copy (whether electronic or printed) should go out with the backup tapes so that the system can be restored in the event of a disaster at the main site. In addition to printing the run book, you could also put the information on a Web site that would be accessible by only authorized users. This could be on an intranet or a secure extranet. For example, you could have a Web page that shows a grid of all the latest service packs, hotfixes, system hardware configuration, and so on. You could also pull that information into a SQL Server database or Extensible Markup Language (XML) and base some self-healing maintenance on that as well. You should also document the organization and procedures for the configuration management of a specific product, project, system, support group, or service.

Items to Place in a Run Book

The following categorized list can be used as the basis for a run book or customized operations guide for your database system. This list is based on Microsoft SQL Server 2000, but it could apply equally to other versions, in concept, and it outlines the configuration items you would use to maintain a high standard of operations support. The following list has been reviewed and approved by operations and field personnel within Microsoft, and it represents the current opinions and best practices of those groups.

> **On the CD**   A sample run book can be found on the CD-ROM in the file Run_Book.doc. This can be used and modified to fit your environment; it serves as a good starting point. In addition, many of the worksheets and templates included for use with other chapters in this book can be used as the starting point for information for your run book.

> **Important**   A few of the items that follow note that you must document passwords. First, make sure this is not in violation of any corporate policy. However, if you cannot document passwords needed for vital accounts during a restore, you must ensure that people who know them can be on site during a recovery operation.

SQL Server Administrative Information   There is a minimum set of information that you must keep to fulfill your responsibilities as database system administrator:

- Maintain information on maintenance plans: all related scripts, how information is transferred for analysis (if it is), how alerts and errors are handled, and remote servers.

■ Maintain information about database backup files such as their location and type (full database, differential, file, filegroup, log) and how current these are, per location. Also record the times that files are backed up to tape (or other removable storage) and where these are stored, and notes on related directories, data, or files that must also be backed up. Remember to include the password for each backup if necessary. All related information should be recorded.

■ From a command line, run Sqldiag.exe and store the result to a text file. Do this on a regular basis, and save the files historically.

> **Important**   Make sure you know what to look for in the output of SQLDIAG. If you or your staff is not familiar with it, script the relevant portions separately.

■ Store your Data Transformation Services (DTS) packages as files to enable an easy modular restore or transfer. Make notes regarding logins and passwords for the packages, and any alternate data sources.

■ Create a script of all system or application users and passwords (including the *sa* account). Create scripts for application roles or passwords and linked or remote servers.

■ Record your software serial number, a copy of the CDs (including all service packs and hotfixes), and a reference to their location on network file shares.

■ Keep a record of all related interconnected systems, including contacts, configuration information, network topology, and documentation of data interfaces.

■ Record any custom-made database administration objects that you depend on to maintain or administer the server.

■ Record hardware and software vendor support phone numbers and account numbers as well as any login/password information for related Web sites.

■ Record contact information for your remote site, if you have one.

■ Record people to notify in the event that you must re-create standard SQL Server users or reset their passwords.

- Use a tool like Microsoft Visual Source Safe to manage script versions (for example, schema, install and rollback scripts, and maintenance scripts, and perhaps even the run book). Scripting is especially important for encrypted objects.

- Write down contact information. Remember to list these by each person's role, so that if the person changes jobs, you can still find the correct contact. Ideally, you should record a group name (department, e-mail discussion list, and so on).

Analysis Services Administrative Information   There is a minimum set of information you must record if you are using Analysis Services in your solutions:

- Information on maintenance plans: all related scripts, how information is transferred for analysis (if it is), how alerts and errors are handled, and any remote servers.

- Setup information about the Analysis Services server. Where is the metadata stored (Microsoft Access database, SQL Server database, or SQL Server Meta Data Services)? Where are the data files located? What are the other configuration parameters for Microsoft SQL Server 2000 Analysis Services?

- As described in the previous sections, store DTS packages that are used to populate Analysis Services cubes as files.

- Any custom-made DBA objects that you depend on to maintain or administer the server.

Application System Information   There is a minimum set of information you must record about the non-SQL Server portions of your solutions:

- List all the applications that must be in place for the system to run (either on the server itself or another system, if that is required). Include custom-built software.

- Document the application's security architecture, including type of logins used, any fixed passwords, and role permissions, and note the process for changing passwords on any multiuser logins.

- Contacts for the application: include developers and anyone else (analysts, testers, managers) who should be involved if a system change is made to the application or to any related system or process.

Database Components   There is a minimum set of information you must record about your databases:

- Script out all database schemas, collations, jobs, and custom error messages. Anything that can be saved in script form should be scripted and stored historically. User-defined functions, user-defined datatypes, custom roles, triggers, indexes, and object permissions are all easy to miss in the scripting process. Be careful if you intend for your disaster recovery scenario to encompass these objects.

- Information related to distributed databases or partitions (if applicable), such as data dependent routing tables and distributed transaction marks.

- Linked server connections.

Server Configuration   There is a minimum set of information you must record about your servers to use during disaster recovery:

- Operating system version, with service pack level and hotfixes.

- Exact list of hardware in use, and how that hardware is configured.

- Processor information (for example, speed and class), RAM (amount, speed, and type), and BIOS (manufacturer and version).

- Dates or version numbers of firmware.

- Physical and logical disk configuration, including redundant array of independent disks (RAID) levels and disk controller information (including write cache settings), disk type and size, any special options used (that is, allocation units, formerly known as block size), and use of each disk (explanation).

- Notes on anything unusual regarding this server, hardware, configuration, or location; for example, if you have disks on different shelves plugged into the same array controller.

SQL Server Configuration   There is a minimum set of information you must record about each SQL Server instance's configuration for use in a disaster recovery scenario:

- SQL Server installation configuration, including the installation and service pack levels, and any hotfixes that were applied.

- SQL Server instance names, IP addresses, ports, configuration options, database file locations, service logins and passwords, e-mail accounts, enabled network protocols, and their order.

- File share information, shares to which the service login must have permission reached by Universal Naming Convention (UNC) names or through any other protocols. This can be a potential nightmare in an off-site disaster recovery scenario, so you need to mitigate this for your environment.

- Configuration information for any other software that runs on the same server. Make sure complete installation and configuration documentation are available and that correct support personnel (or job titles) are listed as contacts. Also list support numbers and Web sites for each piece of software.

- Note any client tools that must be installed for remote database connections (for example, to heterogeneous data sources). Note configuration information such as what data access components must be loaded on clients.

- Document any data source names (DSNs) that exist on the server.

- Setup of SQL Server 2000 failover clustering, replication, log shipping, and a configuration and topology description.

- Multi-instance configuration.

- Notes on anything unusual regarding this server. For example, special features in use such as XML support for Internet Information Services (IIS), Active Directory directory service support, and so on.

Network Information and Configuration   There is a minimum set of information you must record about your network topology for use in a disaster recovery scenario:

- Switch, hub, router, and gateway information.

- Topology graphics or diagrams prepared in tools such as Microsoft Visio.

- Management and configuration utilities for switches, routers, and gateways, and the settings for each; "how-to" instructions or manuals; and scripts.

- Any redundant path information based on multipath routing.

- Notes on anything unusual regarding the network.

Storage Information and Configuration   There is a minimum set of information you must record about your disk subsystem configurations for use in a disaster recovery scenario:

- Switch information.

- Fabric topology graphic or diagrams prepared in tools such as Visio.

- Management and configuration utilities for switches, the settings for each, "how-to" instructions or manuals, scripts, and other items.

- Any redundant path information based on multipathing.

- Impact of clustering on fabric such as zoning or portioning.

- Notes on anything unusual regarding the fabric.

Other Necessary Information   This is a list of other items that should also be recorded that do not fall under one of the preceding categories:

- Complete contact information (home phone, e-mail address, cell phone, pager number—whatever you have) for anyone who might be involved in a disaster recovery. This information might include the following:

  - All of your company's IT resources necessary for the recovery. This would include technical operations manager, DBAs, system administrators, networking people, and so on.

  - All factory support personnel and contract numbers. For example, your Microsoft Premier Product Support Services (PSS) support representative, the hardware vendor sales representative, and your agreement contract numbers.

  - Off-site data storage facility. You need access to the librarian software to prepare a list of which tapes you need to recall.

  - In addition to the off-site data storage facility, you might also need the name of a high-speed transcontinental courier service. For example, if there is a major blackout in the eastern United States, you might need to recover in the Midwest. When time is critical and overnight services are not fast enough, there are options. Airlines have services that can often provide four-hour bonded courier point-to-point delivery. Research this option in advance and have current contact numbers, drop-off times, and prices available.

  - The vendor information for your hot site location.

  - Senior managers who will be responsible for the recovery and their alternates.

  - Telecommunications managers responsible for networking.

  - Other senior management as needed. For example, general manager, chief information officer, and chief financial officer.

  - Work schedules.

- Application dependencies.

- Backup and restore plans.

- Disaster recovery plans.

- Service level agreements (SLAs).

- Like plants, people need care to survive. Two main concerns are sustenance and a place to sleep. You might want to include the following:

  - Phone numbers and addresses of hotels and rental agencies in the area of your recovery site. You should also have back-ups, in case they are full.

  - Location of cots, couches, or sleeping bags for on-site personnel.

  - Phone numbers of restaurants that deliver.

  - Names and locations of 24-hour convenience stores in the area where you can get the basics after other stores are closed.

  - Check and see what type of bathroom facilities are available on site, too. For example, are there showers nearby?

  - Note the policy about food and where it can be eaten, and document the break room locations.

> **Important**   The run book is only useful if it is meticulously kept up to date and stored on a separate system (which must also be treated as highly available). If you can automate the process, do so.

> **Tip**   The run book should be stored both on site and off site, with both copies kept up to date. At least one copy should be a printed document or an encapsulated program or both (not a backup tape or a database that needs a separately installed GUI). Use a versioning tool such as Visual Source Safe to keep track of all changes made to the run book. Also keep a copy of all software installations off site as well in the event systems need to be rebuilt.

SLAs, Risk, and Disaster Recovery

Think back to Chapter 2, "The Basics of Achieving High Availability," and the discussion there of SLAs. As crucial as they are to high availability, they are even more crucial to disaster recovery. This is where the difference in downtime—planned or unplanned—of minutes, hours, or even days comes into play. SLAs, in the form of support contracts, must exist for every physical and software component of a system to ensure that your SLAs with all parties are met. If you cannot meet your end user SLA because, for example, your disk subsystem was down and you did not have a proper SLA in place for it, that could be a problem. Now, in some cases this might not be possible, but you need to try. SLAs typically encompass issues such as physical security, money, uptime, and response times.

Obviously, the cost of buying the right SLA must be considered. Does the risk justify the financial cost of addressing it? For example, your company's off-site data storage facility might have limited hours. This is probably not a wise choice, and you would need to find a better solution. In the meantime, management decides to put their off-site backups in a bank safe deposit box for easy access. This is a cost-effective solution because it costs only $100 per year. However, only certain individuals can get at the tapes and only during banking hours. Alternatively, you might decide to let the DBA on the night rotation take home a set of tapes. This is not only a risk, it might also violate corporate security policy.

When you are purchasing your SLAs, do not take only high availability into account. Remember disaster recovery, too.

Planning Step 1: Assessing Risk and Defining Dependencies

Disaster recovery, like "local" high availability, is about mitigating risk. Risk comes in several varieties, such as risk to the business, risk to human life, and risk to technology. Unfortunately, assessing risk is a complex task and each company's risks and tolerance for those risks will be different. The following steps show you the thought process to follow and how to assess risk in your company.

Example Scenario

You have implemented a customized Microsoft Solution for Internet Business (MSIB). This encompasses IIS, SQL Server 2000, Microsoft BizTalk, and Microsoft Commerce Server. This particular solution involves two SQL Server 2000 failover clusters, each with two instances of SQL Server on them.

First, identify the physical servers that are part of this solution and their names. This extends to not only server functionality, but domain controllers and so on. Missing even one server could prove fatal. Taking an inventory of your environment, you see that you have the following:

- DOMCONT1

- DOMCONT2

- STAGING1

- FIREWALLDOMCONT1

- FIREWALLDOMCONT2

- ISASRV1

- STAGINGSQL1

- SQL1ANODE1

- SQL1ANODE2

- CLU2NODE1

- CLU2NODE2

- MSIB1

- MSIB2

- BIZTALK1

Next, take an inventory of all of the software configured on each server and make a detailed list, including versions. A final list should also include service packs and hotfixes. Here is a preliminary list for the example environment:

- Microsoft BizTalk Server 2002

- Microsoft Commerce Server 2002

- Content Management Server 2001

- Internet Information Server 5.0

- Microsoft Message Queue

- SQL Server 2000

- Microsoft Windows 2000

- Microsoft Windows Server 2003 (for domain controllers)

- Custom applications

Now it is time to gather information about the instances of SQL Server. The instance names are as follows:

- SQL1A

- SQL1B\INST2

- SQL2A

- SQL2B\INST2

- STAGINGSQL1

Table 12-1 lists the databases.

Table 12-1   Databases

Database	SQL Instance	Use
CustomDB3	SQL2A	CustomDB3
CustomDB8	SQL2A	CustomDB3
CustomDB4	SQL2A	CustomDB3
CUSTOMDB1	SQL1B\INST2	CUSTOMDB1
Company_CUSTOMDB1	STAGINGSQL1	CUSTOMDB1
ETSBizTalkReference	SQL1A	BizTalk
CustomDB2	SQL1A	BizTalk
InterchangeBTM	SQL1B\INST2	BizTalk
InterchangeDTA	SQL1B\INST2	BizTalk
InterchangeSQ	SQL1A	BizTalk
MCMS_Data	SQL2A	Content Management Server
MSCS_Admin	SQL2B\INST2	Commerce Server
MSCS_Admin	STAGINGSQL1	Commerce Server
MSCS_BDPermissions	SQL2B\INST2	Commerce Server
MSCS_BDPermissions	STAGINGSQL1	Commerce Server
MSCS_Campaigns	SQL2B\INST2	Commerce Server
MSCS_Campaigns	STAGINGSQL1	Commerce Server
MSCS_CatalogScratch	SQL2B\INST2	Commerce Server
MSCS_CatalogScratch	STAGINGSQL1	Commerce Server
MSCS_EndeavorCE	STAGINGSQL1	Commerce Server
MSCS_ProductCatalog	SQL2B\INST2	Commerce Server
MSCS_ProductCatalog	STAGINGSQL1	Commerce Server
MSCS_Profiles	SQL2B\INST2	Commerce Server
MSCS_Profiles	STAGINGSQL1	Commerce Server
MSCS_TransactionConfig	SQL2B\INST2	Commerce Server
MSCS_TransactionConfig	STAGINGSQL1	Commerce Server
MSCS_Transactions	SQL2B\INST2	Commerce Server
MSCS_Transactions	STAGINGSQL1	Commerce Server
Inventory	SQL2A	CustomDB3
Inventory_Asia	SQL2A	CustomDB3
Inventory_SA	SQL2A	CustomDB3

Table 12-1   **Databases**

Database	SQL Instance	Use
InventoryArchive	SQL2A	CustomDB3
InventoryArchive2	SQL2A	CustomDB3
CustomDB9	SQL2A	CustomDB3
CustomDB2	SQL2A	CustomDB3
CustomDB11	SQL2A	CustomDB3
CustomDB5	SQL2A	CustomDB3
CustomDB7	SQL2A	CustomDB3
XLANG	SQL1A	BizTalk

Table 12-2 lists database dependencies and their impact on availability.

Table 12-2   **Database Dependencies and Impact on Solution Availability**

Database	Impact	Dependencies (N/A if None)
CustomDB6	CustomDB3 (North America) will not work if this database is not running.	Databases: CustomDB1, CustomDB8, Inventory, CustomDB9
CustomDB1 (production)	This is a crucial database for the solution. It will, over time, also contain tables for other applications. It is a central point of integration.	All CustomDB3 databases
CustomDB7	These are the database lookups for BizTalk Server (BTS) maps. Some tolerance where CustomDB1, BTM, DTA, and XLANG die here.	N/A
CustomDB5	Risk is low for losing data because it can be recovered elsewhere, but is part of the whole CustomDB2 process.	N/A
InterchangeBTM	Contains the definition of BTS objects. This will not change often, but is crucial for BTS being up.	N/A

(continued)

Table 12-2 Database Dependencies and Impact on Solution Availability *(continued)*

Database	Impact	Dependencies (N/A if None)
InterchangeDTA	This is the logging database for BTS. The use of the textimage field is configurable, and right now it is turned on. There is a low risk to the solution from a high level if this database fails, and it is used mainly for archiving and reporting purposes. However, it is actually a high risk to the solution because if BTS cannot log, BizTalk will not be able to work. You will not lose transactions if this happens, though.	N/A
InterchangeSQ	Shared Queue database. This is very important, as it contains the state of anything received and recorded. If you lose this database, you lose the transaction. CustomDB2 system dials every 60 minutes, CustomDB3 data (spike between 9 A.M. and 12 P.M. North America and Latin America, Asia 10 hours prior, EMEA 6 hours prior).	N/A
MCMS_Data	Content Management Server will be down if this database is not available, and the entire solution will be down if this database is down because it contains all the site content.	Commerce Server databases (from a restore standpoint)
MSCS_Admin (production)	Will affect Commerce Server as it is the administrative definition database.	MCMS_Data (from a restore standpoint)
MSCS_BDPermissions (production)	Like the MSCS_Admin, this is a configuration database mainly used with BizDesk. BizDesk will be affected if this is down, but site will not go down.	MCMS_Data (from a restore standpoint)
MSCS_Campaigns (production only)	This will not affect solution because it is not in use.	N/A

**Table 12-2   Database Dependencies and
Impact on Solution Availability** *(continued)*

Database	Impact	Dependencies (N/A if None)
MSCS_CatalogScratch (production only)	Used for virtual catalog generation. There is no need to back up or worry about it because it only affects BizDesk.	N/A
MSCS_ProductCatalog (production only)	Although the site will not shut down if this database is unavailable (it is the master product catalog), you cannot navigate the solution. You will still be able to register users as long as other databases are up.	MCMS_Data (from a restore standpoint), MSCS_Transactions (GUID orphans), MSCS_ProductCatalog (staging)
MSCS_ProductCatalog (staging)	Very important to the solution, as it contains the copy of the catalog that is pushed out to the production server.	N/A
MSCS_Profiles (production)	If down, no one will be able to buy anything on the site or register users.	MCMS_Data (from a restore standpoint)
MSCS_TransactionConfig (production)	This contains the definition of all pipeline configurations. It is updated with code push. It is needed for BTS operation, but can be re-created as long as staging is available. If it is down, users will not be able to buy anything on the site.	MSCS_TransactionConfig (staging)
MSCS_Transactions (production)	This is the heart of BTS; it contains all completed transactions and it will definitely affect the solution. If this database is down, users will not be able to buy anything on the site.	MCMS_Data, MSCS_ProductCatalog
Inventory_USA	This has a minimal impact; CustomDB3 will still be up and running if this database is not available.	CustomDB1, CustomDB8, CustomDB6, CustomDB9
Inventory_Asia	This has a minimal impact; CustomDB3 will still be up and running if this database is not available.	CustomDB1, CustomDB10, CustomDB12

(continued)

Table 12-2 Database Dependencies and Impact on Solution Availability *(continued)*

Database	Impact	Dependencies (N/A if None)
Inventory_SA	This has a minimal impact; CustomDB3 will still be up and running if this database is not available.	CustomDB1, CustomDB11, CustomDB13
InventoryArchive	This has a minimal impact on just archived data for CustomDB3.	CustomDB1
InventoryArchive2	This has a minimal impact on just archived data for CustomDB3.	CustomDB1
CustomDB9	CustomDB3 will not work if this database is down. Customers and partners are in here, and it contains all item definitions.	CustomDB1, CustomDB8, CustomDB6, Inventory_USA
CustomDB2	CustomDB3 (Asia) will not work if this database is not running.	CustomDB1, Inventory_Asia, CustomDB12
CustomDB11	CustomDB3 (South America) will not work if this database is not running.	CustomDB1, Inventory_SA, CustomDB13
CustomDB5	CustomDB3 (Asia) will not work if this database is not running.	CustomDB1, Inventory_Asia, CustomDB10
CustomDB7	CustomDB3 (South America) will not work if this database is not running.	CustomDB1, Inventory_SA, CustomDB11
XLANG	Similar to InterchangeSQ, but stores state for orchestration schedules. This is very important to keeping BTS up.	N/A

Once the dependencies are known, you can then establish the facts for each product that will influence any disaster recovery planning.

Known Facts About Servers

The following is a list of facts for each server product.

BizTalk

- CustomDB1, CustomDB2, BizTalk, and Commerce Server are all related.

- If Internet Information Server (IIS), Message Queuing (also known as MSMQ), or Microsoft Distributed Transaction Coordinator (MS DTC) are down, BizTalk will not function.

- If BizTalk is down, the site will still technically be up, but not fully functional, which essentially means it is down.

- If BizTalk and MSMQ are down, the site will not be functional at all.

- If InterchangeDTA is down, you will not be able to report from BizTalk (and BTS will be down because it cannot log). If you restore it to an older time, CustomDB1, CustomDB3, and so on, are interdependent. The issue is that a transaction might exist elsewhere that is not here, and you will need to create a process to get DTA back in sync.

Commerce Server

- CustomDB1, CustomDB2, BizTalk, and Commerce Server are all related.

- Commerce Server is dependent on IIS.

- If you lose your MSCS_ProductCatalog database and need to restore it to an earlier backup, you will invalidate MSCS_Transactions because you will now have orphaned GUIDs.

- If a problem occurs in Content Management Server or Commerce Server, you will have to restore all Commerce Server databases and Content Management Server databases to the same point if (and only if) the products that exist in one place do not exist in the other. This also means that you will probably need another server to restore the older backups on and reconcile the difference, making it a time-consuming process. If you can restore the catalogs back to the same point in time, this should not be a concern. Otherwise, you will get orphaned postings if products were not added to Content Management Server.

- Without Commerce Server, there is no solution, because it controls all buying functionality.

- If Commerce Server order status (that is, MSCS_Transactions) cannot be updated due to Commerce Server being down, the transaction from BTS should roll back if there is a schedule in XLANG, and it might have to be pushed back out. This needs to be addressed.

Content Management Server

- Content Management Server is dependent on IIS.

■ If a problem occurs in Content Management Server or Commerce Server, you have to restore all Commerce Server databases and Content Management Server databases to the same point if (and only if) the products that exist in one place do not exist in the other. This also means that you probably need another server to restore the older backups on and reconcile the difference, making it a time-consuming process. If you can restore the catalogs back to the same point in time, this should not be a concern. Otherwise, you will get orphaned postings if products were not added to Content Management Server.

■ Without Content Management Server, there is no solution, as it is the presentation server for the MSIB site. All permissions and roles are also stored; the site will not work without authentication, and even if you could authenticate, you need the site content (Content Management Server contains 90 percent of the content).

■ Staging Content Management Server is the master for site content and feeds the production Content Management Server, so staging's availability is crucial for the production and external portion of the solution.

■ The Content Management Server site definition object (SDO) file created by staging updates the production Content Management Server daily. You can take backups from staging and then apply them to production, but not vice versa. The SDO itself is more crucial than the database, because it is the mechanism by which you can re-create objects on the site. To ensure that the company is protected, the following should probably happen, in this order:

1. Back up the Content Management Server database currently in production (if not done yet; this would be the previous day's configuration).

2. Back up the staging SQL database prior to generation of the daily SDO file.

3. Generate the new SDO file, immediately back it up, and then apply it to the production environment.

4. Back up the newly updated Content Management Server database in production.

5. If an error is found due to a bad SDO push or inaccurate data in the SDO, the SDO should be repushed to production when it is fixed.

6. Content Management Server has the ability to support release dates for certain content, so what appears to be an error might not be.

CustomDB1, CustomDB2, and CustomDB3

- CustomDB1, CustomDB2, BizTalk, and Commerce Server are all related.

- CustomDB2 uses CustomDB4, which keeps track of all activity for CustomDB2 trading partners. There are file pointers for every interchange received, and they remain until archived. It is hit every 45 minutes when CustomDB2 goes out to get transactions; this activity lasts for approximately 10 minutes. Risk of losing some data is low. Three systems feed CustomDB2: an EDI Value Added Network (which has its own archiving and can go back four days), the back-end SAP system (which can go back one day), and BizTalk (which also comes from SAP).

- CustomDB1 has two transactional tables. If the application cannot identify customers, it goes elsewhere.

- CustomDB1 is hit most heavily in the morning, and that might be a logical time to back the CustomDB1 database up (instead of in the middle of the night).

- CustomDB1 is a central point of integration and, as time goes on, other applications will use it (such as telcom and asset), so it is important to the solution and the company.

- If a transaction is not committed, everything will roll back and go into the retry queue (sits in MSMQ).

- The CustomDB1 and CustomDB3 databases should be restored in a recovery situation at the same time.

- CustomDB3 has triggers on tables, which feed MSMQ, which then feeds CustomDB1. If CustomDB1 needs to be rolled back to an older backup, you will be missing entries from CustomDB3, so you need to establish a process to roll forward entries from CustomDB3.

- SAP is a flat file extract and a daily feed once in the morning. The flow is to the staging table, to MSMQ, and finally, into CustomDB1. If you need to regenerate data from CustomDB1, it is a difficult process because no transaction ID exists, so you need to devise a disaster recovery process for this interaction.

- CustomDB3 is broken out by region: North America, Asia, and South America. All backups of dependent databases (see Table 12-2) must be coordinated, which means that you need separate SQL Server Agent jobs that are scheduled to run at the same time to ensure that all dependent databases can be restored to the same point.

- CustomDB8 might be loaded once or twice a week depending on a reseller sending data. From a recoverability standpoint, the company can go back about a week because the Microsoft Excel spreadsheets are available and the spreadsheet names are stored in the database.

- You might need a separate server to restore older databases to reconcile differences if a problem happens on one or more databases, especially the dependent ones.

Other Servers

- Without the DOMCONT1 and DOMCONT2 domain controllers, the SQL Server clusters will not work, and their absence will most likely affect all other functionality as well (not just from an SQL Server perspective), such as MSMQ.

- MSMQ public queues are dependent on the domain controllers for lookup purposes.

- Without the Internet Security and Acceleration (ISA) Server domain controllers, ISA will not work.

- Without IIS, no one will be able to connect to the solution, and Content Management Server, Commerce Server, and BizTalk will be unable to function.

- If MSMQ is down, BizTalk will not function.

- If MS DTC is down, BizTalk will not function.

- Without ISA and the firewall, the solution will not be protected (but it should function).

- SAP technically has no impact on the site if it is down, but it is part of the solution in one way or another and needs to be brought within its scope. Every message for SAP will be in MSMQ until it can be submitted. Obviously, if MSMQ fails, you cannot send the messages. The data is in Commerce Server, so it could be re-created.

Risks and Unknowns

The following is a list of risks and unknowns that must be accounted for:

- You do not have a backup until you have done a restore. You need to restore all backups made (possibly on a rotational basis) so that you know the backups being made are usable. This requires hardware that might or might not currently exist.

- You need to determine the retention time of backup files. Currently, it is limited by storage space, but that will affect the solution's potential availability if you find all of the needed backups that exist (in the event of an emergency) are bad.

- Schedule fire drills and test the disaster recovery plans and process so that it "feels" like the real thing. Making disaster recovery plans without testing them is not good enough.

- The company needs to create disaster recovery plans based on this document and the Excel spreadsheets containing the backup information.

- What will happen if the hardware load balancer fails? How is that being protected?

- What is the impact of a network failure? How is that being mitigated?

- Is the company stocking hardware, such as additional disks, host bus adapters (HBAs), network cards, and so on, in the event a component fails in one server?

- There is no process to move the staging MSCS_ProductCatalog data to the production environment. You need to test that and initiate a way to re-create it.

- You must revisit the SLAs to ensure that the steps put in place for disaster recovery reflect the time it takes to do the process.

- When figuring out exact steps, document where you would have to start the whole process by reinstalling the operating system versus other methods (such as third-party software).

- Include in this disaster recovery document any relevant support information, such as links to the diagrams for the disk configurations. That will speed up any disaster recovery process.

Planning Step 2: Putting the Plan Together

Once you have assembled your lists of known facts, risks, and dependencies and have all pertinent information in hand (such as SLAs), you can put the plan together. This plan should include the exact steps it will take to recover the system and who is responsible for what task (job roles mainly; a list maintained in the run book should tell you who is currently responsible for the action). Other information that you need to put into your disaster recovery plan includes the following:

- Define a go/no-go point for executing the plan. Many companies like to try to solve the problem on their own before engaging any type of support such as Microsoft's PSS, original equipment manufacturers, and service providers. Keep in mind that seconds and minutes matter with SLAs. If you want to try to diagnose the problem on your own, set a reasonable time frame (say 15 minutes) to solve the problem. If you cannot do it within that time, pick up the phone. Also keep in mind that if you have, say, a four nines SLA (meaning less than 52 minutes of downtime a year), do you really want to try to diagnose the problem yourself? Putting in explicit instructions avoids what can be known as "the hero syndrome." A clear understanding of what skills and knowledge you have in house can make it clear what failures can be addressed internally and which ones must be escalated immediately.

■ Define a chain of command. Chaos can quickly ensue with too many chefs and not enough bottle washers, or plenty of bottle washers but no chef to direct them. Roles and responsibilities should be clear. Even if the people performing the job change, everyone should know how they fit into the works and who reports to whom.

> **Important**   A chain of command can solve a bottleneck when dealing with support. Often, when support professionals are contacted, they require a seemingly large amount of information, potentially including a copy of your database. Constructing barriers that prevent the support professional from helping you only increases your downtime. Remember that reputable support organizations are not there to peruse your potentially sensitive data or steal your trade secrets. They want to help you get up and running. Work out any corporate security issues that relate to external organizations prior to contacting support as part of your SLA. Conversely, if you will never be able to work with a support organization because you cannot divulge certain information, you might want to rethink your strategy. Is it better to be down or up?

■ Define a communications plan. With a chain of command, you must establish clear communications. Communications plans are based partially on being able to reach everyone who needs to be involved, so make sure that any type of contact information is updated in the run book. This also goes for any type of work schedules, on-call schedules, and so on.

■ Define schedules for the recovery plan itself. A recovery is often a 24-hour operation. It is neither practical nor smart to expect one person to oversee or work a particular aspect of the plan from the beginning to the end. People become fatigued after a period of time and might make poor decisions. The correct solution is to define shifts and staff them appropriately.

■ Define milestones. These are events on the critical path that, when complete, represent forward movement. Milestones make it easy to gauge your progress. Some examples follow.

❑ All recovery personnel have been notified.

❑ Personnel have shown up or been called in and are ready.

❑ Call numbers for the site and personnel are physically available in e-mail.

❑ The backup server is physically ready.

❑ Operating systems and service packs are installed.

❑ SQL Server is installed.

❑ Application software is installed.

❑ Tapes have arrived from off-site facilities.

❑ The restoration of the database has begun.

❑ Periodic updates are provided on the restore operation's percentage complete.

❑ The database restore is completed.

❑ Logs have been reviewed.

❑ Results of various diagnostics attest to the health of the database (for example, DBCC CHECKDB).

❑ Applications have been started and connected to the database.

❑ Application test reports confirm validity of the data.

❑ Management has made the go/no–go decision.

■ Define acceptance criteria and a testing suite for a go/no-go decision. The confidence of recovery personnel in the successful accomplishment of milestones is key. For example, if the restore finished, but the DBCC CHECKDB failed, then clearly there is a lack of confidence in the recovery. Problems influencing a decision to go live can be independent of the database recovery, of course. If SQL Server is completely operational, yet the network is not functional at the time, then clearly the users are not going to be coming online.

When All Else Fails, Go to Plan B

Do not be naive and assume that your plan is perfect. There could be something beyond your control (such as data corruption or inability to get a new disk drive) that might mean you are down for a longer time. Always have a trick up your sleeve and create a backup plan so that if your primary plan fails, you can still get up and running sooner rather than much, much later.

> **Tip**   You might even want to execute Plan B in parallel with Plan A so that there is no lag time in the event Plan A fails.

> **More Info**   For links to SQL Server–specific disaster recovery Knowledge Base articles that contain additional information, consult Knowledge Base article 307775, "INF: Disaster Recovery Articles for Microsoft SQL Server." You might also want to print some of these articles and incorporate them into your test plans or run book.

Testing Disaster Recovery Plans

Remember, you have not done a backup until you test the restore. Similarly, you do not have a disaster recovery plan until you test it. Why would you spend time developing a plan if you know it will never be tested? Equate testing to holding a fire drill. Most municipalities around the world insist that all office buildings practice fire drills to ensure that people can get out and that all systems are working. Protecting your SLAs, as well as equipment and human life, is just as vital to your business. A successful test will give you confidence in your plan.

Every company that cares about disaster recovery needs to have a simulated recovery drill at least once a year, preferably more often. This ensures that everyone knows his or her role and responsibilities, and can execute the plan successfully. If plans have not been proactively updated as they should have been and not everything is documented, the mock drill is the time to find out, not during a real disaster.

A drill should start by simulating a system crash or that the primary site has become physically inaccessible. For example, assume that there has been a major accident at a chemical plant and your offices have been completely evacuated. At that point, the team is assembled, responsibilities are handed out, and the team sets out to the recovery site to put the system back together from the ground up. Disaster recovery could also be as simple as rebuilding a database locally.

Figuring out the logistics for the test is the complicated part. For example, is it really a valid test if everyone knows the exact time and date in advance? If you do not want it to be a complete surprise, you might give a vague time. The problem with publishing a time and date is that people can prepare. You must also notify users, management, and vendors if they will be affected or involved in the test. You should even go so far as to book flights and hotels, if necessary. In all regards, this should feel and act like the real thing.

During the drill, make notes about what is working and what is not, or where things are inaccurate. After the drill comes arguably one of the most important activities, the postmortem. This postrecovery meeting assesses what was good and what was bad. This feedback then needs to be incorporated back into the disaster recovery plan and the run book, both of which should be updated immediately so that whoever executes the plan in the future benefits from the experience, even if they were not part of the drill.

Executing Disaster Recovery Plans

At some point, you might be called on to execute the plans you have put into place. Successful execution means more than just the correct bits on the disk. It is about the process and organization of the team to get to that point. If you have not tested your plan and do not have the confidence that you know it will work and how long it will take, you could be in for a rude awakening. It cannot be stressed enough how much preparation shortens downtime. Keep in mind that even with careful planning and tests, you can always encounter a situation that is beyond your control. Even with careful planning and testing, you could still miss the agreed-on timeframes detailed in your SLAs. These are the realities of disaster recovery, as it is by nature a difficult and pressure-filled operation. Do not plan for disaster recovery or go into executing a plan thinking that everything will go as planned; expect the unexpected.

During the execution of the actual recovery, everyone involved should be making notes about what is working and what is not, or where things are inaccurate. These notes can be logged directly into the run book text as each step is executed. Notations such as "This did not work for the following reason ..." and "This is what had to be done to resolve the issue" allow process and procedure improvement. After the fact, recall will not be complete and accurate, so any postmortem used to improve the process and procedures will not be as productive as possible, and could even cause future harm if incorrect information is acted on. This postrecovery meeting will assess what was good and what was bad and the feedback should be reflected in an updated disaster recovery plan.

Example Disaster Recovery Execution

The following is a simple example of a basic recovery plan execution.

Roles and Responsibilities

- Name: Tim
- Role: Operations Manager
- Recovery responsibility: Coordinate resources, interface with management and business users. Responsible for go/no-go decision. Sends out status e-mails.
- Rotation: Watch beginning of recovery. Notified as needed during the restore. End communication with business users.

- Names: Jane and Bill
- Role: DBAs
- Recovery responsibility: Install SQL Server software. Restore SAP, msdb, and master databases. Ensure that SQL Server Agent jobs are running properly. Run DBCC CHECKDB. Review error log and make sure it is clean. Make sure that database network libraries are configured properly. Install SQL Server client on the application servers.
- Rotation: Jane will start the restore. Bill will come on at 2:00 A.M. and finish up the restore, and check the DBCC and logs.

- Name: Doug
- Role: OS administrator
- Recovery responsibility: Install operating system. Apply service packs and security patches. Confirm configurations: disk letters and configuration are as expected, disk is formatted for 64K blocks. Make sure the firmware is correct, network cards are set to proper duplex, and so on. Check event viewer and error logs.
- Rotation: Build the server on the front end. Be on site for any other issues as they arise.

- Name: Shrikant

- Role: SAP basis administrator

- Recovery responsibility: Build SAP instance. Confirm profile parameters. Ensure connectivity to the database. Check that network library configurations are correct. Make sure batch jobs are running appropriately. Confirm the transport paths are in place and operational. Bring SAP up so it is open to the users.

- Rotation: Will configure SAP and check the status at the end. Configure SAP at 11:30 P.M. and check at 6:00 A.M.

Recovery Timeline

- 9:28 P.M. A power surge crashed the storage area network and corrupted the database. The server itself has crashed, and the database is now unavailable. Operations paged the on-call production manager.

- 9:30 P.M. Operations manager receives notification and dials in to check the system. Recovery team called. Disaster recovery plan activated.

- 9:45 P.M. Tim calls the CIO and notifies him or her that a business interruption has occurred. Tim posts the first e-mail to business users about the status and plan as well as notification checkpoints.

- 10:15 P.M. The team starts showing up. Food and beverage orders are taken. Pizza is ordered for team and coffee is put on.

- 10:50 P.M. Off-site backup tapes are recalled.

- 11:00 P.M. Recovery begins. Backup server is confirmed to be on the latest software and firmware revisions. Service packs and security patches are applied. Status e-mail is sent out.

- 11:30 P.M. SQL Server installation begins. Service packs are applied. When this process is complete, a status e-mail is sent out.

- 11:36 P.M. SAP is installed and configured on the central instance. Application servers are recovered and the profiles are adjusted for the new database server.

- 11:45 P.M. Tapes arrive. Contents are confirmed. Another status e-mail is sent.

- Midnight Database restore begins. Master and msdb are restored. Another status e-mail is sent.

- 12:30 A.M. SAP database restoration begins. Another status e-mail is sent.

- 2:00 A.M. Restore is 39 percent complete. Estimated time to completion is 3.5 hours more. A status e-mail is sent out with an estimated completion of 5:30 A.M.

- 4:00 A.M. Restore is 78 percent complete as seen through RESTORE with STATS. Another status e-mail is sent out.

- 5:30 A.M. Restore is complete. DBCC CHECKDB is started. SAP is brought up and locked in single-user mode. SAP diagnostics are begun. Another status e-mail is sent out.

- 6:00 A.M. SAP is confirmed that all is okay.

- 7:18 A.M. DBCC CHECKDB complete and clean. Status e-mail is sent out to technical team.

- 7:20 A.M. Go live decision is made by the operations manager in conjunction with the CIO. A go is given to start up production at half past the hour.

- 7:30 A.M. SAP is started and error logs are checked. Business users are notified. Work can commence.

Each recovery for each company is different. Different personnel and capabilities exist. Hence, each schedule will be different. The idea is that one person cannot be expected to do it all and responsibilities and roles need to be parceled out appropriately.

Disaster Recovery Techniques

Chapters 9 and 10, "Database Environment Basics for Recovery" and "Implementing Backup and Restore," covered backup and restore from a high availability standpoint. One topic not covered, however, was the restore of the system databases, which are critical for the successful recovery of your user databases in a disaster recovery scenario.

> **More Info**   For specific disaster recovery scenarios with clusters, see Chapter 5, "Designing Highly Available Microsoft Windows Servers," Chapter 6, "Microsoft SQL Server 2000 Failover Clustering," and Chapter 8, "Replication." Use that information in conjunction with the information presented here to help recover your systems completely. This section deals mainly with the general SQL Server failure condition.

Warning   Again, it cannot be stressed enough that unless yours is a very experienced shop and you have seen this type of failure before and know with certainty how to handle it, it is crucial to know what procedures to follow. Ultimately, the process is best led by a support professional or senior staff member who knows what he or she is doing. Performing any of the work in the following list improperly could worsen your situation.

You should be aware of some important characteristics of system databases:

- The default recovery model on system databases is Simple. Although this can be changed, you should leave the default unless you have a good reason to change it. Because the recovery model is Simple, you cannot do point-in-time recovery. This is one of the main reasons that anytime you make a system change (for example, adding new logins or adding or growing databases), you should back them up.

- Tempdb is rebuilt every time SQL Server is started, so not only can it not be backed up, but it is not necessary. It will be regenerated to the size specified on configuration.

- It is possible to rebuild master, but not any other database. When you are rebuilding the master database, users cannot be on the system. This is not the case when user databases are being restored.

There are further distinctions, but this list is a brief summary of the basic factors that make a rebuild different from other restores.

As important as your user databases are, the system databases are just as—if not more—important to protect. If you lose your master database, SQL Server ceases to operate correctly. This is one of the most basic premises of proper design in architecting your high availability solution. Just as you should separate your data volumes from your transaction log, you should also separate your system databases (master, msdb) onto a more secure area of your system protected by RAID. Prevention is much easier than a rebuild from the ground up.

Tip   System databases are small in comparison to user databases. They range in size depending on system usage. Due to their smaller size, but their importance to SQL Server availability, you should back them up every night along with your user databases. Additionally, scheduling a DBCC CHECKDB on them periodically helps confirm the overall health of SQL Server, too. The work involved in doing this test is a very small price to pay for the long-term benefits.

Step 1: Assessing Damage

Many times when a system crashes, everything is not completely lost. There are reasonable starting places other than a total flatten and rebuild. It is in your best interests to survey the damage first and then put together a plan of attack.

The five categories that most issues fall into are as follows:

- **Hardware failures** This includes CPU, memory, and a media failure (that is, a disk drive failing, even if you have RAID).

- **Logical failures** This is the human error in which bad data would be inserted or a DBA does something wrong, like accidentally dropping a critical table.

> **Tip** When making large or critical system changes, make sure you not only make a backup prior to starting, but when executing the Transact-SQL statement, begin the SQL command with a BEGIN TRAN. If all is successful, then you can commit the transaction; if something incorrect happened (for example, the DBA forgot to put a WHERE clause on a DELETE statement), you can always rollback the transaction without damage.

- **Operating system failures** This is a problem that you cannot do much about, because it is external to SQL Server. The kernel fails to complete a function. You can only keep up with service packs and appropriate hotfixes for your environment.

- **Device driver failures** A driver for a particular piece of hardware malfunctions. Like an operating system failure, this is external to SQL Server, but affects it. A good example is a bad SAN driver on a cluster.

- **Low-level failures** A low-level failure occurs when something abnormal happens to a SQL Server database. It can be situational and is usually rooted in hardware failure. For example, a power outage could cause a torn page or corruption. You would then need to perform the appropriate action, such as issuing a DBCC CHECKDB or restoring a full, good backup.

> **Tip** Use battery-backed-up controllers to help protect your data from power outages. Many controllers have extensive amounts of cache on them to increase performance. If you lose power, you have lost the data if there is no battery backup. Additionally, an interrupted write due to power loss can cause a torn page.

As part of any good game plan, you should make a backup of the server if possible. This could be a flat file operating system backup and a SQL Server backup. If PSS needs to be engaged, a "before" image of a corrupt database can offer valuable clues for rescuing data. If you destroy the original state of the data by restoring over it before backing it up, you have lost a good starting point for PSS.

In the same vein, people often find out the hard way that the backup they thought was good really was not, so they were in worse shape after the restore than before. If you made a backup at the operating system level with automatic system reconfiguration (ASR) before starting the restore process, you can always restart. Remember, the last good backup you made was the last one that was successfully restored.

> **Tip**   Restore your backups often to help ensure their integrity and make yourself familiar with the restore process. It also helps to know how long a database restore takes. Users often want to know, "Is it finished yet?"

If you have any doubts about the process or do not feel comfortable with recovering your system, stop and engage PSS. Not performing any work can actually be a safer alternative than haphazardly beginning an unsuccessful rebuild.

> **Tip**   Any "ground up" recovery starts with a good backup of the master and msdb databases. Make sure you always have current, known, good backups of your system databases and run health checks against them.

Step 2: Preparing for Reconstruction

Before starting any reconstruction of a server, whether minor or full-blown, there are certain steps that need to be taken and items that need to be in place. First and foremost, ensure that you have the right person in place to execute any actions. Do not leave an important task to a rookie system engineer or DBA who does not know your systems well enough. The following steps offer fallback positions if you need to start over or engage other support personnel. They also help if you need to reconstruct at an off-site recovery location.

1. Refer to the documentation in your run book for your hardware configuration, which should include model numbers, the physical layout (including which card goes in what slot), configuration settings for each component, firmware revisions, driver versions, block size of the file system, and so on.

2. If your server is up, make an operating system-level backup of the server with SQL Server down, including ASR. This allows you to go back to a known state before attempting any rebuilds and gives you the ability to send the damaged data to PSS if needed.

3. After making the operating system backup, back up what you can using the standard SQL Server backup processes. Try and run a full backup, and also grab the tail of the transaction log. These allow you to recover to the point of failure.

4. If the database is accessible, run DBCC CHECKDB to assess the damage.

> **Warning** Running DBCC CHECKDB can take a long time depending on which options you select and the size of your database. This might not be appropriate for all environments and should be done at the recommendation of a support professional.

5. When you want to rebuild SQL Server, as with the server itself, a build sheet should be accessible in your run book. The information that should be included is listed in the section "Run Book" earlier in this chapter.

6. If you are restoring at a remote disaster recovery site, ensure you have compatible tape media hardware and the proper version of the restore software at that location, too. For example, you do not want to find out that your site uses Linear Tape-Open (LTO) technology and the disaster site only has Super DLT technology.

7. Your run book should also include software and license keys for all components (Windows, SQL Server, third-party applications, and so on) that will be rebuilt.

8. A connection to the Internet will help you gather service packs and hotfixes, as well as information such as the Knowledge Base articles

on *http://support.microsoft.com*. You should probably pull all relevant service packs and hotfixes and burn them to a CD or DVD that can be easily accessed in a disaster recovery situation.

9. Reference your vendor call list and contract numbers in the run book. If your support contracts have expired, you might need a credit card handy in case you need to call in other vendors using phone support.

> **Important**   The key to success is having all this in place *prior* to a disaster.

Step 3: Reconstructing a System

The following are the basic steps that should be followed if you need to do a full recovery, or "flatten the system," when all components need to be rebuilt:

1. Rebuild the system, starting with the operating system and any service packs, hotfixes, and so on. This should be done with the proper tools (such as NTBACKUP or a third-party utility, such as Veritas Backup Exec or any number of enterprise backup tools). Depending on the scope of damage, you might even need to low-level format your disks.

2. Test the operating system to ensure that it is configured properly.

3. Follow the steps detailed later to restore or recover system and user databases.

4. Restore full-text indexes (if necessary or possible).

5. Synchronize logins, and perform any other tasks (such as restoring custom objects with scripts) to bring your SQL Server instance to a usable point.

6. Test everything extensively.

> **On the CD**   You can find a flowchart that illustrates the disaster recovery process in the file Disaster_Recovery_Process.pdf.

Restoring the Tempdb Database

You do not need to do anything if tempdb is damaged because tempdb is regenerated each time SQL Server restarts. What you might want to do, for example, if your disk is damaged, is use the ALTER DATABASE statement to move the location of tempdb.

Step 1: Rebuilding and Restoring Master

To put it bluntly, without master, there is no SQL Server, so ensuring that master is up and functioning is paramount to any recovery operation. This is why you must go to great lengths during the planning phases of the system to use techniques like RAID and put the proper backup scheme in place. However, if you lose master, it does not necessarily mean that your user databases are damaged. You can rebuild or reinitialize the server, including the master database only, and then restore the system database backups from your last verified backup files. However, there are some very important requirements to make this work successfully. If planned for properly, this is easy!

> **Tip**   Remember to back up your master database any time you make a change to it.

> **Caution**   You cannot restore a backup of a system database, especially master, from a different build onto another SQL Server with a different build version because there are schema or metadata changes. The following is an example of an error message:
>
> ```
> Server: Msg 3168, Level 16, State 1, Line 1
>
> The backup of the system database on device
> d:\temp\master.bak cannot be restored because it was created
> by a different version of the server (134217904) than this
> server (134217920).
>
> Server: Msg 3013, Level 16, State 1, Line 1
>
> RESTORE DATABASE is terminating abnormally.
> ```
>
> You need to reinstall and apply all service packs, hotfixes, and so on, to be able to use the backup. Go to *http://support.microsoft.com* and consult Knowledge Base article 264474 for information and workarounds. Remember to back up system databases both before and after an application of a SQL Server 2000 hotfix or service pack so you can restore to the proper point in time.

Rebuilding Master for 32-Bit SQL Servers   The tool used for rebuilding the master database is called Rebuildm.exe, a binary executable located in the SQL Server installation's Tools\Binn directory on your hard disk.

> **Caution**   Do not rebuild your master database without knowing the consequences and making absolutely sure you need to do this. Follow the text in this entire section relating to master for more information.

> **Important**   To run REBUILDM, you also need to access the SQL Server installation CD-ROM or installation point because it includes various data files needed for execution of the tool. Because the CD-ROM is read-only, you must copy the CDROM:\x86\Data directory on the CD locally to the server before starting the REBUILDM utility, and change the attribute of all files to be non-read-only. This can be done with the command line `attrib -r *.*` in the directory, or by right-clicking the files, selecting Properties, and clearing the Read-Only check box.
>
> If you have access to a network share installation of SQL Server, that would also be appropriate. However, ensure that the files do not have a read-only attribute (as they would if it was just a copy of the CD-ROM).

Use the following steps to run REBUILDM.

> **Important**   If you are running REBUILDM on a clustered instance of SQL Server 2000, make sure you are on the node that currently owns the SQL Server resources. You can verify this in Cluster Administrator.

1.   Ensure all files are not read-only.

2.   Take SQL Server offline using SQL Server Service Manager.

3.   From a command line, run Rebuildm.exe. When the main dialog box opens, as shown in Figure 12-1, select or enter the name of the SQL Server in the Server drop-down list box, select the directory of the files that you copied from the CD-ROM, and select the proper collation. Click Rebuild to begin the rebuilding process.

> **Warning** Make sure you select the right collation for your SQL Server. It should match the previous setting for this particular instance. If you do not select the right one, you might have some incompatibilities with your user databases.

Rebuild Master

IMPORTANT: Rebuilding the master database will result in the loss of previously created databases.

Enter the location of the data files (*.mdf, *.ldf) which are located on the CD and select the options you want to use for rebuilding the MASTER database.

Server: MCBATH

Source Directory containing Data Files:

C:\TEMP\MASTER   Browse ...

Collation setting ...   Settings ...

Data Directory:

D:\Program Files\Microsoft SQL Server\MSSQL

Help   Rebuild   Cancel

Figure 12-1 The main Rebuild Master dialog box.

The process then copies the data files for master to the right location and configures the server. A successful completion results in the dialog box shown in Figure 12-2.

Rebuild Master

Rebuild Master completed successfully!

OK

Figure 12-2 A successful Rebuild Master completion.

Rebuilding Master for 64-Bit SQL Server   Under the 64-bit edition of SQL Server 2000, you cannot use REBUILDM to rebuild your master database. For a stand-alone instance, follow the instructions outlined in the SQL Server 64-bit Books Online topic "Repairing a SQL Server Installation (64-bit)." On a SQL Server 2000 64-bit virtual server, you must follow the steps outlined here, as the standard process does not work.

> **Note** To rebuild the master database, you need the product Product ID (PID) used to install SQL Server 2000 (64-Bit). The PID is a globally unique identifier (GUID) that is stored in the registry. For a default instance of SQL Server 2000 (64-Bit), the PID is in the registry under HKEY_LOCAL_MACHINE\Software\Microsoft\MSSQLServer\Setup\productID. For a named instance of SQL Server 2000 (64-Bit), the PID is in the registry under HKEY_LOCAL_MACHINE\Software\Microsoft\Microsoft SQL Server\<instance name>\Setup\productID.

When you rebuild the master database, you can configure the *sa* password, collation, cross-database ownership chaining, and error reporting. If you make changes to the authentication mode, they are not reflected after the server is reinstalled. You can change the authentication mode manually after the reinstallation is complete.

You must complete all steps from the cluster node that owns the SQL Server resource.

To rebuild the master database of a default instance of Microsoft SQL Server 2000 (64-Bit), follow these steps:

1. Take the SQL Server virtual server offline.

2. In Registry Editor, under HKEY_LOCAL_MACHINE\Software\Microsoft-Windows\CurrentVersion\Uninstall\<PID>, where <PID> is the PID of the Windows Installer package used to install SQL Server, change the SqlCluster value to 0 and note the value of SqlClusterSec. Then change the value of SqlClusterSec to 0. You will need to restore the value of Sql-ClusterSec after you rebuild the master database.

3. Run Cliconfg.exe to launch the SQL Server Client Network Utility.

4. In the SQL Server Client Network Utility, on the Alias tab, click Add. The Add Network Library Configuration window appears.

5. Under Network Libraries, click Other.

6. In the Server Alias text box, type **<computer name>**. For a named instance, type **<computer name>\<instance name>**, where <computer name> is the name of the local computer and <instance name> is the name of the SQL Server instance. The local computer must be the cluster node that owns the SQL Server resource.

7. In the File Name text box, type **DBNETLIB**.

8. In the Parameters text box, type **LPC:<*virtual server name*>**. For a named instance, type **LPC:<*virtual server name*>\<*virtual server instance name*>**, where <*virtual server name*> is the name of the SQL Server virtual server, and <*virtual server instance name*> is the name of the named instance of the SQL Server 2000 (64-bit) virtual server.

9. Click OK.

10. Run Msiexec.exe to rebuild the master database. Type

    msiexec.exe /i <*PID*> REINSTALL=ALL REINSTALLMODE=amus SQLAUTOSTART=0 /L*v <*path and filename.txt*>

    where <*PID*> is the PID of the Windows Installer package used to install SQL Server, and <*path and filename.txt*> is the location and file name for the verbose log file. For example, type **d:\rebuild_master_verbose_log.txt**.

11. In the Reinstallation dialog box that appears, make any necessary changes to the *sa* password, collation, cross-database ownership chaining, and error reporting. If you make changes to the authentication mode, they are not reflected after the server is reinstalled. You can change the authentication mode after the reinstallation is complete.

> **Note**   In some situations, the computer might display a message stating that file operations are pending and ask you if you want to reboot the computer. Click No.

12. In Registry Editor, under HKEY_LOCAL_MACHINE\Software\ Microsoft\Windows\CurrentVersion\Uninstall\<*PID*>, change the SqlCluster value to 1. Restore the value of SqlClusterSec to the value you noted in Step 2.

13. Run Cliconfg.exe to launch the SQL Server Client Network Utility. On the Alias tab, select the server alias that you created in Step 6, and click Remove.

14. If the computer requests a restart, restart the computer now.

15. Bring the virtual server online.

Restoring the Master Database   As noted earlier, once the master database has been rebuilt, it has no recognition of the user databases or user logins. To finish the recovery process, you need to restore the master database from the most recent available backup by following these steps:

- **Restoring master without a valid backup**   There is no way to restore master in this case other than by using REBUILDM and then going through the steps for the other databases.

- **Restoring master with a valid backup**   The way to restore master in this case is as follows:

  1. Ensure that your SQL Server 2000 installation is at the same version as your backup, including hotfixes and service packs.

  2. Optionally, create a logical backup device to reference the location where the backup of master is located, or you can just point the restore to the physical file. To create the device, use, for example:

     ```
     sp_addumpdevice 'disk', 'master_backup_device',
     'c:\backup\master.bak'
     ```

  3. Take SQL Server offline using SQL Server Service Manager.

  4. If you have changed the recovery model for msdb to Full, save the transaction log before attempting any rebuild process for master; this allows you to back up the tail of the log and have up-to-the-minute recovery. To do this, after SQL Server is offline, you have to go to the location of the transaction log for msdb and rename it in a command window or in Windows Explorer because executing REBUILDM overwrites it.

  5. Rebuild the master database (see the previous section).

  6. In a command window, restart SQL Server in single-user mode from the command line using Sqlservr.exe. This is located in the \80\Binn directory under your SQL Server 2000 installation. The following syntax is an example of a default instance and its resulting output:

     ```
     D:\Program Files\Microsoft SQL Server\MSSQL\Binn> sqlservr.exe
     -c -m
     2003-02-02 15:44:08.43 spid3   SQL Server started in single user
     mode. Updates allowed to system catalogs.
     2003-02-02 15:44:08.46 spid3   Starting up database 'master'.
     ```

This is the syntax for a named instance:

```
D:\Program Files\Microsoft SQL Server\MSSQL$instancename\Binn>
sqlservr.exe -c -m -Sinstancename
```

If you do not bring up SQL Server in single-user mode, you will see the following error when you attempt to restore master:

```
Server: Msg 3108, Level 16, State 1, Line 1
RESTORE DATABASE must be used in single user mode when trying to
restore the master database.
Server: Msg 3013, Level 16, State 1, Line 1
RESTORE DATABASE is terminating abnormally.
```

Do not shut this command window until Step 8 is completed because you are now running SQL Server as a process in that command window.

7. You can now start Enterprise Manager or log into a query tool such as Query Analyzer or OSQL, and log into your instance as system administrator or as a trusted administrator to begin the restore process.

8. Restore the master database from a backup using either the backup device or with disk= syntax. For example:

```
restore database master from master_backup_device
```

When complete, you will see the following output:

```
The master database has been successfully restored. Shutting
down SQL Server.
SQL Server is terminating this process.
```

If you are running Enterprise Manager, you might have to manually terminate it with Task Manager.

9. Bring SQL Server online using SQL Server Service Manager.

10. Back up master.

If you have the ability to back up the tail of the log for msdb, follow these steps:

1. Create a database similar to msdb, with the same number of data and log files.

2. Take SQL Server offline.

3. Delete all of the data files from your newly created database so that it will fail recovery. Replace the log file with the log file you renamed from your original msdb and rename it appropriately.

4. Restart SQL Server.

5. Back up the tail of the transaction log of this database with Enterprise Manager or in a query tool with Transact-SQL. A sample syntax follows:

```
backup log db_name to disk = device_name WITH NO_TRUNCATE
```

6. Use sp_dbremove to remove the temporary database from your new SQL Server. Back up master.

You can now go about restoring other databases, such as msdb, model, and finally, user databases. Then you can worry about tasks such as synchronizing logins and ensuring all objects are there for your use.

> **Tip** As you go through the rest of your recovery process, make frequent backups of master and any other databases as they are restored or at key points of the recovery process.

Step 2: Restoring the Msdb Database

Restoring msdb is the next step in rebuilding your SQL Server instance. If master is the brains and heart of SQL Server, msdb is the soul. It contains much of the status information and other information (such as replication information and definition of all SQL Server Agent jobs) used by SQL Server. It is doubtful that you do not use msdb at all. There are two scenarios for recovering msdb:

- If you did not change the recovery model for msdb, you can only restore the last full backup that is good. This means that you might have lost quite a bit of information if it is a very old backup.

- If you changed the recovery model of msdb to Full and you were able to back up the tail of the transaction log as described in the last section (as long as master was not damaged), you can take your point-in-time backup and restore all the transaction logs, meaning you could have an up-to-the-minute recovery.

> **Tip** It is strongly recommended that you change the recovery of msdb to Full. However, when you stop and restart SQL Server Agent, the recovery model is reset to Simple. You need to create a job that runs on each SQL Server Agent restart that executes two commands:
>
> ```
> ALTER DATABASE msdb SET RECOVERY FULL
> ```
> and `BACKUP DATABASE msdb TO DISK = 'location '`
>
> You should back up msdb's transaction log on a frequent basis.

This is optional, but you might want to stop and restart SQL Server after restoring msdb.

Restoring the Model Database

The model database is used as the basis for all new databases that are created, so you do need to back it up and have a valid backup for a possible disaster recovery scenario. However, unless you make customizations to it that are specific to your environment, you should not need to back up the model database on a very frequent basis. There are two main scenarios for restoring model:

- You have a valid backup of model from that server. If that is the case, you can stop and then restart SQL Server with trace flag 3608. This trace flag has only SQL Server recover master in the startup process. You can then restore model like any other database. Remove the trace flag from the startup parameters in Enterprise Manager, and stop and restart SQL Server.

- You do not have a backup, but do have another SQL Server *with the same code page/collation* in your environment with a valid model database (modified or not modified).

If the latter situation is yours, perform the following steps to restore model:

1. Stop and start the instance you are recovering with trace flag 3608.

2. On the SQL Server instance that has the valid model database, execute the following syntax in a query window:

```
use master
go
sp_detach_db 'model'
go
```

3. Copy the Model.mdf and Modellog.ldf files to the proper location for your damaged instance.

4. Open a query window that is connected to your damaged instance, and execute syntax similar to the following example to attach model:

```
use master
go
sp_attach_db 'model','E:\Sqldata\model.mdf',
'E:\Sqldata\modellog.ldf'
go
```

5. Remove the trace flag from the startup parameters in Enterprise Manager, and stop and restart SQL Server.

Restoring User Databases

When it is time to restore user databases, you have two main options: a traditional restore using backup and restore, or `sp_attach_db`. Restore, as you know, is a straightforward process that can take considerable time depending on the size of your database. However, you might want to consider using `sp_attach_db` if your server has crashed but your disk array is still intact. In this case, you might be able to recover your data in a few minutes instead of hours. This stored procedure allows you to attach database data and log files that exist at the operating system level, but are not yet part of the SQL Server. The corresponding stored procedure to detach a database from SQL Server is `sp_detach_db`. Because the time could be much shorter than doing a full restore, it might be worth trying to attach and then let the database attempt recovery. You should run a DBCC CHECKDB after the `sp_attach_db` to ensure that the database is in proper condition for usage by your users. Additionally, make sure the user logins are mapped properly.

The following is an example of the usage of `sp_attach_db`:

```
EXEC sp_attach_db @dbname = N'PRD',
@filename1 = N'H:\mssql\data\PRD_data1.MDF',
@filename2 = N'U:\mssql\log\PRD_log1.LDF',
@filename3 = N'J:\mssql\data\PRD_data3.NDF',
@filename4 = N'L:\mssql\data\PRD_data5.NDF',
@filename5 = N'I:\mssql\data\PRD_data2.NDF',
@filename6 = N'K:\mssql\data\PRD_data4.NDF',
@filename7 = N'M:\mssql\data\PRD_data6.NDF',
@filename8 = N'N:\mssql\data\PRD_data7.NDF',
@filename9 = N'O:\mssql\data\PRD_data8.NDF',
@filename10 = N'P:\mssql\data\PRD_data9.NDF',
@filename11 = N'Q:\mssql\data\PRD_data10.NDF',
@filename12 = N'R:\mssql\data\PRD_data11.NDF',
@filename13 = N'S:\mssql\data\PRD_data12.NDF'
```

> **Note**   Restoring pubs and Northwind is exactly like restoring a user database.

> **More Info**   For details on the differences between doing a database restore with RESTORE and using `sp_attach_db`, consult Chapter 13, "Highly Available Microsoft SQL Server Upgrades."

Restoring the Full-Text Indexes

If you are using full-text indexing with your user databases, you need to think about how you will restore your indexes if there is a catastrophic failure, as mentioned in earlier chapters such as Chapter 7, "Log Shipping."

> **More Info**   Knowledge Base article 240867, "INF: How to Move, Copy, and Back Up Full-Text Catalog Folders and Files," is a good reference on backing up, copying, and moving full-text indexes.

Synchronizing Logins

If you have successfully restored your master database, you should not need to synchronize logins unless new ones were added after the date and time of the backup that was restored. If that is the case, consult the section "Synchronizing Logins" in Chapter 14, "Administrative Tasks to Increase Availability."

> **Tip**   After the full rebuilding process, back up all system databases because you know they are in a good state.

Summary

No one ever hopes to find themselves in a disaster recovery situation. Unfortunately, however, it is usually a matter of when, rather than if. The best offense is a good defense, and as the old Boy Scout motto states, Be Prepared. Up-front planning, including testing of the plan, will pay huge dividends. If you do not test your plan *before* disaster strikes, all you have is words on a page. Remember that recovering a system is more than performing some steps laid out on a page: it involves people, processes, communication, and technology, among other things. Plans should be executed by qualified individuals only; those with lesser experience or without nerves of steel should not apply. Finally, when the dust settles, do a postmortem on the process so you can learn from the execution of the plan as well as from what went wrong on the servers. Then you can take corrective action and avoid the problem in the future.

13

Highly Available Upgrades

Upgrades present a challenge that all organizations face at some point. Upgrades fall into different categories, such as upgrading versions of Microsoft SQL Server, server consolidation, applying a SQL Server or Microsoft Windows service pack or hotfix, or applying third-party patches for the software you run in your environment. The challenge with upgrades is not so much the upgrade process itself—that is fairly mechanical—it is ensuring that you minimize downtime and the impact on users. If you have specific service level agreements (SLAs) in place, you understand the complexities of maintaining a highly available environment when you need to apply changes to your production environment. This chapter guides you through the process of how to plan and execute highly available upgrades and the considerations you need to take into account.

> **Important** Regardless of any discussion that follows, please keep in mind that only qualified personnel should perform upgrades of any type. Leaving your upgrade to someone who is unfamiliar with your environment could prove costly.

General Upgrade, Consolidation, and Migration Tips

An upgrade or migration is all about having a solid plan, testing it, and developing contingency plans to deal with common problems or possibilities. From a high availability perspective, at some point your upgrade process is likely to incur some downtime. Remember that there are application-specific patches or upgrades as well as ones for operating systems and that the availability of the operating system will absolutely affect the availability of the applications running on the server. Whether you are upgrading for security reasons or to fix another functionality, as you try to minimize the impact take into account the following rules of thumb that apply to all the concepts presented in this chapter:

- **Everything affects everything.** Think about your body. When a doctor prescribes a new medicine for you to take, it is absorbed by your blood and might solve a problem, but it might also have some undesirable side effects that affect you daily. Or it might not have any negative interactions with your internal systems, and you will be just fine.

  From a technology standpoint, if you apply a Windows service pack, assume it will affect SQL Server in some way. There can be no 100 percent guarantee that whatever you do is transparent, and it might even subtly change the behaviors of your application or operating system. The more you have running on one server, the greater the chance of possible interactions. Even doing something as seemingly innocuous as upgrading the BIOS on your system or upgrading to the latest driver or firmware for a specific piece of hardware (such as a SAN)—seemingly unrelated to your application software—can affect your software behaviors or break them completely.

  You should consult the hardware or software manufacturer for any and all available information on their update and what it might do to your systems. However, manufacturers do not have the ability to test all permutations of the effects of their patches (and probably do not have your application code to do so even if they wanted to), so it is your responsibility to ensure that upgrades behave in your environment.

- **Try not to combine multiple updates, especially large ones.** For example, do not upgrade to a higher bandwidth network card and then install various driver updates to existing components in one maintenance window. It is even more important not to perform multiple updates if they were not tested both alone and together. Troubleshooting after simultaneous upgrades is infinitely more difficult than after just one; it is more difficult to determine what is causing the problem because you applied different changes.

  Another example would be if you upgrade the Windows service pack and the SQL service pack at the same time. You probably save some downtime during the upgrades, but if you experience some form of regression you will *more* than lose it in the amount of time it takes you to troubleshoot the problem.

- **Test any patches, driver updates, hotfixes, service packs, and so on *prior* to rolling them out.**   If availability is one of your company's concerns, there is no better time than the present to start testing. The best way to test, should you want to apply a hotfix, is to do it on a dedicated testing or staging environment to determine how it will impact your applications, the server itself, and so on. You do not want to cause a potentially larger availability outage by having to roll back your installation or reinstall from scratch should you encounter a worst-case scenario. You need additional hardware to do these tests, but think about the business case. Is it better to spend some money up front to ensure minimal downtime or to pay an expensive price for being down?

- **Test the patches under your production load.**   Do not test on a server with no or minimal usage. Many companies are great about testing the functionality of what they are upgrading to but neglect to test it under stress. The testing environment must have some method of simulating load on the servers so that you will know there are no issues waiting for you around a "performance" bend in the upcoming road.

    This is especially true with SQL Server because of its self-tuning nature. This internal tuning is incredibly complex but it can also be somewhat fragile in that it is picking a particular plan based on its statistical information and the underlying mathematics. You might be right on the borderline for a particular plan, and the smallest possible change could give you a completely different plan for that subset of queries. The performance difference is probably not noticeable unless this is a plan you happen to use very often and it is also the biggest load point (bottleneck) in your application at the time. The solution might be as simple as a two-word hint for that query to slide things back to the original plan. However, finding the problem during testing allows you to implement this hint *during* your upgrade instead of finding it during your peak load the next day and being unable to do anything about it quickly enough to prevent a negative user experience.

- **How do you build your test platform?**   Your test platforms will prove your deployment. If they are not built in the same manner as the production servers, even small delta could skew the results.

- **Always read the documentation that comes with the upgrade or patch carefully.**   It contains information about the fixes and behaviors, as well as how to install the upgrade or patch. Too often support calls are generated because people skip this step and just click on Setup.exe or Install.bat (or whatever the installation mechanism is) without thinking. If you have any questions or concerns that are not addressed in the documentation, especially in relation to your configurations, call a support professional. This is *your* production environment, not some system that no one is using (if it is, you might want to make it your test server). Although some might see it as a wasted support call, it is better to ensure that the process will go smoothly and properly than to skip that call but spend hours on the phone later, after an unsuccessful installation. Also, keep an eye on newsgroups, magazine articles, and other resources, because your peers might point you to helpful information they have learned through their implementation experiences.

■ **Notify anyone who will be affected by the upgrade and give them plenty of lead time.** The point is to inconvenience others as little as possible. Notifying them five minutes beforehand or killing their session or connection without any warning will not create goodwill. Remember to notify them after the system is available for use again. Give them a solid contact point to notify if they do experience difficulties. You might have been up all night doing the upgrade, and somebody else could try to fix the problem the next day while you are catching up on your sleep without knowing what you were working on or where you left off.

■ **Do not allow user connections to the server while you are applying the upgrade or fix.** The upgrade instructions should include any specific implications and details, but it is best to ensure that nothing or no one can interfere with the installation process. For example, a Microsoft SQL Server 2000 service pack installation puts the server into single-user mode, so no connections can be made unless the user goes in at the right moment, which would ruin the installation.

■ **Prepare a detailed implementation plan and ensure your disaster recovery plans are up to date *prior* to the upgrade or update.** You do not want surprises in the middle of your implementation. As noted earlier in this book, your plan and the way to back out of it will be crucial for your success. Unfortunately, many people still attempt to apply an upgrade or fix to their systems without thinking of the consequences. When availability is one of your main goals, you are asking for trouble if you are without a workable plan.

■ **Consider the time frame within which you will execute your plan.** If you know your business does its monthly sales forecasting the last week of the month and users need access to the sales database at that time, do not perform the upgrade that week, or maybe even not the one before or after. That would leave you, in a four-week month, a one-week window to execute the plan at a time when it would have the least impact on the business and give you the most time to recover should something catastrophic happen.

■ **Make backups of all of your user and system databases prior to performing an update or upgrade.** This is one of the most important things you should do. It ensures (assuming the backups are good) that in a worst-case scenario you can get back to the point in time where you were prior to the bad update or upgrade. If the process goes well, remember to back up the databases afterward so you have a new baseline of good backups for use in a disaster recovery scenario. Finally, you should make another set of backups *after* the upgrade if it involved SQL Server in any way. This way, you can restore to this point in time without restoring the server to the previous state separately from the database.

■ **For SQL-based backups, you should consider your backup strategy carefully.** You should also calculate the effect of both your backup strategy and your current checkpoint timers and how they affect your SQL Server log size. It might be worth a little extra work to quiesce or at least partially quiesce your database if you will be backing it up twice! Think of the time, disk, or tape savings in pure size and time for the backup. Then think also of the restore time savings if things do go wrong in spite of all your careful planning.

Note   Good planning cannot protect you from every problem, but it can give you a solid plan for dealing with most problems.

More Info   For more information on putting plans together and good background information in general for this chapter, consult Chapter 1, "Preparing for High Availability," Chapter 2, "The Basics of Achieving High Availability," Chapter 9, "Database Environment Basics for Recovery," Chapter 10, "Implementing Backup and Restore," and Chapter 12, "Disaster Recovery Techniques for Microsoft SQL Server."

Upgrading, Consolidating, and Migrating to SQL Server 2000

Whether you are just upgrading from another version of SQL Server, consolidating your database environment, or migrating to SQL Server from another platform, you need to be concerned with some basics before you even begin the process. This section focuses primarily on the technical aspects, but it is crucial to understand the business reasons or drivers for undertaking such a project to ensure that the technical meets the business, and vice versa. Follow the guidelines in Chapter 1 and Chapter 2 for setting up a steering committee and so on. Any planning fits squarely within Microsoft Solutions Framework (MSF) and Microsoft Operations Framework (MOF) models.

Your business sponsors should be able to answer the following questions. The information will greatly help you in your technical planning.

- What business value do you believe will be gained from your upgrade, consolidation, or migration effort?

- If you are consolidating, what is the desired consolidation ratio—2:1, 5:1, 10:1, or what? Is it realistic?

- What are the drivers for your effort? Why are you upgrading, consolidating, or migrating?

- Have the IT and business stakeholders bought into and signed off on the effort? Is there adequate funding?

- Is chargeback for resource usage a need or a consideration? Will the tools currently in place to measure chargeback still work?

- How many users are expected to be supported concurrently by this solution? in the short term? in the long term?

- What is the life expectancy of this solution (that is, how long is this solution, along with its systems, supposed to stay in production)?

- How much will the data grow over time? What is projected versus actual growth (if known)?

- What is acceptable performance from end-user, administrative, and management perspectives? Keep in mind that performance is defined differently—it could mean throughput, response time, and so on.

- What is the current availability goal for each individual system? Each solution? Will the availability goal for the component or solution meet the new requirements?

- How is maintenance going to be performed on this system? Will maintenance change due to consolidation?

- How are backups going to be performed on the system and the data? How will this work affect performance?

- What are the security requirements for both the application and the systems for the solution? Are they in line with corporate policies?

- Are there security conflicts between systems and objects that might be consolidated together?

- What is the cost of developing, implementing, and supporting? in the short term? in the long term?

- What is the actual cost of downtime for each individual system or database installation? The entire solution? What is the current cost of administering and running the server?

- What are the dependencies of the components in the solution? For example, are there external data feeds into SQL Server that might fail as the result of an availability problem or move in a system?

- What technologies are currently used in the application, solution, or system, and what is desired? How will a change affect each component of your solution individually and as a whole?

- What is the budget allocation for hardware? What is the available budget for the entire effort?

- If this is an existing SQL Server, is the system already at or exceeding capacity, whether it is processor, memory, or disk?

- What SLAs are in place and how will they be affected?

- Where are the servers located? Are they currently in the same place? If not, how will changing location or geographic placement affect the entire group of users, performance, and the SLA?

- What roles exist within the IT division? Do you have a person who is dedicated solely to capacity management?

- Do you have effective change control processes in place with the existing systems or do you need new ones?

- Do you have proper development, test, and staging environments?

- Do you have a testing or quality assurance team? Are there dedicated DBAs? If so, how many?

- What is the current ratio of SQL Servers and databases to DBAs?

- Do you plan on eliminating or downsizing personnel as a result of this effort?

- What are the different types of systems considered for upgrading, consolidating, or migrating—production, test, and development?

- Will you employ new technologies, such as clustering for high availability? How will that affect your employees from a skills, cost, and training perspective?

- Do you have specific SLAs to maintain with each "application" even after consolidating them onto a single system in a server consolidation effort?

- Are there multiple systems with conflicting SLAs currently or being planned on the same machine?

- Are certain systems required to be separated from others due to things like performance or SLAs?

- What is the desired end date for the project? Are there any constraints that might come into play, such as those posed by hardware or service vendors?

- Do you know if the systems are mission critical? If you are looking to combine certain target servers, how will that affect the other systems?

- How much business, in terms of both actual transactions (not database) and revenue, does each system generate?

- List any reference projects done to date that have influenced your interest.

- State any particular issues or information that must be taken into account, such as the following:

  ❑ Are there any corporate policies that might affect the effort?

  ❑ Such things as "sole source" providers are illegal with some government agencies, so that might restrict consolidation contracts in some way.

  ❑ Corporate security policies might inhibit or change the nature of an effort, such as server consolidation, by requiring physical isolation of systems and data from different departments, as in the case of Limited Liability Partnerships.

Phase 1: Envisioning

While the business side of the house is figuring out the nontechnical drivers for your effort, the administrators (DBAs and non-DBAs, too) must start to gather information for the plan on the technical side. This involves a great deal of information that you should have been gathering all along to establish baselines and make judgments. Ask the following sample questions and document the answers, as each one will influence your planning. Add questions if they are relevant to your environment.

- What technical advantages do you believe you will gain from this effort?

- How did the original deployments occur? What can be learned (good and bad) from those deployments?

- How many servers are going to be part of the effort? Have the servers even been identified? Who is your vendor, and what class will the target servers be?

- How many databases are on the targeted servers?

- Are the servers to be consolidated currently separated geographically?

- What are the usage patterns of the targeted servers, including use of the system databases? Do you have a performance baseline for each server? Is this baseline broken down to business units and their respective systems?

- Do you know the resource utilization of each server? Can you accurately assess if the targeted servers are overutilized or underutilized?

- Are these servers already employing some form of high availability, such as failover clustering or log shipping?

- Is replication configured for any of the databases?

- How do you manage database schemas, including stored procedures and functions? Do you keep them in some form of version control?

- Are security policies and procedures documented for each server (physical hardware, operating system, SQL Server, and the applications)? Are security policies in line with your current corporate policies?

- Do you know all the information about each server (such as service pack levels, disk space usage, SQL Server configuration settings, and so on)?

- Do you know the types of workload on each system (that is, OLTP versus OLAP/Decision-support)?

- Do you use administrative tools such as Alerts and SQL Mail? Do you have standardization between all servers?

- Do you have any custom extended stored procedures that might affect other databases?

- Do you have conflicting objects with the same name?

- Do you have access to all source code for the applications accessing SQL Server as well as stored procedures (especially if you use stored procedure encryption)?

- Do you know how many users, on average, connect to SQL Server? What types of clients connect to SQL Server (such as handheld devices, fat clients, and so on)? How do they connect?

- Do you know the requirements of the third-party applications that might use SQL Server and be consolidated?

- What current backup technologies are used?

- What current high availability technologies are used?

- Have the DBAs in your organization been formally trained on SQL Server in all aspects, including administration, high availability, and performance?

- Are the current servers in different domains?

- What versions of SQL Server are these servers running?

- What versions of the operating system are used on these servers?

- How much will the data grow over time? What is projected versus actual growth (if known)?

- What technologies are currently used in the solution?

Profile Target Systems

The most important component of any upgrade, consolidation, or migration is having adequate technical information about each system. Without this, you cannot proceed successfully with any of your efforts. If you do not know if you can combine a workload, it is impossible to make any decisions.

Each system that is being considered must be profiled, and not for just one day or, sometimes, even just one week. The profile is the result of monitoring over time to gather trends. These trends might be daily or weekly jobs, as well as daily, weekly, and even monthly trends in workload (for example, end-of-month sales reports). Profiling includes much more than just the system name: every important performance aspect of the server must be captured. When figuring out if workloads and systems can be combined, you need to determine if incompatibilities will result from, say, a configuration setting or an application requirement.

Besides capturing general items such as operating system version, service pack levels, IP addresses, and disk configurations through the worksheets, the specific settings for each application also need to be captured. SQL Server provides the following methods to assist in the documentation of your systems:

- Run the system-stored procedure `sp_configure`, which captures all of the configuration settings for SQL Server.

- Run the system-stored procedure `sp_helpstartup` on Microsoft SQL Server 6.5 or `sp_procoption` on Microsoft SQL Server 7.0 and SQL Server 2000. These help determine the startup procedures and settings used by SQL Server.

- Use the command-line Sqldiag.exe utility to capture SQL Server system information. This utility is usually used for diagnostic purposes, but this is one of its side benefits. This is the syntax to use:

```
SQLDIAG.EXE -X -U user_name -P password -I instance_name -O
output_file
```

-*X* skips the error logs; you can use -*C* as well to get cluster information; -*I* is only used if it is not a default instance.

You should also document all of the objects associated with each database. This includes stored procedures, jobs, logins, and system-level logins as well as their corresponding database users, maintenance plans, and so on, even if they reside outside of the database. You will use this information later to determine conflicts, such as duplicate stored procedure names and logins or differences in naming standardizations. If you want, run the same DBCC commands on each system. Document anything and everything, even if you think it might not be relevant. Include linked servers, modified system databases, and so on.

> **More Info**   For more information on gathering information about your systems, consult Chapter 4, "Disk Techniques for High Availability," Chapter 12, and Chapter 15, "Monitoring for High Availability." The run book described in Chapter 12 is a great resource for information. Chapter 4 and Chapter 15 cover monitoring and capacity management from a system performance perspective.

Gathering System Performance Metrics

Gathering performance metrics from your server is more than a one-time event. To truly understand what is going on with your system, performance metrics must be done over a period of time and then analyzed. At a minimum, you should gather statistics about your systems for one business week. During that time, record numbers when there is little to no load, medium load, and heavy load. Gathering numbers only at times that show one extreme or the other does not paint an accurate picture of system use.

Other SQL Server Information to Gather   This section describes the most common data to collate, which should help you plan for the issues that are most commonly encountered when consolidating. Refer to the section on technical considerations under the planning section of this chapter for more information and details on most of these points.

Consolidating System Databases   Be sure to take care of the following:

■   Identify any objects in system tables that are not part of a standard installation.

■   Identify any objects in system tables that have been modified since a base installation.

■   Look for duplicate names.

■   Review each object for relevance in the new environment.

■   Review each object to determine if duplicity exists at a more granular level.

■   Review each object for explicit references, such as path names, server names, and task names.

■   Do not address tasks found in msdb; this will be addressed in the next section.

■   Only search for nondefault objects found in tempdb. Use of tempdb is dealt with later.

Collation and Sort Order   Check out the following:

■   What is the sort order of the source server?

■   Identify any objects that deviate from the collation setting of the server.

Security (Logins, Security, and Permissions)   Be sure you have information about the following items:

■   Collect and identify duplicate logins.

■   Determine whether trusts are required across domains.

- Determine if guest is an active user.

- Collect data of logins with administrative rights.

- Collect security settings and the permission structure for the public group.

- Determine if you will need specific registry permissions.

- Determine what permissions are required for extended stored procedures, particularly xp_cmdshell.

- What accounts are the SQL Server services running under?

- Understand the security model that the client is implementing.

- Compare security models of source servers and target servers.

- Collect database options, to ensure that read-only, single-user, and dbo-only settings are maintained during migration.

- Collect the encrypted passwords to transfer to the new server.

- Compile a list of all Windows Authentication and SQL logins that have administrative access.

- Pay special attention to the scheduled jobs on the system. Not only do these jobs have to be migrated, but they also identify specific workloads that kick off at specific times. They also tell you which user accounts are commonly performing the maintenance for each instance.

Serverwide Configuration Settings   Here are some factors to check out:

- Determine if any SQL Server configurations, such as affinity mask, Address Windowing Extensions (AWE), and so on, have been modified since installation—that is, do they deviate from a standard installation?

- Monitor context switches after migration, mainly to decide if fiber mode is necessary.

- Determine if there are requirements for XML stored procedures and OLE automation objects.

- Establish which statistics are inaccurate when running in fiber mode.

- Monitor the worker threads to see if they are exceeding the maximum value allocated.

- Collect error messages that have been added to sysmessages and sysservermessages.

- Establish if any system-supplied error messages have been modified.

Determining the Existing Environment (Workstations, Servers, Applications, Users, and so on)   Some more information you must gather follows:

■   Verify that clients with older versions of Microsoft Data Access Components (MDAC)—such as MDAC 2.5—can connect to a default or named instance of SQL Server 2000, depending on which you are implementing. Default instances should be fine, but named instance support was introduced with MDAC 2.6.

■   Collect the host names that connect to named instances of SQL Server.

■   Identify applications where the connection string is hard coded. This also includes connection objects, such as COM objects and data source names (DSNs).

■   Identify if any connections are connecting other than TCP/IP. Exclude internal connections that connect using named pipes.

■   Identify all applications that are known to have hard-coded parameters.

■   Identify all applications for which vendors are no longer accessible.

■   Collect information that describes the type of workload the application generates.

■   Determine the domain that the central server will reside in.

■   Identify the domains of the source servers.

■   Identify the domains of the connection sources.

■   Collect the trust relationships between central server and connection sources.

Health Checks   Take care of these, too:

■   Execute DBCC statements and scan logs for errors.

■   Review error logs and event viewers.

■   Determine if any procedures must be added to the cache before opening the environment up to your user community.

Multiple Versions   Take care of this:

■   Collect all versions of servers, binaries, and compatibility modes of the databases.

Excessive Use of Tempdb   Take the following actions:

■   Determine the maximum space used by tempdb for source servers.

- Establish the amount of memory used for procedures.

- Decide if each SQL Server instance should have its own physical place for tempdb or if they should all share a single space.

Database Options   Answer these questions, too:

- How much space has been assigned to devices on source servers?

- How much space is actually used?

- What is the maximum space used for the transaction logs?

- What has the growth rate been like over the last week, month, quarter, six months, and year?

- Is the current backup strategy at source servers in line with the strategy to be used at the target server?

- Are there requirements for connection settings to be other than the default ANSI settings and connection-related properties?

- Collect the current database options.

Phase 2: Technical Considerations for Planning

Once you gather the necessary information, you can then perform the analysis to put the proper plans in place.

Single Instance Versus Multiple Instances

Before you can consider any other technical aspect, you must decide if you will be using one instance with many databases or multiple instances, each with its own set of databases. Instances were first introduced in SQL Server 2000. One instance of SQL Server 2000 equates to one installation of SQL Server on your machine. Prior to SQL Server 2000, you could only have one installation of SQL Server per physical server. There are two types of instances: *default* and *named*. A default instance is analogous to the current functionality of previous versions of SQL Server. A named instance of SQL Server is exactly like it sounds: you name your SQL installation with a unique name. SQL Server 2000 supports up to 16 instances on one physical server or in a single Windows server cluster, regardless of the number of physical nodes comprising the cluster. In other words, you can have 16 named instances or one default and 15 named instances. Consult SQL Server Books Online for any changes in the number of instances supported.

> **Note**   You can only have one default instance, so older applications that cannot handle named instances might have problems. Please test if you are implementing named instances.

Each instance gets its own set of core binaries, but they share underlying components such as MDAC, Microsoft Distributed Transaction Coordinator (MS DTC), and one Microsoft Search service. If there is more than one instance of SQL Server, each has the ability to stay at a certain service pack level, with the exception of any shared components. This is a benefit for a consolidation effort, because you can have instances at the specific levels at which you need them; however, for example, if you need to install a SQL Server 2000 service pack and it for some reason requires a physical reboot, you will affect all other services running on that server. In general, once you have upgraded one instance to that service pack level you will not have to reboot to upgrade the other instances because these shared files have already been replaced. Regardless, your availability and SLAs must be taken into account when designing consolidated SQL Servers.

From a performance perspective, each instance will get its own memory, including cache for stored procedures. Is it better for your endeavor to put hundreds of databases under one instance or to spread them out over more than one? The "Memory and Processor" section later in this chapter delves into this topic in more depth.

In most cases, a single instance means less administrative overhead: with only one instance to manage, the complexity of what goes on in SQL Server can be easily managed and localized. It also ensures that "automatic" settings, such as using dynamic memory, are easier to consider if there are no other processes to contend with. If you have limited hardware, this might be your best option.

Multiple instances allow for each instance to cater to a different set of rules, SLAs, and so on. The biggest advantage is that you can stop the services for each instance individually. Multiple instances also mean more complexity when it comes to system design and management on all levels, but the rewards of dedicated memory and separate processes (with the exception of shared components) might be worth the trade-off.

When thinking about single versus multiple instances—as stated in the introductory paragraph of this section—I/O, processor, and memory are the key considerations.

Application Compatibility with Instances

Because the architecture of SQL Server 2000 is different with instances, in particular named instances, you should test older applications to ensure that they still work properly. Named instances technically require MDAC 2.6 to connect properly. A default instance should be fine. In the event there is a problem if named instances are used, there are a few potential ways to solve any issues if the application cannot connect to a named instance:

- Install MDAC 2.6 or higher on the machine hosting the application or on each client machine if the application is run directly by the client. This is the version of MDAC that ships with SQL Server 2000, and it contains support for named instances. Installing MDAC 2.6 does not guarantee that the application will work with named instances, however. Testing on one or a small number of machines is recommended before rolling this out to large numbers of users.

- If it is not possible to update the client utilities to the SQL Server 2000 versions, do not use the name but rather connect directly to the IP address and port number. Configure that in Client Network Utility.

- Update the client tools to SQL Server 2000. Then use the SQL Server 2000 version of Client Network Utility to create an alias to the named instance.

- Update application code to support named instances. If the application already hard-coded server names, database names, and paths into the application, there are more significant issues than named instances.

Disk Subsystem

The first stop for any SQL Server system should be the architecture of its disk subsystem. If you are looking to combine workloads or to upgrade, it is imperative to know not only how much disk space you will need but, if you are consolidating, what workloads will work well together from an I/O perspective. That is a serious challenge faced by customers both big and small. Read-only reporting databases have different I/O requirements than heavily used OLTP systems with many writes and a smaller number of reads. Do not take this configuration lightly; you might initially save cost by consolidating, but if you have underperforming applications, the consolidated environment will be a failure.

> **More Info**   Disks were covered in great depth in Chapter 4, "Disk Techniques for High Availability." Refer to that chapter for any further discussions relating to disk issues.

Memory and Processor

There are a few important considerations when determining how many processors the new servers will contain. As with disk and memory, prior benchmarking and application and system profiling data will need to exist to help you make a more accurate decision. Here are some of the main issues:

■ Based on your memory or processor needs, you need to choose the appropriate operating system. Do not assume you will be always be able to utilize the same hardware and budget appropriately.

> **More Info** See the topic "Memory Used by SQL Server Objects Specifications" in SQL Server Books Online for more information on how much memory certain types of objects will consume.

■ When it comes to memory and SQL Server usage, the biggest consideration is your procedure cache. This also dictates whether you can use one instance or multiple instances for your consolidation. With 32 bits, you can access at most 2.6 GB of procedure cache (this is also dependent on what memory options you use). If you are now consolidating multiple databases, each with many stored procedures, you might run out of procedure cache. Each stored procedure you have will have a plan in cache so that it runs faster. If you have many databases, and each has the same stored procedures, they are still different to SQL Server because the statistics for each database are potentially different, and therefore the plans are different as well. On top of that, if your server contains more than one processor, you will have *two* plans for every stored procedure, because the SQL Server engine will decide at run time how many processors will be used to run this stored procedure at this moment. Thus you could potentially be trying to cache the number of stored procedures in each database times the number of databases times two. This will definitely affect performance and push you into multiple instances. You might not know this requirement up front, and you might discover it in your testing phase.

■ If you need more than 2 GB of memory for your SQL Server 2000 instance, you will need to use a form of advanced memory, which must be configured properly for SQL Server to recognize it.

> **More Info**   See the section "Memory Management for SQL Server 2000" in Chapter 14, "Administrative Tasks to Increase Availability," for a full description of how SQL Server uses memory, recommendations on tuning memory, and how to configure memory for use with SQL Server 2000.

■ Processor and connection affinity has two effects: it limits the SQL Server instance to using only certain processors instead of using all the processors on the system (which is the default); this is processor affinity. It also ties the user scheduler to each processor, which is connection affinity.

To restrict processor usage for a particular instance, use the *affinity mask* option of SQL Server. The ability to limit which processors are used would be useful if you had an eight-processor system and wished to run two instances such that neither ever affected the processor workload of the other. You would simply configure the first instance to use processors 0, 1, 2, and 3 and the second instance to use processors 4, 5, 6, and 7. This sounds great, but in practice is often less than optimal. For example, when instance 1 is very busy, it cannot use any of the processor time from instance 2, even when instance 2 is idle. A better approach would be to configure instance 1 with processors 0, 1, 2, 3, 4, and 5 and instance 2 with processors 2, 3, 4, 5, 6, and 7. Thus each server has two dedicated processors that it can use and four processors that are shared.

> **Tip**   Windows and other applications can still use all of the processors. This setting affects only SQL Server instances unless you restrict the operating system or other applications as well. For more information, see the topic "Managing SQL Server Resources with Other Tools" in Chapter 14.

Tying user connections, or connection affinity, is not as straightforward. This allows an instance to always direct a set of client connections to a specific SQL Server Scheduler, which in turn manages the dispatching of threads on the available processors.

There is a limited set of conditions under which connection affinity provides a noticeable performance benefit. One of its advantages is that it can increase the number of hits against a Level 2 hardware cache, but it also prevents a task from going to another processor if the processor it is tied to is busy. The disadvantages of using connection affinity are similar to those discussed for processor affinity.

A good example of a disadvantage specific to connection affinity would be a Windows-level memory check that comes up and is assigned to a particular processor. Your Transact-SQL query can no longer jump to another processor for completion and must wait until this check completes. Processors multitask, but they also have a priority component; on occasion, Windows priorities can and need to outrank SQL Server thread priorities.

If misused, connection affinity can prevent one from fully utilizing all available resources. Keep this in mind when evaluating the use of this feature.

> **More Info** For more information on the affinity mask option, see the topic "Affinity Mask Option" in SQL Server Books Online.

■ If you are moving an application from a system of one type—for example, with one or two processors—to one that has six or eight processors to handle the increased load, each query might perform differently because a new execution plan might exist due to the increased number of processors available. If this is the case, you might need to alter the configuration settings of max degree of parallelism, and possibly also affinity mask. The problem with combining multiple workloads is that tuning these two things affects everything running under that instance.

> **Important** Do not use any current tool other than SQL Server to manage your processor resources, such as Process Control under Windows 2000 Datacenter Edition. These other tools might not produce the desired effect. You should do all processor-related tweaking with the SQL Server parameters. Consult updated versions of SQL Server Books Online for any information on other tools as they become available.

Networking

You might now encounter more network traffic flowing to one SQL Server. As with any other planning consideration, do you currently know how many concurrent users are usually connected to the SQL Server at various times, especially under maximum load? From a memory perspective, each connection consumes 12 KB added to the network packet size multiplied by three:

Connection Size = (12 + (3 × packet size))

Therefore, in addition to the memory required for the normal SQL Server usage for things like procedure cache and queries, you need to take into account network connections. This factors into whether you decide to consolidate on one instance or multiple instances.

Once you know how much memory user connections take up for each database, you need to worry about network bandwidth. Can what is coming in and going out be handled by the proposed networking on the server? For example, if you have one 10-Mb card but your overall required throughput is 20 MB, do you add another network card and IP address (both of which add a bit of system overhead) or get a higher bandwidth network card and ensure that the network itself can handle the load?

Other networking issues include the following:

- What port is SQL Server using? On installation, SQL Server 2000 grabs a dynamic port and not necessarily 1433. This is partially due to the instance support, as multiple instances cannot really share the same port. Generally the first instance (whether named or default) is assigned to 1433. Use Server Network Utility to assign a known, static port to each instance.

- Does the SQL Server require domain connectivity (that is, a failover cluster) or have processes that use other SQL Servers (such as log shipping)? Are they all in the same domain? Mixed domains can cause problems in consolidation.

- Do you have a mixture of SQL Servers that use domain accounts for the service accounts? Are they all in the same domain? Do you also have SQL Servers set to use the local service account? This might seem easy to solve when you consolidate because you can standardize; however, when it comes to object ownership and the login that was configured to run SQL Server Agent jobs, it is a different story. You must open the properties SQL Server Agent job and make sure that the Owner is set to the proper SQL Server login.

Security and Logins

Security is an obvious concern. Are there different standards for all of the applications, databases, and servers targeted? If there are, will they be in conflict with one another if they are combined? Or, for example, is something like IPSec required, but you are consolidating to a cluster where IPSec is not designed for failover, meaning the application will need to be changed or possibly not consolidated but put instead on its own instance or server?

Logins and how applications and users actually access SQL Server are the biggest areas of concern for security in a consolidation effort. User migration could consume a great deal of planning time. The "Networking" section earlier in this chapter already mentioned domain connectivity and domain accounts, but here the focus is on the actual logins. Do you have servers that have a mix of both Windows Authentication and mixed mode? Will that introduce risk when workloads are combined?

Also, security has changed a bit if you are only familiar with SQL Server 6.5 and earlier. SQL Server 7.0 introduced the concept of roles, so you might want to rethink how security is done for a particular application. This might become scope creep, so do not consider or implement it if it will impede the consolidation effort.

Here are some issues to consider with logins:

- Plan sufficient time for your login and user migration plan, test, and implementation.

- You have a login named JoeJ at the SQL Server level who has sysadmin privileges on one database server, a generic user on another database server, and dbo on one specific database. JoeJ maps back to one person. The problem in consolidation is that you do not want to accidentally give one user more or less rights than he or she needs, so take that into account when combining workloads.

- You have three different users named JoeJ across different database servers and, until now, this was not a problem. It will take good communication to resolve these types of issues.

- Even worse is the same login for the same person with different passwords across different servers that are now being consolidated. You can either assign a new password, choose one of the two that exist, or ask the user to select which password to use.

- Do you need the Builtin\Administrators login? Do you currently remove it now from all installations? If you do not remove it, but are considering it, what will its impact be? Does a third-party software application require it?

- Because consolidation means that you will more than likely have more users connected to the server, what permissions will you grant to public and guest users?

- Not all logins that exist are in use (for example, old employees, active users versus configured users, and so on). Only migrate logins that are used. Remember that adding and dropping logins impacts the transaction log.

- Do the logins, if Windows Authentication is used, come from different domains? Will you need to set up two-way trusts at the Windows level?

- Does the database, or specifically, the application using it, currently use or require sa access? If so, that should be evaluated.

- Have you locked down Group Policies on Windows Servers since the server was rolled out? How will that impact the new consolidated environment (for example, have you locked down the policies needed for clustering if that is the desired end goal)?

- Did you plan your port assignments for your SQL Server instances, or are you letting SQL Server choose them dynamically? It is best to use static, known ports.

High Availability

Each instance of SQL Server 2000 needs to be made highly available to meet your SLAs. Because this book is all about high availability, putting solutions together, planning, and so on, this section is pretty self-evident.

Replication

If replication is configured on any, or many, of the databases being considered, planning will certainly be impacted. Each database or publisher needs a distributor, and the distributor can live on the publisher, the subscribers, or be hosted on a separate system. Do you plan on having a 1:1 ratio of publishers to distributors? That is probably unrealistic in a consolidated environment, which means that you will need to do some up-front capacity planning to ensure that the distributor can handle multiple publishers. Disk I/O will be impacted greatly, followed by processor and memory, especially depending on the type of replication implemented. This also means that the distributor will have to exist in a completely separate instance or, most likely, on a different server to ensure good performance and high availability. You might consider a remote distributor as well. Remote distributors for various publishers can be consolidated under one SQL Server instance, but distribution databases per publisher should be distinct. One instance with a publisher and distributor might be acceptable in a nonconsolidated environment, but it will not be acceptable in a consolidated environment.

You also have to consider the base snapshot directory and its location per publisher: will you share one per SQL Server instance or use another one?

Also consider the subscribers, as they will be impacted, too, if you move publishers and distributors. This is important if you have to disable replication during the implementation process.

Migrating Objects

One of the hardest tasks for any upgrade, consolidation, or migration effort will be migrating objects, such as alerts, SQL Server Agent jobs, and Data Transformation Services (DTS) packages. For alerts, jobs, and operators, you can easily script them; however, before applying them to the consolidated SQL Server, ensure that there are no naming conflicts and that when you migrate to the new server, the proper user is associated with SQL Server Agent jobs. For DTS packages, you have a few options to migrate the packages to other servers, but once you move them, you might need to make modifications to them. Do not assume that they will run as is. Also ensure that the package is compatible. As of SQL Server 7.0 Service Pack 2, Microsoft changed the format from SQL Server 7.0 RTM and Service Pack 1. In that case, you would have to completely re-create the package under SQL Server 2000. Remember to account for time in your testing phase for testing and possibly fixing these types of issues.

> **Tip**   There is a utility called the Copy Database Wizard included that can help move databases and their corresponding users, jobs, and other elements. An interesting option with this utility is to select the Run Later option and allow it to create five separate DTS tasks to move these pieces. You can then run all five or any combination of them that you need to transfer your database information.
>
> Also, you could consider using the Transfer Databases Task of DTS as well.

Administration

Prior to migration, think about the following considerations that impact the eventual administration of each consolidated SQL Server instance:

- Serverwide server settings definitely need to be reconciled before bringing the new server online. Each individual SQL Server might have its own, and one setting could impact a database in many ways, so coming up with the final set of global server settings is crucial.

- Similarly, if you use any startup options, those also have to be reconciled.

- Do you have any history for objects or technologies configured, such as replication or SQL Server Agent jobs existing in msdb that are still valid and need to be migrated?

- How will your maintenance change as a result of adding multiple databases or instances? For example, how will your entire enterprise backup strategy change? Will one backup now conflict with another and affect performance? Is your maintenance window for the server now smaller because of increased load?

> **Tip**   Be especially careful if you plan to back up to disk, and then from disk to tape. This speeds the backup process but triples the workload on disk spindles (the first operation is the read from the database, the second is the write to disk, and the third is the read from disk to write to tape).

- Watch msdb growth, because with more databases it might increase in size due to more statuses and histories being written (depending on which functionality of SQL Server you are using).

Chargeback

Chargeback is the process of assessing the cost to utilization of the hardware so business units or customers can be charged appropriately. If chargeback is a consideration, you have a few options. One is to use SQL Server. Third-party tools such as ARMTech from Aurema can assist you in your cost accounting for system resource usage.

System Databases

System databases are an important consideration, especially in a consolidation effort. The system databases contain data and structures that are relevant to the entire server installation. Unlike user databases that can exist independently of each other, system databases are closely associated with each other as well as to the user databases from the source server.

How will master, model, and msdb be configured? Because you are now combining multiple servers, each with its own copy of the databases, you cannot just restore multiple copies, as the last restore will overwrite the previous copy. Remember that msdb includes all of your jobs, alerts, and operators (as well as history for some features such as log shipping), so plan on a size of at least 45 MB, and then add the additional amount per instance as well as about 10 percent overage.

Besides these space requirements, you need to analyze master, model, tempdb, and msdb to detect duplicate database objects and document them. This will extend from logins, stored procedures, user-defined data types, and tasks through to the specifics of objects. For instance, an object of the same name will represent or perform actions particular to the source server, or an object of a different name will represent or perform actions that accept modifications at the server level. This becomes particularly difficult when modifications have been made to these databases outside of logins. Remember to include any and all startup stored procedures.

You must identify any elements that are not part of a standard SQL Server build or installation, whether they are modifications or new objects. Review each object for relevance in a consolidated environment. Review each object to determine if duplicity exists at a more granular level. Review each object for explicit references, such as path names, server names, and task names. Do not address tasks found in msdb, as those are handled separately and must be dealt with on their own. Only search for nondefault objects found in tempdb. Also consider in advance how you will respond to application needs for previous compatibility levels. In general, these tips can save you much trouble in having to "update" applications, but remember that being fully on the current version usually minimizes support difficulty and costs.

Collations and Sort Orders

You must also take into account the collations and sort orders between servers. It is more likely that databases of varying collations will coexist in a consolidated environment than in numerous stand-alone servers. You can encounter unexpected results after migrating to a consolidated environment, and you must realize that certain applications depend on the collation and sort order setting of the database. If they are not set properly, the applications will not work after the switch to the consolidated environment.

Temporary tables will be created in tempdb with collation settings of the tempdb if the collation syntax is not included. Passwords in a case-insensitive SQL Server are converted to uppercase before being stored or used. Passwords in a case-sensitive SQL Server are not converted to uppercase. Because of this difference, passwords originally encrypted on a case-sensitive server and later transferred to a case-insensitive server cannot be used unless all alphabetic characters in the password are uppercase.

Similarly, understand how you need NULL to behave in your queries. If you turn the database option ANSI_NULLS on, all comparisons to a null value evaluate to NULL, which equates to unknown. If this option is off, comparisons of non-Unicode data evaluate as true if both values are null (that is, NULL = NULL is true). This is set to Off by default, so you should see the latter behavior. Also look at any other ANSI-related setting that might affect your environment.

> **More Info**   For more information about collations, see the "Effect on Passwords of Changing Sort Orders" topic in either the SQL Server 6.5 Books Online or 7.0 Books Online and "Selecting Collations" in SQL Server Books Online.

Other Technical Considerations

Here are other technical considerations to think about prior to migration:

- Are you currently using linked servers to enable connectivity and queries between servers that might or might not exist any longer? Are you changing domains that might also impact linked servers? If you consolidate, how will it impact the application? Will queries need to be rewritten? How will you migrate your linked server settings?

- As mentioned a few times, certain resources, such as DTC and the underlying Microsoft Search service that powers full text, are shared among all of the instances and even among other applications. That will be a concern in a consolidated environment as you add more databases and resources that use shared resources.

- General application and database upgrade and migration rules apply in a consolidation effort. Remember to take into account running of processes like DBCCs, reviewing logs, updating statistics, and so on, and fix any issues prior to moving the database. Also remember that depending on the physical layout (that is, where you put the data and log files for your consolidated SQL Server), what you do to one database might affect others.

- Have you modified any of the system tables? If so, those modifications might not work with the consolidated SQL Servers. Also, Microsoft does not recommend that you modify the system tables or add objects to databases like msdb or master.

- Are there collation and sort order conflicts between the current SQL servers and the proposed consolidated SQL Server environment? This is an easy item to miss if the planners, implementers, and DBAs are not in touch. Resolve any conflicts prior to consolidating.

- Does the database to be consolidated use extended stored procedures? If so, how will that impact other databases and, potentially, other instances?

- Service packs are a major consideration for a consolidated environment. If you have one SQL Server at one level and another at a different level, is that acceptable? (With SQL Server 2000, you can have this situation.)

- Remember that if you previously implemented SQL Server 7.0 clustering and upgraded to SQL Server 2000, you cannot go back on the same hardware without reinstalling the operating system due to the changes in MDAC that SQL Server 2000 installs. Plan for this.

- XML stored procedures are not supported in fiber mode, so use thread mode or a separate instance to avoid error 6604. Thread mode is excellent for systems performing MS DTC tasks, remote queries, linked servers, and extended stored procedures.

Phase 3: Consolidation Planning—The Server Design and the Test Process

Once the envisioning phase is done and guiding principles are agreed on and documented, work on planning the consolidation can begin. There are two main parts to planning: designing what the consolidated servers will "look" like and testing the implementation process.

Designing the New Production Servers

When you start to design the new environment, you need to take into account every aspect from the ground up: administration and operations (including monitoring), performance, backup and recovery, chargeback (if necessary), disaster recovery, high availability, security, and so forth. Do not assume that you can just use what you have in place for your current system, as the new environment might be different. Also, with more databases and SQL Server instances, you will have different rules and options that need to be reconciled. At this stage, if you identify new tools that need to be either built or acquired, document and plan for those, too.

Migration of Applications, Users, and Data

One of the important factors for the DBA is how the applications, users, and data will be migrated to the new consolidated environment. At this stage, any potential SQL Server 6.5 and SQL Server 7.0 migration issues should be completely isolated and identified, from Transact-SQL incompatibilities to system settings and everything in between. You might also need an intermediate staging server. Determine the order in which you will migrate the applications, users, and data. Resolve any conflicts in object names and location. Worry about the end users' experience and how you will make the effort as transparent as possible for them. Also determine how you will notify your end users about the move. How will business processes be impacted?

Avoid scope creep. You are consolidating, not adding new functionality or enhancements to applications or data schemas. Problems could be identified during the migration planning that, as long as they will not break in the consolidated environment, should be left alone. Once you have consolidated, you might want to consider these problems, but trying to solve them at this stage only causes the consolidation to take much longer than necessary.

Finally, do not waste time adding applications to a consolidation until the application is reasonably stable. Stability is crucial; many of the troubleshooting tools that might be required to diagnose the flaky application (for example extra perfmon counters, debug builds, and so on) could adversely affect the performance of the entire system.

Test the Process

Prior to actually doing the planned upgrade or consolidation in a production environment, you must build and test all of the new procedures, tools, and the entire migration. The capacity and capability of the environment used for testing should be the same as, if not close to, the final production environment. However, you may be constrained by budget, resources, and other limitations. The importance of this stage is to isolate, identify, document, and fix any defects, errors, or problems that you encounter so a production effort will, one hopes, be flawless. Devising the proper test plans will ensure a successful production rollout. The plans should identify the following:

■   Do applications and utilities still function in the same way as before the change, and how that is tested and measured? Remember, it is not just the changed component, but components that have dependencies on it. This can be a large matrix that must be modeled and then tested.

■   Does the system, and subsequently, SQL Server and all related applications still provide the required performance as they did before the change and how that can be tested and measured? This is as difficult to test as functionality. Do you have playback scripts or dummy test loads that you can use to reliably and accurately assess and compare the performance impact of a change?

Building a test platform is not an easy task. In some cases, it does not need to be an identical system or set of systems from the standpoint of number of processors, amount of memory, or total storage accessible by the cluster nodes, but in all other ways the test platform and the production environment should be identical. The ability of the system or systems to be partitioned affects this as well. Partitioned systems can be set up so that a small partition has exactly the same BIOS, chipset, devices (include firmware and BIOS versions), driver versions, kernel components (for example, antivirus, storage management, security monitor, system management utilities, firewall, disk mirroring, and so on), and user mode applications. All versions of all components should match the production environment and configuration, otherwise the confidence gained from testing an update or upgrade is lowered. Systems that do not support partitioning must be mirrored separately, but it is still important to ensure that all the components are identical between the test system and the production system. The same logic applies to clusters.

The most critical factor affecting whether the update or upgrade will be successful (and not cause any unplanned downtime) is interactions between different versions of hardware and software components and not the total size of the system as measured by number of processors, amount of memory, total storage, number of network or storage adapters, and so on. Thus, a test system or partition need not be exactly the same capacity as the production system, but it should be representative. An example for the use of a partitionable system might be that the production environment is 12, 16, or even more processors, but to be representative, the test partition might only need to contain 4 CPUs. Similarly, the production system might include 32 GB, 64 GB, or even more RAM, but to be representative, the test partition might only need to contain 8 GB of RAM.

Continuing with the same logic, it might not be necessary to fully reproduce the storage capacity of the production system, but only to provide the same behavior and characteristics, scaled to match the smaller test configuration. Some storage arrays support multiple systems and provide internal partitioning. The test system could be attached to the same partitionable storage resource as the production system but scaled down, providing the same storage behavior and characteristics for the test system as the production system. Finally, if you are using a server cluster, it is important to model the test cluster to match the production cluster configuration as closely as possible. Doing this ensures that planned and unplanned failovers allow the application or entire solution to function correctly, guaranteeing the highest possible availability. You can accomplish this testing with just two cluster nodes even if you have a four-node cluster in production, but if you do not match capabilities as closely as possible, your testing may be somewhat invalid.

The reasons that versions are the key factor to test, rather than size or capacity, include the following:

- No single vendor can test against all possible permutations that customers might deploy. They number in the millions.

- Quick fix engineering updates (QFEs) are typically less risky than version changes because the architecture of the component (that is, how it functions internally as well as how it interacts with the rest of the hardware components, operating system, the various applications and utilities, and so on) does not change.

- Version changes, even "point" version changes such as a difference between version 1.0 and 1.1, or service packs from hardware and software vendors, might have many small changes compiled together or might include architectural changes. The aggregation of many small changes or the change in architecture might impact other components in the complete configuration or solution and thus need to be more extensively tested.

- Obviously, a full version change of any type, be it for hardware, the operating system, applications, or utilities, requires similar or even larger amounts of testing than that done for service packs.

- From a Windows Datacenter Edition standpoint, certain conditions must be met for a configuration to be considered tested well enough to mitigate the risks inherent in updates and upgrades. These include the support of an original equipment manufacturer (OEM) as part of the Datacenter program, where the customer and the OEM have mutually agreed on configuration management and change control processes and policies as well as the pretesting required for an SLA.

The use of a scaled-down environment is *usually* possible, with the most glaring exception being when the production system is running close to its maximum capacity, as measured in processor utilization, memory utilization, paging activity, network bandwidth, storage queues, and so on. In this case, even small changes in the behavior of components might cause the production system to begin to function noticeably more slowly and not be responsive enough for production use. This is unavoidable and simply a function of how any system responds when the work demand exceeds its ability to complete that work. In a worst case, the system might effectively be unusable. Thus, customers should always leave headroom in the production system that can absorb an unexpected performance impact. This also gives the system the same headroom for spikes in demand. As a rule of thumb, many customers limit average utilizations of various system resources to between 65 percent and 70 percent. This guideline, however, may not apply to your systems at all. There is a difference between peak usage and overall average use of systems. Those same customers begin planning to expand or otherwise upgrade the system capacity when those levels are consistently exceeded.

Once the test systems are built and are "identical" with the production systems, baseline testing should occur to validate functionality and assess performance characteristics and how they scale in comparison to the production systems.

There is some expense involved for the test system or systems, adapters, fabrics, networks, storage, and possible clusters and other hardware components. This is also true for the various software components, such as the applications and utilities that run on the system. However, you need to measure these expenses against the cost of encountering unplanned downtime that results from a failure, or when the update or upgrade goes bad and results in hours—or even more—of downtime. For all of these components, both hardware and software, customers should ask their vendors about costs and licensing, vendor policy on product instances used strictly for testing purposes, and other concerns.

Finally, it might be necessary to have some clients and a small network set up so that loads can be applied to the system or components using synthetic or dummy loads supplied by vendors or built by the customer.

Important   Pay attention to time in your testing. Too often, testing occurs in the weeks before a migration when there is plenty of time. Your staff might kick off jobs and go home. The next morning, the jobs have completed successfully and everybody is happy. However, when you go to migrate production applications in the 8-hour window of downtime you have arranged with users and find out the migration takes 12 hours, you have a problem. Every test task should measure not only the migration function, but also the time it takes to do this function. You might find that your available downtime window limits how much of the task you can accomplish in a night or a weekend.

Determining Risk

It is important to determine the risks—whether based on people, technology, or cost—that will be measured against. The success of a plan depends on knowing where potential failures can occur so you can mitigate them and see if the risks are worth taking. The best thing you can do to determine these risks is to test the entire process. However, you should also discuss the risks with anyone who has migrated these applications in the past. They might save you a lot of trouble by helping you to avoid any problems they encountered.

Phase 4: Developing

The developing stage is when the plans are realized and implemented for the first time in a testing or staging environment. This requires hardware completely separate from the eventual production servers, as it is crucial to work out any potential problems before going live. Ideally, the servers used in this stage have the same capacity and horsepower as their production counterparts, but that might be unrealistic due to budgetary constraints. The bottom line is that the better your testing or staging environments mirror your production environment, the more successful you will be when the actual production migration occurs.

There are at least three steps during this phase: technology validation, proof of concept, and piloting.

Once you decide on and plan for the technology that will be used during this phase, it is time to see if the technology performs as expected or if it is not appropriate at all. This is one of your last chances to modify the consolidation effort's physical design. Once the technology has been proven, it is time to roll out a proof of concept to show that the final environment will work as expected. The proof of concept should mirror the production environment exactly, just on a smaller scale. Finally, choose one of the servers that will be consolidated and make a pilot of it. Even if the technology has been evaluated and the proof of concept was successful, you still need a proper pilot to prove that in a production capacity—unlike the proof of concept, which is on a much smaller scale—the consolidation will benefit the entire business. If the pilot is a failure or is scrapped for other reasons, this is the time to figure things out.

Follow the configuration plans and migration plans as documented. If problems arise, document them, and if there is a fix, document the fix and revise the plans accordingly. After migrating applications, data, and users to the new consolidated SQL Server, put it through its paces—use it as it would be used on a daily basis—and test the servers under load. It is crucial to ensure that the databases that are now consolidated under one SQL Server will work well together when all applications are experiencing high utilization. Otherwise, there will be performance issues in production.

If any issues arise due to coexistence after testing, document the issues, and possibly rethink the strategy for that particular application's databases. Mitigating risk at this stage is crucial. Remember to test not only the migration, but also any administration plans, scripts, procedures, tools and so on that will be used in the eventual production environment. Just testing the migration process is not enough.

Phase 5: Deploying and Stabilizing

There are two main steps in this phase: back-end deployment and application deployment.

Back-end deployment is when the backbone of the system (hardware, operating system, networking, SQL Server, and so on) has been completely configured and tested. Application deployment is just that—configuring the databases and rolling out the applications in the new consolidated environment. At some point, you reach the go/no-go point, beyond which you cannot easily go back to the old environment. Stabilization continues through and beyond this stage.

Once you are confident that the proper hardware designs have been crafted and the migration plans are well tested, it is time to build and deploy the production consolidated SQL Servers. Even if your plans are well tested, do not perform the entire consolidation at once. Take a phased approach: Deploy one consolidated server, migrated server, or upgrade, thoroughly test it, compare it with the original environment, and then finally retire the old environment. Only at this point should you consider consolidating another SQL server, because if you do not completely verify that one effort went as expected and other problems are encountered during another migration, you could obscure and add to the problems. If it was unsuccessful for whatever reason, you can update your plans accordingly. Keep the old environment available until you have completed several or all of the upgrades, just in case.

Windows Version Upgrades

No discussion on highly available upgrades can ignore the operating system. Although you may be a SQL Server DBA, you need to consider that your operating system will need to be upgraded at some point. This is one of the reasons you will need a great working relationship with your systems engineers to ensure that the proper communication flows between groups.

Should You Upgrade Your Version of Windows?

Upgrading to a new version of Windows causes heartache for many administrators because they are changing the foundation of their entire server. Windows is Windows, but as you know, there are differences between Microsoft Windows NT 4.0 Server, Microsoft Windows 2000 Server, and now Microsoft Windows Server 2003. Should you upgrade your operating system? You must answer this question, and the answer here is the same as it was in Chapter 3, "Making a High Availability Technology Choice": *It depends*. If you have a current production system that is running, stable, and has SLAs with valid support contracts in place (that is, the product has not reached the end of its support life from the manufacturer), you might not need to upgrade the operating system. You might want to upgrade it, on the other hand, if your application software (such as SQL Server) has a feature or performance characteristic you need that is dependent on some feature of the new operating system or, say, if you need more scalability, which could be provided by the higher memory and processor capacity of a new operating system. The bottom line is that although you might want to upgrade, you might be able to avoid this for a period of time that you will determine.

If your operating system is near, at, or beyond its supported phase, regardless of the supportability status of your application software, you should consider upgrading your version of Windows. This is not a ploy to trick you into spending money. Microsoft would like you to have stable, available, and supported solutions that you are happy with. It wants you to have the peace of mind that comes from knowing that, should you run into any problems, you can pick up the phone and have someone say, "That product is still supported."

Like many customers, you might have a legacy system with no support, but that system should be fine as long as you and your staff can handle any known issues that come up, understand that the manufacturer might not have fixes for other issues that might arise, and know that any downtime that might occur because of that lack of fixes is acceptable from a total cost of ownership (TCO) perspective. You will be able to handle only problems that fall within the realm of what you can fix for an end-of-life product if no more fixes are available from the manufacturer, so understanding and accepting the risk is crucial for systems that may be mission-critical. If that is the case, ensure that any and all relevant documentation is complete and handy.

Another major factor is the abilities built into each version of the operating system. For example, if you are using SQL Server virtual servers, upgrading from Windows NT 4.0 Enterprise Edition to Windows 2000 Advanced Server or even Windows Server 2003 would be a huge benefit because clustering is greatly improved in those versions. Remember to take into account how the technologies you are using might have been enhanced or changed (possibly impacting you in a negative way) in the upgrade to the next version.

Also remember the hardware platform. At some point, the OEMs and hardware vendors who provide the system, adapters, and other components will cease both production and support on a certain operating system or hardware platform. If you later need a replacement component such as a processor, memory, disk controller, network card, or connector, it might not be in the supply chain, and the system would then have a point of failure from which there is no easy recovery. Also, if the software that controls the hardware component is no longer supported, no fixes will be possible for a recurring problem, even if the underlying hardware still functions.

There are many factors that go into a decision to upgrade your operating system—cost, features, compatibility with your current applications, and so on. Just because an operating system is new does not mean you should wait for one service pack and then upgrade to it automatically, as has been a common practice for years. Windows is tested extremely thoroughly for reliability and stability prior to release, and it gets better with each succeeding release of the operating system. If you need the features or benefits that come with, say, Windows Server 2003, you should definitely consider it for your environment.

Performing a Windows Version Upgrade on a Server

There are really two varieties of Windows upgrades: upgrading stand-alone servers and upgrading clustered servers (that is, server clusters, not Network Load Balancing). When you are running a mission-critical application like SQL Server on your server, minimizing your downtime becomes crucial. The most obvious method of reducing downtime besides planning and testing is to perform your version change onto new hardware and not on your existing servers. Why?

First and foremost, from a contingency standpoint, if something goes wrong on your new hardware during the cutover, your old hardware configuration has not changed, giving you the perfect fallback or rollback plan. In fact, it should be exactly the same as when you stopped allowing traffic to hit it, so you should have zero loss of any data or functionality. If you use the same hardware, your rollback plans might be hard to recover, and if you have to do a complete reinstall, you will never be *exactly* in the same state you were in prior to reconfiguration. Second, you can reduce the amount of downtime if you can start building your system while the other is up, and then just have to do some minor tasks instead of many things after you stop traffic to the current production server. In terms of making an upgrade available—whether Windows or SQL Server—one of the best things you can do is perform it on new hardware. The difference between being down 20 minutes or 20 hours is huge. Last, but not least, you will get the benefits of newer, faster hardware, which should extend the amount of time the system can be kept in production. If you use your existing hardware, which might be more than a few years old, it might work, but how long will you be able to keep it in production? Remember that newer versions of software, including operating systems, require more horse-power. Hardware prices have come down over the past few years and you can get an extremely capable server at a fairly reasonable price.

> **Tip**   In a multiple upgrade scenario, such as upgrading from Windows NT 4.0 to Windows 2000 and SQL Server 7.0 to SQL Server 2000, you should upgrade your operating system first, and then SQL Server.

> **Important**   Remember to test your systems thoroughly after configuration and back them up once you have established that the installation of the new operating system is working properly. This ensures you can recover to the new, known, good configuration. Do not decommission old servers until you know your new ones are working properly!

Upgrading Stand-Alone Servers

Upgrading a stand-alone server is straightforward. If you are using the same hardware, whatever functionality that server hosts will be completely unavailable during the upgrade process. This puts you at risk in the event that things do not go as planned during or after the upgrade and you need to roll back to your previous state. If you are doing this on the same hardware, at that point you will be relying on your backups. It is always best to configure a new server and then decommission the older one after you confirm that it is up and running in the way that it should be.

> **Note**   Doing a version or SKU upgrade can present some challenges if you are a constant consumer of SQL Server or MDAC hotfixes. Be sure to reapply any hotfixes not included in the Windows service pack level on the system if you elect this procedure.

Upgrading Clustered Servers

Upgrading servers in a server cluster is not dissimilar to upgrading stand-alone servers, as each node would individually need to be upgraded. A cluster presents different challenges, however. First and foremost, is your hardware solution still on the cluster Hardware Compatibility List (HCL) for your operating system choice? It might be, but it also might not. If it is not, you will have to buy new hardware. Could you upgrade on your current hardware and have it still work? Maybe, but if problems occur, you will technically have an unsupported solution. The biggest problem would be in terms of driver compatibility for your hardware, especially for components like RAID controllers. Do not put yourself in this situation.

You also now have more than one server that needs to be dealt with because it is an entire solution. How do you handle a multiple-server upgrade and keep your servers somewhat available? The best approach is to use new hardware, but if you are going to utilize the same hardware, the answer is actually easy; perform a rolling upgrade. A rolling upgrade is when you take the resources currently owned by one node and manually fail them over to another node while you are upgrading its operating system. This is where all of your planning comes into place. If you planned your system resource usage properly, you should have no performance impact after a failover and there should be no need to cause another availability interruption by failing the resources back (or to yet another node) until you are going to upgrade the other nodes in the cluster.

Warning   You cannot mix versions of server clusters in a day-to-day production environment. This means that you cannot, say, keep one node at Windows NT 4.0 Enterprise Edition and one at Windows Server 2003 while you are "checking things out." Once you make the decision to upgrade your existing server cluster, all nodes must be upgraded. During a rolling upgrade, this state does occur because not all nodes are upgraded at once. A mixed-mode cluster is fully supported in a rolling upgrade scenario but not as a permanent production platform.

More Info   For detailed information on performing a rolling upgrade to a Windows 2000 server cluster and what versions you can upgrade from and to, see *http://www.microsoft.com/windows2000/ techinfo/planning/incremental/rollupgr.asp for Windows 2000*. For Windows Server 2003, see *http://www.microsoft.com/technet/ treeview/default.asp?url=/technet/prodtechnol/windowsserver2003/ deploy/upgrdmigrate/RollUpNT.asp*.

SQL Server Version Upgrades or Migrations

Upgrading an SQL Server version is something most DBAs have encountered or will encounter at some time in their careers. Whether you are upgrading the legacy Enterprise Resource Planning (ERP) system that was on SQL Server 6.5 and is finally being retired or migrating to a new SQL Server 2000 instance on new hardware because you outgrew capacity on your current server, you have to take into account the amount of downtime that will be caused and what effect it will have on your end users and the SLA.

> **Tip** Much of the information in an earlier section, "Upgrading, Consolidating, and Migrating to SQL Server 2000," is applicable to any upgrade or migration process, including version upgrades for SQL Server. Use that in conjunction with the information in this section to help you plan your upgrades or migrations from another SQL Server version or instance to your target instance of SQL Server 2000.

Depending on which version you are starting from, you will have different options. Regardless of the version, you should have a dedicated testing environment as well as new hardware for the new SQL Server 2000 instances. When you are trying to upgrade on the same server, you increase your risk greatly for a few reasons. The most important reason is that should something go wrong, you might not only ruin the new environment, but also damage the old environment to the point that it can never be a fallback plan. Another reason is that while the upgrade is happening, you might not be able to use the server at all, whereas on different hardware, you might be able to keep things running while you are doing some, if not all, of the upgrade. From an availability perspective, that is crucial.

Another reason to keep the original hardware available is troubleshooting against the perceptions of the occasional change-fearing user. Consider a case in which you performed a flawless migration, only to have users complain about the performance of a particular task a few days, or even a week or two later. Keep in mind that this might be noise, as sometimes hearing that the system changed at all makes users think there actually will be a performance difference, causing perceived problems. Having the ability to run the query on the existing old system and prove that it is just as fast or even faster can save you much time and effort. It can also save your reputation and your performance review.

Depending on which version of SQL Server you are starting from, different native SQL-based tools are available to assist during an upgrade, consolidation, or migration effort. Other requirements also drive the decision process of what to use, such as the window of time that is open to perform the migration. Whatever tool you decide to use, realize that each has its strengths and weaknesses, and you might need to combine tools.

Warning   If you are using replication, it must be disabled or unconfigured prior to the upgrade. It would be necessary to have the replication configuration documented, as well as scripted, so that it can be set up after the upgrade. For more upgrade information with replication, see the topics "Backing Up and Restoring Replication Databases," "Scripting Replication," and "Replication and Upgrading" in SQL Server Books Online.

Caution   Do not assume your application running on a previous version of SQL Server will work or perform better than it did before the upgrade to SQL Server 2000. First, if it is from a third-party manufacturer, make sure the software is supported on SQL Server 2000. Second, make sure that syntax that is used by any application is still valid and that some variables or things like column names that you are using are not now reserved keywords in SQL Server 2000 (see "Reserved Keywords" in SQL Server Books Online under the topic Transact-SQL Reference) or are not being deprecated. The same goes for any applications, as Open Database Connectivity (ODBC) keywords are also listed.

More Info   For more information on upgrading your SQL Server version, some key topics in SQL Server Books Online you can reference (there are more that are not listed here) are "Upgrading an Existing Installation of SQL Server," "Upgrading from SQL Server 7.0 to SQL Server 2000," "Preparing to Upgrade from SQL Server 6.5," and "How to Upgrade from SQL Server 6.5."

Tools for Upgrading from SQL Server 6.5

The database formats of SQL Server 6.5 and SQL Server 2000 are incompatible, so it is not possible to use the backup and restore process to create the database on the target SQL Server 2000 instance, which can also jump start the process. You also cannot apply transaction logs of a SQL Server 6.5 database to a SQL Server 2000 database. There are a few options to consider when planning your upgrade or migration to SQL Server 2000:

- **BCP/BULK INSERT**   One tried-and-true method of migrating data from one platform to another is the use of flat files. BCP has been in SQL Server since version 4.21a, and now there is not only the command-line version, but also a Transact-SQL command BULK INSERT. In some ways, this is easier to plan than using the Upgrade Wizard, and in other ways it is more difficult. For example, you now need to worry about creating all your databases in SQL Server 2000 with the proper size and devising a process to migrate the users. BCP only takes care of the data migration. Any indexes, views, and other elements would need to be re-created after the bulk insert because it might slow the process down if indexes are configured prior to inserting data.

- **SQL Server Upgrade Wizard**   SQL Server 2000 has a built-in wizard to assist you with your migration from SQL Server 6.5. It takes into account all aspects of your SQL Server 6.5 configuration, including users. However, the Upgrade Wizard is not appropriate for all migrations to SQL Server 2000.

> **More Info**   For more information and details about the specifics of using the Upgrade Wizard, see the topic "Upgrading Databases from SQL Server 6.5 (Upgrade Wizard)" in SQL Server Books Online.

Tools for Upgrading from SQL Server 7.0

If you are migrating from SQL Server 7.0 to SQL Server 2000, you have some different options than you would if you started with SQL Server 6.5.

- **Log shipping**   It is possible to send and then apply transaction logs from a SQL Server 7.0 Service Pack 2 database to a SQL Server 2000 database. This is one of the better migration options, if not the best, as it not only provides a fallback plan by leaving the source server in place, but also the amount of downtime incurred will most likely be minimal.

■ **Backup/Restore**   Backup and restore needs no long introduction. It is possible to take a SQL Server 7.0 backup and restore it under SQL Server 2000; the restore process upgrades the database and performs other functions, such as rebuilding statistics.

■ **Copy Database Wizard**   This wizard uses the attach and detach functionality of SQL Server to do the work. The database files will be detached, copied, and then attached to the target server. When going from SQL Server 7.0 to SQL Server 2000, the attach process upgrades the database to SQL Server 2000, but statistics are not automatically rebuilt. That might be a consideration when deciding between backup/restore and the Copy Database Wizard. Also, consider if the collations are different between the SQL Servers, especially if you have an international application. For example, if you use char/varchar data types you could not store and retrieve any data except what can be represented by the code page on the destination SQL Server. Unicode would be a workaround.

> **More Info**   For more information on the differences between attaching and detaching versus backup and restore, see the section "Attaching and Detaching Databases Versus Backup and Restore" later in this chapter.

■ **BCP/BULK INSERT**   BCP or BULK INSERT work the same as they do with a SQL Server 6.5 or SQL Server 2000 database; you take flat files and use them to import data into a database. You would need to find another method to import users, objects, and other items.

Upgrading Between Different Versions of SQL Server 2000

The same options for SQL Server 7.0 are valid for SQL Server 2000 to SQL Server 2000 migrations, and because all databases are at the same version level (sans service pack differences), there is less work that needs to be done because the databases do not need to be upgraded. Concerns about collations and service packs are still valid, but you do not need to worry as much about things like behavior differences and syntax changes.

Upgrading from Previous Versions of SQL Server Clustering

If you are looking to upgrade from previous versions of SQL Server clustering to SQL Server 2000 failover clustering, or even from a stand-alone SQL Server to a failover cluster, this section will help you. The same rules for a standard upgrade apply (such as having to unconfigure replication), but there are other considerations to take into account:

■   You absolutely cannot mix different clustered versions of SQL Server on the same server cluster. If you are currently running SQL Server 6.5 or SQL Server 7.0 clustering, those absolutely cannot coexist with a SQL Server 2000 failover cluster unless they are physically installed on separate server clusters. This means you would potentially need new hardware for your upgrade to SQL Server 2000.

■   If you are upgrading your operating system as well, see the section "Windows Version Upgrades" earlier in this chapter for information about Windows. SQL Server's health and stability in a clustered environment is directly dependent on a properly configured operating system.

■   With SQL Server 6.5 and SQL Server 7.0, the binaries were put on the shared drive and possibly the quorum. Now all binaries will be on the local system drive in the same place on each node. Are the nodes configured the same?

■   Where are the database files physically located on your shared disk array? Does your disk configuration meet your current and future needs? This is probably the most important factor in any SQL Server cluster upgrade, whether it is SQL Server 6.5 or SQL Server 7.0 to SQL Server 2000, or SQL Server 2000 to SQL Server 2000. In SQL Server 6.5 and SQL Server 7.0, files could be placed on the quorum drive with no warnings. In SQL Server 2000 this not a recommended configuration.

As you learned, the quorum drive should be left alone and used only by the server cluster. Nothing else should be placed on it if at all possible. Another potential problem is that even if the data and log files are not on the quorum but on one LUN/drive letter and you are going to be using multiple instances, you now need dedicated drive letters to support each instance. Multiple SQL Server 2000 instances cannot share a drive letter. You need to move the data and log files for the databases that will live on other instances and not on that existing drive and reconfigure your disk subsystem by adding drives. Even with a modern storage area network (SAN), for which adding disks and space are relatively painless, adding additional disks to an existing server cluster is a regimented process detailed elsewhere in this book. Remember to try to add all your disk resources to be used on the server cluster *before* you install clustering to avoid this extra work. Finally, if you are on an old SCSI attached drive array, will it meet your growth needs? Chances are it will not in the long term, so you might even need a new disk subsystem.

> **More Info**   For the exact technical steps for upgrading and more information, see the topics "Upgrading to a SQL Server 2000 Failover Cluster," "How to Upgrade from a Default Instance to a Default Clustered Instance of SQL Server 2000 (Setup)," and "How to Upgrade from a Local Default Instance to a Clustered, Named Instance of SQL Server 2000 (Setup)" in SQL Server Books Online

Attaching and Detaching Databases Versus Backup and Restore

One feature introduced in SQL Server 7.0 was the ability to attach and detach a database. This is a very useful function that you can use in many scenarios, including upgrades and disaster recovery, but what exactly is the difference between detaching and attaching a database and using backup and restore? Both seemingly do the same things. However, in reality, they are different. Detaching and then attaching a database, notwithstanding the physical time it takes to copy the files, can be a relatively quick process in comparison to a straightforward backup and restore. That is one of the reasons many people like to use it as an option for their databases.

If you detach and then attach a database from the same SQL Server version (for example SQL Server 2000 to SQL Server 2000), nothing should really change. The on-page structure of the database will be intact after the move. You might notice performance issues if the server is not exactly the same (capacity, memory, RAID type on the disks). Why? Remember that your statistics, as well as execution plans, are based on a specific configuration. These are not changed or updated in the attach process to match the new server, so you need to ensure that after the database is attached, it performs and behaves as you expect it to.

If you use the detach and attach process or the Copy Database Wizard, which is based on that functionality, to upgrade from SQL Server 7.0 to SQL Server 2000, that is a fully supported method of migration. During the attach process, the database's metadata is upgraded to SQL Server 2000. However, the earlier caveat will become much more important: your statistics are not automatically rebuilt. Although SQL Server 2000 is built on the foundation started by SQL Server 7.0, the engine did change a bit in SQL Server 2000, so statistics that were generated under SQL Server 7.0 are invalid, meaning that the queries do not take advantage of the new optimizer. You should thus ensure that your execution plans and statistics are rebuilt based on the hardware you will now be running.

Take into account when detaching and attaching that your database will be unavailable during the entire process. You are literally detaching the file from SQL Server and can then make a copy, and so on, and then reattach the database after you have your copy. Once you have your copy, or if you plan on using that file and not making a backup, you can move it wherever you want as a function of time, bandwidth, and disk speed. The savings that you might gain in the attach process might therefore be negated by a copy time for a very large database over a WAN.

Tip   One of the keys to good performance with attaching and detaching (and subsequently the Copy Database Wizard) is to copy the files to a different set of disks. When copying from the same physical disk or stripe of disks to the same disk or stripe, you will spend most of your time seeking back and forth for the write location, and therefore your I/O performance will suffer a great deal.

Tip   Remember that you have the ability to use compression with a third-party tool to reduce the size of your files before you copy them over the network. You are in effect trading processor time on both ends for reduced network time in the middle. You also might want to try alternative copy programs such as xcopy or robocopy from the *Windows 2000 Resource Kit* if you have particularly large files to move around. Even if they do not move the data faster for your particular case, the ability to restart at the point at which you left off in the case of a disconnect or timeout can be invaluable.

Backup and restore was discussed in detail in Chapter 10. However, when comparing backup and restore to detaching and attaching a database, why should you consider it? First and foremost, it is tried and true (as is detach and attach at this point). Like the attach process, a restore upgrades a SQL Server 7.0 database when it is restored on an instance of SQL Server 2000. The main difference that you are likely to be concerned with is that statistics are rebuilt automatically during the restore process. All other things being equal, you have two excellent choices for ensuring your database is upgraded and restored on your SQL Server 2000 instance.

> **Note**   Keep in mind that server capacity and configuration on a different server affect your database, whether as the result of an attach or a restore. For example, SQL Server will keep the on-page structures, but if it is on a different disk subsystem (say, RAID 5 versus a striped mirror), your data access might have better (or possibly worse) performance.

Service Packs and Hotfixes

All systems need normal maintenance, which greatly increases your long-term availability. This means that from time to time you need to apply patches and upgrades. Many administrators would consider service packs to be normal maintenance, but in reality, they are a form of upgrade. A service pack for any Microsoft product is a collection of patches, bug fixes, and so on, collectively tested and released as one distribution. Some service packs might enhance functionality, and others might not. Hotfixes are different than an SQL Server 2000 service pack or a service pack for a version of Windows 2000 or Windows 2003 Server. A hotfix is exactly what it sounds like: an issue that needs to be addressed is detected. In this case a patch is made available for you to apply between service pack releases.

The following is a definition of critical hotfixes, which can be defined as those hotfixes that affect the following problems:

- Data is at risk of being corrupted.
- Data is at risk of being lost.
- Security is at risk of being compromised on the system.
- System crashes (blue screens) that are repeatable (same failure) and occur regularly.

- System hangs that are frequent (same criteria as for blue screens) and, if the Dump Switch, Service Processor, or Secure Admin Console is used to create a crash, the resulting dump file indicates a common cause (which would qualify as repeatable).

- System performance is at an unacceptable level, such as data transfers that take hours instead of minutes.

- The customer might have a system usage or configuration that is very similar to customers who have actually experienced one of these problems.

Keep these general rules in mind when applying any type of service pack or hotfix:

- Test, test some more, and then test again. You want to make absolutely sure that when you roll this out in production, you know how it is done and that you will have no problems in terms of compatibility or availability as a result. Create a standard set of tests that are run for base operating system functionality and for application functionality. Record these results for comparison after the upgrade is performed.

- Make backups of everything prior to applying the service pack or hotfix. Remember, system files such as DLLs and binaries are being changed. Should you need to go back to the state of your system if the installation does not work and cannot be backed out cleanly, having backups will save you. For a SQL Server service pack, back up all user databases and system databases before and after the upgrade.

- Make sure your system has enough disk space to meet the requirements of the upgrade. This is sometimes overlooked. You might have to unlock your resources (for example, a read-only database) to run the upgrade scripts or add new procedures.

- Again, as mentioned earlier, read all documentation that comes with the upgrade *carefully*. Do not apply and ask questions later; that could prove costly in both the short term and the long term.

- After the application of the upgrade, test everything thoroughly alone as well as under load. Use the same standard set of tests that are run during the testing phase for base operating system functionality and application functionality so that you can do a before–after comparison. This will, more often than not, tell you if the upgrade was a success or a failure.

- Once you are sure everything is okay, make full backups of your operating system and your databases so that you have a snapshot of a known, good post-upgrade configuration. Do not wait, because if something goes wrong, your backups might be older, and you will need to reapply any upgrades you just performed.

- In terms of all versions of Windows Datacenter Server, these systems are often strictly managed from the standpoint of installing updates, adding enhancements, and making other changes. There are a number of reasons for this, such as the customer having an SLA with another party (for example, an OEM). For this reason and others, it is necessary to have retest requirements for systems and drivers so that the risk of change and possible reliability decrease is mitigated.

  Datacenter Server customers occasionally require hotfixes. However, these should be infrequent and uncommon occurrences. You should apply hotfixes only when customers are actually experiencing problems, with some critical exceptions, as explained in this section.

> **Important**   Hotfixes should not be applied in a preventive manner, except when it is clear you need them based on known issues. In all other cases, if a Datacenter Server system is not exhibiting signs of a failure that is resolved by a hotfix, OEMs and independent software vendors should not recommend that the customer install the hotfix. Remember that this applies to the operating system layer; any support and hotfixes for applications installed on top of Windows Datacenter editions should be cleared for installation to ensure that you will not invalidate your OEM support agreements.

Emergency Hotfixes and Testing Requirements

In some rare cases you might need a fix immediately, even without the delay incurred from update testing. In general, it can be better for your availability to "work around" the problem instead of installing an untested kernel component. Note that because the provided file might be unsigned, the customer is notified in a pop-up message of that fact when the kernel component is installed.

In these cases, even if a hotfix is immediately required and testing cannot be accomplished before delivery to the customer, the responsible party should accomplish the testing as soon as possible to ensure the stability of the system. The driver should be submitted to Windows Update, if appropriate, only after this testing has occurred (see Figure 13-1).

Tip   If you are using Windows Update for operating system hotfixes and critical updates, you might want to disable automatic updates on a server that you want to be highly available to control what is installed. First and foremost, it might or might not be directly connected to the Internet. Second, if you choose to automatically download and apply all fixes that you have not tested, you might unknowingly affect your production server. If you enable automatic updates, the best thing to do would to be to have Windows Update notify you before downloading and installing updates.

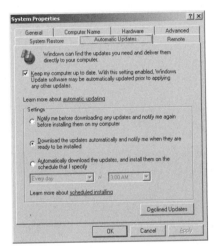

Figure 13-1   Automatic Updates screen in Windows.

More Info   For more information on putting a plan together for your production changes, see Chapters 1 and 2.

Applying a Windows Service Pack

Applying a service pack to your operating system will affect the availability of your SQL Server in one way or another whether it is clustered or not. A Windows service pack is applied per server, or specifically, per instance of Windows (if you have a multiboot system). On a stand-alone system, the process is straightforward in that you install it on the operating system and the server, and its functionality is unavailable during the whole process. Clustered systems are similar, yet different.

Windows Service Packs and Server Clusters

One significant difference between a stand-alone server and a server cluster in terms of an upgrade is that your environment can be a bit more available (depending on how you have things configured). Because a Windows service pack is done per installation of Windows, in an *N*-node cluster, you will hopefully have *N* − *1* nodes still completely up and available (assuming no other problems). Because of this, you use a process similar to that of a rolling upgrade of the operating system. First, notify users that the clustered process (such as SQL Server) will be unavailable at certain specific times. You can then manually fail the resources over to another node and start servicing requests again. At the same time, you can also be upgrading node 1. However, here is where your planning comes into place. If you planned your system resource usage properly, you should have no performance impact after a failover, and there should be no need to cause another availability interruption by failing the resources back (or to yet another node) until you are going to upgrade the other nodes in the cluster.

> **Note**   At the time of the writing of this book, no information about Windows Server 2003 Service Packs was available, so all information is based on Windows 2000.

Applying a SQL Server 2000 Service Pack

Before applying a SQL Server 2000 service pack, you need to understand how it works for both clustered and nonclustered environments. As you know, a single server or a server cluster running SQL Server 2000 supports up to 16 instances per operating system installation. Each installation has some dedicated binaries, as well as a set of shared binaries (including MDAC). The binaries for each instance are usually found on the drive you selected during installation under \Program Files\Microsoft SQL Server. Under that directory, you will find an \80 directory containing any shared binaries for all instances not installed under your Windows directories. You will find the dedicated binaries for a default instance in the \Mssql directory, and you will find the dedicated binaries for a named instance in the \Mssql$*instance_name* directory. What does all of this background mean to you? Microsoft fully supports, should you have multiple instances of SQL Server 2000, a mixed service pack environment. However, consider the ramifications of such an environment: whenever you apply a service pack, you upgrade any shared binaries. So, for example, if you have two instances of SQL Server both at Service Pack 2, and then upgrade one, you now have one at Service Pack 3, one at Service Pack 2, with shared binaries at the Service Pack 3 level. Going back to the idea that everything affects everything, although this is fully supported from a Microsoft standpoint, make sure that it is supported by any third-party software vendors you are using. It also complicates any plan to roll back an environment to a previous version. If your installation of a service pack on one instance fails, and you install, for example, the RTM version of SQL Server 2000, you will have potentially downgraded your shared components until you upgrade to the right patch or service pack level.

A SQL Server 2000 service pack is applied per instance, so if you have five instances, you will have to run the installation process five times. There is no way to install them all at once with one process. You generally only have to reboot after the first one because there are locked files (by the operating system) that require the reboot to upgrade, and files that were not locked before will probably not be locked now, or the files will already have been upgraded and therefore be skipped by the installation. On nonclustered instances, you can script the installation of a SQL Server 2000 service pack.

When a SQL Server 2000 service pack is installed, a log file is created under your Windows installation directory, such as C:\Windows. If there has been more than one execution of a SQL Server 2000 service pack install, the log files are numbered sequentially, such as Sqlsp1.log, Sqlsp2.log, and so on.

> **Note**   There are separate service packs for SQL Server 2000 (including Standard Edition, Enterprise Edition, and Developer Edition), SQL Server 2000 Desktop Engine (MSDE 2000), and SQL Server 2000 Analysis Services. You might need to get different versions of the service pack and apply each of them separately depending on what is installed on your server.
>
> Although there are no 64-bit SQL Server 2000 service packs as of the publication of this edition of the book, the 32-bit and 64-bit service packs should behave the same. If the behavior winds up being different for some reason under the 64-bit version, it will be documented in the information that comes with the service pack and in Knowledge Base articles.

> **Important**   You must install SQL Server 2000 Service Pack 3 (or later) for SQL Server 2000 to work with Windows Server 2003.
>
> Installing a SQL Server 2000 service pack is a *permanent option* for a SQL Server instance. There is no way to revert to the previous version of SQL Server without a complete reinstall from an installation point or CD-ROM, which obviously causes an availability problem. However, keep in mind that rolling back could destroy other things like MDAC versions that were upgraded in the interim and needed for an application, so you must keep track of everything done to the server so that you can put the server back in the state you need it to be in for your applications.

Failover Clustering and SQL Server 2000 Service Packs

Applying SQL Server 2000 service packs is not the same as applying a service pack to a clustered server running SQL Server 7.0. The older process for SQL Server 7.0 involved using a wizard to uncluster SQL Server 7.0. You would then apply the service pack and recluster. It was an awkward procedure at best, and it caused problems for some. With a SQL Server 2000 service pack, as with the main installation process, the service pack is cluster-aware. It will detect that it is going to be applied to a virtual server.

However, there is no concept of a rolling upgrade as there is with the operating system, so SQL Server is unavailable during the entire operation. During the installation process, the installer will then proceed to not only upgrade the database, but all binaries *on each node* defined for that specific virtual server. Therefore, you run the service pack install once and have it applied to all nodes. You do not run the service pack install on each node; however there is *one (and only one)* exception to that rule: should you encounter a catastrophic failure on one node and have to rebuild it (see Chapter 5, "Designing Highly Available Microsoft Windows Servers," and Chapter 6, "Microsoft SQL Server 2000 Failover Clustering," for details), you do not have to rerun the setup to patch all nodes. You can just patch the newly repaired node. This is possible because when the node is added back into the SQL virtual server definition, a registry key of need_sp_key is added to the newly rebuilt node, indicating it needs to have a service pack applied to it. You can now run the SQL Server 2000 service pack installation on the node, and Setup checks for need_sp_key and proceeds to update the binaries on that node only because the databases were already updated. This also allows you to fully service requests from applications or clients because SQL Server 2000 is not put into single-user mode. On the new node you are updating, you will see some entries in the Sqlsp.log file that will look similar to the following:

```
[args]
NumRemoteServers=1
Server.1=<newnodename>
[Server.1]
NumRemoteServices=1
...
```

These entries confirm that the unattended setup processes are running on the one node only. From a GUI standpoint, you will see the standard "Setup Is Performing Required Operations On ..." messages, but behind the scenes, it is doing the right thing.

> **Caution**   If you rerun the SQL Server 2000 service pack installation from the node currently owning the SQL Server resources and not the failed ones added back into the SQL virtual server definition, you will then be reapplying the service pack to all nodes defined for the SQL virtual server. This should be seen as a potential risk, as you have one or more perfectly functioning nodes that are now being affected. Make sure before you start the process that you are on the right node!

> **Warning**   Due to file replacements that need to be registered, the first installation of a SQL Server 2000 service pack usually requires a reboot of all nodes. Once you do this, unless there is some other requirement for a reboot in the service pack, all other instances on the cluster that have the service pack applied should not need a reboot because the shared files are already installed and registered. You can check the HKLM\CCS\Control\Microsoft\Session Manager\PendingFileRenames registry key for a list. By stopping whatever services were using these files before running the upgrade you might avoid the reboot in the future, but perform this procedure with caution. It might just be best to do the reboot. Again, test before doing it in your production environment.

Log Shipping and SQL Server 2000 Service Packs

If you employ log shipping, you must also understand the impact of a SQL Server 2000 service pack. First and foremost, a service pack upgrade does not break log shipping. Setup automatically detects user databases (as well as filegroups) that are not able to be written to and skip those. Because a database that is being log shipped on a secondary is either in NORECOVERY or STANDBY, it cannot be written to or updated. These skipped databases are documented in the Sqlsp.log file mentioned earlier. The following message is also displayed during the process:

```
Setup has detected one or more databases and filegroups which are not writable.
```

It is fully supported to log ship from any version of SQL Server (RTM, Service Pack 1, Service Pack 2, and Service Pack 3 as of the writing of this book) to another because there are no metadata changes that would affect log shipping. If there were to be any metadata changes to the user databases themselves in future service packs, this might require you to have all databases at the same service pack level. Read the documentation that ships with the service pack to see if there are any user database metadata changes that are included.

You should, however, consider service pack upgrades to an instance of SQL Server if your primary is at one level and your secondary is at another.

Important   If you recover a database from secondary status to be the active database servicing requests, you do not need to reapply the SQL Server 2000 service pack to it unless there are metadata changes that would affect the database in question (as noted earlier). This would be clearly documented in whatever comes with the update. The one exception to this rule is if you are using replication and use the keep_replication flag when bringing the database online. Once the database is fully recovered, before opening it up to users and applications, run the stored procedure sp_vupgrade_replication to upgrade the replication metadata. If you do not do this, the replication metadata for that database will be out of sync. If running sp_vupgrade_replication is not necessary, it will be noted in the accompanying documentation.

> **Warning**   Do not apply any SQL Server 2000 service pack prior to Service Pack 2 on a log shipped server. Service Pack 1 would not apply successfully on a server that had databases that could not be written to.

Replication and SQL Server 2000 Service Packs

Replication and SQL Server 2000 service packs are a bit more complicated a combination than log shipping or failover clustering. The order in which you upgrade your instances participating in a replication chain absolutely matters, specifically:

- Distributor has to be upgraded before Publisher. If Publisher and Distributor are on the same instance of SQL Server, this is not a concern, as they will be upgraded together.

- If you are using transactional replication with some read-only Subscribers (that is, they do not participate in replication other than receiving data), the Subscriber can be upgraded before or after you do Publisher and Distributor, so order does not matter for the Subscriber in this case.

- If you are using merge or transactional replication with updating Subscribers (that is, they replicate data elsewhere), you must update the Subscriber after you update Distributor and then Publisher. The order in this case would be Distributor, Publisher, and then all Subscribers.

> **Tip**   In this case, if you have a database that, for example, is a read-only subscriber for one publication but the source for another chain of replication servers, you must know your hierarchy so that you upgrade everything in the proper order.

- If you are using a remote distributor with merge replication, you need to generate a new snapshot after applying SQL Server 2000 Service Pack 3. This might affect the availability of some servers, so you must plan for it.

■   As noted in many places, back up all databases participating in replication after the application of the service pack. This will ensure that you will not have to reapply the service pack if you need to restore the database.

> **Important**   Heed the information in the previous section on log shipping about databases that are recovered and running `sp_vupgrade_replication`. This also applies to purely read-only databases, which are covered in the next section.

Applying a SQL Server Service Pack to a Nonwritable Database or Filegroup

There are cases where you literally have a read-only database (such as in replication) or one that is used for reporting but needs to be upgraded (that is, it is a Subscriber) to the latest service pack. Because read-only databases are skipped in the service pack install for SQL Server, these need to be upgraded. To accomplish this task, follow these steps prior to applying the service pack or after, depending on your needs. It is better to do it beforehand so that you have only one availability outage and not multiple outages:

Nonwritable Database

1.   Alter the state of the database that needs to be modified to make it writable. You can either clear the Read-Only option in the Options tab of the database Properties dialog box or run the following Transact-SQL statement:

    ```
    ALTER DATABASE database_name SET READ_WRITE
    ```

2.   Repeat step 1 for each read-only database on that instance that should be upgraded.

3.   Apply (or reapply) the service pack.

4.   Reselect the Read-Only option, or run the following Transact-SQL statement for each database to make it read-only again:

    ```
    ALTER DATABASE database_name SET READ_ONLY
    ```

Nonwritable Filegroup

1. Alter the state of the filegroup that needs to be modified to make it writable. Run the following Transact-SQL statement:

```
ALTER DATABASE database_name MODIFY FILEGROUP filegroup_name READ
WRITE
```

2. Repeat Step 1 for each read-only filegroup on that instance that should be upgraded.

3. Apply (or reapply) the service pack.

4. Run the following Transact-SQL statement for each database to make it read-only again:

```
ALTER DATABASE database_name MODIFY FILEGROUP filegroup_name READONLY
```

Hotfixes

Hotfixes are ultimately added, in most cases, to the next major service pack. Should you apply a hotfix when it is released? Do you avoid the hotfix? The answer is not clear cut. Not all hotfixes apply to you, so you have to read any relevant Knowledge Base articles. Like anything else, assess the risk and reward of applying the hotfix. Be aware that because they are essentially one-off fixes, and, because of their critical nature, hotfixes might not undergo the rigorous months of regression testing that, say, a service pack is subjected to. They fix a problem, but in doing so, they might affect other applications or processes running on the server.

In addition to individual hotfixes, often bundles or rollups of hotfixes are released from time to time. For example, a common rollup would be security fixes that are wrapped together. These packages sometimes receive additional testing before release to help address some of the more common issues at that moment. Security is very important, of course, and putting off the testing and deployment of these patches could cost you the server, its data, and—in a worst-case scenario—potentially even your job. Finding the correct middle ground between testing and deployment is the only safe way to proceed.

> **Note** As of the release of this book, Microsoft policy is to support the creation of hotfixes on the previous service pack for 60 days after the current service pack ships. For example, hotfixes of any nature (security, bug, and so on) can be made for up to 60 days after SQL Server 2000 Service Pack 3 is released specifically for SQL Server 2000 Service Pack 2.

> **Note** Keep in mind that the next service pack will also contain other enhancements or fixes that might not have been released as a patch for the version of the service pack that you have installed. Once the new service pack is released, you should test your applications against it and upgrade as soon as possible. If you cannot upgrade for other reasons, such as those that are business-related (for example, a third-party application must be certified with it otherwise you will invalidate your support contract), evaluate these situations and take the appropriate actions to ensure that you can upgrade to the latest service pack.
>
> You will be supported on whatever version of a service pack you are using as long as the platform itself is in active support; you just might not be able to get new patches for it. If this policy changes for future service packs, such as when SQL Server 2000 Service Pack 4 is released, please check *http://support.microsoft.com* or consult a Microsoft support professional about the policy for hotfixes and service packs.

Summary

Achieving a highly available upgrade is a challenge for even the best IT shops. Everything about upgrades is ultimately a function of time. Upgrades, highly available or not, require a great deal of planning and testing before you actually implement them in your production environment. Remember to take into account any SLAs when you are planning your upgrades, as there is always a chance that you might not achieve them should the upgrade require you to be down longer than the time allotted in the SLA itself.

Doing your homework should pay off. If no one notices any functionality differences after the upgrade and downtime is minimal, this provides the best situation possible for everyone involved. If you do not do your homework, it could mean a great deal of both short-term and long-term pain. Upgrades of any sort should never be taken lightly. Mitigate your risks and, whenever possible, upgrade to completely new hardware so that your old environments provide the perfect fallback plan.

Part V

Administering Highly Available Microsoft SQL Servers

14
Administrative Tasks for High Availability

Like the human body, Microsoft SQL Server needs care. When the body gets the right nutrition, sleep, and exercise, it performs at a higher level. If you ignore your body's needs, you are at a higher risk of developing problems. Proactive administration of your SQL Servers is like daily exercise: your systems will tend to live longer and stay healthier. The topics in this chapter are there for a reason: in most cases they are not about only the administration of one particular technology related to SQL Server. This chapter addresses security, memory, transferring objects, and normal maintenance tasks, such as rebuilding indexes.

> **Note** Although monitoring is an administrative task, it is covered in its own chapter, Chapter 15, "Monitoring for High Availability." Performance is also an administrative task and is related to availability. For more information, see HA_Perf_And_Scale.doc, available on the CD.

> **On the CD** Examples of the automated tasks run internally in some parts of Microsoft can be found on the CD in DBAScripts.zip.

Security

The most basic—and arguably the most important—thing you can do from an administrative standpoint is to secure your Microsoft SQL Server 2000 instances. Beyond the obvious steps of putting your servers in racks, locking cases, and physically securing data centers (all of which were discussed in Chapter 2, "The Basics of Achieving High Availability"), how can you specifically secure things at the operating system and SQL Server layers? You need to address multiple threats. A few years ago it might have been good enough to throw up a firewall and make sure that your SQL Server was isolated. Unfortunately, the game has changed. Worms, viruses, and denial of service attacks—some of which are directed at your database, others of which are not—can compromise your data's security.

When a Web site pops up on the evening news in a story about how it was hacked, it is a glaring example of how something can be compromised. But how do you measure what was compromised—especially sensitive data? Because many systems now access both internal and external systems, the potential for someone gaining unauthorized access increases dramatically unless you have dedicated security professionals making sure that you are protected. There have recently been cases where hackers have broken into an e-commerce site or into a bank and compromised large numbers of credit cards. Or think about the recent rash of identity theft. Do not assume it cannot happen to you or your systems. As important as your platform's availability is, it is your data's availability and security that you are really protecting. However, the reality is that sometimes security and availability do not always play nicely together in the sandbox, and you might have to make tradeoffs one way or the other.

Securing Your SQL Server Installations

You can do several things to ensure that your physical SQL Server installations are secure.

- Do not use a blank or weak sa password. For obvious reasons, this can compromise your SQL Servers. Even before SQL Server 2000, it was a common practice in testing or development environments to use the SQL Server's sa account with no password in testing or development environments. The unfortunate thing is that the practice followed into production and was never altered.

- Passwords for all accounts—whether or not they are SQL Server and from system administrators on down to users—should not be weak passwords. Since there is no direct way to enforce stronger passwords, a weak or a blank password can be a problem if you configure your instance to only use SQL Server security. The recommended approach is to set SQL Server to use Microsoft Windows Authentication and to require your applications to use it as well. This allows you control at the Windows level. For example, you can create a group in Windows and place users in it. In SQL Server, you can then assign a login to that group and add that login as a user to a database. Now, when you want to have someone gain access to the database, your administrators can do it in a standard way. In addition, you can force your Windows users to change passwords on a periodic basis, you can enforce strong passwords, and you can take other measures to ensure that you are protecting your data.

> **Important** Even if you use Windows Authentication, you must still set a strong password for the sa user. If you just select Windows Authentication, the sa user still exists in SQL Server, but a password is not set. Also, if you later change to Mixed, you might need to use sa.

- The service accounts used in your environments, especially ones for SQL Server, should not have unneeded privileges, nor should SQL Server share the same account (with the same password) with every other application on the server. This means that the use of accounts like LocalSystem or a domain administrator is strongly discouraged. That way, if someone accesses your SQL Server, that person cannot then turn around and use something like xp_cmdshell to attack the rest of your environment.

- Install SQL Server only on NTFS partitions.

- Never install SQL Server 2000 instances on a domain controller unless it is absolutely necessary. Doing so might expose your data to attackers who can gain escalated user permissions through some other method.

- Stay abreast of security patches, hotfixes, and service packs. As noted in Chapter 13, you should evaluate all updates to see if they need to be installed; if they enhance your security, apply them!

- Where possible, set your SQL Server instances only to Windows Authentication, sometimes known as Integrated Security. Doing so permits centralized account management and the use of other protocols such as Kerberos. If you use SQL Server authentication, use

Secure Sockets Layer (SSL), at a minimum, to encrypt the login packets as well as strong passwords (which you must enforce yourself). Never use blank passwords.

■ Turn on auditing in SQL Server. Although this might cause overhead, you can track failed login attempts and then take care of the problem. This is done by setting the Audit Level in the Security tab of your server properties, which is shown in Figure 14-1. Setting it to Success records successful logins. Failure records unsuccessful logins. Setting it to All records both.

> **Note** Turning on the auditing feature will cause you to cycle your SQL Server, causing an availability outage.

■ You are strongly advised to use Enterprise Manager to change your service accounts, as there are file system and registry dependencies that go along with a change in service accounts. You do this in two places:

❑ **SQL Server service account** You change this in the Security tab of your instance's properties.

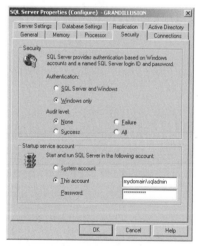

Figure 14-1 Security tab of Properties.

❑ **SQL Server Agent service account** You change this in the General tab of the SQL Server Agent (see Figure 14-2), which is in the Management folder in Enterprise Manager.

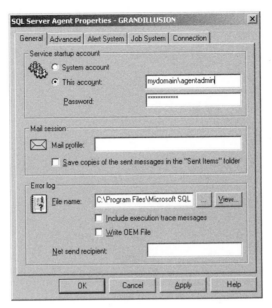

Figure 14-2   The General tab of SQL Server Agent Properties.

If you do not change the passwords in the recommended way in Enterprise Manager, it might be possible to use the Services utility. The problem is that doing it there will not reset the correct registry keys or NTFS permissions in all cases. For a full list of what you would have to alter after using Services, see Knowledge Base article 283811, "HOW TO: Change the SQL Server Service Account Without Using SQL Enterprise Manager in SQL Server 2000" (available at *http://support.microsoft.com/*).

Warning   You can use only the Windows-level Services utility to change password accounts on nonclustered SQL Server instances.

Important   Changing your service account passwords will require you to stop and start the associated SQL Server services. So you must plan for this availability outage.

- Use Server Network Utility to change the port to a static port that is known only to you. By default, the first instance installed on your server or cluster will try to take port 1433, which is a known port for SQL Server and can potentially be exploited. To access Server Network Utility, you can find it in the Microsoft SQL Server folder of the Programs menu. Once it is started, select your instance in the drop-down list, select TCP in the Enabled protocols list, and then click Properties. You can then modify the port number (see Figure 14-3).

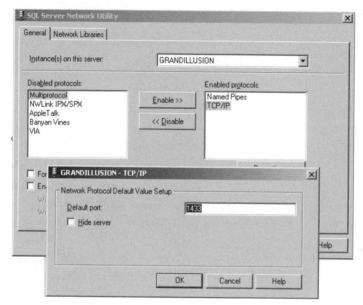

Figure 14-3 Modifying your port.

> **Important** Two instances on the same server cannot share the same port number. If you are using a version of the Microsoft Data Access Components (MDAC) prior to MDAC 2.6, you might need to physically put this port number in the connection string, as it will not be 1433.

- Avoid using User Datagram Protocol (UDP) port 1434 at a firewall if possible. This is the SQL Server listener.

- Use the Microsoft Baseline Security Analyzer (*http://www.microsoft.com/technet/security/tools/Tools/mbsahome.asp*) to help you assess your environment, including SQL Server. It will scan for known things such as blank sa passwords, file and registry permissions, exposure of xp_cmdshell to users who are not system administrators, and more. Version 1.1 or later supports multiple instances of SQL Server.

- Do not configure unnecessary features, tools, and utilities, and do not install more software on your SQL Server machine than you need to.

- Never change the default permissions on xp_cmdshell. Restrict the people who can have access to this extended stored procedure by not configuring users as system administrators.

- Never allow anyone to access your SQL Servers directly. Using a method such as Terminal Server will allow you not only to see who is logging into the machine, but also to prevent physical access to the server.

- You can use SQL Profiler to audit events. For information on how to do this, see SQL Server Books Online, available with the SQL Server installation.

- Scan and remove logins with NULL passwords. On a regular basis, evaluate and remove old and unused logins; this might prevent unauthorized access.

- Make sure that when you are assigning roles, you trust the user that you are giving privileges to. Although this seems obvious, the point is to put thought into what roles you assign to users.

- Secure your startup procedures.

- Always verify your file and registry key permissions, as outlined in the earlier Knowledge Base article 283811.

- After you install a service pack or an instance (or something else), passwords might be exposed in the installation or log files. To scan those files and remove any potential offending exposures, Microsoft Product Support Services (PSS) has a tool called KillPwd that you can download from *http://download.microsoft.com/download/ SQLSVR2000/Utility/2.0/W98NT42KMeXP/EN-US/killpwd.exe*. For instructions on its use, consult Knowledge Base article 263968, "FIX: Service Pack Installation May Save Standard Security Password in File."

- SQL Server supports the encryption of your file system. As of Windows Server 2003, it is also supported with SQL Server 2000 failover clustering. Using it will decrease the chance of someone using a text tool to read your data or backup files, but you must account for any system overhead incurred.

- You can enable C2 security with SQL Server 2000 if it is necessary.

More Info   To see how to use C2 with SQL Server 2000, see the "SQL Server 2000 C2 Administrator's and User's Security Guide" at *http://www.microsoft.com/technet/treeview/default.asp?url=/technet/prodtechnol/sql/maintain/security/sqlc2.asp*.

Securing Your SQL Server–Based Applications

As a database administrator (DBA), or as someone who will be performing database-related tasks, whether you like it or not, you are responsible for every application's database in your environment. Although you might control the back end, developers control the front end. It is in your best interests to validate custom database-specific code and ensure that packaged applications will work with your security model. Here are some tips to consider:

■ When coming up with the architecture for your application, how will you access the database? You have essentially three options: flowing the user to the database, using a single Windows context to the database, and using a single connection to the database using SQL Server authentication.

If you use flowing, all machines must be part of the same domain or be trusted, Kerberos and delegation must be enabled, and impersonation must be enabled in ASP.NET. This will allow you to enforce security for SQL Server and audit all user actions. If, however, you have external components (such as outside vendors accessing the application), this might not be feasible, and connection pooling is limited since you cannot share connections.

If you use Windows Authentication, run ASP.NET as a nondomain administrator. The users would authenticate at the application component, and the connection to the database is made in the context of the ASP.NET account (usually ASPNET user). This account should not have a system administrator role in SQL Server. With this method, you do not have to store passwords or pass any credentials to SQL Server, connection pooling is possible, and running ASP.NET as a low privileged account will minimize risk.

If you are using SQL Server authentication, the application is using SQL Server to authenticate your login. You now need to ensure that all logins have the correct privileges at the SQL-level and to force users to enter strong passwords. You can use secure credentials at the middle tier using data protection application programming interfaces (APIs) to encrypt the credentials, which means that only that account can decrypt. The problem with this method is that you now need to store credentials, and SQL Server authentication, by its nature, might not be as secure as Windows Authentication. But you can work across firewalls and nontrusted domains and use connection pooling. If you do not have a specific limitation in your application, it is highly recommended that you design and deploy using Windows Authentication to grant user access and privileges.

- If your company is writing an application (or has hired contractors to write one), make sure that they have the skill and experience to implement your company's security policies through the use of things like correctly privileged logins and roles. No single user should be doing everything in the application. At the very least, you should have a separate user and administrator account. Since many developers install SQL Server on their machines, they incorrectly assume that all database access requires credentials equivalent to a highly privileged administrator.

- Some developers might hardcode the sa user directly into the application, which is not only bad for security, but which also might hurt you if you need to use another server for a warm standby. Do not allow a developer to hardcode passwords, ever!

- For a security model, Windows Authentication should be your first choice, if possible. Because the control is now at the network level, not in the application, your application is, by default, easier to secure. Passwords are stored in one place (at the domain controller), and you can combine Windows Authentication with some sort of encryption to secure your connections. Active Directory directory service can assist you in centrally managing your passwords.

- If possible, use some form of encryption (Internet Protocol Security [IPSec], SSL, Kerberos, or other forms of encryption, such as data encryption with third-party tools like Protegrity) in your application or database. If you are doing things like passing credit card numbers, performing online bank transactions, sending Social Security numbers, and doing other sensitive operations across a network, you do not want to transmit these as clear text in an HTML stream that could be sniffed or found in a log somewhere.

- Know your connection method. If you do your best to encrypt data, but your underlying protocol winds up sending passwords and SQL statements through text, you need to mitigate this somehow by using another form of encryption like SSL, IPSec, or Kerberos to encrypt the connection as well as the underlying data access protocol.

■ When designing the schema, make sure that roles, and not users, own all objects. If, for some reason, the user is dropped or renamed, you will not have any issues of access to the object.

■ Use ownership chaining to mask or hide the actual schema by using views and stored procedures, and not direct SQL statements, to go against base tables in your database. If the object and the user calling it have the same owner, the underlying permissions check is skipped. This not only makes your code secure, but more efficient. Consider the following example:

You have an Orders table in your sales database created by User1. To access it, User2 creates a stored procedure to retrieve data from the table, which also includes some potentially sensitive information. If User3 tries to execute User2's stored procedure, SQL Server will check both the execute permissions for the procedure as well as the SELECT permissions on the underlying table created by User1. However, if you created the stored procedure with User1 and granted execute permissions to User3, since User1 is the owner of both the table and the stored procedure, only one permissions check is needed.

■ Perform code reviews to ensure that the code is safe to implement (like making sure your application is available and scalable, among other things). A code review should be a formalized, regular process. Similarly, your company should develop coding standards that can govern the creation of code.

■ Developers will often put debugging code used for testing or messages into the application that might be accidentally exposed or be too technically informative to an end user. You should remove the information that is presented (such as account names, passwords, Internet Protocol [IP] addresses) prior to rolling the application out in production.

■ The application should also disallow any ad hoc queries. A savvy person might use a text field he or she knows is issued as part of a SQL statement and use it to do something malicious. You should validate all user input and reject anything that does not meet the standards of your company's security policy. Along the same lines, if you can, attempt to avoid using dynamic SQL statements within a stored procedure.

- Although focusing on code is important, developers need to also think about how the application could be compromised through something like a denial-of-service attack or exposing problems (publicly known or not yet known) through standard interfaces. For example, if a hacker gains access to your Web server, that person might now have access to your entire enterprise. How you have your security model will determine how far the hacker will be able to get. To combat this, ensure that your operations people who are doing monitoring know how to interpret a seemingly harmless blip on the monitor.

Maintenance

Besides backup and restore, there are other tasks that you will need to do from time to time. These will largely involve maintaining your indexes for performance and routine maintenance using DBCC commands. However, some of these maintenance tasks can be intrusive. By *intrusive*, it is meant that it might affect performance, availability, or both.

Table 14-1 shows a list of what to run and what the best practices are for running these commands so that there is minimal impact on online processing.

Table 14-1   Routine Maintenance Commands

DBCC	Note
CHECKDB, CHECKALLOC, CHECKFILE-GROUP, and CHECKTABLE	Does not block updates, with recommended parameters
DBREINDEX (nonclustered index)	Shared lock (used to take an exclusive in previous versions)
SHOWCONTIG	Has an option not to take a shared lock on the base table
DBREINDEX (heap)	Exclusive lock
UPDATEUSAGE	Shared lock
CHECKCONSTRAINTS	Shared lock
DBCC INDEXDEFRAG	Runs while database is fully operational

DBCC CHECK (CHECKDB, CHECKALLOC, CHECKFILEGROUP, and CHECKTABLE) and DBCC INDEXDEFRAG can each be run online without blocking updates, but they do prevent log truncations while running. The impact is minimal when you use the recommended settings. You still have to understand the impact these have on your system. You also should weigh different options and carefully consider what you are getting out of the process.

Perform regular updates to your index schema or statistics. Your goal is to find out how long everything takes, and then decide which action will provide the best benefit. (You can create scripts that keep track of the time elapsed during any maintenance task you do on a regular basis.) Be sure to review the documentation for these traditional maintenance tasks thoroughly before you use them in SQL Server 2000; they have undergone significant improvement and enhancement specifically for the purpose of supporting online maintenance. You cannot use the same cost/benefit grid as you did for Microsoft SQL Server 6.5 or Microsoft SQL Server 7.0.

Calculating the Cost of Maintenance

You might find that your tasks (some or all) are so lightweight (good examples of this include DBCC CHECKDB with the PHYSICAL_ONLY option or DBCC INDEXDEFRAG) that you notice only a minor effect on performance during the scan.

On the other hand, if you drop and recreate an index, the build process will perform faster than a DBCC INDEXDEFRAG (especially if you have Microsoft SQL Server 2000 Enterprise Edition and you take advantage of the parallel index builds). But there is a cost: if it is a vital index, you will still see performance degradation until it is rebuilt, and if it is a clustered index, your data is completely unavailable while the index is rebuilt. In most cases, use the lightweight DBCC INDEXDEFRAG, which might take a little more time to complete because it runs without interfering as much with online processing.

Table 14-2 provides some tips about planning and running these medium impact commands. Run these as a SQL Profiler script on your test server and get a baseline of its performance. Then run each maintenance task and record the results. Compare them to the original and begin to put together a plan for maintenance and administration.

Table 14-2   Medium Impact Commands

Process	Impact	Recommendation
UPDATE STATISTICS	Depends on usage of the command. The higher the sample ratio, the more of an impact this will have. Monitor your system carefully to determine optimal usage.	Use autocreate and autoupdate where possible. (Test this before changing your system's setting.) In high transaction volume systems or any situation where autostats are not used, explicitly update statistics on specific tables at scheduled times. The higher the sample ratio, the more useful your statistics will be, but the longer it will take to build them.
DBCC SHOWCONTIG	Minimal (with the WITH FAST option).	Use this to help you determine if decreasing query performance is linked to fragmentation.
DBCC INDEXDEFRAG	Minimal (system transactions), no blocking.	If you determine you have fragmentation, this is one method you can use to defragment your indexes.
DBCC CHECKDB Note: CHECKDB includes CHECKALLOC	Minimal with PHYSICAL_ONLY, NO_INFOMESSAGES; uses log analysis to get transactional consistency; makes heavy use of CPU and tempdb.	Corruption in the database stems primarily from problems at the hardware layer. Run this periodically and before and after upgrades or hardware changes. Do not run simultaneously with other CPU and disk-intensive tasks.

Another potential problem is any need to truncate and refresh a table in the production system. You can create two tables and alternate between them.

This is just one example, but you can introduce many design changes to make sure that services are not interrupted. The following is a brief history of how things have changed:

- In SQL Server version 6.5, CHECKALLOC had to run offline to avoid spurious errors. In SQL Server 7.0, you could run it with read-only access.

- From SQL Server 7.0 on, CHECKDB, CHECKALLOC, CHECKFILE-GROUP, and CHECKTABLE all became fully online operations.

- A nonclustered index rebuild only takes an S lock on the base table. It used to take an exclusive lock.

Intrusive Maintenance

Some maintenance operations are more intrusive than others. By intrusive, it is meant that a table, or possibly the entire database, will be unavailable while the command is running. Notable ones include create index, rebuild index, full update statistics (auto update statistics does not cover all customer scenarios), and restore database. Customers must plan for these intrusions.

Table 14-3 provides some tips about planning and running these processes should you decide to run them; you should try less intrusive versions before running some of these commands.

Table 14-3   Intrusive Maintenance Commands

Process	Recommendation
UPDATE STATISTICS FULLSCAN	Use autocreate and autoupdate where possible. (Always test changes prior to implementing in production.) In high transaction volume systems, or any situation where autostats are not used, explicitly update statistics on specific tables at scheduled times. The higher the sample ratio, the more useful your statistics will be, but the longer it will take to build them.
DBCC SHOWCONTIG WITH TABLERE-SULTS, ALL_INDEXES	Again, another variation of SHOWCONTIG that can help you determine if you have fragmentation and are seeing poorly performing queries.
DBCC CHECKDB with options other than physical_only Note: CHECKDB includes CHECKALLOC	As with CHECKDB described earlier, this can help you determine things about possible corruption, but if you check more than PHYSICAL_ONLY, this might take some time. Do only as directed by PSS, so as to not cause availability problems.

Table 14-3   Intrusive Maintenance Commands

Process	Recommendation
DBCC DBREINDEX clustered index WITH NO_INFOMSGS or DROP/CREATE INDEX	Do this during the lowest levels of usage. This should be a very infrequent process, and it is covered here because of its former prominence. DBREINDEX is more optimized than drop/create index. Use the white paper mentioned in "Defragmenting Indexes" later in this chapter to determine if you need to run DBREINDEX.
DBCC SHOWCONTIG WITH TABLERESULTS, ALL_INDEXES	Using TABLERESULTS or ALL_INDEXES may take some time, depending on the results.

Defragmenting Indexes

Defragmenting indexes, whether small or large, might become a problem for you at some point. You do have a few options, but you need to weigh them carefully. All of them will have some impact on your system. The size of your database will definitely affect index defragmentation, since the larger the database is, the more complex the solution has to be.

> **More Info**   An excellent resource on defragmenting indexes is the white paper "Microsoft SQL Server 2000 Index Defragmentation Best Practices," which is located at *http://www.microsoft.com/technet/treeview/default.asp?url=/technet/prodtechnol/sql/maintain/Optimize/SS2KIDBP.asp*. Use this section as a primer, but this white paper should be your main guide.

Before you even attempt to defragment an index, you need to determine if you have fragmentation and if you need to actually do something about it. This is documented in the white paper.

If you need to defragment your indexes, one thing you could choose to do is to run a DBCC INDEXDEFRAG, but it might not be optimal for you. It can only defragment a single index. It can span files, but it only does one file at a time if you are using file sand filegroups, although you have to issue only one command. DBCC INDEXDEFRAG is an online operation, which means that you do not have to worry about users affecting the defragmentation process.

DBCC DBREINDEX can rebuild a single or even all indexes for one table. However, it is an offline operation—that is, the underlying tables will be unavailable for use while the DBREINDEX is happening, and you cannot generate any transaction log backups. Its advantage over an explicit DROP INDEX and CREATE INDEX is that you can rebuild indexes enforcing PRIMARY KEY or UNIQUE constraints without worrying about needing to recreate the constraints manually. Statistics are also rebuilt automatically and DBREINDEX will use multiple processors if they are available. You will also need to account for disk space during a DBREINDEX operation.

> **More Info**   The white paper mentioned in the previous reader aid has a good comparison of the two options.

Logical vs. Physical Fragmentation

Logical fragmentation means that you have a fragmented SQL Server file internally where the data is stored but that the physical file on the file system is not fragmented. Your data can also be logically fragmented if you do many inserts and deletes. If your data is fragmented, you will need to find some way to compact your data so that it is contiguous and not fragmented. DBCC SHRINKDATABASE can shrink the database, but it is not coded to know about or reduce fragmentation; it only compacts things. DBCC SHRINKDATABASE will shrink a database even if it spans multiple files. Physical fragmentation can also occur if you are using your server for multiple applications and each one is using the same disk(s).

Physical fragmentation at the disk level can occur for SQL Server. With releases prior to SQL Server 7.0 that could not automatically grow, you physically had to create additional segments for your data or log. This could cause physical fragmentation over time. Now, with SQL Server 7.0 and SQL Server 2000, you can allow your databases to grow or shrink automatically, but you need to realize that these two can cause physical fragmentation at the disk level since you are expanding or shrinking your database files, or both.

This is directly related to placement of your data and log files. If you place all your files on the same spindle, your growth will occur on each database and expand (or contract, if shrinking) to the next available disk block(s). Over time, this can fragment your files. This is one good reason to place your disk files onto separate spindles. If you encounter severe physical fragmentation, you will have to consider defragmenting at the file system level. If you choose to do this, it is recommended that you make sure that no users are connected to SQL Server and possibly that SQL Server is shut down so you do not encounter any potential conflicts while the disk pages are moved around on the disk. It might be easier, however, to use a utility like sp_detach_db to copy and move the data and log files safely, reformat the disk so that it has a clean slate, and then copy the data back and reattach it.

How you approach physical fragmentation will vary depending on the size of your data, on whether other things will be affected, and on how fragmented things are. Make sure you back up your databases prior to initiating such an action.

> **Note**   Because you have fragmentation does not necessarily mean you have to do something about it. Some storage area networks (SANs) actually have logic to prevent such a problem. That said, as part of your monitoring, you need to determine if you are actually having problems that might indicate fragmentation, such as longer average reads and writes per second and poor throughput (disk reads and writes per second).

In the end, you will have to test what works best in your environment to give you availability and performance, as well as the windows of opportunity you will need to perform the necessary maintenance.

Example: Defragmenting a VLDB That Uses Log Shipping

Consider the following scenario: you have a database that log ships to another server every 15 minutes. Once a week, it is necessary to defragment the indexes on the database. Unfortunately, at the end of the process, you now have a 5 GB transaction log that takes too long to send and apply on your warm standby. To make matters worse, the database has 12 files. Also, you cannot control the fill factor directly with INDEXDEFRAG. If you consider DBCC DBREINDEX, you can control fill factor and it will span files, but it will cause a lot of blocking on the database at the time—and that only increases with size.

In this case, you might want to think about the following:

■   Concern yourself with fill factor rather than fragmentation. You would do well to scan the same amount of data with less I/O.

■   You might want to switch the recovery model to BULK_LOGGED, do a SELECT INTO and a rename for the data, and then switch to FULL recovery model. This will keep the integrity of the transaction-log chain, and you get the benefits of minimally logged operations.

- Consider disabling log shipping before the defragmentation, and then resynchronize after the defragmentation. This might potentially take less time; however, you will be exposed during that time.

- DBCC INDEXDEFRAG is definitely slower, but it has less impact on end users. Because the transactions are smaller with INDEXDEFRAG, the transaction logs will be much smaller. It is likely that the latency between the log-shipped database and the production database will be negligible.

- Alternate DBCC INDEXDEFRAG and DBCC DBREINDEX.

Ultimately, the right answer is the one that suits a company's conditions. For the bullets listed previously, messing around with the fill factor of your indexes might be too granular, and, unless you really know what you are doing, you might cause more harm than good. Switching recovery models and moving data around and such is too much movement for some and might be risky for others. Disabling log shipping is a viable option, but you will still have the problem of a large transaction log after the defragmenting is complete. You are also exposed from an availability perspective, so you need to think about that. Alternating between DBCC DBREINDEX and DBCC INDEXDEFRAG is certainly viable, but unless you have a maintenance window to allow for DBREINDEX to happen, just doing DBCC INDEXDEFRAG might be your best option from an availability standpoint. At some point you might have to do a full DBREINDEX or DROP and CREATE INDEX, but you might be able to stave that off.

Database Corruption

Although it is not common, you can still encounter database corruption with SQL Server 2000. Corruption usually happens due to some hardware error (good example: a bad or improper disk driver) that corrupts your SQL Server databases when data is written to them. A good indicator of corruption is 605 errors in your SQL Server error log. If you suspect disk corruption, scour Event Viewer as well as any hardware-specific monitoring tools to find out if you are seeing any errors outside of SQL Server. Whether you are seeing other messages or not, the best way to handle corruption is to call Microsoft PSS to have them help you assess your problems and walk you through the next steps. You do not want to accidentally cause additional problems by running DBCC commands that might not be necessary. At this point, you might be reliant on your backups and disaster recovery plans.

Changing Database Options

You should not change configuration options once a system is in production if you do not have to. However, if you do, some will require you to stop and then restart your SQL Server instance. You must take this into account for your availability. Here are the options in SQL Server 2000 that require a stop and restart (when configuring or changing the option if it is already configured):

- affinity mask
- AWE enabled
- C2 audit mode
- fill factor
- lightweight pooling
- locks
- max worker threads
- media retention
- open objects
- priority boost
- remote access
- scan for startup procs
- set working size
- user connections

Memory Management for SQL Server 2000

One of the most important administrative tasks any DBA or system administrator has to do is manage the memory that an instance of SQL Server 2000 uses. This section covers the various types of operating system memory tuning you can use with SQL Server and offers recommendations on how to use them. Several types of memory tuning are available, and each has its own advantages, disadvantages, and uses.

> **Note**   This is not intended as a complete guide to the operating system memory manager. Rather, this is a brief overview designed to give you enough understanding of the memory manager to comprehend the various memory-tuning techniques available to SQL Server, as well as the implications that can arise from using them.

Before describing the various types of memory tuning, however, here is a brief "tour" of the operating system memory manager. This "tour" will help you understand the hows and the whys of employing the various types of memory tuning.

Understanding the Memory Manager

All versions of Windows up through Microsoft Windows 2000 and some versions of Microsoft Windows Server 2003 were primarily 32-bit operating systems until the release of the 64-bit versions of Windows Server 2003.

The amount of memory the operating system can address is directly tied to how many bits the operating system is. The 32-bit versions of Windows are able to address 2^{32} bytes of physical memory out of the box, or 4,294,967,296 bytes. To put it more plainly, Windows can address 4 GB of physical memory. The obvious implication is that the more address bits your operating system has, the more memory you can address. So a 64-bit operating system would be able to address, at most, 2^{64} bits worth of physical memory (which is 18,446,744,073,709,551,616 bytes—an extremely large number). From this discussion, you would think that 32-bit versions of Windows are limited to supporting only 4 GB of physical memory, but that is not the case.

However, before you get excited and start writing or implementing applications that will require 4 GB of memory just to load, there are a few ground rules about how memory can be used. Windows utilizes something known as a memory split (see Figure 14-4). This means that by default, the kernel can utilize up to 2 GB of memory in its own separate memory space and each application can utilize up to 2 GB of memory in its own private address space.

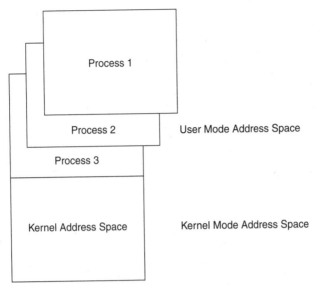

Figure 14-4 An example of a memory split.

The memory manager works this way for two main reasons: self protection and application protection. The kernel mode gets 2 GB all to itself so that it will have enough room to do whatever it needs to do without running out of space. Plain and simple, applications will not run if the kernel space does not have enough memory. Along with this self-protection, user mode applications cannot address kernel mode space and accidentally corrupt kernel mode memory and cause an access violation (AV).

Notice that previously it was noted that *each* application can utilize up to 2 GB of memory. That might seem a little odd given that, natively, the operating system can recognize only 4 GB of total memory. For example, pretend that a server that has 4 GB of RAM (which we will call *myserver* for the purpose of the example), and the kernel mode functions are using 1 GB of memory, leaving 3 GB for all other applications. Now, also imagine that an instance of SQL Server 2000 is active and using its full range of 2 GB of memory, leaving only 1 GB for all other applications. Now add Web services, native user mode applications, management and monitoring processes, and we are running at a full 3.9 GB of memory used. What happens when a new process is started that needs 200 MB of memory? This single request would put the processes over the actual amount of memory that the system has in total. So now, with each application getting its own 2 GB range, the memory picture begins to look a little more like Figure 14-5.

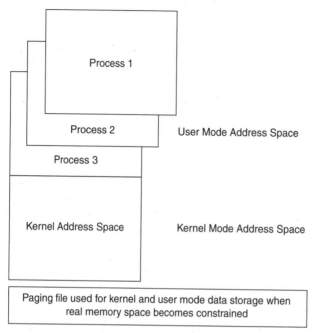

Figure 14-5 Memory split with a paging file in use.

To combat this hard limit of physical memory in the server, the memory manager uses disk space to substitute for physical memory. This disk space is called the paging file (pagefile.sys). Whenever there is not enough physical memory left to satisfy requests, memory that is currently not in use will be written to the paging file on disk, freeing physical memory to satisfy requests (actually, the process is somewhat more complicated than described here, but for this discussion, it is sufficient).

> **Note** *Paging* is a fairly generic term that refers to the memory manager writing from memory to disk. This can be writing data out to a paging file or simply saving a file to disk. In context for this text, we will use the term *paging* to refer to writing to the page file for the purposes of memory management unless otherwise noted.

So far, there can be 4 GB of memory in the operating system with 2 GB available to kernel mode functions and 2 GB available to *each* user mode application. If physical memory becomes constrained, items in memory that have not been recently used will be written out to a pagefile to free physical memory for more pressing needs, and the memory picture looks more like Figure 14-6. So what happens when an application needs some of its memory that has been written out to the paging file?

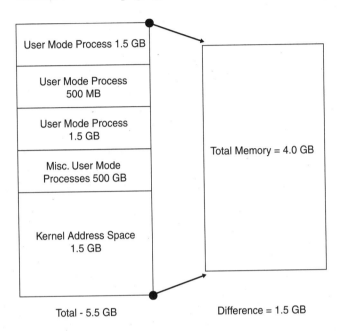

Total - 5.5 GB   Difference = 1.5 GB

Applications (including those in the kernel mode space) are using
5.5 GB of memory, yet Windows can only natively recognize 4 GB.

Figure 14-6   Freeing physical memory.

To enable applications to not have to keep track of memory in case it gets moved or worry about overwriting the memory of other applications and processes, the memory manager *virtualized* all the memory addresses used by user mode applications and processes. For example, imagine that we have two processes, process A and process B, and both ask for 1 MB of memory. Both processes get an answer from the memory manager that they have been allocated 1 MB of memory starting at address 0x28394532. What happens when both applications write to that address? Will one of the processes erroneously overwrite the other's data? Will one of the processes receive an error? Will one or both of the applications crash?

The answer is none of the above. Both processes will be able to write to the same address because of the virtualization that goes on behind the scenes. User mode processes are never able to directly write to physical memory and never actually know where their data resides. A user mode processes and requests a block of memory and writes to it. In the meantime, the memory can be written out to the pagefile, and when the application does something with the memory, the memory manager will go out to the pagefile and retrieve the data from the pagefile for the application. The key thing here is that the application never knew anything about the virtualization process; it simply thinks it is writing to a memory location.

How does an application get its memory back once it is in the paging file? It does not get it back. Whenever an application references memory in the paging file, the memory manager will retrieve the data out of the paging file for the application because, remember, the application is not responsible for keeping track of where the data really is.

Because of this virtualization, each application can write to the virtual locations of 0x00000000 – 0x7fffffff (or 2 GB) without affecting any other process. Each application thinks that *its* memory location 0x38344134 is the only one on the server, when, in fact, many applications are simultaneously using that virtual location. All the while, in the background, the memory manager is writing memory for those applications and keeping track of where they are in physical memory and in the pagefile.

Keeping this in mind, the previous statement that the kernel space and each application could utilize up to 2 GB of memory was somewhat incorrect. Now that we have introduced the concept of virtual memory, it is far more accurate to state that the kernel mode space, as well as each application, can utilize up to 2 GB of virtual memory. Certain portions of the memory manager, however, cannot be paged to disk.

The kernel address space can also use 2 GB of address virtual memory, but the key difference is that all processes in the kernel space share the same 2 GB. Each process does not get its own unique memory space use without affecting other kernel mode processes. Any user mode thread that enters and does its work in this space and then returns will lose access to the memory it just used. Because of this, it is very important for drivers and kernel processes to be very good at handling memory. When rogue processes corrupt or overwrite kernel address space memory, the results are disastrous indeed. Errors in the kernel mode space, where most hardware driver code exists, often lead to a dreaded system crash if the right set of conditions occurs. In Windows 2000 and later, this is less likely to happen due to protection mechanisms built into the operating system.

Most memory in the kernel mode space is virtualized. Some memory, depending on the function, can be paged out to disk as well. There is a special type of memory that cannot be paged out to disk. One of the key items that resides in that space is the portion of the memory manager that handles virtual address translation and its related items and drivers for disk access. Those must remain resident in physical memory at all times (this is addressed later).

Memory access is always slow compared to memory access from physical memory. For example, imagine that an application named memoryhog.exe references three pieces of data it has stored in memory: Mem1, Mem2, and Mem3. Mem1 is right where memoryhog.exe left it. The memory manager has not shuffled it around at all. The memory manger has not moved Mem2 either, but the virtual memory address no longer points to the data that is still in physical memory. The data is not out on the paging file yet. The memory manager, however, has moved Mem3 into the paging file. memoryhog.exe does not know this, of course—it simply references the memory virtual addresses it wrote to in the first place. Which reference will occur faster and why? The answer is Mem1, and here is why.

When memoryhog.exe references Mem1, nothing "extra" happens. It is right where memoryhog.exe left it, and no extra looking and retrieving goes on. When Mem2 is referenced, it is a little slower because the memory manager has to repoint the virtual address to the physical memory, but the performance hit is negligible because the item still remained in physical memory. Mem3, however, must be retrieved from disk, and it is the slowest of all. Disk access times are measured in milliseconds and memory access time is measured in nanoseconds, so every time memory has to be retrieved from disk, it takes approximately *1 million times longer* to retrieve the data than if it had still been resident in physical memory.

Whenever data is not where an application originally left it and the memory manager has to retrieve the data, a page fault—which means that you are now accessing a physical disk—is incurred. You must be aware of two types of page faults: soft page faults, as occurred with Mem2, and hard page faults, as occurred with Mem3.

Because hard page faults are devastating to system performance, operating system–based solutions were developed to help applications use and retain more data in physical memory.

Breaking the 2-GB Barrier Under 32-Bit

Because databases are growing so large and usage is heavy, the default 2 GB that a single user mode process can utilize is often insufficient for real-world needs. In order to combat this and increase performance (or to prevent performance degradation due to increased load), you will need to tune the amount of memory you are using for a given SQL Server 2000 instance.

The following memory tuning options are discussed in this section:

- /3GB switch
- Physical address extensions (PAE)
- Address windowing extensions (AWE)

Each option does not function the same but has the same goal: to increase performance of an application by modifying the way the memory manager works to reduce disk paging.

/3GB boot.ini Switch   /3GB is a switch configured in the boot.ini file read by Windows at startup. This option allows an application such as SQL Server to utilize up to 3 GB of virtual memory in its private address space rather than the default maximum of 2 GB. The memory is virtual and can still be paged out if necessary. Here is an example of a boot.ini entry with the switch:

```
multi(0)disk(0)rdisk(0)partition(1)\WINDOWS='Windows Server 2003, Enterprise'
/fastdetect /3GB
```

The benefits of using /3GB are immediately obvious. An application can map 1 more GB of memory into its private memory space. Specifically, SQL Server is able to map 3 GB of data into its memory space, a gain of 50 percent.

> **Note** Applications have to be compiled specifically with the `IMAGE_FILE_LARGE_ADDRESS_AWARE` flag to take advantage of the /3GB switch. The 32-bit version of SQL Server 2000 is one of these applications.

Applications such as SQL Server that can frequently refer to the same data multiple times to satisfy different requests can greatly benefit from an extra GB of memory to map.

An administrator will need to keep several considerations in mind before enabling the /3GB switch. Usage of this switch will limit the kernel memory space to the remaining 1 GB. In some cases this can cause undesirable results if the kernel mode space is not large enough for the operating system. If the right conditions do not exist, the server's performance can be degraded or possibly result in a system crash. It would never be wise to allow a single application to starve the kernel of memory because it not only could affect other applications but also could cause the kernel to not have enough memory to continue to function at all. Also, because the memory is still virtualized, SQL Server or any other application that uses a 3 GB virtual address space might not necessarily realize a performance benefit.

The /USERVA boot.ini Switch   Because of these possible problems, a new sub-switch has been introduced in Windows 2003 Server (as well as Windows XP Service Pack 1 or later) that can only be used in conjunction with the /3GB switch, the /USERVA switch. The /USERVA switch allows an administrator to determine the size of the user mode virtual address space between 2 GB and 3 GB. For example, assume that an administrator determines (through testing and benchmarks) that the system will perform at its peak with a user mode virtual address space of 2.5 GB and the kernel will be able to work comfortably with a 1.5 GB virtual address space. The administrator could them modify boot.ini to the following:

```
multi(0)disk(0)rdisk(0)partition(1)\WINDOWS='Windows Server 2003, Enterprise'
/fastdetect /3GB /userva=2560
```

In some cases restricting the kernel to only 1 GB of memory might not be desirable, but the kernel might not need 2 GB, either, so the /USERVA switch allows administrators a middle-ground alternative to the all-or-nothing approach of the /3GB switch.

> **Important**   Without the /3GB switch, the /USERVA switch will be ignored if it is put into boot.ini alone.

Despite these concerns, using the /3GB switch is a perfectly valid approach to memory. The key to determining whether or not it will be useful in your environment is testing. Usage trends and performance changes can rarely be predicted; before and after performance benchmarks and tests are essential to determining whether or not memory tuning is beneficial in a particular case.

Physical Address Extensions (PAE)

You might have noticed that we mentioned earlier that a condition might exist where total system memory usage is more than 4 GB. What does an administrator do then, since earlier we pointed out that a 32-bit operating system can only address 4 GB of memory? Simple, make the operating system use more than 32 bits.

PAE is a hardware modification that allows a 32-bit hardware platform to address more than 4 GB. Essentially, PAE changes the addressing from 32-bit to 36-bit addressing mode on an Intel server (37-bit on AMD). The calculation for the amount of memory is 2^n, where n is the number of bits of the operating system. So an Intel-based processor, when PAE is enabled, will allow an operating system to address up to 64 GB of memory, since 2^{36} works out to 64 GB.

Implementing PAE is done through a /PAE switch configured in the startup line for the specific installation of Windows in boot.ini option. Here is an example of a boot.ini entry with the switch; PAE is also enabled by means of a switch in boot.ini. Table 14-4 shows how much memory you can access with /PAE set under the various editions of Windows.

```
multi(0)disk(0)rdisk(0)partition(2)\WINNT='Windows 2000 Advanced Server' /PAE
/basevideo /sos
```

Table 14-4   Memory Supported for 32-Bit Versions of Windows with PAE

Operating System	Maximum Memory (in GB)
Windows 2000 Advanced Server	8
Windows 2000 Datacenter Server	32
Windows 2003 Server Enterprise Edition	32
Windows 2003 Server Datacenter Edition	64

PAE allows the operating system to see and utilize more physical memory than otherwise possible. The obvious benefit to this is that with more physical memory available, the operating system will have less need of a paging file to service memory requests.

For example, a server, named MyServer, has 4 GB of memory. SQL Server is using 2 GB, the various kernel functions are using 1.5 GB, and other applications, such as virus scanners, essential services, and support applications, are using 2 GB of memory. Whoops, that adds up to 5.5 GB of memory. Since normally a server can support only up to 4 GB of memory, this means that at least 1.5 GB worth of data is paged out to disk at any given time (again, this is not strictly true, but this is a simple overview of the memory manager). Constantly swapping 1.5 GB of data in and out of the pagefile is a performance-intensive task, so it would really be beneficial if somehow the system could use more than 4 GB of physical memory to decrease, if not eliminate, the pressure on the paging file.

With PAE, a server can recognize and use more than 4 GB of physical memory. This is a great performance enhancer because, even though all memory is virtualized for applications (remember, this means they never know where it is in physical memory or if it has been pushed out to the pagefile), data does not get pushed out to the pagefile unless there is a deficiency of physical memory. Because of this, increasing the amount of physical memory available *decreases* the amount of pagefile usage that takes place and will therefore *increase* performance.

How does this help SQL Server? It does not help directly. Although applications directly take advantage of the /3GB switch, the performance gains that come from PAE are hidden from the application. In fact, applications are completely unaware of PAE or the amount of physical memory. Applications get an indirect performance boost because more of their data can remain resident in physical memory on a system with >4 GB of memory with PAE enabled. That is good news, because applications do not natively need to do anything to take advantage of PAE; it just happens.

Combining /PAE and /3GB   For some, the better news might be that you can combine the /3GB and /PAE switches to allow applications (correctly compiled, of course) to use up to 3 GB of memory and to allow more of that data to remain resident in physical memory, providing a performance boost from both ends.

Earlier, we mentioned that the memory manager virtualizes memory for applications and for portions of the kernel so they do not have to do the work of keeping track of where their data is located. Because of this, the memory manager must keep track of where data is located, in physical memory or the pagefile, so that when an application asks for the data in location 0x12345678, the memory manager can look in a translation table, find the data, and grab it from the right place, whether it is the pagefile or memory, and send it to the application. One of the structures involved in this translation and lookup process is called a page frame number (PFN).

Because PAE creates a larger range of physical addresses for the memory manager to keep track of and index, the amount of PFN entries that is required grows dramatically. On a system that is booted with both the /PAE and /3GB switches, an interesting thing happens. The amount of memory that must be indexed/translated in a lookup table is dramatically increased, more key data structures involved in that lookup process are used, and the area of memory where that structure is stored, kernel mode memory, is capped at 1 GB.

This combination will exhaust system kernel space much earlier than normal. Because of this, the memory manager imposes a hard cap of 16 GB on a system booted with both the /3GB and /PAE boot options. Even if a system has 32 GB, if it is booted with both options, only 16 GB will be recognized. So if your SQL Server instance requires more than 16 GB of memory, you cannot mix these two memory models.

> **Warning**   Even though the memory manager imposes a hard limit of 16 GB in this configuration, it is possible to encounter problems even with lesser amounts of memory (say, 8 GB or 12 GB), so it is always a good idea to give the kernel as much room as possible either by reducing the memory load or by using the /USERVA subswitch to increase kernel memory.

Address Windowing Extensions (AWE)

What if 3 GB is not enough for an application? What if an application needs to use 5 GB of physical memory and cannot ever have that memory paged out to disk? There is a way to have an application use gigabytes of virtual memory and ensure that data mapped into that physical memory was never written to the pagefile. It is Address Windowing Extensions (AWE), which is enabled in SQL Server 2000. This feature was introduced in SQL Server 2000 and does not exist in earlier versions.

AWE is an API set that compliments PAE. Unlike PAE, AWE is not a boot option. Applications must directly invoke the AWE APIs in order to use them. The specifics of the AWE API are beyond the scope of this book and are not covered here.

More Info   To learn about specific APIs and to get code samples, please see MSDN online at *http://msdn.microsoft.com*.

Since there are no code samples of AWE or even a look at the API set, this section looks at the functionality AWE provides through applications that utilize it, such as SQL Server, and how it affects memory usage.

Because an application virtual address space can be extended only to 3 GB on the Intel 32-bit platform, applications (and database applications in particular, since they deal with such large datasets and do a lot of swapping of data from disk to memory) need a method to map large portions of data into memory and keep that data in physical memory at all times to increase the performance. This also allows an application to map/remap data into its virtual memory space very quickly without failures.

AWE does just that. AWE allows an application to "reserve" chunks of physical memory that cannot be paged out to the paging file or otherwise manipulated except by the reserving application (which will be SQL Server, since that is the topic of discussion). AWE will keep the data in physical memory at all times. Because the memory manager cannot manage this memory, it will never be swapped out to the paging file. The application is now completely responsible for handling the memory in a responsible manner.

Because this technique is only useful if an application is able to reserve large chunks of memory, it is a technology that best compliments existing technology, namely PAE, rather than being a stand-alone memory tuning solution. When you use the combination of PAE and AWE with SQL Server, the instance does not dynamically manage the size of the memory address space used. And once initialized, AWE memory holds all the memory acquired at the instance's startup until the SQL Server is shut down. To enable AWE in SQL Server, you must use the `sp_configure` stored procedure. Here is the syntax to run in a query window to enable AWE:

```
EXEC sp_configure 'awe enabled', 1
RECONFIGURE
```

> **Important**   AWE enabled is not a dynamic configuration change. You must stop and start your SQL Server instance before it takes effect. And if you need to change the settings, you must also go through another stop and start. You must plan for this downtime, which means it might affect any service level agreement (SLA) you have in place.

You must set the Max Server Memory and Set Working Size configuration options when using AWE with SQL Server. If they are not set, SQL Server grabs the total memory available (except 128 MB to allow the base operating system to function). This potentially deprives the operating system—and any other processes that would be running on the same server—of memory.

Because the memory pages used by the instance of SQL Server are taken from the nonpaged pool of Windows memory, none of the memory can be exchanged. This means that if the physical memory is filled up, SQL Server cannot use the page file set up on a physical disk to account for the surplus in memory usage.

In terms of AWE and multiple instances, since the memory allocated to SQL Server is expecting to grab is a static amount to be kept, if the memory you have told SQL Server to take upon startup is greater than the amount of memory that is actually available, SQL Server 2000 automatically changes the mode form AWE to non-AWE (dynamic allocation) for that instance. This means that SQL Server will only use up to 2 GB of memory. This is the case if there are multiple instances on one server or if the node is starting up an instance after a failover in a server cluster. If more than 2 GB of physical memory is available, the AWE-enabled instance will allocate all available memory during the failover startup and will only leave 100–120MB free for the operating system, effectively starving it. However, if other instances that are not using AWE use more memory during the failover situation or are using AWE and consume that memory, *and* the whole system has less than 2 GB of physical memory available, the instance that fails over and starts on the other node will be started in the non-AWE mode.

AWE presents the same dangers as the other memory-tuning techniques. Using any one, or a combination, of these methods to boost SQL Server performance through memory tuning can starve other applications—or even the kernel itself—of memory that they need to perform adequately. In some cases the starvation caused by weighing memory too heavily in favor of SQL Server can cause performance degradation in other areas that is severe enough to cause an instance's performance to drop.

The bottom line is that SQL Server memory tuning can be a really good thing but it also has the potential to cripple a server. As with most things, take time to understand the outcome of server-wide changes such as this *before* you make them.

You might have noticed that in this section we give no hard numbers, examples, or performance charts showing at which point performance drops off. Because performance is such a subjective topic and very dependent upon hardware, installed applications, services, and the configuration of these items, giving hard and fast numbers for performance is practically impossible. The key to finding the best performance for *your* infrastructure is testing and establishing benchmarks to gauge the effects of changes. There are literally mountains of data on this subject in MSDN, TechNet, and in the various resource kits, since a subject that broad is outside the scope of this book.

Paging File Sizing and Location

As noted above, the operating system uses the paging file, which is a physical file located on your disk subsystem, for some memory operations. The general rule of thumb is to size it at 1.5 times the amount of physical memory that you have. However, in Windows 2000, there is a maximum of 4 GB for the page file size. A paging file size of 2050 MB (just over 2 GB) is the minimum file size necessary for computers with 4 GB or more of physical memory. In Windows 2000 and Windows Server 2003 32-bit, there is a maximum file size of 4 GB, but there is no limit in 64-bit versions of the operating system. In Windows Server 2003 64-bit, you can have a paging file size much larger than the 2050 MB, and it is typically three times the physical RAM. To do this, you have two options:

Option 1: Through the Graphical User Interface (GUI)

1. Select My Computer, right-click, and select Properties (in Windows Server 2003 you might need to turn on the Classic view to see My Computer). Or, under Control Panel, select System.

2. Select the Advanced tab. In Windows Server 2003, click Settings under the Performance category. In Windows 2000, click Performance Options.

3. In Windows Server 2003, in Performance Options, select the Advanced tab, and in Virtual Memory, click Change. In Windows 2000, in Performance Options, click Change in Virtual Memory. The Virtual Memory dialog box, as shown in Figure 14-7, will be displayed.

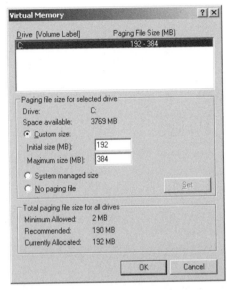

Figure 14-7   Changing your paging file settings.

4. In Virtual Memory, select the drive where you want to place your paging file and an initial and maximum size. You can allow Windows to manage it, but it is recommended that you control this. Click Set when you are finished. Click OK. You will see a message similar to the one shown in Figure 14-8. Click OK three more times.

Figure 14-8   Restart message.

Option 2: Through the Registry

1. In the location where you will create the extra paging files, create folders for each additional paging file.

2. Start the Registry Editor with Regedt32.exe, and find the following registry key:

```
HKEY_LOCAL_MACHINE\System\CurrentControlSet\Control\
SessionManager\MemoryManagement
```

3. Under the key, find the Pagingfiles value, and double-click it. Delete any entries that exist and add entries for each of the files you will be using in the folders you created. For example:

```
c:\pagefile1\pagefile.sys 3000 4000
c:\pagefile2\pagefile.sys 3000 4000
```

4. When you are finished, click OK and exit the Registry Editor. You must restart the operating system for the new changes to take effect; this is not a dynamic change.

5. After the system is rebooted, verify the new settings using the instructions for the GUI to see the changes in the Virtual Memory dialog box.

In terms of placing the pagefile.sys, it is recommended that you do not place it on any disk that will have SQL Server databases, because if you run out of memory and start paging, you could have serious I/O contention with your SQL Server databases and have a double performance problem (memory and disk). You might choose to use a form of redundant array of independent disks (RAID) to protect your paging files, and that is absolutely required if you split your paging files among multiple disks. RAID 1 would work well.

Also, how you configure your paging file is directly related to how you set the Startup and Recovery settings in Computer Management, which you can find in the Advanced tab when you right-click Computer Management (Local) and select the Properties. If you choose either the Kernel Memory Dump or Complete Memory Dump option and select the option Overwrite Any Existing File, Windows will write over any existing dump file and use the same name. If you do not select Overwrite Any Existing File, you will have the ability to save all your memory dumps, but you will have to account for the space. See Figure 14-9 for the Startup and Recovery settings in Computer Management.

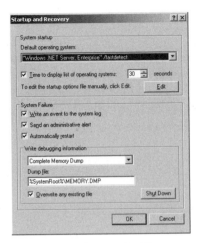

Figure 14-9   Startup And Recovery dialog box from Computer Management.

If you want to get full memory dumps after a crash with 32-bit systems larger than 4 GB, you must add the /MAXMEM switch in boot.ini like this:

```
multi(0)disk(0)rdisk(0)partition(1)\WINDOWS='Windows 2000 Advanced Server'
/fastdetect /MAXMEM=n
```

where n is the amount of memory you are specifying as the maximum amount of memory that the operating system can use.

> **Caution**   /MAXMEM was originally designed for stress testing and debugging, so use this with extreme caution.

For example, if you put /MAXMEM=128, you would be restricting the operating system to only 128 MB of memory, and no matter how much more memory you have in your server, that is all it would see. Do not set this lower than 128 MB for Windows 2000 versions of the server or for Windows Server 2003, Enterprise Edition. Windows Server 2003, Datacenter Edition, has a minimum requirement of 512 MB of memory. Realistically, if you use /MAXMEM, you should set it to the minimum *recommended* RAM, not the bare minimum needed.

> **Important**   Using /MAXMEM requires that one of the paging files on the system must be at least 1 MB larger than your physical memory; otherwise you will not get a full memory dump.

> **Warning** /MAXMEM is an undocumented boot.ini switch that you can find in Volume 3 of the Windows NT Resource Kit. It is meant only for specific configurations, and the memory you specify must be contiguous. This option is valid through Windows 2000 and is not guaranteed to be in future operating systems. Do not use the /MAXMEM option without careful consideration and thorough testing.

SQL Server Memory Recommendations

The toughest part about understanding the memory models is putting it into practice. What do you do for your SQL Server instances? This becomes more glaring on a server cluster where you are trying to implement more than one instance or where you are trying to consolidate multiple SQL Servers onto one or more instances, possibly on a single server or a cluster. Use Table 14-4 as well as Table 14-5 for 64-bit versions to see how much memory you can use under your operating system of choice.

> **Note** If your hardware as well as your operating system choice supports hot swap memory, you might be able to add more physical memory to your server without incurring downtime. However, to use the memory, you would need to allocate it in an application such as SQL Server, which might require a reconfiguration that necessitates downtime of some sort.

Table 14-5 Memory Supported for 64-bit Versions of Windows (No Boot.ini Modifications Necessary)

Operating System	Maximum Memory (in GB)
Windows Server 2003, Enterprise Edition	64
Windows Server 2003, Datacenter Edition	512

> **Important**   Although you can expand beyond 4 GB of memory in SQL Server, the 32-bit version of SQL Server 2000 will always be limited to 2.6 GB of procedure cache. If you have multiple workloads, you will need to test whether they can all coexist and one will not exhaust the procedure cache. If so, you might need multiple instances as each instance gets its own procedure cache; it is not shared between instances.

64-bit SQL Server 2000 changes the rules a bit. All memory under 64-bit is dynamic, and you have much more available to you. In this case, whether you are on a cluster or using a stand-alone server, you can allow SQL Server to manage its own memory, and you can set the MIN SERVER MEMORY option of SQL Server to set the minimum amount of memory for each instance. To set this through Transact-SQL, here is the syntax:

```
EXEC sp_configure 'min server memory', 8000
GO
```

Conversely, you can also set your memory settings in Enterprise Manager in the Memory tab of the instance's properties, as shown in Figure 14-10.

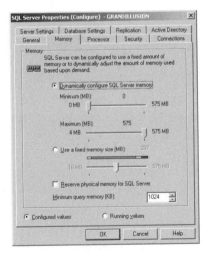

Figure 14-10   Memory tab of an instance's properties.

Using the Memory tab, you can set the following: if you select Dynamically Configure SQL Server Memory, you can set a maximum or minimum amount of memory, or both, that the SQL Server instance can use. By default, the maximum is set to the total amount of memory SQL Server can use and the minimum is set to 0, meaning SQL Server can use up to every amount of available memory. If you are using this option, when you set Minimum (MB) on the screen, it corresponds to executing sp_configure with MIN SERVER MEMORY, and Maximum (MB) is the same as issuing sp_configure with MAX SERVER MEMORY.

If you select the option Reserve Physical Memory For SQL Server, this will physically reserve that amount of memory for SQL Server and not let it go until you reconfigure (and subsequently restart) SQL Server. You should be setting this option only when you also select the option Use A Fixed Memory Size (MB) with an appropriate number. Behind the scenes, when this combination is set, SQL Server is issuing sp_configure twice, once with MAX SERVER MEMORY, and once with SET WORKING SET SIZE (setting that to 1). Setting this option also requires a stop and a restart of SQL Server, as shown in the prompt in Figure 14-11.

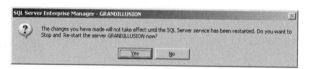

Figure 14-11   Prompt after selecting Reserve Physical Memory For SQL Server.

> **Tip**   It is not a good idea to select Reserve Physical Memory For SQL Server along with Dynamically Configure SQL Server Memory. They are, in essence, conflicting options, and you would be telling SQL Server to dynamically manage memory but grab a fixed amount. If you set Set Working Set Size with dynamic memory, it might cause problems. The Enterprise Manager GUI does not prevent you from combining these options.

If you are using /3GB only, you can allow SQL Server to manage memory dynamically up to 3 GB, or you can set a static amount. Nothing special is required. However, if you are using AWE memory, as mentioned earlier, you *must* set the option awe enabled to 1, as well as set working set size to 1 to allow SQL Server to physically reserve the amount of memory. Here is what the syntax looks like:

```
EXEC sp_configure 'awe enabled', 1
RECONFIGURE
EXEC sp_configure 'set working set size', 1
RECONFIGURE
```

Then you will need to set the options Max Server Memory and Min Server Memory to the same number.

```
EXEC sp_configure 'min server memory', 8000
RECONFIGURE
EXEC sp_configure 'max server memory', 8000
RECONFIGURE
```

Once all this is done and you restart your SQL Server instance, you will be able to take advantage of your memory above 4 GB with AWE.

When you are looking to tune your memory used for SQL Server, when can you combine /3GB with AWE under 32-bit? Follow Table 14-6.

Table 14-6   Memory Recommendations for a 32-Bit SQL Server 2000 Instance

Amount of Physical Memory	Recommendation
Up to 4 GB	No switches (each instance can use only up to 2 GB of memory) or /3GB (each instance can use up to 3 GB of memory dynamically or statically, reserving 1 GB for Windows). No real benefit from setting AWE with this small amount of memory. /3GB is used for plan cache.
4 GB to 16 GB	Can combine /3GB and /PAE with AWE, but you would need to test the use of both to see if any benefit is gained. /3GB can help with plan cache, and AWE for data cache.
More than 16 GB	/PAE with AWE only; /3GB is useless. If combining instances for consolidation or failover clustering, make sure the instances do not rely on /3GB.

> **Note**   It is possible to use AWE memory without having more than 4 GB of memory, but you will get very little benefit from setting a server to use AWE and be able to grab only 2 GB of memory. You might as well just set working set size to 1 (or select Reserve ... from the GUI) and select the amount of memory. They will have basically the same effect.

> **Warning**   Do attempt to deploy AWE, PAE, or /3GB in a production environment without testing the configuration first. You do not want any surprises awaiting you. Also, remember to take into account room for the operating system. The rule of thumb is to leave at least 1 GB for Windows "just in case," as long as you can spare it.

Memory and Multiple Instances on the Same Server or Server Cluster

One thing many people struggle with is how to set memory for a clustered instance or multiple clustered instances running as part of a server cluster or if you have multiple instances on one Windows installation. In addition to the considerations listed in the previous section, for a cluster you now need to take failover into account. If you have a single instance cluster, assuming all nodes are equal in capacity and are configured the same, you will not have to worry about anything. During a failover, the SQL Server should start up and behave exactly the same way.

Multiple instances are different. Why? In a failover, your goal should be to ensure that during the failover, when the instance is restarted on another node, it will have the correct capacity from a processor and memory standpoint (this section will deal only with memory; see Chapter 6, "Microsoft SQL Server 2000 Failover Clustering," for details on processors). Here is where the version of your operating system greatly plays into how you ultimately configure your memory for each SQL Server virtual server. For example, if you are using Windows 2000 Advanced Server, you are limited to 8 GB of memory, eight processors, and two nodes. If you need two, three, four, or even more instances, this could be challenging to say the least, especially if they all need more than 4 GB of memory each! Switching to Windows Server 2003 Enterprise Edition, you can now have up to 32 GB of memory (not to mention two more nodes that would be available to you).

With multiple instances on a stand-alone server, all instances need to play well together in the proverbial sandbox. Although you do not need to worry about failover, you do need to worry about performance and about ensuring that you are not starving one instance to feed another. Your operating choice and the amount of memory it can handle will influence the design of your instances, and, specifically, the amount of memory you can allocate.

Think of your instances as glasses of liquid. If you have two glasses that are half-full, you can pour the contents of one into the other. If you have two full glasses, you cannot combine them. This is how your SQL Servers will behave in a failover or when you combine instances on one server. To prevent this, no matter what you employ (PAE/AWE or /3GB), you should set the Max Server Memory option on each instance to physically cap the amount of memory each instance will get.

Consider this example: you have a two-node cluster with three SQL Server instances. Instance 1, which currently resides on Node 1, has 7 GB of memory configured using AWE. Node 2 houses Instance 2, which has 5 GB of memory allocated with AWE, and one instance that is not using any advanced options and is currently using 1.5 GB of memory. Each node individually has a total of 8 GB of physical memory. This is shown in Figure 14-12.

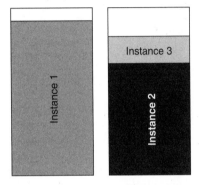

Figure 14-12   Nodes prior to failover.

A problem occurs on Node 1, causing a failover. The instance tries to restart on Node 2, but it cannot. You now have a failed set of SQL Server resources that cannot come online, causing an availability problem. Why? Well, to use AWE, you need to *guarantee* that the memory you told SQL Server to use will be there. A failover is basically a stop and start on another server. In this case, you were already using 6.5 of the available 8 GB of memory. 6.5 + 7 does not equal 8, and it does not matter how big your page file is. Your instance will not grab the memory for AWE. It might, however, start up, but it will only grab the amount of memory that it can up to 2 GB (see earlier for how AWE behaves in a failover). Now you are risking memory starvation of the operating system, and this can affect *all* instances. This is shown in Figure 14-13.

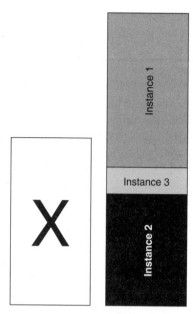

Figure 14-13   Nodes after failover.

So how do you prevent this? By planning, these are the types of scenarios you need to play out in your head when proposing the number of instances on a cluster. Your management might see a two-node cluster and say, "Hey, why is this second server doing nothing? Get something on there!", leaving you in the state of the previous example.

The way you can balance memory in this case would be to give two instances that need a fixed amount of memory 3 GB each and let the other one be dynamic (or set it to 1 GB or 1.5 GB to allow room for the operating system). If you cannot live with this, you will need another cluster or set of servers to handle this workload. The recommendation was basically to halve the memory, which might lead some to believe that you are wasting resources, but again, is performance or availability your goal? By definition, if you are reading this book and implementing things like a cluster, you are probably saying that availability is your highest priority. If you never have to failover and you left the instances at 7 GB, 5 GB, and dynamic, things would work great. But once a failover happened, all bets would be off.

64-bit does change the rules, as stated above. Because all memory is dynamic and you have much more available to you, you should set a fixed minimum amount of memory that SQL Server will need to use and let SQL Server manage anything else it needs. This way, you will always guarantee that your instance will have enough memory to do what it needs to do, but you are giving it the option of grabbing more memory if necessary.

> **Important**   When employing AWE, using 64-bit, or setting a fixed amount of memory, the SQL Server instance upon startup will need to physically reserve the configured amount of physical memory. This process is not instantaneous. The more memory you allocate to SQL Server, the more time it will take to start. In a failover scenario, it will definitely increase your failover time, so take that into account. It is usually measured in minutes, rather than seconds.

Managing SQL Server Resources with Other Tools

Other applications might have the ability to control the amount of memory, or, say, processor that your SQL Server instance can utilize. Is this recommended? In most cases, the answer is no. SQL Server does a good job of managing its own resources, and in some cases it has to. However, in Windows Server 2003, you can use a new feature called Windows System Resource Manager (WSRM). WSRM is supported in both stand-alone and clustered environments, although in a clustered environment, you will need to create or export the settings on one node and apply them to others. WSRM is a nonintrusive tool. You should use SQL Server's interfaces to manage processor affinity and memory, but using WSRM, you can allocate processor percentage for systems with multiple applications (such as a machine with SQL Server, Internet Information Services [IIS], and Microsoft Operations Manager [MOM]) or multiple SQL Server instances. You cannot do this amount of granular control through existing SQL Server-based tools. Do not use WSRM to do anything related to processor affinity or memory management for SQL Server.

Transferring Logins, Users, and Other Objects to the Standby

When you are looking to have a server function as a standby, it needs to be functionally in sync with your production database. This means that logins and any other objects that exist on your primary database have to be on your standby. With failover clustering, that is not a worry, as the entire instance moves to another node, so you get not only the same database, but also essentially the same server. With log shipping, replication, and possibly backup and restore, you are not guaranteed to get all objects on your standby, and you will have to institute processes to ensure that in the event of a problem, you can flip the switch and users will not notice any difference in your standby.

Transferring Logins, Users, and Other Objects Between Instances

Although this topic was somewhat covered in Chapter 7, "Log Shipping," with a more focused approach on log shipping, this is a generic problem that you will have with warm standbys. You have two levels to worry about: the server-level login, as well as the user that is in the database. If you transfer just the database login, your users might not be able to connect because the login it is associated with does not exist in SQL Server.

Transferring Logins and Users

Moving logins from one instance to another is perhaps the easiest problem to tackle. One method, which is covered in the first task in section entitled "Step 3: Post-Wizard Configuration Tasks" in Chapter 7, is to use the DTS Transfer Logins task, with its corresponding task, to move the users by BCPing data out of syslogins.

If you do not move your logins, you will see an error similar to the following when applications or users try to access the database:

```
Msg 18456, Level 16, State 1
Login failed for user '%ls'.
```

Orphaned Users

When you move over your logins, you might have what is known as an orphaned user. An orphaned user is one that exists in the database but whose system identifier (SID) does not match a login or exist as a login on the new server. To see if you have any orphaned users, you can execute the following Transact-SQL statement to give you a list of all orphaned users:

```
exec sp_change_users_login 'Report'
```

Sp_helplogins might also assist you in your debugging process, as it will show you all information about a specific login. Another procedure that might help you is sp_validatelogins, which will tell you if you have Windows users or groups that no longer exist but are mapped to logins in SQL Server.

If you do have orphaned users, they should be able to access the new server, but they will not be able to access the database. This means that the SID is not matching, and you should see this error:

```
Server: Msg 916, Level 14, State 1, Line1
Server user '%.*ls' is not a valid user in database '%.*ls'.
```

To map your logins, you can use a tool provided by Microsoft Support Services named MapSids, which can be found at *http://download.microsoft.com/download/ sqlsvr2000/utility/5.0/win98me/en-us/Mapsids.exe*. This will create two stored procedures on your SQL Server. Follow the instructions found in Knowledge Base articles 240872, "HOW TO: Resolve Permission Issues When You Move a Database Between Servers That Are Running SQL Server" and 298897, "SAMPLE: Mapsids.exe Helps Map SIDs Between User and Master Databases When Database Is Moved" on how to map your SIDs using these stored procedures.

Another method you can do once you have generated a report with `sp_change_users_login` is to use that stored procedure to try to fix your problems. Sp_change_users_login can take the following parameters:

- *@Action*, which can have the values of Auto_Fix, Report, and Update_One. As of SQL Server Service Pack 3, Auto_Fix does require a password.

- *@UserNamePattern*, which is the user in the database.

- *@LoginName*, which is the SQL Server-level login.

For example, if you wanted to change the database login that the database user Fred is mapped to, you would execute the statement below. However, as of SP3, you cannot create logins with NULL passwords, so you will have to ensure that the login you are mapping to has a password.

```
Exec sp_change_users_login 'Update_One', 'Fred', 'FredNewLogin'
```

> **Note**   Keep in mind that transferring logins will not solve issues external to SQL Server. For example, if your standby is not in the same domain and you are using Windows Authentication, you need to ensure that the logins you are transferring will actually work on the standby. You might need to work with your network administrators to put things in place, such as two-way trusts between domains.

Transferring Objects

There are two ways to move objects between instances: SQL scripts and Data Transformation Services (DTS) packages.

Generating SQL Scripts

Database objects come in a variety of categories—stored procedures, table definitions, permissions, jobs, triggers, and so on. One of the easiest and most recommended ways of moving objects is to generate a SQL script. The script would be one that you coded to initially get the object into SQL Server, or, if you used the GUI of Enterprise Manager, using Enterprise Manager to generate the script. You can script most objects created within Enterprise Manager directly by selecting it, right-clicking, selecting All Tasks, and then selecting Generate SQL Script. Three tabs are in the Generate SQL Scripts dialog box.

Tip SQL Server Agent jobs, Alerts, and Operators can also be scripted this way. Scripting replication was covered in Chapter 8, "Replication."

The first tab of the Generate SQL Scripts dialog box, General, is where you select the objects that will be scripted. An example is shown in Figure 14-14.

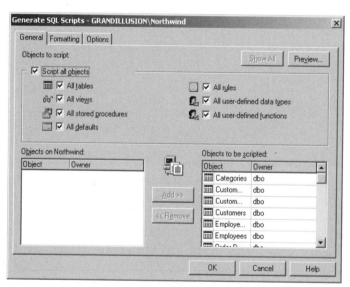

Figure 14-14 General tab of Generate SQL Scripts.

The Formatting tab, shown in Figure 14-15, allows you to control how your files look after they are scripted.

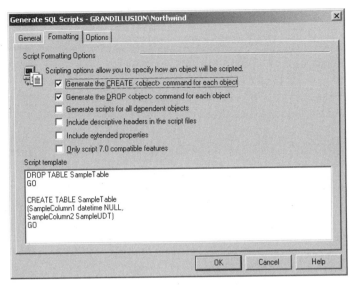

Figure 14-15 Formatting tab of Generate SQL Scripts.

The Options tab shown in Figure 14-16 is an important tab. It is where you select primary/foreign keys, permissions, logins, and such to be included in the .sql file. If you do not select options such as Script Object-Level Permissions, you might not be able to correctly use the script if you ever need to use it as, say, part of a disaster recovery plan.

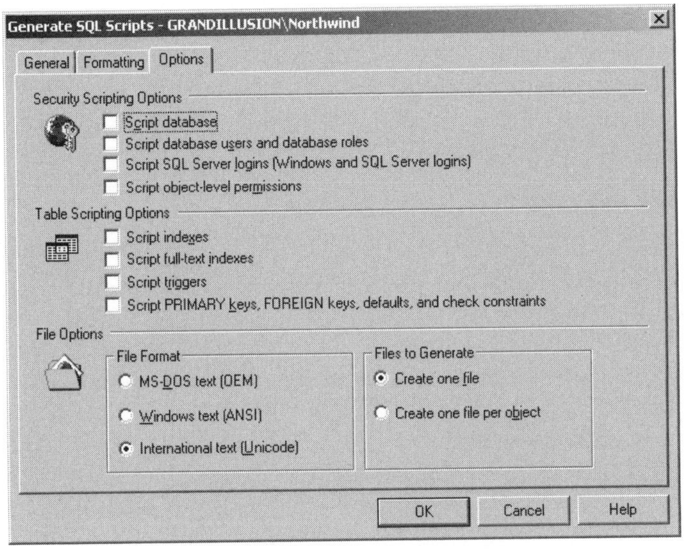

Figure 14-16 Options tab of Generate SQL Scripts.

When you are done, click OK, and you will be prompted for a location in which to save your .sql file.

If you are scripting SQL Server Agent Jobs, Alerts, or Operators, the dialog box is a bit different. The three are nearly identical, and the Jobs dialog box is shown in Figure 14-17. However, unlike generating scripts for all jobs at once, you do it for each job. You can then combine the output scripts into one master script, but there is no way through the GUI to select more than one job at once.

Figure 14-17   Generate SQL Scripts windows for SQL Server Agent Jobs.

> **Note**   If you are employing log shipping, all objects captured in the transaction log will be automatically transferred to the warm standby. See Chapter 7 for more details.

Using a DTS Package to Transfer Objects

You can use a Data Transformation Services (DTS) package to send certain objects to another SQL Server. In SQL Server 2000, you can transfer logins (as covered in Chapter 7; this is represented by a small gray server icon with a person's head on it), jobs (represented by a miniature dialog box with a small circle, or clock, in it), error messages (represented by a person's head and a small thing that looks like a piece of paper with an *x* in it), and objects (represented by two gray servers with a red arrow pointing from one to the other). You can see these in Figure 14-18.

Figure 14-18   DTS package with transfer tasks.

Important DTS packages do not run, and Dtsrun.exe was not ported to SQL Server 2000 64-bit. Under 64-bit, you have the option to create and run DTS packages on 32-bit that can take data from and send data to 64-bit. You can save a DTS package to a 64-bit SQL Server 2000 instance, but you cannot run it on 64-bit. If you have SQL Server 2000 Service Pack 3 or later installed, the option to schedule the package is disabled since you cannot run the package under 64-bit.

The Transfer Logins Task, Transfer Jobs Task, and the Transfer Error Messages Task all have similar dialog boxes: they have three tabs—Source, Destination, and a tab to select the login(s)/job(s)/or message(s) you want to send. An example is shown in Figure 14-19.

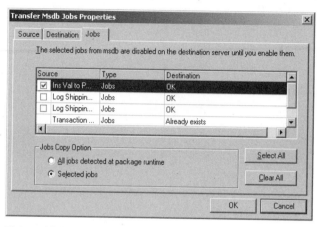

Figure 14-19   Transfer Jobs Task dialog box—Jobs Tab.

The Copy SQL Server Objects Task dialog box is different. It also has three tabs, but the third tab, Copy, is more like the Generate SQL Scripts dialog box. An example is shown in Figure 14-20. By default, this task will also copy your data. You will want to deselect the Copy Data option. By default, it will also copy all objects and use default options. If you want to send only selected objects, clear Copy All Objects and click Select Objects. You will then be presented with the Select Objects dialog box to choose what you want. Similarly, if you want to control the default options that will govern the task, clear Use Default Options and click Options. You will see the Advanced Copy Options dialog box.

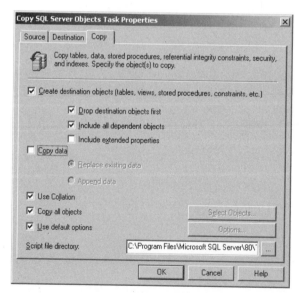

Figure 14-20   Copy SQL Server Objects Task—Copy tab.

To create a DTS package, do the following:

1. Select the Data Transformation Services folder in Enterprise Manager, right-click, and select the New Package option.

2. Select the tasks you want to add to your DTS package from the icons at the left side of the DTS Package dialog box, or select them from the Task menu.

3. Once you are finished adding and configuring your tasks, save the package by selecting the Save or Save As options from the Package menu. You can now schedule this package to run on a regular basis.

DTS Packages

DTS packages are a bit different. They are not transferred through the transaction log. To move a DTS package, follow these steps:

1. Select the package and open it by double-clicking.

2. Under the Package menu, select Save As.

3. In the Save DTS Package dialog box shown in Figure 14-21, enter a name if one does not exist (that is, it was not previously saved), a password, and select where you want the DTS package to go. If you select Meta Data Services or SQL Server, the package will be saved to the msdb database of the SQL Server you designate in the Server drop-down list. You will then need to back up msdb. However, remember that you cannot restore another server's msdb database to another server unless you rename the server itself.

   If you select Structured Storage File or Visual Basic File, you will be prompted to enter a file name with a .dts or .bas extension, respectively. If you do not put a path name, the package will be saved to your My Documents directory. For transporting packages between servers, saving the package as one of these two options is the preferred method.

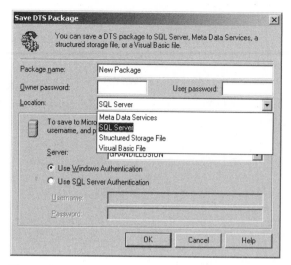

Figure 14-21   Save DTS Package dialog box with Locations expanded.

4.   Click OK.

> **Tip**   Remember that DTS packages can be versioned and that after loading the packages onto another server, you might need to modify it, as some of the source or destination properties of some tasks will be assigned to the wrong server(s).

Summary

Correct administration and maintenance will go a long way in the battle to keep your servers up—and this means more than performing regular backups. Whether it is securing your instance, performing proactive index maintenance, tuning memory, or moving objects, the little things make a big difference. You should definitely not implement or change your current administrative procedures without correct testing and commitment.

Now that you have learned what it takes to administer your SQL Servers for high availability, it is time look at how you can be proactive in understanding the health of your SQL Server through monitoring.

15

Monitoring for High Availability

One of the challenges of making your systems highly available is ensuring the capability to verify your environment's health in terms of its current availability. Because it is always better to be proactive than reactive, you should be alerted when something occurs. Ultimately, management will want reports of your system's availability and possibly performance statistics—such as number of users per hour—so it is in your best interests to have the tools and information to be able to generate these reports. You never want to be in a position where you have to scramble to collect that information or, worse, come up empty handed with simply verbal assurances that your systems really are available.

This chapter walks you through the approaches and processes of monitoring, based on the internal systems monitoring experience at Microsoft. Keep in mind that every environment has different experiences and capabilities for its approach to monitoring and reporting.

> **On the CD** For more information on monitoring disks, turn back to Chapter 4, "Disk Configurations for High Availability." For performance tuning and scalability information, see the document HA_Perf_And_Scale.doc.

Monitoring Basics

When you begin to look at how you will monitor your enterprise, if you spend most of your time performing database administrator (DBA) work, you will immediately think of monitoring the primary SQL Server and databases associated with the specific application. However, monitoring for availability is more complicated than that. An application or solution is made of multiple layers, including the network, possibly the firewall, application servers, associated infrastructure servers (such as Microsoft Exchange or domain controllers), and the code components themselves (for example, middle-tier Microsoft .NET Web Services). To claim that the whole system is available, you must take into account, monitor, and report on every "moving part."

Most monitoring documents focus on one specific aspect, such as Microsoft SQL Server. There is simply not enough space to cover all aspects of monitoring an entire application chain in depth in only one chapter. Because this book focuses on SQL Server, the discussion is mostly limited to SQL Server–specific monitoring. For a SQL Server database chained to an application that is expected to be highly available, the following items are mandatory for monitoring:

- The SQL Server service, and connectivity to that instance

- The primary databases on the primary instance

- Crucial working parts of the database system (network cards, disk adapters, memory, processor)

- The operating system on the primary instance

- The operating system on your standby server, whether hot, warm, or cold

- Key functionality within each database

You should make every effort to incorporate similar monitoring in your test and development platforms. This will serve you well if you decide to introduce a change to your monitoring system, because you can see how it behaves in the relative safety of a test environment first. Your highly available application is relying on a highly available monitoring system; therefore you should have a standby system for your monitoring database repository. If the monitoring system goes down, how will you know if your primary system is running or not?

Monitoring generally has two forms: systems that are monitored and managed in near real time, and systems that are monitored only when there appears to be a problem. For highly available systems, you will need to ensure that you are indeed capable of monitoring your systems in near real time so that your response to issues minimizes outages. In either case, it is imperative that you monitor the proper details so that you can base your response to changes on data you have at hand. It is easy to go "over the top" with monitoring.

You could collect information on everything, but what would you do with it all? With just the standard counters, monitoring everything at a 15-second interval would yield 250 MB of data per day per server. In SQL Server Profiler, on a system running 1000 transactions per second, you would generate about 86 million entries per day. That is a lot of data, and unless you employ a small army of people to analyze your data, odds are you will never go through it on a regular basis to identify trends. This is not to say that there is actually anything wrong with collecting all that information if you have the bandwidth, storage space, and ability to put it to work. However, gigabytes or terabytes of collected data will not necessarily result in more available systems, and in some cases, depending on the system load that monitoring adds, you might skew the numbers generated.

This chapter presents the approach of minimal monitoring, which means monitoring in a lightweight manner with a specific goal. It is a bit new in relation to other documentation on monitoring, but it is what is used internally at Microsoft. The approach is deceptively simple:

- Look for known conditions.

- Look for common issues.

- Look for early warning signs.

- Collect only what you can use.

Monitoring everything over time is pointless and potentially destructive to your service level agreements (SLAs). Monitor only what you are using. Even if you choose to monitor at a granular level, there is no real need to store all of that data over a long period of time. Instead, aggregate the data, or save smaller, more specific subsets of it. Trends that can be utilized to your benefit emerge over time. You can monitor more aggressively when the occasion calls for it, but long-term monitoring must be more lightweight.

Do not just look at the data generated by monitoring. Look for meaning *in* the data. Have a question or problem in mind, decide which factors will produce an answer, and look for the answer where you expect to find it. When you detect a problem, and you then begin monitoring for troubleshooting purposes, you will be collecting significantly more data and looking through it for patterns you expected. If that fails, you might find yourself collecting additional data in search of a pattern.

Counters, events (measurements) for system health, and day-to-day alerts and actions might provide you with data that you want to store for capacity planning over the long term. In some cases monitoring might provide you with data that you could use to answer a business or application behavior question. For example, how many failed searches were issued in 1998 and were they all similar?

With SQL Server in particular, there is no shortage of data to analyze. If you do not start with what you want to know, you can end up looking through everything available to see what piques your interest. This random approach can consume many hours of interesting activity and discussion. Ultimately, however, it fails to improve availability on a consistent basis.

Table 15-1 gives you some ideas of the types of questions you might try to answer through monitoring. Some of these relate to availability and some do not.

Table 15-1   What Do You Want to Know Now?

System Health	Planning
■ Is the service up?	■ What is our availability per our SLA?
■ Is response time slow?	■ Is the system performing properly?
■ Are there any errors?	■ When will I need a higher capacity design or new hardware?
■ Is it being properly monitored?	■ When is the system in use?
Application	**Business**
■ Did all required processes complete?	■ How many function X occurred per hour?
■ How fast is it?	■ What items are most popular?
■ Is any condition detected that causes issues I have solved already?	■ What items were searched for and not found?
■ How is this month different from last month?	■ How effective is this business component?

You must also answer questions regarding what you want to know from a reporting perspective, such as those shown in Table 15-2.

Table 15-2   What Do You Want to Know Later?

In Six Months?	In a Year?
■ Response time variation	■ Response time variation
■ Function *X* per month	■ Performance changes
■ Revenue that could have been made on items searched but not found	■ Orders per quarter
	■ Errors resolved
■ Usage patterns	■ Change in usage
■ Buying patterns	■ Resource and space utilization

Monitor in layers. Monitoring is like a layered cake—once you get through one layer, there is another (and possibly even another flavor). Instead of one gargantuan monitoring system, use smaller concurrent monitoring processes, each one lightweight and specifically targeted. You can use the tools listed in Table 15-3 to monitor the various layers of your systems.

Table 15-3   Monitoring Tools for System Layers

Tools	Monitoring Layer
Profiler	SQL Server
Auditing, and so on	Customized monitoring
System Monitor	Application
	Operating system
Desktop Management Interface (DMI) tool	CPU, RAM, disk, host bus adapter (HBA), SCSI, NIC, network

When available, you should always choose to use the hardware vendor's DMI tools. In most cases these tools are free. Even more important, these tools return information on predictive failure much sooner than errors show up in the Windows Event Log. Simply put, this is a required level of monitoring if you are serious about availability. Hardware failures in general are a primary cause of outages, and DMI tools help to predict these failures. In general, these tools can be set up so a central monitoring station collects information on many servers.

You can also set up a great deal of customized monitoring. Obviously there is a lot of variety implicit in customizing your own program for this, but for our purposes this is intended as a general label of everything that does not fall into the category of System Monitor or SQL Server Profiler.

Setting Ground Rules

The question then becomes, what do you set up in Profiler and System Monitor? Before getting down to specific examples, you must first understand fundamentals for monitoring. Listed next are a few terms of engagement you should memorize, along with being proactive and practicing due diligence.

> **Tip** Perhaps the most important ground rule is that the monitoring tools that you decide to leverage should be selected keeping in mind that this is something you are going to have to maintain going forward. Your solution should be as hands-off as possible and should require minimal effort on the part of your team as your environment changes. Manually configured custom tools might be just the thing for a small environment or for unique situations. Large environments, however, require monitoring solutions that are easily managed, fault tolerant, and capable of self-monitoring. Monitoring should not add to your daily workload, and if implemented correctly can actually reduce it, freeing up valuable time for more productive activities.

1. You are creating history. When you monitor, you are creating a time-line of events. A counter value is an event, a query is an event, an error is an event, and a change is an event. To make the monitoring data meaningful, record the following events:

    ❑   Change in software version

    ❑   Difference in edition

    ❑   Application of service packs

    ❑   Change in hardware

    ❑   Change to the application

    ❑   Change in usage

    ❑   Change in priorities

    Whenever anything on this list changes, be sure to reevaluate your monitoring methodology. In some cases, such as a difference between version, edition, or service pack of SQL Server (or hotfixes), SQL Server's behavior might change. If you cannot compare behavior before and after such changes, for example, you will not know if a phone call from an end user complaining about performance is valid or not. You should always be able to say empirically how things worked before so you can figure out what the delta of change is.

The same would go for a new version of the front-end application, or hardware changes of any type, Windows update, new drivers, new firmware, and so on. Record it all. Make things easier for yourself by storing it in a table in a format that joins easily with the data you are already collecting. That way, when you issue a report or create a timeline, it will be a relatively painless process.

Most important, record a baseline. Make one at the beginning and then again after every major system change. This is critical: without a history of what has happened before, you have no way to meaningfully interpret the data you collect. Trying to track developing problems is a complete waste of time without a baseline. It is difficult to state that there is a change in behavior if you only have the ability to observe the current behavior without being able to compare it to anything. Raw data becomes useful in relation to other counters, other events, or real-world activity. Therefore, the same measurement (counter, event) can be used more than once to answer an entirely different question. The same measurement can also shift in interpretation over time, especially if the system being measured is changed in some fundamental way. For example, if you added more processors to your system, the counter % Processor Time found in System Monitor would go down. If you did not record the addition of processors and make a correlation to this increase in processing ability, it might later be difficult to explain to others why the server appears to be "underutilized." The same goes for application changes.

2.   If a server goes down in the middle of your data center, no one cares how many PCI slots it had. Availability monitoring is about knowing if the trees and the forest are still standing, not if each leaf is turning brown or fallen. You do not want to collect minute details or data at too granular a level. Doing so generates a lot of what is referred to as "noise," and it can also have a serious performance impact on your system.

This by itself is a vague recommendation. There is obviously going to be a lot of monitoring you can implement if you follow all the recommendations in this chapter. Does that mean this is all a big example? Not at all. Everything suggested in this chapter is actually running together simultaneously on some of Microsoft's most heavily used internal systems. The key is being lightweight so it all works well together. To succeed, you have to make sure that your monitoring is not negatively impacting your systems. Plan it that way, and then turn more things on to monitor gradually. Throughout you need to monitor resource usage to measure and report on the impact of monitoring, because there is always a cost associated with monitoring.

> **Tip**   If you want to find out if your system gets the same light-weight impact received for the same monitoring strategy, do not add more counters because you think they might be useful. Test the original versions listed here first, then test any changes you make. For example, you could probably make an argument for measuring the disk impact based on the idea that you are writing information to a disk somewhere. However, if monitoring your system in a responsible and *minimal* fashion has a severe detrimental impact, then you have larger problems to deal with before implementing this kind of a system.

3. Push, pull, and call names. In some circles you can get into a discussion over whether it is better to push monitoring data to a central area or to pull it instead. Arguments can be made for keeping some information locally, replicating information, or storing it in a customized manner. Either way, make sure you can immediately detect the absence of a particular server name in a stream of information. A server that goes down or gets bumped off a network node most certainly stops delivering information about itself. Therefore absence of information associated with a particular name should trigger an alert.

4. Bring it on. That is the attitude you want to see in a server. You are not off the hook for monitoring performance and scalability, but sometimes you just want to know if the system is available. However, you also want to know if the server will be available tomorrow, too. Some performance or scalability issues can take your server offline very abruptly and if this happens it can take a team precious minutes or hours to bring it back online. You do not have to be a programming genius to keep an eye on the most common trends that impact performance and scalability. A few simple, well-monitored items can give you the opportunity to address issues long before users start to grumble about response time. To be very clear, part of your baseline (which is the keystone of your entire monitoring effort) should include performance and scalability information. If the numbers point to decay in this area, your monitoring solution should trigger an alert. What you do when that alert is received depends on your skill level, application policies and procedures, and other resources.

> **On the CD**   For performance tuning and scalability informa-
> tion, see the document HA_Perf_And_Scale.doc.

5.   "We are already aware of the problem." This should be one of your
trademark phrases, and this should be impressed on every member of
your team. Do not wait for the user, the help desk, or an application
administrator to complain. Do not wait until you read your e-mail
tomorrow, the error logs tomorrow morning, or the event log (which
you should monitor even if some other group does that regularly). Automate all of your alerts. To go one step further, once you can successfully
automate the process and detect a problem, you can then revise your
phrase to "We are already aware of the problem, and based on our previous experience it will take X minutes to fix." This would simply
require you to record problems and resolutions as events (or link to the
problems) in your monitoring database. On systems you are responsible
for monitoring, you should never learn of a monitored issue from anyone outside your team. Every problem should be detected in an automated fashion or by human eyes trained to notice it.

How Available Is Available?

Instead of looking at whether or not something is available, consider the measurement of monitoring data to be an indicator of how quickly users can get to
the data. If you look at it this way, you can see that this adds a useful dimension
to availability monitoring. You will be able to see impending availability problems before they occur if you begin with a baseline and chart the time intervals
related to response time.

On a very simple level, you could create a set of queries (that do not change
any data) based on the top n queries, or "heavy hitters" in the system. These are the
10 or 20 most important questions that you ask your data to retrieve from the application. These can be deliberately chosen based on business importance, or they
can be the most frequently executed queries with a duration above an arbitrary
interval, such as 5 seconds. These queries can then be used for tuning the system
or measuring performance (or lack thereof). Once you have this list of queries, you
can create a monitoring script or a trace that does something like the following:

1.   Record start time.

2.   Execute query. If you like, also record the Show Plan ALL output.

3. Record end time and number of records returned.

4. Store this information to a table.

Ideally, you would also collect System Monitor counters at the same time. SQL Server provides the option of creating custom counters through a User Settable object. If you set off a counter log based on an alert in Perfmon (SQLServer: User Settable Performance Object) on one of the instances of the query counter of the SQL Server User Settable object (mundanely known as user counters 1–10), you can change the value of the user counter and trigger the alert. For instance, by executing the sp_user_counter1 procedure to change the value for User Counter 1 in Perfmon prior to executing your set of queries you are able to trigger collection of other System Monitor counters as a result. Obviously, your script or trace would work into this plan quite easily (just allow a delay that equals the delay interval that the alert polls the value of the counter, to ensure everything is running at once).

Information collected this way is very simple to report on. If you also store basic SLA information, you can easily create some very useful information. Consider the reports shown in Table 15-4, which could be set up as part of a Web site.

Table 15-4   Sample Reports

Region	Status	Deviation from SLA	Last 24 Hours	Last 7 Days	Last 30 Days
East	Green	–0.16	98.19%	98.45%	98.52%
West	Yellow	–3.3	87.80%	91.10%	91.00%

In Table 15-4, the availability information is separated by region. The Status column is a quick visual indicator of whether the availability falls within acceptable ranges. Deviation from SLA indicates how much deviance is measured from the SLA. The last three columns provide numbers showing the percentage of monitoring queries that produced results that fell within the SLA. For this to work, you must define exactly how available "available" is. The easiest and most productive way to do this is not to simply record if the resource was responsive to an inquiry, but to define how responsive it should be. Have the users tell you what their expectations are to work effectively. If they expect something to respond in 60 seconds, record the availability as just that: responds within 60 seconds. This number is an availability target, even though it clearly incorporates the idea that the query must perform well and that the design must scale. This approach helps tell you when your availability is at risk due to response time decreases.

If you combine this with a report that shows you how much of your downtime was incurred based on hardware failures and operational issues, you will have a report that helps you manage your system and drive necessary process change. You will also have data to support any incident of not meeting your "nines" goal. This is far more effective than simply reporting that your system was online for a percentage of time.

To take this example a little further, look at this not by region, but by functional component or workflow. Using the top n queries approach, you can create a list that shows which functional components are significant to your users. As part of an extended SLA, you might list "My Order Status" as requiring availability with a response time of 5 seconds. You would record the workflow description of this in terms of the front-end activity, for example, "Click on Order Status || My Orders." Then you would need to design a mechanism for verifying the response time, as shown in Table 15-5.

Table 15-5   Availability by Function

Function	My Order Status		
SLA in Seconds	5		
Description	Click on Orders || My Orders		
	Last 24 Hours	**Last 7 Days**	**Last 30 Days**
Number of Attempts	939	6860	38,347
Attempts Met SLA	583	4391	24,903
Max Duration	132.48	476.65	839.68
Avg Duration	4.23	4.17	3.99
Avg Duration (Met SLA)	1.51	1.40	1.42
Avg Duration (Not Met SLA)	8.69	9.08	8.76

Table 15-5 shows one way you could report on this information. To do this you could take a lightweight profiler that included the queries sent and their duration, and map the results to specific functionality. With some simple calculations, you have a valuable report. Remember the goal is to consider availability as how quickly the users were able to get to the data.

Implementing a Monitoring Solution

At some point you have to put theory into practice. This section walks you through the various methods of implementing a monitoring solution. No matter what technology you employ, the process is going to be the same. The first step is to create a baseline. Once you have a good idea of what you are going to need to collect, you can create a good baseline with that in mind. Note that what you need to baseline will undoubtedly change over time, so it is essential with this (as with any other system) to design it so it is relatively flexible to change as your needs change.

What exactly is a baseline? This simply means setting down a record of how things look now, not unlike a photograph. When you run the same monitoring you plan to run in the future, save it and call it a baseline. You then are able to compare historical data with current data. The idea is that later on, you can compare things to this baseline to see what has changed. Later, you might find that you need to create a new baseline based on a change to the system or usage. That gives you two baselines for analysis and comparison purposes.

For example, if you monitor your transaction log file growth on a regular basis, you can start to see trends. If your starting size was 200 MB as a baseline, and you monitor the file size and record it daily, over time, you can calculate the percentage of growth and correlate it to changes to the system, such as higher usage, new users, or different work patterns.

Much more could be discussed about what exactly to save, in what format, how to report on it, and so on. Because this book has a finite amount of space, you will get a foundation you can build on. Interpretation of data will also be customized to every environment; no two numbers that might be the same can be interpreted in the same way because of the surrounding environment.

> **More Info**   The best resources are Windows Resource Kits, the SQL Server Resource Kits, and the *SQL Server 2000 Operations Guide*, which can be found at *http://www.microsoft.com/technet/treeview/ default.asp?url=/technet/prodtechnol/sql/maintain/operate/opsguide/ default.asp*.

Hardware Layer Monitoring

Hardware monitoring is required for anyone serious about maintaining availability. Obtain your hardware vendor's monitoring tool for a specific component, install it, and configure it to monitor the right servers. In most cases you can set the tool to alert you if there is a problem. Collecting this information should never be optional. However, you can monitor it through a more customized DMI tool. You can gather this information using tools such as Microsoft Operations Manager (MOM) or Microsoft Windows Management Instrumentation (WMI). Here is a list of standard information that should be checked:

- Hardware error messages
- Hardware error timestamps
- CPU cache sizes, model name, and speed
- Disk drive capacities, firmware revisions, and models
- IP numbers
- Memory sizing: total, individual application, and type of memory used
- Network interface descriptions
- PCI board names
- ROM version
- Serial number, model name, and server name

> **Tip** Note that the preceding list includes more than error messages. With the information collected from this list, you could begin to collect information for a configuration management database or a run book. For more information, read Chapter 2, "The Basics of Achieving High Availability," as well as Chapter 2 of the *SQL Server 2000 Operations Guide*.

Monitoring Windows and SQL Server Events

Once you have the hardware layer sufficiently monitored, you need to look to the software layers, namely SQL Server, Windows, and anything else running on a specific server. Ultimately, you want proactive monitoring that alerts you using e-mail, pager, or phone that there is a problem based on an event or rule. Sometimes even with minimal monitoring, there can be too much for any one person to look at everything.

Tools for Monitoring and Alerting

You can use various tools to monitor events, alert someone or something, and in some cases provide an action based on an event. Relevant Microsoft tools are described here, but you can also use capable third-party tools that might be employed in your enterprise.

> **Tip**   Prior to setting up any formal monitoring, you should set up alerts for all known failure types. You can set up SQL Server to forward events or perform alerts, but you might also consider setting up an enterprise management tool such as MOM.

Sqldiag.exe   Sqldiag.exe ships with Microsoft SQL Server 2000 and is located in the shared Binn subdirectory. You can use it to retrieve information on the current state of your SQL Server, including user information, DLL versions, configuration information, and database size information. On completion, this tool creates an output file with detailed information about your SQL Server. The file is overwritten each time you run the tool, so if you would like to archive the information, rename the output file and archive it to another location.

System Monitor   System Monitor, otherwise known as Perfmon, is the most common way of monitoring system events over time. It is found under the Start menu in Administrative Tools. You can log your results to disk or, as of Microsoft Windows Server 2003, you can also log the data captured to a SQL Server database file using a standard Open Database Connectivity (ODBC) connection. This can prove to be a very useful feature, because if you are looking to track trend information over time, you could then feed that information into Analysis Services or perform a custom analysis to provide your company with a wealth of information about your systems that was previously difficult to mine. Its usage is profiled later in this chapter.

Event Viewer   Event Viewer, which can be found under the Start menu in Administrative Tools, is generally the first place you would monitor for all types of events outside of System Monitor. There are different types of logs in Event Viewer, such as application, security, and system logs.

Log Files   Simply looking at the log files generated by an application or the operating system can provide you with invaluable information that might not be found elsewhere.

SQL Server Profiler   SQL Server Profiler can be a useful monitoring tool, especially for auditing events within SQL Server. Its use is detailed later in this chapter.

WMI   WMI is a standard programming interface like ASP.NET that lets you work with aspects of your applications so that you can create your own applications, ASP or ASP.NET pages, and so on, that can be used for monitoring or performing management tasks. For SQL Server 2000, the WMI provider is built on SQL-DMO, so it cannot do anything that DMO cannot do. There are many Windows-level events that can be tracked and acted on through WMI. Beginning with Windows Server 2003, you can also use WMI with Windows Clustering. WMI can be accessed many different ways (programs, command-line tools such as Wmic.exe, and so on), which is also a positive.

WMI is very useful for creating an in-house monitoring tool, but you must be careful. From a security perspective, you must ensure that no one who does not need access would have access to the namespace. Because there is no granularity of security privileges in WMI, once someone has access to the namespace, he or she can do anything allowed in that namespace. WMI might not work for some because the WMI provider and DMO are run in the same process space as that of the WMI management service.

> **More Info**   For more information on WMI, look at the Windows Management Instrumentation section in MSDN (*http://msdn.microsoft.com/ library/default.asp?url=/library/en-us/wmisdk/wmi/wmi_start_page.asp*), TechNet Script Center (*http://www.microsoft.com/technet/scriptcenter*), and books published on the topic, such as *Microsoft Windows 2000 Scripting Guide* (Microsoft Press, 2002).

Microsoft Operations Manager   Microsoft Operations Manager (MOM) can capture a wide variety of system and application events from distributed Windows-based systems. It is also capable of aggregating them into a central event repository. You can consolidate these events for an overall view of your enterprise, server, and service availability, or you can obtain specific information from the detailed event stream.

MOM includes a series of plug-ins, or management packs, geared toward a specific piece of functionality. Management packs exist for SQL Server and Windows Clustering. As with all other forms of monitoring, monitor only as much as you need. When you install the SQL Server management pack, all objects it monitors are enabled for monitoring by default. You should disable them and add them in one by one as you determine your monitoring needs. MOM brings a centralized management structure to your environment. MOM can monitor your servers in many different ways (for example, event logs, WMI, Simple Network Management Protocol [SNMP], log files, service status changes, and System Monitor thresholds). It can also detect when a scheduled event, such as a database backup, has been missed. Reporting is another time-saving feature that MOM provides.

Finally, and most important, MOM provides a "hands-off" monitoring solution. Once you have defined your monitoring for SQL Server (or other types of servers), those monitoring rules are automatically applied to the server based on the products that are running on it. For example, if you introduce a new SQL Server to your environment, MOM automatically recognizes that the server is running SQL Server and deploys the appropriate agent and rules. This saves you a lot of time because there is no manual setup or maintenance as servers move in and out of your environment.

MOM has a maintenance requirement for its databases because it logs all information to a SQL Server database. Also, if you want to install MOM on a clustered SQL Server 2000 instance, you need at least Microsoft Operations Manager 2000 Service Pack 1.

More Info   An in-depth discussion of MOM is largely out of scope for this book. For more information, see *http://www.microsoft.com/mom*, which includes links to documentation, including the Microsoft Operations Manager 2000 Service Pack 1 Deployment Guide at *http://www.microsoft.com/mom/techinfo/deployment/guide.asp*.

SQL Server Alerts   All versions of SQL Server include the ability to create alerts. You can create an alert as part of a SQL Server Agent job to notify you of its success or failure, or you can set up generic alerts based on certain events. You can find alerts under the SQL Server Agent tree on the Management tab in Enterprise Manager. When you create an alert, you will see the dialog boxes shown in Figures 15-1 and 15-2.

On the General tab, enter the name for the alert and select what type of alert you are creating. You can base the alert on a specific error number you know might happen, or, more broadly, you can use the severity of an event to trigger an alert. Most Microsoft production systems prefer to use the more targeted error number to associate very specific actions with unique events. You can also select the database or databases to affect by this alert. As a matter of management, you should probably create an alert, even if it is the same type, for each database you need to monitor.

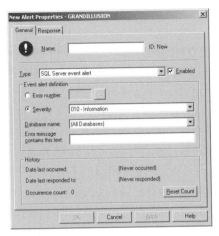

Figure 15-1   New Alert Properties dialog box General tab.

On the Response tab, you specify what to do if the alert happens. If it is something you can automate and you wish to run a specific SQL Server Agent job, select the Execute Job check box, and then select the appropriate job. Whether you automate corrective action or not, you should always notify. Creating an alert without notifying anyone is like a tree falling in the forest and no one hearing it. To notify using an e-mail alias, you must create an operator, which is then linked to a specific e-mail name. To complete the implementation you will be using the underlying SQL Mail component of SQL Server, which requires the Microsoft Outlook or compatible Messaging Application Programming Interface (MAPI) client to be installed on the box.

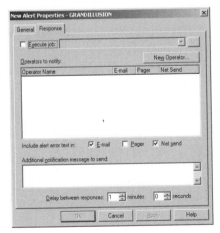

Figure 15-2   New Alert Properties dialog box Response tab.

SQL Server Notification Services   SQL Server Notification Services is an add-on product for SQL Server 2000. Although you would need to create your own solution based on Notification Services, you can create one that exactly meets your enterprise monitoring needs.

More Info   For more information on SQL Server Notification Services, see the information posted at *http://www.microsoft.com/sql/ns/default.asp*.

Monitoring System Uptime

In its most basic form, system uptime can be calculated by identifying outages and subtracting the length of those outages from a predefined window of time. This window might be every minute between 8:00 A.M. and 6:00 P.M. In some cases it could be 24 hours a day, 365 days a year.

If you really want to monitor your exact uptime number (for example, 99.983 percent), then you need to do two things:

- Decide what part of your system will be measured for availability. This would usually be from an application perspective. For a Web site, a company might define that its customer account page must be accessible, and then base its availability measurement on whether that page was available every time the monitoring tool queried it within certain windows of time.

- Decide what tool you will use to do this (and where you will store the information). Third parties that specialize in availability monitoring can monitor many enterprise-level applications that have public presence. If you are going to do it yourself, then you will need to either create a tool, using WMI for example, or MOM.

Doing these two things are good ideas for measuring your uptime in an objective way. However from a database perspective, it does not help you solve the problem if your numbers are not what you hoped they would be. Additionally, an overall availability number is good from a higher-level viewpoint, but it does not detail exactly where barriers to availability lie. If you design your own tool, make sure that you also can report on the various components of the system, and assign separate availability numbers to each. This way you can more easily identify where to spend your time eliminating barriers to availability.

Using System Monitor

System Monitor plays an important part in availability. For best results, collect the counters from the server you are monitoring, not over the network from another server. Although System Monitor is capable of monitoring over the network, you can load your network down and cause delays, depending on the speed of your network. Also, you would need to ensure that both machines involved are capable of keeping their times synchronized; otherwise, in the event of a problem, coordinating information will be extremely difficult. Unless you have a viable reason not to monitor on the server itself, avoid monitoring remotely.

> **More Info**   Chapter 4 discusses System Monitor counters you can use to monitor your disk subsystem.

Listed next are specific recommended availability counters. You could limit these to a particular process (for example, sqlservr) or a specific disk (the disk holding the data files). However if you have multiple instances on the server, you need to collect them all. On the other hand, if a separate process is monitoring at that level, then by all means focus only on SQL Server.

- **Processor\% Processor Time**   This counter is considered high if all processors are consistently above about 90 percent in most environments, and is considered low if consistently below 30 percent in most environments. Your values will vary. You can monitor total processor usage by selecting _Total, or by the individual processor number. It is not necessary to run individual processor counters over the long haul. Turn on this level when you notice the total processor time peaking in the 80 percent range.

- **Process\Various Counters**   Under Process, there are many counters that show the usage of a specific process, such as SQL Serve. Some examples are % Processor Time, IO Write Operations/sec, IO Read Operations/sec, Thread Count, and Working Set (good for Address Windowing Extensions [AWE] usage).

> **Tip**   SQL Server instances will appear as sqlservr, SQL Server Agent instances as sqlagent, and SQL Manager instances as sql-mangr. If you have multiple instances, these will be enumerated. However, keep in mind that the enumerations are in the order in which your instances were started, not in the order in which you actually installed them onto your system. There is no good way to ensure that your SQL Server instances are started in a consistent manner, because if you start them all in parallel, some might start quicker than others. The only way to ensure that the instances are in the same order is to start them one by one.

- **Memory\Available Mbytes**   This tells you how much physical memory is actually free on the system.

- **Memory\Pages/sec**   This counter should be very low (under 10 or 20), and none of the paging should be associated with the sqlservr process. Of course, if you are using AWE memory, that comes from the nonpageable pool so you would expect this counter to always be zero (or close to it). You can use DBCC MEMORYSTATUS to provide a snapshot of the current memory status of SQL Server. The output shows distribution of 8 K pages among the various components of SQL Server. It contains sections for stolen memory (the lazywriter is not allowed to flush stolen buffers, which include most of the buffers that are in use), free memory (buffers not currently in use), procedures (compiled stored procedures and ad hoc plans), InRam (that is, pinned tables), dirty (pages not yet flushed to disk), kept (temporarily pinned in-use pages), I/O (waiting on pending I/O), latched (pages being scanned), and other (data pages not currently in use).

- **PhysicalDisk\Avg. Disk sec/Transfer**   This counter is more useful than the disk queue length for seeing exactly how long you are waiting on the disk to respond. Because response time is made up of service time and queuing time, as queue lengths increase the response time becomes dominated by queuing time. Longer queue lengths therefore translate directly to longer response times. If you are seeing response times greater than 25 msec for random requests or 2 msec for sequential requests, you probably have some nontrivial queuing delays (but not necessarily a cause for alarm). Certainly if you exceed 50 msec average response time you should be concerned. This counter in particular is a great baseline counter to use over time.

The following counters are related to a particular SQL Server instance, so you need to gather information on all the instances currently running on that server. All of the SQL Server counter information also appears in the system table master..sysperfinfo, so you might wish to instead collect that information from within SQL Server. More information on how to do that is provided in the next section. Using sysperinfo might benefit you.

- **SQLServer: Buffer Manager\Buffer cache hit ratio**   The Buffer cache hit ratio tells you, in a percentage format, how much SQL Server could use the pages in memory versus having to read from the disk. This number will vary, because if you have a heavy write and not a heavy read application, you will not be keeping many things in memory.

- **SQLServer: SQL Statistics\Batch Requests/sec** The Batch Requests/sec counter reveals the incoming workload for prepared statements, but if your application uses stored procedures it might not be a good counter to use because a procedure might have many statements in a single batch. The value of this counter should be high (reflecting high usage of the system), and is only a matter of concern when it is very low (below 100 or so), but even that might not represent a problem if you have large stored procedures.

- **SQLServer: Databases\Transactions/sec**   If you have a lot of writes to your database, this counter might be a better indicator of how much work is being done in a unit of time. This is also another great baseline counter.

  If neither Batch Requests/sec nor Transactions/sec is a really good indicator of workload, you might have to rely on an application-specific metric to determine your throughput.

- **SQLServer: General Statistics\User Connections**   By itself, this counter does not indicate much, but it can be useful when evaluated over time and in comparison with the other counters.

- **SQLServer: SQL Statistics\SQL Compilations/sec**   This counter is considered high if consistently above 10 or so at steady state; ideally the value should be zero.

- **SQLServer: Memory Manager\Connection Memory (KB)**   This tells you how much memory the sum of the user connections for that instance is consuming.

- **SQLServer: Memory Manager\Total Server Memory (KB)**   This tells you how much memory the instance is consuming.

- **SQLServer: General Statistics\Logins/sec and Logouts/sec**   These tell you how many logins or logouts you are having. If there is an excessive amount of either, you could be getting hacked.

- **SQLServer: General Statistics\User Connections**   This tells you the total number of users at any given point for an instance.

- **SQLServer: Buffer Manager\AWE counters**   There are various counters for monitoring AWE usage.

Make sure your collection interval is not more frequent than once every 15 seconds (it can be a much wider interval, up to 15 minutes). When you choose to archive the information for later use, such as deriving a new baseline value, you should only keep an average over a period of time to cut down on the amount of data you are storing.

Automated Collection of Data

There are several ways to automate the collection of information from System Monitor (or other aspects of the operating system). One is to use MOM; another is to create your own monitoring collection agent using WMI.

> **More Info**   There is a lot more information available about WMI in the TechNet Script Center online at *http://www.microsoft.com/technet/ scriptcenter*, or you can simply navigate to it from the main menu tree on TechNet. Also, there are some code samples on the CD that accompanies this book.

You can use simpler, old-fashioned methods for automating the collection of this information. First, you should be aware that System Monitor Perfmon is an ActiveX object and can be started from HTML.

> **More Info**   Using HTML to monitor with System Monitor is included as part of the *SQL Server 2000 Resource Kit* in the automatic System Monitor generation tool that is on the *SQL Server 2000 Resource Kit* CD under DBManagement. You could also code your own solution, but this provides a good base to start from.

Another way is to set it up through the System Monitor interface. To do this, simply navigate to counter logs in System Monitor, right-click, and select New Log Settings from the shortcut menu. Add the counters in question and set the collection interval to something reasonable. In Microsoft Windows 2000, set it up to save the output to a .csv file, and then save it.

> **Tip**   Never use a Universal Naming Convention (UNC) path to a log file. The overhead is far too high for the volume of information that needs to be logged.

If you choose to log data to a file, you can set a maximum limit on the file size. You can also schedule it to start a new log file when one of them is full (which breaks it into easy-to-import chunks). You need to decide how long the log should collect data once it is started by the alert, unless you opted to store it to a SQL table. You might schedule it to stop the log after 3 hours, for example, or at a specific time. You can set it to run a command every time a log file closes, so you could actually have it import the data as it goes.

In Windows Server 2003, you have the option of saving the output to a SQL Server database. This is a good solution for some things, and there will be some overhead, but this is lightweight monitoring, and you are going to observe the impact before running it all the time, as discussed earlier in the chapter. You might drop entries if you are using tables, so be careful when using this approach.

Then, go to System Monitor alerts, create a new one, and add a counter to it. This counter sets off the alert. To find this counter, select the SQL Server performance object named User Settable; there is only one counter for this one (Query), so just select the instance you want to use, such as User Counter 1. Set the alert to occur when the value is over the limit of, for example, 0. Then set the sample interval to every 30 to 60 seconds (or whatever seems reasonable to you); this number reflects how much of a delay there can be between turning on the counter and triggering the alert. Next, set up the action the alert will take. In this case we want it to start a performance log; choose the one you just created.

Inside of SQL Server, create a job that will run the following commands as steps:

```
EXECUTE sp_user_counter1 1
WAITFOR DELAY '00:05:00'
EXECUTE sp_user_counter1 0
```

This way you can execute the job on demand to set off the monitoring from within SQL Server, if you wish. You could set it off without making the alert and job to do it. You also want to collect information from a trace at the same time.

Next, you need a script to import the Perfmon data. The easiest way to do this is to import the first one so you can get your table created correctly. The table always defaults to varchar columns unless you format it yourself to match your counter data. This is where this process can get difficult. If your filename is always the same, you are all set. However, if it is a rollover file that appends numbers, or if it simply appends the date, then the filename is different, and you run into a problem of automating the load. This is easy enough to solve if you have the coding knowledge, and you might want to learn this to broaden your horizons. There are numerous sample scripts available online in developer communities that could assist with this task.

Once the information is imported, you can query it and report on it like any other data in a table. One huge benefit of having this information in the database is having the full facility of Transact-SQL at your disposal to be able to easily find out precisely what was occurring in a certain time range.

Using Sysperfinfo

Sysperfinfo is a system table, and its contents are described in Table 15-6. Normally, you should not use system tables, but this is a table used for read-only information that can prove very useful. Because System Monitor essentially gets its values from sysperfinfo, you can create your own management tool that might be more natural for you to work with as a database developer than System Monitor.

> **Note** There are a few caveats to be aware of before you use sysperfinfo directly. First, it only captures information for the first 99 databases on an instance. Any databases beyond those 99 are not in the system table. It impacts your system's processor, memory, and disk I/O to some small degree. Take these factors into account if monitoring Processor Time, Pages per sec, and Disk sec/Transfer information. Also, because sysperfinfo is for dynamic data, it does not store the information historically. You would need your own mechanism to save the information to another table. Finally, remember that that these counters are not persistent, so they reset every time the instance restarts. If you end up with data that does not seem correct, remember that the counter values roll over when they pass the limit of the column data type.

Table 15-6 **Sysperfinfo Table Contents**

Sysperfinfo Column Name	Description	Sample Value
object_name	Performance object name, such as SQL Server: Lock Manager or SQL Server: Buffer Manager.	SQLServer: Cache Manager
Counter_name	Name of the performance counter within the object, such as Page Requests or Locks Requested.	Cache hit ratio
instance_name	Named instance of the counter. For example, there are counters maintained for each type of lock, such as Table, Page, Key, and so on. The instance name distinguishes between similar counters. The instance name can also be the name of a database where a counter can be viewed at that level.	_Total
Cntr_value	Actual counter value. In most cases, this will be a level or monotonically increasing counter that counts occurrences of the instance event.	175
Cntr_type	Type of counter as defined by the Microsoft Windows NT 4.0 performance architecture.	537003008

There are a few types of counters represented in sysperfinfo. In some cases, you cannot just select a counter and use its value directly. For example, to calculate a percentage (such as the buffer cache hit ratio), you need to take two values, which are the main value itself (such as Buffer cache hit ratio) and the base value that is the number used to divide by. This is usually denoted with the word *base* added to the associated counter value. All base counters have a cntr_type value of 1073939459, and the number used as the upper number has a cntr_type value of 537003008. Examples are shown here:

```
-- Instance-wide counter
SELECT (CAST(a.cntr_value as NUMERIC(20,4)))/(CAST(b.cntr_value AS
NUMERIC(20,4))) AS 'Buffer cache hit ratio'
FROM master..sysperfinfo a, master..sysperfinfo b
WHERE a.counter_name ='Buffer cache hit ratio'
AND b.counter_name ='Buffer cache hit ratio base'
```

```
-- Example for a specific instance_name
SELECT (CAST(a.cntr_value AS NUMERIC(20,4)))/(CAST(b.cntr_value AS
NUMERIC(20,4))) as 'Cache Hit Ratio'
FROM master..sysperfinfo a, master..sysperfinfo b
WHERE a.counter_name ='Cache Hit Ratio'
AND b.counter_name ='Cache Hit Ratio Base'
AND a.instance_name = '_Total'
AND b.instance_name = '_Total'
```

Other counters, such as those with averages, need to be calculated as well. This means that you need to store the value for a counter and then perform math to get the average value based on the current value and the last value. That is how it is displayed in System Monitor. However, tracking it over time, you can get longer averages than you might be able to get with a normal System Monitor trace. Usually the counters that are averaged are cumulative ones, such as Transactions/sec, which is available to different instance_name values. All cumulative counters have a cntr_type value of 272696320. By themselves, cumulative counters are only snapshots of the moments in time they are measuring. The following is an example of grabbing one point in time for the counter Transactions/sec for all databases:

```
SELECTinstance_name,
'Transactions/sec' = cntr_value
FROM master..sysperfinfo
WHERE object_name = 'SQLServer:Databases'
ANDcounter_name = 'Transactions/sec'
ORDER BY instance_name
```

If you want to get the average, you need to be able to store these to a table or somewhere else that you can average two numbers. The following example takes the values from a table called average_values. The table is populated by an application that runs the following statement to populate the table (it can be explicit Transact-SQL or run as a stored procedure):

```
INSERT INTO average_values
SELECTobject_name, counter_name, instance_name, cntr_value, GETDATE()
FROM master..sysperfinfo
WHEREcounter_name = 'Transactions/sec'
ORDER BY instance_name
```

If you now want to average the last two values, here is one way to do it:

```
SELECT TOP 2 *
INTO #tmp_tran_avg
FROM average_values
WHERE instance_name = '_Total'
ANDcounter_name = 'Transactions/sec'
ORDER BY time_inserted DESC
```

```
SELECT SUM(cntr_value)/2 AS 'Average Transactions/sec for two consecutive
readings'
FROM #tmp_tran_avg

DROP TABLE #tmp_tran_avg
```

If you want to average all data captured over a specific period of time, you can do that as well. The following example calculates averages for all data captured over a one-minute period. Remember that this number, unless you are capturing the data at each time interval (say every second), might not be a complete reflection of an average, but it represents a good approximation.

```
DECLARE @max_time DATETIME

DECLARE @max_time_less_1_min DATETIME

SET @max_time = (SELECT MAX(time_inserted) FROM average_values WHERE
instance_name = '_Total')
SET @max_time_less_1_min = DATEADD(mi,-1,@max_time)

SELECT avg_val_id, instance_name, cntr_value, time_inserted
INTO #tmp_tran_avg
FROM average_values
WHERE instance_name = '_Total'
AND counter_name = 'Transactions/sec'
GROUP BY avg_val_id, instance_name, cntr_value, time_inserted
HAVING time_inserted >= @max_time_less_1_min
ORDER BY time_inserted DESC

SELECT SUM(cntr_value)/count(cntr_value) AS 'Average Transactions/sec over a 1
minute period'
FROM #tmp_tran_avg

DROP TABLE #tmp_tran_avg
```

Finally, you can average all values you have captured over the lifetime of monitoring to get a picture of a certain counter. The following are two examples:

```
SELECT SUM(cntr_value)/COUNT(cntr_value) AS 'Instance Average Transactions/sec'
FROM average_values
WHERE instance_name = '_Total'
AND counter_name = 'Transactions/sec'

SELECT SUM(cntr_value)/COUNT(cntr_value) AS 'MSDB Average Transactions/sec'
FROM average_values
WHERE instance_name = 'msdb'
AND counter_name = 'Transactions/sec'
```

More monolithic counters, such as Percent Log Used or Active Transactions, are also only snapshots of the time being observed. These have a cntr_type value of 65536. An example of a monolithic counter query is as follows:

```
SELECT cntr_value AS 'User Connections'
FROM master..sysperfinfo
WHERE object_name = 'SQLServer:General Statistics'
AND counter_name = 'User Connections'
```

On the CD   The preceding Transact-SQL statements can be found in the file Sysperfinfo_Examples.sql.

Caution   Compilations can be a significant detrimental factor, typically characterized by high CPU usage and low throughput, and can be viewed directly through the SQLServer: SQL Statistics\SQL Compilations/sec counter. If you monitor and find this issue, see Knowledge Base articles 243588, "INF: Troubleshooting Performance of Ad-Hoc Queries," and 243586, "INF: Troubleshooting Stored Procedure Recompilation" available at *http://support.microsoft.com/* for helpful information.

Profiler/Trace Core

SQL Server Profiler actually runs a trace in SQL Server and makes it easier for you to manipulate it graphically. However, running SQL Server Profiler as a graphic utility incurs system overhead that might be better utilized for servicing database requests. Set up a trace the hard way (using script) and you can easily control it from a job while getting the same results.

On the CD   There is a stored procedure, LRQ_Trace_Start, in the file LRQ.zip that performs this function. It also imports the trace file automatically and stores it to a table.

One of the more interesting features of this `LRQ_Trace_Start` is the use of `::fn_trace_gettable`, a function that allows you to directly query a trace file, even one that has multiple rollover files, and view it as you would a table. The script, LRQ_permanent_trace.sql, also contains more code that manages the process and allows it to work properly in a production environment.

The interesting thing about this script is its reusability. There are a couple of common reasons that people run a trace. One is to audit security or audit changes to system objects, usually with a very tightly focused trace. Another is for performance tuning. A great deal of the tracing that goes on with Microsoft's own internal systems is of this variety. If there is a performance problem, the DBAs that are put in charge of these systems usually want to be the first to know. In the second case, a trace is run as far as it can go at full bore during a crisis. Because there is seemingly a problem, SQL Server Profiler is started to see if anything looks wrong. DBAs who use SQL Server Profiler very effectively are unfortunately in the minority.

By providing this script, you should run a lightweight, tightly focused trace to help you identify queries with response times that stray into the unacceptable range. The sample trace that is provided is run permanently on many critical production SQL Servers at Microsoft. The traces are made permanent by SQL Server Agent jobs that restart them if they are stopped. Daily reports highlighting the previous day's performance are sent out in e-mails to the application owners. The report also shows performance trends over the last 30 days for comparative purposes. This helps with performance tuning efforts, and if you archive the data you can chart degradations in performance and act on them before they impact availability. Knowing the trend in advance of the end users "feeling" the trend is the sign of a sophisticated operations organization. It really does not require high-powered monitoring tools to adopt and implement best practices like this.

It is important to note that this trace is designed specifically to mitigate the performance impact on the server. To this end, the events include *only* the Transact-SQL batch completed and remote procedure call (RPC) statement completed. Do not add more events to this trace, such as statement starting or stored procedure statements. Although they are useful, they increase the impact on the server and are not something you want in a *permanently* running trace.

Filter the trace to queries with durations greater than 10 seconds to also limit the performance impact. This is meant for OLTP systems; reporting systems with a longer standard for queries would probably require a higher duration filter. By limiting the events captured and by using a duration filter, you should experience negligible performance impact on the server.

> **On the CD**   To examine trace data, you can use the procedure `Monitor_LRQ`, which is created by the file LRQ_Monitor.sql in LRQ.zip. Another useful script in LRQ.zip is Performance_Trend.sql, which reports on output duration trends over specific time periods ranging back to 30 days.

A by-product of a good application is unavoidable database growth. As databases become larger there will always be some tuning and tweaking that can produce better performance. Some of this takes the form of reoptimizing queries and indexes. Having this report and historical comparisons can help you identify where you can best spend your time optimizing queries.

The approach of monitoring for response time shows you how a SQL Server trace can be used to record baseline performance of the database itself and detect significant deviations in response times expected by the user community.

Those of you who are paying sharp attention will realize that the scripts provided do not monitor response time of all functional pieces of the system (see the earlier section "How Available Is Available?"). The reason for this is that we do not recommend that you do this on every server you have. You *can* do that with the permanent trace example.

To create a full-scale trace of response times for purposes of availability, you can take one of several approaches. First, you could simply define a metric such as "all queries run in less than 10 seconds, except for these." The advantage of that is that you could run the permanent trace for it. The caveat is that you would have to both make sure it is understood that from the database side you can monitor only query duration, not the actual time it takes to return to the user's desktop, and make a report on duration that excludes the queries your users agree will take longer than the blanket duration number (10 seconds in this case).

Another way to approach it, based on exactly what is running on some of Microsoft's internal servers, is to select specific servers that are targets for high availability measured by response time. Set up a permanent trace on those *without* the duration filter. You will collect a significantly greater amount of data with this method, so you might want to run it for an hour during peak time and then calculate how much data you expect to get back and how you will accommodate it from a storage perspective. For example, you could immediately archive it to your centralized administration SQL Server or a server that is not so heavily used.

You can also experiment with specific filters, such as those that record only queries with text data you are monitoring for, for example, select, insert, update, and delete, or names of specific procedures. Or you can exclude text data you are *not* looking for in the permanent trace by filtering out specific tables or procedures such as exec sp_cursorfetch. To do this intelligently, you first need to define which items you are going to watch for (specific queries that map to functional areas). This requires some meticulous work, and we suggest you start with a one functional workflow. Once you are very comfortable with this, consider others.

Monitoring Extended Blocking and Deadlocks

Extended blocking and deadlocking indicates a design issue in your application that needs to be resolved. This could be due to poorly written statements that escalate to table locks, slow hardware, long transactions that must complete before others can use a column, and more. If you have an application that shows symptoms of blocking and locking, such as low CPU utilization combined with low throughput, you need to capture these problems to decide what actions to take. There are several methods documented on the Microsoft site, including Knowledge Base article 224453 "INF: Understanding and Resolving SQL Server 7.0 or 2000 Blocking Problems," as well as elsewhere. Choose the approach that you feel most comfortable with and implement it. Just be sure it has a way to map any issues that occur to queries that were running.

> **Tip**   Beware of using DBCC INPUTBUFFER to capture running queries, because when your application uses sp_executesql, that is all you will see in the input buffer.

> **On the CD**   There is a tool to assist you in monitoring blocked processes in SQL. Use the file Blocking_Monitor.sql in Blocking_Monitor.zip. Should you need to ever call Microsoft Product Support Services for a blocking and deadlocking problem with your queries, they will require that you use Knowledge Base article 271509 "INF: How to Monitor SQL Server 2000 Blocking."

Monitoring Database and Transaction Log Space

If your files fill up and cannot grow further, this directly impacts your availability. Of course, you do not want them growing during production hours either, if you can help it, because if a database is growing, it cannot service requests during the expansion. It is a good idea to keep tabs on the space remaining. Here is a sample using sysperfinfo for programmatically obtaining that information:

```
SELECT'Log File(s) Used Size (KB)' = a.cntr_value,
'Log File(s) Size (KB)' = b.cntr_value,
'Log File Space remaining' =
b.cntr_value - a.cntr_value,
'Database' = a.instance_name
FROM master..sysperfinfo a
JOIN master..sysperfinfo b
ON a.object_name = b.object_name
AND a.instance_name = b.instance_name
WHERE a.object_name = 'SQLServer:Databases'
AND a.counter_name = 'Log File(s) Used Size (KB)'
AND b.counter_name = 'Log File(s) Size (KB)'
```

On the CD   Some tools that might help you with monitoring your database space and disk usage are included in Database_Capacity_ and_Disk_Capacity_Monitor.zip.

Monitoring Index Fragmentation

Properly tuned and managed indexes are crucial to good performance. Incorrect indexing might show up in symptoms such as high processor usage with low throughput, table scans, and queries that initiate a high number of reads and have long duration. Keep your statistics up to date, either by using update statistics or updating them later. Keep them defragmented as well.

More Info   See Knowledge Base article 243589, "HOW TO: Troubleshoot Slow-Running Queries on SQL Server 7.0 or Later," for some information on index tuning, and also refer to HA_Perf_and_Scale.doc on the accompanying CD. For more information on indexes and fragmentation, see Chapter 14, "Administrative Tasks to Increase Availability."

> **On the CD**   For scripts that might help you deal with your fragmen-
> tation, see Index_Analysis_Tool.sql and IndexDefrag_Tool.sql in
> Defrag.zip.

Monitoring Read/Write Statistics per File

This type of information can be useful when you want to look at your
read:write ratio, or when you are tracking usage of a particular database or of
each database file separately:

```
SELECT dats.name,
stats.FileId,
stats.NumberReads,
stats.NumberWrites,
stats.BytesRead,
stats.BytesWritten,
'UserWaitTime(ms)' = stats.IoStallMS,
BytesPerRead = CASE WHEN ISNULL(stats.NumberReads,0) > 0
THEN stats.BytesRead/stats.NumberReads
ELSE 0 END,
BytesPerWrite = CASE WHEN ISNULL(stats.NumberWrites,0) > 0
THEN stats.BytesWritten/stats.NumberWrites
ELSE 0 END,
WaitPerRead = CASE WHEN ISNULL (stats.NumberReads,0) > 0
THEN stats.IoStallMS/stats.NumberReads
ELSE 0 END,
WaitPerWrite = CASE WHEN ISNULL (stats.NumberWrites,0) > 0
THEN stats.IOStallMS/stats.NumberWrites
ELSE 0 END
FROM ::fn_virtualfilestats(-1,-1) AS stats
JOIN master.dbo.sysdatabases dats ON stats.DBId = dats.dbid
```

This can become important when you need to track usage of each file separately either to determine where a problem lies, or to help you redesign your
database file layout.

Monitoring Your Monitor and Other Critical Services

One important aspect of monitoring overlooked in most environments is ensuring that the tools you are using to monitor are up and running. In the event of
a problem with your monitor tools, how will you monitor your environment?
Remember that essential Windows services, such as RPC for a server cluster,

must be monitored to ensure that they are available. Monitoring these things goes beyond the normal monitoring of a database or a server for performance through System Monitor or SQL Server Profiler. You need to have redundant monitoring systems in place so that your monitoring center will never miss a beat. There is nothing worse than end users' or customers' experiencing a problem when the people on the other end are unaware because they do not even know the monitoring system is down.

Capacity Planning and Monitoring

Until now, the discussion on monitoring has been largely focused on being proactive and reactive in a production environment. However, if you have the proper monitoring, you can use it for much more than your 24-hour operations: you can use it like a crystal ball to help you predict the future.

In numerous places in this book, capacity planning has been mentioned as a success factor in helping you with your solutions. The only way to achieve any reasonable form of capacity planning is with data gathered through monitoring. If you are carefully tracking each system's usage over time, you are actually painting an accurate picture of its life. Much like medical records and family history are leading indicators of an individual's health future, these reports and collected data can help you predict things such as usage, rate of growth, potential bottlenecks, system life cycles, availability potential, and more. Look back at Chapter 4 and Chapter 11, "Real-World High Availability Solutions," for planning your disk capacity, where ways to arrive at an intelligent guess based on pure data consumption were discussed. But what if you knew things like how many new users you would add per month or per year? How much better would your "guess" be if you knew what the trends for index growth and usage patterns were? Some would argue that disk space is cheap and quite available. However, disks become increasingly slower when data is being put close to the spindle. Sizing right in the beginning is another sign of a sophisticated operations team.

Summary

There is no such thing as a /monitoring startup switch for SQL Server, and there is no magic potion that cures all ills, either. The only trick is the monitoring system that you create for your environment. Monitoring represents the final piece of the puzzle. Up until this point, you have planned and designed for availability and put people, systems, and processes in place. Monitoring is the bow on the package that tells you after the solution is in place that it is healthy, available, and performing as expected. Your monitoring solutions can range from simple to complex, but without monitoring, you will never achieve high availability because your environment will lack the underlying base of information that all highly available systems require. Monitoring also facilitates capacity management by capturing trends over time. This information is useful in any planning stage where hardware needs to be purchased for a future solution. In the end, though, it all comes down to devising a monitoring scheme that works for your environment so you have the information to make decisions with confidence.

Glossary

active/active cluster A configuration of two SQL Server installations in a clustered environment where each node is initially configured with one SQL Server installation but where either node can host both "active" SQL Servers. This term applies to SQL Server 6.5 and SQL Server 7.0 clusters only. It has been replaced by a multiple-instance cluster for SQL Server 2000.

active/passive cluster A configuration with one SQL Server installation in a clustered environment where one "active" node runs the SQL Server resources, and the other is waiting for a potential failover. This term applies to SQL Server 6.5 and SQL Server 7.0 clusters only. It has been replaced by a single-instance cluster for SQL Server 2000.

change management The process allowing changes to applications to occur in a predictable fashion with minimal or no impact on the service. Change management applies to all phases of a lifecycle.

client/application redirection The process of diverting client or application usage to another SQL Server database in the event of a replication failure—if replication is the high-availability method employed—or in the event of a role change.

cluster group A collection of cluster resources analogous to a folder on your hard drive that contains multiple files.

cluster node A physical server participating in a cluster.

cluster resource Object types which may be added to cluster resource groups to provide a specific type of cluster functionality that can be utilized by the cluster. Default cluster resource types include DHCP servers, MSDTC, file shares, generic applications/services, servers running IIS, IP addresses, network names, MSMQ, physical disks, print spoolers, and time services.

cluster resource group See *cluster group.*

cluster-aware application An application that runs on a node, is managed as a cluster resource, and is designed to be aware of and interact with the server cluster environment. SQL Server 2000 is an example of a cluster-aware application. The clustering application program interface provides the programming elements necessary to work directly with cluster objects and to interact with the Cluster Service service.

clustering   Connecting two or more computers in such a way that they behave like a single computer to an application or client. Clustering is used for parallel processing, load balancing, and fault tolerance.

convergence   The process used by Network Load Balancing to reach consensus on what the Network Load Balancing cluster looks like. See *Network Load Balancing*.

DAS   See *direct attached storage*.

default instance   An installation of SQL Server 2000 that generally uses the name of the underlying server, or a specific name in a server cluster that is the name of neither an individual node nor the server cluster itself. A default instance is similar to the experience of having one installation of SQL Server 7.0 or earlier per server. There can only be one default instance of SQL Server on an individual standalone server or a single server cluster. All other instances must be named instances.

differential database backup   A type of database backup that only backs up changes made to the database since the last full database backup.

direct attached storage   An external disk array connected to one or more servers via traditional disk protocols such as SCSI.

disaster recovery   The process of executing documented procedures to restore a server or an entire environment after a catastrophic problem occurs.

disk page   The fundamental unit of data storage for SQL Server. The page size in SQL Server 2000 is 8192 bytes, or 8 KB.

downtime   The amount of time that a given system or solution is not available for servicing requests.

extent   The basic unit by which space is allocated to a table or an index. An extent is eight continuous disk pages, which equates to 64 KB.

failover   The process in which, in response to a node or resource failure, resources in a cluster switch ownership and start on another node in the server cluster. This term applies to a server cluster/failover cluster combination only. In log shipping implementations, the similar terms *switch* and *role change* are used to describe the change in ownership that occurs between primary and secondary servers.

failover clustering   The SQL Server 2000 implementation of clustering for availability that is built on a Windows Server Cluster.

federated cluster   A grouping of SQL servers used together to achieve scalability by employing a distributed partition view. A federated cluster is not used for availability, only for achieving scalability through scale out.

filegroup   A named collection of one or more disk files that represent a single allocation on or for administration of a database. A database can have more than one filegroup.

five nines   Shorthand for a system's being available, or having uptime, 99.999 percent of the time.

full database backup   A complete point-in-time backup of a database.

heartbeat network   See *private network*.

IsAlive process   A check in the server cluster, run after LooksAlive, that is an application-specific health check. For SQL Server 2000, this issues a SELECT @@*Servername* query to determine if the SQL Server instance can handle requests.

load testing   The process of testing an application, entire solution, or hardware component under realistic conditions, or load, to ensure that it will behave properly in a highly utilized production environment.

Log Sequence Number (LSN)   A unique identifier assigned to a record in the transaction log that is incremented automatically.

log shipping   The process of backing up a transaction log on one SQL Server, copying it, and then applying it to another SQL Server where a full database backup of that original database has been applied with the proper settings.

log shipping pair   The log shipping primary/secondary combination.

log shipping primary   The server containing the database source of the transaction logs.

log shipping secondary   The server containing the database recipient of the transaction logs in a log-shipping pair.

logical disk   See *logical drive*.

logical drive   Any volume created that Windows can see, after it has been formatted and assigned a drive letter. You can have multiple logical drives per volume.

logical unit (LUN)   See *volume*.

LooksAlive process   A specifically coded application-level health check in a server cluster to ensure that the application is up and running. For SQL Server, this is a lightweight check.

LSN   See *log sequence number*.

LUN   See *volume*.

LUN masking   A relationship between a specific volume and a host at the disk controller level.

mean time between failures (MTBF)   The average expected time between failures of a specific component.

mean time to recovery (MTTR)   The average time it takes to recover from a failure.

Microsoft Cluster Service (MSCS)   The original name for a server cluster under Windows NT 4.0.

MSCS   See *Microsoft Cluster Service.*

MTBF   See *mean time between failures.*

MTTR   See *mean time to recovery.*

multiple-instance cluster   A SQL Server 2000 failover cluster with more than one SQL Server virtual server.

named instance   An installation of SQL Server 2000 that has a unique name to differentiate itself from other SQL Server instances. The name must be unique for both the server as well as the domain. There can be multiple named instances of SQL Server on an individual standalone server or a single server cluster.

Network-Attached Storage   Low-cost, high-density storage generally used to store files; generally not used with databases.

Network Load Balancing   The type of clustering under Windows Clustering that provides scalability and availability for IP-based services and some SQL Server uses.

nine   Refers to the digit 9 in a percentage that represents availability. For example, three nines is 99.9 percent.

node   See *cluster node.*

perceived downtime/unavailability   The amount of time that a system or application is unavailable to those who normally access it from a business standpoint, although the server itself may be up and running and having normal maintenance performed on it, or one part of the overall solution is down, preventing access to that server.

physical disk   The actual disk used internally in a system or as part of a disk array.

primary   See *log shipping primary.*

private network   In a cluster, the dedicated intra-cluster network used to run processes that check to see if the cluster is up and running. For non-clustered machines or other uses, a private network is one that is segmented off from the public network on a different subnet to offload tasks such as large file copies.

public network   On a standalone server or a cluster, the network that allows clients and applications to access the server itself.

quorum   In a server cluster, contains the master copy of the server cluster's configuration and is also used as a tie-breaker if all network communication fails between the nodes. Depending on the type of server cluster implemented, this may or may not be a physical disk on the shared cluster disk array.

RAID   See *redundant array of independent disks*.

recovery model   The database-level setting—either Bulk-Logged, Full, or Simple under SQL Server 2000—that controls the amount of logging that occurs.

redundant array of independent disks (RAID)   A specific fault-tolerant disk array system design strategy that takes into account issues of cost benefit, reliability, and performance. It can be implemented at a hardware or a software level; each provides a different profile of cost, reliability, and performance. Depending on the person defining RAID, the word *independent* may be substituted with *inexpensive*.

resource group   See *cluster resource group*.

role change   The process of switching from the log shipping primary to the secondary; applies to log shipping only. This is a manual process.

run book   A centralized and continually updated collection of information such as contacts, phone numbers, disaster recovery plans, software license information, support information, and so on. It is used in the event of an emergency to ensure the system can be brought back online in a timely fashion.

SAN   See *storage area network*.

secondary   See *log shipping secondary*.

server cluster   The type of Windows Clustering that provides availability only. It is a collection of nodes that allow resources to be failed over to another node in the event of a problem. SQL Server 2000 failover clustering is installed and configured on top of a server cluster.

service level agreement (SLA)   A signed agreement of system service requirements between two parties (such as your company and an ASP or between your department and end users) that defines the guidelines, response times, actions, and so on, that will be adhered to for the life of the agreement.

shared cluster disk array   In a server cluster, the DAS or SAN that contains the disks used by the nodes.

single-instance cluster   This is a SQL Server 2000 failover cluster configured with only one SQL Server virtual server. This replaces the term active/passive.

SLA   See *service level agreement.*

spindle   Another name for an individual physical disk.

standby server   A server configured to be brought online in the event of a failure of the current server used in production. Standby servers are commonly referred to as "hot" or "warm" standby servers to reflect how quickly the server can be pressed into production.

storage area network (SAN)   An external disk array connected to one or more servers via underlying networking protocols, such as fibre, and requiring specialized hardware. SANs provide flexibility, availability, scalability, reliability, and ease of configuration.

switch   The process of switching from one server to another in the event of a problem. This is usually used for non-clustered implementations where a manual process is implied.

transaction log backup   A backup of the transaction log that flushes the transactions from the transaction log to a file. To have transaction log backup integrity, each consecutive file must not break the LSN chain.

uptime   The amount of time that a given system or solution is available for servicing requests.

virtual server   The combination of the network name and IP address that makes up the clustered application or server that a client or application will access. This appears as a normal application or server. Both the server cluster itself, and a SQL Server 2000 instance installed on a cluster, can be considered virtual servers.

volume   The amount of physical disk that Windows recognizes after the storage is configured at a hardware level (whether one individual disk or a RAID subsystem). The volume is then formatted and configured in other ways so Windows and applications can use it in different ways.

warm standby   A server waiting to be brought online; generally refers to the secondary in a log shipping pair.

Windows Clustering   The umbrella group of clustering technologies for the Windows platform, which currently includes a server cluster and Network Load Balancing.

zoning   Isolating volumes on a SAN so that only designated computers that have access to the zone can see them and activity in that zone will not affect other volumes and users on the SAN.

Index

Symbols and Numbers

(continued)

(continued)

striping with parity (RAID 5), 117–19, 133–37, 523
transaction logs and, 390
RAISERROR, 384
random I/O, 112
raw disk space, 87–88
readahead I/O, 112
read-only access, 274–75
read-only database, 43–44, 68–69
read-only SQL Servers, 205–6
read-only tables, 441
read/write statistics, 723
read-write tables, 441
REBUILDM command-line utility, 125
reconstruction, 563–65
recovery. *See also* backup and restore; disaster recovery
  paths, 436
  up-to-the-minute recovery, 442
  Windows Server 2003 enhancements, 155
RECOVERY completion state, 483–84
recovery models, 404–16
  Bulk-Logged recovery model, 409–12
  choosing, 407–8, 413–14
  Full recovery model, 408–9
  functions of, 406
  log shipping, 283–85
  overview of, 404–6
  settings, 400
  Simple recovery model, 412–13
  switching between, 414–16
  tail of the log and, 407
redo phase, database recovery, 483
redundancy. *See also* RAID (redundant array of independent disks)
  backup strategies and, 443
  booting Windows from SANs, 145
  prevention and, 4–5
registry
  page files, 671–72
  permissions, 645
Registry Editor, 259
release readiness review, 45
Remote Administration mode, Terminal Services, 147
Remote Distributor, 356–57
remote mirroring, 119–20
remote procedure calls (RPCs), 165
remote sites, 536
replication, 345–77
  agents, 353–55
  architecture, 352
  database availability and, 345–46
  database schema and, 348–52
  database synchronization and, 517
  disk capacity and, 360–63
  distribution database and, 124–25
  Distributors and, 356–58
  failover clusters compared with, 77–78
  file types, 354
  logins and, 348

log shipping and, 74–77, 372–75
merge replication, 346
overview of, 69–71
primary database and, 278
Publishers and, 356–58
Republishers, 358–59
role changes and, 375–77
service packs and, 360, 633–34
snapshot replication, 347
transactional replication, 74–77, 347–48
upgrades and, 601–2, 618
replication, disaster recovery, 363–72
  backing up replicated database, 364–65
  Distributors, 366
  overview of, 363–64
  Publishers, 365–66
  scenarios, 370–72
  Subscribers, 367–69
  sync with backup option, 366–67
  system databases, 369–70
Replication folder, Enterprise Manager, 364
reporting server, 522
reports, monitoring
  baseline, 702
  overview of, 696–97
  sample, 700–701
Republishers, 358–59
requirements set, high availability solutions, 515–16
resources
  failover clustering and wasted, 67
  failover preferences, 237–40
  management, 681
  ownership preferences, 236–37
restore. *See* backup and restore
RESTORE, 485–86
RESTORE FILELISTONLY, 477–78, 487, 498
RESTORE HEADERONLY, 451, 476
RESTORE LABELONLY, 476
RESTORE VERIFYONLY, 478
retention period, backups, 433–34, 553
risk assessment, 542–53
  BizTalk servers, 548–49
  Commerce Server, 549
  Content Management Server, 549–50
  CustomDB1, CustomDB2, and CustomDB3, 551–52
  database dependencies, 545–49
  database inventory, 544–45
  environment inventory, 542–43
  instances of SQL Server, 543
  list of risks and unknowns, 552–53
  servers, 552
  software inventory, 543
  upgrades, 610–11
risk identification, 9–10
role changes, 311–16
  demoting primary, 311–13
  options for, 290
  performing, 335–38
  promoting secondary, 313–15

(continued)

(continued)

(continued)

Allan Hirt

Allan Hirt is a consultant for Microsoft Consulting Services based in the Boston, Massachusetts, area and has more than 10 years of enterprise relational database experience. He has authored numerous white papers and training courses for Microsoft (including the white paper "Microsoft SQL Server 2000 Failover Clustering") and has contributed to other documents about high availability. Allan has presented at various conferences, including SQL Pass, TechEd, Microsoft Global Briefing, and a spotlight session at the November 2002 SQL Pass conference.

When he is not working, Allan is the main composer and arranger and the bass player for a jazz ensemble that has a few released CDs, and the bass player and keyboardist for a Rush tribute band. He is currently writing and arranging for a big band recording project scheduled for the fall of 2003. As if he were not busy enough, Allan is also the co-Webmaster of *http://www.styxcollector.com* and the Webmaster of *http://www.bobmintzer.com*.

Cathan Cook

Cathan Cook provides strategic consulting about large system architecture and management. She works for Microsoft Enterprise Services and has an extensive background in managing projects through the full life cycle of planning, development, testing, operations, and optimization.

Her technical focus is on data-centric or information-sharing systems that must be highly available, scalable, and manageable; her nontechnical focus includes the process- and people-related issues that affect these systems and the management techniques that make them successful. Cathan is a coauthor of several books, including Microsoft SQL Server 2000 Resource Kit, and of many white papers, including "SQL Server 2000 Operations Guide" and "Internet Data Center Reference Architecture."

As a work hobby, she experiments with finding better or more useful ways to design systems and has a particular interest in research projects such as

SDSS SkyServer. In her Spare Time™, she pursues activities such as scuba-diving, tai chi, theater arts, and maintaining a collection of animated foreign films, self-reflective artwork, and Hispanic artifacts from the Caribbean. Her pastimes include studying technology as culture, interpreting opera, and reading about philosophy and science. She is currently working on a novel and is planning to resume work on her Ph.D. next year.

Frank McBath

Frank McBath has worked in IT for more than 15 years and extensively with SQL Server for the last decade. Currently he is working on the Microsoft-Siebel Global Alliance team for creating the next generation of technologies. Prior to joining Microsoft, he worked for several major enterprise software companies, Fortune 100 firms, and consulting houses. Frank has extensive experience in enterprise implementations, upgrades, deployments, and production support. In 2000, Frank was named the Microsoft Distinguished Consultant of the Year.

Kimberly L. Tripp

Kimberly L. Tripp, a SQL Server MVP, began working in the database field in 1989. Since 1995, Kimberly has worked as a speaker, writer, trainer, and consultant for her own company, SYSolutions, Inc. In 2002 she joined six other SQL Server specialists to form Solid Quality Learning, a high-end training and consulting firm with more than 100 years of combined database expertise.

Kimberly frequently writes for SQL Server Magazine and was a technical contributor for the Microsoft SQL Server 2000 Resource Kit. She has lectured for Microsoft TechEd, PASS, SQLLive, and SQLMagazineConnections, where she is consistently a top-rated speaker.

Additionally, Kimberly works closely with Microsoft to provide new and interesting technical resources, including the SQL Server 2000 High Availability

Overview DVD, which features more than nine hours of in-depth technical content, demos, and peer chats with MVPs. Currently, Kimberly is working to help create Yukon content, including labs and white papers.

Prior to starting her own company, Kimberly held positions at Microsoft including Subject Matter Expert/Trainer for Microsoft University and Technical Writer for the SQL Server Development Team. You can get more information about Kimberly at *http://www.SQLSkills.com*. When Kimberly is not working she enjoys scuba diving, underwater photography, playing with her dog, and relaxing with her friends.

Get a **Free**
e-mail newsletter, updates,
special offers, links to related books,
and more when you

register online!

Register your Microsoft Press® title on our Web site and you'll get a FREE subscription to our e-mail newsletter, *Microsoft Press Book Connections.* You'll find out about newly released and upcoming books and learning tools, online events, software downloads, special offers and coupons for Microsoft Press customers, and information about major Microsoft® product releases. You can also read useful additional information about all the titles we publish, such as detailed book descriptions, tables of contents and indexes, sample chapters, links to related books and book series, author biographies, and reviews by other customers.

Registration is easy. Just visit this Web page and fill in your information:

http://www.microsoft.com/mspress/register

Microsoft®

- -

System Requirements

Microsoft SQL Server 2000 120-day Evaluation Edition CD

- Intel Pentium or compatible 166-megahertz (MHz) or higher processor.

- Microsoft Windows Server 2003, Microsoft Windows 2000 Server, Microsoft Windows NT Server 4.0 with Service Pack 5 (SP5) or later, Microsoft Windows NT Workstation 4.0 with SP5 or later, Microsoft Windows XP Professional, Microsoft Windows XP Home Edition, or Microsoft Windows 2000 Professional.

- 64 megabytes (MB) of RAM; 128 MB recommended.

- 95 to 270 MB of available hard disk space for the server; 250 MB for a typical installation. 50 MB of available hard disk space for a minimum installation of Analysis Services; 130 MB for a typical installation; 80 MB of available hard disk space for English Query. MSDE requires 44 MB of available hard disk space.

- CD-ROM drive.

- VGA or higher-resolution monitor.

- Microsoft Internet Explorer version 5.0 or later.

- Microsoft Windows 95, Microsoft Windows 98, Microsoft Windows Me, Microsoft Windows NT 4.0, Microsoft Windows 2000, and Microsoft Windows XP have built-in network software. Additional network software is required if you are using Banyan VINES or AppleTalk ADSP. Novell NetWare IPX/SPX client support is provided by the NWLink protocol of Windows-based networking.

Microsoft SQL Server 2000 High Availability Companion CD

- The SQL Server–based utilities and scripts (job aids) require SQL Server 2000.

- The job aids will take up about 20 MB of disk space if copied to hard disk.

- The .zip files require decompression software such as WinZip or PKUnzip.

- The .pdf files require the Adobe Acrobat Reader (link supplied on CD) or Adobe Acrobat; the .doc files require the Microsoft Word viewer (supplied on CD) or Microsoft Word; the .xls files require the Microsoft Excel viewer (supplied on CD) or Microsoft Excel.